E INSTI

FILM FACTS

First published in Great Britain
2001 by Aurum Press Ltd
25 Bedford Avenue, London WC1B 3AT

ISBN 1 85410 654 6

10 9 8 7 6 5 4 3 2 1
2005 2004 2003 2002 2001

Design by Don Macpherson
Printed in Singapore by Imago

COUNTRY ABBREVIATIONS

Afghanistan	Afg	Ghana	Gha	Poland	Pol
Algeria	Alg	Greece	Gre	Portugal	Por
Argentina	Arg	Gabon	Gab	Romania	Rom
Australia	Aus	Hong Kong	HK	Russia	Rus
Austria	Aut	Hungary	Hun	Singapore	Sin
Bangladesh	Ban	India	Ind	South Africa	SA
Belgium	Bel	Iceland	Ice	Spain	Sp
Brazil	Bra	Ireland	Ire	Sweden	Swe
Bulgaria	Bul	Israel	Isr	Switzerland	Swz
Canada	Can	Italy	It	Syria	Syr
China	Chn	Ivory Coast	IvC	Senegal	Sen
Colombia	Col	Jamaica	Jam	South Korea	S. Kor
Commonwealth of		Japan	Jap	Taiwan	Tai
Independent States	CIS	Kenya	Ken	Thailand	Tha
Czechoslovakia	Cz	Korea	Kor	Tunisia	Tun
Cayman Islands	Cayl	Libya	Lby	Turkey	Tur
Curacao	Cur	Mexico	Mex	United States	US
Denmark	Den	Morocco	Mor	Uruguay	Uru
Egypt	Egy	Mozambique	Moz	Venezuela	Ven
Finland	Fin	Mauretania	Mau	Yugoslavia	Yug
France	Fr	Netherlands	Neth	
Germany	Ger	New Zealand	NZ	
Germany, East	GDR	Norway	Nor	*The abbreviation i.p. after a film title*
Germany, West	FRG	Philippines	Phi	*instead of a date signifies 'in production'.*

FILM FACTS

PATRICK ROBERTSON

AURUM PRESS

CONTENTS

CHAPTER 1
Fade in

The first motion picture films were taken with a camera patented in Britain by French-born Louis Aimé Augustin Le Prince (1842–90?) in November 1888. Two fragments survive: one taken at a speed of 10–12 frames per second early in October 1888 in the garden of his father-in-law, Mr Joseph Whitley, at Roundhay, Leeds; the other taken at 20 frames per second later in the month and showing traffic crossing Leeds Bridge. According to Le Prince's mechanic, James Longley, the latter film was shown on a projector incorporating a Maltese cross for intermittent picture shift. He claimed that the image obtained was sufficiently clear for smoke to be visible rising from the pipe of a lounger on the bridge. Both films were made on sensitised paper rolls 2⅛ in wide and it was not until a year later that Le Prince was able to obtain Eastman celluloid roll film, which had just been introduced into Britain. This provided a far more suitable support material and it seems likely that the inventor was able to start the commercial development of his motion-picture process by the beginning of 1890. A new projector was built so that a demonstration could be given to M. Mobisson, the Secretary of the Paris Opera. On 16 September 1890 Le Prince boarded a train at Dijon bound for Paris, en route to New York where he intended to present his invention in public for the first time. He never arrived in the French capital. No trace of his body was ever found and after exhaustive enquiries the police were unable to offer any rational explanation for his disappearance. The mystery has never been solved.

The fullest account of Le Prince's life and his mysterious disappearance is Christopher Rawlence's *The Missing Reel* (Collins, 1990), described by *Variety* as 'an important rewriting of film history'.

The Le Prince camera of 1888.

The first commercially developed motion picture process was instigated by Thomas Alva Edison (1847–1931), American electrical engineer. His initial attempt to produce an illusion of movement, by means of an apparatus called the 'optical phonograph', resulted in failure, and in January 1889 Edison assigned William Kennedy Laurie Dickson (1860–1935), an assistant at his laboratories in West Orange, NJ, to work on the development of what was to become the Kinetoscope, a film-viewing machine designed for use in amusement arcades. Dickson, the French-born son of English parents, had early training as a photographer and was better suited to this kind of research than his mentor, who knew little of optics. Abandoning the use of rectangular sheets of celluloid for camera work, he substituted 50ft lengths of celluloid film produced by the firm of Merwin Hulbert. These long rolls were first purchased on 18 March 1891, which is the earliest date at which it seems likely that Dickson could have made successful films for viewing in the peep-show Kinetoscope apparatus.

The first public demonstration of motion pictures took place at the Edison Laboratories at West Orange, NJ, on 22 May 1891, when 147 representatives of the National Federation of Women's Clubs, having lunched with Mrs Edison at Glenmont, were taken over to her husband's workshops and allowed to view the new Kinetoscope. The *New York Sun* reported: 'The surprised and pleased clubwomen saw a small pine box standing on the floor. There were some wheels and belts near the box, and a workman who had them in charge. In the top of the box was a hole perhaps an inch in diameter. As they looked through the hole they saw the picture of a man. It was a most marvellous picture. It bowed and smiled and waved its hands and took off its hat with the most perfect naturalness and grace. Every motion was perfect . . .'. The film used for this demonstration appears to have been taken with a horizontal-feed camera without sprockets. This would have been an imperfect apparatus at best, and not until October 1892 is there evidence that William Dickson had built an effective vertical-feed camera using perforated film. In that month the *Phonogram* published an illustration showing sequences from four films evidently taken with such a device. These included pictures of Dickson himself, together with his helper, William Heise, and also shots of wrestling and fencing. By this date, then, it can be positively asserted that Dickson had overcome all the obstacles that had stood in the way of making films suitable for commercial exhibition. He was to receive little thanks for his work. After Dickson left West Orange in 1895, following a dispute with his employer, Edison steadfastly refused to concede that anyone but himself was responsible for bringing the invention to fruition. Most historians were content to accept Edison's own version of events until the appearance in 1961 of a painstaking work of scholarship titled *The Edison Motion*

The earliest known motion-picture film—Traffic Crossing Leeds
Bridge *(GB 88).*

Picture Myth. The author, Gordon Hendricks, demonstrates by reference to hitherto unpublished papers in the Edison archives that all the experimental work on the Kinetoscope was conducted by Dickson, or under his direction, and that Edison himself can be credited with little more than instigating the research programme and providing facilities for carrying it out.

The practical development of motion pictures in Britain can be dated from a camera built in 1895 by Birt Acres (1854–1918) and R. W. Paul (1869–1943) at the latter's optical instrument works in Saffron Hill. Paul's interest in films had been aroused the previous October when he was approached by a Greek showman, George Trajedis, with a request to manufacture some Edison Kinetoscopes. This Paul agreed to do on learning that Edison had omitted to patent the machine in Britain. Since Edison's agents understandably refused to sell films for the pirated machines, Paul approached Acres with the suggestion that they should construct a camera together (later each claimed to have been the only begetter of the apparatus) so that they could make their own Kinetoscope subjects. Acres was to be cameraman. Using film obtained from the American Celluloid Co. of Newark, NJ, Acres tried out the camera for the first time in March 1885 with a scene of a cricketer (his assistant, Henry Short) coming out of Acres' home, Clovelly Cottage, in Barnet. This was followed by what Paul described as 'our first saleable film', *The Oxford and Cambridge University Boat Race,* shot on 30 March, which was premièred on a Kinetoscope at the India Exhibition, Earls Court, on 27 May 1895. This film, together with *The Derby* and *The Opening of the Kiel Canal* (see p. 000), formed the first programme presented on screen in Britain since Le Prince's experiments, when Acres gave a private show with his Kine-opticon projector in a coach-house at Wrotham Cottage, Barnet in August 1895. Acres was also the first to give a public screening (see below), while Paul became the first manufacturer of projectors and Britain's pioneer film producer.

The first commercial presentation of motion pictures took place at Holland Bros' Kinetoscope Parlor, 1155 Broadway, New York, which opened for business on 14 April 1894. The Kinetoscopes were arranged in two rows of five, and for 25c viewers were allowed to watch five films—to see the whole programme they had to pay double entrance money. The first day's take of $120 suggests that this first 'cinema audience' totalled nearly 500. The films, made in the Edison 'Black Maria' (see p. 000) at West Orange, were titled: *Sandow, Bertholdi (mouth support), Horse Shoeing, Bertholdi (table contortion), Barber Shop, Blacksmiths, Cock Fight, Highland Dance, Wrestling, Trapeze.*

The first commercial presentation of films in Britain took place at The Kinetoscope Parlour opened by the Continental Commerce Co. of New York at 70 Oxford Street, London, on 18 October 1894. The 12 machines offered such titillating delights as *Carmencita* (a buxom vaudeville artiste) and *Annabelle Serpentine Dance,* as well as more prosaic fare like *Blacksmith Shop, Wrestling Match* and *The Bar Room.*

The first film presented publicly on screen was *La*

HOW THE CINEMA SPREAD AROUND THE WORLD

Few inventions have spread more rapidly than cinematography. By the end of 1896, a mere 12 months after the real start of commercial cinema in France, nearly all the major countries of the western world had witnessed their first demonstration of the new art. It is clear from the following chronology that the Lumière brothers of Lyon were the most positive force in introducing motion pictures to the world. (The designation 'Lumière' below signifies that the programme was made up of Lumière films.) The presentations listed were public shows before a paying audience unless otherwise indicated.

1895
22 March FRANCE *La Sortie des Ouvriers des l'Usine Lumière* (Fr 1894), presented by Louis and Auguste Lumière before the Société d'Encouragement pour l'Industrie Nationale at 44 rue de Rennes, Paris (see below).
20 May UNITED STATES *Young Griffo v. Battling Charles Barnett* (US 1895) presented before paying audience at 153 Broadway, New York (see p. 8).
1 November GERMANY Eight short films (for subjects, see Production: firsts by countries, p. 8) presented by Max and Emil Skladanowski at Berlin Wintergarten.
10 November BELGIUM Lumière programme before invited audience of scientists etc., in Brussels. First before paying audience at 7 de la Galerie du Roi, Brussels, 1 Mar 1896.

1896
10 January UNITED KINGDOM Programme (subjects see p. 8) presented by Birt Acres before Lyonsdown Photographic Club, Barnet. First before paying audience: Lumière programme by F. Trewey at Regent Street Polytechnic, London, 20 Feb 1896.
?? February ITALY Lumière presented by Vittorio Calcina at the Ospedale di Carita, Turin.
19 March AUSTRIA Lumière presented by E. J. Dupont at the Graphic Arts Teaching & Research Centre, Vienna.
6 April NORWAY Skladanowski programme presented at Circus Variété, Oslo.
7 April SPAIN R. W. Paul's Theatrograph presented Circus Parish, Madrid.
20 April IRELAND Unidentified programme presented at Star of Erin Variety Theatre, Dublin.
4 May RUSSIA Lumière presented by Francis Doublier at Aquarium Theatre, St Petersburg.
6 May SOUTH AFRICA R. W. Paul's Theatrograph programme—*Highland Dancers* (GB 1896), *Street Scenes in London* (GB 1896), *Trilby Dance* (GB 1896), *A Military Parade* (GB 1896), *The Soldier's Courtship* (GB 1896)—presented at Empire Theatre of Varieties, Johannesburg.
10 May HUNGARY Lumière presented at Royal Hotel, Budapest. Included street scenes taken in front of Opera House and Chain Bridge, Budapest, and Hungarian Millenary Procession.
21 May NETHERLANDS Skladanowski (see Germany) presented Amsterdam.
27 May ROMANIA Lumière presented at Salon l'Independenta Romana, Bucharest.
7 June SERBIA Lumière presented at Kod Zlatnog Krsta Café, Belgrade.
7 June DENMARK Lumière presented by Vilhelm Pacht in Raadhuspladsen, Copenhagen.
18 June PORTUGAL R. W. Paul programme presented by Erwin Rousby at Real Coliseu, Rua da Palma, Lisbon.
28 June SWEDEN Lumière presented by C. V. Roikjer at the Industrial Exhibition, Malmö.
28 June FINLAND Lumière presented at the Societetshuset, Helsinki.
28 June CANADA Lumière presented by Louis Minier and Louis Pupier at Palace Theatre, Montreal.
7 July INDIA Lumière presented at Watson's Hotel, Bombay.
8 July BRAZIL 'Omniographo' (probably Lumière) presented at 57 Rua do Ouvidor, Rio de Janiero.
15 July CZECH REPUBLIC Lumière presented at the Lázensky dum, Karlovy Vary.
23 July URUGUAY Lumiere presented at Salon Rouge, Montevideo.
28 July ARGENTINA Lumière presented by Francisco Pastos and Eustaquio Pellier at Colón Theatre, Buenos Aires.
11 August CHINA French programme (negative evidence suggests not Lumière) presented as act of variety show at Hsu Gardens, Shanghai.
15 August MEXICO Lumière presented by engineering student Salvador Toscano Barragan at 17 Calle de Jesus, Mexico City.
22 August AUSTRALIA R. W. Paul programme presented by conjurer Carl Hertz at Melbourne Opera House.
25 August CHILE Lumière presented by Julio Prá, Santiago.
26 September GUATEMALA Lumière presented by Arnold Tobler at 11 Passage Aycinena, Guatemala City.
13 October NEW ZEALAND R. W. Paul (?) programme of English films presented by Profs Hausmann and Gow at Auckland Opera House.
?? October POLAND Edison programme presented at Lvov.
Date unknown EGYPT unidentified pro gramme at Zavani Café, Alexandria.
Date unknown SLOVENIA unidentified programme presented by Charles Crassé at Celje, Ljubljana and Maribor.

1897
24 January CUBA Lumière presented by Gabriel Veyre at Teatro Tacón, Havana.
28 January VENEZUELA Edison presented by Manuel Trujillo at Teatro Baralt, Maracaibo.
15 February JAPAN Lumière presented by Inkato Shotaro and Francois-Constant Girel, Nanchi Theatre, Osaka.
?? February/March BULGARIA Lumière presented in port town of Russe.
2 March PERU Edison Vitascope presented on the Plaza de Armas, Lima.
10 June THAILAND Lumière presented by S. G. Marchovsky in Bangkok.
Date unknown PHILLIPINES Lumière presented by Antonio Ramos, Manila and on tour.
Date unknown TUNISIA Lumière at store show established by Albert Samama on rue Es-Sadika, Tunis.

1898
Spring GREECE Lumière at Place Kolokotronis, Athens.
25 March ZIMBABWE (Rhodesia) Edison at Empire Theatre, Bulawayo.

1899
Date unknown TURKEY unidentified programme presented privately before Sultan by Spaniard Don Ramirez and then publicly at his Electric Circus, Constantinople.

1900
30 (?) November INDONESIA Nederlandsche Bioscope Maatschappij presented at Batavia.
Date unknown KOREA free film show sponsored by Anglo-American Tobacco Co. of Shanghai. Admission in exchange for cigarette coupons.
Date unknown SENEGAL Lumière presented at Dakar.
Date unknown IRAN unidentified programme presented before Shah by Mirza Ebrahim Khan at Royal Palace, Teheran. First public show opened in Avenue Cheraq Gaz, TEHRAN, by Sahâf Bâshi in 1905.

Sortie des Ouvriers de l'Usine Lumière (Fr 1894) which was shown before members of the Société d'Encouragement pour l'Industrie Nationale by Auguste and Louis Lumière at 44 rue de Rennes, Paris, on 22 March 1895. Believed to have been taken in August or September 1894, the film showed workers leaving the Lumière photographic factory at Lyons for their dinner-hour.

The first public screening in Britain of which there is documentary evidence was given by Birt Acres before members of the Lyonsdown Photographic Club at Lyonsdown, near Barnet, Herts on 10 January 1896. The films shown were probably the same as those presented before the Royal Photographic Society at 12 Hanover Square, London four days later, usually, and erroneously, described as the first public screening in Britain. Shot by Acres himself, they were *The Opening of the Kiel Canal, The Derby, Boxers, The Skirt Dancers* and *Rough Seas at Dover*, comprising the first news film, the first film of a scheduled sporting event to be shown on screen, the first British film featuring professional artistes and the first

British 'documentary'. Acres claimed to have given public performances during August and September 1895. Although there is no direct evidence of these, the development of his projector was sufficiently advanced by then for performances to have been practicable.

The first film to be screened before a paying audience was a four-minute boxing subject, *Young Griffo v. Battling Charles Barnett*, presented by Major Woodville Latham of the Lamda Co. at 153 Broadway, New York on 20 May 1895. The projector was a primitive and imperfect machine called the Eidoloscope, designed for the Lamda Co. (the first film company established as such) by former Edison employee Eugene Lauste. Although some authorities have cast doubt on the Eidoloscope's ability to create an illusion of movement on a screen, it must have achieved a sufficient level of technical acceptability, however jerky and inadequate the picture, for Latham to have attracted paying customers. Another commercial show was given by C. Francis Jenkins and Thomas Armat, using a projector they had designed themselves, at a purpose-built temporary cinema at the Cotton States Exposition at Atlanta, Ga., in September 1895. After making various improvements to the machine, Armat came to an arrangement with Thomas Edison, who had failed to produce a workable projector himself, by which the celebrated inventor would be allowed to exploit it as his own. As the Edison Vitascope, the improved machine was debuted at Koster and Bial's Music Hall on Broadway on 23 April 1896, an occasion which has often, and erroneously, been heralded as the first time that motion pictures were presented on a screen to a paying audience.

The first screening before a paying audience in Europe was given by Max and Emil Skladanowski with a projector of their own invention at the Berlin Wintergarten on 1 November 1895. The films were made up of endless loops and the action lasted only a few seconds before it was repeated. Taken at the rate of eight pictures a second, the films were flickering and jerky, but the fact that there was movement on the screen at all was sufficient for the Nazis to claim, some forty years later, that Germany was the cradle of the cinema industry. In fact neither the work of Lauste and Latham in America, nor that of the Skladanowskis in Germany was destined to have any lasting effect on the development of the cinema. It is generally agreed that the première of the Lumière brothers' show, before a paying audience at the Grand Café, 14 Boulevard des Capucines, Paris, on 28 December 1895, marks the debut of the motion picture as a regular entertainment medium. Their projector was the first to advance beyond the experimental stage and the first to be offered for sale.

The first screening before a paying audience in Britain took place at the Regent Street Polytechnic on 20 February 1896, when the French magician Felicien Trewey exhibited the Lumière Cinématographe with accompanying commentary by M. Francis Pochet. Admission was 1s and the engagement lasted three weeks, hours 2–4 p.m. The opening programme included the Lumière films *Arrival of a Train at a Station*, *The Baby and the Goldfish*, *The Family Tea Table* and *M. Trewey: Prestigidateur*. The first commercial show outside London was by Birt Acres at Cardiff Town Hall on 5 May 1896.

The oldest production company in the world is Paris-based Gaumont, founded by Léon Gaumont on 10 August 1895 when he bought out the optical company Comptoir Général de la Photographie and renamed it Societé Léon Gaumont & Cie. Manufacture of projectors started the following year and film production began in 1897 with short actualities to help sell the projectors. Early productions included the first film directed by a woman (q.v.), *La Fée aux choux* (Fr 1900), and the first European cartoon, Emile Cohl's *Fantasmagorie* (Fr 07). The Gaumont archive is one of the most abundant in the world, with 7000 hours of 1910–74 newsreels as well as hundreds of dramatic subjects. A recent discovery was three hours of colour film made in Gaumont's Trichone process prior to World War I, located in the Kodak Archives. And reaching back to the very beginning of Gaumont's production history was footage of the Place de la Concorde shot by a Gaumont cameraman in 1897, revealed by a private collector and now copied for the archive. Currently production runs at eight to 12 pictures a year, with plans to produce one English-language film annually for the international market. Recent successes have included the box office hit *Les Visiteurs* (Fr 93), about a 12th-century knight who time travels to modern France, which sold 13 million tickets in its home territory and became the most successful French film in 25 years.

CHAPTER 2

The Industry

Feature Films

The first feature film, according to the Cinématheque Française definition of a feature, that is 'a commercially made film over one hour duration', was Charles Tait's *The Story of the Kelly Gang* (Aus 06), which was 4000ft long and had a running time of 60–70 minutes. A biopic of Victoria's notorious bushranger Ned Kelly (1855–80), the film was produced by the theatrical company J. & N. Tait of Melbourne, Victoria, and shot on location over a period of about six months at Whitehorse Road, Mitcham (Glenrowan Hotel scenes, including the last stand of the Kelly Gang); at Rosanna (railway scenes); and on Charles Tait's property at Heidelberg, Victoria (all other scenes). The actual armour which had belonged to Ned Kelly—a bullet-proof helmet and jerkin fashioned from ploughshares—was borrowed from the Victorian Museum and worn by the actor playing the role, an unidentified Canadian from the Bland Holt touring company who disappeared before the film was finished. It had to be completed with an extra standing in as Ned, all these scenes being taken in long shot. Elizabeth Veitch played Kate Kelly, and others in the cast included Ollie Wilson, Frank Mills, Bella Cole and Vera Linden.

Made on a budget of £450, *The Story of the Kelly Gang* was premièred at the Athenaeum Hall, Melbourne, on 24 December 1906 and recovered its cost within a week, eventually grossing some £25,000, including receipts from the English release. No complete print survives but stills from the film were issued as picture postcards and give the impression of a vigorous, all-action drama made with imaginative use of outdoor locations—a significant advance on the studio-bound one-reelers being turned out in Europe and America at this time. It was long believed that the film had been totally lost, but recently a 210ft-long fragment was discovered in Melbourne. Other versions of the Ned Kelly story survive. There were remakes in 1910, 1917, 1920, 1923, 1934, 1951 and 1970, all of them Australian productions except the last, a British film with Mick Jagger in the title role.

Australia was the only country in the world to have established regular production of feature-length films prior to 1911. For figures on early output, see Production: World Output (pp. 16–17).

The first feature-length film made in Europe was Michel Carré's 90-minute-long production *L'Enfant prodigue* (Fr 07), premièred at the Théâtre des Variétés in the Boulevard Montmartre, Paris, on 20 June 1907. This was a screen representation of a stage play, with little or no adaptation.

The first European feature film scripted for the screen was a four-reel version of *Les Misérables* (Fr 09), produced by Pathé from the novel by Victor Hugo.

The first feature film exhibited in the United Kingdom was Charles Tait's *The Story of the Kelly Gang* (Aus 06), which had its British première at the Assembly Rooms, Bath, in January 1908. The film was released by the Colonial Picture Combine.

The first feature film produced in the United Kingdom was Thomas Bentley's *Oliver Twist* (GB 12), a Hepworth production in four reels starring ex-beauty queen Ivy Millais as Oliver Twist, Alma Taylor as Nancy and John McMahon as Fagin. It was released in August 1912, two months after Vitagraph's version in America (see below).

The first feature film produced in the United States was Vitagraph's four-reel production of *Les Misérables* (US 09), released in separate one-reel parts between 18 September and 27 November 1909. Charles Kent's Vitagraph production of *The Life of Moses* (US 09), in five reels, was also released in separate parts (4 December

The world's first full-length film was The Story of the Kelly Gang *(Aus 06), made in Australia in 1906. No other country established regular production of features until 1911. (Backnumbers)*

PIONEER PRODUCTIONS

THE FIRST TWELVE FEATURE FILMS PRODUCED IN THE USA

May 1912 *Oliver Twist* (5 reels) H. A. Spanuth
Oct 1912 *From the Manger to the Cross* (6 reels) Kalem Co.
Oct 1912 *Richard III* (4 reels) Sterling Camera & Film Co.
Nov 1912 *Cleopatra* (6 reels) Helen Gardner Picture Plays
Nov 1912 *The Adventures of Lieutenant Petrosino* Feature Photoplay Co.
Feb 1913 *One Hundred Years of Mormonism* (6 reels) Utah Moving Picture Co.; Ellay Co.
Feb 1913 *A Prisoner of Zenda* (4 reels) Famous Players Film Co.
March (?) 1913 *Hiawatha* (4 reels) Frank E. Moore
June 1913 *The Battle of Gettysburg* (5 reels) NY Motion Picture Co.
July 1913 *The Seed of the Fathers* (6 reels) Monopol Film Co.
Aug (?) 1913 *Victory* (5 reels) Victory Co.
Sept 1913 *Tess of the D'Urbervilles* (5 reels) Famous Players Film Co.

It is worthy of note that neither Cecil B. DeMille's *The Squaw Man* (US 14) nor D. W. Griffith's *Judith of Bethulia* (US 14), each of which has been cited as the first feature produced in the US, appears above.

THE FIRST 12 FEATURE FILMS PRODUCED IN THE UK

Aug 1912 *Oliver Twist* (4 reels) Hepworth
Dec 1912 *Lorna Doone* (5 reels) Clarendon
May 1913 *East Lynne* (6 reels) Barker
July 1913 *The Battle of Waterloo* (5 reels) British & Colonial
July 1913 *Ivanhoe* (6 reels) Zenith Films
July 1913 *A Message from Mars* (4 reels) United Kingdom Films
Aug 1913 *David Copperfield* (8 reels) Hepworth
Sept 1913 *King Charles* (4 reels) Clarendon
Sept 1913 *A Cigarette-Maker's Romance* (4 reels) Hepworth
Sept 1913 *The House of Temperley* (5 reels) London Films
Oct 1913 *The Grip* (4 reels) Britannic Films
Oct 1913 *Hamlet* (6 reels) Hepworth

COUNTRIES PRODUCING FEATURE FILMS BY 1914

By the outbreak of World War I, the following countries had commenced feature-film production:

1906	Australia
1909	France
1911	Denmark, Germany, Italy, Poland, Russia, Serbia, Spain
1912	Austria, Greece, Hungary, Japan, Norway, Romania, United Kingdom, United States
1913	Brazil, Finland, India, Netherlands, Sweden, Venezuela, Canada
1914	Argentina

FILM-PRODUCING NATIONS

The following list chronicles, wherever known, the first motion-picture production, the first dramatised (i.e. acted) production, the first feature film (over one hour duration) and the first talkie feature of each of the film-producing countries of the world, signified by the abbreviations Film, Drama, Feature, Talkie. The first feature film in natural colour is included for major film-producing nations.

The first motion-picture production means a film made by a native or permanent resident of the country, as opposed to a visiting cameraman or non-resident producer. Where a category has been omitted no information is available. Drama/Feature and Feature/Talkie signify respectively that the first feature-length film was also the first dramatic production of any length and that the first talkie was also the first feature-length production.

Other abbreviations: doc.=documentary; f.=filmed; d.=directed; pr.=première; prod.=produced.

ALBANIA
Feature/Talkie: *Tana* (1958), d. Kristaq Dhano, starring Tinka Kurti.

ALGERIA
Film: *La Prière du muezzin* (1906), d. Felix Mesguich.
Drama: *Ali Bouf a l'huile* (1907), d. Felix Mesguich.
Feature/Talkie: *Peuple en marche* (1963), d. Ahmed Rachedi and René Vautier.

ANGOLA
Film: *Monangambé* (1968), d. Sarah Maldoror.
Feature/Talkie: *Des fusils pour Banta* (1970), d. Sarah Maldoror.

ARGENTINA
Film: *La Bandera Argentina* (1897), d. Eugenio Py.
Drama: *El Fusilamiento de Dorrego* (1908), d. Mario Gallo and Salvador Rosich.
Feature: *Amalia* (1914), d. Enrique Garcia Velloso.
Talkie: *Muñequitas porteñas* (1931), with Maria Turguenova—Vitaphone system.

AUSTRALIA
Film: *Passengers Alighting from Ferry 'Brighton' at Manly*, (pr. 27 Oct 1896), d. Marius Sestier.
Drama: untitled 75ft drama by Joseph Perry of the Salvation Army about man sent to gaol for stealing bread and helped by Army's 'prisongate brigade' on release, c. 1897.
Feature: *The Story of the Kelly Gang* (pr. 26 Dec 1906), d. Charles Tait. (NB: First feature film (q.v.) in world.)
Talkie: *Fellers* (press shown 23 May 1930), d. Arthur Higgins and Austin Fay, prod. Artaus Films, starring Arthur Tauchert.

AUSTRIA
Drama: *Ein Walzertraum* (scene from opera) f. 2 Mar 1907.
Feature: *Zweierlei Blut* (1912), starring Luise Kohn and Jakob Fleck.
Talkie: *G'schichten aus der Steiermark* (pr. 23 Aug 1929), d. Hans Otto Löwenstein, prod. Eagle Film and Ottoton film, starring Hilde Maria and Anny Burg.

BANGLADESH
Feature/Talkie: *Mukh O Mukhosh* (1956), d. Jabbar Khan.

BELGIUM
Film: *Le Marché aux poissons de Bruxelles* (1897) and other actualities, d. M. Alexandre.
Drama: *'chand d'habits* (1897), d. M. Alexandre.
Feature: *Belgique meurtrie* (1920), d. Paul Flon.

Talkie: *La Famille Klepkens* (1930), d. Gaston Schoukens and Paul Flon.

BHUTAN
Feature/Talkie: *Phorpa/The Cup* (1999), d. Khyentse Norba in Tibetan, starring Jamyang Lodro and Orgyen Tobgyal with the monks of Chokling Monastery.

BOLIVIA
Film: actualities by Luis Castillo, 1913.
Feature: *La Profecia del Lago* (1923), d. José Maria Velasco Maidana (film banned).
Talkie: *La Guerra del Chaco* (1936), d. José Luis Bazoberry.

BRAZIL
Film: *View of Guanabara Bay* (f. 19 July 1898), d. Affonso Segreto.
Drama: *Os Estranguladores* (1906)—crime film based on true story in police files, d. Isaac Sandenberg.
Feature: *O Crime dos Banhados* (1913), d. Francisco Santos, prod. Guarany Film.
Talkie: *Acabaram-se os Otarios* (1930), country comedy d. Luis de Barros, starring Genésio Arruda and Tom Bill.

BULGARIA
Film: actuality about Bulgarian army, 1910.
Drama: *Such is the War* (1914).
Feature: *The Bulgar is a Gentleman* (1915), satire about Sofia snobbery, d. Vassil Guendov, starring ditto and Mara Lipina.
Talkie: *A Song of the Balkan Mountains* (1934), d. Peter Stoychev.

BURKINA FASO
Film: *A Minuit . . . l'Independence* (1960).
Feature/Talkie: *Le Sang des parias* (1973), d. Mamadou Djim Kolas.

BURMA
Film: *The Funeral of U Tun Shein* (1920) actuality made by U Ohn Maung.
Feature: *Dana Pratap* (1925), prod. London Art Photo Co. of Rangoon.
Talkie: *Shwe ein the* (1932), prod. British Burma Film Co.

BURUNDI
Feature/Talkie: *Gito, L'Ingrat* (1992), d. Léonce Ngabo, co-prod. Cinematographiques du Burundi, starring Joseph Kumbela.

CAMEROON
Film: *L'Aventure en France* (1962), d. Jean-Paul N'Gassa.
Feature/Talkie (doc.): *Une Nation est née* (1972).
Feature/Talkie (drama): *Pousse-pousse* (1975), d. Daniel Karawa.

CANADA
Film: actualities of life on the prairies made by James Freer of Brandon, Manitoba, 1897.
Drama: *The Great Unknown* (1913), d. Oscar Lund, starring Barbara Tennent and Fred Truesdell.
Feature: *Evangeline* (1913), d. E. P. Sullivan and W. H. Cavanaugh, prod. Canadian Bioscope Co., starring Laura Lyman and John F. Carleton.
Talkie (English): *North of '49* (1929), d. Neal Hart, prod. British Canadian Pictures.
Talkie (French): *Notre-dame de la Mouise* (1941).
Colour: *Talbot of Canada* (1938), Kodachrome.

PIONEER PRODUCTIONS (continued)

CAPE VERDE ISLANDS
Feature/Talkie: *Os Flagelados do Vento Leste* (1988), d. António Faria, starring Carlos Alhinho and Arciolinda Almeida.

CHILE
Film: *Un Ejercicio General de Bomberos*, pr. 26 May 1902.
Drama: *Manuel Rodriquez* (1910) (includes shots of soldiers firing single-shot muskets repeatedly without reloading)
Feature: *La Baraja de la muerte* (1916), d. Salvador Giambastiane.
Talkie: *Norte y Sur* (1934), d. Jorge Délano.

CHINA
Film/Drama: *Tingchun Mountain* (1908), d. Lin Tenlun of the Feng Tai Photo Shop, Peking, starring Tan Hsin-pei.
Feature: *Yen Rei-sun* (1921), about embezzler who murders prostitute, d. Ren Pun-yen, prod. China Film Research Society, starring Chun Tso-Tze and Wang Tsai-yun.
Talkie: *Singsong Girl Red Peony* (1930), d. Chang Shih-chuan, prod. Star Film Co., starring Butterfly Wu.

COLOMBIA
Film/Drama: *The Life of General Rafael Uribe* (1914), d. Di Domenico brothers.
Feature: *La Maria* (1922), d. Alfredo Del Diestro.
Talkie: *Flowers of the Valley* (1939), d. Pedro Moreno Garzón.

CONGO
Film: *Kayako* (c. 1967), d. Sébastien Kamba.
Feature/Talkie: *La Rançon d'une alliance* (1973), d. Sébastien Kamba.

COSTA RICA
Drama: *El Retorno* (1926), d. Romulo Bertoni.
Feature: *La Segua* (1984), d. Antonio Yglesias.

CUBA
Film : *El Brujo desapareciendo* (1898), d. José E. Casasús.
Drama: *El Cabildo de ña Romualda* (1908), d. Enrique Diaz Quesada, prod. Metropolitan Films.
Feature: *El Rey de los campos de Cuba* (1913), d. Enrique Diaz Quesada, starring Gerardo Artecona and Evangelina Adams.
Talkie: *El Caballero de Max* (1930), d. Jaime San-Andrews, starring Nancy Norton and Wilfredo Genier—Vitaphone. (The Cuban government had made a sound-on-film documentary by the Phonofilm process in 1926.)

CURAÇAO
Feature/Talkie: *Ava & Gabriel. Un Historia di Amor* (1990), d. Felix de Rooy, starring Nashaira Desbarida and Cliff San-A-Jong.

CYPRUS
Feature/Talkie: *Avrianos Polemistis/ Tomorrow's Warrior* (1981), d. Michael Papas, prod. Cyprian (MP) Films, starring Christos Zannidea.

CZECH REPUBLIC
Film/Drama: *Vystavní Párkar a Lepic Plakátu* (1898), *Dostavencícko Ve Mlynici* (1898), *Plác a Smích* (1898), etc., actualities and short comedies featuring Bohemian cabaret artiste Josef Sváb-Malostransky, d. Prague student Jan Krízenecky.

Feature: *Prazstí Adamité* (1917), d. Antonín Fencl, prod. Lucernafilm, starring Josef Vosalik.
Talkie: *Tonka of the Gallows* (1930), d. Karel Anton.
Colour: *Jan Rohác of Duba* (1947), d. Vladamír Borsky.

DAHOMEY (BENIN)
Film: *Ganvié, mon village* (1966), d. Pascal Abikanlou.
Feature/Talkie: *Sous le signe du Vaudoun* (1974), d. Pascal Abikanlou.

DENMARK
Film: *Korsel med gronlandske Hunde* (1896), d. Peter Elfelt.
Drama: *Henrettelsen* (1903), d. Peter Elfelt, starring Francesca Nathansen and Victor Betzonich.
Feature: *Den sorte Drom* (pr. 4 Sept 1911), circus drama, d. Urban Gad, starring Valdemar Psilander and Asta Nielsen.
Talkie: *Eskimo* (pr. 9 Oct 1930), d. G. Schneevogt, starring Mona Martenson and Paul Richter.
Colour: *Tricks* (pr. 7 May 1956), d. Erik Balling.

DOMINICAN REPUBLIC
Drama: *Las Emboscados de Cupido* (1924), d. Francisco Palau.
Feature/Talkie: *La Serpiente de la Luna de los Piratas* (1972), d. Jean-Louis Jorge.

ECUADOR
Feature/Talkie: *Se Conocieron en Guayaquil* (1949), d. Alberto Sanatana, prod. Ecuador Sono Films.

EGYPT
Film: *Dans les rues d'Alexandrie* (1912), d. M. de Lagarne.
Drama: *Sharaf el Badawi* (1918), prod. Italo-Egyptian Cinematographic Co.
Feature: *Koubla Fil Sahara'a* (1927), d. Ibrahim Lama, prod. Condor Film. (NB: Shooting on *Laila* (1927), generally credited as first Egyptian feature, started earlier, but the film was released later.)
Talkie: *Onchoudet el Fouad* (pr. 14 Apr 1932), d. Mario Volpi.

FAROE ISLANDS
Feature/Talkie: *Atlantic Rhapsody* (1989), d. Katrin Ottarsdottir, starring Erling Eysturoy and Katrin Ottarsdottir, prod. Kaledidoskop.

FINLAND
Film: *Pupils of Nikolai Street School during Break* (1904).
Drama: *Salaviinanpolttajat* (1907), d. Louis Sparre, starring Teuvo Puro and Jussi Snellman.
Feature: *Kun Onni Pettää* (pr. 23 Nov 1913), d. Konrad Tallroth, starring Axel Precht and Sigrid Precht.
Talkie: *The Log-Driver's Bride* (1931), d. Erkki Karu.

FRANCE
Film: *La Sortie des Usines* (1894), d. Louis Lumière.
Drama: *L'Arroseur arrosé* (1895), d. Louis Lumière, starring Lumière's gardener M. Clerc and apprentice boy Duval.
Feature: *L'Enfant prodigue* (pr. 20 June 1907), d. Michel Carré.
Talkie: *Les Trois masques* (1929), d. André Hugon, prod. Pathé-Natan, starring

Renée Heribel and Marcel Vibert.
Colour: *L'Eternal amour* (1921), d. Gaston Colombani in Héraute Colour.
Colour talkie: *Le Mariage de Ramuntcho* (1947), d. Max de Vaucorbeil—Agfacolor.

GABON
Film: *M'Bolo Gabon* (1967).
Feature/Talkie: *Où vas-tu Koumba* (1971), d. Alain Ferrari and Simon Auré.

GERMANY
Films: *Italian Dance*, *Kangaroo Boxer*, *Juggler*, *Acrobats*, *Russian Dance*, *Serpentine Dance*, *Lutte*, *Apothéose* (all pr. 1 Nov 1895), d. Max and Emil Skladanowski.
Feature: *In dem grossen Augenblick* (pr. 11 Aug 1911), d. Urban Gad, prod. Deutsche Bioscop GmbH, starring Asta Nielsen and Hugo Hink.
Talkie: *Melodie der Welt* (pr. 12 Mar 1929), d. Walter Ruttman, starring J. Kowal Samborsky and Renée Stobrawa.
Colour: *Beauty Spot* (1936)—Agfacolor.

GHANA
Drama: *Amenu's Child* (1949), d. Sean Graham.
Feature/Talkie: *Boy Kumasenu* (1951), d. Sean Graham.

GIBRALTAR
Feature/Talkie: *Instant Justice* (1985), d. Denis Amar, prod. Mulloway Ltd, starring Michael Paré and Tawny Kitaen.

GREECE
Film: Olympic Games actuality (1906).
Drama: *Quo Vadis Spiridion* (1911), comedy, d. Spiros Dimitracopoulos, prod. Athina Films.
Feature: *Golfo* (1912), d. Costas Bahatoris from Spiros Peressiadis' folk-story play.
Talkie: *Les Apaches d'Athenes* (1930), musical, d. D. Gaziadis, prod. Dag Films, starring Mary Sayannou and Petros Epitropakis.

GREENLAND
Feature/Talkie: *Lysets Hjerte/Hearts of Light* (Greenland/Den/Nor/Swe 99), d. Jacob Grønlykke, starrring Rasmus Lyberth and Vivi Nielsen (in Greenlandish).

GUATEMALA
Drama: *Agent No. 13* (1912), d. Alberto de la Riva.
Feature/Talkie: *El Sombreron* (1950).

GUINEA
Film: *Mouramani Mamadou Touré* (1953).
Feature/Talkie: *Sergeant Bakary Woolén* (1966), d. Lamine Akin.

GUINEA-BISSAU
Feature/Talkie: *Ntturudu* (1986), d. Umban U'Kset, prod. Republic of Guinea-Bissau, starring Mario Acqlino.

GUYANA
Feature/Talkie: *Aggro Seizeman* (1975), d. James Mannas and Brian Stuart-Young, starring Gordon Case and Martha Gonsalves.

HONG KONG
Dramas: *The Widowed Empress*, *The Unfilial Son*, *Revealed by the Pot*, *Stealing the Cooked Ducks* (all 1909), d. Benjamin

PIONEER PRODUCTIONS (continued)

Polaski, prod. Asia Film Co.
Feature: *Yanzhi/Rouge* (pr. 20 Feb 1925), d. Li Beihai, starring Li Minwei an Lin Chuchu, contemporary melodrama prod. Minxin Co.
Talkie: *Shazai Dongang/The Idiot's Wedding Night* (pr. 20 Sept 1933), d. Li Behei, starring Liu Mung-Kok and Yeung Sin-Nung, Cantonese comedy prod. Zhonghua Co.

HUNGARY
Film: *The Emperor Franz Josef Opening the Millenial Exhibition* (1896), d. Arnold Sziklay.
Drama: *Siófoki kaland* (pr. 29 Apr 1898)— shown as sequence in stage production *Mozgáfényképek/Moving Pictures*.
Feature: *Ma és holnap* (1912), d. Mihály Kertész (Michael Curtiz).
Talkie: *A Kék Bálvány* (pr. 25 Sept 1931), d. Lajos Lázár, starring Pál Jávor.
Colour: *Ludas Matyi* (1949), d. K. Nádasdy.

ICELAND
Film: various short subjects shot 1904.
Drama: *Aevintyri Jóns og Gvendar/The Adventures of Jön and Gvendur* (1923), d. Loftur Gudmundsson.
Feature/Talkie: *Milli fjalls og fjöru/Between Mountain and Shore* (1948), d. Loftur Gudmundsson.

INDIA
Film: *Cocoanut Fair* (1897), maker unknown, probably English. First by Indian: *Dancing Scenes from the Flower of Persia* (1898), d. Hiralel Sen.
Drama: *Alibaba and the Forty Thieves* (1898), d. Hiralel Sen.
Feature: *Raja Harischandra* (pr. 17 May 1913), d. D. G. Phalke of Bombay.
Talkie (Hindi): *Alam Ara* (pr. 14 Mar 1931), d. A. M. Irani, prod. Imperial Film Co., starring Master Vithal and Zubeida.
Talkie (Bengali): *Jamai Sasthi* (1931), prod. Madan Theatres.
Colour: *Sairandhri* (1933), prod. Pune by Prabhat Studio (processed and printed Germany).

INDONESIA
Feature: *Loetoeng Kasaroeng* (1927), d. G. Kruger at Bandung.
Talkie: *Njai Dasima* (1931), d. Lie Tek Soi and Bakhtiar Effendi, prod. Tan's Film.

IRAN
Film: scenes of religious procession and of Shah's private zoo, d. Mirza Ebrahim Khan (court photographer to Shah Mozaffareddin) 1900.
Drama/Feature: *Abi and Rabi* (1932), comedy, d. Oranes Ohanian.
Talkie: *Dokhta Lor* (1934), d. Abdol Hoseyn Sepenta (made in India). In Iran: *The Tempest of Life* (1948), d. Ali Daria Baigi.

IRAQ
Drama/Feature/Talkie: *Leila in Iraq* (1949).

IRELAND
Film: Visit of King Edward VII to Lismore Castle 2 May 1904, f. by Thos Horgan of Youghal.
Drama: *Fun at Finglas Fair* (1915), d. F. J. McCormick. Never released, as all prints destroyed in Easter Rising.
Feature: *A Girl of Glenbeigh* (1917), starring Kathleen O'Connor, prod. Film Co. of

Ireland.
Talkie (English): *The Voice of Ireland* (1932), d. Col Victor Haddick. Talkie (Irish): see Languages: Irish Gaelic (p. 000).

ISRAEL
Film: documentary about Jewish settlement in Palestine (1913), d. Akiva Arie Weiss.
Drama: *Yerahmiel the Shlemiel and other short comedies* (1926), d. Nathan Axelrod.
Feature: *Oded Hanoded* (1933), d. Nathan Axelrod.
Talkie: *Me'al Hekhoravot* (1936), d. Nathan Axelrod.

ITALY
Film: *Arrivo del treno nello stazione di Milano* (1896), d. Italo Pacchioni.
Drama: *La Presa di Roma* (1905), d. Filoteo Albernini, starring Carlo Rosaspina.
Feature: *La Portatrice di pane* (1911), d. S. De Montépin, prod. Vesuvio Films, Naples.
Colour Feature: *Cyrano de Bergerac* (1925), d. Augusto Genina, prod. Unione Cinematographica Italia, starring Pierre Magnier.
Talkie: *La Canzone dell' amore* (1930), d. Genarro Righelli.

IVORY COAST
Film: *Sur la dune de la solitude* (1964), d. Timité Bassori.
Feature/Talkie: *Korogo* (1964), d. Georges Keita.

JAMAICA
Feature/Talkie: *The Harder They Come* (1972), d. Perry Henzell, starring Jimmy Cliff and Janet Bartley.

JAPAN
Film: street scenes in Tokyo's Ginza and shots of geisha from Shimbasi and Gion districts, d. Tsunekichi Shibata of the Mitsukoshi Department Store's photo dept., 1897.
Drama: *Inazuma goto Hobaku no Ba/The Lightning Robber is Arrested* (1899), d. Shibata Tsunekichi, starring Yokoyama Umpei as the detective and Sakamato Keijiro as the robber, prod. Koyo Komada.
Feature: *The Life Story of Tasuke Shiobara* (1912).
Talkie: *Taii no Musume* (1929), prod. Nikkatsu Co.
Colour: *Karumen Kokyo ni Kaeru* (1951), d. Keisuke Kinoshita, starring Hideko Takamine.

JORDAN
Feature/Talkie: *Watani Habibi* (1964).

KENYA
Feature/Talkie: *The Bride Price* (1992), d. Shatru Jit Paul, prod. in Swahili and English versions by Malaika Films.

KOREA
Drama: *The Righteous Revenge* (1919), d. Kim Do-san.
Feature: *A Pledge in the Moonlight* (1923), morality tale about importance of keeping money in banks, d. Yun Paek-nam.
Talkie: *Chun Hyang-jon* (1935), d. Yi Pil-u and Yi Myong-u.

KUWAIT
Feature/Talkie: *Bas Ya Bahar* (1972), d.

Khaled el Seddik, starring Mohamad Monsour and Amal Baker.

LAOS
Feature/Talkie: *Gun Shots in the Valley of the Jugs* (1983).

LEBANON
Drama/Feature: *The Adventures of Elias Mabrouk* (1929), comedy about Lebanese emigrant returning from US, d. Jordano Pidutti.
Talkie: *In the Ruins of Ba'albak* (1936), d. George Costi, prod. Lumnar Film Co.

LIBYA
Feature/Talkie: *Lorsque le destin s'acharne* (1972), d. A. Zarrouk.

LIECHTENSTEIN
Feature/Talkie: *Kinder der Berge* (1958), d. Georg Tressler, prod. Rialto-Filmproduktions-Anstalt of Vaduz, starring Maximilian Schell and Barbara Rütting with Prince Constantin and Princess Monika of Liechtenstein as themselves.

LUXEMBOURG
Feature/Talkie: *Wât huet e gesôt?* (1980), d. Paul Scheuer, prod. AFO-Film.

MALAGASY REPUBLIC
Film: Centenary celebrations of martyrdom of Malagasy hero Rasalama, d. M. Raberono 1937.
Feature/Talkie: *Le Retour* (1973), d. Randrasana Ignace Solo.

MALAYSIA (MALAYA)
Talkie: *Chandu* (1939), prod. Malayan Films Inc.

MALI
Drama: *Bambo* (1968).
Feature/Talkie: *Les Wandyalankas* (1973), d. Alkaly Kaba.

MALTA
Feature/Talkie: *Katarin* (1977), d. Cecil Satariano, starring Anna Stafrace.

MAURITANIA
Feature/Talkie: *Soleil O* (1971), d. Med Hondo.

MEXICO
Drama: *Don Juan Tenorio* (1898), d. Salvador Barragan, starring Paco Gavilanes Toscano.
Feature: *Fatal Orgullo* (1916), prod. México Lux.
Talkie: *Más fuerte que el deber* (1930), d. Raphael J. Sevilla.
Colour: *Novillero* (1936), d. Boris Maicon— Cinecolor.

MOROCCO
Feature/Talkie: *Itto* (1934), d. Jean Benoit-Levy.

NEPAL
Feature/Talkie: *Harischandra* (1951).

NETHERLANDS
Drama: *Muis Hamel bij den Criffeur* (1904), d. Albert and Willy Mullens.
Feature: *De Levende Ladder* (1913), d. Maurits H. Binger, prod. Hollandia.
Talkie: *Vader des Vaderlands* (1933), d. G. J. Teunissen.

PIONEER PRODUCTIONS (continued)

NEW ZEALAND
Film: *Opening of the Auckland Exhibition* (f. 1 Dec 1898), d. A. E. Whitehouse.
Drama: *A Message from Mars* (1903), d. W. F. Brown.
Feature: *The Test* (1916), d. and starring Rawdon Blandford.
Talkie: *Down on the Farm* (1935), d. Lee Hill and Stuart Pitt, prod. Sound Film Productions Ltd.

NICARAGUA
Feature/Talkie: *Alsino y el Condor* (1982), d. Miguel Littin.

NIGER
Film: *Aouré* (1962), d. Mustapha Allasane.
Feature/Talkie: *FVVA* (1971), d. Mustapha Allasane.

NIGERIA
Drama: *My Father's Burden* (1961), d. Segun Olusola.
Feature/Talkie: *Two Men and a Goat* (1966), d. Edward Jones Horatio.

NORWAY
Film: reception of the newly elected King Haakon VII in Oslo, 1905.
Drama: *The Dangerous Life of a Fisherman* (1907), prod. Norsk Kinematograf A/S, starring Alma Lund.
Feature: *Anny—Story of a Prostitute* (1912), d. Adam Eriksen, starring Julie Jansen.
Talkie: *The Great Christening* (pr. 26 Dec 1931), d. Einar Sissener and Tancred Ibsen, starring Einar Sissener.

OUTER MONGOLIA
Feature/Talkie: *At the Frontier* (1937).

PAKISTAN
Feature/Talkie: *Teri Yaad* (1948), prod. Dewan Pictures, d. Dawood Chand, starring Asha Posley and Nasir Khan. Urdu.

PAPUA NEW GUINEA
Feature/Talkie: *Tinpis Run* (1991), d. and prod. Pengau Nengo, starring Leo Konga and Oscar Wenu. (Second film in Pidgin English—see p. 174.)

PARAGUAY
Feature/Talkie: *Cerro Cora* (1978), starring Rosa Ros and Roberto de Felice, d. Ladislao Gonzalez.

PERU
Film: *Peruvian Centaurs* (1908), actuality of cavalry manoeuvres.
Drama: *Negocio al Agua* (1913), d. Frederico Blume.
Feature: *Luis Pardo* (1927), biopic of brigand of that name, d. and starred Enrique Cornejo Villanueva.
Talkie: *Resaca* (1934), d. Alberto Santana.

PHILIPPINES
Film: *El Fusilamiento de Rizal* (1908).
Feature: *Dalagang Bukid* (1919), d. José Nepomuceno.
Talkie: *Ang Aswang/The Vampire* (1932).

POLAND
Film: actualities made by Kazimierz Proszynski with a camera of his own invention—the 'pleograph'—1894.
Drama: *His First Visit to Warsaw* (1908), comedy starring Antoni Fertner.
Feature: *Dzieje Grzechu* (pr. 26 Aug 1911), d.

Antoni Bednarczyk, starring Maria Mirska and Teodor Roland.
Talkie: *The Morals of Madame Dulska* (1930), d. B. Newolyn.

PORTUGAL
Film: *Workers Leaving the Confiança Factory*, pr. Oporto 12 Nov 1896, d. Aurélio Da Paz Dos Reis.
Drama: *Rapto duma Actriz* (1907), d. Lino Ferreira, starring Carlos Leal and Luz Velozo.
Feature: *A Rosa do Adro* (1919).
Talkie: *A Severa* (pr. 17 June 1931), d. Jose Leitao de Barros, prod. Super-Filmes, starring Dina Teresa and Conde Marialava.

PUERTO RICO
Drama: *Por la Hembra y el Gallo/For Women and Fighting Cocks* (1916), prod. Rafael Colorado and Antonio Capella for Sociedad Industrial Cine Puerto Rico.
Talkie: *Romance Tropical* (1934), about a lovesick young musician who seeks fortune at sea, scripted by the poet Luis Palés Matos, d. Juan Emilio Viguié Cajas.

ROMANIA
Film: *HM the King Riding to the Palace, Escorted by his General Staff and by the Foreign Military Attachés* (f. 10 May 1897) and actualities of Bucharest racecourse, a fair and the Capsa coffee house (1897), d. Paul Menu.
Drama: *Amor fatal* (pr. 26 Sept 1911), d. Grigore Brezeanu, starring Lucia Sturdza and Tony Bulandra.
Feature: *Razboiul Independentei* (pr. 1 Sept 1912), d. Grigore Brezeanu, starring C. Nottra and Ar. Demetriade.
Talkie: *Ciuleandra* (pr. 30 Oct 1930), d. Martin Berger, starring Jeana Popovici-Voinea.

RUSSIA
Film: *The Religious Procession Carrying Over the Miraculous Icon of the Virgin in the Kharkov Kuryazh Monastery*, f. 19 Sept 1896 by A. P. Fedeksky at Kharkov, Ukraine (then part of Russia).
Drama: *Boris Gudonov* (1907), d. A. O. Drankov, starring F. G. Martini and Z. Lopanskaya.
Feature: *The Defence of Sebastopol* (pr. 15 October 1911), d. Vasili Goncharov and Aleksandr Khanzhonkov, starring Andrei Gromov.
Talkie: *The Earth Thirsts* (1930), d. Yuli Raizman.
Colour: *Nightingale, Little Nightingale* (1936), d. Nikolai Ekk.

SAUDI ARABIA
Feature/Talkie: *Sinbad, the Little Sailor* (1990).

SENEGAL
Film: *C'était il y a 4 ans* (1955), d. Paulin Vieyra.
Feature/Talkie: *La Noire de . . .* (1967), d. Ousmane Sembene.

SINGAPORE
Feature/Talkie: *White Golden Dragon* (1936).

SLOVAKIA
Feature: *Janosik* (1921) d. and pr. Jaroslav Sinkel and Frantisek Holivy.

SLOVENIA
Film: *Sejem v Ljutomeru/Ljutomer's Fair*

(1905), d. Karol Grossmann.

SOMALIA
Film/Drama: *The Love that Knows no Barrier* (1961), d. Hossein Manrok.
Feature/Talkie: *Town and Village* (1968), d. El Hadji Mohamed Giumale.

SOUTH AFRICA
Film: scene taken from front of tram travelling down Commissioner Street, Johannesburg, d. Edgar Hyman, 1896.
Drama: *The Star of the South* (1911), about theft of diamond found on banks of Vaal by a Hottentot, prod. Springbok Film Co.
Feature: *Die Voortrekkers* (pr. 16 Dec 1916), d. Harold Shaw, prod. African Film Productions Ltd, starring Dick Cruickshanks and Zulu actor Goba as Dingaan. Claimed (in S. Africa) that *The Covered Wagon* (US 23) was inspired by this film.
Talkie (Afrikaans): *Moedertjie* (1931), d. Joseph Albrecht, starring Carl Richter and Joan du Toit.
Talkie (English): *They Built a Nation* (1938), d. Joseph Albrecht, prod. African Film Productions Ltd.

SPAIN
Film: *Salida de misa de doce en la Iglesia del Pilar en Zaragoza* (1896), d. Eduardo Jimeno.
Drama: *Riña en un Café* (1897), d. Fructuoso Gelabert.
Feature: *Lucha por la herencia* (1911), d. Otto Mulhauser, prod. Alhambra Films.
Talkie: *Yo quiero que me lleven a Hollywood* (pr. 20 June 1932), d. Edgar Neville.
Colour: *En un rincon de España* (1949), d. Jerónimo Mihura.

SRI LANKA
Feature/Talkie: *Banda Nagarayata Pemineema* (1953).

SUDAN
Feature/Talkie: *Hopes and Dreams* (1969), d. Al Rachid Mehdi.

SURINAM
Feature/Talkie: *Wan Pipel* (1976), d. Pim de la Parra, starring Borger Breeveld and Diana Gangaram.

SWEDEN
Film/Drama: *Slagsmål i Gamla Stockholm* (pr. 3 July 1897), two 17th-century cavaliers fighting over a girl, d. Ernest Florman, prod. Numa Handels & Fabriks AB.
Feature: *Blodets Röst* (pr. 20 Oct 1913), d. Victor Sjöström, prod. Svenska Biografteatern, starring Victor Sjöström and Ragna Wettergreen.
Talkie: *Konstgjorda Svensson* (pr. 14 Oct 1929), d. Gustaf Edgren, prod. Film AB Minerva, starring Fridolf Rhudin and Brita Apelgren.
Colour: *The Bells in Old Town* (1947), d. Ragnar Hylton-Cavallier, prod. Europa Film—Cinecolor, starring Edvard Person.

SWITZERLAND
Films: *Exposition Nationale Suisse, Genève; men bathing; smoker; man drinking from bottle* d. Casimir Sivan mid-1896; *Laveuses; Défilé de 8ème Bataillon; Cortège Arabe; Danse Egyptienne* d. 1896–97 by Henri Lavanchy-Clarke, Lever Bros representative in Geneva – many contained product placement for

PIONEER PRODUCTIONS (continued)

Sunlight Soap.

Drama: *Une Adventure de Redzipet* (1908), d. Albert Roth-de-Markus, starring Paul Marville.

Feature: *Le Spectre de minuit/Lo Spettro di mezzanotte* (1915), d. Giovanni Zannini, prod. Talia-Film, starring Giovanni Zannini and Lina Pellegrini.

Talkie: *Bünzli's Grosstadtabenteuer* (1930), d. Robert Wohlmut, starring Freddy Scheim.

SYRIA

Drama/Feature: *Al Moutaham al Bari* (1928), gangster movie, d. and starring Ayoub Badri, prod. Hermon Film.

Talkie: *Leila Al-Amira* (1947), d. Niazi Mustafa.

TADZHIKISTAN

Feature/Talkie: *Flight of the Bee* (1998), d. and prod. Jamshed Usmanov and Min Biong Hun (S. Korea) – won top award 16th Turin Festival.

TAIWAN

Drama/Feature: *Eyes of the Buddha* (1922), d. Tanaka King on behalf of Japanese occupying authorities as pro-Japanese propaganda.

Talkie: *Awakening from Nightmare* (1950), d. Zhong You, prod. Central Motion Picture Co.

TANZANIA

Feature/Talkie: *Gumu* (1935).

THAILAND

Drama/Feature: *Miss Suwan* (1922), d. and prod. Henry McRay and the Wasuvati family. Performers were 'noble families and high-ranking government officials'.

TRINIDAD

Drama: *Callaloo* (1937), starring Ursula Johnson.

Feature/Talkie: *The Right and Wrong* (1970), d. Harbance Kumar, prod. De Luxe Films, starring Ralph Maharaj and Jesse Macdonald.

TUNISIA

Drama: *Ain el Ghezal* (1924), d. Haydée Samama-Chikly, starring Si Haj Hadi Djeheli.

Feature: *The Secret of Fatouma* (1928), d. Dedoncloit, starring Véra de Yourgaince.

Talkie: *Tergui* (1935), d. Abdelaziz Hassine.

TURKEY

Film: *Collapse of the Russian Monument in Ayestafanos* (1914), d. Fuat Uzkinay.

Drama: *The Wedding of Himmet Aga* (1916).

Feature: *Pençe* (1917), d. Sedat Simavi.

Talkie: *Istanbul Sokaklarinda* (1931), d. Muhsin Ertugrul, prod. Ipek Film.

The first and only feature film from Vatican State—the world's smallest sovereign nation—was *The Gates of Heaven* (Vat 44), which its director Vittorio De Sica declared to have been 'one of the finest films I ever made'. Completed the day the Americans arrived in Rome, the 'Open City', it was never released as the Vatican, according to De Sica, found his view of miracles 'too unorthodox'. One of the officials responsible for overseeing the production was Monsignor Giovanni Battista Montini of the Vatican Diplomatic Service, later to become Pope Paul VI. 'I can still remember him looking through my camera,' De Sica recalled. 'In Italy there is a custom that whenever anyone looks through a camera for the first time, he must buy drinks for everyone. So Paul bought us all drinks down at the Rome railway terminal.'

UK

Film: *Traffic Crossing Leeds Bridge* (1888), d. Louis Aimé Augustin Le Prince.

Drama: *The Soldier's Courtship* (f. Apr 1896), d. Robert Paul, starring Fred Storey.

Feature: *Oliver Twist* (1912), d. Thomas Bentley, prod. Hepworth, starring Ivy Millais and Alma Taylor.

Colour Feature: *The World, the Flesh and the Devil* (1914), d. F. Martin Thornton, prod. Union Jack Photoplays and Natural Colour Kinematograph Co., starring Frank Esmond.

Talkie: *Blackmail* (pr. 21 June 1929), d. Alfred Hitchcock, prod. British International Pictures, starring Anny Ondra and John Longden.

URUGUAY

Film: *Una Carrera de Ciclismo en el Velodrome de Arroyo Seco* (1898), d. Felix Oliver.

Drama: *Oliver, Juncal 108* (1900), d. and starring Felix Oliver.

Feature: *Del Pingo al Volante* (1928), d. Roberto Kouri, prod. Bonne Garde.

Talkie: *Dos Destinos* (1936), d. Juan Etchebchere, prod. Estudios Ciclolux, starring Pepe Corbi.

USA

Film: actualities of fencers and wrestlers, etc., d. W. K. L. Dickson, prod. Edison Co., 1892.

Drama: *The Execution of Mary Queen of Scots* (f. 28 Aug 1895), d. Alfred Clark, prod. Raff & Gammon and Edison Co., starring Mr R. L. Thomas (as Mary!).

Feature: *Oliver Twist* (pr. 20 May 1912), prod. H. A. Spanuth, starring Nat C. Goodwin and Winnie Burns.

Colour Feature: *The Gulf Between* (pr. 21 Sept 1917), prod. Technicolor Motion Picture Corp., starring Grace Darmond and Niles Welch.

Talkie: *The Jazz Singer* (pr. 6 Oct 1927), d. Alan Crosland, prod. Warner Bros, starring Al Jolson.

VENEZUELA

Film: *Muchachas bañádose en el Lago* (1897) and *Un gran especialista sacando muelas en el Hotel Europa* (1897), d. Manuel Trujillo Durán at Maracaibo.

Drama: *Carnival in Caracas* (1909), d. Augusto Gonzalez Vidal and M. A. Gonham.

Feature: *The Lady of Cayenas* (1913), parody of *Camille*, d. E. Zimmerman.

Talkie: *El Rompimiento* (1938), d. Antonio Delgado Gomez, starring Rafael Guinard.

VIETNAM

Drama: *Vie du Detham* (1910), biopic of guerilla leader, d. Rene Batisson.

Talkie: *The Flower from the Cemetery* (1939), prod. Société Indochine Films et Cinéma.

YUGOSLAVIA

Film: *Odhod od mase v Ljutomeru* (1905), made in 17.5mm by Ljutomer lawyer Karl Grossman.

Drama/Feature: *Zivot i Dela Besmrtnog Vozda Karadjordje* (pr. 17 Nov 1911), biopic of 'Immortal Leader Karadjordje', d. I. Stojadinovic, starring M. Petrovic.

Talkie: *Nevinost Bez Zastite* (1939), d. D. Aleksic.

ZAIRE

Feature/Talkie: *La Nièce captive* (1969), d. Luc Michez.

ZIMBABWE

Feature/Talkie: *Jit* (1991), d. Michael Raeburn, starring Dominic Makuvachuma and Sibongile Nene.

1909–19 February 1910) because the producers did not consider that the American public were prepared to sit through a film that lasted over an hour. The first feature film to be released in its entirety in the USA was *Dante's Inferno* (It 11) in August 1911. *Queen Elizabeth* (Fr 12), which is nearly always cited as the first feature film shown in America, was in fact the third, because in the meantime the first domestic feature-length production to be shown whole had been released. This was *Oliver Twist* (US 12), produced by H. A. Spanuth and starring Nat C. Goodwin and Winnie Burns, which was premièred on 20 May 1912, seven weeks before *Queen Elizabeth* (12 July 1912). However, the prejudice against long films was so insistent in America (at least among producers and distributors) that even in 1913 the major European success of that year,

August Blom's feature *Atlantis* (Den 13), had to be compressed into a half-length version for US release.

The earliest surviving American feature film is James Keene's *Richard III* (US 12), starring Frederick Warde as Shakespeare's usurping king, which had been originally released in October 1912. The third full-length feature produced and shown as such in the US, the pioneer production was long considered lost to posterity. It was rediscovered only in 1996, when retired Oregon projectionist William Buffum, preparing to move house, found the five faded reels of nitrate film in his attic. He donated them to the American Film Institute, one of its most important acquisitions ever.

Domestic production was a modest five in 1912 and 12 in 1913, the real watershed being in 1914, when no less than 212 features were produced. The delay in going over to feature-film making suggests that the impact of *Queen Elizabeth*'s successful exploitation by Adolph Zukor in 1912 may not have been so influential as historians of the cinema have generally believed. Competition from the major European film-producing nations, most of whom had a two-year lead on America in feature production (see p. 10), may in fact have been the deciding factor.

Production Output

Total world output of feature films is nearly 4000 annually. Asian countries (including Australasia) account for approx. 50% of output, European countries (including Russia) for approx. 33%, the Middle East and Africa for approx. 5.5%, North America for approx. 6%, and Latin America for approx. 5.5%.

The country with the largest production output in the world is India, with a peak of 948 full-length feature releases in 1990 and an annual output that has exceeded 680 each year since 1979.

India has also produced **more feature films than any other country**, a total of over 30,000 from 1913 to 2000 inclusive.

The twelve major film-producing countries of the 1990s in terms of output are the following (approximate average annual output in brackets): India (789); USA (328); Japan (256); Hong Kong (155); France (148); Philippines (142); Bangladesh (120); China (120); Russia (107); Italy (104); Pakistan (72); Germany (64).

FEATURE-FILM PRODUCTION

The following countries have held the production record since the inception of feature films:

1906–11	Australia	1922–32	Japan	1940	Japan
1912	Hungary	1933–35	USA	1941–53	USA
1913	Germany	1936–38	Japan	1954–70	Japan
1914–22	USA	1939	USA	1971–99	India

The smallest country with an established film industry is Iceland, whose population of 251,000 are among the most frequent filmgoers in the world with an average of 4.5 visits a year (about three times the Scandinavian average). Feature production began in 1948 with Loftur Gudmundsson's *Between Mountain and Shore* and continued sporadically through the next three decades with a dozen features made up to 1977. The breakthrough for the establishment of a permanent film industry came in 1978 with the setting up of the Icelandic Film Fund by an act of Parliament. The first grants from the fund were made the following year and three full-length features went into production immediately. The number of features released annually since then has fluctuated between two and seven, and it is estimated that the more successful productions are seen by as many as a quarter of the population of the nation. Remarkably, Iceland's biggest box-office success, August Gadmundson's *On Top* (Ice 83), achieved an audience of 120,000 – nearly half the population.

Iceland's first full-scale film studio able to accommodate the making of feature films was built in 1988 by Jon Thor Hannesson and Snorri Thorisson. The following year Icelandic cinema, once regarded as a curiosity, achieved international recognition when Gudny Halldorsdottir's *Under the Glacier* (Ice 89) won the Lübecker Lens, top prize at Lübeck's annual Nordic Film Days Festival.

The best year for UK film production was 1936, with 192 features released. The most productive year of the silent era was 1920, with 155 features.

The worst year for UK film production (since 1914) was 1988 when only 27 features were released. The worst years of silent pictures were 1925 and 1926 with 33 releases. On two occasions in the past 85 years, production in Britain has come to a total halt. No films were made during November 1924 and for a three-week period in 1975.

The best year for US film production was 1921 with 854 feature releases.

The worst year for US film production (since 1913) was 1963 with 121 feature releases.

The highest output of any Hollywood studio was 101 features from Paramount in 1921; highest of the sound era was 68 by Paramount in 1936 and the same number from Warner's in 1937.

The largest number of foreign films released in the USA in any one year was 361 in 1964. The number of domestic releases was 141. The lowest number of foreign films was 30 in 1943, against 397 Hollywood productions.

Worldwide Feature Film Production 1906–99

The figures given in the chart on pp. 16–17 refer to feature films of an hour or more in length, including co-productions and feature-length documentaries. Television movies (TVMs) are excluded unless they have had a theatrical release. Production is attributed to the country in which the production company is registered. It should be noted that figures are for the number of new pictures released, which in many cases is not far short of the number produced. In the case of the USA, however, the gap has been widening considerably in recent years. The number of American films which failed to make it into the cinemas went over the 50% mark for the first time in 1988, up from 27% only four years earlier.

WORLDWIDE FEATURE FILM PRODUCTION 1906–1999

	Algeria	Argentina	Australia	Austria	Bangladesh	Belgium	Brazil	Bulgaria	Canada[1]	China[4]	Cuba	Cz	Denmark	Egypt	Eire	Finland	France	Germany[5]	E.Germany	Greece	Hong Kong[3]	Hungary	India	Indonesia[2]	Israel
1906	0	0	1	0		0	0	0	0	0	0	0	0	0	0	0	0	0		0	—	0	0	0	0
1907	0	0	2	0		0	0	0	0	0	0	0	0	0	0	0	1	0		0	—	0	0	0	0
1908	0	0	0	0		0	0	0	0	0	0	0	0	0	0	0	0	0		0	—	0	0	0	0
1909	0	0	0	0		0	0	0	0	0	0	0	0	0	0	0	1	0		0	—	0	0	0	0
1910	0	0	3	0		0	0	0	0	0	0	0	0	0	0	0	—	0		0	—	0	0	0	0
1911	0	0	16	0		0	0	0	0	0	0	0	1	0	0	0	—	1		0	—	0	0	0	0
1912	0	0	8	1		0	0	0	0	0	0	0	2	0	0	0	—	3		1	—	14	0	0	0
1913	0	0	4	6		3	2	0	1	0	1	0	13	0	0	1	—	49		0	—	11	3	0	0
1914	0	0	3	9		0	—	0	0	0	1	0	16	0	0	1	—	29		0	—	19	1	0	0
1915	0	4	8	10		0	3	1	1	0	1	0	24	0	0	0	—	60		0	—	27	0	0	0
1916	0	12	15	7		0	6	0	2	0	1	0	34	0	0	1	—	107		1	—	52	0	0	0
1917	0	16	6	9		0	4	2	2	0	3	1	40	0	1	0	—	117		0	—	77	3	0	0
1918	0	2	13	40		0	2	0	1	0	1	13	21	0	0	0	—	211		1	—	107	7	0	0
1919	0	15	16	56		1	6	0	2	0	2	23	20	0	0	0	—	345		0	—	48	8	0	0
1920	0	5	10	48		1	6	0	2	0	5	17	8	0	3	1	—	485		0	—	54	27	0	0
1921	0	11	15	47		7	2	3	0	—	8	25	10	0	0	2	—	646		0	—	25	44	0	0
1922	0	10	7	64		8	4	3	8	—	5	30	8	0	3	3	—	474		3	—	6	64	0	0
1923	0	15	7	45		3	6	1	2	—	0	18	15	0	0	3	—	347		2	—	13	52	0	0
1924	0	13	10	30		4	4	0	0	—	0	8	9	0	0	4	68	271		1	—	9	54	0	0
1925	0	15	9	24		10	12	1	0	—	1	17	8	0	2	2	73	228		2	—	3	86	0	0
1926	0	7	16	17		2	12	0	0	80	3	31	7	0	0	2	55	195		2	—	3	94	1	1
1927	0	6	4	18		2	10	2	2	75	2	24	6	1	0	6	74	241		2	—	8	90	1	—
1928	0	6	13	19		1	10	2	3	50	1	16	4	4	0	3	94	226		2	—	2	109	2	—
1929	0	4	3	22		4	13	7	0	40	3	35	3	2	0	7	52	194		4	—	5	140	5	—
1930	0	5	3	17		3	14	3	1	—	2	23	5	4	0	2	98	180		13	—	3	194	7	—
1931	0	4	6	9		3	4	2	0	—	0	23	4	2	0	7	157	199		6	—	3	228	5	—
1932	0	2	4	11		5	8	0	0	60	0	24	6	6	1	3	156	150		6	—	8	148	5	—
1933	0	6	7	18		1	6	2	1	—	0	44	10	6	0	5	152	129		2	—	9	144	1	—
1934	0	6	9	17		6	2	2	2	69	0	34	8	7	0	4	119	142		1	—	12	171	3	—
1935	0	13	3	32		5	2	0	3	80	0	34	11	12	1	5	128	111		0	—	18	233	3	—
1936	0	15	6	25		3	3	1	5	—	0	31	6	13	1	9	145	128		0	—	28	217	2	—
1937	0	28	5	18		7	0	1	6	75	1	49	13	17	0	12	124	108		1	150	36	179	3	—
1938	0	41	7	11		5	3	1	0	86	2	41	10	10	2	20	122	113		3	55	35	172	4	—
1939	0	50	4	11		3	2	1	1	58	8	41	9	15	0	21	94	118		1	100	27	165	4	—
1940	0	49	3	10		2	7	2	0	—	2	31	12	12	0	22	40	89		0	—	39	170	13	—
1941	0	47	3	5		3	1	4	0	—	1	21	16	12	0	15	41	71		1	—	41	167	31	—
1942	0	56	1	6		5	1	1	0	—	1	11	18	22	0	18	74	64		0	—	48	173	1	—
1943	0	36	0	10		1	1	3	0	—	3	10	18	15	0	22	81	83		3	—	53	161	0	—
1944	0	24	1	8		1	7	1	1	—	1	9	18	23	0	16	27	75		2	—	22	127	6	—
1945	0	23	1	1		9	5	2	0	—	2	3	10	42	0	20	50	72		5	—	3	99	0	—
1946	0	32	3	4		8	11	4	3	—	1	11	13	52	0	16	81	1	(3)	4	—	2	200	0	—
1947	0	38	1	13	0	3	9	3	0	—	2	19	13	55	0	15	88	6	(4)	6	—	4	281	0	—
1948	0	41	1	25	0	3	14	0	2	—	2	17	10	49	0	16	84	21	(7)	6	—	5	263	3	—
1949	0	47	4	25	0	1	18	0	5	10	4	20	8	44	0	16	97	56	(12)	8	256	7	291	8	—
1950	0	56	1	17	0	2	30	1	3	26	10	20	14	48	0	14	104	61	(10)	6	202	4	241	23	—
1951	0	53	3	28	0	1	22	2	3	17	5	8	18	52	0	19	109	69	(8)	12	192	9	221	40	—
1952	0	35	1	19	0	2	31	2	1	8	5	16	12	59	0	28	100	73	(6)	17	259	5	233	42	—
1953	0	37	1	28	0	4	31	1	2	10	4	18	12	62	0	25	111	103	(7)	19	188	6	260	50	—
1954	0	45	2	22	0	5	25	4	2	24	11	14	13	65	0	28	98	109	(9)	19	167	8	278	59	—
1955	0	43	2	28	0	5	24	2	0	23	7	16	13	51	0	30	110	128	(13)	16	235	10	289	64	—
1956	0	36	2	37	1	8	21	9	2	40	5	21	13	39	0	18	129	122	(19)	26	311	10	295	36	—
1957	0	15	3	26	0	3	36	5	3	41	3	25	16	40	1	21	142	107	(22)	28	223	15	294	21	—
1958	0	32	1	23	0	12	41	9	3	101	6	29	16	55	3	17	126	115	(17)	38	237	13	294	19	—
1959	0	22	2	19	3	6	30	3	4	79	5	33	14	58	2	15	133	106	(28)	59	239	18	304	16	—
1960	0	31	2	20	2	9	29	10	2	59	2	30	19	59	0	18	158	94	(24)	68	293	14	318	38	—
1961	0	25	1	23	5	9	36	9	5	26	2	39	22	52	1	18	167	80	(27)	56	303	19	298	37	3
1962	0	32	1	20	5	11	28	8	4	33	2	35	23	49	0	21	125	61	(24)	78	261	17	315	12	4
1963	1	27	0	15	4	4	21	9	5	39	4	36	21	48	0	14	141	66	(20)	66	260	21	302	19	5
1964	0	37	0	19	17	2	23	10	14	28	6	38	19	45	0	6	148	77	(16)	94	235	18	310	19	6
1965	3	30	0	16	12	5	26	8	15	43	4	40	16	43	0	9	142	69	(14)	96	204	20	322	15	7
1966	1	34	3	18	24	3	30	12	10	12	2	31	18	39	0	7	130	60	(16)	106	171	20	311	13	6
1967	2	27	2	12	22	31	41	15	11	0	3	40	20	33	0	3	120	96	(20)	76	169	22	329	13	10
1968	4	32	1	7	34	10	47	6	13	0	4	36	19	40	1	12	117	107	(16)	95	156	21	349	8	11
1969	2	29	6	3	30	15	46	14	25	0	1	25	23	44	0	9	154	12	(13)	88	158	20	379	9	10
1970	8	28	14	7	41	12	70	25	46	2	0	38	28	48	0	13	138	113	(—)	86	138	20	398	21	9
1971	1	38	10	5	6	16	69	18	32	2	4	37	33	46	0	9	127	99	(12)	83	127	20	432	52	14
1972	9	32	7	9	28	20	81	22	32	5	2	35	17	41	1	6	169	85	(17)	63	133	21	411	50	15
1973	6	39	12	6	31	27	58	18	43	4	3	36	12	43	0	8	200	98	(16)	63	201	18	448	58	14
1974	10	38	11	8	30	16	82	19	41	17	2	38	14	44	0	3	234	80	(15)	38	147	19	432	84	9
1975	3	33	24	6	34	21	90	25	39	25	2	39	17	49	0	5	222	80	(16)	47	109	19	470	39	9
1976	4	21	16	5	44	11	78	20	30	37	5	46	20	47	0	9	214	61	(17)	38	112	17	507	58	11
1977	1	21	17	8	31	30	73	21	39	19	3	42	20	50	1	7	142	60	(15)	21	116	19	555	124	14
1978	5	22	10	3	42	20	101	21	39	45	3	46	16	51	2	10	227	64	(17)	18	135	23	612	81	11
1979	2	33	18	9	52	10	93	22	55	62	6	46	11	39	0	9	234	66	(17)	27	145	25	714	51	13
1980	0	34	12	8	44	21	102	21	54	83	4	45	12	34	5	11	189	49	(15)	26	132	21	742	68	13
1981	0	24	17	11	39	9	80	—	33	105	0	44	12	43	2	16	231	76	(16)	25	127	24	737	71	12
1982	5	17	26	13	42	5	86	17	27	114	3	44	7	41	1	19	164	70	(16)	46	126	27	763	52	12
1983	3	17	20	11	45	11	84	22	34	127	8	41	12	46	2	17	131	77	(16)	48	114	26	741	74	14
1984	3	31	19	14	50	8	90	20	27	143	6	34	13	63	3	20	161	77	(—)	37	125	23	800*	78	16
1985	5	24	17	18	63	7	83	17	58	127	7	44	8	75	2	15	151	77	(19)	23	105	27	912	62	11
1986	3	37	25	12	70	6	79	23	63	125	12	56	10	91	2	29	134	73	(16)	26	109	26	840	64	17
1987	4	33	22	14	65	12	60	26	61	142	10	39	11	70	2	15	133	74	(5)	22	113	24	806	54	14
1988	—	32	23	9	—	15	—	15	—	158	10	42	15	58	1	9	137	57	(—)	13	151	19	773	83	16
1989	—	32	23	16	—	—	25	20	—	146	6	41	17	65	2	10	137	68	(—)	14	199	18	781	104	20
1990	—	9	18	14	—	—	—	19	—	135	10	54	13	67	3	13	144	48		10	272	30	948	115	8
1991	—	17	15	15	—	—	7	16	—	140	—	18	12	56	0	12	156	72		15	274	19	910	57	—
1992	—	10	23	10	—	10	—	14	—	128	—	15	10	66	2	11	155	63		10	160	25	838	31	—
1993	—	13	19	18	130	—	—	8	—	154	—	18	11	72	6	20	133	67		18	154	25	812	27	12
1994	—	10	20	17	—	9	8	5	—	148	—	15	14	21	8	11	138	57		17	140	15	754	32	—
1995	1	23	13	20	—	7	20	—	—	144	—	22	13	25	6	8	141	84		24	154	—	795	30	—
1996	—	32	20	16	—	8	25	10	—	—	—	19	20	28	20	10	134	64		20	116	—	681	26	—
1997	—	28	25	14	—	7	27	—	—	—	—	18	24	16	25	14	151	61		16	94	16	697	24	—
1998	0	36	19	21	—	10	26	—	20	80	—	15	18	16	12	13	147	50		14	92	13	693	8	—
1999	13	31	21	19	—	14	34	—	—	—	—	18	16	19	30	12	181	74		16	95	17	764	—	—

— No data available. 1. Completions per year. 2. Starts per year. 3. Financial year April–March. 4. Excludes co-productions. 5. Figures in brackets for 1946–1991 refer to East Germany.

WORLDWIDE FEATURE FILM PRODUCTION 1906–1999

Italy	Japan	Korea, S.	Malaysia	Mexico	Neths[1]	NZ	Norway	Pakistan	Philippines	Poland	Portugal	Romania	Russia/USSR	Singapore	S. Africa	Spain	Sri Lanka	Sweden[3]	Swz	Thailand	Tunisia	Turkey	UK	USA	Ven	Yug
0	0	0	0	0	0	0	0	0	0	0	0	0	0	0	0	0	0	0	0	0	0	0	0	0	0	0
0	0	0	0	0	0	0	0	0	0	0	0	0	0	0	0	0	0	0	0	0	0	0	0	0	0	0
0	0	0	0	0	0	0	0	0	0	0	0	0	0	0	0	0	0	0	0	0	0	0	0	0	0	0
0	0	0	0	0	0	0	0	0	0	0	0	0	0	0	0	0	0	0	0	0	0	0	0	0	0	0
0	0	0	0	0	0	0	0	0	0	0	0	0	0	0	0	0	0	0	0	0	0	0	0	0	0	0
2	0	0	0	0	0	0	0	0	3	3	0	0	1	0	0	—	0	0	0	0	0	0	0	0	0	1
5	2	0	0	0	0	0	1	0	2	2	0	1	9	0	0	—	0	0	0	0	0	0	2	2	0	—
29	0	0	0	0	1	0	0	0	5	5	0	10	31	0	0	—	0	4	0	0	0	0	18	12	1	—
16	5	0	0	0	5	0	0	0	5	5	0	0	17	0	0	—	0	5	0	0	0	0	15	212	0	—
39	3	0	0	0	7	0	0	0	0	3	0	0	44	0	0	—	0	2	1	0	0	0	73	419	1	—
57	—	0	0	1	9	1	2	0	0	5	0	0	74	0	14	—	0	4	0	0	0	0	107	677	0	—
37	—	0	0	11	5	0	3	—	—	7	0	0	57	0	7	—	0	7	1	0	0	2	66	687	0	—
46	—	0	0	6	10	0	3	—	—	6	0	0	27	0	5	—	0	6	1	0	0	1	76	841	0	6
51	—	0	0	13	5	0	2	—	—	7	4	0	12	0	6	17	0	11	2	0	0	3	122	646	0	—
52	—	0	0	7	10	0	2	—	—	8	2	2	8	0	4	12	0	20	0	0	0	0	155	797	0	—
56	—	0	0	8	10	0	3	—	—	17	3	1	5	0	2	8	0	7	3	0	1	3	137	854	0	—
34	—	0	0	4	11	2	3	—	—	15	2	0	9	0	3	4	0	11	4	1	2	2	110	748	0	—
38	—	3	0	3	6	0	1	—	—	11	7	1	12	0	1	8	0	23	5	1	0	3	68	576	0	—
35	875	4	0	0	6	1	1	—	—	8	3	1	41	0	1	10	0	16	3	1	1	1	49	579	1	—
16	—	8	0	7	2	1	2	—	—	5	0	6	76	0	1	38	0	18	5	2	0	0	33	579	0	—
10	—	7	0	4	4	0	5	—	3	8	1	4	77	0	0	39	0	18	1	3	0	0	33	740	1	—
15	648	14	0	2	1	2	5	—	4	12	1	3	106	0	0	25	0	11	2	3	2	0	48	678	0	—
22	798	13	0	2	1	1	3	—	—	12	1	4	125	0	0	12	0	6	2	8	2	1	80	641	3	0
10	850	—	0	2	1	0	2	—	—	16	1	5	103	0	0	21	0	6	2	—	1	1	81	562	1	—
6	—	—	0	1	1	0	2	—	—	12	5	3	123	0	0	8	0	13	2	—	1	0	75	509	0	—
12	—	—	0	1	0	0	1	—	16	10	2	3	88	0	2	2	0	24	4	—	0	1	93	501	1	—
20	498	—	0	6	1	0	5	—	20	14	0	1	67	0	0	9	0	22	4	—	0	1	110	489	1	4
34	450	—	0	21	0	0	3	—	—	11	0	0	35	0	0	17	0	22	3	—	0	7	115	507	3	2
35	413	—	0	23	8	0	2	—	—	14	3	2	59	0	0	23	0	19	7	—	0	3	145	480	0	0
21	470	—	0	22	9	1	1	—	—	14	1	0	34	0	0	44	0	20	7	—	2	0	165	525	0	0
37	558	—	0	25	11	3	1	—	15	24	1	0	49	1	1	19	0	28	9	—	0	0	192	522	0	0
32	583	5	0	38	5	0	2	—	32	28	3	1	45	—	0	10	0	22	1	—	1	1	176	538	1	0
68	554	—	0	57	3	0	5	—	55	21	4	0	41	—	1	4	0	27	5	10	1	1	134	455	0	0
79	437	—	0	37	4	0	4	—	—	18	1	3	52	—	1	20	0	30	7	12	0	4	84	483	2	1
85	497	—	6	29	2	1	4	—	—	0	3	0	50	0	3	40	0	36	11	—	0	4	50	477	1	0
89	232	—	0	37	—	1	4	—	—	0	2	0	50	0	0	33	0	34	14	—	0	1	46	492	1	0
19	87	—	1	47	—	0	5	—	—	0	4	1	26	0	0	49	0	34	12	—	0	4	39	488	2	0
70	61	—	0	70	—	0	4	—	—	0	4	2	27	0	0	53	0	43	5	—	0	2	47	397	0	0
19	46	—	0	73	—	0	3	—	—	0	3	0	21	0	1	34	0	43	2	—	0	2	35	401	0	0
28	38	—	0	82	2	0	4	—	—	0	4	1	20	0	0	33	0	44	2	—	0	3	39	350	4	0
66	57	4	0	72	1	0	6	—	10	1	6	4	19	—	4	41	0	36	1	—	0	6	41	378	1	0
69	97	13	2	58	0	0	1	0	24	2	7	0	22	—	2	48	0	43	2	—	0	12	58	369	0	2
49	123	22	3	81	2	0	4	0	—	2	4	0	22	—	1	44	0	40	2	—	1	16	74	366	3	4
95	156	20	3	108	2	0	3	4	—	3	7	1	13	—	4	37	0	34	4	10	0	18	101	356	4	3
74	215	5	8	124	0	0	2	15	—	4	2	0	14	—	2	49	0	25	3	—	0	21	81	383	4	4
13	212	5	11	101	1	0	7	10	—	2	2	2	10	15	5	41	0	31	1	—	1	32	75	391	1	6
42	258	—	18	99	1	1	7	7	—	4	8	1	20	14	1	41	0	25	3	—	0	52	101	324	3	5
70	302	—	16	83	2	0	6	10	—	3	4	2	42	21	5	43	6	31	3	—	0	50	102	344	1	9
45	370	18	11	105	0	0	9	7	—	10	3	3	35	13	5	69	5	30	2	—	1	53	110	253	1	7
33	423	15	9	84	2	0	9	19	—	8	0	4	84	20	4	56	7	30	3	—	0	64	95	254	2	14
14	514	42	9	87	0	0	8	31	—	6	4	3	98	12	2	75	7	34	3	—	0	52	91	272	3	10
155	443	44	16	106	3	0	9	27	—	16	1	8	144	13	2	72	8	32	5	—	0	60	115	300	2	15
137	516	80	23	92	4	0	9	33	97	16	4	4	130	19	5	75	9	29	7	—	1	80	111	241	1	15
160	500	109	28	84	1	0	8	34	92	16	5	4	145	17	6	68	9	24	6	50	1	71	99	187	1	14
29	555	85	13	64	6	0	6	38	112	21	2	9	139	12	8	73	9	23	4	43	0	68	110	154	1	14
200	537	91	19	49	1	0	6	34	108	23	2	10	137	19	19	91	8	18	7	35	1	116	109	131	0	32
197	378	115	18	—	5	0	5	34	152	23	5	8	97	27	13	89	6	17	6	96	0	127	126	147	3	22
254	363	146	15	—	2	0	6	46	142	26	8	10	96	21	7	113	11	18	4	48	0	125	107	121	4	18
245	346	148	13	—	3	1	6	67	161	25	8	11	108	19	8	123	15	24	1	44	0	178	75	141	9	17
206	487	189	12	52	1	0	8	54	161	20	6	14	127	11	6	133	15	19	2	44	1	214	80	153	3	20
217	442	124	9	—	6	1	7	72	201	26	5	15	131	12	10	152	20	25	1	54	2	238	69	156	3	21
280	410	155	10	48	7	0	6	66	180	21	7	14	136	10	9	138	21	27	4	51	7	206	89	178	2	31
297	494	219	11	90	4	0	6	99	175	18	4	7	121	5	12	117	20	34	7	52	3	177	73	180	5	36
246	494	229	11	93	6	0	5	91	169	22	4	12	141	5	12	123	20	24	5	64	5	229	85	177	1	29
228	423	209	9	—	3	0	11	85	194	25	4	8	130	4	17	105	17	20	7	73	4	225	103	231	4	23
223	421	202	2	—	4	1	6	79	253	25	7	13	133	3	17	107	14	19	6	74	2	266	97	223	4	23
316	400	122	2	81	6	0	8	99	181	20	8	16	127	3	24	104	20	14	8	70	4	298	90	224	1	21
207	405	125	3	48	11	1	12	93	146	25	6	16	150	4	22	112	18	18	18	81	2	208	80	201	5	16
265	333	141	6	44	9	0	12	107	120	31	11	18	140	1	34	115	41	24	15	83	2	188	81	179	3	11
58	333	94	4	40	14	1	14	111	143	36	10	23	148	4	30	102	31	20	15	90	3	124	80	161	5	19
223	356	134	4	43	8	0	12	109	174	28	18	22	149	2	25	90	30	16	10	130	1	164	64	188	13	18
56	337	102	3	59	8	4	10	74	141	32	19	20	143	2	24	97	75	22	17	98	2	225	43	157	29	15
23	326	117	4	63	9	2	6	87	135	27	5	23	141	0	19	79	35	17	10	148	3	123	49	162	12	16
41	335	96	5	85	14	3	13	80	170	32	6	28	151	0	22	73	29	18	—	150	2	195	38	167	9	24
63	320	91	9	108	7	2	10	58	173	37	13	32	151	0	20	110	75	26	13	142	4	68	41	200	5	26
03	332	87	14	87	11	5	10	84	179	41	8	31	145	0	20	92	56	25	16	138	3	72	32	181	4	24
14	322	97	13	74	13	5	10	66	149	33	7	30	158	0	15	146	65	18	13	117	3	66	37	187	7	32
10	363	91	15	80	15	4	7	85	143	32	4	32	148	0	35	99	33	23	17	109	3	78	33	231	9	28
03	379	81	13	77	12	8	7	82	138	32	8	26	150	0	80	75	34	23	17	141	3	124	42	262	15	34
89	329	80	8	73	16	12	10	92	158	27	2	26	142	0	85	77	26	20	21	134	—	127	47	264	15	30
09	311	73	10	88	13	5	10	106	177	33	4	30	142	0	56	60	18	27	28	102	—	185	30	311	16	24
15	286	90	13	82	17	6	8	76	167	35	5	26	151	0	78	69	18	25	36	130	—	185	30	332	14	26
24	265	—	—	112	10	8	9	88	—	42	9	23	171	0	52	63	—	20	18	—	—	117	27	325	7	35
17	255	—	—	99	13	9	11	101	162	35	7	23	138	0	19	47	—	17	16	—	—	117	38	276	—	33
19	239	—	—	72	13	9	8	84	—	27	4	9	215	0	12	36	11	21	24	—	—	75	29	304	—	25
29	230	—	18	36	12	5	10	91	130	23	9	19	221	0	9	64	24	20	17	—	—	33	31	279	—	—
27	240	—	—	47	13	5	7	91	120	17	8	18	178	—	6	35	—	20	9	96	—	38	37	263	7	3
06	238	65	14	47	16	6	9	88	123	21	14	15	152	—	6	56	—	30	16	64	—	83	33	267	2	—
95	251	64	—	34	16	2	10	76	130	—	12	—	60	—	12	44	26	19	—	57	—	16	37	335	2	—
75	289	64	—	37	18	—	10	64	141	28	9	—	47	1	—	59	24	17	—	41	—	16	46	339	4	—
99	278	64	16	19	18	—	8	63	161	19	4	3	53	1	6	91	26	28	—	40	—	—	55	366	2	5
87	278	59	—	16	13	4	11	66	204	20	8	—	52	3	3	80	—	32	—	30	—	—	72	379	9	—
92	249	43	11	10	22	—	10	51	130	14	16	—	45	4	6	65	—	34	—	13	—	12	73	357	4	10
08	270	49	—	15	22	7	10	49	—	24	—	2	37	8	6	82	20	23	—	9	1	—	83	395	4	4

The other figures for these years refer to West Germany. * Estimated.

Accidents

The largest number of fatalities incurred in the production of a film took place in 1989 when fire engulfed the set of Indian TVM *The Sword of Tipu Sultan*, killing over 40 people.

Reports of prodigious death tolls on Hollywood movies tend to be exaggerated. Neither version of *Ben Hur* (US 25 and US 59) resulted in any deaths, except of horses. **Hollywood's worst accident** took place during production of *Such Men Are Dangerous* (US 30), when two planes collided on the way to shoot a scene. Ten members of the film crew were killed.

Deaths in the course of production have a macabre tendency to come in threes. A helicopter crash during the making of *Twilight Zone* (US 82) resulted in three dead, two of them child actors; three stuntmen were killed on *Hell's Angels* (US 30), though only one of them while actually filming; three horsemen died in the cavalry charge in *They Died with Their Boots On* (US 41). One of the latter was Bill Mead, whose horse tripped as he rode by the side of Errol Flynn. He had the presence of mind to fling his sword forward to avoid falling with it, but by incredible mischance the hilt stuck in the ground and Mead fell on the tip of the blade, impaling himself.

Greater safety precautions on Hollywood sets since the *Twilight Zone* disaster noted above resulted in a sharp decline in accidents. In 1982 there were 214 accidents involving members of the Screen Actors Guild; in 1986 the figure was down to 65, though this included two deaths—stuntmen Dar Robinson and Vic Magnotta.

Sadly, the improved record has been marred by the death of two prominent actors on set. In 1988 British comic actor Roy Kinnear, an inexperienced rider, fell from a mettlesome horse while galloping across a drawbridge during the filming of *The Return of the Three Musketeers* (US 89). His widow won a $1 million settlement from the production company following charges of negligence.

There was a particularly bitter twist to the tragedy that occurred on the set of *The Crow* (US 94) at Wilmington, NC, on 31 March 1993. Actor Brandon Lee, son of the late martial arts star Bruce Lee, was mortally wounded by a supposedly blank shot from a pistol fired by another actor. By a sad irony the scene was intended to show the character played by Lee being killed by what turned out to be a fatal shot in stark reality. Another macabre note was struck by the fact that when Lee's father, Bruce, died in 1973 of a brain disorder while working on *Game of Death* (HK 78), he was playing the role of an actor who is slain on set by a gangster who had replaced the dummy bullets in a prop pistol with real ones. *The Crow* was completed with the aid of a powerful computer which lifted the image of Lee out of several scenes already shot and transposed the moving figure into newly filmed scenes.

Probably the only instance when a director has been killed on set occurred in 1994 when Iranian filmmaker Ali Sajjaji was shot accidentally by an actor while making a war film with the sadly apt title, *The Line of Fire* (Iran 95).

It is rare for scenes of actual deaths during filming to be retained in the completed picture, but one known example is the anti-British propaganda drama *Mein Leben für Irland* (Ger 41). In the final battle scene several extras were killed when one stepped on a live land-mine, and the footage was included in the release prints.

Archives

The first film archive was the Danish Statens Arkiv for historiske Film og Stemmer, which had its origins in the spring of 1910 when Anker Kirkeby of the Copenhagen newspaper *Politiken* approached Ole Olsen of Nordisk Films with the idea of preserving a selection of films likely to be of historic interest in the future. During the ensuing three years a collection of films was assembled, including a number specially taken for the archive, which showed Danish writers, scientists, politicians, etc., and shots of parts of old Copenhagen due for redevelopment. The archive was formally established at the Royal Library in Copenhagen on 9 April 1913.

By the outbreak of war in 1914, film collections had been formed at the Louvre in Paris, the National Records Office in Madrid, the New York Public Library, and in Brussels, Rome, Berlin, and the Indian state of Baroda. These pioneer efforts, and those that followed in the 1920s, were generally concerned with the preservation of films as a record of national or civic history.

The first National Film Archive formed as a record of the film industry, rather than as a retrospective of public events, was the Reichsfilmarchiv established in Germany at the instigation of Arnold Raether on 4 February 1935. The Svenska Filminstituter Archive claims an earlier date of foundation, but it originated with the Filmhistorika Samlingarna, a private collection formed in 1933 by Einar Lauritzen.

Two other major archives were founded in 1935. The British Film Institute (founded 1933) set up the National Film Archive under Ernest Lindgren in May, and in New York, Iris Barry and John Abbott established the Museum of Modern Art Film Library. The following year, Henri Langlois formed the Cinémathèque Française from his own private film collection and this rapidly grew into a national institution, though the government support enjoyed since the end of World War II was withdrawn in 1969 when the French government established its own archive. Russia's giant Gosfilmofond, which occupies a 150-acre site at Bielye Stolbi near Moscow and used to employ a staff of 600, was not founded until 1948.

The world's largest service film archive is Britain's National Film Archive with 161,000 films, of which 45,000 are available for viewing by the general public. The Centre Nationale de la Cinématographie in Paris holds 95,000 films, while Russia's Gosfilmofond has about 45,000.

The smallest national archive is the Icelandic Film Archive, which contains some 400 films about or made in Iceland.

The country with the most complete visual record of its cinema heritage is the Czech Republic, whose Prague Film Archive holds an estimated 95% of all the Czech fiction films made since production began. Britain's National Film Archive holds 79% of all British feature films made since the advent of talkies in 1929. Elsewhere the picture

MISSING ... BELIEVED LOST

In 1993 the British Film Institute launched its Missing Believed Lost campaign in an effort to find a hundred historically important British feature films of which no known copies had been traced. Successes have included spy drama *Secret Lives* (GB 37), located in a Swiss archive, the Conrad Veidt melodrama *Bella Donna* (GB 34), found in the Czech Republic, speedway drama *Money for Speed* (GB 39), edited by the young David Lean, which turned up in Paris, and two Walter Forde comedies, *Bed and Breakfast* (GB 30) and *Lord Babs* (GB 33), with Bobby Howes, retrieved from a vault at Pinewood Studios. Michael Powell's *The Man Behind the Mask* (GB 36) was identified in New York and a private collector in Leeds was able to furnish a print of *Schweik's New Adventures* (GB 43) featuring a very juvenile Richard Attenborough. Two on the missing list with special priority and yet to be found are *A Study in Scarlet* (GB 14), the first Sherlock Holmes feature film, and the only lost Alfred Hitchcock movie, his early silent *The Mountain Eagle* (GB 26).

Similar quests have been conducted on the other side of the Atlantic, but in August 1994 the Library of Congress received an unexpected bonanza when 2000 'lost films' were shipped to Washington from the Australian Film & Sound Archive. Dating from the 1890s to the early 1950s, this treasure trove of nitrate stock movies, which the Australians did not have the resources to convert to acetate stock for preservation, included some of the earliest films of Bronco Billy Anderson (see First Western Star), comedian Harold Lloyd and pioneer directors Rex Ingram and Allan Dwan. How had so many classics of the silent screen and rare early talkies, some of them the only known copies in existence, ended up down under? In those days Australia was traditionally the last stop for worldwide distribution of American pictures. As they had reached the end of their distribution cycle, it was seldom worth the cost of shipping them back across the Pacific Ocean.

is bleaker. Worldwide it is estimated that half of all the feature films made before 1951 have been irretrievably lost; three out of every four feature films made before 1930; and four out of every five features made before 1920.

The largest private collection of historic films belongs to Jeff Aikman of Osterville, Cape Cod, Mass., who started it at the age of 13 in 1974 and has now amassed 35,000 different titles dating from Edison's *The Kiss* (US 1896) to the present. He recently refused an offer of $35 million for the whole collection.

The biggest single loss of archive film occurred in March 1982 when 6506 films were destroyed by fire and explosions at the Cineteca Nacional in Mexico City. A commentator described the disaster as 'the most terrible cultural loss in modern Mexican history—the filmic memory of our country is erased'.

The largest collection of film stills in the world is the National Film Archive Stills Collection in London, which consists of 6.5 million black-and-white stills and over a million colour transparencies from over 80,000 films.

Co-productions

The first co-production was *Das Geheimnis der Lüfte* (Aut/Fr 13), a full-length feature thriller starring Julius Brandt. The Austrian production company was Wiener Autorenfilm; the French company is believed to have been Pathé.

The first Anglo-American co-production was *Charley's Aunt* (US/GB 25), starring Syd Chaplin, a Christie comedy co-produced with Ideal Films Ltd of London, which opened at the Colony Theater, New York, on 8 February 1925.

The first Anglo-Russian co-production was *Anna Pavlova* (USSR/GB 85), made by Mosfilm (Moscow) and Poseidon films (London) and starring Galina Belayeva as Pavlova, Martin Scorsese and James Fox.

The first US–Russian co-production was *The Blue Bird* (US/USSR 76), based on Maurice Maeterlinck's fantasy about a dream trip in search of the elusive bluebird of happiness. The cast was predominately American (Elizabeth Taylor, Jane Fonda, Ava Gardner and Cicely Tyson as a cat) and British (Robert Morley, Harry Andrews, George Cole and a very young Patsy Kensit). The Russians, including prima ballerina Nadejda Pavlova as the Blue Bird, were consigned to the bottom half of the bill.

Soviet production facilities came as something of a rude shock to the visiting Hollywood film-makers. When director George Cukor arrived in Leningrad with Elizabeth Taylor and Ava Gardner he remarked to the Soviet studio head what an honour it was to be filming in the very studio where Eisenstein had shot his classic *The Battleship Potemkin* in 1925. 'Yes,' beamed their proud host, 'and with the very same equipment.'

The first US–Chinese co-production was *A Great Wall* (US/China 85), made by W & S Productions of New York and the Nanhai Film Co. of Beijing. It starred Chinese-American actor Peter Wang, who also directed, as a San Francisco computer executive experiencing culture shock on a visit to relatives in the old country.

The most cosmopolitan co-production was Lars von Trier's 11-nation *Dancer in the Dark* (Den/Fr/Swe/Ger /Nor/Neths/Ice/Fin/GB/US 00), with no fewer than 36 production companies or institutions participating. Icelandic pop singer Björk, playing a Czech, starred with French diva Catherine Deneuve in a film by a Danish director and a Swedish producer set in the USA and shot by a German director of photography. The distributor was British.

Hollywood

The first European inhabitant of the area now known as Hollywood, then called Nopalera, was Mexican-born Don Tomas Urquidez, who built an adobe dwelling in 1853 at what is now the north-west corner of Franklin and Sycamore Avenues.

The name 'Hollywood' was conferred on her

Cahuenga Valley ranch by Mrs Harvey Henderson Wilcox, wife of one of the district's earliest real-estate developers, in 1886. The name had nothing to do with holly-bushes imported from England, as some accounts have it. Mrs Wilcox had been travelling by train to her old home in the east when she met a lady with a summer home near Chicago called 'Hollywood'. She was so charmed by the name that she decided to borrow it for her own property. In 1903 the village of Hollywood and its environs were incorporated as a municipality, but in 1910 the citizens voted to become a district of Los Angeles in order to secure water supplies. At that time the population was 5000; by 1919 it was 35,000 and by 1925 it had grown to 130,000.

> The only other Hollywood to have made its mark on the movies is Hollywood, Co. Wicklow. It is there that the scene of the assassination of Michael Collins (Liam Neeson) was filmed for *Michael Collins* (US 96).

The largest private house in the Hollywood area is producer Aaron Spelling's 123-room 'The Manor' in Holmby Hills. Built on the site of Bing Crosby's former home, which Spelling bought for $10 million and demolished, the house is in the style of a French château and contains a theatre, gymnasium, four bars, three kitchens, an Olympic-size swimming pool, a doll museum, eight two-car garages, 12 fountains, a bowling alley and a bomb-proof anti-terrorist room. It was completed in 1990 at an estimated cost of $45 million.

BEVERLY HILLS
The exodus of Hollywood's upper crust to Beverly Hills began when Douglas Fairbanks rented sports goods manufacturer Syl Spaulding's 36-room house on Summit Drive in 1919. At that time Beverly Hills was mainly agricultural land given over to the cultivation of beans and there was only one house between Fairbanks' rented property and the sea, 7 miles away. Early in 1920 he bought a hunting lodge adjacent to the Spaulding man-sion and rebuilt it in a style befitting his new bride, Mary Pickford, and gave it to her as a wedding gift. Named 'Pickfair' after the first syllables of their names, Doug's wedding gift to Mary was, and remained, Beverly Hills' most regal establishment, a magnet that drew the elite of the film colony to what was soon to become America's richest suburb. In 1980, following the death of Mary Pickford, the 45-room mansion was put up for sale, but it was not until 1988 that international financier Meshulam Riklis paid the equivalent of £12 million for it as a home for his diminutive actress wife Pia Zadora. Riklis announced that he would spend another £3.5 million to 'spruce it up'

... AND MALIBU
The first film star to settle in Malibu Beach was Anna Q. Nilsson, who built a house on a sandy strip of deserted beach just north of Malibu Creek in 1928. Clara Bow, Gloria Swanson, Ronald Colman and Frank Capra soon followed her and within two years the area had been dubbed the Malibu Motion Picture Colony.

The first dramatic film made in the Los Angeles area was Francis Boggs' *The Count of Monte Cristo* (US 08), a Selig production made partly in Colorado and partly in the Laguna and Venice districts of what is now Greater Los Angeles. The first made wholly in LA was Francis Boggs' *The Power of the Sultan* (US 09), starring Hobart Bosworth, a Broadway actor who had lost his voice through tuberculosis and was seeking recuperative sunshine. The movie was shot in three days, 8–10 May 1909,

Hollywood stars headed for the beach after Anna Q. Nilsson set the trend by building a house at Malibu in 1928. The largest and most palatial beach house of all was built for Marion Davies in the '30s by her lover Randolph Hearst (the original of Citizen Kane*). Key: (1) Guest house for 50, (2) two tennis courts, (3) orchid house, (4) swimming pool with bridge, (5) Miss Davies' living quarters, (6) games room, (7) kitchen with capacity of 200-room hotel, (8) staff quarters for 18.* (Backnumbers)

Filming at the first studio in California, established by the Selig Co. in 1909.

on a rented lot next to a Chinese laundry on Olive and Seventh Streets, Los Angeles. Boggs, who might have become prominent as California's pioneer director, was unfortunately cut down in his prime, murdered by a crazed Japanese studio gardener in 1911.

At the 1984 American Film Institute Life Achievement Award presentation to 90-year-old Lillian Gish, John Houseman recalled that many years earlier Miss Gish and her sister Dorothy were offered the chance of buying the Sunset Strip in Hollywood for $300. The Gish sisters talked the matter over, weighing the pros and cons. They then went down to fashionable Bullock's and bought a dress each instead.

The first studio in the Los Angeles area was established by the Selig Co. at 1845 Allesandro Street, Edendale. Construction began in August 1909 and enlargements were made in 1910 and again in 1911, so that within two years of opening it was occupying a 230 x 220ft building.

The first film made in Hollywood was D. W. Griffith's *In Old California* (US 10), a Biograph melodrama about the liaison between a Spanish maiden (Marion Leonard) and a dashing hero, destined to become Governor of California (Frank Grandin), who have an illegitimate wastrel son (Arthur Johnson). It was shot in two days, 2–3 February 1910, and released on 10 March.

The first studio in Hollywood was established there as the result of a toss of a coin. Al Christie, chief director of the Centaur Co., wanted to make westerns in California, since he was tired of having to simulate sagebrush country in New Jersey. Centaur's owner, David Horsley, thought that Florida would be better, but agreed to abide by a heads-or-tails decision. Christie tossed and won. After viewing various possible sites in Southern California, he found a derelict roadhouse at 6121 Sunset Boulevard which looked suitable and cost only $40 a month to rent. This building was converted into a studio in October 1911. It was called the Nestor Studio, after the name of the western branch of the company. Today the

site is occupied by the West Coast headquarters of CBS. By the end of the following year there were 15 film companies operating in Hollywood. Uninterrupted sunshine and a comforting distance from the agents of the Patents Co. were not the only attractions of Southern California as a film-making base. The astonishing range and variety of its scenery enabled locations to be found that could reasonably represent any terrain from Cornwall to the Urals; westerns could be located in the real West rather than New Jersey, South Sea island pictures could be shot on Catalina and neighbouring islands, an oil field in Los Angeles itself served for Texan oilman dramas, Spanish missions set the scene for old Mexico, and there were even sufficient baronial mansions to cater for the needs of pictures playing in Hollywood's England. Only a jungle was missing, but studios like Selig and Universal established their own zoos and built their African locales on the back-lot.

The first talking picture made in Hollywood was a Fox Movietone short *They're Coming to Get Me* (US 26), with comedian Chic Sale, released in May 1926.

THE CELEBRATED HOLLYWOOD SIGN
The sign was erected on Hollywood Hills in 1923 at a cost of $21,000. Originally it spelt out the word HOLLYWOOD-LAND, in letters 30ft wide and 50ft tall and built up from 3 x 9ft sheet metal panels attached to a scaffolding frame. Each letter was studded with 20-watt light bulbs at 8-inch intervals. A man called Albert Kothe, who lived on the job—in a hut behind one of the 'L's'—was employed full time to change the bulbs when they burned out. The sign has often been featured in movies as a means of establishing locale, for example as shown in *The Day of the Locust* (US 75), *1941* (US 79) in *Double Dragon* (US 94), set in an earthquake-ravaged LA, in which it is seen half-submerged in flood-water (how did they do that?). It has been put to more macabre use for frequent suicide attempts. First to take a death dive from the top of the sign was failed starlet Peg Entwhistle in 1932 (an episode dramatised in *Stand-Ins* (US 97) – her only on-screen epitaph.

Declared an historic landmark in 1973, the original and much dilapidated sign was replaced five years later after a fund for this purpose had been established by Gene Autry, Alice Cooper and *Playboy* chief Hugh Hefner. The new sign cost $27,000 for each letter. The remains of the old one were sold to a Mr Hank Berger, who cut the scrap metal into 1-inch squares and retailed them to the more obsessive nostalgia buffs at $29.95 a time.

A group calling themselves 'The Environmental Pranksters' made newspaper headlines by their depredations on the famous sign. Using black plastic sheeting to cover up whole letters, or parts of letters, they converted HOLLYWOOD to HOLYWOOD to celebrate the Pope's visit in 1987, to HOLLYWEED after laws on marijuana possession had been relaxed, and to OLLYWOOD in tribute to Col. 'Olly' North's performance at the Senate's Irangate hearings.

The first footprints outside Grauman's Chinese Theater in Hollywood were Norma Talmadge's on 18 May 1927. Legend has it that she stepped on the wet cement by accident, thereby giving Sid Grauman the idea for his celebrated and still continuing publicity stunt.

BITING THE HAND

- 'A town that has to be seen to be disbelieved'—Walter Winchell
- 'It's a great place to live—if you're an orange'—Fred Allen
- 'Just a small town with notions'—Theodore Dreiser in 1931
- 'A small-minded little town in the middle of nowhere'—Marlon Brando
- 'Hollywood is a sewer—with service from the Ritz Carlton'—Wilson Mizner
- 'There is one word which aptly describes Hollywood—nervous!'—Frank Capra
- 'Hollywood is the only community in the world where the entire population is suffering from rumourtism'—Bert Lahr
- 'They've great respect for the dead in Hollywood, but none for the living'—Errol Flynn
- 'Hollywood is pretty painful even in small quantities'—Constance Bennett. (It grew a little less painful when her salary leapt from $8000 a week to $30,000 a week—the highest in Hollywood—shortly after saying this.)
- 'It's somehow symbolic of Hollywood that Tara was just a façade, with no rooms inside'—David O Selznick
- 'Hollywood stinks'—Frank Sinatra
- 'I saw Hollywood born and I've seen it die …'—Mary Pickford in old age
- 'Hollywood is a place where they'll pay you $50,000 for a kiss and 50c for your soul'—Marilyn Monroe
- 'Hollywood is where, if you don't have happiness, you send out for it'—Rex Reed
- 'This town's motivated by fear—the fear of failure'—Amanda Donohoe
- 'Here, it is boring, incredibly boring, so boring I can't believe it is true'—Greta Garbo in 1926
- 'Hollywood doesn't destroy you. But it certainly gives you the opportunity to destroy yourself.'—Martin Sheen
- 'Hollywood is another planet … They do things differently there.'—Carol White, who went from stardom in Britain to bit parts in Hollywood, drug abuse, alcoholism and an early death.
- 'It's an opportunity to fly first-class, be treated like a celebrity, sit around the pool and be betrayed.'—Ian McEwan
- 'Hollywood's a place where they shoot too many pictures and not enough actors'—Walter Winchell again

Cinema Museums

The first cinema museum was the Czeskoslovenské Filmové Museum, founded by Jindrrich Brichta at Prague in 1923.

The first cinema museum in America was the Crocker Museum which Charles Chaplin's assistant Harry Crocker, who had a mania for collecting movie memorabilia, established on Sunset Boulevard, Hollywood in 1928. The exhibits consisted of props and costumes from silent movies, including Chaplin's original tramp costume, Harold Lloyd's glasses, William S. Hart's first leather chaps, Keaton's pancake boater, Gloria Swanson's 'Sadie Thompson' costume, the cabin that tottered on the brink from *The Gold Rush* (US 24), and the winning chariot from *Ben Hur* (US 26).

Longest and Shortest Films

The longest film ever made was the 85-hour *The Cure for Insomnia* (US 87), directed by John Henry Timmis IV and premièred in its entirety at the School of Art Institute of Chicago from 31 Jan to 3 Feb 1987. Much of the film consists of L. D. Groban reading his own 4080-page poem, also titled *The Cure for Insomnia*, interspersed with scenes of rock band J.T.4 and Cosmic Lightning and what the makers describe as some 'X-rated footage'. A short 'clean' version lasting a mere 80 hours is available without the erotic scenes.

The longest commercially made film was *The Burning of the Red Lotus Temple* (Chn 28–31), adapted by the Star Film Co. from a newspaper serial *Strange Tales of the Adventurer in the Wild Country* by Shang K'ai-jan. It was released in 18 feature-length parts over a period of three years. Although never shown publicly in its 27-hour entirety, some cinemas would put on all-day performances of half-a-dozen parts in sequence.

The longest commercially made film to be shown in its entirety was Edgar Reitz's 25-hour and 32-minute *Die Zweite Heimat* (Ger 92), premièred at Munich, starting at 2. p.m. on Saturday 5 September 1992 and continuing (with intervals) until 1.30 a.m. on Wednesday 9 September. The sequel to the 15-hour and 40-minute *Heimat* (FRG 84), it told the story of Hermann (Henry Arnold), Maria's youngest son in the earlier film. An earlier première had begun at the Venice Film Festival on 1 September, but finished later on 12 September.

When Fellini's three-hour *La Dolce Vita* (It 60) was premiered at Cannes, Luis Buñuel was asked his opinion of what was to become an Italian classic. 'Quite good,' returned the great surrealist cautiously, then added 'insofar as a film lasting over 90 minutes can be said to be good.'

The longest commercially made American movie to be released uncut was Erich von Stroheim's *Foolish Wives* (US 22), which was distributed to Latin American countries in its original six-hour and 24-minute version. In the United States, however, it was seen only in a severely cut form, a 12-reel version for the road show and a ten-reel version for general release.

The 42-reel version of von Stroheim's masterpiece *Greed* (US 24)—**Hollywood's longest-ever film in its original form**—was shown only once at a nine-hour screening at MGM on 12 January 1924. Idwal Jones, drama critic of the *San Francisco Daily News*, who was present, commented that it had 'every comma of the book put in'.

Richard Attenborough's tour de force *Gandhi* (GB 82) ran for three hours and eight minutes—unbeknown to 150 patrons of a cinema in Cleveland who had parked their cars in a two-hour zone. A benevolent mayor, in an act perhaps unprecedented in the history of municipal endeavour, later voided the parking tickets. (London's new mayor please note.)

CINEMA MUSEUMS

The following museums are either wholly devoted to cinema or have substantial cinema collections. Film archives are only included if they also administer a museum.

ARGENTINA
Museo Municipal de Arte Moderno, Mendoza.

AUSTRALIA
Australian Film Institute Museum, Canberra.
Movie Museum, Buderim.

AUSTRIA
Österreichisches Filmmuseum, Vienna.

BELGIUM
Cinémathèque Royal de Belgique, Brussels (early equipment).
Foto en Kinematografie Museum Sterckshof, Antwerp.
Musée de la Photographie et du Cinéma, Brussels.
Provinciaal Museum voor Kunstambachten het Sterckshof, Deurne.

BRAZIL
Carmen Miranda Museum, Parque de Flamengo, Rio de Janeiro.
Embrafilme Cinema Museum, Rio de Janeiro.
The Cinema Museum, Sao Paulo.

CANADA
The Marie Dressler Museum, Cobourg, Ontario (birthplace).

CZECH REPUBLIC
Museum of Animated and Puppet Films, Kratochvile Castle, Bohemia.

DENMARK
Det Danske Filmmuseum, Copenhagen.

FRANCE
Musée du Cinéma Henri Langlois, Palais de Chaillot, Paris.
Musée du Cinéma, Rue de Courcelles, Paris.
Musée du Cinéma, Lyons (Lumière collection), at the splendid address: 1 rue du Premier Film.
Pirates Galleon Museum, Cannes. Housed in the galleon built at a cost of £7m for Roman Polanski's Pirates (US/Tun 86).

GEORGIA
Cinema History Museum, Odessa (history of cinema in Georgia).

GERMANY
Filmmuseum, Potsdam.
Filmmuseum, Düsseldorf.
Kreismuseum, Bitterfeld.
Munich City Museum (Film and Photography Department).
Deutsches Film Museum, Frankfurt-am-Main.
Woltersdorf, nr Berlin. 'When Woltersdorf was Hollywood' Museum, devoted to 1912–23 period when 31 silent features were made locally. Housed in observation tower in forest, accessible only on foot.

GREAT BRITAIN
Barnes Museum of Cinematography, St Ives, Cornwall.
The National Museum of Photography, Film and Television, Bradford.
Bill Douglas Centre Museum, University of Exeter.
Kay Kendall Memorial Museum, Withernsea Lighthouse, Yorks.
Laurel and Hardy Museum, Ulverston, Cumbria (birthplace of Stan Laurel).
Hove Museum, Sussex: permanent display commemorating the work of pioneer film-makers George Albert Smith (1864–1959) and James Williamson (1855–1933), the most prominent members of the 'Brighton school'.
The Museum of the Moving Image, South Bank, London.
The Cinema Museum, Effra Road, Brixton.
Cars of the Stars, Standish St., Keswick Cumbria. Famous cars from films and TV series, including Bond's Aston Martin, Herbie and Chitty Chitty Bang Bang.

HUNGARY
The Ciné-Museum, Kaposvár.

IRELAND
White O'Mornin' Cottage Heritage Centre, Cong, Co. Mayo. Rare example of museum devoted to single film—John Ford's The Quiet Man (US 52) in which an ex-boxer (John Wayne) returns from America to reclaim the cottage where he was born.

ITALY
Museo Michaelangelo Antonioni, Palazzo dei Diamanto, Ferrara.
Museo del Cinema/MICS, Rome.
Museo Nazionale del Cinema, Turin.

JAPAN
Masei University Gone With the Wind display—2000 items on the book and the film.

MEXICO
Cinematica Luis Buñuel, Puebla.
Cinematica Mexicana, Mexico City.
Anda Museum, Mexico City. Established 1987 by actors' union Anda to preserve mementos of Mexican stars.

NETHERLANDS
Stichting Nederlands Filmmuseum, Amsterdam.

NORWAY
Norsk Filminstitutt, Oslo—over 500 pieces of early cinema apparatus.

POLAND
Muzeum Kinematografii, Lódz.

RUSSIA
The Eisenstein Museum, Moscow (housed in Eisenstein's widow's small apartment).

SERBIA
Muzej Jugoslavenske Kinoteke, Belgrade.

SOUTH KOREA
Cheju Island Movie Town Museum.

SWEDEN
Asta Nielsen Filmmuseum, Lund.

SWITZERLAND
Museum des Films, Basel.

THAILAND
Movie Walk, Bangkok, The world's only movie-themed art gallery, part of the Entertainment Golden Village seven-screen multiplex.

UKRAINE
Ukrainian State Museum of Theatrical, Musical and Cinema Art, Kiev.

USA
James Dean Museum, Fairmount, Indiana (birthplace).
Roy Rogers Museum, Portsmouth, Ohio (contains stuffed Trigger).
Tom Mix Museum, Dewey, Oklahoma.
Laurel and Hardy Museum, Harlem, Ga. (birthplace of Oliver Hardy).
Will Rogers Memorial, Claremore, Oklahoma.
International Museum of Photography, George Eastman House, Rochester, NY.
Museum of Modern Art, New York.
Hollywood Stuntmen's Hall of Fame, Mojave, California.
The Hollywood Museum, 7051 Hollywood Boulevard.
Hollywood Studio Museum, opened 1987 in what was formerly known as the De Mille Barn, site of the original Lasky Studio where Cecil B. De Mille filmed The Squaw Man in 1913.
American Museum of the Moving Image, Kaufman Astoria Studios, Queens, New York. Billed as first museum in the US devoted to 'the art, history and technology of motion pictures and television'.
International Cinema Museum, 319 W. Erie, Chicago.
The Movie Museum, Las Vegas (Ann Miller Collection).
Autry Museum of Western Heritage, Los Angeles. Named after singin' cowboy Gene Autry, the museum is a celebration of the Old West in fact and fiction, but with special attention to the history of the Western.
Warner Bros Museum, Burbank, Ca. Opened June 1996 with 650 artefacts in 7000 sq ft, this was the first studio museum—most Hollywood studios had long since consigned their heritage to the skip. Includes shooting script of Casablanca (US 42), showing that wherever the celebrated closing scene came from, it had not been scripted.
Movie Museum, Hawaii.

It was subsequently cut to 24 reels by an aggrieved von Stroheim, who had already spent four unpaid months editing the original footage down to 48 reels; then to 18 reels by Rex Ingram, and finally ten reels by Joe Farnham. The 32 reels of cut negative were melted down by MGM to retrieve the minute quantity of silver nitrate they contained.

The longest commercially made American movie

released in America was the ill-fated $43 million epic Cleopatra (US 63) at a seemingly endless four hours and three minutes. The only other Hollywood productions longer than Gone with the Wind (US 39), which ran for three hours and 40 minutes, were The Greatest Story Ever Told (US 65) at three hours and 45 minutes, Bob Dylan's three-hour and 55 minute Renaldo and Clara (US 77) and Kenneth Branagh's Anglo-American co-produc-

FILMS RUNNING FOUR HOURS

The following are films shown in public in a version lasting four hours or longer. The list includes films issued in parts, but not serials. The duration of the silent films listed is calculated on the assumption that they were projected at 16 fps.

HOURS	FILM	HOURS	FILM	HOURS	FILM
4 hr	Chusingura (Jap 55)	4 hr 58 min	Percal (Mex 50)	12 hr 43 min	Comment Yukong deplace les
	Mera Naam Joker (Ind 70)	5 hr	Damnation (Hun 88)		montagnes (Fr 76)
	Gosta Berlings Saga (Swe 24)	5 hr 2 min	Winifred Wagner und die	13 hr	The Old Testament (It 22)
	Heaven's Gate (US 81)[1]		Geschichte des Hauses	14 hr 33 min	The Journey (Can 87)
	The Iron Curtain (Rus 95)		Wahnfried (FRG 75)	15 hr 21 min	Berlin Alexanderplatz (FRG/It
	Ludwig (It/Fr/FRG 73)[2]	5 hr 5 min	Les Misérables (Fr 27)		80)
	Manon des Sources (Fr 54)	5 hr 6 min	Petersburgskije truscoby (Rus	15 hr 40 min	Heimat (FRG 84)
4 hr 2 min	Hamlet (US/GB 96)		15)	24 hr	* * * * (US 67)[11]
4 hr 3 min	Cleopatra (US 63)	5 hr 14 min	Potop/The Deluge (Pol 74)	25 hr 32 min	Die Zweite Heimat (Ger 92)
4 hr 5 min	The Keys of Happiness (Rus 13)	5 hr 16 min	1900 (It 78)	27 hr	The Burning of the Red Lotus
	Siberiade (USSR 79)	5 hr 20 min	Vindicta (Fr 23)		Temple (Chn 28–31)
4 hr 12 min	L'Amour Fou (Fr 68)	5 hr 32 min	Les Misérables (Fr 33)	42 hr	Cinématon Part 1 (Fr 86)
4 hr 15 min	Parsifal (FRG/Fr 82)	5 hr 36 min	Jeanne la Pucelle (Fr 94)	48 hr	The Longest Most Meaningless
	Paths of Life (GDR 81)	5 hr 37 min	La Révolution Française		Movie in the World (GB 70)[12]
	Molière (Fr 78)		(Fr/GDR/It/Can 89)	50 hr	Mondo Teeth (US 70)
	Out 1: Spectre (Fr 72)	5 hr 50 min	Fanny and Alexander (Swe 83)[4]	85 hr	The Cure for Insomnia (US 87)
4 hr 16 min	The Age of Cosimo de Medici (It	5 hr 54 min	Soldati Svobodi		
	72)		(USSR/Bul/Hun/Cz/		
	Gustaf Wasa (Swe 28)		GDR/Rom/Pol 77)		1. Long version shown Venice Film Festival
4 hr 17 min	Les Plouffe (Can 81)	5 hr 57 min	Little Dorrit (GB 87)		1982 and elsewhere.
4 hr 20 min	Amor der Perdicao (Por 80)	6 hr	Charles XII (Swe 27)		2. General release print 3 hr; 4-hr version
	Boris I (Bul 85)		Idade de Terra (Bra 79)		shown Rome 1980, Paris 1983.
	The Greatest Story Ever Told		Khan Asparouch (Bul 82)		3. At première only. Release prints were 3 hr
	(US 62)[3]		Monte Cristo (Fr 28)		58 min.
	Rubens (Neth 78)		Babel: Letter to My Friends		4. Long version shown at Venice Film
4 hr 25 min	The Idiot (Jap 51)		Remaining in Belgium (Bel 93)		Festival 1983.
	The Tokyo Trial (Jap 85)		Legend of the Cixi Tomb		5. Released at this length in South America
4 hr 27 min	Hotel Terminus: The Life and		Treasure (Chn 86–87)		only. US general release: 10 reels.
	Times of Klaus Barbie (Fr 88)	6 hr 10 min	Die Nibelungen (Ger 24)		6. Russian-language version. English-
4 hr 30 min	Measure for Measure (Bul 81)	6 hr 24 min	Foolish Wives (US 22)[5]		language version 6 hr 13 min.
	Imagen de Caracas (Ven 68)	6 hr 30 min	Sleep (US 63)		7. Released in 4-hr version, but VGIK in
	The Great Citizen (USSR 38)	6 hr 40 min	Hitler: a Film from Germany		Moscow has print of 8½-hr original.
	Time of Violence (Bul 87)		(FRG 77)		8. Premièred in 9-hr entirety at Dominion,
	Le Chagrin et la Pitié (Fr 70)	7 hr	Der Hund von Baskerville (Ger		Tottenham Court Road, May 1983.
	La Hora de los Hornos (Arg 68)		14–15)		Release version 5 hr.
4 hr 34 min	Atvaltozas/Point of Departure	7 hr 30 min	Satan's Tango (Hun 93)		9. Abel Gance's 42-reel version définitive;
	(Hun 84)	7 hr 45 min	Français si vous savez (Fr 73)		trade and press shown at the Apollo,
4 hr 38 min	The Memory of Justice (FRG	7 hr 58 min	Iskry Plamja (Rus 25)		Paris in 1927 and believed to have been
	76)	8 hr	Empire (US 64)		shown commercially in Nice and other
4 hr 39 min	The Kingdom (Den 95)	8 hr 27 min	War and Peace (USSR 63–67)[6]		provincial centres. The version shown at
4 hr 40 min	Amerikanske Billeder (Den 81)	8 hr 32 min	La Roue (Fr 21)[7]		the Paris première was 3 hr 40 min. The
	The Prodigal Son (GB 23)	9 hr	Wagner (GB/Hun/Aut 83)[8]		7½-hr version reconstructed by Kevin
	A Dream of Red Mansions (Chn		Napoleon (Fr 27)[9]		Brownlow was first shown at Don Bosch,
	88–89)	9 hr 21 min	Shoah (Fr/Swz 85)		Netherlands on 24 November 1984.
4 hr 45 min	Rameau's Nephew by Diderot	9 hr 29 min	The Human Condition (Jap		10. Shown only once at this length, then re-
	(Can 74)		58–60)		edited as 4¼-hr Out 1: Spectre.
4 hr 53 min	Smoking/No Smoking (Fr 93)	11 hr	Decisive Battle (Chn 93)		11. Shown only once, then re-edited as two
4 hr 57 min	Darkness (Fr 88)	12 hr 40 min	Out 1: Noli me Tangerey (Fr		features of conventional length.
	The Kingdom (Den 94)		71)[10]		12. Premièred at this length, then cut to 1½ hr.

---

tion of *Hamlet* (US/GB 96) at four hours and two minutes.

Otto Preminger's *Exodus* (US 60) was exactly the same length as *Gone with the Wind*. Prior to *Gone with the Wind* the record for the longest Hollywood talkie was held by MGM's *The Great Ziegfeld* (US 36), which ran for two hours and 59 minutes.

A 24-hour version of Hitchcock's *Psycho* (US 60) was presented at London's Hayward Gallery as part of its 'Spellbound: Art & Film' exhibition in March 1996 to celebrate the centenary of cinema in Britain. This was not some hitherto undiscovered 'director's cut'. The film was projected at 2fps instead of the normal 24fps, transforming it into what the presenters described as 'a strange sequence of lingering stills'.

The longest commercially made British film was Christine Edzard's monumental screen adaptation of Charles Dickens's *Little Dorrit* (GB 87), starring Sir Alec Guinness, Derek Jacobi and talented newcomer Sarah Pickering in the title role. With a total running time of five hours and 57 minutes, the film was released in two parts, playing on alternate days, the first part of two-hour and 56-minute duration, the second three hours and one minute.

The shortest film was a TV commercial for Bon Marché's Frango candy, aired on King-TV in the US on 29 November 1993. It comprised just four frames of film and lasted for 0.133 seconds.

Publicity

The largest publicity budget was the $68 million spent

by Universal and licensed merchandisers on promoting Steven Spielberg's *Jurassic Park* (US 93) in the US. This was $8 million more than the cost of the film.

The average publicity budget for films made by members of the Motion Picture Association of America (i.e. the mainstream studios) was $24.5 million in 1999, bringing the total average cost of a picture to $76 million.

SLOGANS

Slogans extolling movies have tended towards hyperbole ever since impresario George Belmont announced his presentation of the 'Theatrograph' at Sadler's Wells in 1896 with the words: 'A mighty mirror of Promethean Photographs and a superb, brilliant, and electrifying entertainment specially adapted to cheer the toiling millions'.

A travelling bioscope showman encountered by a correspondent of the *Pelican* in a Kentish village in 1908 stretched credulity with a sign proclaiming: 'The most extraordinary invention of modern times, as presented before the Emperor Napoleon!'

Innocence of a different type during the early years of the movies is represented by a local billsheet for a Mary Fuller serial showing in Haddington, Scotland. It proffered 'What Happened to Mary Twice Nightly'. Somewhat later, but still in Scotland, a Glasgow exhibitor announced on his marquee in foot-high letters 'GEORGE WASHINGTON SLEPT HERE WITH ANN SHERIDAN'.

Impressive figures have often engaged the attention of publicists. India's first feature film *Raja Harischandra* (Ind 12) was advertised as 'a performance with 57,000 photographs ... a picture 2 miles in length ... all for only three annas!' *After Rain, Clear Sky* (Chn 31), one of China's earliest all-talkies, was promoted with the information that 'on the 977 occasions for dialogue, 6935 sentences are spoken'. The quantitative attractions of Twentieth Century Fox's *The Egyptian* (US 54) stimulated a slogan writer to even greater flights of figurative fancy with the claim that it had '10,965 pyramids, 5337 dancing girls, one million swaying bulrushes, 802 sacred bulls'.

Promoting a film to the wrong audience may be deliberate, in the case of a weak attraction, or perpetrated through sheer ignorance. In 1918 a Chicago theater urged: 'Tomorrow—Ibsen's Doll's House—Bring the Kiddies!' Equally inappropriate was a Toronto cinema's slogan for David Lean's gentle evocation of middle-aged suburban romance *Brief Encounter* (GB 45): 'Girls who live dangerously'. A cinema on New York's 42nd Street, an area noted for vice, booked a nature film titled *The Love Life of a Gorilla* (US 37) and brought the crowds flocking in with a poster asking the searing question 'Do native women live with apes?' Anyone paying good money to see the film was rewarded with the answer—no, they don't.

Carl Laemmle knew that what audiences really want is escapist nonsense and signalled the fact loud and clear by billing his *Fighting American* (US 24) as the picture 'guaranteed not to make you think'.

The slogan used to boost the Joan Crawford starrer *Mildred Pierce* (US 45) entreated moviegoers 'Don't tell what Mildred Pierce did!'. The line was parodied all over. A diner in downtown Los Angeles put up a sign reading: 'For 65c we'll not only serve you a swell blue plate—we'll tell you what Mildred Pierce did.'

Attempts to summarise the story in a phrase could involve criminal assault on the English language. *Bridal Suite* (US 39) was encapsulated: 'Howl Bent for Laugh Heaven, Four Zanies Tangle with Cock-Eyed Love'. Real extravagance of prose style, though, was reserved for the epics. Cecil B. De Mille's *King of Kings* (US 27) was advertised in New York as abounding in 'Dramatic Magnificence, Spectacular Splendor, Riotous Joy, Tigerish Rage, Undying Love, Terrifying Tempests, Appalling Earthquakes' (audiences might be forgiven for not recognising this as the story of the Gospels).

In contrast, publicity could hardly be more downbeat than the announcement on the marquee of a drive-in in Cleveland County, NC, in 1960: 'Two Features'. The manager explained that he never advertised the titles of the films because 'the people who patronise this drive-in don't care what's playing'.

Devastating honesty was seldom an attribute of movie publicists, but individual cinema managers would occasionally give a frank opinion of their offerings. Ray S. Hanson broke the house record for his Fox Theater in Fertile, Minnesota, in November 1940 when he advertised *Windjammer* (US 40) with the slogan 'See a lousy show and win $70'. In 1947 an exhibitor in Hastings, Neb., announced: 'Double Feature—One Good Show and One Stinker'.

> Humphrey Bogart recalled that his mother had been unhappy with a promotion for *King of the Underworld* (US 39), in which he had the title role. An enterprising California cinema manager had plastered the sides of an automobile with pictures of Bogart in character and a loudspeaker blared 'Who is King of the Underworld? Who is this loathsome character? Who is this despoiler of the home?'
>
> 'Humphrey,' his proud parent protested, 'why don't they say it is you?'

Slogans could be used to take a side-swipe at another star. Fox's advertising to promote George O'Brien in *The Iron Horse* (US 24), which declared 'He's not a Sheik or a Caveman or a Lounge Lizard—He is a Man's Man and An Idol of Women', was clearly meant to draw a denigratory comparison with Latin lover Rudolph Valentino.

If the star was not the main attraction, someone else might be. When Oscar, the well-known negro boot-black on the Paramount lot, played a bit part in *Gambling Ship* (US 33), a black cinema on Los Angeles' Central Avenue billed the film with the legend: 'Sensational star in Gambling Ship, Oscar supported by Cary Grant'. The pictures outside were entirely of Oscar.

There is nothing like a good scandal to hype an indifferent picture. Released at the time of the Profumo affair, *The Man who Couldn't Walk* (US/Can 64) was billed as 'the story behind the scandal that shocked London ... baring untold secrets of vice, intrigue and international party girls'. What was actually delivered on screen amounted to no more than a routine meller about safe-crackers. There was no character remotely resembling the Defence Minister and none that bore any connection with Miss Keeler.

Another attempt at topicality was made by the British

Billboard in Peoria, Illinois, advertising D. W. Griffith's epic
The Birth of a Nation *(US 15) in 1916. The fact that no less than*
six different poster designs were used underlined the
*importance of the event. (*Kobal Collection)

distributors of a florid Indian romance titled *Red Rose* (Ind
82). The original slogan ran 'Petals from a beautiful film
flower named Red Rose', to which some enterprising publicist had added 'Adapted from "The Yorkshire Ripper"'.

Howard Hughes made immediate impact with the
posters promoting his controversial picture *The Outlaw*
(US 43) when it was briefly released in 1943 before being
withdrawn again. The slogan—'Mean, Moody and
Magnificent'—was spread below a picture of a rampant-
breasted Jane Russell standing bare-legged bestride a
haystack with a pistol in each fist. When released in 1946
a far more decorous though equally striking copy-line
had taken its place, a quote from Judge Twain Michelsen,
who had tried the film for indecency: 'We have seen Jane
Russell. She is an attractive specimen of American womanhood. God made her what she is.'

The *Los Angeles Times* banned an ad for *The Trip* (US
67) because it contained a quote from a review
which mentioned LSD. The source of the quote ... er, the
Los Angeles Times.

Briefer, but equally apt, was the slogan promoting
Tony Richardson's *The Loved One* (US 65): 'The Picture
with Something to Offend Everyone'. Briefer still and perhaps even more effective was the slogan accompanying
Baby Doll (US 56): 'Condemned by Cardinal Spellman'.

Today movie publicity in America and Western
Europe has lost some of the panache that characterised
its outrageous claims in a more credulous age. The skills
of the old-style huckster, however, are still being honed
in some emergent nations. When Bjorndal's *Nightwatch*
(Den 93) was released in Slovenia, its imaginative promot-
ers lured in patrons with the promise: "The largest number of bodies per square metre of film screen!" This was
literally true. The film was set in an overcrowded mortu-
rary.

MGM plumbed new depths of insensitivity with a huge
poster for *Turbulence* (US 97) positioned at the entrance to
Burbank Airport. It showed a plane careering out of control, with the strap-line "Can you survive the ride?"

The first colour stills were taken in the Uvachrome
process by Max Hofstetter of the Powers Photo
Engraving Co. of New York on the set of the Rudolph
Valentino movie *Monsieur Beaucaire* (US 24) at the
Paramount Astoria Studio on Long Island, NY. Hofstetter
had great difficulty taking the pictures, partly because
nobody could understand his broken English, but more

particularly on account of the yellow make-up used by the cast to counteract the effect of the blue light radiated from the Cooper-Hewitt mercury vapour lamps with which the set was illuminated. Despite the producers' objections that it would cost $10,000 an hour to make up the cast again, and the need to scout the town for incandescent floodlights to supplement the mercury vapour lamps, Hofstetter succeeded in getting his shots. Later, one of them became the first colour photograph transmitted by wire when it was sent from Chicago to New York by Dr Hubert E. Ives of the Bell Telephone Laboratories.

The most valuable movie poster sold at auction was for Universal's *The Mummy* (US 32), starring Boris Karloff, which fetched $450,000 at Christie's New York in 1997. The British and European record was established on 27 March 2000 when Ohio surgeon Dr Mark Swift paid £54,300 at Christie's, South Kensington, for a French poster advertising *Casablanca* (US 42). Dr Swift, who left his operating theatre to bid by telephone, already had 50 other posters for the Warner Bros classic.

The first trailers were clips of film which Georges Méliès projected on a screen above the entrance of his Théâtre Robert Houdin, Paris in 1898 to give passers-by an idea of the delights awaiting them within. The modern trailer originated in September 1916 when Famous Players issued 'an advance strip of film' to promote *The Quest of Life* (US 16). The first sound trailer was for gangster pic *Tenderloin* (US 28), starring Dolores Costello and Conrad Nagel, which opened at the Warner Theatre in New York on 14 March 1928.

Nowadays, there are twenty major specialist production houses providing the Hollywood studios with trailers for their films and cost per trailer is in the region of $125,000, exclusive of prints—these can run to as many as 6000. Standard length was 90 seconds until 1990, when by agreement with the Motion Picture Producers Association it was increased to 120 seconds.

Some movies have more than one trailer and in the case of the kidpic *Teenage Mutant Ninja Turtles* (US 90) there were no fewer than five. One was targeted at young males, a 'sweet one' at young females, another was for family viewing, an alternative consisted of funny one-liners, and the fifth was for Hispanics. The specialist trailer houses aim for a creative angle the studios might miss. In the words of one New York-based creative director: 'The trailer should always be better than the movie.'

Perhaps the most daring use of a trailer was the one used to promote *Austin Powers: The Spy who Shagged Me* (US 99). It started with a novel proposition: 'If you see one movie this summer, see *Star Wars*. But if you see two movies, see *Austin Powers*.' And the audience did just that, racking up a shagadelic $70m gross for the picture in its first five days of release.

The first neon sign promoting a film and its star was erected in July 1923 on the marquee of the Cosmopolitan Theatre at Columbus Circle, New York City to publicise *Little Old New York* (US 23) with Marion Davies.

The first licenses for merchandising a film character were issued in the US and UK in 1924 in respect of Pat Sullivan's phenomenally successful cartoon creation Felix the Cat. At first the licences, issued by 27-year-old producer Margaret Winler, were for Felix images on packaging, but two years later merchandising hit its stride when the cat who 'kept on walking' was manufactured as a cuddly toy. Merchandising of Mickey Mouse began almost as soon as the world's most celebrated rodent made his screen debut in 1928, followed by the rest of the burgeoning Disney stable. In March 1934 Walt Disney revealed in an interview with the *New York Times* that he made more money from the licensing of his characters than from the films in which they appeared. Citing as an example *The Three Little Pigs* (US 33), at that date his most successful film at the box office, he said that the cartoon had cost $60,000 to produce and had returned $64,000 in theatrical rentals. The 500 items bearing Disney images then on sale were the real earners for the Disney studio. The first time merchandising licences were issued in respect of a feature film was for Disney's *Snow White and the Seven Dwarfs* (US 38). A total of 147 manufacturers were licenced to produce 2183 different novelty products. Sales of character dolls topped 2 million and eager fans purchased no fewer than 16,500,000 Snow White drinking glasses. The few that survive today command the prices of rare antique crystal.

PUBLICITY STUNTS

These began decorously enough in the early days of cinema and became progressively more outrageous during the days of Hollywood's greatest extravagances, the

'Is it a Man or Machine?' asked the placard billing this publicity stunt at the La Porte cinema in Laporte, Indiana, in 1937. Anyone making the dummy smile got a free pass for Double or Nothing *(US 37); anyone failing to laugh at the picture got a double free pass. But if they didn't find it funny the first time, why would they want to see it again?*

1920s. Initially, a little ingenuity was made to go a long way. One of the earliest stunts, reported by *Kinematograph Weekly* in 1907, was dreamed up by the proprietor of a Chicago nickelodeon who had letters printed in simulated handwriting purporting to be from a girl called Lizzie, on a visit to the city, writing to her friend Mary about an exciting excursion to the cinema. They were scattered in the streets and the advertiser relied on the baser human impulse to read other people's letters. Other gimmicks employed in the USA prior to World War I included making arrangements with grocers to give 13 eggs for every dozen ordered, the extra egg being paid for by the cinema and stamped with details of the next attraction; distributing oversized neckties of a garish hue and offering free seats to any man willing to wear one throughout the performance; and giving free admission to anyone slender enough to pass through a narrow wicket set up in the lobby or alternatively short enough to pass under a low bar.

The Vaudette Theater of West Point, Ga., announced that they would be giving away a free 'one-piece coat and garment hanger' to every patron on an advertised date in 1914. Those who attended were handed a very small envelope which contained a 2-inch nail. The distributors of *Neptune's Daughter* (US 14), in which Annette Kellerman was clad in rather less than that customary for the period, sent out 36-inch tape measures which bore, at appropriate intervals, Miss Kellerman's vital statistics.

When Kalem reissued *The Colleen Bawn* (US 11), they had several tons of earth shipped from Killarney to New York and made up into 4-foot-square sods for distribution to cinemas exhibiting the film. For the price of a theatre ticket, Irish immigrants could savour the pleasure of once again standing on Irish soil.

One of the most sure-fire stunts, repeated in small towns all over the USA from about 1912, was known as 'Giving Away a Baby'. The exhibitor announced that a baby would be given away on the stage on a certain day. He then arranged for someone to write to the local newspaper deploring this act of inhumanity, to which the cinema manager would reply in a hurt tone saying that the baby had made no objection and the mother was indifferent to its fate. This would provoke a shoal of letters, a lively public debate in the community, and threats of police prosecution. On the appointed night a packed house, usually including a contingent of police, would see the manager give away a baby pig.

As a promotion for the serial *Bride 13* (US 20), the manager of the Lyric Theater at Easley, S. Carolina persuaded an engaged couple to be married in front of the screen immediately following the first episode. A capacity audience watched the event, which included an unscheduled moment of drama when the bride's mother, who was present but had no idea that her daughter was involved in the stunt, shouted 'Stop!' from the stalls. She was persuaded, in the interests of her daughter's happiness and the manager's profits, to let the show go on.

Hollywood's csars were not above a little stunt work themselves. Carl Laemmle turned the expensive luxury of employing Erich von Stroheim as a director to good account by erecting a mammoth electric sign on Broadway flashing out the prodigious budget allocated for *Foolish Wives* (US 22), then in the course of its year-

long shooting schedule. As von Stroheim's extravagances pushed the budget ever higher, Laemmle arranged for the New York Fire Brigade to tear down Broadway every Wednesday to change the light bulbs to the latest spiralling figure. The 'S' in Stroheim was replaced on the billboard by a $ sign.

It was about this period that publicity stunts involving stars reached their apogee. During a dip in Valentino's popularity, Harry Reichenbach, arch-exponent of ballyhoo, persuaded the great lover to grow a beard, and then proceeded to orchestrate a chorus of protest from outraged legions of female fans and the proprietors of barber shops. A few months later he arranged a ceremonial debearding by experts nominated by the Master Barbers of America.

To promote Raoul Walsh's *The Honor System* (US 25), the producers arranged for a practical demonstration of the 'honor' system in action, with a prisoner being released for a single day on his honour to return. Alas, he was not seen again.

Another stunt that backfired was the misguided one perpetrated by Universal when *The Phantom of the Opera* (US 25) was brought to England. By some means the studio publicity department persuaded Lt. Col. W. H. Barrell, Commanding Officer of the 153rd Heavy Brigade of the Royal Artillery, to give the English release prints a military escort from Southampton docks to the station and from Waterloo to Wardour Street. For the ceremonial march through London, the prints were preceded not only by troops but also an armoured car and a full regimental band. Press and public were equally scandalised by the vulgarity of the operation and the 'outrage on British troops', as one newspaper put it. There was a full-scale War Office enquiry and questions were asked in the House. To make matters worse, Universal's English representative, James Bryson, confessed that the military had been escorting empty boxes, since the prints of *The Phantom of the Opera* had been left safely in his trunks on the Berengaria, the liner which had brought them from New York. The uproar was so great that the film

---

D e Laurentis Entertainment Group offered a $1 million prize to the theater patron who guessed where the hidden cash was located in *Million Dollar Mystery* (US 87). The picture, which cost $10 million to make, grossed less than the value of the prize.

---

was never released in Britain and when, some years later, there was a second and more discreet attempt to bring it over, permission was flatly refused.

When *The Man I Killed* (US 32) went on release, an American exhibitor engaged a man to be buried alive for 24 hours. Unfortunately, a storm during the night obliterated the grave marker and long after the 24 hours were up, a team of 30 rescuers were desperately digging to release the entombed man. His first demand on being brought to the surface was for overtime pay.

Publicist Pete Smith was inspired with the idea of getting Sam Goldwyn to say that there were only 13 real actors in Hollywood and to name them. Goldwyn liked the stunt, but for the fact that he felt that as a result he would only be on speaking terms with 13 actors. He found the solution himself, naming 12 of the actors and leaving Hollywood to guess the name of the 13th.

Mom and Dad aka *A Family Story* (US 47), an exploitation movie with a live childbirth scene, was shown to sexually segregated audiences. According to publicity, this was 'so as not to offend the delicate'. To improve the effect, promotional manager Joe Solomon arranged to have a nauseous chemical put into the ventilation system and then called the local press to take pictures of the women reeling and retching out of the cinema. This ensured a full house of men in the evening.

As producer-director of *Psycho* (US 60) Alfred Hitchcock had it written into every booking contract that no one was to be admitted into the cinema after the film began. The master showman created a publicity gimmick that was actually enforceable in law. When one cinema manager called the studio to complain about angry patrons forced to wait in the rain until the next show, Hitchcock intercepted the call and told him 'Buy them umbrellas.'

The distributors of *Snuff* (Arg/US 74), a tasteless exploitation movie based on the unfounded rumours then circulating that young girls were being killed for real on camera in Latin America sex pix, hired rentamob teams to picket cinemas showing the film in order to attract adverse but none the less beneficial publicity.

In 1939 the US Post Office calculated that the average weight of a bundle made up of a single copy of each of the Hollywood studios' press releases issued in a week was 20lb. Or as the *New York Times* expressed it, 'Twenty pounds of piffle'.

Rather more tasteful in both senses was the tie-in with Gabriel Axel's *Babette's Feast* (Den 88) when it opened in New York at the Lincoln Plaza Cinema. Patrons were able to carry on to the Petrossian restaurant afterwards to partake of the magnificent gourmet dinner they had just witnessed on screen.

When *Too Scared to Scream* (US 85) premièred at Hollywood's Paramount Theater a contest was held on the sidewalk outside to find the girl who could scream loudest and most frighteningly. One hundred contestants were judged for howl quality by the picture's producer and star Mike Connors.

While the real 24-carat hype seems to have gone out of movie promotion, some publicists succeed in preserving their cherished tradition of plumbing the depths of bad taste and insensitivity. French video distributors GCR excelled with their giveaway promo for *Mississippi Burning* (US 86)—free Ku Klux Klan masks.

Gramercy Pictures marketing department went one better in the sick idea stakes with a promotional item for *Fargo* (US/GB 96). It was a snow globe—one of those innocent toys which sprinkle a miniature blizzard over an idyllic winter scene when you shake it—with a difference. This one sprinkled snow over a scene derived from the film's opening shot: dead bodies spilling blood beside an overturned auto.

Remakes

The story which has been remade the most times is *Cinderella*, of which there have been 103 productions, spanning 103 years, including cartoon, modern, ballet, operatic, pornographic and parody versions, from *Cinderella and the Fairy Godmother* (GB 1898), starring Laura Bayley, to *Cinderella—The Movie* (GB 00, TVM) with Marcella Plunkett as Cinders, Kathleen Turner as the Wicked Stepmother and Jane Birkin as the Fairy Godmother. The most recent big-screen version was Andy Tennant's feminist reworking *Ever After* (US 98), starring Drew Barrymore as a funky Cinders confronting a male chauvinist Prince Charming (Dougray Scott). The previous year another PC version, *Rodgers and Hammerstein's Cinderella* (US 97, TVM), introduced the first black Cinderella on screen, Brandy (with Whitney Houston as the Fairy Godmother). Neither version was able to use the traditional title: that has been trademarked by Disney.

In addition to *Cinderella*, the following works have been the subject of 12 or more movie remakes: Shakespeare's *Hamlet*—80 including modern versions and parodies; *Carmen* (Merimée's story and Bizet's opera)—60 plus two parodies; R. L. Stevenson's *Dr Jekyll and Mr Hyde*—61 (including parodies and variants); *Faust* (Marlow, Goethe and Gounod's opera)—60; Shakespeare's *Romeo and Juliet*—37 plus eight modern and 12 parodies; Defoe's *Robinson Crusoe*—48 including two pornographic; Cervantes's *Don Quixote*—43; Dumas *père's The Three Musketeers*—39 and 13 variants featuring the character d'Artagnan; Shakespeare's *Macbeth*—30 plus six modern and two parody; Dumas *fils' La Dame aux camélias*—37; Hugo's *Les Misérables*—33; Dickens's *A Christmas Carol*—28; Shakespeare's *A Midsummer Night's Dream*—27; Dumas *père's The Count of Monte Cristo*—27 plus 13 variants featuring the character Edmund Dantes; the Hindu epic *Harischandra*—25 in nine different languages; Tolstoy's *Resurrection*—24; Dickens's *Oliver Twist*—24, including Seth Michael Domsky's gay version *Twisted* (US 96); R. L. Stevenson's *Treasure Island*—23; Tolstoy's *Anna Karenina*—21; Lewis Carroll's *Alice in Wonderland*—20; Dostoevsky's *Crime and Punishment*—20; *Othello* (Shakespeare and Verdi's opera)—20; Shakespeare's *King Lear*—19 including Godard's 'free' version (the director admitted he had not read the play); Shakespeare's *Julius Caesar*—18 plus one modern; *William Tell* (Schiller and legend)—17; Hugo's *The Hunchback of Notre Dame*—17; Brandon Thomas's *Charley's Aunt*—15; Dumas *père's The Corsican Brothers*—15; Sir Arthur Conan Doyle's *The Hound of the Baskervilles*—14; Tolstoy's *The Living Corpse*—13; Kalidasa's Sanskrit play *Shakuntala*—13; Mrs Henry Wood's *East Lynne*—13; Hugo's *Lucretia Borgia*—12; Charlotte Brontë's *Jane Eyre*—12; Henryk Sienkiewicz's *Quo Vadis*—12.

The first remake was the Lubin Co.'s *The Great Train Robbery* (US 04), described as a frame-by-frame reproduction of the Edison Co.'s phenomenally successful *The Great Train Robbery* (US 03). It was released seven months after the original. The Lubin production, at 600ft, was shorter than Edwin S. Porter's classic by 140ft. At this time there was no intellectual copyright on original film scenarios and pioneer production companies replicated their competitors' successes with no fear of reprisal, other than to have their own box-office successes similarly ripped off.

The first director to make a remake of his own original was Cecil B. De Mille with the second, 1918 version of *The Squaw Man*, which he had first filmed in 1913. He had a third go at it as a talkie in 1931.

The longest interval between the original version of a film and the remake was 72 years in the case of *Camila* (Arg 12), starring Bianca Podestá in the title role, and *Camila* (Arg/Sp 84) with Susú Pecoraro. The real-life story of aristocratic young beauty Camila O'Gorman, both films related how she fell in love with a Jesuit priest, their elopement and their tragic end before a firing squad. Although the events had taken place in the 1840s, passions about the affair still ran so high a century later that all attempts to bring it to the screen again between 1912 and 1984 were blocked either by open censorship or by political manoeuvring.

The longest interval between the original version of a film and the remake with the same actor playing the same role was 34 years in the case of Tito Lusiardo's performances in *El Dia que me Quitas/The Day You Leave Me* (US 35 and Arg 69). The longest interval for an actress was 28 years between Sophia Loren's performances as the mother in *Two Women* (It 61 and It 89).

The distinguished German actress Lil Dagover appeared in the remake of *The Spiders* (FRG 79), 60 years after performing (in a different role) in the 1919 original. Jean Simmons played Miss Havisham's ward Estella in David Lean's *Great Expectations* (GB 46) and Miss Havisham in the 1989 remake. Jane Greer played the heroine in *Out of the Past* (US 47) and the heroine's mother in the remake *Against All Odds* (US 85). Magda Schneider starred in *Liebelei* (Aut 32); her daughter Romy Schneider in the remake *Christine* (Fr 59). Barry Norton played a leading role in *What Price Glory?* (US 26) and a bit part in the 1952 remake; Jack Pennick played a bit in the silent original and a leading role in the talkie.

The shortest interval between the original version of a film and the remake with the same actor playing the same role was three years in the case of Gérard Lauzier's *Mon père, ce héros* (Fr 91) and Steve Miner's *My Father, the Hero* (US 94), with Gérard Depardieu as the estranged father seeking to win the affection of his teenage daughter, Marie Gillain in the French version and Katherine Heigl in the American remake.

The most versions of a film to be shown collectively were 11 *Les Misérables* (out of a total of 32) during a season of Victor Hugo adaptations at the Cinémathèque Française in 1985. They included the French versions of 1912, 1925, 1933, 1957, 1971 and 1982, the Hollywood versions of 1918, 1935 and 1952, the Italian version of 1947 and the 1937 Soviet version titled *Garoche*.

> '**I**f I had my life to live over I would do everything the exact same way—with the possible exception of seeing the movie remake of *Lost Horizon*.'—Woody Allen.

Sequels

The longest interval between a sequel and its original was 46 years in the case of Walt Disney Productions' *Return to Oz* (US 85), starring Fairuza Balk as Dorothy, which resumed the story six months after the previous Dorothy (Judy Garland) had returned to Kansas in MGM's *The Wizard of Oz* (US 39). The sequel was based on the second and third of Frank Baum's 14 Oz books, *The Land of Oz* and *Ozma of Oz*.

The longest interval between a sequel and its original with the same stars was 30 years in the case of Neil Simon's *The Odd Couple II* (US 98), released in March 1998, nearly 30 years after the April 1968 release of *The Odd Couple* (US 68). Both pictures centred on the fractious relationship of total opposites, cigar chomping slobbish sportwriter Oscar Madison (Walter Matthau) and the excessively fastidious and obsessively neat Felix Unger (Jack Lemmon). In the original both men's wives have walked out on them and they find themselves cohabiting uneasily in Matthau's debris-strewn New York appartment. The sequel reunites them 17 years after they last saw each other as they share a rental car to attend the wedding of Oscar's son to Felix's daughter.

Lee Patrick exceeded this time span as a featured player when she made a welcome return as Effie, Sam Spade's secretary in *The Maltese Falcon* (US 41), in the sequel *The Black Bird* (US 75). Thirty-four years on, Spade's son (George Segal) had inherited her along with his father's detective agency.

The shortest interval between a movie and its sequel was four months in the case of The Kodakawa Shoten Co's Japanese animated sci-fi actioner *Evangelion* (Jap 97) and *Evangelion II* (Jap 97), the former released in March 1997 and the latter on 19 July.

The most successful sequel in terms of box office ratio was *Austin Powers: The Spy Who Shagged Me* (US 99), the Mike Myers spoof of '60s spyaramas, which exceeded the total domestic box office of the original *Austin Powers: International Man of Mystery* (US 97) in its first three days of release. It took $205 million at the North American box office, compared to a total of $54 million for its predecessor, a ratio of 3.8:1. On average sequels expect to earn about 60% of the gross of the original.

The highest-grossing sequel was Universal's *The Lost World: Jurassic Park* (US 97), which took $611 million, compared with $913 million for *Jurassic Park*. Or Fox's *Star Wars: Episode 1—The Phantom Menace* (US 99) at $927 million—the second highest-grossing film of all time—if prequels are considered eligible for the record.

CHAPTER 3
Box Office and Budgets

Box Office

The film with the highest earnings at the box office is Twentieth Century Fox and Paramount Pictures' *Titanic* (US 97), directed, scripted and co-produced by James Cameron and starring Leonardo DiCaprio opposite British thesp Kate Winslet. Budgeted at a record $200 million, *Titanic* became the first ever billion-dollar movie on 1 March 1998. It went on to achieve $1,834 million in world-wide ticket sales, of which $600.8 million was in the North American market. This was over twice the gross of the previous box-office champion, *Jurassic Park* (US 93), at $913.3 million.

Box-office champions before *Titanic* and since the advent of talkies were as follows: *Snow White and the Seven Dwarfs* (US 37), which was the first talkie to over-take the record for silent pictures set by *The Big Parade* (US 25) (see below); *Gone with the Wind* (US 39), which held the record from 1940 until overtaken by *The Sound*

of Music (US 65) in August 1966 and again in 1971–2 as the result of a reissue; *The Godfather* (US 72), which set a new record the year of its release; and *Jaws* (US 75), also a record-breaker in its first year and box-office champion until surpassed by *Star Wars* in 1977. The crown passed to Steven Spielberg's *E.T. The Extra-Terrestrial* (US 82) in January 1983, 31 weeks after its release, and then to another Spielberg epic, *Jurassic Park* (US 93), over ten years later.

The top grossing silent film was King Vidor's *The Big Parade* (US 25), with worldwide rentals of $22 million. No exact figure is available for D. W. Griffith's *The Birth of a Nation* (US 15), which was long thought of as the top gross-ing silent, with estimates of up to $50 million receipts in the domestic market alone. This is now considered to be a wildly exaggerated figure, and *Variety* quotes $5 million as a reasonable 'guesstimate'. Griffith himself stated in 1929 that the film had earned $10 million worldwide.

The highest grossing film from outside the USA was the phenomenal Australian success *Crocodile Dundee* (Aus 86), starring Paul Hogan as the irrepressible croco-dile hunter from the Northern Territory who takes on New York and wins hands down. It earned a worldwide gross of $328 million.

The most successful all-British film was the PolyGram and Channel 4 production *Four Weddings and a Funeral* (GB 94), directed by Mike Newell and starring Hugh Grant and Andie MacDowell, which has grossed $257.4 million worldwide. BBC commissioning editor Nick Elliott admit-ted he had turned the script down because he 'thought it was just a lot of jokes'. *Notting Hill* (US/GB 99) outgrossed *Four Weddings and a Funeral* at $363 million, but was an Anglo-American co-production.

The highest grossing foreign-language film in North America was Roberto Benigni's concentration camp tragi-comedy *Life is Beautiful* (It 98) with a gross of $57.6 million.

The highest opening gross for a film was the $92.7 million earned in North America by Universal's *The Lost World: Jurassic Park* (US 97), directed by Steven Spielberg, over the four-day Memorial Day weekend of 23–26 May 1997. The highest single day's gross of all time was $28.5 million for the Lucas Film/Fox's *Star Wars: Episode I—The Phantom Menace* (US 99) on its opening day, Wednesday, 19 May 1999, aided by the fact that the first shows started at 12.01 a.m. and continued non-stop night and day.

The highest loss on any film was incurred by

THE TWENTY TOP GROSSING FILMS

This list has been compiled from data published in the American trade paper *Variety* and ranks the 20 most successful films at the box office by their worldwide grosses at end 2000. The figures represent the total value of the tickets sold, as opposed to the rentals returned to the distributors. All the productions listed are American.

		million $
1	*Titanic* (Fox/Paramount 97)	1,834
2	*Star Wars: Episode I—The Phantom Menace* (Fox 99)	927
3	*Jurassic Park* (Universal 93)	913
4	*The Lion King* (Buena Vista 94)	772
5	*Independence Day* (Fox 96)	789
6	*E.T. The Extra-Terrestrial* (Universal 82)	701
7	*The Sixth Sense* (Buena Vista/Spyglass 99)	679
8	*Forrest Gump* (Paramount 94)	674
9	*The Lost World: Jurassic Park* (Universal 97)	611
10	*Star Wars* (Fox 77)	590
11	*Men in Black* (Sony 97)	584
12	*Home Alone* (Fox 90)	534
13	*Mission: Impossible 2* (Paramount 00)	525
14	*Ghost* (Paramount 90)	518
15	*True Lies* (Fox 96)	514
16	*The Bodyguard* (Warner 92)	507
17	*Aladdin* (Buena Vista 92)	498
18	*Indiana Jones and the Last Crusade* (Paramount 89)	495
18	*Twister* (Warner/Universal 96)	494
20	*Terminator 2* (Tristar/Carolco 91)	490

BOX OFFICE

ANNUAL TOP MONEYMAKERS USA

The following pictures were top moneymaker of the year in the domestic market (US and Canada). Where the top moneymaker is a non-American production, the top American grosser is listed second.

1930	Whoopee
1931	Cimarron
1932	The Kid from Spain
1933	King Kong
1934	It Happened One Night
1935	Mutiny on the Bounty
1936	San Francisco
1937	N/A
1938	Snow White and the Seven Dwarfs
1939	N/A
1940	Gone with the Wind
1941	N/A
1942	Mrs Miniver
1943	This Is the Navy
1944	Going My Way
1945	Leave Her to Heaven
1946	The Bells of St Mary's
1947	The Best Years of Our Lives
1948	The Road to Rio
1949	Jolson Sings Again
1950	Samson and Delilah
1951	David and Bathsheba
1952	The Greatest Show on Earth
1953	The Robe
1954	White Christmas
1955	Cinerama Holiday
1956	Guys and Dolls
1957	The Ten Commandments
1958	The Bridge on the River Kwai (GB)
	Peyton Place (US)
1959	Auntie Mame
1960	Ben Hur
1961	The Guns of Navarone (GB)
	The Absent-Minded Professor (US)
1962	Spartacus
1963	Cleopatra
1964	The Carpetbaggers
1965	Mary Poppins
1966	Thunderball (GB)
	Doctor Zhivago (US)
1967	The Dirty Dozen
1968	The Graduate
1969	The Love Bug
1970	Airport
1971	Love Story
1972	The Godfather
1973	The Poseidon Adventure
1974	The Sting
1975	Jaws
1976	One Flew Over the Cuckoo's Nest
1977	Star Wars
1978	Grease
1979	Superman (GB)
	Every Which Way But Loose (US)
1980	The Empire Strikes Back

1981	Raiders of the Lost Ark
1982	E. T. The Extra-Terrestrial
1983	Ghostbusters
1985	Back to the Future
1986	Top Gun
1987	Beverly Hills Cop II
1988	Who Framed Roger Rabbit
1989	Batman
1990	Ghost
1991	Terminator 2
1992	Home Alone 2: Lost in New York
1993	Jurassic Park
1994	The Lion King
1995	Batman Forever
1996	Independence Day
1997	The Lost World: Jurassic Park
1998	Titanic
1999	Star Wars: Episode 1— The Phantom Menace
2000	Mission: Impossible 2

Of the 72 top grossers listed above, 13 were comedies, 12 were period dramas, 11 were contemporary dramas, 11 were science-fiction/fantasy, seven were musicals, six were war films, three were adventure films, two were animated, one was a Bond movie and one a Cinerama travelogue. Only one was a straight crime drama (*The Godfather*).

Usually the top grosser in the US is also the top grosser worldwide. A notable exception occurred in 1986, when *Top Gun* wasn't; it was outgunned by Australia's all-time sleeper *Crocodile Dundee*. And in 1990, despite *Ghost*'s spirited performance at home, it was unable to match the charms of *Pretty Woman* worldwide.

The Lion King's number one spot in 1994 is dependent on the accountants having got the figures right. According to the data, the Disney blockbuster roared home with a gross of $298.88 million—but only a whisker ahead of *Forrest Gump* at $298.10 million.

ANNUAL TOP MONEYMAKER GB

The following have been the annual top moneymaking British films in the domestic market:

1936	The Ghost Goes West
1937	Good Morning Boys
1938	A Yank at Oxford
1939	Pygmalion
1940	Convoy
1941	49th Parallel
1942	The First of the Few
1943	In Which We Serve
1944	This Happy Breed
1945	The Seventh Veil
1946	The Wicked Lady
1947	The Courtneys of Curzon Street

1948	Spring in Park Lane
1949	The Third Man
1950	The Blue Lamp
1951	Laughter in Paradise
1952	Where No Vultures Fly
1953	The Cruel Sea
1954	Doctor in the House
1955	The Dam Busters
1956	Reach for the Sky
1957	Doctor at Large
1958	The Bridge on the River Kwai
1959	Carry on Nurse
1960	Doctor in Love
1961	The Swiss Family Robinson
1962	The Young Ones
1963	From Russia with Love
1964	Goldfinger
1965	Help!
1966	Thunderball
1967	You Only Live Twice
1968	Up the Junction
1969	Oliver!
1970	Battle of Britain
1971	On the Buses
1972	Diamonds are Forever
1973	Live and Let Die
1974	Confessions of a Window Cleaner
1975	The Man with the Golden Gun
1976	The Return of the Pink Panther
1977	The Spy Who Loved Me
1978	The Revenge of the Pink Panther
1979	Moonraker
1980	Monty Python's Life of Brian
1981	Superman II
1982	Chariots of Fire
1983	Octopussy
1984	Never Say Never Again
1985	A View to a Kill
1986	Santa Claus—The Movie
1987	The Living Daylights
1988	A Fish Called Wanda
1989	Scandal
1990	Memphis Belle
1991	The Commitments
1992	Howards End
1993	The Crying Game
1994	Four Weddings and a Funeral
1995	Goldeneye
1996	Sense and Sensibility
1997	The Full Monty
1998	Sliding Doors
1999	Notting Hill
2000	Chicken Run

Of the 65 films listed, 24 were comedies, 14 were Bond movies, ten were war films, nine were contemporary dramas, four were historical, two were musicals, one was science-fiction, and one was an animated picture. Significantly, as in the list of US annual top money-makers, only one straight crime drama (*The Blue Lamp*) is included.

Columbia's *Last Action Hero* (US 93), starring Arnold Schwarzenegger, which cost a total of $124,053,994 to produce, promote and distribute. It earned $26.8 million in North American rentals and an estimated $44 million worldwide—a loss of some $80 million. There were 'too many guns, too many cars, too many explosives and not enough heart,' concluded *Variety*. One of the few to have admitted to actually enjoying the picture was Arkansas's own movie buff, William Jefferson Clinton.

The lowest box-office gross of any Hollywood studio production of recent years was the $17,650 returned on MGM's *Molly* (US 99), starring Elizabeth Shue. Unusually the picture had been released for in-flight showings before its theatrical release, scoring a much larger audience at 35,000 feet than at ground level.

Budgets

The most expensive film was Fox/Paramount's epic *Titanic* (US 97), with a reported negative cost of exactly $200 million. By comparison the average negative cost of the films made by the Hollywood majors in 1996/97 was just over $40 million. Dire predictions that director/producer/screenwriter James Cameron (whose cavalier approach to production budgets was said to match an ego monumental even by Hollywood standards) had finally reached his nemesis, were to prove unfounded. *Titanic* was the first picture to gross $1 billion, became all-time box-office champion with double the gross of the previous record holder and won 11 Oscars to boot, including Best Picture. Remarkably, this, the first $200 million production, followed only three years after the first $100 million picture, *True Lies* (US 94), also directed by James Cameron.

The previous highest budgeted movie had not fared so well. Universal's Kevin Costner starrer *Waterwold* (US 95) had a negative cost of $172 million and a bottom line, including distribution, marketing and interest costs, of $232 million. Despite doom-laden forecasts that it would be the greatest loss-maker of all time, *Waterworld* grossed $285 million worldwide, of which about half represented earnings to the studio. When video and TV rights are taken into account, Universal probably turned a modest profit.

The most expensive silent film was Fred Niblo's *Ben Hur* (US 25), produced by MGM at $3.9 million.

The record for the most expensive production has been held successively by the films listed below. Figures quoted are those reported at the time the films were produced and in many cases are impossible to verify.

$30,000 *Napoleon* (US 08)	$4,250,000 *Gone with the Wind* (US 39)
$34,000 *For the Term of his Natural Life* (Aus 08)	$5,200,000 *Wilson* (US 44)
$47,500 *Queen Elizabeth* (Fr 12)	$6,000,000 *Duel in the Sun* (US 46)
$50,000 *The Prisoner of Zenda* (US 13)	$8,700,000 *Joan of Arc* (US 48)
$210,000 *Cabiria* (It 14)	$13,500,000 *The Ten Commandments* (US 56)
$575,000 *Intolerance* (US 16)	$15,000,000 *Ben Hur* (US 59)
$1,000,000 *A Daughter of the Gods* (US 16)	$19,000,000 *Mutiny on the Bounty* (US 62)
$1,100,000 *Foolish Wives* (US 22)	$44,000,000 *Cleopatra* (US 63)
$1,500,000 *When Knighthood was in Flower* (US 22)	$55,000,000 *Superman* (GB 78)
$1,800,000 *The Ten Commandments* (US 23)	$63,000,000 *Rambo III* (US 88)
$2,000,000 *The Thief of Baghdad* (US 24)	$70,000,000 *Who Framed Roger Rabbit* (US 88)
$3,900,000 *Ben Hur* (US 25)	$95,000,000 *Terminator 2: Judgement Day* (US 91)
$3,950,000 *Hell's Angels* (US 30)	$115,000,000 *True Lies* (US 94)
	$172,000,000 *Waterworld* (US 95)
	$200,000,000 *Titanic* (US 97)

The highest budgeted film by an independent producer was *1492: Conquest of Paradise* (Fr/GB/Sp 92), starring Gérard Depardieu as Christopher Columbus, which was produced by French film-maker Alain Goldman and British film-maker Ridley Scott, who also directed, at a cost of $45 million.

The least expensive full-length feature film (shot on film) on record is Victorian Film Productions' part-colour *The Shattered Illusion* (Aus 27), which took 12 months to complete and included spectacular scenes of a ship being overwhelmed by a storm. Total cost of production was £300 ($1460).

The least expensive all-colour talkie (shot on film) was Pat Rocco's 80-minute psychological drama *Someone* (US 65), with Joe Adair and four other paid performers, which was made on an eight-day schedule for $1200 (£500). The cheapest feature shot on video, Stefan Avalos's and Lance Weiler's *The Last Broadcast* (US 99), was also the first film made and presented in digital. Coming in at just $900, the picture was produced at the same time as *The Blair Witch Project* (US 99) and bears a striking similarity—after the disappearance of a group of men seeking the legendary Jersey Devil in the New Jersey Woods, an independent film-maker makes a documentary about the incident using footage shot by the victims. When the film was shown in London, Dublin, Stockholm and the Cannes Film Festival it was beamed from America by satellite and then screened with digital projection equipment.

The least expensive talking picture ever released by a major studio was Robert Rodriguez's good-natured crime drama *El Mariachi* (US 92). Shot in two weeks in the Mexican border town of Acuna, the Spanish-language pic was made by the 24-year-old helmer with a hand-held 16mm camera and non-synch sound at a bargain basement $7000. The original budget was $9000, raised by Rodriguez and his friend and leading man Carlos Gallardo, but with the director doubling as producer, co-writer, camera operator, soundman and editor, they found that they had $2000 over on completion of the picture. Budgeting restraint was assisted by the fact that Mr Galladro brought his mother along to cook for the crew, for which she was rewarded with an Associate Producer credit. Other cost-cutting measures included saving on the cost of a dolly for tracking shots by placing the camera on a wheelchair borrowed from the local hospital. It was rated one of the best films at the 19th Teluride Film Festival when it had its world première there in September 1992. After El Mariachi had won the Audience Award at the prestigious Sundance Festival, Columbia Pictures paid for the film to be blown up to 35mm and a Dolby soundtrack to be added. Under the Columbia banner it was distributed throughout the US and internationally, winning box-office success as well as critical plaudits.

The lowest budgeted British film to win an international release was Bill Forsyth's *That Sinking Feeling* (GB 79), made for £6000. Cost of dubbing new voices for the North American release in 1983—the original Glaswegian accents were impenetrable to US audiences—exceeded the budget of the picture.

The average negative cost of Hollywood major studio productions in 1999 was $51.5 million, slightly down on the previous year. With marketing costs averaging $24.5 million, cost per release was $76 million.

The record budget/box office ratio was 1:1150 in the

case of black and white horror picture *The Blair Witch Project* (US 99), shot on a mixture of video and 16mm film by five friends from Orlando, Florida calling themselves Hoxan Films at a cost of $25,000, raised mainly on credit cards. The film starts with a caption saying that in 1994 three student film-makers had hiked into Maryland woods to make a documentary about a local occult legend called 'Blair Witch' and had never returned. A year later, footage of the uncompleted film and a video diary were found. What follows purports to be an edited version of the footage. The beauty of this concept was that lack of production values and imperfect technique only added to the picture's verisimilitude, but it was the fact that it succeeded in being genuinely terrifying without special effects that impressed those who attended its first public screening at the Sundance Film Festival. Among them were three young women co-directors of acquisitions from Artisan Entertainment, who despite interest from Fine Line, Trimark and Miramax, had bought the film for $1.1 million by the following morning. Cost of transferring the footage to 35mm film and enhancing the sound was several times more than the original cost of production and the final negative cost was variously estimated at $100,000 (per *Variety*) and $200,000 (per Artisan). Even assuming the latter, the worldwide gross of $230 million, of which $140 million was in the domestic market, made it the most profitable film of all time on a cost-to-gross ratio. (The ratio of 1:1150 is based on the Artisan figure).

RAISING COIN

Finding finance for films is never easy in India, but director John Abraham literally drummed up the money for his award-winning *Amma Ariyan* (Ind 87). He spent six years touring round remote villages soliciting funds by banging a drum as he went. Master film-maker Shyam Benegal also believed in involving the common people. When he made a film called *Manthan* (Ind 76) that was set in a milk co-operative, the money came from the co-op's own members. His acclaimed *Susman* (Ind 87), about the handloom weavers of Andra Pradesh, was financed by the weavers themselves.

The budget for *The Diary of a Madman* (Fr 87), from Gogol's short story, was mustered by producers Fanny Cotençon and Roger Coggio, who also starred in the film, by the simple device of selling tickets in advance. Six months before release they had managed to sell 300,000 tickets at 23fr (about £2.85) apiece.

Debut black helmer Robert Townsend raised the seed coin for his comedy *Hollywood Shuffle* (US 87), about Hollywood's perceptions of blacks, by using ten different unsolicited credit cards to charge up $40,000 of expenses. The film stock came free when he succeeded in begging the short-ends from two films he was acting in, *Ratboy* and *Odd Jobs*. Using his salary from these performances, plus the money he earned as a stand-up comic, he was able to finance the film entirely from his own resources—a total of some $100,000—but the seventeen days of shooting had to be spread over two years to enable him to take to the road again whenever funds ran low. His efforts paid off when the picture grossed $5 million.

Miguel Pereira hustled the money for his powerful film *The Debt* (Arg 88), winner of the Silver Bear at the Berlin Film Festival and the grand jury prize at the Chicago Film Festival, by getting up early every morning and begging donations from local merchants in the remote Andes township where they were filming. 'No one denied me anything,' he recalled, 'but by the end of filming people were crossing the street to avoid me ...'.

Journalist Michael Moore's idiosyncratic *Roger and Me* (US 90) became the third most successful feature-length documentary, grossing over $6.7 million at the US box office. It told of his quest to interview Roger Smith, the General Motors chairman who had closed down the auto factories in the company's birthplace of Flint, Michigan, leaving 30,000 unemployed. Moore, also unemployed and himself born in Flint, set about raising a $250,000 budget from scratch by running Saturday-night bingo games in the town. When the money from the bingo games ran out, he started scouring the streets for empty soda pop bottles on which he could claim the deposit.

Similarly tyro helmer Jean-Francois Richet, a 26-year-old unemployed factory worker, raised the coin for his gritty drama of working-class life in an outer Paris high-rise apartment block, *Etat des Lieux* (Fr 95), by gambling with his dole money in casinos over an eight-month period.

The completion of Diego Kaplan's *Sabes Nadar* (Arg 99) was dependent on the soft-heartedness of a black-jack dealer. Down to his last $100, Kaplan decided to play the tables in gambling resort Mar del Plata. He lost, but the dealer, accustomed as he was to hard-luck stories, was genuinely moved by Kaplan's tale of woe and paid out what he had aimed to win. It enabled Kaplan to finish his film in time for its debut at the inaugural Buenos Aires Independent Film Festival.

Japanese producers Yatuka Osawa and Mitsuo Okamura found a sure-fire way of persuading 1421 investors to put up $740 each towards the cost of their $3.7 million production *Senso to Seishin/War and Love* (Jap 91). They promised each one an end credit as a 'citi-

> The hazards of raising film funding include the totally unpredictable. In June 1998 Australian production company, Energee Entertainment issued a public prospectus inviting investment in its projected animated film of Norman Lindsay's children's classic *The Magic Pudding* on the same day as Australian tax commissioner Michael Carmody gave a speech on tax evasion scams under the title 'Beware of the Magic Pudding'. Carmody knew nothing of the film, but the share issue promptly bombed. Over the next few months the $12 million budget was painstakingly put together from 20 private investors and their faith in the film was rewarded when Energee succeeded in selling worldwide distribution rights at the 1999 Cannes Film Festival.

zen producer'. The makers of *Staggered* (GB 94) also felt that investors needed an inducement. Backers buying shares of £500 or more were allowed to appear as guests in the big wedding scene which is the climax of the film.

The idea was picked up by MGM, with the added touch of offering screen immortality by mail order. In their MGM Star catalogue, issued in association with top retailer Neiman-Marcus, they offered a bit part in the Pierce Brosnan/Rene Russo remake of *The Thomas Crown Affair* (US 99) to the highest bidder over $10,000. Anything over $10,000 was to be donated to research into ovarian cancer.

BUDGET BREAKDOWN

In Hollywood's so-called 'Golden Age' at the end of the 1930s, the average cost of an 'A' picture was $1.1 million and of a 'B' picture $300,000. Here is how the budgets broke down:

	'A' picture	'B' picture
Rights	$50,000	$10,000
Script	$40,000	$5000
Leading player	$100,000	$35,000
Other players	$150,000	$25,000
Extras	$15,000	$9000
Director	$50,000	$15,000
Director's assistants	$7500	$1250
Camera team	$12,000	$4000
Props men	$7500	$2800
Costume designer	$5000	$850
Hairdressing/make-up	$5000	$875
Editors	$7500	$3500
Sets	$50,000	$25,000
Music	$50,000	$5000
	$1,100,000	$300,000

With the added cost of promotion and distribution, the 'A' picture would need to earn $1.5 million in rentals to break even. This would require the circulation of 250 prints to 10,000 cinemas to achieve a break-even audience of 23 million at an average ticket price of 22c. Anything earned from overseas release was pure profit.

The inducement offered to investors in the Christopher Lee/Edward Fox film *A Feast at Midnight* (GB 95) by producer Yoshi Nishio, a former Goldman Sachs trader, was the right to have characters in the film named after them

In 1937 a producer of Poverty Row westerns revealed to the *New York Times* how he made a profit on films which he sold to the distributors for $8000 outright—this at a time when the average budget for 'B' pictures was $300,000. Largest outlay was the fee for the hard-ridin' star, who received $1000—the heroine, usually an unknown willing to work for very little in the forlorn hope of being spotted by one of the major studios, got only $75. Second highest paid was the director at $400. The completed script cost $250 and this would often include the lyrics for a song or two. Everyone on the film was hired for a single week, with four days on location and one day in the studio for interiors. To achieve such a compressed shooting schedule, the troupe was on call at 4 a.m. and carried on working until 7 p.m. According to the anonymous producer, the biggest margin of profit he ever made on these quickies was 10% or $800; but often it was less and sometimes nothing at all.

in return of a £10,000 stake. Nishio took the project to Goldman Sachs and no fewer than 12 of his former colleagues on the trading floor were persuaded to put up their own money in addition to their clients'.

Not all newcomers have to exercise such ingenuity. According to Paul Hogan, when he decided it was 'time to have a go at this film-making business', Aussie investors were so eager to put up coin for *Crocodile Dundee* (Aus 86) that 'we had to send $3,500,000 back'. Speculators fortunate enough to receive the shares they applied for saw a return of 1000% on their investment.

CHAPTER 4
Story and Script

Authors

Producers began turning to literature for their plots soon after the turn of the century. In 1902 Ferdinand Zecca of Pathé succeeded in compressing Zola's *L'Assommoir* into five minutes of screen time as *Les Victimes d l'Alcolisme* (Fr 02), while Edwin S. Porter of the Edison Co. presented *Uncle Tom's Cabin* (US 02) in 14 'tableaux' lasting some 17 minutes. Probably the first novel to be adapted at sufficient length for an adequate presentation of the story was *Robbery Under Arms*, by Rolf Boldrewood, which was brought to the screen by the Australian producer C. McMahon in a five-reel version premièred at the Athenaeum Theatre, Melbourne, on 2 November 1907. The first in Europe was Viggo Larsen's three-reel version of Guy Boothby's *Dr Nicola* (Den 09), starring August Blom. In America the same year Vitagraph produced a four-reel version of Dickens' *Oliver Twist* (US 09) and soon found they had set a trend, eight versions of the story appearing in various countries during the following three years. Among them was Britain's first essay at a 'full-length' screen adaptation, Thomas Bentley's *Oliver Twist* (GB 12), with Ivy Millais in the title role.

FILM RIGHTS

The payment of film rights was first arranged on an organised basis in France, where the Société Cinématographique des Auteurs et Gens de Lettres was established in 1908 to act as a performing rights society interceding between companies like Film d'Art—who based all their films on works of literature—and the members of the two leading literary associations, the Société des Auteurs and the Société des Gens de Lettres.

It was only the previous year that the matter of film rights to an author's work had arisen for the first time, when the Kalem Co. produced a one-reel version of *Ben Hur* (US 07). The publishers of Lew Wallace's novel, Harper's, and the producers of the very successful play based on the book, promptly sued. Kalem defended themselves on the grounds that neither publisher nor author had suffered damage and that the film was a good advertisement for the book and the play. The case lasted four years, Kalem finally conceding defeat and settling for $25,000.

The first copyright fee paid in the US for film rights had been negotiated in the meantime between Biograph and Little, Brown & Co., publishers of Helen Hunt Jackson's *Ramona*, a bestselling romance about an Indian maiden, originally published in 1884. The film of *Ramona* (US 10) was directed by D. W. Griffith with Mary Pickford in the title role. The fee was $100 and the authoress received the rare distinction of a credit following the main title.

Film rights were not to remain on this modest level for long. In Italy Gabriele D'Annunzio (1863–1938) signed

Orson Welles based The Lady from Shanghai *(US 48) on a book he had not read and knew nothing about (see below).*

Some books have been turned into movies for the unlikeliest of reasons. Orson Welles decided to make a movie of Sherwood King's novel *If I Die Before I Wake* without having read so much as a synopsis. In a desperate financial situation over a stage play he was producing in Boston, Welles called Harry Cohn of Columbia to ask him for a $50,000 loan. When Cohn sounded reluctant, Welles offered to direct a film for him and added that he had an excellent thriller in mind which could be produced very inexpensively. The director was momentarily nonplussed when Cohn asked the title, but glancing over his shoulder he noticed that the wardrobe mistress was reading a paperback and signalled to her to hold it up so that he could see the cover. He told Cohn the title was *If I Die Before I Wake* and was promised a loan in exchange for making the film. It was released as *The Lady from Shanghai* (US 48) with Welles himself playing opposite Rita Hayworth.

an historic contract with Ambrosio-Films in May 1911 disposing of rights to six of his works at 40,000 lire each, equivalent to $7845 at the then rate of exchange. Ambrosio later bought eight more, but far from delighting in this good fortune D'Annunzio displayed only contempt for the medium which had so wholeheartedly embraced his work. He saw only one of the films, *La Leda senza cigno* (It 12), which he dismissed as 'childish and grotesque'. So far as the 40,000 lire fees were concerned, he declared that they were just a means of buying meat for his dogs.

The record fees noted below do not take account of *The Birth of a Nation* (US 15), for which the copyright fee was paid on a royalty basis. The film was based on a disagreeably racist novel called *The Clansman*, for which author Thomas Dixon had demanded an unprecedented (for the US) rights fee of $25,000. Producer-director D. W. Griffith was unable to raise such a sum and offered him a $2000 advance against a 25% royalty instead. Dixon ultimately received some $750,000, the highest sum made by the author of any silent film property.

The highest sum paid for rights during the silent era was $600,000 (£170,000) by the Classical Cinematograph Corporation in 1921 for *Ben Hur*, the Lew Wallace novel made into a 1925 movie.

The first million-dollar properties were Mary Chase's comedy play *Harvey*, made into a 1950 film with James Stewart by Universal-International; and Garson Kanin's Broadway show *Born Yesterday*. Kanin had instructed his agent to refuse any offers from Columbia, owing to a long-standing feud with production chief Harry Cohn. The munificence of the offer undermined Kanin's resolve and Columbia made the 1950 picture with Judy Holliday and Broderick Crawford. The first book to be bought for a seven-figure sum was Charles Lindbergh's *The Spirit of St Louis*, acquired by Broadway producer Leland Hayward and Hollywood director Billy Wilder in January 1954 for a sum said to be in excess of $1 million. The film, starring James Stewart as the Atlantic aviator, was released under the same title in 1957.

> George S. Kaufman was a writer's writer who hated Hollywood and never underestimated his own worth. Once in the early 1930s Paramount chairman Adolph Zukor cabled him in New York offering $30,000 for the screen rights to his latest Broadway play. Kaufman telegraphed Zukor in reply with an offer to buy Paramount Pictures for $40,000.

The highest ratio of rights to budget was 78% in the case of Pathé's *Les Misérables* (Fr 11). The film had a budget of 230,000fr, of which 180,000fr was paid to the Victor Hugo estate for the rights.

The highest price ever paid for film rights is the $9,500,000 (£4,950,000) by Columbia in 1978 for Charles Strouse's Broadway musical *Annie*. When the $35 million picture was eventually released in 1982, *Variety* remarked in a thumbs-down review that the price of the rights was 'about what the whole film should have cost'.

The highest sum made by any novelist in film history has almost certainly accrued to William Peter Blatty, author of *The Exorcist*. The amount of money involved is indeterminate, since Mr Blatty, as producer of the film,

> Sam Spiegel considered it essential that his epic production *Lawrence of Arabia* (GB 62) should be based on Lawrence's own poetic account of the World War I Arab revolt against the Turks, *Seven Pillars of Wisdom*. Many had tried and failed to wrest the rights from the zealous guardianship of the enigmatic hero's literary executor, his brother Professor A. W. Lawrence. Len Deighton has since revealed how Spiegel succeeded in achieving what other producers had reluctantly concluded was impossible. Spiegel went to Professor Lawrence and said that he was so convinced that his sensitive treatment of the story would satisfy the trustees of his brother's estate that if he was wrong they could withdraw the right to use the title *Seven Pillars of Wisdom*. When Harry Saltzman related this to Deighton at the time the rights were under negotiation, he laughed hugely. Deighton recalls that he was totally perplexed until Saltzman said 'Can you imagine the title *Seven Pillars of Wisdom* above a marquee in Omaha?'. On completion, Professor Lawrence was shown the film and, hating it, withdrew the rights to the title. But as Len Deighton observed, had he visited any of the locations during filming, the professor would have seen that all the signs identifying the production were labelled *Lawrence of Arabia*.

was on 40% of the gross. *The Exorcist* (US 73) grossed over $89 million in North American rentals alone.

The highest reported fee for the rights to a novel was the $9 million-plus reportedly paid by Dino de Laurentis for Thomas Harris's *Hannibal*, his 1999 sequel to *The Silence of the Lambs* (US 91) in which Anthony Hopkins chilled audiences as 'Hannibal the Cannibal'.

The highest fee earned by a British novelist was the $3 million paid by Robert Redford and Hollywood Pictures for former journalist and TV reporter Nicholas Evans' *The Horse Whisperer* (US 98). Evans had asked Caradoc King of literary agents A. P. Watt to read the first half of the unfinished book and fully intended to throw the manuscript away if he did not think it was any good. Fortunately, King saw the story's merit. When A. P. Watt offered screen rights at a flat fee of $1 million, they were amazed to receive three immediate and unconditional offers. By the time the subsequent bidding closed at $3 million there were four finalists, all of whom were invited to pitch to the author by transatlantic conference call at his home in far-from-fashionable Stockwell in deepest South London. 'That evening was so daft,' reported a bemused Evans. 'My kids and my wife were downstairs, and upstairs I had some of the biggest names in the business asking my permission to take $3 million from them. It was absurd.' Having sold the movie rights to Redford, and with another 180 pages still to write, Evans proceeded to pick up another $3.15 million from Dell Publishing for the US book rights. UK rights of £357,000 were the icing on the cake. Both were record-breaking advances for a first novel.

The highest fee for a non-fiction book, as well as **the highest fee for a book that failed to become a film**, was the $2.5 million paid to Gay Talese in 1979 by United Artists for *Thy Neighbour's Wife*. Based on Talese's nine-year investigation into sexual behaviour, the book quickly dated because of the revolution in sexual mores—much of it AIDS-related—during the 1980s. The fee would be worth nearly $8 million in year 2000 inflation-adjusted dollars, but William Morris agent Marty Bauer, who helped to negotiate the deal, is on record as saying: 'Nobody would buy that book today. You couldn't get a $25,000 option.'

STARRING...THE AUTHOR

Novelists and playwrights have occasionally appeared in the screen versions of their own works, the earliest known example being Jean Richepin's starring role as the Count de la Roque in *Gypsy Passion* (Fr 22), from his story *Miarka, the Child of the Bear*. Elinor Glyn, the one who preferred to sin on a tiger skin, played herself in her own *It* (US 27), overshadowed only by the 'It Girl' herself, Clara Bow. With the coming of sound Peter Frauchen, author of bestseller *Der Eskimo*, featured as the villain in MGM's *Eskimo* (US 33), but no other examples are noted until after the war, when Sir Compton Mackenzie played Captain Buncher in *Whisky Galore!* (GB 49), from his popular novel of the same name—for US release the picture was retitled *Tight Little Island*—and author Birgit Tengroth took a leading role in Ingmar Bergman's sombre rendering of *Törst/Thirst* (Swe 49). The first American writer to literally get into the act was black novelist Richard Wright, who took the lead in an Argentinian film, *Native Son* (Arg 50), from his story about a black youth afflicted by racism in the Chicago ghetto. Desmond Young, author of the biography of Rommel, *The Desert Fox*, played himself in the 1951 picture, though his voice was dubbed by Michael Rennie.

Eynon Evans was cast as Amos in *The Happiness of Three Women* (GB 54), based on his play *The Wishing Well,* and a few years later Erich Maria Remarque, author of *All Quiet on the Western Front*, put in a distinguished performance as the schoolmaster Pohlmann in the film of his novel *A Time to Love and a Time to Die* (US 58). Donn Pearce, author of the novel filmed as *Cool Hand Luke* (US 67), played the chain-gang convict Sailor in the Paul Newman picture. Pearce brought personal experience to the role. He was a former safecracker who had done time.

The role of private eye Mike Hammer was played by his creator Mickey Spillane in *The Girl Hunters* (US 63) and paperback queen Jacqueline Susann did a bit part as an interviewer in her own *Valley of the Dolls* (US 67). Another cameo role by the author was Peter Benchley as the reporter in his mighty *Jaws* (US 75). He also appeared in *The Deep* (US 77), from his novel of that name, as the first mate who had served aboard the *Goliath*. Gore Vidal appeared as a senator in the film of his play *The Best Man* (US 64). Anne-Cath Vestly starred in *Mormor og de Atte Ungene I Byen* (Nor 76), based on her own short stories, while another Norwegian film, *Anette* (Nor 80), not only featured the author of the novel, Astri Nustad, but was directed by her son. Amos Kolek, son of the Mayor of Jerusalem, had the satisfaction of playing a character based on himself in the film of his autobiographical novel *Don't Ask Me Why I Love* (Isr 79). Another autobiographical novel brought to the screen was Vergilio Ferreira's *Manha Submersa* (Por 80), in which the author played the rector of a seminary to which a boy is sent against his will

to train for the priesthood. The boy's experiences were based on Ferreira's own. Similarly Gavino Ledda, the shepherd lad whose deprived childhood was so movingly portrayed in *Padre Padrone* (It 77), starred in as well as wrote and directed the autobiographical *Ybris/Habris* (It 84), which recounted the story of the scholar shepherd grown to manhood.

Other examples of authors performing in the films of their own works have come from Switzerland, where Ingrid Puganigg played the title role in *Martha Dubronski* (Swz 85), and Canada, where Gordon Pinsent directed and starred in the film of his novel *John and the Missus* (Can 87), a mining drama set in the economically depressed Newfoundland of the early '60s. *Last Exit to Brooklyn* author Hubert Rechy played a hit-and-run driver in the 1987 West German film of his novel and Tama Janowitz had a small speaking part in the 1989 Merchant-Ivory adaptation of her anecdotal stories *Slaves of New York*. In *Pet Sematory* (US 89), based on Stephen King's bestseller of the same title, the much-filmed novelist had a cameo role as a minister presiding over a funeral. Over 40 years after the publication of his classic 1949 novel *The Sheltering Sky*, 80-year-old Paul Bowles appeared in Bernardo Bertolucci's 1990 film version observing the protagonists (John Malkovich and Debra Winger) from a sidewalk café in Tangiers. The low-life drunken Jimmy the Skite in Neil Jordan's acclaimed *The Butcher Boy* (US/Ire 98) was played by the author of the novel of the same title, Patrick McCabe.

The hugely successful French AIDS drama *Les Nuits Fauves/Savage Nights* (Fr 93) was derived from Cyril Collard's autobiographical novel. The author not only starred in the film as the HIV-positive bisexual lead but also directed it. Tragically he died of AIDS three days before the picture won four César awards, the French Oscars, including Best Film.

Norman Mailer put in a distinguished performance as magician Harry Houdini in Matthew Barney's extraordinary and compelling exercise in surrealism

Stephen King made a personal appearance as a minister at a funeral in Pet Sematory *(US 89), from his own bestselling novel.*

HAMLET FILMOGRAPHY

Fr 00 with Sarah Bernhardt
Fr 07 with Georges Méliès
Fr 08 with Haques Gretillat
It 08 (Cornerio)
It 08 (Milano)
It 08 (Cines)
Fr 09 with Mounet-Sulley
It 10 with Dante Capelli
It 10 with Amleto Palermi
Fr 10 with Jacques Grétillat
Den 10 with Alwin Neuss
Nor 11
GB 12 with Charles Raymond
Fr 13 with Paul Mounet-Sully
GB 13 with Sir Johnston Forbes-Robertson
US 13 with Maurice Costello
It 14 with Hamilton A. Revelle
US 14 with James Young
GB 14 with Eric Williams
US 14 with Alla Nazimova (there is some
    doubt whether this film was ever made,
    nor is it known whether Nazimova played
    Hamlet or Ophelia if it was)
It 17 with Ruggero Ruggeri
Ger 20 with Asta Nielsen
Blood for Blood (Ind 27)
Khun-E-Nahak (Ind 28)
US 33 with John Barrymore (test reel of Act I
    Scene v and Act II Scene ii)
Khoon Ka Khoon (Ind 35) with Sohrab Modi
Strange Illusion (US 45)
GB 48 with Sir Laurence Olivier

I, Hamlet (It 52) with Erminio Macario
Ind 54 with Kishore Sahu
US 58 (Baylor Theater production)
US 59 (Encyclopaedia Britannica 16mm
    production)
Ger 60 with Maximillian Schell
Pol 60 (short directed by Jerzy Skolimowski)
The Bad Sleep Well (Jap 60)
US 64 with Richard Burton
USSR 64 with Innokenti Smoktunowski
Hamile aka the Tongo Hamlet (Gha 65) with
    Kofi Middleton-Mends
Hun 65 (animated)
GB 69 with Nicole Williamson
US 70 with Richard Chamberlain (TVM)
Heranca aka Hamlet (Bra 70) with David
    Cardaso
US 71 with David Suchet (16mm)
Can 71 (musical) with Rick McKenna and
    Caroline Johnson, both playing the Prince
GB 72 with Ian McKellen (TVM)
Un Amleto di meno (It 73) with Carmelo Bene
A Gay Hamlet (GB 76)
Dogg's Troupe Hamlet (GB 77)
Female Hamlet (Tur 77) with Fatma Girik
GB 78 with twins Anthony and David Meyer
    interchangeably as the Prince
Dome to Elsinore (USSR 78)—made by work-
    ers of the Paris Commune Shoe Factory,
    Moscow
GB 80 with Derek Jacobi
Act V (GB 81) animated

Den 85 with Stine Bierlick—at 18 the
    youngest screen Hamlet
US 90 with Mel Gibson
US 90 with Kevin Kline (TVM)
US/GB 97 with Kenneth Branagh
US 00 with Ethan Hawke

LOOSELY-BASED VERSIONS
Der Rest ist Schweigen (Ger 59) with Hardy
    Kruger
Ophelia (Fr 61) with André Jocelyn
Ithele na yini vasilas/He Wanted to be King
    (Gre 67) with Angelos Theodoropoulos
Quella sporca storia del West (It 68) with Enio
    Girolami
Johnny Hamlet (It 72) with Chip Corman
Hamlet Goes Business (Fin 87) with Pirkka-
    Pekka Petelius
Rosencrantz and Guildenstern Are Dead (GB
    90) from Tom Stoppard's play. Hamlet
    (Iain Glen) is a background character.
GB/Rus 92—animated
Motello (Den 97) with Allan Olsen—Hamlet
    combined with *Macbeth* and *Othello*.

PARODIES	
GB 15	GB 19
US 16	US 19
US 16	Den 22
It 16	Den 32
GB 19	US 37
GB 19	It 73

Cremaster 2 (US 99). It was based on Mailer's *The Executioner's Song*, about murderer Gary Gilmore (played by Barney), who refused to appeal against execution in accordance with his belief, as a devout Mormon, that it was an atonement for the crime he had committed.

The first black writer to sell film rights to a novel was Georgia-born Frank Yerby, whose 1946 novel of the ante-bellum South *The Foxes of Harrow* sold over 1 million copies and was acquired by Twentieth Century Fox. In the 1947 film Rex Harrison played opposite Maureen O'Hara, who had to utter such deathless lines as 'I don't care what they call you! I only care that you are all man—and all mine!'.

The youngest author whose book has been filmed was 14-year-old Gideon Sams, whose school composition about punk rockers living in a Notting Hill Gate squat was published as *The Punk* in 1976. It was adapted for the screen by Mike Sarne as *The Punk and the Princess* (GB 83), but sadly Sams did not live to see the film version. He had died alone in his unheated New York apartment at the age of 21.

The most filmed author is William Shakespeare (1564–1616), whose plays have been presented in 344 straight or relatively straight film versions, 55 'modern versions' (where the story line has been loosely based on Shakespeare, e.g. *West Side Story*) and innumerable parodies. Not surprisingly *Hamlet* has appealed most to film-makers, with 80 movie versions (see above), followed by *Romeo and Juliet*, which has been filmed 57 times, and

Macbeth, filmed 37 times.

It will be noted from the checklist above that on four occasions *Hamlet* has been played by a woman: Sarah Bernhardt in a French synchronised sound short of 1900; the great Danish star Asta Nielsen in a German version of 1920 where Hamlet is revealed at the very end to have been a girl raised as a boy; Caroline Johnson, who interchanged with male thespian Rick McKenna in the 1971 film version of Toronto's Theatre of God production; and Fatma Girik in the explicitly titled *Female Hamlet* (Tur 77).

One version of *Hamlet* not included in the filmography of Shakespeare's greatest work (see above) is *Prinsen af Jylland/Prince of Jutland* (Neths/Fr/Den/GB 94). Starring Christian Bale as the Prince, it is based on the story by the 13th-century Danish historian Saxo Grammaticus which was later used by Shakespeare as the inspiration for *Hamlet*.

Among the more bizarre film versions of Shakespeare's greatest play is one in which the Prince of Denmark has undergone a metamorphosis into a gunslinger in the Wild West—*Quella sporca storia del West* (It 68). Hamlet has yet to meet Frankenstein's Monster, but one fears this is only a matter of time. Even the most well-intentioned treatment of Shakespeare's work can be subject to the grossest liberties. One of the most inexplicable is the translation of the subtitles on the US/GB release prints of Grigori Kozintsev's *Hamlet* (USSR 64), intended as a word-for-word film version of the play. The title-writer has given a modern English rendering of Boris Pasternak's scrupulous Russian translation of Shakespeare's original text. Other debasements of the Bard's work have been more deliberate. We may be thankful that there has been no follow-up to the soft-porn British film *The Secret Sex Life of Romeo and Juliet* (GB 70) and even more so that among the many projected Shakespeare films that have failed to go into production was Joseph Goebbels' viciously anti-Semitic version of *The Merchant of Venice*.

The early 1990s were a relatively fallow period for Shakespeare at the movies, noted only for Mel Gibson's *Hamlet* (US 90) and Kenneth Branagh's *Much Ado About Nothing* (GB/US 93). The second half of the decade, however, saw a veritable explosion of screen versions of the Bard's plays. The cycle started with the Laurence Fishburne and Kenneth Branagh *Othello* (US 95). Ian McKellen starred in an innovative *Richard III* (GB 96), with the King as a fascistic 1930s dictator, while Al Pacino brought his own take on the controversial monarch in his drama-documentary *Looking for Richard* (US 96). The same year Lloyd *Class of Nuke Em High* Kaufman delivered his toxic-monster movie version of Shakespeare's greatest romance as *Tromeo and Juliet* (US 96), while Leonardo DiCaprio played Romeo to popular acclaim in *Romeo + Juliet* (US 96), also targeted at the teen market and set in modern Los Angeles, though with the original Elizabethan text.

Trevor Nunn's *Twelfth Night* (GB/US 96) presented Richard E. Grant and Nigel Hawthorne playing opposite Helena Bonham Carter and Imogen Stubbs. Kenneth Branagh turned in a bravura performance as *Hamlet* (US/GB 97) in a year that also brought Deborah Warner's National Theatre production of *Richard II* (GB 97, TVM), in which Fiona Shaw became the first actress to portray the king on screen, and *Macbeth* (GB 97) with Jason Connery and Helen Baxendale. Three modern versions of 'the Scottish play' followed, *Macbeth in Manhattan* (US 99); *Macbeth in Africa* (Senegal(?) 99); and *Sangrados* (Ven 99), *Macbeth* set in the Andes.

Other unconventional productions were the modern Hungarian version of *King Lear* titled *Romani Kris/Gypsy Love* (Hun 98) and *The Tempest* (US 98), with Peter Fonda, set in Mississippi in 1851. *The Taming of the Shrew* also took on a wholly new look in US high school-set *10 Things I Hate About You* (US 99).

The Malayalam language *Kalliyattam/The Play of God* (Ind 97) was an adaptation of *Othello* to Kerala's ritual Temple dance *Theyyam*, while perhaps the oddest Shakespearean adaptation of the decade was Danish contempo comedy *Motello* (Den 97), which mixed elements of *Hamlet*, *Othello* and *Macbeth*. Another *Othello* (SA 99), directed by Eubulus Timothy, came from South Africa.

There were two incarnations of *A Midsummer Night's Dream*, a classic 1996 British version with Lindsay Duncan as Hippolyta and Titania, adapted from the Royal Shakespeare Company stage production, and in striking contrast a 1999 star-studded Hollywood outing with Michelle Pfeiffer, Kevin Kline, Rupert Everett and Calista Flockhart, set in Tuscany in the 1890s. The decade came to an end with *Titus* (US 99), the first large screen production of *Titus Andronicus*, directed by Broadway's

Julie Taymor with Anthony Hopkins and Jessica Lange.

The new millennium opened appropriately with the 80th motion picture rendering of the world's most oft performed drama, with Ethan Hawke as the Prince of Denmark in a version by Michael Almereyda set in a modern Gotham City lookalike; and Kenneth Branagh's lively and audacious musical adaptation of *Love's Labours Lost* (GB 00) with an Anglo-American cast including Branagh himself, Alicia Silverstone, Richard Briers and Geraldine McEwan.

The most filmed novelist is Edgar Wallace (1875–1932), whose books and short stories have been made into at least 179 British, American and German films. In addition there have been other films based on Edgar Wallace plays, scripts and unidentified sources, making him the most filmed 20th-century writer. The first movie derived from one of Wallace's works of fiction was *The Man who Bought London* (GB 16), from his novel of the same name. Despite the royalties from his prodigious literary output, his film rights (over 50 of the films were made in his lifetime), and fees for scriptwriting, directing and chairing the board of British Lion, Edgar Wallace died owing $315,000.

The most filmed American writer is Edgar Allen Poe (1809–49), with 114 films of his works. Apart from Shakespeare and Edgar Wallace, the only writers who have been filmed more often than Poe are Alexander Dumas (*père*) (1802–70), author *of The Count of Monte Cristo* and *The Three Musketeers*, whose works have been brought to the screen in 126 films, and Charles Dickens (1812–70), with 132 films to his credit. (NB: It has not been possible to determine how many of over 200 films featuring Sherlock Holmes—see pp. 51–2—were based on actual stories by Sir Arthur Conan Doyle.)

The most filmed living writer is the Swedish children's novelist Astrid Lindgren (b. 1907), whose works have been adapted for 40 movies. Most recent are two versions of her ever popular *Pippi Longstocking*, one a German/Canadian/Swedish live-action film of 1997, and the other an animated Swedish feature of 1999. The 41st film of her work, the Swedish-Dutch-Norwegian *Karlsson on the Roof*, will be released in 2001. The most filmed living American writer is Stephen King with 32 adaptations, including *Carrie* (US 76), *Misery* (US 90), *The Shawshank Redemption* (US 94) and *The Green Mile* (US 99).

Clashes

The simultaneous release of Gregory Ratoff's *Oscar Wilde* (GB 60), with Robert Morley, and Ken Hughes's *The Trials of Oscar Wilde* (GB 60), with Peter Finch, drew attention to a phenomenon which has been commoner in the history of movies than is generally realised. As early as 1912 the first feature film made in Britain and the first feature film made in America were rival versions of *Oliver Twist* and that same year no less than three different productions of *The Last Days of Pompeii* were made in Italy. Here are some of the more notable examples of movie 'clashes':

- Two Russian adaptations of *War and Peace* were actually released on the same day, 13 February 1915, and the same thing happened the next year in America when both the Francis X. Bushman-Beverly Bayne and Harry Hilliard-Theda Bara versions of *Romeo and Juliet* were premièred on 22 October 1916.

- As many as eight biopics of the rascally monk Rasputin were made in 1917, four in Russia, three in the USA and one in Germany.

- Two versions of Max Marcin and Charles Guernon's play *Eyes of Youth* were made in 1919, one with an all-white cast headed by Clara Kimball Young, the other with an all-black cast headed by Abbie Mitchell.

- In 1934 Marlene Dietrich's bravura performance in and as *The Scarlet Empress* (US 34) eclipsed Elizabeth Bergner's less vibrant interpretation of *Catherine the Great* (GB 34).

- The following year there was another clash of costume dramas with Josef von Sternberg's American version of *Crime and Punishment*, starring Peter Lorre, and Pierre Chanal's French production with Pierre Blanchar.

- America and France clashed again in 1936 when audiences could choose between the Hollywood biopic *Louis Pasteur* with Paul Muni or the more authentic portrayal of the great scientist by Sacha Guitry in the version titled simply *Pasteur*.

- Two feature-length cartoon versions of *Cinderella* appeared in 1950, one from Walt Disney in America, the other from Estela Film in Spain.

- Disney had competition again the following year when his cartoon version of *Alice in Wonderland* was on release at the same time as Lou Bunin's puppet and live-action version with Carol Marsh as Alice.

- Twin films about the July plot to kill Hitler, *The 20th July*, and *It Happened on 20th July*, were released in Germany on successive days in 1955.

- Mario Lanza was not the only actor to play *The Great Caruso* (US) in 1951. Ermanno Randi starred in a rival biopic, *Enrico Caruso, Legend of a Voice* (It).

- When the Italian director Franco Zeffirelli made a British production of *Romeo and Juliet* in 1968 with Leonard Whiting and Olivia Hussey, an Italian production of the great love story was made by Ricardo Freda with Gerald Meynier and Rosemarie Dexter. This version was brought to London for dubbing, but hoping to penetrate the lucrative American market, Signor Freda chose to have it done in that most unromantic of accents, Brooklynese!

- Another clash of classics—this time with some real competition at the box office—came in 1975 with the simultaneous release of Patrick Garland's *A Doll's House*, with Claire Bloom as Nora, and Joseph Losey's *A Doll's House* with Jane Fonda. Both these were British productions, but there was also a German version the same year, directed by Rainer Werner Fassbinder and starring Margit Carstensen.

- Two biopics titled *Harlow* (US 65), one with Carroll Baker as the 1930s star, the other with Carol Lynley, were joined by a third from the Andy Warhol stable titled *Harlot* (US 65). In this rather unconventional

version, the Blonde Venus was portrayed by Mario Montez in drag.

- The well-loved children's classic *The Little Mermaid* appeared in three different versions in 1976—a Czech production, a Finnish production, and a USSR-Bulgarian co-production. There were another two in 1990, both of them cartoon features: Disney's *The Little Mermaid* (US 90) and Saban's *Adventures of The Little Mermaid* (Swz 90).

- *The Elephant Man* (GB 80), with John Hurt, was one of the box-office successes of 1980, but not many people were aware of the Canadian version produced the same year.

- Released within 12 months of each other, if not the same year, were the three treatments of the Entebbe Raid story, *Victory at Entebbe* (US 76), *Raid on Entebbe* (US 76), and the most accurate version of the events, *Operation Thunderbolt* (Isr 77).

- Opera buffs were confronted with no fewer than seven versions of *Carmen* in 1984, albeit three of them from the same director. Peter Brook filmed his French stage production with three different casts, the title role being taken by Helene Delavault, Zehava Gal and Eva Saurova. Julia Migenes-Johnson took the part in Francesco Rossi's Italian-French co-production, Anne-Marie Mühle in Roland Sterner's Swedish production, Stefania Toczyska in Mate Rabinovski's French production and Laura del Sol in Carlos Saura's Spanish production. An eighth version of *Carmen*, based on Merimée's story rather than Bizet's opera, was *Carmen Nue* (It 84) with Pamela Prati in the title role.

- *Wills and Burke* (Aus 85) was released a week before *Burke and Wills* (Aus 85). The latter is a straight presentation of the story of Australia's most celebrated explorers, the former a parody. Uniquely in a clash situation there were two actors, Peter Collingwood and Chris Haywood, who appeared in both versions. (Any listing of either actor's credits is going to read like a mistake.)

- Raymond Radiguet's novel *Le Diable au corps*, about a love affair between a 17-year-old boy and a married woman, was filmed by Scott Murray with a World War II Australian setting as *Devil in the Flesh* (Aus 86) and by Marco Bellocchio with a 1985 Rome setting as *Il Diavolo in Corpo* (It 86). The Australian version did not contain the fellatio scene which caused Bellocchio censorship problems in the Italian version.

- In 1987 both mainland China and Taiwan produced rival biopics of the leader of the 1911 revolution and 'Father of modern China' Dr Sun Yat-Sen. As the two films had the same booking dates, audiences were confused as to which version was which. There were also two biopics of China's last Emperor, Pu Yi, Bertolucci's *The Last Emperor* (It/GB/Chn 87) and the Chinese production *The Last Empress* (Chn 87). The latter concentrates mainly on Pu Yi's relationship with his official wife Wanrong and his two concubines Wenxlu and Tan Yuling.

- Stephen Frears' *Dangerous Liaisons* (US 88) and Milos Forman's *Valmont* (Fr/GB 89), each based on Choderlos de Laclos' 18th-century French novel of high-class sexual shenanigans, were both on general release in 1989. The Valmont role was played by John Malkovich in the Frears version, by Colin Firth in

Forman's version; the Marquise de Merteuil by Glenn Close and Annette Bening respectively; Madame de Tourvel by Michelle Pfeiffer and Meg Tilly; and 15-year-old Cécile by Uma Thurman and Fairuza Balk. Frears, a British director, had his 18th-century French aristocrats speaking in uncompromising American; Forman, a Czech, in the Queen's English.

- Morgan Creek's $50 million *Robin Hood Prince of Thieves* starring Kevin Costner and Twentieth Century Fox's more modestly budgeted $15 million *Robin Hood* with Patrick Bergin were both shot in England at the same time, both claimed to be the first historically accurate rendering and both were released in the summer of 1991.

- The 500th anniversary of Columbus's voyage to the Americas in 1492 saw two straight dramatised versions of the story, one comic send-up and one animated film. First to be released was John Glen's *Christopher Columbus: The Discovery* (US 92), with George Corraface as the explorer, Marlon Brando as Torquemada, Tom Selleck as King Ferdinand and Rachel Ward as Queen Isabella. Some winsome pulchritude was contributed by Catherine Zeta Jones, better known at the time to British TV audiences in her role as Mariette Larkin. Gerald Thomas's ribald *Carry on Columbus* (GB 92) had the Philadelphia cheese TV commercial's blonde airhead Sara Crowe in a comparable role, while *Carry On* veteran Jim Dale played the title role with lascivious aplomb, with Leslie Phillips and June Whitfield portraying Ferdinand and Isabella. Reverting to historical reality, Ridley Scott's sumptuous $45 million *1492: Conquest of Paradise* (GB/Fr/Sp 92) offered Gérard Depardieu in a penetrating performance as Columbus and Sigourney Weaver as Queen Isabella. In the cartoon feature *The Adventures of Pico and Columbus* (Ger 92), the discovery of the New World was seen from the viewpoint of a woodworm accompanying the navigator on his voyage.

- Two off-beat versions of Chekhov's *Uncle Vanya* surfaced in 1994 from as far apart as the Big Apple and Australia's Hunter Valley. Louis Malle's *Vanya on 42nd Street* (US 94) was about a theatre company staging the classic drama in a derelict 42nd Street theatre (actually the New Amsterdam, former home of the *Ziegfeld Follies*), with Wallace Shawn as Vanya and André Gregory (of *My Dinner with André* (US 81)) playing himself. Michael Blakemore transposed this exploration of the Russian soul to rural New South Wales in *Country Life* (Aus 94) with himself in the Vanya role, supported by Sam Neill, Greta Scacchi and veteran Googie Withers celebrating 60 years on screen.

- Twin biopics of Native American warrior Geronimo, Ted Turner's gung-ho TVM and Walter Hill's earnest PC theatrical version, debuted in the same month, December 1994. The former scored the highest rating ever for the Turner channel; the $40 million cinema film, despite stand-out performances from Gene Hackman and Robert Duvall, bombed at the box office.

- Eva Perón was limned by Madonna, with Jonathan Pryce as Juan Perón, in Alan Parker's mega-budgeted musical *Evita* (Arg 96), while the Argentines responded with their own, straight biopic *Eva Perón* (Arg 96). Starring Esther Goris and Victor Laplace, this was made from a leftist, Perónist perspective, far removed from the razzle-dazzle of the Andrew Lloyd Webber movie version, and yet succeeded, probably against the intentions of its director, in revealing the resentment, spite and small-mindedness of its heroine.

- *Fairy Tale: A True Story* (US 97) and *Photographing Fairies* (GB 97) were both based on a true incident in 1917, known as 'the Cottingley Fairies', when two young girls succeeded in hoaxing the public, photographic experts and scientists with photographs purporting to be of fairies in their Yorkshire garden. Although most of the characters were fictionalised, Sherlock Holmes creator Sir Arthur Conan Doyle, a spiritualist and firm believer in the original fairy photographs, is portrayed in both pictures: by Edward Hardwicke in the British version and by Peter O'Toole in the American one.

- The first and second screen versions of eighth-century Saxon epic *Beowulf* opened within weeks of each other in April and August 1999. *Beowolf* (US/GB 99) starred Christopher Lambert as the eponymous wandering knight, while Vladamir Kullich essayed the role in Disney's *The 13th Warrior* (US 99).

- Miranda Richardson voiced Anna Leonowens in Warner Bros' animated *The King and I* (US 99), while Jodie Foster played the role live in Fox's *Anna and the King* (US 99).

Script

The first scriptwriter was New York journalist Roy McCardell, who was hired in 1900 by Henry Marvin of the American Mutoscope & Biograph Co. to write ten scenarios a week at $15 each. Since most of the films made by Biograph at that time were 50–100 ft in length (about 1½ minutes), McCardell found he was able to complete his first week's assignment in a single afternoon.

The first contract writer (i.e. full-time employee of a studio) was Louis Feuillade, who joined the Gaumont Studios in Paris in 1905.

Britain's first regular scriptwriter was Harold Brett, engaged by H. O. Martinek of the British & Colonial Kinematograph Co., whose earliest known scenario was for a spy picture called *A Soldier's Honour* (GB 11). Previously it had been the custom of British film producers to shoot without a script or write their own screenplays.

The first writer of literary distinction to be engaged to produce a scenario was the French playwright Henri Lavedan, whose *L'Assassination du Duc de Guise* (Fr 08) was made by Film d'Art. In the USA the first eminent writer under contract was Emmett Campbell Hall, who was engaged by D. W. Griffith to script the Biograph pictures *His Trust* (US 11) and *His Trust Fulfilled* (US 11), a two-part story of the American Civil War.

The first scriptwriter to 'have his name in lights'—in other words, to be credited on a cinema marquee—was

H. H. Van Loon, author and adaptor of *The Virgin of Stamboul* (US 20), who was afforded this tribute by the Strand Theater, San Francisco, in November 1920.

Spencer Tracy was asked what qualities he sought in a film script. The laconic reply was: 'Days off.'

The first scriptwriters to write dialogue for a sound feature film were Joseph Jackson and Edward T. Lowe Jr, who composed the four talking sequences of Warner Bros' crime melodrama *Tenderloin* (US 28). The dialogue was so ludicrous that two of the sequences were cut after the first week of the film's run. (The dialogue sequences in *The Jazz Singer* (US 27) had been ad libbed by Al Jolson in the title role.)

The shortest dialogue script since the introduction of talkies was written for Mel Brooks' *Silent Movie* (US 76), which had only one spoken word throughout. The dialogue sequence in the otherwise silent movie occurs when mime artist Marcel Marceau, having been invited by telephone (silently) to appear in a silent movie, replies (audibly) 'Non!'. The person making the call is asked (according to the inter-title) 'What did he say?' Response, also by inter-title: 'I don't know. I don't understand French.'

The only other film with but a single word of dialogue, Paul Fejos's *Marie, A Hungarian Legend* (Hun 32), used a longer word—the name 'Marie'.

The most co-writers employed on any film was 35 in the case of *The Flintstones* (US 94), breaking the 47-year record held by *A Yank at Oxford* (GB 38) with its mere 31. The first draft was penned by a single scribe in September 1987, followed by another five from seven other writers. At that point Universal gagged and went back to first base with a four-page outline by Michael Wilson. A two-man script team then produced another two drafts, after which a fresh team of five literati was commissioned to come up with new ideas. One of these, plus seven neophytes, delivered a revised script, which was then rewritten by three of these eight and another four scribes. The next version employed four scripters formerly involved and three brand-new faces. This was then changed into a different storyline by an assortment of the above and another three rookies. The following script retained just two of these veterans and added three hopefuls who may have thought they were on to a job for life. Not so. A 34th wholly independent and free-standing certified creative genius was hired to polish this definitive ... practically definitive script. The result was so close to perfection that it took only one more, a 35th, screenwriter to deliver unto the producers a work of cinematic literature which even they felt was now ready to be consigned to the rigours of the camera.

Unfortunately for those of this numerous company who expected to be immortalised in the credits, there is now a law in Hollywood which decrees that no more than three writers can receive screen credit. In the event those whose names are recorded in the annals of Hollywood as the official begetters of *The Flintstones* screenplay are Tom S Parker, Jim Jennewein and Steven E. de Souza.

Screenwriters, who have long bemoaned their lowly place in the Hollywood hierarchy, have now secured a tangible recognition of their creative contribution. In 1995 the Writers Guild negotiated the studio's agreement to a change in the pecking order of the final end-credits. Traditionally the final three titles had been, in ascending order of priority, Writer, Producer, Director. Now the order is Producer, Writer, Director. The auteurist concept of the creative merits of a film being wholly attributable to the director is, however, unlikely to give way to a more even distribution of credit where it is due. Novelist and scriptwriter William Boyd reported an occasion when he visited one of London's leading bookshops to buy a published screenplay. In the film section the sign on the bookshelf read: 'Screenplays listed A–Z under Director'.

The highest fee ever paid for a speculative script was $5 million paid by Disney to Pennsylvania-based 28-year-old Indian-born screenwriter M. Night Shyamalan for his suspense thriller *Unbreakable* (US 00), starring Bruce Willis and Samuel L. Jackson. Shyamalan's calling card was sleeper *The Sixth Sense* (US 99), which came out of nowhere to gross $673 million worldwide. On top of his script fee, he garnered another $5 million for taking on directing chores. The former record had been held by Shane Black, paid $4.5 million for the script of *The Long Kiss Goodnight* (US 96). Shyamalan saw a report of the sale in *Time* magazine and clipped the story to keep, vowing to himself 'That has to be me one day'.

Art mirrors life and sometimes life mirrors art, or movie scripts. In the Hemdale production *Irreconcilable Differences* (US 84), Drew Barrymore played a nine-year-old who hires a lawyer to obtain a divorce from her neglectful parents, played by Ryan O'Neal and Shelley Long. Wildly improbable as this seemed in 1984, only eight years later, 12-year-old Gregory Kingsley brought a successful suit in the Florida courts to divorce his parents on grounds of neglect, abuse and abandonment.

The lowest fee paid for the script of a major Hollywood feature was the $10 earned by Preston Sturges for *The Great McGinty* (US 40). Sturges was a scriptwriter who wanted to direct. The deal with Paramount was that he should be given the opportunity in return for doing the script for a nominal fee.

Outside Hollywood, fees have been known to be even lower. Bruce Robinson, Oscar nominated for his script for *The Killing Fields* (GB 84), was paid £1 for adapting his novel *Withnail and I* into the screenplay of the 1986 cult movie starring Richard E. Grant. He claims he had to pay it back when the film ran over budget.

The longest delay between the completion of a movie script and the making of the movie was nearly 44 years in the case of Dylan Thomas's screenplay for *Rebecca's Daughters* (GB/Ger 92). Directed by Karl Francis, the picture starred Peter O'Toole as a drunken lord in South Wales in 1843 and Joely Richardson as the love interest.

PROFANITIES, OBSCENITIES AND EXPLETIVES

It is Hollywood myth that Clark Gable's celebrated closing line in *Gone with the Wind* (US 39)—'Frankly, my dear, I don't give a damn'—was the first occasion on which the word 'damn' had been spoken on the screen. It was said by both Leslie Howard and Marie Lohr in *Pygmalion* (GB 38) and had featured in several earlier Hollywood pictures. Fred Stone said 'Damn you!' to the heroine's boss (who had wronged her) in *Alice Adams* (US 35) and three years before that Emma Dunn had exclaimed 'Well, I'll be damned' in *Blessed Event* (US 32). Even at the beginning of the talkie era there were three 'damns' in *Glorifying The American Girl* (US 29) and 'It's me, goddamnit' could be heard in *Hell's Angels* (US 30), as well as 'What the hell', 'For Chrissake', 'Jesus!' and 'That son-of-a-bitch!'. Nothing stronger, however, was allowed until the 1960s, the obscenities voiced by Mickey Shaughnessy in *Don't Go Near the Water* (US 56) being bleeped out. A similar device had been used a generation earlier in the Astaire-Rogers musical *Swing Time* (US 36). Victor Moore's angry response to a street cop was deliberately rendered inaudible by the honking of a motor horn. Little skill in lip-reading is needed to discern that the words spoken were 'Motherfucking son-of-a-bitch!'.

British censors had less reserve about the use of realistic language where it was appropriate. 'Bloody' was heard for the first time in *Pygmalion* (GB 38), 'fanny' in *Convoy* (GB 40), 'arse' in *The Guinea Pig* (GB 49) and 'bastard' in *The Blue Lamp* (GB 49). The British also pioneered the on-screen use of the most over-used four-letter word in *I'll Never Forget Whatshisname* (GB 68), in which Marianne Faithfull made a little piece of film history by breaking the ultimate 'word barrier'. (Critic Kenneth Tynan had, though, said it earlier on television.) The Americans were first, however, with 'shit', which was heard in *In Cold Blood* (US 67) a year earlier than its first appearance on a British soundtrack in *Boom!* (GB 68), and also 'bugger' in Mike Nichols' *Who's Afraid of Virginia Woolf* (US 66), while the permissive Danes led with the first on-screen use of a four-letter word in reference to female genitalia in *Quiet Days in Clichy* (Den 69). This was the era of the permissive society and the breakdown of old taboos, aptly summed up by Bob Hope in 1968: 'Last year Hollywood made the first pictures with dirty words. This year we made the pictures to go with them.'

By the late 1970s language in theatrical movies had become so free that it presented problems for the American TV networks, committed to running only the kind of programming suitable for family viewing. Technology came to the rescue with a computer software package called Automatic Replacement System or ARDS. This would automatically transform every 'shit' into 'shoot' and every 'fucking' into 'freaking'.

In other countries the problem may be overcome in translation, the subtitles to American films not always rendering the words as spoken. When Michael Cimino's *The Deer Hunter* (US 78) was shown on Egyptian TV in 1997, the injunction from one character to another to 'Go fuck yourself' appeared in Arabic as 'You're not nice'.

The film with the doubtful distinction of over-using the f-word the most times was Quentin Tarantino's *Reservoir Dogs* (US 92), in which it is uttered 254 times by the all-male cast, or an average of once every 24.6 seconds. The record for foul language in general is held by

animated TV spin-off *South Park: Bigger Longer and Uncut* (US 99), which had 399 swear words spewing from the mouths of its infant protagonists in a running time of 81 minutes—one every 12.2 seconds.

The longest film script was Edgar Reitz's 2143 pages of high drama of life in Munich in the '60s and '70s for *Die Zweite Heimat* (Ger 92). Reitz also produced and directed the 25½-hour film.

> There were three scripted endings to Robert Redford's *The Horse Whisperer* (US 98), one with two f-words, another with one and the other with none. None won.

The most hackneyed line in movie scripts is 'Let's get outta here'. A survey of 350 American features of the period 1938–85 showed that it was used at least once in 81% of Hollywood productions and more than once in 17%. Film critic David McGillivray disputes this finding with the assertion that no single phrase has been so overworked in movie scripts as 'Try to get some sleep now'.

The most clichéd saying of the Western genre, 'A man's gotta do what a man's gotta do', did not originate with a cowboy hero, first appearing in print in John Steinbeck's 1939 novel about the Depression, *The Grapes of Wrath*. It was not spoken in the film version. The first actor to speak the line on screen was Alan Ladd in *Shane* (US 53).

The fastest time for writing the script of a full-length feature film was two days for *Weird Science* (US 85) by John Hughes, who also directed. This was an improvement on previous efforts—it had taken him three days to script *The Breakfast Club* (US 84), a full four days for *National Lampoon's Vacation* (US 83), and no less than a week for *Mr Mom* (US 83). Although he failed to break his own record with the script of *Home Alone* (US 90), he did manage to write the whole of the second half in just eight hours. 'The faster I go, the better it is,' Hughes declares.

The longest uninterrupted monologue in a dramatic film is a 20-minute speech by Edwige Feuillère in *L'Aigle à deux têtes/The Eagle has Two Heads* (Fr 48).

The longest uninterrupted monologue in a Hollywood movie is by Lionel Barrymore in *A Free Soul* (US 31). Six cameras were used to film the 14-minute speech in one take, since sound editing had yet to be perfected.

In *JFK* (US 91), Kevin Costner as Jim Garrison delivers a courtroom summing-up which lasts for 31 min 34 sec with occasional interventions and brief flashbacks.

STATESMEN AS SCRIPTWRITERS

A number of statesmen have turned their hands to scriptwriting, including Sir Winston Churchill, who was under contract to London Films from 1934 until the war and worked on such films as *The Twenty-Five Year Reign of King George V* (uncompleted) and *Conquest of the Air* (GB 38). He is also said to have contributed a speech to the script of *Lady Hamilton* (US)/*That Hamilton Woman* (GB 42). On the other side of the Atlantic, President Roosevelt wrote the original scenario for *The President's Mystery* (US 36), about a lawyer (Henry Wilcoxson) who fakes his own death so that he can right the wrongs he did in the name of big business. His wife Eleanor wrote the commentary for *Women in Defense* (US 41), a documentary about women helping America to prepare for war which had just been released when the Japanese bombed Pearl Harbor. Katharine Hepburn spoke the First Lady's words.

Carmine Gallone's vast and sprawling epic *Scipio Africanus* (It 37), a story of Roman victories in Africa intended to parallel Mussolini's contemporary victories in Abyssinia, was alleged to have been written by *Il Duce* himself. Some years earlier Mussolini's melodrama *The Cardinal's Mistress* had been made into a successful silent movie. Another dictator with a screenplay to his credit was General Franco, who wrote the scenario for *The Spirit of Race* (Sp 41), an adaptation of his own novel, under the pen-name Jaime de Andrade. He also scripted and shot his own animated cartoons. U Nu, Prime Minister of Burma in the 1950s, used his scripting talents on the side of democracy. His *Rebellion* (Burma 51) described the disillusionment of a young intellectual who espoused communism only to discover it was a false philosophy.

In more recent times former Thai Prime Minister Kukrit Pramoj wrote *Fai Dang/The Red Bamboo* (Phi 79). Field Marshal Idi Amin Dada, before he was deposed as President-for-Life of Uganda, scripted an adulatory biopic of himself, but happily this was never made. India's former premier Moraji Desai was one of only two world leaders to have scripted a film while in office. Having committed himself to producer J. G. Mohla before being jailed under Mrs Gandhi's State of Emergency, and finding himself Prime Minister shortly after his release, he nevertheless felt under an obligation to fulfil his undertaking. Working in the early mornings he completed his English-language script of *Yogeshwar Krishna* (Ind 79), the story of Lord Krishna, a few months later. The other was Hrafn Gunnlaugsson, Prime Minister of Iceland, author of a Christmas telefilm with the politically charged title *Everything is Fine* (Ice 91).

Edvard Shevardnadze, first President of independent Georgia and former Foreign Minister of the USSR, co-scripted *Repentance* (USSR 84) with the director Tengiz Abuladze while serving as Georgian Interior Minister and head of the KGB in 1981. Although hardliner Brezhnev was still in power, this was the film which is now seen as a harbinger of the 'Perestroika' movement which was to revitalise the Soviet Union's stagnant culture under Mikhail Gorbachev. Set in 1937, at the height of the great purges, it was the first film to confront Stalinism in its full horror. 'The year 1937 was in my home too,' Shevardnadze observed at the time.

The only head of state to have been a professional scriptwriter is former President Ranasinghe Premadasa of Sri Lanka, who is also a poet and novelist and has done much to revive Sri Lankan film production as well as setting up a National Film Archive.

Originally written as a play, Pope John Paul II's *The Jeweller's Shop*, first performed in Poland in 1960, was filmed in Montreal in 1987 with Burt Lancaster, Ben Cross and Olivia Hussey in the leading roles. His 1949 play *Our God's Brother* was brought to the screen by Krysztof Zanussi in a 1997 Italian/Polish/German production using the original text for a script.

Royalty has also turned a hand to scriptwriting, HRH Prince Charles assisting John Cleese with the dialogue of environmental comedy *Grimes Goes Green* (GB 90), in which he and the hero of *A Fish Called Wanda* co-star. He also co-scripted the 25-minute cartoon telefilm *The Legend of Lochnagar* (GB 93), based on his bestselling children's book. Made for STV and S4C, the picture was originally produced in three versions, English, Gaelic and Welsh. It has now been dubbed into French.

Sources of Hollywood Movies 1914-94

Not since the 1960s have plays, novels and short stories been the predominant source of Hollywood movies. In the mid-1980s nearly 80% of scripts were original—i.e. not based on a primary source—and by the mid-1990s the figure still stood at over 75%. It was not always so. In 1914, at the outset of feature-film production, plays were the chief source of material. Perhaps surprisingly, considering that the play is heavily dependent on spoken dialogue, 120 of these silent pictures took stage productions as their source against 74 based on novels and ten on short stories. Less than a third of the 1914 output was original material.

Ten years later, still in the silent era, the balance had shifted significantly, with 67 films based on novels, no fewer than 94 on short stories—demonstrating the importance of mass-circulation family weeklies like the *Saturday Evening Post* and *Collier's* as sources. The proportion of original scripts had increased by half to 45%, probably reflecting the fact that by the 1920s most studios retained their own stable of highly paid, professional scenario writers. With the exception of the war years, which saw another temporary surge of original scripts, this figure was to remain fairly constant until the 1970s.

The coming of sound is usually said to have stimulated a rush to buy up successful Broadway and West End productions and transfer them with little adaptation direct to the talking screen. This may have been so during the brief pioneering period when the chief attribute of a talkie was considered to be relentless, unrelieved dialogue, but by 1934 novels and short stories were again in

> 'Not many executives actually read books in Hollywood. Their lips get tired after ten pages.'
> —senior v.p. at Paramount.

the ascendant, outnumbering plays by 138 to 69. The '50s were the sunset years of the magazine short story. In 1954 the number of films based on this source outnumbered novels and plays combined. Ten years later the proportion had dwindled from nearly 25% of all films to less than 6%. This was partly a reflection of the decline of the mass-circulation weeklies, as TV became the primary entertainment medium, and partly the total demise of B westerns, many of which were founded on stories from Wild West pulp-fiction magazines.

The novel as source of material peaked in the 1960s, with a third of all movies made in 1964 derived from full-length works of fiction. As the number of films based on original scripts rose in the 1970s and again in the 1980s, so

SOURCES OF HOLLYWOOD MOVIES 1914–94

	1914		1924		1934		1944		1954		1964		1974		1984		1994	
	No.	%	No.	%	No.	%	No.	%	No.	%	No.	%	No.	%	No.	%	No.	%
Original	97	29.5	187	45.1	191	46.1	234	68.6	107	46.7	71	45.8	89	62.2	189	79.1	246	75.5
Plays	120	36.5	59	14.2	69	16.7	28	8.2	10	4.4	17	11.0	8	5.6	6	2.5	15	4.3
Novels	74	22.5	67	16.1	81	19.6	37	10.9	43	18.8	52	33.6	31	21.7	26	10.9	39	12.0
Biography/History	13	4.0	2	—	7	1.7	9	2.6	9	3.9	5	3.2	6	4.2	4	1.7	7	2.1
Short stories	10	3.0	94	22.7	57	13.8	22	6.5	56	24.5	9	5.8	6	4.2	1	—	4	1.2
Songs & Poems	6	1.8	4	—	0	—	1	—	0	—	0	—	0	—	1	—	0	—
Biblical	4	1.2	0	—	0	—	0	—	0	—	0	—	1	—	0	—	0	—
Legends & Fables	3	—	1	—	0	—	1	—	1	—	1	—	0	—	0	—	0	—
Cartoons & Comics	1	—	0	—	2	—	0	—	2	—	0	—	1	—	5	2.1	4	1.2
News stories	1	—	0	—	1	—	4	1.2	0	—	0	—	1	—	0	—	0	—
Opera	1	—	1	—	3	—	0	—	3	1.3	0	—	0	—	0	—	0	—
Foreign films	0	—	0	—	3	—	0	—	0	—	0	—	0	—	2	—	6	1.8
Magazine/ Newspaper features	0	—	0	—	0	—	1	—	2	—	0	—	0	—	1	—	1	—
Radio/TV Progs	0	—	0	—	0	—	4	1.2	1	—	2	1.3	0	—	2	—	3	—
Non-fiction books*	0	—	0	—	0	—	1	—	0	—	1	—	3	—	2	—	1	—
Diaries	0	—	0	—	0	—	0	—	1	—	1	—	0	—	0	—	0	—
Video games	0	—	0	—	0	—	0	—	0	—	0	—	0	—	0	—	1	—

* Excluding biography & history (see separate category)

the proportion of novel-based movies declined—down to under 22% in 1974, then halving again to under 11% in 1984. In 1994, with screen rights to works of fiction fetching up to $6 million, one in eight movies was novel-based. A preponderance were of the action/adventure and thriller genres represented by the works of such luminaries of the airport novel as Stephen King, John Grisham and Tom Clancy.

The chart above shows that Hollywood has been surprisingly unadventurous in looking to sources outside popular literature and drama, even biography and history never rising above 4% of the total. For the immediate future it seems that comic-book characters and video games will be a strong minority source and there is an increasing trend towards Americanised remakes of popular French (and occasionally Italian) movies, usually comedy-dramas of the *Scent of a Woman* (US 92) kind or family-fare like *My Father the Hero* (US 94). Independent producers, disadvantaged by the prodigious cost of acquiring rights to popular fiction, will doubtless continue to look to unusual sources of story material in the future as they have in the past (see below).

UNUSUAL SOURCES

● Louis Malle's *Pretty Baby* (US 78), in which Brooke Shields played Violet, the 12-year-old inmate of a New Orleans bordello, is probably the only major film whose story was based on a series of historic photographs. They were taken by E. J. Bellocq, who photographed the whores of the notorious Storyville red-light district of New Orleans in the years before it was shut down by the police authorities in 1917. In the film, Keith Carradine played Bellocq, who in Malle's fictitious version of his life in Storyville falls in love with the child prostitute, marries her, and then loses her when she is 'rescued' and given a respectable middle-class upbringing. The character of Violet was based on a real-life whore of that name, who was interviewed by Al Rose for the book *Storyville, New Orleans* in which he reproduced the Bellocq photographs. She was a 'trick baby', the offspring of a whore and a 'John', who was born in the attic of Hilma Burt's brothel on Basin Street. Like the character played by Brooke Shields, Violet was not traumatised by growing up in such a milieu and having her virginity sold to a client. 'I know it'd be good if I could say how awful it was and like crime didn't pay,' she told Al Rose. 'But to me it seems just like anything else—like a kid whose father owns a grocery store. He helps him in the store. Well, my mother didn't sell groceries.'

● Snapshots have also provided the basis for a film. Cebrie Baril's *L'Absent* (Can 97), about one man's quest for his family's past, developed from her chance find of a dusty old family album of black and white photographs in a Paris flea market.

● While a number of silent pictures were inspired by paintings, probably the only feature film since the introduction of talkies to have been directly derived from a canvas is Norman Rockwell's *Breaking Home Ties* (US 87 TVM). The Rockwell painting, one of his most evocative, was commissioned by the *Saturday Evening Post* and used on the cover of the issue for 25 September 1954. Set in 1950s rural America and starring Jason Robards, Doug McKeon and Eva Marie Saint, the film followed the passage of a young farm boy through his college years to adulthood, and his final leaving home when his life is shattered by his mother's premature death.

- A ten-minute segment of CBS News was the basis of Phil Karlson's *Walking Tall* (US 74). It reported the story of a peaceful citizen, Buford Pusser, in a small Tennessee town whose life was turned upside down when local heavies threatened him and his family. First Pusser turned on the crime syndicate, literally armed with a bit stick, and broke both their heads and their operation. Then he got himself elected sheriff and ran them out of town. When Karlson decided to make the news report into a film, however, they ventured back, dynamited Pusser's house, and then tried to close the town to the film-makers. Virtue triumphed in real life as it did in the film: Pusser's deputies succeeded in sweeping them out again and the whole town appeared as extras in the picture.

- David Puttnam was inspired with the idea of *Chariots of Fire* (GB 81) after being confined to bed ill at a friend's house in Los Angeles. The friend, not of a literary bent, had few books and dull ones at that. Puttnam was reduced to reading a history of the Olympic Games, a subject in which he had little interest. When he reached the 1924 Games his health returned and he abandoned the book, but the last paragraph he had read stuck in his mind. It recounted that Britain's gold medallists had included one, Harold Abrahams, who was driven to succeed because he was an outsider, a Jew; and another, Scots athlete Eric Liddell, who had refused to run on Sunday because of his Calvinist religious principles. Five years later Puttnam's screen embodiment of Olympic glory was to take him to Oscar glory, with awards for Best Film, Screenplay, Music and Costume Design. Colin Welland's screenplay drew extensively on the letters home of another member of the British Olympic team, Aubrey Montague (played by Nick Farrell). In the film's narration many of Montague's own words were left intact.

- Another film based on letters was *Take Her, She's Mine* (US 63), which Phoebe and Henry Ephron scripted with their beloved daughter Nora's letters home from university as the principal source. Sandra Dee played the Nora character as a featherbrain highly unlikely to become the Hollywood icon the real Nora became—scriptwriter of *Silkwood* (US 83), *Heartburn* (US 86) (see next entry)—and her triumphant *When Harry Met Sally* (US 89).

- Nora Ephron's script for *Heartburn* (US 86) may have been derived from a novel—her own—but it was also based on a characteristically Jewish-New York slice of life—also her own. The film reflected the pain and heartbreak Ephron suffered when her husband, *Watergate* investigator Carl Bernstein (played by Dustin Hoffman in *All the President's Men* (US 76)), had an affair with Margaret Jay, daughter of British

Prime Minister James Callaghan and husband of British Ambassador Peter Jay—now Leader of the House of Lords Baroness Jay. In the film the Bernstein character, described by Ephron as 'capable of having sex with a Venetian blind', was played by Jack Nicholson, Ephron's character by Meryl Streep and the temptress by Maureen Stapleton. For once, though, the fictional version underplayed the real story. No one would have believed such an improbable tale of high jinx in high places had Ephron brought it to the screen in its original lurid detail.

- Other film-makers have also drawn on personal experiences. The source for Bob Fosse's *All That Jazz* (US 79), a study of a talented man hell-bent on self-destruction (Roy Scheider), was the director's own life story. Two of his ex-girlfriends were cast in the picture—Ann Reinking, with whom Fosse had had a six-year affair, who played Scheider's girlfriend, and Jessica Lange in the somewhat unusual role of the Angel of Death. Among the scenes which were straight out of Fosse's personal experience was the

Louis Malle's Pretty Baby *(US 78) was the only major film derived from a series of historic photographs. Studies of whores taken by E. J. Bellocq in the notorious Storyville district of New Orleans, like the one above, inspired the story of a photographer who falls in love with a child prostitute.*

open-heart surgery sequence.

Bertrand Tavernier's remarkable story of the Paris drug squad, *L.627* (Fr 92), had its origin in the brief involvement with drugs of the director's son Nils. Tavernier scripted together with a genuine Paris flic of 15 years' service, Michel Alexandre. The odd title refers to a French drug law.

The principal source for the story of Jessie Nelson's *Corrina, Corrina* (US 94), about a child who will not speak following the death of her mother until the advent of sympathetic nanny Whoopi Goldberg, lay in the producer-director-writer's own childhood. After her mother died, Jessie Nelson was brought up by no fewer than 35 nannies.

● Luis Buñuel's and Salvadore Dali's controversial surrealist film *Un Chien Andalou* (Fr 28) was inspired by twin dreams they had while staying at Dali's house in Figueros. Dali had dreamed obsessively of a hand crawling with ants. Buñuel dreamed that 'a long tapering cloud sliced the moon in half like a razor blade slicing through an eye'. It was the latter image that Buñuel chose for the shock opening to the film, with the slicing of the eye of a young woman rendered in such graphic detail that it still causes some viewers to pass out. (In fact the actual eyeball sliced was that of a dead ox.) 'We wrote the script by associating images and eliminating anything which had a political, historical, aesthetic or moral connotation,' Buñuel explained. 'Critics have invented a thousand interpretations. In fact *Un Chien Andalou* is a desperate appeal to violence and crime.'

● Jack Nicholson starrer *The Wolf* (US 94) had its origin in a 'lycanthropic' nightmare which scriptwriter Jim Harrison had at his home in the dense forests of Michigan's Upper Peninsular, wolf country. He dreamed that he picked up the corpse of a wolf hit by a car and that it entered his body, causing his face to sprout hair and taking over his personality. During an aeroplane flight he happened to recount the dream to producer Douglas Wick, who urged Harrison to make it into a screenplay for him to produce.

● Federico Fellini found the inspiration for his classic *La Dolce Vita* (It 59) from a miscellany of mainly Italian newspaper stories. One episode after another—the false miracle, the striptease orgy, the dawn dip at the Trevi Fountain—were plucked straight from the headlines. Fellini picked up the Steiner episode, wherein a prosperous intellectual pointlessly kills his two children and then himself, from a cause célèbre reported in a French newspaper.

● The idea for *The Black Pirate* (US 26) was given to Douglas Fairbanks by 11-year-old Jackie Coogan, star of Chaplin's *The Kid* (US 21). The youngster had attended the Photoplay Awards with Doug and his wife Mary Pickford and afterwards was invited back to their sumptuous mansion Pickfair. Over dinner Jackie told his mentor, then Hollywood's number-one box-office star, that he had just read Howard Pyle's *Book of Pirates* and thought it would be material for a film. After dinner Doug took the book and started on an outline. Meanwhile, Jackie was too busy having a pillow fight with Mary to participate in the creative process. Nevertheless, Fairbanks acknowledged his indebtedness to the child star with a cheque for

$10,000—a not ungenerous recompense, representing, as it did, about ten times what a store clerk would earn in a year. Unfortunately, his father would not let him keep it, on the grounds that nobody should take money from a personal friend. Jackie returned the cheque to Doug and *The Black Pirate* justified its star's faith in his young friend's judgement of good source material by becoming the highest grossing picture of 1926.

● Photo-novels, enormously popular on the Continent, are often regarded as the lowest form of creative endeavour. Spain's enfant terrible Pedro Almodovar got his break in movies when he was commissioned to produce a 'really dirty' photo-novel for a fanzine and used it as the basis of his debut picture, the summery, joyous and hugely popular pop farce *Pepi, Luci, Bom . . .* (Sp 80).

● Peter Weir's critically acclaimed *The Last Wave* (Aus 77), which he described as a film 'about the spiritual lives of different creatures', had its genesis in a premonition he himself experienced in North Africa and in a conversation he later had with an Aboriginal in a Sydney bar. The premonition occurred during a package holiday in Tunisia in 1971 when he and his wife were exploring Roman ruins with the rest of the tour party. They were about to depart when Weir was suddenly seized by a feeling that just below the surface of where he stood lay a sculpture. Scrabbling in the dirt he unearthed a small carved stone head, possibly a cupid. Afterwards he began to wonder about the experience in filmic terms—'What if someone with a very pragmatic approach to life experienced a premonition. How would he absorb it?'. Three years later he was working with the Aborigine actor David Gumpilil, star of Nicholas Roeg's *Walkabout* (Aus 70), and they were relaxing in a bar after the day's work when his companion remarked: 'Last week my wife was very upset with me because the great space had left me, and there I stood, and that was because the moon was there . . .'. Weir asked him to repeat this, thinking that he had misheard, and then repeat it again. 'Though it turned out that premonitory things were very ordinary for Gumpilil, I became very excited,' Weir recalled. 'I was confronted by a basic error I'd made in my assessment of tribal Aboriginals—namely, that they perceived life the way I did.' The story that emerged from these two events was of a Sydney lawyer 'with a very pragmatic approach to life' (played by Richard Chamberlain) whose recurrent dreams during a spell of torrential rain gives him the key to an Aboriginal prophecy about the world being destroyed by flood.

● Liliana Cavani's *The Night Porter* (It 74), about a former concentration-camp guard (Dirk Bogarde) resuming a sado-masochistic relationship with a former inmate (Charlotte Rampling) 15 years after the war, was also based on a personal encounter which profoundly moved and intrigued her. Researching a documentary on women of the Resistance, she met a woman whose late adolescence had been spent in Dachau. 'After the war she tried to insert herself back to normalcy,' Miss Cavani told Grace Lichtenstein of the *New York Times*, 'but she confided that she spent all her summer holidays in Dachau. I asked her why she didn't go to Hawaii or some place else, instead. She couldn't explain. It was the victim returning to the scene of the crime.' A similar victim impelled to relive her torment became the theme of Cavani's controversial film.

- The primary source for Sir Carol Reed's classic *The Third Man* (GB 49) was simply a city. There was no specific story idea when executive producer Sir Alexander Korda sent Graham Greene to Vienna in February 1948 to soak up the atmosphere of the still war-torn city governed by an uneasy alliance of the four powers, Russia, the US, Britain and France. Greene himself set out on the journey with only the opening paragraph of a story which he had scribbled on the back of an envelope: 'I had paid my last respects to Harry a week ago, when his coffin was lowered into the frozen February ground, so that it was with incredulity that I saw him pass by, without a sign of recognition, among the host of strangers in the Strand.' For two weeks Greene stalked the city, impressed by its sinister ambience but unable to find any way of disinterring the character Harry from his grave. On his penultimate day in Vienna, he had lunch with a British intelligence officer who told him that when the British had taken control of the city he had seen a list of Viennese law officers which had contained a section headed 'Underground Police'. The British officer had commanded that they be disbanded, as a harbinger of the democratic way of life. When a month later the list still recorded their existence, he reacted furiously until it was explained that they were not secret policemen, but patrols guarding the enormous network of underground sewers lying beneath Vienna. Then, as the intelligence officer went on to tell him of the illegal trade in contraband penicillin, which the racketeers diluted, often killing those treated with it, Greene found that he had the two basic elements of Harry Lime's story—the penicillin racketeer who fakes his own death and evades arrest by moving around the sewers—to add to his Vienna setting.
- Mike Sarne's *The Punk and the Princess* (GB 94) was based on a story written as a school assignment by Gideon Sams, who was only fourteen when his 'prep' was published as *The Punk* in 1976.
- Tim Robbins' *Bob Roberts* (US 92), which he also wrote and starred in, is a dark comedy about a candidate for the Presidency which exposes the ever-widening gap between image and substance in American politics. Its complex spoof-documentary form, elaborate sets and huge cost belie the fact that it began as a three-minute sketch devised in 1966 for the TV show *Saturday Night Live*.
- Although *The Exorcist* (US 73) was based on William Peter Blatty's novel of the same name, the inspiration for the story was a real case of demonic possession which occurred in 1949 when the author was a student at Georgetown University in Washington DC. The child possessed was a 14-year-old boy, whom Blatty changed to a girl (Linda Blair in the film) to protect the original victim. Many of the episodes in the film happened in reality: furniture and household objects careering around the room without human agency and the child growling and snarling like a wild beast. On one occasion, before witnesses, the boy was barricaded in his bedroom by a table which flew in front of the door and could not be moved. Eventually he was exorcised by Catholic priests, as a result of which his father, a member of the anti-catholic Ku Klux Klan, converted to the faith. Afterwards the youngster grew up normally, married and had children of his own. He had no recollection of the awful events which had afflicted his adolescence.

- A number of Ingmar Bergman's films have been stimulated by a chance observation. The idea for *Persona* (Swe 66) came to him when he saw two women sitting together comparing hands. 'I thought to myself that one of them is mute and the other one speaks,' he recalled. It was on a hospital visit that an incident occurred which gave him the kernel of *The Silence* (Swe 63). 'I noticed from a window a very old man, enormously fat and paralysed, sitting in a chair under a tree in the park,' he told American critic Charles Marowitz. 'As I watched, four jolly, good-natured nurses came marching out, lifted him up, chair and all, and carried him back to the hospital. The image of being carried away like a dummy stayed in my mind.'

  On a somewhat lighter note, a vignette of ordinary life also provided Billy Wilder with the idea for *The Fortune Cookie* (US 66), his comedy hit about an insurance scam involving Jack Lemmon pretending to have a permanent disability at the instigation of wily bent lawyer Walter Matthau. The germ of it had come to the veteran writer-director after he had attended a football game where a hefty player fell heavily on to a diminutive spectator on the sideline.

- Jonathan Lynn's *Clue* (GB 95), a murder mystery set in a gothic mansion in the 1950s, is the only full-length feature film based on a board game. The inspiration was *Cluedo*. And like the game, there was no definitive solution to whodunit because the film offered a choice of three different endings.

- *The Towering Inferno* (US 74) was based on two different novels and produced and distributed by two different studios. The novels were *The Tower* by Richard Martin Stern and *The Glass Inferno* by Frank Robinson and Tom Scortia. The studios were Warner Bros, who paid $390,000 for *The Tower*, and Fox, underbidders for Stern's novel, who had second thoughts and were prepared to outbid Warner but found they were too late. Dismay turned to delight eight weeks later when they were shown the unpublished manuscript by Robinson and Scortia, which told an almost identical story to Stern's, about a holocaust in a skyscraper, and snapped it up for $400,000. Then the reality of the situation intruded. There have been numerous examples of twin films of the same story made at the same time (see pp. 40–2), but never was each successful and often both failed. Executives at Warner Bros and their opposite numbers at Fox contemplated the risk they were taking and finally decided to tread where no two major Hollywood studios had trod before: a co-production. All expenses were split down the middle, as were the considerable profits. Fox had distribution rights for North America, Warner's for the rest of the world and for TV sales. As for the two books, apart from amalgamating the titles, the co-producers even decided to split the characters' names—in one instance they took the first name Craig, a character in one novel and the last name Wilson from his counterpart in the other, and combined them as Craig Wilson. For the storyline scriptwriter Stirling Silliphant was able to draw on the best from each, though for the climax he decided to use both of the ingenious twin methods by which those in the blazing building are eventually saved.

- Films based on diaries have been rare, though one obvious example is *The Diary of Anne Frank* (US 59). A notable addition to the genre was Peter Jackson's *Heavenly Creatures* (NZ 94), a remarkable exposition of an intense relationship between two teenage girls in New Zealand in the early 1950s which led to tragedy when they bludgeoned the mother of one of them to death in a public park. Much of the story was pieced together from the diary of the daughter of the victim, Pauline Parker, a solitary girl of working-class background who had been friendless at Christchurch Girls High School until the advent of a spirited upper-middle-class girl from England, Juliet Hulme (Kate Winslet). It recounted the fantasy world they isolated themselves within and the growing despair they felt when faced with the prospect of separation. Irrationally they sought a solution by plotting the death of Pauline's mother, recorded in daily detail in the diary. When the horrifying deed was done, it was the discovery of the diary by the police which led to the rapid arrest of both girls. At their trial a plea that they were mentally unbalanced when they committed the crime was dismissed and they were detained at Her Majesty's Pleasure. They were released in 1959 on the condition that they never saw each other again. Shortly before the film was released an investigative journalist in New Zealand revealed that the well-known British writer of crime fiction Anne Perry was the former Juliet Hulme. The title *Heavenly Creatures* was taken directly from Pauline's diary; she had used it to describe herself and Juliet as people set apart.

- *Sergeant Pepper's Lonely Hearts Club Band* (US 78) took the seminal Beatles LP as its source, but writer Henry Edwards only accepted the assignment provided it was not set in the 1960s, nor in England (where's that?), and that the Beatles did not feature in it. Instead he wove a story around the 25 songs of the album, creating a mythical idealised American small town called Heartland whose motto was 'Kindness Above All Else'. Embodying the music were the town's four favourite sons, The Lonely Hearts Club Band, played by Peter Frampton and the Bee Gees. The plot turned on what happened when they were lured away from Heartland for the bright lights of the big, evil city and the debilitating delights of stardom. The

only speaking role was that of the kind, elderly mayor of Heartland, Mr Kite, played by George Burns. The story was framed in the songs, which were used either to reveal character ('Mean Mr Mustard', 'Maxwell's Silver Hammer') or to take the action forward ('She's Leaving Home', 'Being for the Benefit of Mr Kite'). But Henry Edwards never explained why he was so opposed to the Beatles appearing in the picture, nor why England in the swinging '60s should be such a turn-off.

Rolf Schubel's *Gloomy Sunday* (Ger/Hun 99) was based on a single song of the same name. It was composed in 1933 by a pianist at the Kispipa restaurant in Budapest called Rezso Seress and rapidly acquired a cult status as 'The Suicides Hymn' after five people had committed suicide listening to it. As the song spread across Europe and America, over a hundred further fatalities were attributed to it; a band leader in Paris would prelude its nightly performance by reading out the melancholy roll. The film weaves a fictitious tale around the song, set in the restaurant where it was composed. In this the composer himself commits suicide during World War II; in reality Reszo Seress did become the last of the suicides associated with the doom-laden song, though not until 1968.

- The first movie based on a computer game (there had been many computer games based on movies) was *Super Mario Brothers* (US 93), derived from Nintendo's Donkey Kong and Gameboy. According to production designer David Snyder, there were 'more than a hundred game elements in the film, waiting to be counted by keen-eyed and dedicated fans'. The character of the Italian plumber Mario Mario, played by Bob Hoskins, was inspired by the Italian landlord of Nintendo's New York office. Hoskins, an archetypal Cockney from the 'Cally Road' district of North London, may not have been a wholly convincing Italian-American, but he knew how to play a plumber with conviction—he was one before becoming an actor.

- Warner Bros' *Mars Attacks!* (US 96), starring Jack Nicholson, Pierce Brosnan and Glenn Close, was based on some rare Topps bubblegum cards issued under that title in 1962.

- The only film derived from a circus performance was *Alegria* (Can/Fr/Neths 99), loosely based on the Montreal-based *Cirque du Soleil*'s 1994 production of the same name.

- Blur Productions claim that their *The Blur of Insanity* (US 99) was the first movie to be based directly on the content of a website (blurofinsanity.com), modestly proclaimed by its proprietors as the 'top college entertainment website in America'.

CHAPTER 5
Character and Themes

Screen Characters

The character most often portrayed on screen since the inception of the story film has been Sherlock Holmes, the master detective created by Sir Arthur Conan Doyle (1859–1930), who has been played by 79 actors, including one black (Sam Robinson) and one Chinese (Fan Aili), in 215 films produced between 1900 and 1999 (see filmography). The only actor to have played both Sherlock Holmes and Dr Watson was Reginald Owen, who was Watson in *Sherlock Holmes* (US 32) and Holmes in *A Study in Scarlet* (US 33). Apart from the heroes or heroines featuring in films listed under Remakes (see p. 29) the other fictitious or legendary characters most frequently represented on screen have been Count Dracula—167 films; Lord Krishna—127: Frankenstein's Monster—121; Tarzan—102; Zorro—74; Hopalong Cassidy—66 (see p. 116); the Durango Kid—64; Robin Hood—61; Charlie Chan—49; Ali Baba—34

> **W**hen the Allies reached Berlin in 1945, the contents of Hitler's bunker revealed a number of interesting clues to his character and tastes. The two movies they found were both Sherlock Holmes adventures—*The Hound of the Baskervilles* (Ger 37) and *The Man Who Was Sherlock Holmes* (Ger 37).

Biopics

The historical character who has been represented mot often on screen is Napoléon Bonaparte (1769–1821), Emperor of the French. The role has been played in 205 films from Pathé's *Épopée Napoleon/Life of Napoleon* (Fr 04) to *The Emperor's New Clothes* (GB 01) starring Ian Holm and *Sabotage* (GB 01) with David Suchet.

Other historical characters most often represented on screen include Jesus Christ, of whom there are 168 recorded film portrayals, including one by a woman (Ina-Miriam Rosenbaum in *Johannes' Hemmelighed* (Den 85)); Vladymir Ilich Lenin (1870–1924)—92; Adolf Hitler (1889–1945)—81; Josef Stalin (1879–1953)—50; Cleopatra (69–30 BC)—43; Queen Victoria (1819–1901)—39; St Joan of Arc (c. 1412–31)—37; Henry VIII (1491–1547)—35; Queen Elizabeth I (1553–1603)—35; Pancho Villa (1877–1923)—33; Grigori Rasputin (1871?– 1916)—32; Sir Winston Churchill (1874–1965)—22. The US President most often portrayed on screen has been Abraham Lincoln in 142 films. See also Western characters, p. 76. Queen Elizabeth II (b. 1926) was portrayed for the first time by Huguette Funfrock in *Bons baisers de Hong Kong* (Fr 72) and subsequently by Jeanette Charles in *Marcia* (GB 77), by Dana Winter in

Above: Is this the real Sherlock Holmes—suave, sophisticated, a mental giant? Fear not—Mr Caine is masquerading as an actor who is masquerading as the Great Detective in the aptly titled Without a Clue *(US 88).* (British Film Institute)

The Royal Romance of Charles and Diana (US 82, TVM), by Vanessa Redgrave, 8 ins taller than QEII and arch-republican, in *Sing Sing* (It 84), by Jeanette Charles again in *The Naked Gun* (US 89), by Mary Reynolds in *Bullseye!* (US 90), by Huguette Funfrock again in *Le Grand secret* (Fr 90, TVM), by Prunella Scales, even more queenly than her memorable Mrs Basil Fawlty, in *A Question of Attribution* (GB 91, TVM), by Amanda Walker in *Charles and Diana: Unhappily Ever After* (US 92, TVM); and by Anne Stallybrass in *Diana: Her True Story* (US 92, TVM).

Black Films

The first black film was *The Railroad Porter* (US 12), a chase comedy with an all-black cast directed by pioneer black film-maker Bill Foster.

The first black production company was the Lincoln Motion Picture Co., founded in Los Angeles in 1915 by

SHERLOCK HOLMES FILMOGRAPHY

The filmography below includes feature-length TVMs, but excludes filmed television series. Where known, the actor playing Sherlock Holmes is included.

Sherlock Holmes Baffled (US 1900)
Maurice Costello *The Adventures of Sherlock Holmes* (US 05)
Sherlock Holmes Returns (US? 06?)
Bauman Károly *Sherlock Holmes* (Hun 08)
Viggo Larsen *Sherlock Holmes I Livsfare* (Den 08); *Sherlock Holmes II* (Den 08); *Sherlock Holmes III* (Den 08)
Sherlock Holmes in the Great Murder Mystery (US 09)
Viggo Larsen *Sangerindens Diamanter* (Den 09)
August Blom *Droske No 519* (Den 09)
Viggo Larsen *Den Graa Dame* (Den 09)
The Latest Triumph of Sherlock Holmes (Fr 09)
Sherlock Holmes (It 09?)
Viggo Larsen *Der Alte Sekretar* (Ger 10); *Der Blaue Diamant* (Ger 10); *Die Falschen Rembrandts* (Ger 10); *Die Flucht* (Ger 10)
Otto Lagoni *Sherlock Holmes I Bondefangerklor* (Den 10)
Forrect Holger-Madsen (?) *Forklaedte Barnepige* (Den 11)
Holger Rasmussen *Medlem af den Sorte Hand* (Den 11)
Alwin Neuss *Millionobligation* (Den 11)
Hotel Mysterierne (Den 11)
Viggo Larsen *Arsène Lupins Ende* (Ger 11); *Sherlock Holmes contra Professor Moryarty* (Ger 11)
Henri Gouget *Les Aventures de Sherlock Holmes* (Fr 11)
Schlau, Schlauer, am Schlauesten (Fr 12) French title unknown
Georges Treville *The Speckled Band* (GB 12); *The Reigate Squires* (GB 12); *The Beryl Coronet* (GB 12); *The Adventure of the Copper Beeches* (GB 12); *A Mystery of Boscombe Vale* (GB 12); *The Stolen Papers* (GB 12); *Silver Blaze* (GB 12); *The Musgrave Ritual* (GB 13)
Verrater Zigarette (Ger 13)
Schwarze Kappe (Ger 13)
Gli artigli di griffard (It 13)
Forte di Sherlock Holmes (It 13)
Harry Benham *Sherlock Holmes Solves the Sign of Four* (US 13)
Ferdinand Bonn *Sherlock Holmes contra Dr Mors* (Ger 14)
En Raedsom Nat (Den 14)
Em Gregers (?) *Hvem er Hun?* (Den 14)
James Bragington *A Study in Scarlet* (GB 14)
Francis Ford *A Study in Scarlet* (US 14)
Alwin Neuss *Der Hund von Baskerville* (Ger 14); *Der Hund von Baskerville II* (Ger 14); *Der Hund von Baskerville III* (Ger 15); *Der Hund von Baskerville IV* (Ger 15)
Eugen Burg *Der Hund von Baskerville V* (Ger 15)
Alwin Neuss *Ein Schrei in der Nacht* (Ger 15)
Bloomer Tricks Sherlock Holmes (It 15)
Alwin Neuss *William Voss* (Ger 15)
William Gillette *Sherlock Holmes* (US 16)
H. A. Saintsbury *The Valley of Fear* (GB 16)
Alwin Neuss *Sherlock Holmes auf Urlaub* (Ger 16); *Sherlock Holmes Nächtliche Begegnung* (Ger 16)
Hugo Flink *Der Erstrommotor* (Ger 17); *Die Kasette* (Ger 17); *Der Schlangenring* (Ger 17); *Die Indische Spinne* (Ger 18)
Viggo Larsen *Rotterdam-Amsterdam* (Ger 18)
Ferdinand Bonn *Was er im Spiegel sar* (Ger

18); *Die Giftplombe* (Ger 18*); Das Schicksal der Renate Yongk* (Ger 18); *Die Dose des Kardinals* (Ger 18)
Sam Robinson *Black Sherlock Holmes* (US 18) only time Holmes has been played by a named black
Viggo Larsen *Drei Tage Tot* (Ger 19)
Kurt Brenkendorff *Der Mord im Splendid Hotel* (Ger 19)
Erich Kaiser-Titz (?) *Dr Macdonald's Sanatorium* (Ger 20)
Adolf D'Arnaz (?) *Harry Hill contra Sherlock Holmes* (Ger 20)
Lu Jurgens (?) *Das Haus ohne Fenster* (Ger 20)
Eille Norwood *The Dying Detective* (GB 21); *The Devil's Foot* (GB 21); *A Case of Identity* (GB 21); *The Yellow Face* (GB 21); *The Red-Headed League* (GB 21); *The Resident Patient* (GB 21); *A Scandal in Bohemia* (GB 21); *The Man with the Twisted Lip* (GB 21); *The Beryl Coronet* (GB 21); *The Noble Bachelor* (GB 21); *The Copper Beeches* (GB 21); *The Empty House* (GB 21); *The Tiger of San Pedro* (GB 21); *The Priory School* (GB 21); *The Solitary Cyclist* (GB 21); *The Hound of the Baskervilles* (GB 21); *Charles Augustus Milverton* (GB 22); *The Abbey Grange* (GB 22); *The Norwood Builder* (GB 22); *The Reigate Squires* (GB 22); *The Naval Treaty* (GB 22); *The Second Stain* (GB 22); *The Red Circle* (GB 22); *The Six Napoleons* (GB 22); *Black Peter* (GB 22); *The Bruce-Partington Plans* (GB 22); *The Stockbroker's Clerk* (GB 22); *The Boscombe Valley Mystery* (GB 22); *The Musgrave Ritual* (GB 22); *The Golden Pinz-Nez* (GB 22); *The Greek Interpreter* (GB 22)
John Barrymore *Sherlock Holmes* (US 22)
Eman Fiala *The Abduction of Banker Fusee* (Cz 23)
Eille Norwood *Silver Blaze* (GB 23); *The Speckled Band* (GB 23); *The Gloria Scott* (GB 23); *The Blue Carbuncle* (GB 23); *The Engineer's Thumb* (GB 23*); His Last Bow* (GB 23); *The Cardboard Box* (GB 23); *Lady Frances Carfax* (GB 23); *The Three Students* (GB 23); *The Missing Three-Quarters* (GB 23); *Thor Bridge* (GB 23); *The Stone of Mazarin* (GB 23); *The Dancing Men* (GB 23); *The Crooked Man* (GB 23); *The Final Problem* (GB 23); *The Sign of Four* (GB 23)
Philip Beck *Kobenhavns Sherlock Holmes* (Den 25)
Carlyle Blackwell *Der Hund von Baskerville* (Ger 29)
Clive Brook *The Return of Sherlock Holmes* (US 29); *Paramount on Parade* (US 30)
Arthur Wontner *The Sleeping Cardinal* (GB 31)
Raymond Massey *The Speckled Band* (GB 31)
Robert Rendel *The Hound of the Baskervilles* (GB 32)
Clive Brook *Sherlock Holmes* (US 32)
Arthur Wontner *The Sign of Four* (GB 32); *The Missing Rembrandt* (GB 32)
Martin Fric *Lelicek ve Sluzbach Sherlocka Holmese* (Cz 32)

Richard Gordon *The Radio Murder Mystery* (US 33)
Reginald Owen *A Study in Scarlet* (US 33)
Arthur Wontner *The Triumph of Sherlock Holmes* (GB 35); *Silver Blaze* (GB 37)
Bruno Güttner *Der Hund von Baskerville* (Ger 37)
Hermann Speelmans *Die Graue Dame* (Ger 37)
Hans Albers *Der Mann, der Sherlock Holmes War* (Ger 37)
Basil Rathbone *The Hound of the Baskervilles* (US 39); *The Adventures of Sherlock Holmes* (US 39); *Sherlock Holmes and the Voice of Terror* (US 42); *Sherlock Holmes and the Secret Weapon* (US 42) (cameo role); *Crazy House* (US 43); *Sherlock Holmes in Washington* (US 43); *Sherlock Holmes Faces Death* (US 43); *Sherlock Holmes and the Spider Woman* (US 44); *The Scarlet Claw* (US 44); *The Pearl of Death* (US 44); *The House of Fear* (US 45); *The Woman in Green* (US 45); *Pursuit to Algiers* (US 45); *Terror by Night* (US 45); *Dressed to Kill* (US 45)
John Longden *The Man with the Twisted Lip* (GB 51)
Peter Cushing *The Hound of the Baskervilles* (GB 59)
Christopher Lee *Sherlock Holmes und das Halsband des Todes* (FRG 62)
Jerome Raphel *The Double-Barrelled Detective Story* (US 65)
John Neville *A Study in Terror* (GB 65)
Nando Gazzolo *La Valle della paura* (It 68, TVM); *L'Ultimo dei Baskerville* (It 68)
Uncredited *The Best House in London* (GB 69)
Robert Stephens *The Private Life of Sherlock Holmes* (GB 70)
Radovan Lukavsky Touha *Sherlocka Holmese* (Cz 71)
George C. Scott *They Might Be Giants* (US 72) (as character who thinks he is S.H.)
The Case of the Metal-Sheathed Elements (GB 72) cartoon
Stewart Granger *The Hound of the Baskervilles* (US 72, TVM)
Keith McConnell *Murder in Northumberland* (GB 74)
Rolf Becker *Monsieur Sherlock Holmes* (Fr 74, TVM)
Harry Reems *Sherlock Holmes* (US 75) porno
Douglas Wilmer *The Adventure of Sherlock Holmes' Smarter Brother* (GB 75)
Roger Moore *Sherlock Holmes in New York* (US 76, TVM) released theatrically in Europe
Keith McConnell *Murder by Death* (US 76) S.H. role cut in some release prints
Sherlock Holmes (Swz 76)
A Case of Royal Murder (GB 77)
The Case of the Exhumed Client (GB 77)
Nicol Williamson *The Seven-Per-Cent Solution* (GB 77)
Trevor Ainsley *The Case of the Mounting Fortune* (GB 78)
Peter Cook *The Hound of the Baskervilles* (GB 78)
Vassily Livanov *Sherlock Holmes and Doctor Watson* (USSR 79); *The Adventures of Sherlock Holmes and Doctor Watson* (USSR 80); *The Hound of the Baskervilles* (USSR 81); *The Treasure of

SHERLOCK HOLMES FILMOGRAPHY (continued)

Agra (USSR 83); *The Sign of Four* (USSR 83); *Trouble in Bohemia* (USSR 83); *The Twentieth Century is Starting* (USSR 86)—all TVMs

Christopher Plummer *Murder by Decree* (GB/Can 79)

Jeremy Young *The Case of the Fantastical Passbook* (GB 79)

Aljgis Masjulis *The Blue Carbuncle* (USSR 80, TVM)

Peter O'Toole (voice) *Sherlock Holmes and the Baskerville Curse* (Aus 81); *The Sign of Four* (Aus 81); *A Study in Scarlet* (Aus 81); *A Valley of Fear* (Aus 81)—all animated

Ian Richardson *The Hound of the Baskervilles* (GB 83); *The Sign of Four* (GB 83)

Guy Rolfe *The Case of Marcel Duchamp* (Fr 83)

Peter Cushing *The Masks of Death* (GB 84, TVM)

Nicholas Rowe *Young Sherlock Holmes* (GB 86)

Vassily Livanov (voice) *Sherlock Holmes and I* (USSR 86)—animated

Basil Rathbone (voice—posthumously) *The Great Mouse Detective* (US 86)—animated

Michael Pennington *The Return of Sherlock Holmes* (US 87, TVM)

Jeremy Brett *The Sign of Four* (GB 87)

Michael Caine *Without a Clue* (US 88) (NB: Caine character is imposter)

Jeremy Brett *The Hound of the Baskervilles* (GB 88, TVM)

Rodney Litchfield *Testimony* (GB 88)

Edward Woodward *Hands of a Murderer* (GB/US 90, TVM)

Charlton Heston *The Crucifer of Blood* (US 91)

Christopher Lee *Sherlock Holmes and The Leading Lady* (US/Lux 91, TVM)

Christopher Lee *Sherlock Holmes: Incident at Victoria Falls* (US/Lux 91, TVM)

Jeremy Brett *The Master Blackmailer* (GB 91, TVM)

Ian Richardson *The Hound of the Baskervilles* (US 92, TVM)

Ian Richardson *The Sign of Four* (US 92, TVM)

Jean Manuel *Montesinos Sherlock Holmes in Caracas* (Ven 92)

Jeremy Brett *The Last Vampyre* (GB 93, TVM)

Jeremy Brett *The Eligible Bachelor* (GB 93, TVM)

Fan Aili *Fu Er Mo Si Yu Zhong Guo Nu Xia/Sherlock Holmes in China* (Chn 94)

Sherlock Hornie (US 96)–all-black porno movie

Patrick MacNee *Sherlock Holmes: The Case of the Temporal Nexus* (US 96)

Joaquim de Almeida *The Xango of Baker Street* (Br/US 99)

---

black actors Clarence Brooks and Noble Johnson, a prosperous black druggist called James T. Smith and white cameraman Harry Grant. The company's first release was *The Realisation of a Negro's Ambition* (US 16), with Noble Johnson starring as an oil engineer who makes good.

The first black feature film was the Frederick Douglass Film Co.'s six-reel *The Coloured American Winning his Suit* (US 16), which was premièred at Jersey City on 14 July 1916. The all-black cast was largely amateur, made up of 'young men and women of the race from . . . the best families in New Jersey'.

The first black talkie was Christie Comedies' two-reel *Melancholy Dame* (US 28), featuring Roberta Hyson and Spencer Williams. The picture was about black 'high society' in Birmingham, Ala.

The first feature-length black talkie was Fox's *Hearts in Dixie* (US 29), directed by Paul Sloane with Clarence Muse and Stepin Fetchit starring. **The first made by a black production company** was the Oscar Micheaux Corporation's *The Exile* (US 31), directed by Oscar Micheaux and starring Stanley Murrell.

The first feature film produced by blacks in Britain was Horace Ove's *Pressure*, made on location in the Ladbroke Grove area of London in 1974, but not released until February 1978. Originally commissioned by the BBC, but rejected as 'too heavy', the film told the story of a British-born younger son (Herbert Norville) of an immigrant family from Trinidad who finds himself adrift between two cultures. **The first black feature released in Britain** was *Black Joy* (GB 77), a delightful comedy about an innocent and unsophisticated Guyanan immigrant (Trevor Thomas) exposed to the hustlin' way of life of the Brixton ghetto.

Below: A courtly Leslie Nielsen bows to the waist in this close encounter with HM Queen Elizabeth II (Jeannette Charles) in The Naked Gun *(US 89)*. (British Film Institute)

US PRESIDENTS

The President of the United States most often portrayed on film, as well as **America's most oft portrayed historical character**, is Abraham Lincoln (1809–65). The role has been played in the 142 films listed, as well as a quantity of educational subjects. This filmography of representations of US Presidents cites the actor playing the presidential role where known, though in some films the actor has been uncredited. The date preceding the presidents' names is the year of their first inauguration.

1789 GEORGE WASHINGTON (1732–99)
Washington at Valley Forge (US 08)
Barbara Freitchie (US 08)
Washington (US 09)
Benedict Arnold and Major Andre (US 09)
Phillips Smalley *A Heroine of '76* (US 11)
Peter Leon *Washington at Valley Forge* (US 14)
William Worthington *The Spy* (US 14)
Charles Ogle *Molly, the Drummer Boy* (US 14)
Joseph Kilgour *The Battle Cry of Peace* (US 15)
Joseph Kilgour *The Dawn of Freedom* (US 16)
George MacQuarrie *Betsy Ross* (US 17)
Noah Beery *The Spirit of '76* (US 17)
A Daughter of War (US 17)
George MacQuarrie *The Beautiful Mrs Reynolds* (US 18)
Harold Judson *Deliverence* (US 19)
Schoolmaster Matsumoto (Jap 19)
Arthur Dewey *America* (US 24)
Joseph Kilgour *Janice Meredith* (US 24)
Francis X. Bushman *The Flag* (US 27)
Edward Hern *The Winners of the Wilderness* (US 27)
Alan Mowbray *Alexander Hamilton* (US 31); *The Phantom President* (US 32)
Aaron Edwards *Are We Civilized?* (US 34)
George Houston *The Howards of Virginia* (US 40)
Montague Love *Remarkable Andrew* (US 42)
Alan Mowbray *Where Do We Go From Here?* (US 45)
Douglass Dumbrille *Monsieur Beaucaire* (US 46)
Robert Barrat *The Time of their Lives* (US 46)
Richard Gaines *Unconquered* (US 47)
James Seay *When the Redskins Rode* (US 51)
John Crawford *John Paul Jones* (US 59)
Howard St John *Lafayette* (Fr 62)
Washington at Valley Forge (US 71)
Lorne Green *Washington—The Man* (US c. 75)
Patrick O'Neal *Independence* (US 76)
Barry Bostwick *George Washington* (US 84, TVM); *George Washington II: The Forging of a Nation* (US 86, TVM)
Frank Windsor *Revolution* (GB 86)
Jeff Daniels *The Crossing* (US 00, TVM)
Terry Layman *The Patriot* (US/Ger 00)

1797 JOHN ADAMS (1735–1826)
Jack Drumier *The Beautiful Mrs Reynolds* (US 18)
The Phantom President (US 32)
John Paul Jones (US 59)
William Daniels 1776 (US 72)
Pat Hingle *Independence* (US 76)
Hal Holbrook *George Washington* (US 84, TVM)
Paul Collins *George Washington II: The Forging of a Nation* (US 86, TVM)

1801 THOMAS JEFFERSON (1743–1826)
A Continental Girl (US 15)
Charles Jackson *The Heart of a Hero* (US 16)
Albert Hart *The Beautiful Mrs Reynolds* (US 18)P. R. Scammon *My Own United*

States (US 18)
Lionel Adams *Janice Meredith* (US 24)
Frank Walsh *America* (US 24)
Albert Hart *The Man Without a Country* (US 25)
Old Ironsides (US 26)
Montague Love *Alexander Hamilton* (US 31)
The Phantom President (US 32)
George Irving *Hearts Divided* (US 36)
Guy Bates *Post Maytime* (US 37)
The Howards of Virginia (US 40)
Gilbert Emery *The Remarkable Andrew* (US 42); *The Loves of Edgar Allan Poe* (US 42)
Grandon Rhodes *The Magnificent Doll* (US 46)
Holmes Herbert *Barbary Pirate* (US 49)
Herbert Heyes *The Far Horizons* (US 55)
John Paul Jones (US 59)
Ken Howard *1776* (US 72); *Independence* (US 76)
Jeffrey Jones *George Washington II: The Forging of a Nation* (US 86, TVM)
Nick Nolte *Jefferson in Paris* (US 95)
Sam Neill *Sally Hemings: An American Scandal* (US 00, TVM)

1809 JAMES MADISON (1751–1836)
Burgess Meredith *The Magnificent Doll* (US 46)
Guy Paul *George Washington II: The Forging of a Nation* (US 86, TVM)
Reno Roop *Sally Hemings: An American Scandal* (US 00, TVM)

1817 JAMES MONROE (1758–1831)
Charles Brandt *The Beautiful Mrs Reynolds* (US 18)
The Spirit of Lafayette (US 19)
Emmett King *The Man Without a Country* (US 25)
Morgan Wallace *Alexander Hamilton* (US 31)
The Kentuckian (US 55)
Robert Kelly *George Washington II: The Forging of a Nation* (US 86, TVM)

1825 JOHN QUINCY ADAMS (1767–1848)
Anthony Hopkins *Amistad* (US 97)

1829 ANDREW JACKSON (1767–1845)
F. C. Earle *My Own United States* (US 18)
George Irving *The Eagle of the Sea* (US 26)
Russell Simpson *The Frontiersman* (US 27)
Lionel Barrymore *The Gorgeous Hussy* (US 36)
Hugh Sothern *The Buccaneer* (US 38)
Edward Ellis *Man of Conquest* (US 39)
Brian Donlevy *The Remarkable Andrew* (US 42)
Der unendliche Weg (Ger 43)
Lionel Barrymore *Lone Star* (US 52)
Charlton Heston *The President's Lady* (US 53)
Basil Ruysdael *Davy Crockett, King of the Wild Frontier* (US 55)
Carl Brenton Reid *The First Texan* (US 56)
Charlton Heston *The Buccaneer* (US 58)
John Anderson *Bridger* (US 76, TVM)
G. D. Spradlin *Houston: The Legend of Texas*

(US 86, TVM)
Matt Salinger (young Jackson) and David Hemmings (older Jackson) *Davy Crockett: Rainbow in the Thunder* (US 88, TVM)

1837 MARTIN VAN BUREN (1782–1862)
Charles Trowbridge *The Gorgeous Hussy* (US 36)
Nigel Hawthorne *Amistad* (US 97)

1841 WILLIAM HENRY HARRISON (1773–1841)
Douglass Dumbrille *Ten Gentlemen from West Point* (US 42)
George Eldredge *Brave Warrior* (US 52)
David Clennon *Tecumseh: The Last Warrior* (US 95, TVM)

1841 JOHN TYLER (1790–1862)
No portrayals on screen

1845 JAMES KNOX POLK (1795–1849)
Addison Richards *The Oregon Trail* (US 59)
Noble Willingham *Dream West* (US 86, TVM)

1849 ZACHARY TAYLOR (1784–1850)
The Fall of Black Hawk (US 12)
Harry Holden *The Yankee Clipper* (US 27)
Robert Barrat *Distant Drums* (US 51)
Fay Roope *Seminole* (US 53)
James Gammon *One Man's Hero* (US 99)

1850 MILLARD FILLMORE (1800–74)
No portrayals on screen

1853 FRANKLIN PIERCE (1804–69)
Porter Hall *The Great Moment* (US 44)

1857 JAMES BUCHANAN (1791–1868)
Henry B. Walthall *Hearts in Bondage* (US 36)

1861 ABRAHAM LINCOLN (1809–65)
Uncle Tom's Cabin (US 03)
The Blue and the Grey (US 08)
The Reprieve (US 08)
The Life of Abraham Lincoln (US 08)
Lincoln's Speech at Gettysburg (Fr 08)— Gaumont talking picture
The Assassination of Abraham Lincoln (US 09)
Stirring Days in Old Virginia (US 09)
George Stelle *The Sleeping Sentinel* (US 10)
Abraham Lincoln's Clemency (US 11)
The Old Man and Jim (US 11)
The Fortunes of War (US 11)
James Dayton *Lieutenant Grey* (US 11)
Ralph Ince *Under One Flag* (US 11)
A Romance of the '60's (US 11)
Ralph Ince *The Battle Hymn of the Republic* (US 11)
Grant and Lincoln (US 11)
Ralph Ince *The Seventh Son* (US 12)
H. G. Lonsdale *The Fall of Black Hawk* (US 12)
Ralph Ince *Lincoln's Gettysburg Address* (US12)
Francis Ford *On Secret Service* (US 12); *When Lincoln Paid* (US 12)
When Lincoln was President (US 13)
Hugh Ford *With Lee in Virginia* (US 13)

US PRESIDENTS (continued)

From Rail Splitter to President (US 13)
William Clifford The Toll of War (US 13)
Lincoln for the Defense (US 13)
Ralph Ince Songbird of the North (US 13)
Willard Mack The Battle of Gettysburg (US 13)
Ralph Ince Lincoln the Lover (US 14); The Man Who Knew Lincoln (US 14)
The Sleeping Sentinel (US 14)
Benjamin Chapin Old Abe (US 15)
The Magistrate's Story (US 15)
Joseph Henabery The Birth of a Nation (US 15)
Francis Ford The Heart of Lincoln (US 15)
William Ferguson The Battle Cry of Peace (US 15)
Frank McGlynn The Life of Abraham Lincoln (US 15)
The Heart of Maryland (US 15)
Samuel Drane The Crisis (US 16)
Benjamin Chapin Ten one-reelers collectively known as The Lincoln Cycle (US 17)
Ralph Ince Battle Hymn of the Republic (US 17)
Clarence Barr Madame Who (US 18)
Gerald Day My Own United States (US 18)
Rolf Leslie Victory and Peace (GB 18)
Benjamin Chapin Lincoln's Thanksgiving Story (US 18); Children of Democracy (US 18); Son of Democracy (US 18); Down the River (US 18)
Meyer F. Stroell The Copperhead (US 19)
The Land of Opportunity (US 20)
Ralph Ince The Highest Law (US 21)
Ellery Paine Lincoln's Gettysburg Address (US 22) talkie
Wild Bill Hickock (US 23)
The Heart of Abraham Lincoln (US 24)
Ellery Paine (?) An Episode in the Life of Abraham Lincoln (US 24) talkie
George A. Billings Barbara Freitchie (US 24); The Dramatic Life of Abraham Lincoln (US 24)
Charles E. Bull The Iron Horse (US 24)
George A. Billings The Man Without a Country (US 25); Hands Up (US 26)
Charles E. Bull The Heart of Maryland (US 27)
Rev. Lincoln Caswell Lincoln's Gettysburg Address (US 27) talkie
Uncle Tom's Cabin (US 27)
The Heart of Lincoln (US 27)
Frank Austin Court Martial (US 28)
Walter Houston Two Americans (US 29)
George A. Billings Lincoln's Gettysburg Address (US 30)
Only the Brave (US 30)
Walter Houston Abraham Lincoln (US 30)
The Phantom President (US 32)
Frank McGlynn Abraham Lincoln, the Pioneer (US 33); Abraham Lincoln, the Statesman (US 33); Are We Civilized? (US 34); The Littlest Rebel (US 35); Roaring West (US 35)
Chic Sale The Perfect Tribute (US 35)
Frank McGlynn The Prisoner of Shark Island (US 36); Hearts in Bondage (US 36)
Segraren Vid Hampton Roads (Swe c. 36)
Bud Buster Cavalry (US 36)
Frank McGlynn Western Gold (US 37); Wells Fargo (US 37); The Man Without a Country (US 37); The Plainsman (US 37)
Albert Russell Courage of the West (US 37)
Triumph (GB? 37)
Percy Parsons Victoria the Great (GB 37)
Frank McGlynn The Lone Ranger (US 37); The Mad Empress (Mex 39)

A Failure at Fifty (US 39)
Frank McGlynn Lincoln in the White House (US 39)
Frank McGlynn and Walter Huston Land of Liberty (US 39) compilation film
John Carradine Of Human Hearts (US 39)
Henry Fonda Young Mr Lincoln (US 39)
Raymond Massey Abe Lincoln in Illinois (US 39)
Gene Reynolds The Blue Bird (US 40)
Victor Killain Virginia City (US 40)
Charles Middleton Sante Fé Trail (US 40)
A Dispatch from Reuters (US 40)
Dreams (US 40)
Not Long Remember (US 41)
Charles Middleton They Died With Their Boots On (US 41)
Ed O'Neill Tennessee Johnson (US 42)
Joel Day The Days of Buffalo Bill (US 46)
Charles Middleton The Decision of Christopher Blake (US 48)
Jeff Corey Rock Island Trail (US 50); Transcontinent Express (US 50)
G. William Horsley Lincoln in Illinois (US 50)
Hans Conreid New Mexico (US 51)
Leslie Kimmell The Tall Target (US 51)
Thomas Mitchell (?) The Lincoln-Holmes Incident, a Folktale (US 52)
Richard Hale San Antone (US 53)
Suddenly (US 54)
James Griffith Apache Ambush (US 55)
Stanley Hall The Prince of Players (US 55)
The Palmetto Conspiracy (US 55)
Tom Tryon Springfield Incident (US 55)
The Abductors (US 57) corpse only
Austin Green The Story of Mankind (US 57)
Royal Dano Lincoln: The Young Years (US c. 59, TVM)
Lincoln at Gettysburg (US 60)
The Boyhood of Abraham Lincoln (US 62)
Raymond Massey How the West was Won (US 63)
Uncle Tom's Cabin (FRG 65)
Jeff Corey Der Schatz der Azteken (FRG/Fr/It/Yug 65)
Dennis Weaver The Great Man's Whiskers (US 71)
Charlton Heston Lincoln's Gettysburg Address (US 73)
Arthur Hill The Rivalry (US 75)
William Deprato The Faking of the President (US 76)
John Anderson The Lincoln Conspiracy (US 77)
Ford Rainey Guardian of the Wilderness (US 77)
Gregory Peck The Blue and the Gray (US 82, TVM)
Hal Holbrook North and South (US 85, TVM); North and South Book II (US 86, TVM)
F. Murray Abraham Dream West (US 86, TVM)
Sam Waterston Gore Vidal's Lincoln (US 88, TVM)
Robert V. Barron Bill and Ted's Excellent Adventure (US 89)
The Rose and the Jackal (US 90, TVM)
Richard Blake The Big Picture (US 90)
Jason Robards The Perfect Tribute (US 91, TVM)
Kris Kristofferson Tad (US 95, TVM)
The Seven Mysteries of Life (US 95)
Charles L. Brame Happy Gilmore (US 96)
Brendan Fraser Bedazzled (US 00)

1865 ANDREW JOHNSON (1808–75)
Van Heflin Tennessee Johnson (US 42)
Bill Hindman The Ordeal of Dr Mudd (US 80, TVM)

1869 ULYSSES SIMPSON GRANT (1822–85)
Barbara Freitchie (US 08)
Stirring Days in Old Virginia (US 08)
The Blue and the Gray (US 08)
The Old Soldier's Story (US 09)
The Bugle Call (US 09)
From Wallace to Grant (US 11)
Alvin Wyckoff Lieutenant Grey of the Confederacy (US 11)
Grant and Lincoln (US 11)
With Lee in Virginia (US 13)
John Smiley The Battle of Shiloh (US 13)
The Littlest Rebel (US 14)
Paul Scardon The Battle Cry of Peace (US 15)
Donald Crisp The Birth of a Nation (US 15)
Frank Murray My Own United States (US 18)
Wilbur J. Fox The Warrens of Virginia (US 24)
Walter Rogers Abraham Lincoln (US 24)
Dixie (US 24)
Walter Rogers Flaming Frontier (US 26); The Heart of Maryland (US 27); The Little Shepherd of Kingdom Come (US 28)
Court-Martial (US 28)
Fred Warren Abraham Lincoln (US 30)
Guy Oliver Only the Brave (US 30)
Fred Warren Secret Service (US 31)
Walter Rogers Silver Dollar (US 32)
Fred Warren Operator 13 (US 34)
Gold is Where You Find It (US 38)
Joseph Crehan Union Pacific (US 39); Geronimo (US 39)
Harrison Greene The Son of Davy Crockett (US 41); Tennessee Johnson (US 42)
Joseph Crehan They Died With Their Boots On (US 42); The Adventures of Mark Twain (US 44)
Reginald Sheffield Centennial Summer (US 46)
John Hamilton The Fabulous Texan (US 47)
Joseph Crehan Silver River (US 48)
Sunset at Appotomax (US 53)
John Hamilton Sitting Bull (US 54)
Hayden Rorke Drum Beat (US 54)
Morris Ankrum From the Earth to the Moon (US 58)
Stan Jones The Horse Soldiers (US 59)
Henry Morgan How the West was Won (US 63)
Buffalo Bill, l'eroe del Far West (It/Fr/FRG 65)
Antonio Albaisin (?) Ringo e Gringo contro tutti (It 66)
John McLiam Freedom Road (US 79, TVM)
Jason Robards The Legend of the Lone Ranger (US 81)
Rip Torn The Blue and the Gray (US 82, TVM)
Mark Moses North and South (US 85, TVM)
Anthony Zerbe North and South, Book II (US 86, TVM)
Alan North Liberty (US 86, TVM)
James Gamman Gore Vidal's Lincoln (US 88, TVM)
Stanley Anderson Son of the Morning Star (US 91, TVM)
Kevin Kline Wild Wild West (US 99)

1877 RUTHERFORD BIRCHARD HAYES (1822–93)
John Dilson Buffalo Bill (US 44)

US PRESIDENTS (continued)

1881 JAMES ABRAM GARFIELD
(1831–81)
Night Raiders (US 39)
Lawrence Wolf *No More Excuses* (US 68)
Van Johnson *Il prezzo del potere* (It/Sp 69)

1881 CHESTER ALAN ARTHUR (1831–86)
Emmett Corrigan *Silver Dollar* (US 32)
Larry Gates *Cattle King* (US 63)

1885 STEPHEN GROVER CLEVELAND
(1837–1908)
Topack *Lively Political Debate* (US 1894)
William B. Davison *Lillian Russell* (US 40)
Pat McCormick *Buffalo Bill and the Indians*
(US 76)
Wilford A. Brimley *The Wild Wild West
Revisited* (US 79, TVM)
Haji Washington (Iran 83)

1889 BENJAMIN HARRISON (1833–1901)
Steele *Lively Political Debate* (US 1894)
Roy Gordon *Stars and Stripes Forever* (US
52)

1897 WILLIAM MCKINLEY (1843–1901)
A Message to Garcia (US 16)
Del Henderson *A Message to Garcia* (US 36)
Frank Conroy *This is My Affair* (US 37)

1901 THEODORE ROOSEVELT
(1858–1919)
Terrible Teddy, The Grizzly King (US 01)
The 'Teddy' Bears (US 07)
Big Game Hunting in Africa (US 09) recon-
struction newsfilm with actor portraying
T.R.
Up San Juan Hill (US 09)
T.R. as himself in unidentified one-reel com-
edy starring Matty Roubert (US 14)
T.R. himself in *Womanhood, the Glory of a
Nation* (US 17)
W. E. Whittle *Why America Will Win* (US 18)
W. E. Whittle *General Pershing* (US 19)
Francis J. Noonan (boy), Herbert Bradshaw
(young man), E. J. Ratcliffe *The Fighting
Roosevelts* (US 19)
Jack Ridgeway *The Copperhead* (US 19)
E. J. Radcliffe *Sundown* (US 24)
Buck Black *Lights of Old Broadway* (US 25)
Frank Hopper *The Rough Riders* (US 27)
The Phantom President (US 32)
The Man Who Dared (US 33)
I Loved a Woman (US 33)
Erle C. Kent *The End of the Trail* (US 36)
Sidney Blackmer *This Is My Affair* (US 37)
Wallis Clark *Jack London* (US 43)
Sidney Blackmer *In Old Oklahoma* (US 43);
Buffalo Bill (US 44)
John Merton *I Wonder Who's Kissing Her
Now?* (US 47)
Sidney Blackmer *My Girl Tisa* (US 48)
Take Me Out to the Ballgame (US 49)
John Alexander *Fancy Pants* (US 50)
Edward Cassidy *The First Travelling Saleslady*
(US 56)
Karl Swenson *Brighty of the Grand Canyon*
(US 66)
Brian Keith *The Wind and the Lion* (US 75)
William Phipps *Eleanor and Franklin* (US 76,
TVM)
David Healy *Eleanor and Franklin: The White
House Years* (US 77, TVM)
James Whitmore *Bully* (US 78)
Robert Boyd *Ragtime* (US 81)
Walter Massey *Cook and Peary: The Race to*

the Pole (US 83, TVM)
Bob Boyd *The Indominatable Teddy
Roosevelt* (US 85)
David James *Alexander Newsies* (US 92)
Ray Geer *Geronimo* (US 94, TVM)

1909 WILLIAM HOWARD TAFT
(1857–1930)
The Sculptor's Nightmare (US 08)
Ross Durfee *The Winds of Kitty Hawk* (US 78,
TVM)

1913 THOMAS WOODROW WILSON
(1856–1924)
himself in introduction to *The Battle Cry of
Peace* (US 15)
himself *The Adventures of a Boy Scout* (US
15)
himself *Womanhood, the Glory of a Nation*
(US 17)
Ralph C. Faulkner *Why America Will Win* (US
18)
Ralph C. Faulkner *On the Dump* (US 18)
Ralph C. Faulkner *The Prussian Cur* (US 18)
Orlo Eastman *The Kaiser, The Beast of Berlin*
(US 18)
Fred C. Truesdell *The Great Victory* (US 19)
Ralph C. Faulkner *General Pershing* (US 19)
Turn Back the Clock (US 33)
Alexander Knox *Wilson* (US 44)
Earl Lee *The Story of Will Rogers* (US 52)
L. Kovsakov *The Unforgettable Year 1919*
(USSR 52)
Frank Forsyth *Oh! What a Lovely War* (GB 69)
Jerzy Kaliszewski *Polonia Restituta*
(Pol/USSR/Hun/Cz/GDR 81)
Robert Webber *Shooting Star* (US 83, TVM)

1921 WARREN GAMALIEL HARDING
(1865–1923)
No portrayals on screen

1923 JOHN CALVIN COOLIDGE
(1872–1933)
The Adventures of Oktyabrina (USSR 24)
Ian Wolfe *The Court Martial of Billy Mitchell*
(US 55)

1929 HERBERT CLARK HOOVER
(1874–1964)
Tom Jensen *Fires of Youth* (US 31)
Franklin Cover *The Day the Bubble Burst* (US
82, TVM)

1933 FRANKLIN DELANO ROOSEVELT
(1882–1945)
himself (Assistant Secretary to the Navy) *The
Battle Cry of Peace* (US 15)
Capt. Jack Young *Yankee Doodle Dandy* (US
42); *This Is the Army* (US 43)
Herr Roosevelt Plaudert (Ger 43)
Jack Young *Mission to Moscow* (US 43)
Oleg Ervelich *The Fall of Berlin* (USSR 46)
Godfrey Tearle *The Beginning or the End?*
(US 47)
Nikolai Cherkasov *The First Front* (USSR 49)
Secret Mission (USSR 50)
Beau James (US 57)
Ralph Bellamy *Sunrise at Campobello* (US 60)
Richard Nelson *The Pigeon that Took Rome*
(US 62)
McHale's Navy Joins the Air Force (US 68)
Stephen Roberts *First to Fight* (US 67)
Stanislav Jaskevik *Liberation* (USSR 70–71)
Edward Herrmann *Eleanor and Franklin* (US
76, TVM)

Dan O'Herlihy *MacArthur—The Rebel General*
(US 77)
Stephen Roberts *Ring of Passion* (US 77,
TVM)
Edward Herrmann *Eleanor and Franklin: The
White House Years* (US 77, TVM)
Howard Da Silva *The Private Files of J. Edgar
Hoover* (US 78)
Stephen Roberts *Ike* (US 79, TVM)
Jason Robards *F.D.R.: The Last Year* (US 80,
TVM)
Stephen Roberts *Enola Gay* (US 80, TVM)
Teheran '43 (USSR/Fr/Swz 81)
Edward Herrmann *Annie* (US 82)
Ralph Bellamy *The Winds of War* (US 83,
TVM)
Robert Vaughan *Murrow* (US/GB 86, TVM)
Jack Denton *Crossings* (US 86, TVM)
David Ogden Stiers *J. Edgar Hoover* (US 87,
TVM)
Margaret Bourke-White (US 89, TVM)
Bob Gunton *Kingfish: A Story of Huey P.
Long* (US 95, TVM)
Truman (US 95, TVM)
Christopher Plummer *Winchell* (US 98, TVM)

1945 HARRY S. TRUMAN (1884–1972)
Art Baker *The Beginning or the End?* (US 47)
Secret Mission (USSR 50)
Call Me Madam (US 53)
uncredited child *Alias Jesse James* (US 59)
James Whitmore *Give 'Em Hell, Harry!* (US
75)
E. G. Marshall *Collision Course* (US 76)
Ed Flanders *MacArthur—The Rebel General*
(US 77)
Robert Symonds *Tail Gunner Joe* (US 77,
TVM)
Enola Gay (US 80, TVM)
Richard McKenzie *Eleanor, First Lady of the
World* (US 82)
Algimantas Masiulis *Victory* (USSR 86)
Ed Nelson *Brenda Starr* (US 92)
Gary Sinise *Truman* (US 95, TVM)
Kenneth Welsh *Hiroshima* (Can/Jap 95, TVM)

1953 DWIGHT DAVID EISENHOWER
(1890–1969)
Willis Bouchey *Red Planet Mars* (US 52)
The Outsider (US 61)
Harry Carey Jr *The Long Gray Line* (US 55)
Henry Grace *The Longest Day* (US 72)
James Flavin *Francis Gary Powers* (US 76,
TVM)
Andrew Duggan *Tail Gunner Joe* (US 77,
TVM)
Robert Duvall *Ike* (US 79, TVM)
Robert Beer *The Right Stuff* (US 83)
Richard Dysart *The Last Days of Patton* (US
86, TVM)
Keene Curtis *IQ* (US 94)
Truman (US 95, TVM)

1961 JOHN FITZGERALD KENNEDY
(1917–63)
Kennedy in his True Colours (Chn 62)
Cliff Robertson *PT 109* (US 63)
Gas-s-s-s (US 70)
Martin Sheen *The Missiles of October* (US 74,
TVM)
William Jordan *The Private Files of J. Edgar
Hoover* (US 77)
Sam Chew Young *Joe, the Forgotten
Kennedy* (US 77, TVM)
Paul Rudd *Johnny We Hardly Knew Ye* (US
77, TVM)

US PRESIDENTS (continued)

William Jordan *King* (US 78, TVM)
James Franciscus *Jacqueline Bouvier Kennedy* (US 82, TVM)
Sam Groom *Blood Feud* (US 83, TVM)
Martin Sheen *Kennedy* (GB 83, TVM)
Robert Hogan *Prince Jack* (US 84, TVM)
Cliff DeYoung *Robert Kennedy and His Times* (US 85, TVM)
Charles Frank *LBJ The Early Years* (US 87, TVM)
Steve Reed *JFK* (US 91)
Love Field (US 91)
Stephen Collins *A Woman Called Jackie* (US 92, TVM)
Gerard Davy (as JFK in Las Vegas) Kevin Wiggins (as JFK in Dallas) *Ruby* (US 92)
Patrick Dempsey *JFK Reckless Youth* (US 93, TVM)
Jed Gillin (voice only) *Forrest Gump* (US 94)
Perry Stephens *Norma Jean and Marilyn* (US 96, TVM)
William Petersen *The Rat Pack* (US 98, TVM)
Company Man (US 00)
Michael Murphy *Norma-Jean, Jack and Me* (US 00)
Tim Matheson *Jackie Bouvier Kennedy Onassis* (US 00, TVM)

1963 LYNDON BAINES JOHNSON (1908–73)
Ivan Treisault *How to Succeed in Business without Really Trying* (US 67)
Hanoi, Martes 13 (Cuba 67)
Colpo di Stato (It 68)
The Wrecking Crew (US 69)
Andrew Duggan *The Private Files of J. Edgar Hoover* (US 77)
Warren Kemmerling *King* (US 78, TVM)
Nesbitt Blaisdell *Kennedy* (GB 83, TVM)
Forrest Tucker *Blood Feud* (US 83, TVM)
Donald Moffat *The Right Stuff* (US 83)
Kenneth Mars *Prince Jack* (US 84, TVM)
GD Spradlin *Robert Kennedy and His Times*

(US 87, TVM)
Rip Torn *J. Edgar Hoover* (US 87, TVM)
Randy Quaid *LBJ The Early Years* (US 87, TVM)
Tom Howard *JFK* (US 91)
John William Galt (voice only) *Forrest Gump* (US 94)

1969 RICHARD MILHOUS NIXON (1913–1993)
Jean-Pierre Biesse *Made in USA* (Fr 67)
The Statue (GB 70)
Cold Turkey (US 71)
Million Dollar Duck (US 71)
Jim Dixon *Is There Sex After Death?* (US 71)
Bons baisers de Hong Kong (Fr 72)
Dan Resin as young Nixon and Richard Dixon as older Nixon in *Richard* (US 72)
Richard Dixon *The Faking of the President 1974* (US 76); *The Private Files of J. Edgar Hoover* (US 77); *Tail Gunner Joe* (US 77, TVM)
Anderson Humphreys *The Cayman Triangle* (Cayman Isles 77)
Harry Spillman *Born Again* (US 78)
Richard M. Dixon *Hopscotch* (US 80); *Where the Buffalo Roam* (US 80)
Philip Baker Hall *Secret Honor: The Last Testament of Richard M. Nixon* (US 84, TVM)
Anthony Palmer *J. Edgar Hoover* (US 87, TVM)
Joe Alaskey (voice only) *Forrest Gump* (US 94)
Sir Anthony Hopkins *Nixon* (US 95)
Beau Bridges *Kissinger and Nixon* (US 95, TVM)
Bob Gunton *Elvis Meets Nixon* (US 97, TVM)
Dan Hadaya *Dick* (US 99)

1974 GERALD RUDOLPH FORD (1913–)
Dick Crockett *The Pink Panther Strikes Again* (GB 76)

1977 JAMES EARL CARTER (1924–)
Ed Beheler *The Cayman Triangle* (Cayman Isles 77)
Black Sunday (US 77)
Walt Hanna *Sadat* (US 83, TVM)
The Lonely Guy (US 84)
himself *Special Counsel* (US 88)
Ken Jenkins *The Final Days* (US 90, TVM)
Georges Griegegard *Iran: Days of Crisis* (US 91, TVM)

1981 RONALD REAGAN (1911–)
himself in *It's a Great Feeling* (US 49)
Bryan Clark *Without Warning: The James Brady Story* (US 91, TVM)
Bryan Clark *Pizza Man* (US 91)
Jay Koch *Panther* (US 95)

1989 GEORGE BUSH (1924–)
Fred Travelena *Comedy in the Oval Office* (US 89, TVM)
John Roarke *The Naked Gun 2½: The Smell of Fear* (US 91)
El Viaje (Arg/Fr 92)
Lloyd Bridges *Hot Shots: Part Deux* (US 93)
John Roarke *The Silence of the Hams* (It/US 94)
John Roarke *Courage Under Fire* (US 96)

1993 WILLIAM JEFFERSON CLINTON (1946–)
The Beverly Hillbillies (US 93)
Pat Rick *The Silence of the Hams* (It/US 94)
Timothy Watters *Naked Gun 33⅓ The Final Insult* (US 94)
Bruce Gray *Spy Hard* (US 96)
Dale Reeves (voice) *Beavis and Butthead Do America* (US 97)
John Travolta (as Jack Stanton, thinly fictionalised portrait of Clinton) *Primary Colours* (US 98)

The only archive in the world devoted exclusively to films with black casts and films made by blacks is the Black Film Collection at Tyler, Texas.

MAINSTREAM BLACK MOVIES

During the silent period the 'majors' showed little or no interest in black movies and even when black characters were required they were generally played by white actors in black-face. D. W. Griffith's *The Birth of a Nation* (US 15) had a large cast of black roles, since the controversial plot revolved round the black 'takeover' of the South following the Civil War, yet only one genuine black—the curiously named Madame Sul-Te-Wan—was employed on the film.

The coming of sound altered the picture, since the trend towards greater realism demanded that blacks be played by blacks, though their roles were generally confined to the menial or the comic (usually both combined). At the same time the major studios began to turn out the occasional all-black picture, most of them dependent upon the vocal talents of the black American and aimed principally at white audiences. Those made prior to the

sudden explosion of 'superspade' black exploitation pictures in the late '60s were as follows: *Hearts in Dixie* (Fox 29) with Clarence Muse—the first all-black musical and the film which brought Stepin Fetchit to the fore as the first black comedy player to become a household name; *Hallelujah!* (MGM 29) with Daniel Haynes; *Green Pastures* (Warner 36) with Rex Ingram; *Stormy Weather* (TCF 43) with Bill Robinson, Lena Horne; *Cabin in the Sky* (MGM 43) with Eddie Anderson, Lena Horne; *Bright Road* (MGM 51) with Dorothy Dandridge; *Carmen Jones* (TCF 54) with Harry Belafonte, Dorothy Dandridge; *Anna Lucasta* (United Artists 58) with Sammy Davis Jr; *St Louis Blues* (Par 58) with Nat King Cole; *Porgy and Bess* (Goldwyn 59) with Sidney Poitier, Dorothy Dandridge.

No Hollywood films took the subject of contemporary race relations as a main theme until 1949, when three such films came to the screen almost simultaneously, led by *Home of the Brave*, the story of a black veteran (James Edwards) undergoing psychiatric treatment following traumatic war experiences. The other two films, *Pinky* and *Lost Boundaries*, dealt with light-skinned blacks passing for white.

The Hays Code ban on miscegenation as a theme was breached by *Island in the Sun* (US 59), which offered twin romances between John Justin and Dorothy

COMIC-STRIP CHARACTERS

A host of comic-strip characters have been portrayed on screen in live-action feature-length movies. This list is confined to English-language films. The name following the abbreviation 'Orig' is that of the originator of the comic strip.

- Ginger Meggs, cartoon larrikin in Australian newspapers, was played by Ray Griffin in *Those Terrible Twins* (Aus 25). Orig: James Bancks.
- *Ella Cinders* (US 26) with Colleen Moore. Orig: William Counselman and Charles Plumb.
- Fatty Finn, an urchin of the backstreets of Sydney, was played by 'Pop' Ordell in *The Kid Stakes* (Aus 26). Orig: Syd Nicholls.
- *Tillie the Toiler* (US 27) with Marion Davies as the office-girl heroine. Orig: Russ Westover in the New York *American*.
- *Harold Teen* (US 28) with Arthur Lake. Orig: Carl Ed.
- J. Farrell MacDonald played Jiggs and Polly Moran played Maggie in *Bringing Up Father* (US 28). Orig: George McManus.
- *Skippy* (US 30) with Jackie Cooper. Orig: Percy Crosby.
- *Sooky* (US 31) with Robert Coogan in the title role and Jackie Cooper as Skippy. Orig: Percy Crosby.
- *Little Orphan Annie* (US 32) with Mitzi Green. Orig: Harold Gray and Al Lowenthal.
- *Harold Teen* (US 34) with Hal LeRoy. Orig: Carl Ed.
- *Tailspin Tommy* (US 34) with Maurice Murphy as the young flying ace. First serial based on comic strip. Orig: Hal Forrest.
- *Palooka* (US 34) with Stuart Erwin. Orig: Ham Fisher.
- *Tailspin Tommy and the Great Air Mystery* (US 35) with Clark Williams. Orig: Hal Forrest.
- *Flash Gordon* (US 36) with Buster Crabbe. Serial. Orig: Alex Raymond.
- *Jungle Jim* (US 37) with Grant Withers. Serial. Orig: Alex Raymond.
- *Tim Tyler's Luck* (US 37) with Frankie Thomas. Serial. Orig: Lyman Young.
- *Dick Tracy* (US 37) with Ralph Byrd. Serial. Orig: Chester Gould.
- *Radio Patrol* (US 37) with Grant Withers. Serial. Orig: Eddie Sullivan and Charles Schmidt.
- *Blondie* (US 38) with Penny Singleton in the title role and Arthur Lake as Dagwood. First of a series of 28 supporting features made by Columbia 1938–50. Orig: Chic Young.
- *Little Orphan Annie* (US 38) with Ann Gillis. Orig: Harold Gray and Al Lowenthal.
- *Flash Gordon's Trip to Mars* (US 38) with Buster Crabbe. Serial. Orig: Alex Raymond.
- *Dick Tracy Returns* (US 38) with Ralph Byrd. Serial. *Tracy's G-Men* (US 39). Orig: Chester Gould.
- John Trent as Tailspin Tommy in *Sky Patrol* (US 39). Serial. Orig: Hal Forrest.
- *Planet Outlaws* (US 39) with Buster Crabbe as Buck Rogers. Orig: Dick Calkins and Phil Nolan.
- *Buck Rogers* (US 39) with Buster Crabbe. Serial. Orig: Dick Calkins and Phil Nolan.
- *Mandrake the Magician* (US 39) with Warren Hull. Serial. Orig: Lee Falk and

Arnold Schwarzenegger personified the archetypal comic-book hero in Conan the Destroyer *(US 84).* (Kobal Collection)

Phil Davis.
- *Li'l Abner* (US 40) with Granville Owen. Orig: Al Capp.
- *Flash Gordon Conquers the Universe* (US 40) with Buster Crabbe. Serial. Orig: Alex Raymond.
- *Adventures of Captain Marvel* (US 41) with Tom Tyler. Orig: C. C. Beck.
- *Tillie the Toiler* (US 41) with Kay Harris. Orig: Russ Westover.
- *Private Snuffy Smith* (US 42) with Bud Duncan. Orig: Billy de Beck.
- Bud Duncan *as Snuffy Smith in Hillbilly Blitzkrieg* (US 42). Orig: Billy de Beck.
- *Winslow of the Navy* (US 42) with Don Terry. Serial. Orig: Lt Com Frank Martinek.
- *Batman* (US 43) with Lewis Wilson as Batman, Douglas Croft as Robin. Serial. Orig: Bob Kane.
- *Don Winslow of the Coastguard* (US 43) with Don Terry. Serial. Orig: Lt Com Frank Martinek.
- *The Phantom* (US 43) with Tom Tyler. Serial. Orig: Lee Falk.
- *Dixie Dugan* (US 43) with Lois Andrews. Orig: Joseph McEvoy. In this case McEvoy's strip had itself been based on a film—*Show Girl* (US 28).
- *Captain America* (US 44) with Dick Purcell. Orig: Jack Kirby and Joe Simon.
- *Dick Tracy* (US 45) with Morgan Conway. Orig: Chester Gould.
- *Joe Palooka, Champ* (US 46) with Joe Kirkwood, who also starred in eight other Palooka movies 1947–51. Orig: Ham Fisher.
- Joe Yule as Jiggs and Renie Riano as Maggie in *Bringing Up Father* (US 46);

also in *Jiggs and Maggie in Society* (US 48) and *Jiggs and Maggie Out West* (US 50). Orig: George McManus.
- *Dick Tracy vs Cueball* (US 46) with Morgan Conway. Orig: Chester Gould.
- *Dick Tracy's Dilemma* (US 47) and *Dick Tracy Meets Gruesome* (US 47) with Ralph Byrd. Orig: Chester Gould.
- *Superman* (US 48) with Kirk Alyn. Serial. Orig: Jerry Siegel and Joe Schuster.
- *Jungle Jim* (US 48) with Johnny Weissmuller in this and seven other Columbia low budgeters. Orig: Alex Raymond.
- *Bomba the Jungle Boy* (US 49) with Johnny Sheffield; first of series of 12 which continued to 1955. Orig: Roy Rockwell.
- *Batman and Robin* (US 49) with Robert Lowery as Batman, John Duncan as Robin. Serial. Orig: Bob Kane.
- *The Adventures of Jane* (GB 49) with Christabel Leighton-Porter. Orig: Norman Pett.
- *Atom Man vs Superman* (US 50) with Kirk Alyn as Superman. Serial. Orig: Jerry Siegel and Joe Schuster.
- Scotty Beckett as Corky and Jimmy Lydon as Skeezix in *Gasoline Alley* and *Corky of Gasoline Alley* (both US 51). Orig: Frank O. King.
- *Superman and the Mole Men* (US 51) with George Reeves. Orig: Jerry Siegel and Joe Schuster.
- *Blackhawk* (US 52) with Kirk Alyn. Orig: Reed Crandall and Charles Guidera.
- *Prince Valiant* (US 54) with Robert Wagner. Produced in colour and Cinemascope. Orig: Hal Foster.
- *The Sad Sack* (US 57) with Jerry Lewis. Orig: George Baker.
- *Li'l Abner* (US 59) with Peter Palmer. Orig: Al Capp.
- *Dondi* (US 61) with David Kory. Orig: Gus Edson and Irwin Hasen.
- *Modesty Blaise* (GB 66) with Monica Vitti in title role and Terence Stamp as Willie Garvin. Orig: Peter O'Donnell and Jim Holdaway.
- *Batman* (US 66) with Adam West in title role and Burt Ward as Robin. Orig: Bob Kane.
- *Barbarella* (Fr/It 67) with Jane Fonda. Orig: Jean-Claude Forest.
- *The Adventures of Barry McKenzie* (Aus 72) with Barry Crocker; sequel *Barry McKenzie Holds His Own* (Aus 74). Orig: Barry Humphries in *Private Eye*—the only comic-strip artist to have played featured roles in the films based on his strip.
- *Tiffany Jones* (GB 73) with Anouska Hempel. Orig: Pat Tourret and Jenny Butterworth.
- *Wonder Woman* (US 74, TVM) with tennis star Cathy Lee Crosby and *The New, Original Wonder Woman* (US 75, TVM) with Lynda Carter. Orig: Charles Moulton.
- *Friday Foster* (US 75) with Pam Grier, based on first comic strip with black heroine. Orig: Jorge Langaron.
- *Brenda Starr* (US 75, TVM) with Jill St

COMIC-STRIP CHARACTERS (continued)

John. Orig: Dale Messick.
- *The Incredible Hulk* (US 77, TVM) with Lou Ferrigno. Orig: Stan Lee.
- *Spider-Man* (US 77, TVM), Spider-*Man Strikes Back* (US 78) and *The Dragon's Challenge* (US 80) with Nicholas Hammond. Orig: Stan Lee.
- *Dr Strange* (US 78, TVM), with Peter Hooten. Orig: Stan Lee.
- *Superman* (US 78) with Christopher Reeve; followed by *Superman II* (GB 81), *Superman III* (GB 84) and *Superman IV* (US 87). Orig: Jerry Siegel and Joe Schuster.
- *Captain America* (US 79, TVM) and *Captain America II* (US 79, TVM) with Reb Brown. Orig: Jack Kirby and Joe Simon.
- *H Mandrake* (US 79, TVM) with Anthony Herrerra. Orig: Lee Falk and Phil Davis.
- *Buck Rogers* (US 79) with Gil Gerard. Orig: Dick Calkins.
- *Fatty Finn* (Aus 80) with Ben Oxenbould. Orig: Syd Nicholls.
- *Flash Gordon* (GB 80) with Sam J. Jones. Orig: Alex Raymond.
- *Popeye* (US 80) with Robin Williams and Shelley Duvall as Olive Oyl. Orig: Elzie Crisler Segar.
- *Swamp Thing* (US 82) with Dick Durock as the Thing. Orig: DC Comics.
- *Conan the Barbarian* (82) with Arnold Schwarzenegger. Orig: Robert E. Howard.
- *Annie* (US 82) with Aileen Quinn as Little Orphan Annie. Orig: Harold Gray and Al Lowenthal.
- *Ginger Meggs* (Aus 82) with Paul Daniel. Orig: James Bancks.
- *Supergirl* (GB 84) with Helen Slater. Orig: Otto Binder.
- *Conan the Destroyer* (US 84) with Arnold Schwarzenegger. Orig: Robert E. Howard.
- *Sheena Queen of the Jungle* (US 84) with Tanya Roberts. Orig: Sam Iger and Will Eisner.
- *Howard the Duck* (US 86) with Ed Gale, Chip Zien, Tim Rose, Steve Sleap, Peter Baird, Mary Wells, Lisa Sturz and Jordan Prentice taking it in turns to play the eponymous hero. Orig: Steve Gerber.
- *Jane and the Lost City* (GB 87) with Kirsten Hughes. Orig: Norman Pett.
- *The Spirit* (US 87, TVM) with Sam Jones. Orig: Will Eisner.
- *The Incredible Hulk Returns* (US 88, TVM), *The Trial of the Incredible Hulk* (US 89, TVM), *The Death of the Incredible Hulk* (US 90, TVM) with Lou Ferrigno as Hulk, Bill Bixby as alter ego David Banner. Orig: Stan Lee.
- *Batman* (US 89) with Michael Keaton. Orig: Bob Kane.
- *The Return of Swamp Thing* (US 89) with Dick Durock. Orig: DC Comics.
- *Spider-Man* (US 89) with Don Michael Paul. Orig: Stan Lee.
- *The Punisher* (Aus 90) with Dolph Lundgren as Frank Castle. Orig: Marvel Comics.
- *Archie: To Riverdale and Back Again* (US 90, TVM) with Christopher Rich. Orig: John L. Goldwater.
- *The Flash* (US 90, TVM) with John Wesley Shipp. Orig: Harry Lampert.

- *Dick Tracy* (US 90) with Warren Beatty. Orig: Chester Gould.
- *Teenage Mutant Ninja Turtles* (US 90) with Josh Pais as Raphael, Michelan Sisti as Michelangelo, Leif Tilden as Donatello, David Forman as Leonardo. *Teenage Mutant Ninja Turtles II: The Secret of Ooze* (US 91) with Ken Troum and Mark Caso. *Teenage Mutant Ninja Turtles III: The Turtles are Back . . . In Time* (US 93) with Matt Hill, David Fraser, Jim Raposa, Mark Caso. Orig: Kevin Eastman and Peter Laird.
- *The Rocketeer* (US 91) with Bill Campbell. Orig: Dave Stevens.
- *Brenda Starr* (US 92) with Brooke Shields. Orig: Dale Messick.
- *Batman Returns* (US 92) and so does Michael Keaton. Orig: Bob Kane.
- *Captain America* (US 92) with Matt Salinger. Orig: Joe Simon, Jack Kirby. Video release only.
- *Dennis the Menace* (US 93) with Mason Gamble as Dennis, Walter Matthau as grouchy Mr Wilson. Orig: Hank Ketcham.
- *Lois and Clark: The New Adventures of Superman* (US 93, TVM) with Dean Cain. Orig: Jerry Siegel and Joe Schuster.
- *The Crow* (US 94) with Brandon Lee (accidentally shot on set, see p. 18) as Eric Draven. Orig: James O'Barr.
- *Timecop* (US 94) with Jean-Claude Van Damme as Walker. Orig: Mike Richardson and Mark Verheiden.
- *Richie Rich* (US 94) with Macaulay Culkin. Orig: Harvey Comics.
- *Tank Girl* (US 95) with Lori Petty as the eponymous, foul-mouthed feminist superheroine of the year 2033. Orig: Jamie Hewlett and Alan Martin for Deadline Comics.
- *Batman Forever* (US 95) with Val Kilmer. Orig: Bob Kane.
- *Palookaville* (US 95) with Billy Hopkins as Joe Palooka. Orig: Ham Fisher.

- *Caspar* (US 95) with computer-generated Casper the Friendly Ghost in otherwise live-action movie. Orig: Joseph Oriolo.
- *Judge Dredd* (US 95) with Sylvester Stallone. Orig. John Wagner, Carlos Ezguerra for 1977 British comic book *2000 AD*.
- *The Phantom* (US/Aus 96) with Billy Zane. Orig: Lee Falk.
- *Prince Valiant* (Ger/GB/Ire/US 97) with Stephen Moyer. Orig. Bob Kane.
- *Batman and Robin* (US 97) with George Clooney. Orig: Bob Kane.
- *George of the Jungle* (US 97) with Brendan Foster. Orig. Jay Ward.
- *Steel* (US 97) with Shaquille O'Neal as John Henry Irons. Orig. Louise Simonson, Jon Bognadove.
- *Spawn* (US 97) with Michael S. White as Spawn/Al Simmons. Orig. Todd McFarlane.
- *Men in Black* (US 97) with Tommy Lee Jones and Will Smith as the eponymous men. Orig: Lowell Cunningham for Malibu Comics.
- *Blade* (US 98) with Wesley Snipes as caped black vampire-slayer superhero Blade. Orig. Marv Wollman and Gene Colan for Marvel Comics.
- *Mystery Men* (US 99) with Hank Azira as The Blue Raja, William H. Macy as The Shoveller and Ben Stiller as The Furious. Orig: Bob Burden for Dark Horse Comics.
- *X-Men* (US 00) with Hugh Jackman, Famke Janssen, James Marsden and Halle Berry as the X-Men. Orig: Stan Lee and Jack Kirby for Marvel Comics. (Stan Lee appears as a hot-dog vendor.)
- *Ghost World* (US 00) with Thora Birch as Enid Coleslaw. Orig: Daniel Clowes.

Dick Tracy returned long before Warren Beatty. The year was 1938 and war had broken out—on the streets of comic-strip Hollywood. (Kobal)

Romance between white and black was shown for the first time in Pool of London *(GB 50) with Susan Shaw and Earl Cameron. Miscegenation was banned in Hollywood films under the Hays Code.*

Dandridge (who marry in the end) and Harry Belafonte and Joan Fontaine (who part). In Britain the subject had been tackled much earlier in *Pool of London* (GB 50), which depicted the relationship between a Jamaican ship's steward (Earl Cameron) and a white cinema cashier (Susan Shaw).

It was not until 1961 that the even more delicate matter of racially mixed couples having offspring was confronted. In Shelagh Delaney's hit play *A Taste of Honey* the white girl Jo and her black lover Jimmy have a baby out of wedlock. The film rights were owned by John Osborne and Tony Richardson, who did not have enough money to produce the picture themselves and offered it to the major studios. One distinguished American producer was content to make the picture without a 'name' star, as Richardson insisted. 'But took it for granted,' Richardson recalled, 'we would agree to an upbeat ending. By that he meant that Jo shouldn't have the coloured boy's baby. Unless it miscarried or was stillborn, he said, he couldn't sell it in the South.' Unwilling to accept such

strictures, Osborne and Richardson made the film independently on a shoestring budget of £96,000 and were able to preserve the integrity of the original story.

During the 1970s the so-called 'blaxploitation' movies, violent, hip, ghetto fantasies derived from the current sub-genre of Bond film imitations, came and happily went. It was only in the 1990s that a new kind of black movie, made by black directors with 'attitude', began to win not only critical plaudits but also substantial box-office returns. Appealing to a broad audience, white as well as black, they were modestly budgeted but capable of bringing in substantial returns. Doug McHenry's and George Jackson's *House Party 2* (US 91) cost $4 million but took $19.2 million at the domestic box office; Spike Lee's *Jungle Fever* (US 91) cost $14 million and took $32 million; Mario Van Peebles' *New Jack City* (US 91) realised $47 million for a budget of $8.5 million; and John Singleton's *Boyz 'N the Hood* (US 91) led the pack with a $56 million return for an outlay of only $6 million. For the first time in Hollywood history raw, realistic portrayals of black experience were becoming part of the mainstream. The trend continued through the '90s, with steadily increasing budgets.

Production output: A total of 49 all-black silent features are recorded in the US for the period 1917–30; exactly 150 all-black talkies were made in the US 1931–50.

The first black film with an all-African cast was the Stoll Co.'s *Nionga* (GB 25), about a young betrothed couple in Central Africa and the tragic ending to their romance, the man being accidentally killed and the bride burned alive in her hut according to local custom. Such films were rare, the only other pre-war examples on record being *Zeliv* (It 28), a story of tribal life enacted entirely by Zulus, *Samba* (Ger 28) and *Stampede* (GB 30). All these films were aimed at white audiences, a fact made abun-

Molly Picon, seen here in Joseph Green's Mamele/Little Mother *(Pol c. 37), was the Yiddish cinema's foremost star.*

dantly clear in the subtitles to *Nionga*, which referred to its protagonists as 'the savages'.

The first African film drama made by a black African was Ousmane Sembene's *La Noire de . . .* (Sen 67), premiered at the Théâtre Sorano in Dakar on 4 February 1967.

Jewish Films

The first Jewish film with an all-Jewish cast was Stanislaw Sebel's screen version of Gordin's *Satan* (Pol 12), produced by Madame Yelizariantz's Sila Co. with a cast drawn from Warsaw's Fishon Theatre. Within a year there were four Polish companies specialising in Jewish films, Sila having been joined by Variag (also run by a woman, Madame Stern), Mintus and Kosmofilm.

The first British example was *The Jewish King Lear* (GB 12), filmed at the Pavilion Theatre and premiered at New King's Hall in the Commercial Road. America's first Jewish picture was *A Passover Miracle* (US 14), released by Kalem in two versions, one with English subtitles, the other with Yiddish.

The first talkie in Yiddish was Sidney M. Goldin's *Style and Class* (US 29), a Judea Films production with Goldie Eisenman and Marty Baratz.

PRODUCTION OUTPUT
According to Rob Edelman's filmography of feature films in Yiddish (*Films in Review* June/July 1978), there were 53 produced in America 1924–61, 17 in Poland pre-1940, four in Russia 1925–33 and solitary examples from West Germany in 1948 and Italy in 1949. Mr Edelman believes there may also have been Romanian and Hungarian Yiddish features.

After *Three Daughters* (US 61), production ceased entirely for nearly 20 years. Then in 1980 came Samy Szlingerbaum's *Brussels-Transit* (Bel 80), a story of Polish-born survivors of the Holocaust settling in Brussels after World War II. The film, which had a Yiddish commentary and part-Yiddish dialogue, was followed by *The Dybbuk* (Pol 82), a Jewish State Theatre of Poland production from the play by Syymon Szurmiez, and an Israeli offering called *If They Give, Take* (Isr 82). A short directed by David Greenwald, *The Well* (US 84), renewed production of Yiddish films in America.

The revival of interest in Yiddish films was stimulated by the founding of the National Centre for Jewish Film at Brandeis University, Waltham, Mass., established in 1976 with 30 mainly incomplete films from the estate of producer Joseph Seiden. It now houses over 2000 films on Jewish subjects as well as an extensive photo and rare book collection. Despite the lack of any recent products, a Yiddish Film Festival was held in New York in 1978 and the following year a season of Yiddish films ran at Cineplex in Toronto. In Europe, retrospectives of Yiddish cinema were held in Frankfurt by Walter Schobert in 1980, 1982 and 1984. Two feature-length documentaries, *Das Jiddische Kino* (FRG 83) and *Almonds and Raisins* (GB 84), have also been made on the history of Yiddish

films. The former introduced a season of Yiddish features on West Germany's ZDF television station in April 1983. As part of London's 1987 Jewish East End celebration, the National Film Theatre presented a retrospective of Yiddish films dating back to the Molly Picon comedy *East and West* (Aut 23).

Yiddish films, after their tentative revival on the festival circuit, became available to the living-room audience when the National Centre for Jewish Film began releasing pre-World War II classics on video cassette in late 1989. Inaugural titles included *Green Fields* (US 37), *Jolly Paupers* (Pol 37), *Tevye* (US 39) and a poignant documentary *Jewish Life in Vilna* (Lithuania 39), depicting a community about to be destroyed for ever.

When *Solomon a Gaenor* (GB 99) received an Oscar nomination for Best Foreign Film in the Academy Awards 2000, it was remarkable not only for the fact that Britain had been able to enter a non-English language film, but that the dialogue was in a combination of Welsh and Yiddish.

ANTI-SEMITIC FILMS
Happily these have been rare. In 1935, when Joseph Goebbels ordered a search to be made for foreign anti-Semitic films that could be released in Germany, the only example that could be obtained was a primitive Swedish talkie called *Pettersson and Bendel* (Swe 33). Curiously the Nazi-controlled film industry of the Third Reich made no overtly anti-Semitic pictures until just before the war, when Hans Heinz Zerlett directed *Robert und Bertram* (Ger 39), a comedy about two German tramps who get the better of a rascally Jew and save the innkeeper's lovely Aryan daughter from the fate of marrying him. The following year cinematic Jew-baiting began in earnest with *Jud Süss* (Ger 40), *Die Rothschilds* (Ger 40) and *Der ewige Jude* (Ger 40), three films whose virulent hatred was a presage of the vengeance to be wreaked on the race they vilified. Of these *Jud Süss* is undoubtedly the most notorious; it is also the only one to have been released since the war. Dubbed in Arabic, it was distributed in the Arab states in 1955 by the USSR agency Sovexport.

Following the fall of France, collaborators brought shame on their nation by producing the first French anti-Semitic feature film, Paul Riche's *Forces Occultes* (Fr 42). Its theme was principally the evils of freemasonry, but the Jews were shown explicitly as the hidden force behind the hidden force. Riche, an ultra-rightist journalist, real name Jean Mamy, was sentenced to death in 1945, mainly for his pro-Nazi writings.

After the collapse of the Third Reich, anti-Semitic films were mercifully sparse, but in 1952 the semi-official Cifesca company of Spain produced Luis Marquina's *Amaya* (Sp 52). This film blamed the Muslim conquest of Spain on treacherous Jews who were portrayed as funding the invasion in order to make more profit as part of the Islamic empire. One of the characters states that to the Jews, a Christian is no different from a Muslim, simply someone to be exploited for profit. The Jews in the film are depicted as rascally, cunning and devious; the Spanish characters are not unlike the Nordic heroes and heroines in similar types of Nazi film.

Leon Liebgold and Lili Liliana, foremost stars of pre-war Yiddish cinema in Poland—they co-starred as husband and wife (which they were in real life) in the classic and uncharacteristically lavish production *The Dybbuk* (Pol 38)—owed their survival to the exigencies of movie making. The couple were in New York with their theatre troupe in 1939 when Liebgold was approached by the great Yiddish actor/director Maurice Schwartz to appear in his film *Tevye* (US 39). Liebgold agreed, provided shooting of his scenes could be completed in ten days, as he had tickets for his and Lili's return to Poland. Despite Schwartz's best efforts to keep to schedule, shooting was constantly interrupted by the buzzing of aeroplanes over their Long Island location. The day of the sailing came and went with Liebgold's scenes uncompleted and he booked for the next sailing instead, but he and Lili never boarded. Two days later Germany invaded Poland. The two stars, who would otherwise have been part of the grim harvest of the Holocaust, remained in New York, where they lived until Leon's death at the age of 83 in 1993.

Horror

The character most frequently portrayed in horror films is Count Dracula, the creation of the Irish writer *Bram Stoker* (1847–1912), whose novel *Dracula* was published in 1897. Representations of the Count or his immediate descendants on screen number 167 up to and including *Dracula 2000* aka *Wes Craven Presents Dracula* (US 00), while there have been 121 movies featuring his closest rival, Frankenstein's Monster.

The peak year for production of horror films was 1972, with a world total of 189. Of these, 83 emanated from the USA. The horror boom rapidly abated, with only 58 screamers going into production worldwide in 1975. Nevertheless, this was the year in which horror pictures

Dracula has been portrayed in 166 movies to date. Having a bad time on the end of the traditional stake is Japan's Mori Kishida in Lake of Dracula *(Jap 71). (Dracula Films)*

garnered the largest share of the North American box office, with 22% of all motion-picture rentals. The upsurge was largely due to the overwhelming success of *Jaws* (US 75) and a strong performance by Mel Brooks' horror-spoof *Young Frankenstein* (US 74).

The list below records the **most successful horror film** each year since 1970. The top rankings are based on North American rentals, though in practice this almost invariably reflects worldwide box-office performance. All films listed are US productions except *Alien* (GB 79).

1970	*House of Dark Shadows*
1971	*Willard*
1972	*Frenzy*
1973	*Legend of Hell House*
1974	*The Exorcist*
1975	*Jaws*
1976	*The Omen*
1977	*King Kong*
1978	*Jaws II*
1979	*Alien/Amityville Horror*
1980	*The Shining*
1981	*An American Werewolf in London*
1982	*Poltergeist*
1983	*Jaws 3-D*
1984	*Gremlins*
1985	*Teen Wolf*
1986	*Aliens*
1987	*Witches of Eastwick/Predator*
1988	*A Nightmare on Elm Street 4*
1989	*Pet Sematory*
1990	*Arachnophobia*
1991	*Terminator 2*
1992	*Alien 3*
1993	*Bram Stoker's Dracula*
1994	*Interview with the Vampire*
1995	*Vampire in Brooklyn*
1996	*Scream*
1997	*I Know What You Did Last Summer*
1998	*Scream 2*
1999	*The Sixth Sense*
2000	*Scary Movie*

Musicals

The first musical with an original score was MGM's *The Broadway Melody* (US 29), with Bessie Love, Anita Page and Charles King, which was premièred at Grauman's Chinese Theatre in Hollywood on 1 February 1929. The songs were: 'Give My Regards to Broadway' (George M. Cohan); 'The Wedding Day of the Painted Doll'; 'Love Boat'; 'Broadway Melody'; 'Boy Friend'; 'You Were Meant For Me' (Arthur Freed and Nacio Herb Brown); and 'Truthful Deacon Brown' (Willard Robison).

The first British musical was BIP's *Raise the Roof* (GB 30), directed by Walter Summers with Betty Balfour as an actress bribed by a rich man to ruin his son's touring review.

The first musical wholly in colour was Warner Bros' *On With the Show*, directed by Alan Crosland in two-colour Technicolor with Betty Compson and Joe E. Brown and premièred in New York on 28 May 1929. The first

British colour musical was BIP's *Harmony Heaven* (GB 30) with Polly Ward and Stuart Hall.

> The Koreans decided that *The Sound of Music* (US 65) was too long. They shortened it without too much difficulty—by cutting out all the songs.

The musical with the most song numbers was Madan Theatres' *Indra Sabha* (Ind 32), a Hindi movie with 71 songs. The songs were adapted from earlier stage productions of Sayed Aga Hasan Amanat's 1853 classic and scored by Najardas Nayak in a style said to be reminiscent of 'an Indian equivalent of the *Ziegfeld Follies*'.

The Hollywood musical with the most songs was RKO's *The Story of Vernon and Irene Castle* (US 39). In the course of its 93-minute running time the film proffered, in the words of *Variety*, 'one original song and 40 old pop songs by diverse tunesmiths'.

Series

The longest series of films is the 104 Hong Kong-made features about the 19th-century martial arts hero Huang Fei-Hong, starting with *The True Story of Huang Fei-Hong* (HK 49) and continuing to the latest episode *Once Upon a Time in China VI* (HK/US 97), starring Li Lianjie (aka Jet Li). Of the total, 77 starred Kwan Tak-Hing (see p. 116) and no fewer than 25 of the films premièred in a single year, 1956. All but five have been in Cantonese, the others, all made in the 1970s, being in Mandarin.

The longest all-British series was the *Carry On* films, which began with *Carry On Sergeant* (GB 58) and ended with *Carry On Columbus* (GB 92), the 30th in the series following a 14-year gap after *Carry On Emmanuelle* (GB 78). All 30 were produced by John Goldstone. The *Columbus* cast brought together a number of survivors from the earlier films, including Bernard Cribbins, Jack Douglas, Leslie Phillips and June Whitfield. The title role was played by Jim Dale, the good-looking straightman in ten *Carry Ons*. The most enduring performer in the series was the late Kenneth Williams, with 25 *Carry On* roles to his credit, but definitely not a straight man.

Sex

Sex on screen followed rapidly on the emergence of cinema as a public entertainment. The pioneer producer of sex films was Eugène Pirou, beginning with a three-minute long production titled *Le Coucher de la mariée* (Fr 96), starring blonde and chubby Louise Willy. Based on an act performed by Mlle Willy at the Olympia music hall in Paris the previous year, the film showed a newly wed couple preparing for bed. The girl's husband removes her satin slipper and presses it ecstatically to his lips, then she disrobes and puts on her night attire while her husband watches with evident desire. Finally Mlle Willy does a provocative little dance before the couple retire to bed. The film caused a sensation when it was premièred in the

Probably the earliest surviving still from a pornographic film. Title and date unknown but probably French, c. 1900. (Kobal)

basement of the Café de Paris in November 1896 and was soon showing at two other *salles* as well, one in the boulevard Bonne-Nouvelle and the other at 86 rue de Clichy. Pirou followed this success with other sex subjects, such as *Bain de la Parisienne* (Fr 1897), *Lever de la Parisienne* (Fr 1897) and *La Puce* (Fr 1897), most of them based on striptease acts playing in the Paris music halls. *La Puce*, for example, showed a maiden afflicted with a flea who removes her garments one by one to locate the offending insect.

> Former British Board of Film Censors Secretary John Trevelyan recalled an occasion when Customs officers seized an imported film titled *Games in Bed*. On screening the film they found it was about ways of entertaining a sick child.

Pirou's chief rival in the blue-movie field was Georges Méliès, whose *Les Indiscrets/The Peeping Toms* (Fr 1896) came out at the end of 1896. Méliès was the man who brought nudity to the screen in *Après le bal* (Fr 1897) and won a wide following with such sensational subjects as *En Cabinet particulier/A Private Dinner* (Fr 1897), *L'Indiscret aux Bains de mer/Peeping Tom at the Seaside* (Fr 1897) and *La Modèle irascible/An Irritable Model* (Fr 1897). In England these films were distributed by the Warwick Trading Co., who described them as 'welcome at any smoking concert or stag party'.

The earliest known American film on a sexual theme is American Mutoscope & Biograph's *The Downward Path* (US 02), a five-scene melodrama about a sharecropper's daughter who follows a downward path to prostitution—in one of the scenes she is encountered soliciting in the streets.

While most of the above films were very much of the 'What the Butler Saw' genre, the longer sex drama designed for general release emerged with Fotorama's *The White Slave Traffic* (Den 10), a two-reel shocker of such drawing power at the box office that within a few months Nordisk had produced a rival version with the same name. It was no less sensational. A publicity still shows a scene of a kidnapped girl being savagely beaten. Ole Olsen of Nordisk recalled that at the trade show in Berlin, the German cinema managers all clambered on to their seats for a better view. It was the success of these Danish sexploitation films—other titles included *The Last Victim of the White Slave Traffic* (Den 11) and *Dealer in Girls* (Den 12)—that inspired George Loane Tucker to make the first American feature-length sex picture, *Traffic in Souls* (US 13), starring Jane Gail and Matt Moore. Made clandestinely—not because of the subject, but because Universal did not believe that the American public were ready for feature films—Tucker's $5700 movie garnered record earnings of $450,000.

NUDITY ON SCREEN
The first leading lady to appear nude on screen was

As early as 1915 Audrey Munson braved the wrath of America's moral guardians to become the first star to appear on screen in the nude.

Audrey Munson in George Foster Platt's *Inspiration* (US 15), a Thanhouser production released by the Mutual Film Corporation on 18 November 1915. It related the story of an inexperienced country girl who becomes a 'life model' for a sculptor with whom she falls in love. The nude scenes aroused opposition from some, others considered them 'artistic' and 'educational'. Audrey Munson was a well-known artist's model in real life. She performed in two other films: *Purity* (US 16), in which she was also seen naked, and *The Girl O' Dreams* (US 16).

The sensation caused in the 1930s by Hedy Lamarr's nude bathing scenes in *Extase* (Cz 33) has given wide currency to the mistaken idea that Miss Lamarr was the first nude actress on screen. She was not even the first nude in Czech movies, a distinction earned by Ira Rina in Gustav Muchaty's *Eroticon* (Cz 29).

Other nude scenes of the pre-*Extase* period were legion. Celio Film's *Idolo Infranto* (It 13) contained a scene set in an artist's studio with a nude model. 'The Naked Truth' was represented by a nude girl in woman director Lois Weber's *The Hypocrites* (US 15). This Paramount release was banned in Ohio and the Mayor of Boston demanded that clothes be painted on to the image of 'The Naked Truth', frame by frame. The nude was uncredited, but has been variously claimed as a Miss Margaret Edwards and Lois Weber herself.

> Romain Gary shot two versions of *Kill* (Fr 71), one clothed and the other unclothed. The undraped version, he explained, was for Protestant countries and the other for Catholic countries.

D. W. Griffith hired a number of prostitutes to appear naked in the Belshazar's Feast sequence of *Intolerance* (US 16). Joseph Hanabery, Griffith's assistant, had been ordered to shoot nude scenes, but decided it was more than he could get away with and had his actresses lightly draped for the orgy. Meanwhile Griffith, who was back in New York, did some close shots of nude prostitutes and these were intercut with Hanabery's more discreet scenes. When the film was reissued, in 1942, the New York Censor Board insisted that Griffith's nude inserts be cut.

The same year saw no less than three films in which the leading lady appeared in the nude. Apart from Audrey Munson's second nude role in *Purity* (US 16)—see above—the nymph-like Australian swimming star turned actress Annette Kellerman was seen as nature intended in Fox's *Daughter of the Gods* (US 16) and winsome 16-year-old blue-eyed newcomer June Caprice was filmed running naked through the woods in *The Ragged Princess* (US 16). Miss Kellerman, the Esther Williams of silent movies, had been the centre of controversy five years earlier when she had worn the first one-piece bathing suit, though strangely when she wore nothing at all it aroused far less indignation. Esther Williams played Miss Kellerman in *Million Dollar Mermaid* (US 52), but by that date the austere provisions of the Hays Code precluded any presentation of the naked human form.

A nude girl on a crucifix was portrayed in *The Penitentes* (US 16) and a 'Miss Ray' appeared nude in *Le Film du Diable* (Bra 17). In *The Tree of Knowledge* (US 20),

Yvonne Gardelle appeared naked as Lillith, the temptress who seeks to seduce Adam in the Garden of Eden before the creation of Eve. There were nude bathing scenes in *The Branding Iron* (US 20), *Isle of Love* (US 22)—in the nightclub scene naked girls threw themselves into a swimming pool as midnight struck—and in Henry Hathaway's *To the Last Man* (US 33), with Esther Ralston as one of the participants. Clara Bow took to nude bathing in *Hula* (US 27).

Lili Damita was seen in the buff in *Red Heels* (US 26) and Hope Hampton in *Lovers' Island* (US 26), while in *In Line of Duty* (US 32), a picture set in Arctic regions, Sue Carol bravely stripped off twice. Sally Rand performed an alfresco dance wearing nothing but a pair of shoes in *Paris at Midnight* (US 26) and a rather more circumspect Elissa Landi played a naked Christian girl bound to the stake in a Roman arena in *The Sign of the Cross* (US 32). Jean Vigo's *A Propos de Nice* (Fr 30) contains a scene of a nude sitting at a café table. The 35mm prints of the film imported into Britain had the scene cut, but the sub-standard gauge prints retained it, since 16mm film is not subject to censorship in Britain. A full-length nude is observed in the prison scene in *The Yellow Ticket* (US 31), about prostitution in Czarist Russia. The first nude scene in a Russian film, of a widow hysterically mourning in *Earth* (USSR 30), was cut by order of the authorities.

Nude scenes also appeared in *A Man's World* (US 18), *Man, Woman and Marriage* (US 21), *Heedless Moths* (US 21)—the earliest known instance of a nude stand-in being used for the star, Jane Thomas—*Quo Vadis* (Ger/It 24), *Dante's Inferno* (US 24), *Wege zur Kraft und Schönheit* (Ger 25), *Metropolis* (Ger 26), *Beatrice Cenci* (It 26), *Casanova* (Fr/It 26), *Faust* (Ger 26), *Mandrin* (Fr 28?) and *Secrets of the Orient* (Ger/Fr 28). In most of these films the nakedness was tastefully discreet. Stefan and Franciszka Themerson's *Europa* (Pol 30) had what has been claimed as 'the first full-frontal nude'. The censor demanded that the scene should be cut, but Stefan neglected to do so and the film was released intact.

Following the introduction of the 1934 Hays Code, nudity disappeared from the Hollywood screen for 30 years. The first picture to bypass the ban was Sidney Lumet's *The Pawnbroker* (US 64), in which a woman was shown naked to the waist. The film was passed uncut by the Production Code Administration on the grounds that the scene was an essential element in the narrative. This decision opened the way for artistically valid scenes of nudity and sexual explicitness; it also hastened the end of the Administration itself, since a more liberal attitude towards sex on screen was difficult to accommodate within a code of prohibitions, and a ratings system was adopted instead.

The first film containing nude scenes to be passed by the British Board of Film Censors was *One Summer of Happiness* (Swe 51), in which a young couple were seen embracing in a pool of bulrushes. The decision was based on the fact that, in the words of former BBFC Secretary John Trevelyan, 'it was generally accepted in this country that in Scandinavia people bathed in the nude'. The prohibition of nudity, which had remained absolute since the founding of the Board in 1913 until this breach in 1952, was abandoned for good the following year after a naturist movie called *The Garden of Eden* (US 53) was banned by the BBFC but certified for exhibition by over 180 local authorities including the LCC. Some even gave it a U certificate. The Board wisely decided that its original decision had been out of keeping with changing social attitudes and modified its policy on nudity. Another 14 years were to pass, however, before the Board felt the public was ready to accept a full-frontal nude, and again it was a Swedish film which stimulated the change. *Hugs and Kisses* (Swe 66) was passed by the BBFC in 1967 complete with a scene in which a girl undressed in front of a full-length mirror. This was also the first time that pubic hair was displayed so forthrightly, though there had been some revealing 'flashes' during the scene in *Blow Up* (GB 67) in which David Hemmings wrestles on the floor with Jane Birkin and Gillian Hills.

The cinema of the Eastern world took longer to come to terms with nudity. The same year that *The Pawnbroker* (US 64) was restoring bare bosoms to the American screen, the first Indian films were released in which girls were permitted to be seen in bathing costumes—*April Fool* (Ind 64) and *Sangam* (Ind 64). In Japan, however, nudity made a tentative arrival on screen in the '50s, with a scene in *The Princess Yang* (Jap 55) where the heroine enters the bath. Since the heroine was the distinguished dramatic actress Machiko Kyo, it was unthinkable that she should be seen in person in the nude, so a stripper was hired from the Ginza to double for her. Foreign films continued to be subject to strict censorship, though not always simply by cutting. In the Japanese release prints of *A Clockwork Orange* (GB 71) the nude scenes went out of focus, while *Woodstock* (US 69) had the emulsion scraped off the footage containing nudes. Since 1993 nudity has been permitted in films shown in Japan—but only if the revelation of the unclothed human form is in a non-sexual context. Nevertheless, Japan has come a long way since a scene of Cary Grant embracing Sylvia Sidney in *Madame Butterfly* (US 32) was cut by the Japanese censor because Miss Sidney's elbow was exposed. Among the last of the Far Eastern countries to succumb was Red China, where nudity reached the screen in 1985 with a picture called *The Rickshaw Boy* (Chn 85). In this a girl was seen totally naked—but from the rear only.

Full-frontal nudity came to Soviet cinema in 1990 with the Odessa Filmstudio's *The Weakness Syndrome* (USSR 90). A seemingly impregnable bastion was breached the same year when Ferid Boughedir's *Halfouine—Child of the Terraces* (Tunisia 90) became the first film from a Muslim country to strip away the veils and reveal the naked female form.

India finally succumbed in 1996 with the release of three films featuring full-frontal nudity by Indian performers (an earlier film had shown European actresses nude)—*Bandit Queen*, *English August* and *Divine Lovers*. First to be shown was *Bandit Queen*, in which bandit queen Phoolan Devi is depicted being paraded naked in front of a large crowd after her capture. It was reported that the scene was met with outraged catcalls in some cinemas and the film was subsequently banned.

The first full-frontal male nudity to be seen on screen appeared fleetingly in *Dante's Inferno* (It 12). The first explicit scene revealing male genitalia in a commercial feature was the nude wrestling match between Alan Bates and Oliver Reed in Ken Russell's *Women in Love* (GB 69).

The naked form in serious films is usually justified on 'artistic' grounds. Derek Jarman, director of the all-male *Sebastiane* (GB 75), vouchsafed a refreshingly practical explanation for the abundant nudity in this study of religious sexuality in Romano-Britain: 'the budget wouldn't run to authentic costumes'.

The first film made for theatrical release in which the sex act was depicted was *Extase* (Cz 33). The young heroine (Hedwig Kiesler, later known as Hedy Lamarr), who has flown from an impotent husband, runs naked through the woods, bathes, and then has sex with a young engineer in a hut. Curiously *Extase* is celebrated as the first motion picture containing a nude scene, which it was not, rather than the first to show sexual intercourse, which it was.

The first theatrical release to contain a scene of unsimulated sexual intercourse was Jan Lindqvist and Stefan Jarl's Dom Kallar *Oss Mods/They Call Us Misfits* (Swe 67), starring Kenta Gustafsson and Stoffe Svensson. The first in an English-language film occurred between Donald Sutherland and Julie Christie in Nicolas Roeg's *Don't Look Now* (GB 73), though not in North America. The version released in Britain contained what one critic called 'the most sensuous and disturbing erotic sequence since Resnais' *Hiroshima Mon Amour*', but the US print was re-edited in order to secure an R-rating and did not reveal the coupling in its full graphic reality.

The earliest known pornographic film which can definitely be dated is *A l'Ecu d'Or ou la bonne auberge* (Fr 08). Ado Kyrou, writing in the film journal *Positif*, describes the story thus: 'During wartime, a valiant musketeer presents himself famished at the door of an inn. "Nothing to eat" answers the innkeeper. Happily, thanks to an accommodating servant girl, an amorous meal is offered to him. He enjoys it so much that, on the appearance of another girl, he enjoys a second helping.'

There is no doubt that pornographic film-making was well established even by this early date, though for obvious reasons records are sparse. It was in the same year as *A l'Ecu d'Or* was released, 1908, that Russia enacted a law against obscene movies, known there as 'the Paris Genre'. In Moscow the Mephistopholes Kino decided to test its enforcement by presenting a full programme of such films and was promptly closed down.

The oldest surviving pornographic films are contained in America's Kinsey Collection. *Am Abend* (Ger c. 10) is a ten-minute film which begins with a woman masturbating alone in her bedroom and progresses to scenes of her with a man performing straight sex, fellatio and anal penetration. An Argentinian film believed to date from 1907–12, *El Satario*, opens with a group of women bathing in a river in savannah country—probably filmed at Tigre, near Buenos Aires. One of their number is abducted by a satyr, who performs a wide variety of unmentionable acts with her, which she apparently enjoys. Eventually they are disturbed by the other women and the satyr flees back into the forest.

The first full-length erotic cartoon film was Osamu Tezuka's *A Thousand and One Nights* (Jap 69)—claimed (inaccurately) as 'the first animated film for adults'. David

Grant's *Sinderella* (GB 72) was declared obscene by both Bow Street Magistrates' Court and the High Court of Appeal, but later passed by the British Board of Film Censors with cuts amounting to only 26 seconds.

> Among the luminaries of the silver screen who started their career in porno movies was Sylvester Stalone, who exhibited his plexes and quite a lot else in *A Party at Kitty and Stud's* (US 70). Roll on seven years and the pic was being rented out as *The Italian Stallion* for private parties at $10,000 a pop. The star of *Rocky* (US 76), by now the hottest new name in Hollywood, was unfazed when doorstepped by reporters. "Hell, for $10,000 forget the film," he grunted. "I'll be there myself."

'Soft porn' for theatrical release first started in Japan in 1950 with a wave of teenage sexploitation films with titles like *Teenager's Sex-Manual*, *Virgin's Clinic*, *A Virgin's Sex Manual*, *Bitch* and *Bad Girl*. The title role in the latter was played by the aristocratic Yoshiko Kuga, daughter of a Japanese peer, which gave it an added piquancy for some. The films reflected—and exploited—the revolution in social values of post-war Japan, where a confused generation of teenagers was apt to identify freedom with license. Remarkably the production of these movies began only three years after the first Japanese screen kiss.

The genesis of the American 'skinflick' is generally attributed to ex-Signal Corps cameraman Russ Meyer, who made his soft-porn debut with *The Immoral Mr Teas* (US 59), a comedy about a man with the unusual ability to undress girls mentally. This modest pioneer effort, shot on a budget of $24,000 in four days, inspired no less than 150 imitations within a year of its release.

The first hardcore pornographic feature film to be shown in public cinemas in the US was Mike Henderson's *Electro-Sex '75* (US 70). Within ten years there were 800 cinemas in America showing hardcore porn and box-office gross exceeded $500 million. The thriving exhibition industry died as rapidly as it had risen with the advent of the porno video c. 1980.

Although sexploitation movies are generally profitable in relation to their modest budgets, the first to achieve an outstanding box-office success, even by comparison with major studio productions, was *Emmanuelle* (Fr 74). Of the 607 new films released in Paris in 1974 *Emmanuelle* scored the highest number of admissions (1,342,921), ahead of such notable box-office draws as *The Sting* (US 73)—1,154,952 admissions and *The Exorcist* (US 73)—655,092 admissions.

The most prolific producer of pornographic films was the Nikkatsu Company of Tokyo, Japan, which made over 1100 softcore films between 1971 and 1988. The studio went 'straight' under a new name, Ropponica, after deciding that video had killed off the market for theatrical porno movies.

The first film about overt homosexuality was Richard Oswald's *Anders als die Andern* (Ger 19), starring Conrad Veidt, which dared to confront the cinema-going public with a subject still proscribed in literature. Following the resumption of censorship in post-war Germany, male homosexuality received no further attention until Gustaf Gründgens' *Zwei Welten* (Ger 40). The story by Felix Lutzkendorff was an innocuous romance about two boys and two girls working together on a farm in the summer holidays. Under the direction of Gründgens it became transformed into an idyll between the two boys.

Elsewhere the theme attracted less sympathetic treatment. During the Japanese occupation of Shanghai, the Japanese made a film in China for native consumption called *Chu Hai-tang* (Jap/Chn 43), which attempted to propagate the idea of the Chinese as a decadent race with the story of a Chinese General embroiled with a female impersonator from the Peking Opera.

In Britain the subject remained unbroached on screen until Terence Young's *Serious Charge* (GB 59), about a priest (Anthony Quayle) falsely accused by a youth (Andrew Ray) of making homosexual advances. This made relatively little impact, and it was left to Basil Deardon to make a film sufficiently explicit to actually use the word 'homosexual' in the dialogue. The picture was *Victim* (GB 61), in which Dirk Bogarde portrayed a respected barrister who becomes the victim of blackmail as a result of his relationship with a young vagrant (Peter McEnery). In the meantime American director Joseph Mankiewicz had directed Gore Vidal's screen adaptation of the Tennessee Williams play *Suddenly, Last Summer* (GB 59), the story of a homosexual poet whose beautiful cousin (Elizabeth Taylor) lures Italian beach boys for his delectation. Other British films on homosexual themes followed *Victim* in fairly quick succession, including *A Taste of Honey* (GB 61), *The Leather Boys* (GB 63) and *The Servant* (GB 63), but there was little further development of the theme by American film-makers between *Suddenly, Last Summer* and John Huston's *Reflections in a Golden Eye* (US 67), again with Elizabeth Taylor, this time as the wife of an army officer (Marlon Brando) infatuated with a young recruit.

> The earliest gay gag in a movie features in Mutual's Charlie Chaplin comedy *Behind the Screen* (US 16). Eric Campbell as the heavy, thinking the heroine Edna Purviance, dressed in male clothing, is a boy, goes all coy and twee, protruding his bottom provocatively.

Lesbian love was treated with delicacy and discretion in Leontine *Sagan's Mädchen in Uniform* (Ger 31), a tender study of a girl's infatuation for a teacher in a repressive Prussian boarding school. The film's two principals, Dorothea Wieck and Hertha Thiele, were reunited two years later in a homo-erotic melodrama *Anna and Elizabeth* (Ger 33), in which the older, wealthy Elizabeth becomes possessively dependent on the sensual Anna when cured of her lameness by the younger woman's seemingly miraculous powers.

It was another 30 years before Hollywood broached the subject. In *Walk on the Wild Side* (US 62) Barbara Stanwyck played the madam of a brothel who looks to inmate Capucine for the 'affection' she cannot receive from her maimed husband. Rather more explicit in treatment—*Wild Side* took a fairly oblique look at the relationship—was *The Children's Hour* (US 62), the second film version of Lillian Hellman's play of the same name. Both pictures were directed by William Wyler, but in the earlier version, titled *These Three* (US 36), the original story of two schoolmistresses having an affair was changed to a heterosexual triangle involving two female teachers and a man. Wyler's remake had Shirley Maclaine and Audrey Hepburn in a sensitively handled adaptation true to the spirit and the purpose of the play.

KISSING

The first screen kiss was performed in close-up by May Irwin and John Rice in a filmed scene from the stage play *The Widow Jones* (US 1896) and was described by a contemporary journal, *The Chap Book*, as 'absolutely disgusting'.

The first French kiss in a Hollywood movie was between Natalie Wood and Warren Beatty in *Splendor in the Grass* (US 61).

The first erotic kiss between two members of the same sex occurs during the orgy scene in Cecil B. DeMille's *Manslaughter* (US 22). The first leading lady to kiss another woman on screen was Marlene Dietrich, provocatively dressed in a white tuxedo, in Josef von Sternberg's *Morocco* (US 30).

The first erotic kiss between two men was bestowed on Murray Head by Peter Finch in *Sunday Bloody Sunday* (GB 71), John Schlesinger's study of a bisexual love triangle. Originally the intention was to show an embrace in long shot, but the scene developed from there. Schlesinger remarked that the two actors 'were considerably less shocked by the kiss than the technicians on the set were'. The fiercely hetero Finch, on being asked by a TV interviewer how he had coped with this histrionic challenge, responded with admirable *sang froid*, 'I did it for England'.

The most kisses in a single film were the 127 bestowed by John Barrymore on Mary Astor and Estelle Taylor in *Don Juan* (US 26).

The first Far Eastern country to permit kissing in films was China, the first oriental screen kiss being bestowed on Miss Mamie Lee in *Two Women in the House* (Chn 26). In Japan, where kissing was considered 'unclean, immodest, indecorous, ungraceful and likely to spread disease'—at least by Tokyo's Prefect of Police—some 800,000ft of kissing scenes were cut from American movies that same year. Indians reacted much the same way, though with less rigour about cuts. According to *The Report of the Indian Cinematograph Committee* (1928), during foreign films 'when a kissing scene is shown, the ladies turn their heads away'.

Japan's first screen kiss was seen in *Hatachi no Seishun/Twenty-Year-Old Youth* (Jap 46), directed by Yasushi Sasaki. The honour of directing the inaugural kiss should have gone to Yasuki Chiba, who was planning to introduce the daring innovation in his aptly titled *Aru Yo no Seppun/A Certain Night's Kiss* (Jap 46), but he lost his nerve at the last moment and the big clinch between the two lovers was discreetly obscured by an open umbrella. Only four years later the sex act itself was brought to the Japanese screen in *Yuki Fujin Ezu/Picture of Madame Yuki* (Jap 50).

The first screen kiss in a movie from a Muslim country took place in *The Blazing Sun* (Egypt 53), in which Omar Sharif made his second screen appearance.

> Only two Hollywood leading ladies never kissed their leading men on screen. One was Mae West, who exuded such powerful sexuality that actual physical contact would have seemed like overkill. The other was the Chinese-American star Anna May Wong (1907–61). She nearly achieved it in *The Road to Dishonour* (GB 29); indeed her kissing scene with John Longden was shot, but cut by the censor on the grounds that inter-racial love would be offensive to some patrons. One other heroine of the American screen also faced a kissing ban: Marguerite Clark (1881–1940), at one time Mary Pickford's chief rival as 'America's Sweetheart'. In this case the ban was imposed by her husband Harry Palmerson-Williams, whom she married in 1918. Although she made another dozen films, her career was severely damaged by the marital edict and she retired in 1921

The longest screen kiss took place between Steve McQueen and Faye Dunaway in *The Thomas Crown Affair* (US 68) and lasted for 55 seconds.

The last major film-producing country still banning kissing in films is Iran.

Singapore has special rules about 'suggestive prolonged kissing': it is not allowed in Malay-language films, but is acceptable in others. In Pennsylvania in the 1930s, horizontal screen kisses were banned, vertical allowed.

KISSING IN INDIAN FILMS

Kissing was voluntarily renounced by the film producers themselves in the mid-1930s on the grounds that Indians did not kiss in public, and to see them doing so on the screen was pandering to an alien custom. After Independence, when the producers decided that there were sound commercial reasons for a little occidental decadence, they found themselves up against the stern morality of the censors. Some latitude was permitted, however, if at least one of the partners in the act was a foreigner, or in the case of 'international' versions of films for overseas release only. In one instance two Indians were allowed to be seen kissing each other because the girl was playing the part of a Portuguese. The breakthrough came only in 1977, when for the first time in over 40 years two Indians playing Indians were able to kiss in a major film shown in their own country. The historic embrace took place between Zeenat Aman, a former Miss Asia, and the sub-continent's most romantic leading man, Shashi Kapoor, in Raj Kapoor's *Satyam Shivam Sundaram* (Ind 77), a musical melodrama about a man who falls in love with the compelling voice of an adivasi girl and only learns on their wedding night that half of her face is hideously disfigured by a burn.

Sport

Hollywood had made a total of 891 feature films with a sports background up to the end of 2000. The most popular sport as a subject for screen drama is boxing, with 22.8% of the total, followed by horse racing with 15.6%, American football with 13.8% and baseball and motor racing with 9.6%. The number of films devoted to each sport in each decade is listed opposite, with the various sports in rank order according to their individual totals. Only films about competitive sport have been included, so few of the films of Esther Williams, for example, have been counted under swimming.

The most successful sports movie of all time was MGM-UA's *Rocky IV* (US 85), directed by and starring Sylvester Stallone, which grossed $300.4 million worldwide, of which $127.8 million was in North America. Significantly this was about a universal sport: boxing. Most successful on American turf was *The Waterboy* (US 99) about gridiron football, with a domestic gross of $161.4 million, but an overseas box-office taking of under $40 million. The pigskin don't travel.

Sylvester Stallone in Rocky *(US 76). Hollywood has made more films about boxing than any other sport.*

HOLLYWOOD AND SPORT — THE LEAGUE TABLE

	1910–19	1920–29	1930–39	1940–49	1950–59	1960–69	1970–79	1980–89	1990–99	2000	Total
Boxing	7	61	39	29	28	4	11	14	7	4	204
Horse Racing	20	32	44	21	11	5	3	2	1	–	139
American Football	2	23	38	14	10	5	8	8	12	3	123
Baseball	8	9	7	7	13	1	7	14	19	–	85
Motor Racing	2	23	20	3	10	16	8	2	1	–	85
Basketball	–	2	2	–	3	2	12	3	16	1	41
Athletics	–	8	2	–	3	3	8	5	4	–	33
Golf	1	1	4	–	3	4	1	4	5	1	24
Wrestling	–	–	2	1	–	–	7	9	–	1	20
Motor Cycle Racing	–	2	1	–	1	3	6	2	–	–	15
Ice Hockey	–	–	3	1	1	–	1	1	5	–	13
Rowing	1	5	4	–	–	–	–	–	1	–	11
Polo	–	6	4	–	–	–	–	–	–	–	10
Skiing	–	–	1	1	–	2	2	4	–	–	10
Speedboat Racing	–	1	6	–	–	–	2	–	–	–	9
Cycle Racing	–	–	1	–	–	–	1	6	–	–	8
Swimming	–	2	–	–	1	–	1	2	1	–	7
Tennis	–	1	1	–	1	–	3	1	–	–	7
Roller Skating	–	–	–	–	1	–	4	–	1	–	6
Soccer	–	–	–	–	–	–	1	2	1	1	6
Skateboarding	–	–	–	–	–	–	2	2	1	–	5
Pool	–	–	–	–	–	1	1	2	–	–	4
Kickboxing	–	–	–	–	–	–	–	1	3	–	4
Yacht Racing	–	–	1	–	–	1	–	–	1	–	3
Ice Skating	–	–	1	–	–	–	1	–	1	–	3
Gymnastics	–	–	–	–	–	–	–	2	–	–	2
Showjumping	–	–	–	–	–	1	–	1	–	–	2
Volleyball	–	–	–	–	–	–	–	1	1	–	2
Angling	–	–	–	–	–	1	–	–	1	–	2
Bowling	–	–	–	–	–	–	1	–	1	–	2
Fencing	–	1	–	–	–	–	–	–	1	–	2
Cockfighting	–	–	–	–	–	–	1	–	–	–	1
Dog Racing	–	–	1	–	–	–	–	–	–	–	1
Ice Yachting	–	1	–	–	–	–	–	–	–	–	1
Weightlifting	–	–	–	–	–	–	1	–	–	–	1

SOCCER FILMOGRAPHY

Soccer is not only the most popular spectator sport in the world, it is also the most international of all sports in film terms. Although fewer feature films have been made about soccer than about boxing or horse racing, they emanate from a much wider range of countries. No other sport has produced fiction features from as many countries as these: Argentina, Australia, Austria, Belgium, Bhutan, Brazil, Britain, Bulgaria, Cape Verde Is, China, Colombia, Czechoslovakia, Denmark, Ecuador, Egypt, France, Germany, Guinea, Hong Kong, Hungary, Iceland, India, Iran, Ireland, Israel, Italy, Japan, Korea, Netherlands, Norway, Poland, Portugal, Romania, Senegal, Spain, Sweden, Switzerland, Tunisia, Uruguay, USA, USSR, Yugoslavia. The filmography below contains the titles of all known soccer films to end 2000.

The Winning Goal (GB 20)
The Ball of Fortune (GB 26)
Monsieur mon chauffeur (Bel 28)
Der König der Mittelstürmer (Ger 28)
Die Elf Teufel (Ger 28)
The Great Game (GB 30)
Soccerfans (Cz 31)
Up for the Cup (GB 31)
Our Football Eleven (Cz 36)
Goal! (Arg 36)
The Goalkeeper (USSR 36)
The Klapzuba Football Eleven (Cz 38)
Alma e Corpo de Uma Raca (Bra 38)

The Arsenal Stadium Mystery (GB 39)
Bola ao Centro (Por 47)
Plavi (Yug 50)
The Football Parson (Den 51)
The Merry Duel (Cz 51)
In the Penalty Area (Cz 51)
Women Who Have Run Off-Side (Cz 51)
The Great Game (GB 53)
Small Town Story (GB 53)
11:1 (GDR 55)
Two Little Soccer Teams (Chn 56)
A Football Star (Hun 56)
Saeta Rubia (Sp 56)
The Goalkeeper Lives in our Street (Cz 57)
Favourite No. 13 (Bul 58)
Gambe d'oro (It 58)
Il Nemico di mia moglie/My Wife's Enemy (It 59)
Our Lads (Rom 59)
Los Economicamente debiles (Sp 60)
Football Fans (Cz 60)
The Last Goal (Hun 61)
A través del fútbal (Sp 62)
Comrade President the Centre-Forward (Yug 62)
Two Half Times in Hell (Hun 62)
Ivana in the Forward Line (Cz 63)
Pelota de cuerco (Arg 63)
Third Time (USSR 63)
Soccer Fans (Chn 63)
Allez France (Fr 64)
Fadni odpoledne (Cz 65)

Little Soccer Team (Chn 65)
Let's Go Wakadaisho (Jap 67)
Somos los mejores! (Arg 67)
Same Player Shoots Again (FRG 68)
Fish, Football and Girls (Isr 68)
Volver a vivi (Sp 68)
Fish for the Glory (Jap 69)
Aconteceu no Maracna (Bra 69)
Il Presidente del Borgorosso Football Club (It 70)
Shoot Paragon! (Pol 70)
Sekundomer/Stop Watch (USSR 70)
Women Offside (Cz 71)
The Goalkeeper's Fear of the Penalty (FRG/Aut 71)
Bloomfield (Isr 71)
I Due maghi de pallone (It 71)
Mother Love (S.Kor 72)
Willi wird das Kschon schaukeln (FRG 72)
Tochka, Tochka, Zapiataia/Dot, Dot, a Comma (USSR 72)
Football Champion (Ind 73)
A Goal, Another Goal (USSR 73)
Stubby (Swe 74)
Pandhattan/Play Ball (Ind 74)
Pirveli Mertskhali/The First Swallow (USSR 75)
Eleven Hopefuls (USSR 76)
Furia Española (Sp 76)
The Memorable Day (Bul 76)
Takaya Ona, Igra (USSR 77)
The Boys in Company C (HK 77)
Striker (Ind 78)
Trener/The Coach (Yug 78)
Yesterday's Hero (GB 79)
Everything for Football (Rom 79)
Coup de Tête (Fr 80)
Ace! Soccer (Chn 80)
Mundita lito (Uru 81)
The Match (Hun 81)
Gregory's Girl (GB 81)
Escape to Victory (US 81)
At Start of Play (USSR 82)
Football (Ind 82)
Pra Frente Brazil (Bra 82)
Eccezzziunale . . . Veramente (It 82)
White Wing (Bra 82)
Referees, Fans and Soccer Players (It 82)
Copa de Ora (Uru 82)
Soccer Attack Centre (It 83)
El Harrif/Street Player (Egypt 83)
Was Kosted Sieg/What Price Victory (Aut 83)
The Champions (HK 83)
Those Glory, Glory Days (GB 83)
Young Giants (US 83)
Excuse Me—Are You Watching Football? (GDR 83)
The Football Master (It 84)
Hip Hip Hooray (Ind 84)
A Mort l'Arbitre (Fr 84)
Come On, Team China (Chn 85)
The Cup (Tun 86)
Ultimo Momento (It 87)
Hotshot (US 87)
Virile Games (Cz 88)
Football Poker (Pol 88)
The Firm (GB 89)
Silence (Iran 90)
Struck by Lightning (Aus 90)

Shooting Stars (GB 90)
Ladybugs (US 92)
Cup Final (Israel 92)
Born Kicking (GB 92, TVM)
Nordkurve (Ger 92)
A Soccer Fan's Obsession (Chn 92)
The Heartbreak Kid (Aus 93)
Le Ballon d'Or (Fr/Guinea 94)
Ti Kniver/Hjertet (Nor 94)
Darebat Gazaa/Penalty (Egypt 94)
Shoot! (Jap 94)
ID (GB 95)
Le Voyage de Baba (Fr/Senegal 95)
Matias, juez de linea (Sp 95)
Viva Jan Isidro (It 95)
The Big Green (US 95)
L'Estate di Bobby Charlton (It 95)
Pon un Hombre en tu Vida (Sp 96)
The Van (Ire 96)
All Stars (Neths 96)
When Saturday Comes (GB 96)
Hillsborough (GB 96, TVM)
Fever Pitch (GB 97)
Didier (Fr 97)
Historias de Futbol (Chile 97)
Golpe de Estadio (Col 98)
Fintar O Destino (Por/Cape Verde Is/Fr 98)
Una Aventura de Zico (Bra/Ecuador 98)
Boleiros (Bra 98)
Mad About Mambo (US 99)
Bank, Boom, Bank (Ger 99)
Soccer Fans (It 99)
Pros Brazilian Football Rivisted (Bra 99)
6:3 (Hun 99)
The Match (GB/US/Ire 99)
Home Team (US 99)
The Cup (Aus/Bhutan 99)
Air Bud, World Pup (US 99)
Stadium Cup (Sp/It/Col 99)
El Portero (Sp 00)
Extra Time (GB 00)
Un Derangement Considerable (Fr 00)
There Is Only One Jimmy Grimble (GB/Fr 00)
A Shot at Glory (US/GB 00)
Purely Belter (GB 00)
Fussball ist Unser Leben/Soccer is Our Life (Ger 00)
Season Ticket (GB 00)
The Cup (US/GB 00)
The Last Yugoslavian Football Team (Yug 00)
Mondialito (Swz/Fr 00)
Best (GB 01)
The Icelandic Dream (Ice 01)
The Footballers (Iran 01)
Penalty (GB i.p.)

Themes

The chart overleaf shows the number of feature films produced in the USA and UK respectively on each of the major themes, and the percentage of total production repres-ented by that figure, at each ten-year point from 1914 to 1994 inclusive. Films belonging to more than one theme have been credited to each as appropriate, so the percentages do not add up to 100. For example, a backstage crime melodrama set in the 19th century would be counted under Showbusiness, Crime and Historical.

THE FILMS OF 1914

This was the year in which the feature-length film took hold in the USA. By far the greater proportion of features were based on stage plays, which is indicative of the fact that the screen was still regarded as a form of 'silent theatre'. In some cases, though by no means all, the story was opened out to take advantage of the opportunity to shoot outdoor scenes and show action which would not have been possible within the confines of a theatre stage. Since the theatre of the day was dominated by melodrama, the stage-derived features also tended towards a mixture of sensation and sentiment, with sex as a distinct, albeit discreet, ingredient. Favourite themes of 1914 were 'the sins of society', heroes or heroines suffering from amnesia, heirs or more often heiresses being abducted by gypsies, and morality stories about the dreadful consequences of drink, drugs and pre-marital sex. The dreadful consequence of the latter was generally syphilis—one 1914 melodrama even included shots of ravaged patients taken in a genuine VD clinic. The other sexual theme presented in terms of a 'warning to the innocent' was white slavery, the Americans following the European lead in exploiting the subject for all it was worth—and it was worth a lot to producers and exhibitors alike. Foreign locales were comparatively few, though there was a sub-genre of films set in Russia (usually shot in New Jersey) about nihilists, Cossacks and noble heroes unjustly consigned to Siberia. This was a time when the Russian immigrant population of New York included many anarchists and other dissidents, including Trotsky, who played bit parts in two such films released in 1914 and 1915.

British feature production of 1914 consisted mainly of crime melodrama, usually centering around titled people in opulent settings.

THE FILMS OF 1924

The most recurring theme in the Hollywood productions of 1924 was physical and/or sexual conflict in the Far North. Variously set in lumber camps or simply the snowy wastes, the locale was sometimes Alaska, sometimes the Yukon, but more often an unidentified region of mountains and forests in which men battled against the elements and each other, and women, few in number but invariably fair of face, battled for the love of a good man. Other popular themes of the year were romance in the South Seas and the thrills of the circus. A particular plot device used unsparingly in the melodramas of 1924 was the effects of bootleg gin—wood alcohol—on those who sought solace from the rigours of prohibition. The victim was invariably the girlfriend, led into the paths of unrighteousness by the heavy and struck blind as a result. The remainder of the story was generally to do with how the romantic lead obtained the services of a famed Viennese specialist to restore her sight, and about something worse than being struck blind—usually being struck dead—happening to the heavy. Audiences of 1924 were predominately female, which doubtless accounted for the volume of romantic subjects, represented by no fewer than 120 films or over 28% of the total.

British films of 1924 were still in their 'lost heiress' phase—there had been little progress towards more sophisticated themes since the inception of the feature film.

THE FILMS OF 1934

Hollywood production at this period was dominated by the newspaper story, reflecting how the coming of sound had tended to move the action indoors with a corresponding shift from rural to urban locales. Most were about a newspaperman solving a crime and winning the girl—usually a girl who had been framed or the daughter of an upright citizen who had been framed—in the process. While adultery probably occupied more footage in both the films of the '20s and '30s than any other single topic, there was a significant change of emphasis after the introduction of the Hays code. In the 'eternal triangle' films of 1924 it was usually the woman who made the running, often in the guise of a neglected wife or bored daughter 'vamping' a married man. The films of 1934 were much more circumspect in their treatment of infidelity, the man always cast in the role of seducer and the act of adultery scarcely ever reaching consummation.

Apart from the perennial cops and robbers quota quickies, the dominant themes of the early talkies period in Britain were rhythm, romance and Ruritania. No fewer than 34 musicals were released in 1934, many of them in a Viennese or Balkan setting. The 'I know! We'll put on a show!' type of musical was also to the fore. Statistically comedy was king, with films that ranged from the music-hall humour of George Formby to the sophisticated wit of Noel Coward representing over 31% of the total.

THE FILMS OF 1944

Not surprisingly, wartime movies tended towards escapist fare. Comedies, westerns and musicals were the staple, with most of the musicals set against a showbusiness background—one of the 56 fims on this theme was even titled *Show Business.*

With the decline of production in wartime Britain, few discernible trends are apparent, though as in America, popular taste demanded lighthearted films.

THE FILMS OF 1954

This was a year so dominated by westerns that even Joan Crawford slipped off her mink to go riding the range in an oater called *Johnny Guitar.* A total of 55 films, more than one in every five features produced, were horse operas. The rest tended mainly in the direction of light romance of the Doris Day type and big-budget colour musicals, with only a few distinctive pictures like Hitchcock's *Rear Window* and Elia Kazan's *On the Waterfront* standing out from the general dross.

In Britain the year 1954 saw a return to the predominance of crime films, though the majority were B pictures (soon to disappear). Comedy was in the ascendant, with *Doctor in the House* the top moneymaker of the year and *Hobson's Choice* winner of the BFA's Best British Film award.

THE FILMS OF 1964

Youth pictures became big in the early '60s with a short-lived sub-genre of 'beach movies' that retain a cult following on both sides of the Atlantic even today.

	1914 US		1914 UK		1924 US		1924 UK		1934 US		1934 UK		1944 US		1944 UK	
	No	%	No	%	No	%	No	%	No	%	No	%	No	%	No	%
Action/Adventure	39	16.0	–	–	40	7.1	6	10.3	10	2.3	5	2.9	7	1.9	–	–
Animals	1	–	–	–	7	1.6	1	1.7	7	1.6	1	–	4	1.1	1	2.5
Animated	–	–	–	–	–	–	–	–	–	–	–	–	1	–	–	–
Biopics	1	–	1	3.3	2	–	1	1.7	7	1.6	6	3.5	11	3.0	–	–
Black	–	–	–	–	1	–	–	–	2	–	–	–	1	–	–	–
Comedy	25	10.3	1	3.3	53	12.5	5	8.6	85	19.6	54	31.2	56	15.1	11	27.5
Contemporary issues	6	2.5	–	–	3	–	–	–	4	–	–	–	3	–	–	–
Crime	48	19.8	13	43.3	54	12.7	20	34.4	101	23.3	64	37.0	62	16.8	7	17.5
Documentary	9	3.7	2	6.6	2	–	5	8.6	5	1.2	1	–	7	1.9	3	7.5
Drama	49	20.2	5	16.6	103	24.2	7	12.0	63	14.6	8	4.6			5	12.5
Fantasy[1]	12	4.9	3	10.0	3	–	2	3.4	4	–	2	1.2	21	5.7	5	12.5
Historical[2]	28	11.5	5	16.6	16	3.8	7	12.0	22	5.1	14	8.1	19	5.1	4	10.0
Horror	1	–	–	–	–	–	–	–	2	–	2	1.2	11	3.0	–	–
Literary[3]	12	4.9	6	20.0	6	1.4	3	5.1	13	3.0	3	1.7	6	1.6	–	–
Musicals[4]	–	–	–	–	–	–	–	–	32	7.4	34	19.7	73	19.7	8	20.0
Romance	27	11.1	2	6.6	120	28.2	14	24.1	79	18.2	46	26.6	53	14.3	9	22.5
Science-fiction	–	–	–	–	–	–	–	–	–	–	–	–	–	–	–	–
Sex	7	2.9	1	3.3	17	4.0	4	6.8	2	–	–	–	–	–	1	2.5
Showbusiness	10	4.1	1	3.3	21	4.9	–	–	20	4.6	13	7.5	56	15.1	1	2.5
Spies	3	1.2	–	–	3	–	–	–	5	1.2	3	1.2	15	4.1	–	–
Sport	5	2.1	–	–	12	2.8	4	6.8	14	3.2	3	1.7	6	1.6	–	–
War[5]	8	3.3	–	–	1	–	–	–	11	2.5	–	–	32	8.6	3	7.5
Westerns[6]	13	5.3	–	–	59	13.9	–	–	30	6.9	–	–	51	13.8	–	–
Youth[7]	1	–	–	–	7	1.6	–	–	8	1.9	–	–	17	4.6	–	–

1 Includes ghosts, dreams, time-warps, sorcery and fairy stories, as well as horror of the *Frankenstein* genre.
2 Means any period film in which the action is set more than 40 years before it was made.
3 Denotes films based on famous works of literature.
4 Includes concert movies.

Permissiveness and the counterculture were still two or three years away; in the meantime Sandra Dee epitomised teenage USA with wholesome winsomeness. Comedy was enjoying a revival, represented by nearly 30% of all productions compared to less than 10% a decade earlier. Out of fashion was the crime drama, registering only 23 films and 15.6% of production—ten years later, in 1974, there would be nearly three times as many with double the percentage.

Britain was also beginning to discover the charms of youth, symptomatic of the fact that older audiences were staying at home to watch television. Most of the films for this newly affluent teenage market were about pop musicians—Cliff Richard and the Shadows starred in *Wonderful Life*, Gerry and the Pacemakers in *Ferry Across the Mersey* and Freddy and the Dreamers in *Every Day's a Holiday*. Horror had also become a staple of British production, with Hammer riding high.

THE FILMS OF 1974

The year was notable for the virtual extinction of the western, after a 15-year decline, and the paucity of romance. Newspaper films, prolific until the 1950s, had also all but disappeared—the only 1974 movie set in a newspaper office was a remake of *The Front Page* with Walter Matthau and Jack Lemmon. Sex had become a major genre, with pornography making up the greater proportion of the total of 37 sex films reviewed—doubtless there were many more that had failed to attract the attention of *Variety*'s critics. Two new genres just starting to emerge were concert films (mainly rock festivals) and disaster movies. The two examples of the latter released in 1974, *Earthquake* and *The Towering Inferno*, were among the most successful of this 1970s phenomenon. Horror, with the accent on blood and gore rather than monsters, was becoming a cult. Typical, and perhaps the most enduring, of these violent films, was *The Texas Chainsaw Massacre*. The short-lived spate of black exploitation movies peaked in 1974, most of the 29 films featuring black leading players being of the 'superspade' type and conforming to the modish taste for sex and violence.

It is remarkable that the proportion of crime films made in Britain had always been higher than in the USA, but in 1974 the British percentage of 19.1 fell way below the American percentage of 31.6. Sex, with a nil rating in 1964, had reared its ugly head to score more than 20% in 1974, making it equally as prolific as horror. More surprisingly there were three British-made westerns, exactly the same number as Hollywood's meagre output for the year.

THE FILMS OF 1984

The youth movie had made a comeback in America, though the genre had moved onward from the cheerful romps on the beach of the 1960s, through the rock 'n' roll high-school phase of the '70s, to a strong blend of pubescent sex 'n' violence in the '80s. Sleeper of the year was *Angel*, about a 15-year-old 'honor student by day, Hollywood hooker by night', which matched the adolescent appeal of *Porky's* and the *Lemon Popsicle* movies with the sure-fire attention-grabber of a psycho-on-the-loose. Transvestism and Hare Krishna were thrown in for

1954				1964				1974				1984				1994			
US		UK		US		UK		US		UK		US		UK		US		UK	
No	%	No	%	No	%	No	%	No	%	No	%	NO	No	No	%	No	%	No	%
27	10.5	9	7.8	7	4.7	9	12.0	8	3.8	2	2.9	20	7.6	7	16.7	22	6.6	0	–
9	3.5	–	–	6	4.1	1	1.3	8	3.8	–	–	3	1.1	1	2.4	10	3.3	1	2.9
1	–	–	–	1	–	–	–	2	–	–	–	2	0.8	0	–	4	1.2	0	–
8	3.1	1	–	3	2.0	1	1.3	11	5.3	3	4.4	8	3.1	1	4.8	14	4.2	9	25.7
1	–	–	–	3	2.0	2	2.6	29	13.9	–	–	4	1.5	0	–	11	3.0	2	5.7
25	9.7	29	25.0	44	29.7	12	16.0	31	14.8	13	19.1	71	27.1	16	38.1	98	29.3	8	22.8
3	1.2	–	–	2	1.4	1	1.3	8	3.8	–	–	7	2.7	5	11.9	16	4.8	4	11.4
44	17.1	48	41.4	23	15.6	29	38.7	66	31.6	13	19.1	39	14.9	5	11.9	94	28.1	8	22.8
15	5.8	4	3.4	5	3.4	2	2.6	19	9.1	I	1.5	18	6.9	1	2.4	12	3.6	1	2.9
6	2.3	7	6.0	15	10.1	4	5.3	11	5.3	2	2.9	19	7.3	3	7.1	42	12.5	3	8.5
8	3.1	6	5.2	12	8.1	3	4.0	11	5.3	3	4.4	21	8.0	10	23.8	24	7.2	2	5.7
30	11.7	14	12.1	9	6.1	11	14.7	15	7.2	9	13.2	13	5.0	9	21.4	29	8.7	8	22.8
7	2.7	–	–	10	6.8	9	12.0	11	5.3	14	20.1	26	9.9	1	2.4	10	3.0	2	5.7
5	1.9	4	3.4	4	2.7	1	1.3	4	1.9	4	5.9	2	0.8	3	7.1	6	1.6	1	2.9
24	9.3	1	–	16	10.8	7	9.3	11	5.3	3	4.4	10	3.8	3	7.1	0	–	0	–
51	19.8	8	6.8	24	16.2	5	6.7	6	2.9	3	4.4	20	7.6	4	9.5	19	5.7	2	5.7
7	2.7	2	1.7	2	1.4	3	4.0	4	1.9	4	5.9	15	5.7	1	2.4	12	3.6	1	2.9
2	–	1	–	10	6.8	–	–	37	17.7	14	20.1	22	8.4	2	4.8	11	3.3	1	2.9
13	5.1	4	3.4	6	4.1	3	4.0	4	1.9	1	1.5	7	2.7	2	4.8	12	3.6	2	5.7
5	1.9	4	3.4	1	–	5	6.7	1	–	4	5.9	5	1.9	0	–	4	1.2	1	2.9
7	2.7	4	3.4	6	4.1	–	–	9	4.3	1	1.5	8	3.1	3	7.1	11	3.3	1	2.9
8	3.1	5	4.3	11	7.4	5	6.7	2	–	1	1.5	5	1.9	1	2.4	3	0.9	1	2.9
55	21.4	–	–	15	10.1	–	–	3	1.4	3	4.4	3	1.1	0	–	10	3.0	0	–
2	–	–	–	13	8.8	6	8.0	11	5.3	–	–	37	14.1	3	7.1	34	10.1	6	17.1

5. Refers to 20th-century wars only.
6. Not double-counted under 'Historical' unless the film is about actual historical events, nor double-counted under 'Crime'.
7. Signifies movies for or about teenagers or college students. 'Drama' is a category exclusive of any other category.

good measure and the kids loved it. Comedy enjoyed a resurgence with hits like *Splash*, continuing a success formula set by earlier '80s films like *Arthur* (US 81) and *Tootsie* (US 82) in which charm took over from sex. Science-fiction and horror continued their upward surge, the comparatively small number of films produced in these genres bearing no relation to their enormous box office impact. Fantasy was represented by megabuck blockbusters *Gremlins* and *Ghostbusters*, as well as a string of Santa Claus movies, including one in which the children's favourite was revealed to be a manic axeman.

British films of the '80s ran the gamut from megabuck movies like *Gandhi* (GB 82) and *Greystoke* (GB 84), through medium-budget prestige successes like Oscar-winning *Chariots of Fire* (GB 81), to low-budget Channel 4 backed art movies like *The Draughtsman's*

THE TOP 6 HOLLYWOOD THEMES 1914–94

	1914	1924	1934	1944	1954	1964	1974	1984	1994
1.	Drama 20.2%	Romance 28.2%	Crime 23.3%	Musicals 19.7%	Westerns 21.4%	Comedy 29.7%	Crime 31.6%	Comedy 27.1%	Comedy 29.3%
2.	Crime 19.8%	Drama 24.2%	Comedy 19.6%	Crime 16.8%	Romance 19.8%	Romance 16.2%	Sex 17.7%	Crime 14.9%	Crime 28.1%
3.	Action/Adventure 16.0%	Westerns 13.9%	Romance 18.2%	Show-business 15.1%	Crime 17.1%	Crime 15.6%	Comedy 14.8%	Youth 14.1%	Drama 12.5%
4.	Historical 11.5%	Crime 12.7%	Drama 14.6%	Comedy 15.1%	Historical 11.7%	Musicals 10.8%	Black 13.9%	Horror 9.9%	Youth 10.1%
5.	Romance 11.1%	Comedy 12.5%	Musicals 7.4%	Romance 14.3%	Action/Adventure 10.5%	Westerns 10.1%	Documentary 9.1%	Sex 8.4%	Historical 8.7%
6.	Comedy 10.3%	Action/Adventure 7.1%	Westerns 6.9%	Westerns 13.8%	Comedy 9.7%	Drama 10.1%	Historical 7.2%	Fantasy 8.0%	Fantasy 7.2%

Note: Drama excludes all other categories.

Contract (GB 83). The two pictures of 1984 which typify the return to indigenous themes—an enticing combination of the past, privilege and perversion—were *An Englishman Abroad* and *Another Country*, both based on the character of upper-class traitor and homosexual Guy Burgess. British cinema appeared by 1984 to be drawing on a rich store of theatrical talent and themes proven on 'the world's least worst television' to consolidate a modest renaissance.

THE FILMS OF 1994

Crime made a comeback—over 28% of US films were in this genre. Not only had the proportion nearly doubled since 1984, but the mood was much blacker—pictures like Quentin Tarantino's *Pulp Fiction* and Oliver Stone's *Natural Born Killers* seemed to be extolling violence as an art form. Comedy was the largest category, slightly higher than crime at nearly 30%, with films ranging from the infantile, as represented by the critically panned but enormously successful *The Flintstones,* to the Capra-esque, as represented by the critically acclaimed and even more enormously successful *Forrest Gump.*

Weirdness was to the fore in a number of manifestations, not least from Tom Cruise in fangs (*Interview With the Vampire*), Johnny Depp in drag (*Ed Wood*) and Rosie O'Donnell and Dan Aykroyd in bondage (*Exit to Eden*). Kurt Russell was seen as an astronaut landed on a planet peopled by Ancient Egyptians (*Stargate*) and Sir Anthony Hopkins as the cinema-fixated Dr John Harvey Kellogg, complete with chipmunk teeth, in *The Road to Wellville.*

Also fairly weird was a western in which all the lead players were women—*Bad Girls*—though as one English critic observed, the title would have been more accurate had it been 'Girls Who Are Quite Nice Really'. The number of westerns was on the rise for the first time in a generation, probably encouraged by Best Picture Oscars for *Dances With Wolves* and *Unforgiven* in 1991 and 1993 respectively. The total of ten, though not large, included big-budget star vehicles such as *Maverick* with Mel Gibson, *Tombstone* with Kurt Russell as Wyatt Earp and *Wyatt Earp* with Kevin Costner in the same role.

Another neglected genre showing a modest revival was films based on classic works of literature, represented by such diverse subjects as Rudyard Kipling's *The Jungle Book* (Disney's politically correct version, which critics declared owed little to Kipling), Mary Shelley's *Frankenstein*, Louis Malle's *Vanya on 42nd Street*, from Chekhov's *Uncle Vanya*, a modern version of George Eliot's *Silas Marner* titled *A Simple Twist of Fate*, *Black Beauty* from Anna Sewell's children's favourite, and a lavish remake of Louisa M. Alcott's *Little Women*. Historical and period pictures had also made a comeback, with a total triple the 1984 figure, including—unusually—two films about America's earliest settlers: *Kilian's Chronicle,* about the Viking landfalls of the 11th century, and *Squanto: A Warrior's Tale,* about the Plymouth Pilgrims' relations with the Native Americans.

Dropping out of the chart entirely for the first time since the advent of sound was the Hollywood musical. Significantly, war films had all but ceased since Oliver Stone finished working his Vietnam lode, while spy films had also dwindled away with the ending of the Cold War. Action/adventure movies, often decried for catering to the lowest common denominator, had also dropped out of the Top Six Hollywood Themes chart.

British cinema in 1994 will be remembered for the stunning international success of Mike Newell's *Four Weddings and a Funeral*, predictably sneered at by the post-Marxist semiologists of *Sight & Sound* but acclaimed elsewhere for its wry portrayal of contemporary middle-class mores. It cannot, however, be said to typify British film-making of the first half of the 1990s, which was still suffering from the 1980s preoccupation with 'the evils of Thatcherism' and a relentlessly downbeat, pessimistic view of British society of nil interest to overseas audiences and appealing only to a niche home audience (and *Sight & Sound*) who rate movies for their value as agitprop. Exceptions to the general gloom-and-doom theme of inner-city deprivation were the cheerfully outrageous comedy *Staggered*, with the flap-eared Martin Clunes making a happy transition from the small screen, an excellent remake of *The Browning Version* with Albert Finney and Greta Scaachi, T. S. Eliot biopic *Tom and Viv*, and Sir Richard Attenborough's deeply moving *Shadowlands* about the autumnal romance of Oxford professor C. S. Lewis (Anthony Hopkins) and the terminally ill Joy Gresham (Debra Winger).

Westerns

The earliest subjects of western interest were *Sioux Indian Ghost Dance, Indian War Council* and *Buffalo Dance*, made by the Edison Co. at West Orange, NJ on 24 September 1894. *Bucking Broncho* followed on 16 October and is notable for the first appearance of a cowboy in a film—Lee Martin of Colorado, who is seen riding Sunfish in a corral, while his 'pardner' Frank Hammit stands on the rails and discharges the first of many tens

> There has been at least one western in which not a single gunshot is heard. *They Passed This Way* aka *Four Faces West* (US 48) starred Joel McCrea as a bank robber on the run from Charles Bickford's Pat Garrett. Strong characterisation and suspense proved no substitute for the traditional showdown in Main Street as far as the fans were concerned and the film bombed at the box office.

of thousands of pistol shots that were to be seen (and later heard) in almost every western that followed. Annie Oakley, immortalised in *Annie Get Your Gun* (US 50), made her film debut a fortnight later on 1 November 1894. **The first westerns** were copyrighted by the American Mutoscope & Biograph Co. on 21 September 1903. One was titled *Kit Carson* (US 03) and related the story of its hero's capture by Indians and subsequent escape through the agency of a beautiful Indian maiden. There were 11 scenes and the film had a running time of 21 minutes, making it the longest dramatic picture (other than Passion Plays) produced in America at that time. The other film, titled *The Pioneers* (US 03), showed the burning of a settler's homestead by Indians, who kill the homesteader and his wife and carry off his daughter. The picture ends with the dramatic rescue of the child by frontiersmen who have found the bodies of her parents. Running time was approximately 15 minutes. Both pictures were directed by Wallace McCutcheon and filmed on location in the

Adirondack Mountains of New York State. *Kit Carson* was made on 8 September 1903 and *The Pioneers* two days later.

The more celebrated *The Great Train Robbery* (US 03), generally and erroneously described as the first western and often as the first film to tell a story, was copyrighted by the Edison Co. some six weeks later, on 1 December 1903.

The earliest westerns were shot in the Eastern states, generally in New Jersey. **The first western made in the West** was *The Hold-Up of the Leadville Stage* (US 05), directed by Harry Buckwalter for the Selby Polyscope Co in October 1904 and advertised in the trade press on 29 April 1905. Shot on the old Leadville stage road through the Gardens of the Gods and the Ute Pass in Colorado, this reconstruction of an event which had taken place 25 years earlier had been filmed with the original Leadville stage coach and featured the actual driver on the occasion of the hold-up, Old Butch White. The stage, which disintegrated shortly after the film 'wrapped', had the distinction of being lined throughout in chilled steel to withstand both Indian arrows and the bullets of desperados.

The first western to feature real Red Indians was the Lubin production *A Western Romance in the Days of '49* (US 08), about a cowboy captured by Indians who falls in love with a beautiful Indian maid.

The first feature-length film with an all-Indian cast was Frank E. Moore's *Hiawatha* (US 13), starring Soon-goot as Minnehaha and a cast of 150 American Indians from New York State, Canada and the Dakotas. It was filmed in New York State and near Lake Superior.

The first western in colour was a British production by a Dutch director, Theo Bouwmeester's *Fate* (GB 11), made in Kinemacolor by the Natural Colour Kinematograph Co. Set in Texas, it was about an Englishman who becomes leader of a tribe of renegade Indians.

The first feature-length western was Lawrence B. McGill's *Arizona* (US 13), an All Star Feature Corporation production with Cyril Scott and Gertrude Shipman. It was released in August 1913, six months before Cecil B. DeMille's *The Squaw Man* (US 14), usually credited as the first western feature.

The first feature-length colour western was the Famous Players-Lasky production *Wanderer of the Wasteland* (US 24), a Zane Grey horse opera from the novel of the same name. Photographed in two-colour Technicolor by Arthur Ball, it was directed by Irvin Willar, starred Jack Holt, Noah Beery and Billie Dove, and was premièred in Los Angeles on 21 June 1924.

The first in three-strip Technicolor was Henry King's *Ramona* (US 36), from Helen Hunt Jackson's five-handkerchief novel about forbidden love, which opened at the Criterion in New York on 6 October 1936. The Fox release starred Don Ameche as the tragic Allessandro and Loretta Young in the title role as the beautiful Indian maiden. *Variety* praised William V. Skall and Chester Lyons' camerawork, but opined that *Ramona* 'still leaves screen color in need of a story'.

The first all-talking western. (Christie's New York)

The first western talkie was Fox-Movietone's *In Old Arizona* (US 28), directed by Raoul Walsh and Irving Cummings and starring Edmund Lowe, Warner Baxter and Dorothy Burgess. It was premièred at the Criterion Theater, Los Angeles, on 25 December 1928.

The first western with Indian dialogue was Universal's talkie serial *The Indians Are Coming* (US 31), in which Chief Thunderbird spoke in his native Sioux. In 1970 Dame Judith Anderson, an Australian, successfully coped with all-Sioux dialogue in her role as Buffalo Cow Head in *A Man Called Horse* (US 70).

The highest-earning western was Kevin Costner's *Dances with Wolves* (US 90), which grossed $394.2 million worldwide. The previous record was held for 21 years by *Butch Cassidy and the Sundance Kid* (US 69). The extraordinary success of Costner's film, after Hollywood had dismissed the western genre as box-office poison, was all the more remarkable for the fact that much of the dialogue was in the Sioux language Lakota. It was also the first western to win the Oscar for Best Film since *Cimarron* in 1931.

The first western star was G. M. 'Broncho Billy' Anderson (1881–1971), who was to have been cast as one of the villains for his western debut in *The Great Train Robbery* (US 03), but proved so inept on a horse that he had to be relegated to extra work. Notwithstanding this inauspicious start to a career dedicated to the relationship of man and horse, Anderson starred in *Life of an*

American Cowboy (US 06) and then went west with a Selig location crew to make one of the earliest westerns shot in the real west—*The Girl from Montana* (US 07). The following year he established a West Coast studio for Essany at Niles, California, and decided to embark on a series of one-reelers based on a central character, reasoning that the weakness of the Edison, Selig and Essany westerns he had played in was that they lacked clearly defined heroes. His original intention had been to find an actor expert in horsemanship whom he could direct, but actors of any kind being in short supply in California, he eventually decided to cast himself in the role. *Broncho Billy and the Baby* (US 10), a sentimental story of a man-gone-wrong who is reformed by the love of a good woman, was the first in a series of nearly 400 Broncho Billy pictures which established Anderson as a major star. A curious feature of the films was their total lack of continuity. If Broncho Billy married in one picture, he would be a bachelor again in the next; he would be reformed inexhaustibly by a succession of good women; and death would only interrupt his career in the saddle until the opening scenes of the next one-reeler. Anderson turned to features in 1918, but competition from his successors, Tom Mix and W. S. Hart, was too strong. After a period of producing Stan Laurel comedies for Metro, he retired in 1923. Nearly half a century after his last silent western role in *The Son of a Gun* (US 18), he made a single excursion into talkies with a guest appearance in *The Bounty Killer* (US 67).

The most popular western star was determined annually with a poll of exhibitors conducted by *Motion Picture Herald* between 1936 and 1954 (when the B western ended). Buck Jones won in 1936, Gene Autry each year from 1937–42, and Roy Rogers from 1943–54 inclusive.

The western hero most often portrayed on screen has been William Frederick Cody (1846–1917), otherwise known as 'Buffalo Bill', a character who has appeared in 54 dramatic films to date. He was most recently portrayed by Keith Carradine in *Wild Bill* (US 95). William Bonney (1860–81), alias Billy the Kid, has been portrayed in 49 films; Jesse James (1847–82) in 38 films; Wild Bill Hickock (1837–76) in 38 films; General George Armstrong Custer (1839–76) in 35 films; and Wyatt Earp (1848–1929) in 26 films.

The most prolific western directors were Lesley Selander (1900–79), with at least 107 known feature-length westerns made between 1935 and 1967, and Lambert Hillyer (1893–?), with 106 recorded titles between 1917 and 1949.

The only western directed by a woman was Ruth Ann Baldwin's curiously titled Universal production *'49-'17* (US 17).

WESTERN OUTPUT
It is estimated that there have been over 3500 multi-reel westerns made since the first two-reeler, the Oklahoma Natural Mutoscene Co.'s *The Bank Robbery* (US 08).

Cinema and the Call of Nature

It was sometimes remarked, in the days before stark realism invaded the screen, that nobody in films ever seemed to feel the call of nature. As early as 1912, though, a Hungarian company called Hunnia had made a film titled *Bitter Love or Hunyadi János* (Hun 12) which was entirely about going to the lavatory—the plot centering round an aperient water called Hunyadi János which had an extraordinarily stimulating effect on the bowels. Not surprisingly, Hollywood was a good deal more reticent on the subject and it was not until 1928 that King Vidor's *The Crowd* (US 28), better remembered as the first feature film to make extensive use of outdoor New York locations, pioneered in another direction with a bathroom set which actually showed a lavatory bowl. Luis Buñuel advanced scatological film-making when he showed a woman sitting on the lavatory in his controversial *L'Age d'or* (Fr 30). It was the down-to-earth Russians, though, who were the first to depict people performing the natural functions. This was in Alexander Dovzhenko's *Earth* (US 30). Like most Soviet films of the period it was about tractors, and during the scene in question one of them runs out of water and peasants urinate in the radiator. Nothing so overt was permitted in the Land of the Free. In 1950 what threatened to become an international incident between America and Italy occurred over a brief scene in De Sica's classic *Bicycle Thieves* (It 49) in which a small boy prepares to relieve himself against a wall. The Italians were outraged by the MPAA's decision to refuse the film a seal of approval unless the few seconds of footage were cut for exhibition in the US.

Many years were to pass before the bowel action was depicted on screen and it was Orson Welles, always a pioneer and always of regal bearing, who led the way when he was found on the throne in *Catch-22* (US 70). Maria Schneider could have been performing either function as she squatted on the lavatory in *Last Tango in Paris* (Fr 72), but there was no room for doubt when a girl was seen performing the golden shower on her lesbian lover in Pedro Almodóvor's outrageous first feature *Pepi, Luci, Bom and the Other Girls* (Sp 80).

Meanwhile, in *La Grande Bouffe* (Fr 72) Michel Piccoli had perished in his own excrement as a result of overeating. This was also the first film in which a character audibly breaks wind, a theme pursued by Dustin Hoffman in the close confines of a telephone box also containing Tom Cruise in *Rain Man* (US 89). This incident was unscripted. Although this film was garlanded with awards, it was the rather less celebrated *Silent But Deadly* (US 89) which won *Variety's* Gone With the Wind New Genre Citation at the 1989 MIFED sales convention. The genre was flatulence.

The quirky Canadian film *Urinal* (Can 88) was about 'cottaging' rather than urinating, but contained informative asides on the history of the toilet seat and the first public lavatories. The 1990s offered a number of new perspectives, literally so in the case of *I Bought a Vampire Motorcycle* (GB 90) with a shot taken from inside a lavatory bowl on which someone is going about their business. This film also introduced the novelty of a talking turd. Jaime Humberto Hermosillo's *Bathroom Intimacies* (Mex 90) took place entirely in a bathroom while the fixed camera, standing in for the bathroom mirror, records the movements—in more than one sense of the word—of a family of four and their maid.

Probably the most cherished scene for scatology buffs is the one in *The War of the Roses* (US 90) in which a vengeful Michael Douglas urinates into an elaborate fish dish estranged wife Kathleen Turner is about to serve to important business associates.

The only film since Hungary's pioneering *Bitter Love* of 1912 which has been almost entirely about bodily func-

tions is Alan Parker's much reviled *The Road to Wellville* (US 94), which one outraged American critic denounced as a '30-million-dollar bowel movement'. Anthony Hopkins plays Dr John Harvey Kellogg of cornflake celebrity, the highly idiosyncratic and autocratic proprietor of Battle Creek Sanitorium who rejoiced in his personal regimen of five Bulgarian yoghurt enemas a day and sought to impose it upon his hapless patients. One of his choicer observations, delivered by Sir Anthony with all the grandiloquence at his command, runs: 'My own stools, Sir, are gigantic and have no more odour than a hot biscuit.'

CHAPTER 6
Performers

The first motion picture film to employ the use of actors was a brief costume drama, *The Execution of Mary Queen of Scots* (US 1895), which was shot by Alfred Clark of Raff & Gammon, Kinetoscope proprietors, at West Orange, NJ on 28 August 1895. The part of Mary was played by Mr R. L. Thomas, secretary and treasurer of the Kinetoscope Co. After approaching the block and laying his head on it, Thomas removed himself, the camera was stopped, and a dummy substituted. The camera was then started again for the decapitation scene. This was the first use of trick photography or special-effect work in a film.

The first person employed to play a comedy role in a film was M. Clerc, a gardener employed by Mme Lumière at Lyon, France. He was aptly cast in the part of the gardener in the Lumière production *L'Arroseur arrosé* (Fr 1895), a film premièred at the Grand Café in Paris on 28 December 1895. Clerc is seen watering flowerbeds with a hose. A mischievous boy, played by a 14-year-old Lumière apprentice called Duval, creeps up behind the gardener and places his foot on the hose to stop the flow of water. As the perplexed gardener holds the nozzle up to his eye to see if there is a blockage, young Duval removes his foot and capers with joy as a burst of water gushes into M. Clerc's face. Clerc and Duval were the first performers to be seen on the screen, as *The Execution of Mary Queen of Scots* had been made for viewing in Edison's 'peep-show' Kinetoscope.

The first professional actors to perform in movies made their screen debuts almost simultaneously on either side of the Atlantic. In America John Rice and May Irwin performed the first screen kiss in *The Widow Jones* aka *May Irwin Kiss* (US 1896), which was a scene from the Broadway comedy *The Widow Jones* filmed by Raff and Gammon in April 1896. At about the same time in Britain, Fred Storey played the title role in R. W. Paul's *The Soldier's Courtship* (GB 1896), a short comedy made on the roof of the Alhambra Theatre, Leicester Square, and premièred underneath. Storey also got to kiss the heroine, Julie Seale of the Alhambra Ballet. Performers of established reputation rarely appeared in films prior to about 1908 in France and Britain and later elsewhere. There were, however, a few notable exceptions during the primitive period, including Auguste van Biene's role as the cellist in Esme Collings' *The Broken Melody* (GB 1896), from the play of the same name; Joseph Jefferson's performance in American Mutoscope & Biograph's *Rip Van Winkle* (US 1896); Beerbohm Tree and Julia Neilson in *King John* (GB 1899); Sarah Bernhardt in *Hamlet* (Fr 1900); Coquelin in *Cyrano de Bergerac* (Fr 1900); Marie Tempest and Hayden Coffin in *San Toy* (GB 1900); and Marie Tempest, Ben Webster and H. B. Warner in *English Nell*

(GB 1900). The only one of these to make a career as a screen actor was H. B. Warner (1876–1958), whose most notable performances were in *King of Kings* (US 27) as Jesus Christ, *Mr Deeds Goes to Town* (US 36), *Lost Horizon* (US 37) and *Victoria the Great* (GB 37).

The Star System

This emerged in the United States and Europe simultaneously. Previous to 1910 it was the deliberate policy of filmmakers not to give their lead players any star billing, lest they should overvalue their services. First to break with this was the American production company Kalem, which in January 1910 began issuing star portraits and posters with the artistes' names credited. A few weeks later Carl Laemmle, who had succeeded in luring the still anonymous Florence Lawrence away from Biograph to work for IMP, pulled the kind of outrageous publicity stunt that has enlivened and bedevilled the industry ever since, and in the process created the first real movie star.

> The earliest recorded use of the word 'star' in print in respect of film actors preceded the emergence of the star system. A letter from a Brooklyn reader appeared under the heading 'Moving Picture "Stars"' in the 11 March 1909 issue of the *New York Times*. It said: 'The art of posing for moving pictures has in some cases reached a state of development where individual recognition should be given because intelligence, industry, and ability are evident in the acting of those who pose for these pictures. With regard to some, at least, as to facial expression, gesture, and grace of carriage, it might be said that their work is of exceptional merit, and comparable to the work of many dramatic "stars".'

He began by arranging for a story to break in the St Louis papers that the actress had been killed in a street-car accident. Public interest in the supposed tragedy having been fully aroused, Laemmle placed the following advertisement in the same papers on 10 March 1910: 'The blackest and at the same time the silliest lie yet circulated by the enemies of IMP was the story foisted on the public of St Louis last week to the effect that Miss Lawrence, "The Imp Girl", formerly known as "The Biograph Girl", had been killed by a street car. It was a black lie so cowardly. We now announce our next film *The Broken Path*.' This was followed up with personal appearances by Miss Lawrence and a long interview in the St Louis Post-Dispatch; within a year her name was appearing on film posters in larger type than the title.

In Europe the practice of publicising star names

began the same year with the outstanding success of two films, one from Denmark, the other from Germany. Asta Nielsen's bravura performance in *The Abyss* (Den 10), one of the first long films to demonstrate a true sense of dramatic construction, brought a hitherto little-known actress almost immediate international recognition and the first of the really prodigious star salaries (see Artistes' Earnings, below). Germany's box-office success of the year was *Das Liebesglück der Blinden/The Love of the Blind Girl* (Ger 10), starring 'The Messter Girl', a designation that cloaked the identity of Oskar Messter's leading player Henny Porten, who had also scripted the picture. It was received with such acclaim by filmgoers that Messter was persuaded to reveal her name. Once her name was on the credits, Henny proceeded to justify the producers' worst fears by demanding an increase in salary—from the equivalent of $50 a month to $56. Messter refused and she walked straight out of the studio. Having failed to call what he thought was a bluff, the producer sent his assistant, Kurt Stark, to fetch the girl back with a promise that she could have the raise. Henny returned to the studio, married Stark, and went on to become Germany's idol of the silent screen.

Artistes' Earnings

Earnings which have now reached as much as $25 million-plus for a single film began at a level commensurate with the penny gaff milieu of early film-making. The earliest known wage rate was the gold Louis ($4.30 or 17s) per day paid in the late 1890s by Star Films of Paris, but not all production companies were so generous. Gene Gauntier was offered $3 to play the lead in Biograph's *The Paymaster* (US 06), the story of a mill-girl in love with the manly young paymaster of the mill. Miss Gauntier was required to be thrown into the millstream by the villain, which she allowed him to do, not liking to mention that she was unable to swim. The producer was so pleased with her pluck that the $3 fee was raised to $5. Alma Lund, who played the female lead in the first film drama made in Norway—*Dangerous Life of a Fisherman* (Nor 07)—was paid the equivalent of $1.50 for her part; the boy who played her son got 75c. R. W. Paul paid Britain's first professional film actor, Johnny Butt, a daily wage of 5s ($1.25) in 1899, which was rather better than the 4s ($1) a day accorded to Chrissie White when she joined the Hepworth Co. at Walton-on-Thames in 1908. 'When I really got on,' she recalled, 'I received 8s a day, and when I was a star they paid me 50—shillings, not pounds.' Dave Aylott, who joined Cricks & Martin of Mitcham in 1909, remembered that their terms were 7s 6d a day for principal parts, 5s for minor parts, plus 1s 6d travelling expenses to Mitcham and a bread and cheese lunch with beer. In America at this time the $5 a day received by Mary Pickford when she joined Biograph in 1909 seems to have become standard throughout the industry, nothing extra being paid for 'star' roles.

The escalation in salaries, when it came, was rapid and had to do with two factors: the use of major names from the stage, who had to be paid highly to demean themselves in this way; and the introduction of the 'star' system (see above) from 1910 onwards. The change

began with Film d'Art in Paris, a company established in 1908 to produce prestige films with prestige players. Their leading artistes were paid the equivalent of $40 for each rehearsal and $200 for the actual shoot. Featured players, however, received as little as $2 to $3 a day for services in a major film like *Germinal* (Fr 13), for which the star, Henry Krauss, was paid $700. In England Will Barker paid Sir Herbert Beerbohm Tree a record £1000 to play Wolsey in *Henry VIII* (GB 11), a two-reeler which was shot in a single day. How far this was from the norm is indicated by the fact that the following year Barker was able to secure the lead player of his *Hamlet* (GB 12), Charles Raymond, for just 10s—which included his services as director of the film!

The first superstar salary was earned not by any of the rising American players, but by Denmark's Asta Nielsen. For her debut in *The Abyss* (Den 10) she was paid a modest 200kr ($53.60), but the film rocketed her to stardom and by the end of 1912 she was under contract to Berlin producer Paul Davidson with guaranteed annual earnings of $80,000. Compared to Asta Nielsen's salary of over $1500 a week, the highest paid stars in America were Gene Gauntier at $200 a week and Florence Lawrence at $250 a week. At this time Mary Pickford, who was soon to eclipse them all, was trailing at $175 a week at Biograph. The following year, however, Adolph Zukor lured her to Famous Players at $500 a week and this was doubled in 1914 and doubled again in 1915. Already the highest-paid woman in the world, on 24 June 1916 she signed a new contract that put her on a par with the highest-paid man in the world—Charles Chaplin, who had contracted with Mutual earlier in the year at a salary of $670,000. Miss Pickford's earnings were now half the profits of all her pictures, with a $10,000 p.w. minimum, plus a $300,000 single payment bonus, plus $150,000 p.a. to her mother for 'goodwill', plus $40,000 for examining scenarios prior to signing.

In the meantime Francesca Bertini, Italian 'diva', had become Europe's highest-paid star in 1915 at $175,000 p.a., only slightly behind the $200,000 p.a. that Mary Pickford was then earning. European earnings, however, were never to rise above this before World War II, apart from the $450,000 that Alexander Korda paid Marlene Dietrich to star in *Knight Without Armour* (GB 37). American earnings continued to spiral upward, but with the three highest-paid stars—Mary Pickford, Charlie Chaplin and Douglas Fairbanks—combined together as producers

> Samuel Goldwyn on doing business with Mary Pickford: 'It took longer to make one of Mary's contracts than it did to make one of Mary's pictures.'

under the distribution banner of United Artists from 1919 onwards, it is hard to assess their new earning power. In that same year Roscoe 'Fatty' Arbuckle had become the first star with a guaranteed minimum of $1 million a year, but his contract with Paramount only lasted until scandal destroyed his career in 1922 and he became the first star to be formally banned.

No other star of the silent era matched Arbuckle's salary, but Nazimova was reported to be the highest-salaried woman star in 1920 at $13,000 p.w., Tom Mix, the most popular cowboy star of the silents, was earning $17,500 p.w. in 1925 and Harold Lloyd's weekly wage was

> Edna Purviance, Chaplin's 'star soubrette' of the 1915–23 period, made no films after 1926, yet remained under contract to Chaplin on full salary until her death 32 years later.

reported to be $40,000 p.w. in 1926. Salaries in Britain were a sad contrast. Alma Taylor, the most popular female star of the early 1920s, was paid £60 p.w. by the Hepworth Co., but they were less generous with their leading male actor, Stewart Rome, who earned only £10 p.w. Ivor Novello, a matinée idol with a strong stage reputation, could command £3000–£4000 per film at his height in the late 1920s, while the highest sum for a silent film was the £10,000 paid to music-hall artiste Sir Harry Lauder for his role as a retired grocer in George Pearson's *Huntingtower* (GB 27).

The coming of sound and the Depression almost simultaneously forced most star salaries downward. In 1927 over 40 stars were reputedly earning $5000 or more a week. By 1931 only 23 stars had salaries of $3500 or more. Top earners in that year were Constance Bennett and John Barrymore at $30,000 p.w., a sum soon to be matched by Greta Garbo, who earned $250,000 for *The Painted Veil* (US 34) and the same for *Anna Karenina* (US 35). Highest earnings of 1935 were the $480,833 reported by Mae West to the tax authorities, well in excess of the highest earnings of 1938—Shirley Temple's $307,014, or 1939—James Cagney's $368,333, or even 1946 when Bing Crosby topped both at the box office (rated No. 1 in the Quigley Poll) and at the bank with $325,000. During the 1940s and 1950s top star salaries per film were generally in the $250,000–$400,000 region, with a new peak of $500,000 for a British film—Elizabeth Taylor in *Suddenly Last Summer* (GB 59)—and $750,000 for an American production, earned by both John Wayne and William Holden (plus 20% of the net) on *The Horse Soldiers* (US 59). The 1960s saw the era of the $1 million star salary for single pictures and in the 1970s the multi-million dollar contract. In the mid-1970s Charles Bronson was reported to be earning $20,000–$30,000, plus $2500 living allowance, per day. However, this was far exceeded by Marlon Brando's reputed $3.5 million for 12 days shooting on *Superman* (GB 78), which works out at $290,000 per day. According to a special *Newsweek* report on Hollywood in 1978, the world's highest-paid stars were Paul Newman, Robert Redford and Steve McQueen, commanding some $3 million per picture. Each had turned down a $4 million offer to take the starring role in *Superman* (GB 78). Dustin Hoffman accepted precisely that amount for his transvestite role in *Tootsie* (US 82), but an even higher figure of $5 million plus percentage had already been paid to Burt Reynolds for *The Cannonball Run* (US 81). Sean Connery became the highest-paid British star when he was lured back into Bond movies with a $5 million bait for *Never Say Never Again* (GB 83).

Barbra Streisand became the first woman to reach the $5 million plateau with the less than sensational *Nuts* (US 88), then headed upwards again with $6 million for *Prince of Tides* (US 91). Sharon Stone—after years playing minor roles in big movies or leading roles in minor movies—suddenly struck lucky with *Basic Instinct* (US 91) and was signed for *Sliver* (US 93) at the highest-ever fee for an actress of $7 million. Two years later Julia Roberts became the first actress to command double-digit millions when she was contracted for the title role of *Mary Reilly* (US 95) at $10 million. This, her 12th film, earned her exactly 10,000 times as much as her first, *Blood Red* (US 86). In spring 1995 Demi Moore, following successes in

> Donald Sutherland's fortune was based on one very salient fact in addition to his talent—he is a Canadian. Until 1976 there was virtually no Canadian film industry to speak of. Then in an effort to create one, the Canadian government passed a law allowing 100% tax write-offs for investors in productions certified as 'Canadian'. Certification involved having a Canadian producer, spending 75% of the budget in Canada and—the most difficult bit—casting a certain number of Canadian stars. The problem was that there were very few actors from north of the border that anyone in the US—the primary market—had ever heard of. But they had heard of Donald Sutherland, then a Hollywood B-list star earning $500,000 a picture. Mr Sutherland could be enticed back to his native land to make movies, but at a price. Knowing his value to any producer seeking certification, Canada's number one star asked for—and received—an A-list $1 million a picture.

Indecent Proposal (US 93) and *Disclosure* (US 94), wrapped a deal with Castle Rock Entertainment to star in *Striptease* (US 96) at a fee of $12.5 million. The picture bombed. Other actresses now able to command $10 million-plus are Sandra Bullock, Jodie Foster, Meg Ryan, Sigourney Weaver and Michelle Pfeiffer.

The first actor to crash the $20 million-upfront barrier was Jim Carrey in Columbia/Tristar's *The Cable Guy* (US 96). This also created a new record for the leading player's salary as a proportion of the budget, 42% of a relatively modest $48 million.

Carrey has since been joined in the $20 million-plus club by Tom Cruise, Tom Hanks, Bruce Willis, Harrison Ford, Mel Gibson, Sylvester Stallone and Carrey's fellow Canadian Mike Myers, who inked a deal with Universal for the magic figure following his success in *Austin Powers: The Spy Who Shagged Me* (US 99). The only 'juve lead' among this mature company is Generation X-er Leonardo Di Caprio (b. 1976)—his $20 million for *The Beach* (US/GB 00) broke Carrey's fee-to-budget record, rep-resenting as it did nearly half the total budget of the film.Willis and Ford went to the top of the upfront-fee

> 'I'm a sensitive writer, actor and director. Talking business disgusts me. If you want to do business, call my disgusting personal manager.'—Sylvester Stallone, whose sensitivity commands over $20 million a picture.

table in late 2000, the former signing a $22.5 million deal for *Hart's War* and the latter with an even more munificent $25 million contract to star in submarine thriller *K-19*.

Cruise is the highest earner for a single film, with a points deal on *Mission: Impossible* (US 96) which netted him $70 million, a figure expected to be exceeded by his just under 30% of the gross for the sequel, *Mission: Impossible 2* (US 00). Julia Roberts is the only female member, scaling the $20 million peak with *Erin Brockovich* (US 00), following box-office successes in *Notting Hill* (US/GB 99) and *The Runaway Bride* (US 99). Her advance up the salary ladder, often at the heels of Demi 'Gimme' Moore and now triumphantly passing her, is chronicled below.

Blood Red (US 86) $1000
Baja Oklahoma (US 87, TVM) $5000
Satisfaction (US 88) $12,000
Mystic Pizza (US 88) $50,000
Steel Magnolias (US 89) $90,000
Pretty Woman (US 90) $300,000
Flatliners (US 90) $550,000
Sleeping with the Enemy (US 91) $1,000,000
Hook (US 91) $2,000,000
Dying Young (US 91) $3,000,000
The Pelican Brief (US 93) $6,000,000
I Love Trouble (US 94) $8,000,000
Mary Reilly (US 95) $10,000,000
Conspiracy Theory (US 97) $12,000,000
Stepmom (US 98) $17,000,000
The Runaway Bride (US 99) $17,500,000
Erin Brockovich (US 00) $20,000,000

The highest reported fee for voiceover was Bruce Willis's $10 million for articulating the eponymous baby in *Look Who's Talking Too* (US 90)

The lowest salaries of the last 30 years or so have seldom fallen below the £1500 that Olivia Hussey claimed she was paid for 11 months work while she was playing the female lead in Zeffirelli's *Romeo and Juliet* (GB 68)— at least in the west. In eastern countries and even Eastern Europe, different standards prevail. Teresa Izewska, star of the award-winning *Kanal* (Pol 57), revealed at the Cannes Film Festival that she earned the equivalent of $12 a month and that the Polish authorities had bought her one dress and one pair of shoes in order to represent them at the festival. In 1973 *Variety* reported that China's biggest box-office star, Shih Chung-chin, drew a salary of $20 a month. She slept in a communal dormitory with other actresses. By 1980 a top Chinese star could earn a maximum of 250 yuan ($168) a month, though not all

were so generously recompensed. Joan Chen, star of the first Anglo-Chinese co-production *The Last Emperor* (It/GB/Chn 88) and latterly of TV's *Twin Peaks*, was earning less than $8 a month in 1980 when she won the 100 Blossoms award as most popular actress. Her salary then went up to $24 a month. Currently Chinese stars earn an average of 10,000 yuan per annum (£770), or about two-and-a-half times as much as a taxi-driver. Top-class chefs can command ten times as much as a film star.

The lowest-paid players in American pictures were found in black movies. White director Edgar G. Ulmer recalls paying the 50 chorus girls in *Moon Over Harlem* (US 39) 25c a day each. The shooting schedule was four days and the girls had to pay their car fares from Harlem to the studio in Jersey out of the $1 they earned for a week's work. A record zero budget for an entire cast was achieved by Action Pictures Co. for their all-black feature *Sugar Hill Baby* (US 38). The casting director announced with disarming frankness that there was no money available for salaries, the only inducement offered being the somewhat doubtful 'chance to continue to work in future in productions at good salaries'.

Leading players in Hollywood films expect rather more immediate rewards, but even for major motion pictures salaries may, on occasion, be modest. For what many fans reckon to be the most memorable role in movie history, that of Scarlett O'Hara in *Gone With the Wind* (US 39), Vivien Leigh (by no means a newcomer to the screen) was paid a not very princely $15,000. This was less than ice-skating champion turned film star Sonja Henie was then being paid for a week's work. Frank Sinatra earned only $8000 for his Oscar-winning performance in *From Here to Eternity* (US 53). Nodules on his throat had brought his singing career to a temporary halt and he was desperate to get back into movies at any price. A few years later his co-star in *The Man with the Golden Arm* (US 56), Kim Novak, was hired at her regular salary from Columbia of $100 a week, though producer Otto Preminger had to pay the studio $100,000 for her services. In the mid-1950s Paul Newman was getting a relatively meagre $17,500 for each of his Warner Bros' pictures; by the mid-1960s he was on $750,000 a film plus percentage. In the same kind of price bracket was James Dean, paid $18,000 for his outstanding performance in *East of Eden* (US 55). It was his fifth film but his first starring role and it rocketed him to instant stardom.

Perhaps the last of the great western stars, Clint Eastwood had already been in movies for ten not very productive years when he was offered $15,000 to appear in a spaghetti western called *A Fistful of Dollars* (It 64). By 1972 he was the number-one star at the box office and between the mid-70s and mid-80s his pictures grossed a record $1400 million. Another star who found fame and fortune in the 60s was Dustin Hoffman. His worth was rated at $17,000 for the smash hit *The Graduate* (US 67) and $425,000 a couple of years later for the floppo *John and Mary* (US 69).

All of these stars were generously remunerated in comparison with Steve McQueen, whose total reward for playing the lead in tacky horror movie *The Blob* (US 58) was $3000. He was not invited to appear in the sequel, *Son of Blob* (US 71). By that time his fee would have been several times the whole budget of the movie. According to Sylvester Stallone, recently the world's highest-paid

The biggest comeback as represented by a salary hike must surely be that of John Travolta. In his glory days following his standout performance in *Saturday Night Fever* (US 77) he was commanding $3 million a picture, putting him in the same league as top-dollar performers Robert Redford, Steve McQueen and Paul Newman. A string of box-office failures sent his earning power spiralling downward, so that when Quentin Tarantino was casting for *Pulp Fiction* (US 94) he was delighted to be offered a starring role at $150,000, the kind of money paid to minor featured players—and has-beens. His success in the picture was so phenomenal that by early 1996 *Variety* was reporting his asking price at $18 million.

film star, the only recompense he received for playing a leading role in *The Lords of Flatbush* (US 74) was 25 free T-shirts. A performer may still be bargain basement one moment and in the megabuck league the next. One Stephen J. Lewicki cast an unknown rock singer for the lead in *A Certain Feeling* (US 84) and has since been able to congratulate himself all the way to the bank that he secured the services of Madonna for $100 all in.

Unfortunately it is still true that the performance which wins at the wickets does not always command the highest pay cheque. Andie McDowell, whose limp portrayal of the gooey-eyed romantic interest in *Four Weddings and a Funeral* (GB 94) was the only piece of weak casting in an otherwise outstanding ensemble, earned some $3 million from her points-related contract. Hugh Grant, generally acknowledged as the critical factor in the picture's worldwide success, had to be content with a flat-rate fee of $60,000.

Some megastars display a becoming modesty if they believe in the film. Bruce Willis, one of a handful of actors now in the $20-million-a-picture bracket, worked for scale—$1500 a week—on *Nobody's Fool* (US 94), *North* (US 94) and Quentin Tarantino's hit *Pulp Fiction* (US 94). When the latter won the Palme d'Or at Cannes, Willis signed the cheque for the celebration banquet at the Hotel du Cap, which insiders reckoned had cost him $100,000 more than he made on the picture.

The lure of working for Al Pacino on his idiosyncratic Richard III docudrama *Looking for Richard* (US 96) was sufficient to attract the talent he needed – including Harris Yulin, Alec Baldwin, Kevin Spacey, Winona Ryder and Aiden Quinn – at the rate he was prepared to pay. His take-it or leave-it offer: '$40 a day and all the doughnuts you can eat.'

The most highly paid stars have sometimes been victims of ingenious attempts by the unscrupulous to benefit from their box-office drawing power without the formality of payment. In 1917 a film processor in Chicago created his own Chaplin feature film—at a time when Chaplin was the highest-paid star in the world—by matching together shots from his old comedies and then interpolating material from Fox's sensational *A Daughter of the Gods* (US 16), in which Australian star Annette Kellerman appeared in the nude. By clever optical work, he succeeded in creating scenes in which Chaplin and the naked Antipodean beauty appeared to be performing together. The film was released to the underground trade as *Charlie, Son of the Gods*

Even more audacious was Soviet director Sergei Komarov's deception that secured him the gratuitous services of not one but two superstars, Mary Pickford and Douglas Fairbanks. During the visit of the couple to Moscow in July 1926, Komarov posed as a newsreel cameraman and followed them round with a camera, shooting enough footage to piece together a full-length comedy feature after their departure. Titled *The Kiss of Mary Pickford* (USSR 26), it was an engaging tale of a film extra who is determined to kiss the 'world's sweetheart'—and succeeds! Most remarkable of all was the climactic sequence of the close embrace between Soviet hero and Hollywood heroine. Although the film has now been shown publicly in the west, no one has been able to offer a convincing explanation of how Komarov managed to contrive this scene.

The first screen artiste to work on percentage was Nellie Stewart, who was paid £1000 plus a percentage of the gross for her role in *Sweet Nell of Old Drury* (Aus 11).

The first American artiste to receive a percentage deal was James O'Neill (father of Eugene), who played the wronged Edmond Dantes in Famous Players' maiden production *The Count of Monte Cristo* (US 13). O'Neill had played the part on stage no less than 4000 times over a period of 30 years and was both too old (65) and too ham for the screen version, but Daniel Frohman knew that his was the name which would draw theatregoers to the cinema and he offered the star 20% of the net profits as an inducement. Returns were undermined by a rival Selig version of *The Count of Monte Cristo*, but the Famous Players version eventually grossed $45,539.32, of which O'Neill received $3813.32.

Percentage deals were anathema to the Hollywood moguls throughout the great days of the studio system. There may have been the occasional exception. RKO producer Pandro S. Berman has attested that Fred Astaire received a percentage of the profits on several of his RKO musicals of the 1930s, though this was kept a closely guarded secret at the time. The breakthrough came with the deal negotiated with Universal by James Stewart's agent Lew Wasserman for *Winchester 73* (US 50). Stewart was able to command up to $250,000 as a fixed fee for a picture, but this was beyond the resources of Universal after a series of flops. It was agreed that Stewart should receive a 45% share of the picture's net profits. These were to be defined as starting when gross receipts were twice the negative cost of the film. If *Winchester 73* had earned less than this figure, Stewart would not have earned anything. As it turned out his share of the profits was $600,000, rather more than 'The King of Hollywood', Clark Gable, was paid by MGM for a year's work. For subsequent films Stewart received his standard $250,000 upfront plus 10% of the gross.

After three months of tracking the desert wastes of the Kalahari to find the star of his comedy hit *The Gods Must Be Crazy* (Botswana 81), director Jamie Uys knew that he had found his perfect leading man when he encountered N!Xau (the '!' signifies a pronunciation in the Bushman language impossible to render in our alphabet). It is not unusual in the process of film-making for stars to demand more than producers are willing or able to pay. In N!Xau's case, the problem was the other way about. On receiving his salary after the first ten days of filming, he threw the banknotes to the winds. The realisation that Bushmen have no use for money prompted Uys to renegotiate the contract. N! was paid 12 head of cattle. Unfortunately, lions killed eight of them, but four survived long enough to be slaughtered to provide a feast for the Bushman star and his tribe.

Extras

The first film with a 'cast of thousands' in a literal sense was Luigi Maggi's Napoleonic epic *Il Granatiere Rolland* (It 10), for which 2000 extras were employed. A similar number participated in Britain's first extravaganza,

The largest crowd ever assembled for a movie: some of the 300,000 extras recruited by Richard Attenborough for the funeral scene in his epic Gandhi *(GB 82).*

Charles Weston's feature-length *The Battle of Waterloo* (GB 13).

The largest number of extras employed on a film appeared in the funeral scene of Sir Richard Attenborough's *Gandhi* (GB 82) and comprised a crowd believed to have been in excess of 300,000. Announcements by loudspeaker van, in newspapers and on television and radio summoned over 200,000 volunteer extras to Delhi's ceremonial mall, the Raj-path, where they were supplemented by another 94,560 contracted performers, the majority of whom were paid a fee equivalent to 40p each. The sequence had to be shot in a single morning, that of Saturday 31 January 1981, the 33rd anniversary of Gandhi's funeral. Eleven camera crews shot 20,000ft of film, more than the total footage of the 188-minute release print of the movie. The edited funeral sequence with its 300,000 performers ran for only 125 seconds of screen time.

The largest number of soldiers used as extras was 187,000 in the last Nazi-made motion-picture epic *Kolberg* (Ger 45). For this story about Napoleon's siege of Kolberg, whole army divisions were diverted from the front to play Napoleonic soldiers at a time when Germany was facing the prospect of her defeat. The film was started in 1943 and completed at the end of the following year, with drafts of fresh extras continuously replacing those who had to return to more earnest military duties. Released in January 1945, at a time when few Berlin cinemas were still functioning, *Kolberg* was seen by a considerably smaller total audience than the number which had appeared in it.

Other considerable casts include: 157,000 for monster movie *Wang Ma Gwi/Monster Wang-magwi* (S.Kor 67); 120,000 for *War and Peace* (USSR 67); 106,000 for *Ilya Muromets* (USSR 56); over 100,000 on *Tonko* (Jap 88), claimed to be 'the most expensive film ever made in Japan'; 80,000 for *The War of Independence* (Rom 12); 68,894 for *Around the World in 80 Days* (US 56); 60,000 for *Intolerance* (US 16)—publicity for the picture claimed 125,000; 60,000 for *Dny Zrady* (Cz 72); 50,000 for *Ben Hur* (US 59), *Exodus* (US 60), *Inchon* (Kor/US 81) and *Khan Asparouch* (Bul 82); 36,000 in *Metropolis* (Ger 26), includ-

ing 1100 bald men in the Tower of Babel sequence; and 30,000 in *Michael the Brave* (Rom 70).

The year that the largest number of extras were employed in Hollywood was 1927, when a total of 330,397 days were worked (227,415 by men, 102,892 by women), an average daily call of 1056. Since there were 14,000 extras registered with Central Casting that year, average employment rate was approximately one day in 14.

EXTRAS WHO BECAME STARS

Comparatively few major stars began their film careers as extras, the majority having had stage or, latterly, television experience before entering movies. Those who did do extra work include Theda Bara, Gary Cooper, Marlene Dietrich, Clark Gable, Janet Gaynor, John Gilbert, Paulette Goddard, Stewart Granger, Jean Harlow, Harold Lloyd, Sophia Loren, Marilyn Monroe, David Niven, Ramon Novarro, Merle Oberon, Norma Shearer, Erich von Stroheim, Constance Talmadge, Rudolph Valentino, Michael Wilding and Loretta Young.

Sadly the reverse process could also apply. Leading players who ended their careers as extras were King Baggot, Mae Busch, Ethel Clayton, Grace Cunard, western star Franklyn Farnum, Flora Finch, Francis Ford (brother of John Ford and a leading man in the late teens), John Ince (brother of early mogul Thomas Ince), Douglas Fairbanks' leading lady Julanne Johnston, Alice Lake, original 'Biograph Girl' Florence Lawrence, western star

> Despite the fact that he was registered at Central Casting as 'Anglo-Saxon type 2008', David Niven's first role was as a Mexican in a blanket in a Hopalong Cassidy oater. He was subsequently an extra in 26 other westerns.

Kermit Maynard, Marshall Neilan, who had once commanded $125,000 per picture, Florence Turner, who was the first star to be put under contract, and 'country boy' hero Charles Ray. May McAvoy, romantic lead of the 1920s who played opposite Al Jolson in *The Jazz Singer* (US 27), retired when talkies took over but later tried to make a comeback as a character actress. She never succeeded in securing a speaking part and ended her career as an extra with MGM in the 1940s.

The dream of stardom via Central Casting occasionally comes true even today. Sixteen-year-old French schoolgirl Sandrine Bonnaire applied for a role as an extra in Maurice Pialat's *A Nos Amours* (Fr 83). She was given the lead instead, winning plaudits from the critics for her performance and sharing in the accolade of a César award, the French Oscar, for 'Best Film' of the year.

BLACK EXTRAS

Demand for black extras in the USA began with the flood of Civil War movies that followed the 50th anniversary in 1911. Tarzan and other jungle movies, together with epics of the ancient world, maintained a steady flow of work and the number of blacks registered with Central Casting peaked at 6816 in 1926. The following year was the best for employment, with some 10,000 black roles cast—the

The cast of Metropolis (Ger 26) included 1100 bald extras in the Tower of Babel sequence. (Kobal)

total for the previous three years had been 17,000. There was a decline with the coming of talkies and generally the films of the '30s were more confined in their settings than those of the silent era, requiring smaller crowd

---

Political correctness was alive and well long before it was named as such. When Steven Spielberg and his associates were casting for Universal's *I Wanna Hold Your Hand* (US 78), about the outbreak of Beatlemania that hit New York as the mop-headed quartet made their 1964 Stateside bow on *The Ed Sullivan Show*, they ran copious reels of news footage to capture the look of the teenage hordes who invaded Manhattan to picket the Plaza Hotel and the CBS Studios. To their dismay they discovered that the fans were almost exclusively white. Universal decreed that every crowd scene must have a quota of blacks proportionate to the population—one in eight—regardless of historical actuality. None of this caused the film-makers a moment of unease until a particular mob scene found a solid phalanx of black extras bunched directly in front of the camera. Veteran assistant director Newton Arnold wrestled with the conflicting dictates of his employers' liberal instincts and a representation of recent events which was patently untrue before deciding that he would risk the wrath of the committed. The black artistes were discreetly asked to disperse among the rest of the crowd.

---

scenes. World War II brought an almost complete stop to black casting; despite the million black Americans under arms, Hollywood's doughboy was resolutely white. After the war there was little improvement—in 1948 only 130 black roles were cast in pictures.

EXTRA, EXTRA!

- Extras in the 1930s were paid $8.25 for a non-speaking role and $16.50 for a bit part with dialogue. In Republic's *Man of Conquest* (US 39), the Native American extras were required to use the Indian sign language. The studio turned down their request for the higher pay scale, whereupon they appealed to the Screen Actors Guild. The union ruled that they were speaking, even if not orally. They won their $16.50.

- On the set of *Reds* (US 81), the story of Marxist journalist John Reed and the Bolshevik Revolution, director Warren Beatty lectured the extras on Reed's theories about capitalist exploitation of labour. The extras listened attentively, went away to discuss what they had been told, and decided unanimously to go on strike for higher wages. Beatty, hoist by his own petard, gave in and met their demand.

- In Samuel Fuller's war picture *Big Red One* (US 80), all the Nazi concentration camp guards were played by Jews. The location was a military base in Israel and the jackbooted jailers were Israeli soldiers lent for the production.

- When Mario Mattoli was filming his comedy *Imputato, alzateri!/Defendant Stand Up!* (It 39) at Cinecitta Studios in Rome, he was dismayed to hear that on the last day of shooting he had to play host to 200 Japanese tourists. Knowing that it would be all but impossible to control such a herd of non-Italian speaking oriental 'shutterbugs', he made the best of a bad job. Hastily rewriting the script, Mattoli devised an end scene involving a mob of Japanese tourists and filmed his 200 unpaid extras to hilarious effect.

- In 1935 Central Casting installed a mechanical Hollerith computer to handle the selection of extras for speciality roles. Formerly, if a combination of skills and physical attributes were required in an extra, locating such a person among the 12,500 hopefuls registered with the agency depended on the ability of the casting officials to memorise their individual characteristics. Under the new system the particulars of every registered applicant were recorded on 3 x 7 in punched cards, each detailing physical features, wardrobe available, experience, language spoken and other special abilities under 450 different classifications. Lawyers, for example, were subdivided into Shrewd, Dixie, Hawk-faced, Inquisitor and Benevolent. When the new system was unveiled before the press, the operator was asked to produce ten Englishmen, 6ft tall, blue-eyed, possessed of full evening dress, and able to play polo. The cards of all 600 male dress extras were run through the machine to reveal that there were only two such paragons on the books of Central Casting.

- In most countries and most cities casting bit parts is a cinch—everybody wants to be in the movies. Not so in Venice, as David Lean found on location for *Summertime* (US 55). When he needed 45 American tourists for crowd scenes, nobody responded to the notice he posted in the American Express office and the required number of extras had to be rounded up in hotel lobbies. But the biggest challenge came in casting the roles of Giovanna, the maid at the Pensione Fiora, and the young boy who befriends Katharine Hepburn. After weeks of searching for suitable aspirants, an advertisement was placed in Venice's daily newspaper. There was not a single reply. Eventually, Lean persuaded a ten-year-old Neapolitan boy, Gaitano Audiero, into playing the role opposite Miss Hepburn. Giovanna was found waiting tables in a local restaurant. Nevertheless, it took two weeks of wrangling, cajoling and pleading with her boyfriend, who did not want his inamorata's charms exposed to the world, before she was eventually persuaded to sign.

- The highest-paid extra in Hollywood during 1934, according to a contemporary report in the *New York Times*, was one Oliver Cross, whose total earnings for the year amounted to $2846.25. Mr Cross was a 'Class A dress extra' (i.e. he provided his own full evening dress), as were the other five men and the single woman extra to earn more than $2500. Of the 12,416 extras registered with Central Casting that year, only a round dozen succeeded in making a 'living wage', defined by the *New York Times* as $40 a week. The average, at a time when Greta Garbo earned $25,000 a week, was $8.97.

- Between 1923 and 1940 ex-Sergeant Carl Voss commanded a private army. With a strength of 2112 former World War I servicemen when it first appeared in the field as opposing American and German troops in *The Big Parade* (US 25), the Voss Brigade took up arms again as Riff warriors, Hessians, Senegalese, Revolutionary Americans, Chinese, Romans, Maoris and Crusaders in the years that followed. They would not only fight on both sides, but were equally adept as foot soldiers and cavalry, and as artillerymen it was said that there was no piece of ordnance they could not handle from the Roman catapult to Big Bertha. Following a stint as Fascist troops in Chaplin's *The Great Dictator* (US 40), their last battle was fought in *Four Sons* (US 40), some ending as they had begun as German soldiery, others as Czechs. On the eve of America's entry into World War II, the band of veterans was finally routed by the forces of bureaucracy. The Screen Actors Guild decreed that no agent could accept commission from an extra and their commander Sergeant Voss was decreed to be acting as such. After 232 engagements without a serious casualty, the old soldiers faded away.

- By the late 1950s the pay scale of Hollywood extras was graded by skill and by type. Sheep shearers, barbers and crooked card dealers earned a daily minimum of $29.04, nearly $7 more than a general crowd extra, while amputees found fortune in their misfortune at $39.80 a day.

- Payment of the Polynesians of Samoa who worked as extras on John Ford's *Hurricane* (US 37) was in the form of chewing gum, striped candy, canned salmon and chewing tobacco. The US Navy Department, which administered American Samoa, forbade cash payment lest the money be spent on strong liquor, although the studio was required to hand over to the authorities $2 per diem for each extra to be spent on community projects. Half a century later Karla Ehrlich, line producer of Michael Gill's *Gauguin—The Savage Dream* (GB 87), prepared for location shooting in the remote Marquesas, a group of French controlled Pacific islands scattered over an area nearly the size of Europe, where there were no cinemas, no made-up roads, no hotels, no newspapers and but one restaurant. She bought a load of trinkets in London's Oxford Street of a kind she thought would appeal to the Polynesians she intended to recruit as extras. On arrival in the South Seas paradise she found that the treasures of Oxford Street held little allure to natives accustomed to ordering life's little luxuries direct from Paris. They would perform, but only if paid in American dollars—and for not a cent below the Screen Actors Guild minimum rate.

- School, college and regimental reunions are commonplace, but a reunion of film extras? Veteran Australian producer-director Ken Hall organised, at the age of 89, what is believed to have been the first such event when he brought together the surviving walk-ons from his 1931 classic *On Our Selection* (Aus 31) nearly 60 years later. All those who had appeared in the Picnic Race scenes were invited to attend the reunion at Agnes Bank, NSW, which was held on 10 June 1990 together with the outback town's annual Picnic Race.

- Probably for the first time in the history of moviemaking, in Luc Besson's *The Messenger: The Joan of Arc Story* (Fr 99), the number of extras in a battle scene—in this case the Battle of Orleans in 1429—tallied exactly with the number of soldiers reported to have been engaged in the conflict.

- In one of the scenes in François Truffaut's *Day for Night* (Fr 73), his classic film about the process of film-making, the extras playing extras were told to mill around chatting, murmuring, clapping their hands or anything else that would create a realistic background noise. But they were warned 'Don't talk about cinema!'. Like many episodes in Truffaut films, this was based on personal experience. At the age of seventeen he and his close friends Jean-Luc Godard and Jacques Rivette, all three destined to become founders of the *nouvelle vague*, were engaged as extras in a René Clément picture. The three teenagers had to descend from a train at the same time as the star, Michelle Morgan, and walk across the platform to hand in their tickets to a ticket collector. As usual, the trio of young cinéastes were so engrossed in animated discussion of their shared passion, the movies, that they failed to achieve the casual, unassuming saunter required of them. After several failed takes, an exasperated Clément pronounced an edict: 'Don't talk about cinema!'.

- Socialite Amber Gill set up a special casting agency to recruit real-life aristos for the various wedding scenes in *Four Weddings and a Funeral* (GB 94). Such luminaries of the London scene as Lord Burlington (whose hair is even floppier than Hugh Grant's), Constantine Guppy (brother of convicted confidence trickster Darius Guppy) and sculptress Katie Braine were paid £90 a day conditional on the men supplying their own morning dress and the gels their own couture frocks and outrageous hats. The professional extras, sniffed Ms Gill, were 'a sea of C & A'. The 40 or so uppercrust wedding guests she provided were placed in the foreground, their social inferiors as far out of focus as possible.

Contracts, Legal and Binding

In the days when studios 'owned' stars, the price of security and gigantic salaries was often freedom of behaviour. All big stars had morality clauses in their contracts (first to sign had been Maryon Aye in 1922), but Joan Crawford's with MGM in 1930 even specified the hour by which she had to be in bed. Mary Miles Minter's contract with the Realart Co. in 1919 was dependent upon her remaining unmarried for three and a half years. Others enjoined to remain single were Clara Bow, at Paramount's insistence, and Alice White, whose contract with First National further obliged her to learn two languages during the course of 1930, preferably French and Spanish. Walter Pidgeon, much in demand for musicals before he became a father

---

When Johnny Weissmuller was dropped from the *Tarzan* pictures because he had put on too much weight, he was signed by Sam Katzman for a low-budget series of *Jungle Jim* B-movies. The contract stipulated that Weissmuller had to weigh in for each picture at 190 lb or less. For every pound over, his salary of $75,000 was subject to a deduction of $5000 up to 10 lb, maximum $50,000. After the ex-Olympic medallist had performed in the first two *Jungle Jim* films at exactly 189 lb, Katzman observed of the success of his contractual penalty system: 'If Johnny can't take it off by exercise, he takes it off by worry.'

---

figure, was forbidden to sing tenor lest he impair his rich baritone voice. Buster Keaton's famous unsmiling face was a contractual obligation. His contract with MGM in the '20s precluded him from smiling on screen, while Charles Butterworth's with Warner Bros prevented him from smiling in public. Similarly, Roscoe Ates's stutter was legally binding in his contract with RKO. First National demanded of Douglas Fairbanks Jr that he never travel in planes. Joe E. Brown was forbidden to grow a moustache. A clause in teetotaller Frank McHugh's contract with First National required that he play drunkards whenever required, while Maurice Chevalier's with Paramount, signed as talkies were coming in, insisted that he remain in character—it was rendered invalid if he ever lost his French accent. In 1931 boxing fan Vivienne Segal was directed by her contract with Warner's not to yell at prize fights in case she strained her voice.

During the '60s and '70s there was an increasing trend towards stars demanding creative control—and getting it. One who had no desire for such a privilege was that most laconic and laid-back of actors Robert Mitchum. 'Control is marvellous,' he commented in an interview with the *New York Times.* 'You get a white chair with your name on it in lieu of salary. I don't want control like that. There is a very simple way to get control any time: just forget your lines. When the cost of a scene is up to $40,000, they come over and say, "What's the problem?" "Oh, I have this *idée fixe* that it could be better." Believe me, they listen. I think it's a much simpler system than having control.'

Possibly the most difficult contractual obligation to enforce was the one enjoined on Lois Moran not to grow sophisticated for a year after the release of *Stella Dallas* (US 26). Clara Bow was offered a $500,000 bonus by Paramount in 1926 provided she kept herself free of scandal during its tenure. She failed to collect. All the cast of Cecil B. DeMille's reverential life of Christ, *King of Kings* (US 27), were bound by contract not to accept any roles without DeMille's consent for ten years after the film's release. Dorothy Cummings, who played the Madonna, was further denied the right to divorce, which she promptly did three months after the première.

THE CRYING GAME

Not all actresses can cry to order and some directors have been known to resort to less than gentle measures to coax tears from the dry-eyed. Maureen O'Sullivan's tear ducts failed to respond in her deathbed scene as Dora in *David Copperfield* (US 35) until director George Cukor positioned himself out of camera range at the end of the bed and twisted her feet sharply and painfully. Victor Fleming achieved the same effect with Lana Turner, never noted as one of Hollywood's most accomplished thespians, by jerking her arm behind her back and giving it a vicious twist.

Kim Novak, unable to produce tears on demand in the waterfall scene with William Holden in *Picnic* (US 55), asked director Joshua Logan to pinch her arms hard enough to make her cry. The scene took seven takes and after each one a make-up artist swabbed Novak's arms to cover up the marks. Logan was so distressed by the need to inflict physical hurt on his star that he threw up afterwards. Later Ms Novak was to accuse him of unprompted physical abuse when she recalled the episode.

Gregory La Cava was able to obtain convincing tears from Ginger Rogers in response to Katharine Hepburn's calla lilies speech in *Stage Door* (US 37) only when he announced to her that a message had just come through to say that her home had been burned to the ground.

Norman Taurog directed his own nephew, Jackie Cooper, in *Skippy* (US 31). When he was unable to get the ten-year-old to cry on cue, he told him that he would have his dog shot. The ensuing waterworks helped young Cooper on his way to what would be the youngest Oscar nomination for the next 40 years.

Otto Preminger stooped even lower when he needed spontaneous tears from a dozen small Israeli children in a scene in *Exodus* (US 60) to show their fear at an imminent Arab attack. He told them that their mothers no longer wanted them and had gone away never to return.

On one notable occasion, however, a burst of spontaneous tears ruined an otherwise satisfactory take. James Cagney could always cry on cue. But in his role as George M. Cohan in *Yankee Doodle Dandy* (US 42), Cagney's anguished tears at the deathbed of his father so affected director Michael Curtiz that he burst into loud and uncontrollable sobs while the camera was still running.

Whatever the vicissitudes of Hollywood, things were worse for child stars in Hong Kong. Veteran actress Josephine Siao Fong-fond recalled of her days as the colony's most famous juvenile of the 1950s: 'If you were shooting a scene where you had to cry, and they were afraid you wouldn't be able to deliver, they simply beat you with a rattan cane till you did.'

STARS PLAYING THEMSELVES IN FILMS

* signifies starring role

Isabelle Adjani *Paparazzi* (Fr 98)
Anouk Aimée *A Hundred and One Nights* (Fr/GB 95); *L.A. Without a Map* (GB/Fr/Fin 98)
June Allyson *Words and Music* (US 48)
Eddie 'Rochester' Anderson *Star Spangled Rhythm* (US 42)
Woody Allen *Sweet and Lowdown* (US 99)
Fanny Ardant *A Hundred and One Nights* (Fr/GB 95)
Arletty *L'Amour Madame* (Fr 52)
Rosanna Arquette *La Cité de la jeur* (Fr 94)
Fred Astaire *Dancing Lady* (US 33)
Steve Astin *Without You I'm Nothing* (US 90)
Mary Astor *Hollywood* (US 23)
Stephane Audran *Le Fils de Gascogne* (Fr 95)
Lew Ayres *The Cohens and the Kellys in Hollywood* (US 32)
Lauren Bacall *Two Guys from Milwaukee* (US 46)
Carroll Baker *Jack of Diamonds* (US/FRG 67)
Anne Bancroft *Silent Movie* (US 76)
Tallulah Bankhead *Stage Door Canteen* (US 43); *Main Street to Broadway* (US 53)
Brigitte Bardot *Dear Brigitte* (US 65)
Wendy Barrie *It Should Happen to You* (US 54)
Ethel Barrymore *Main Street to Broadway* (US 53)
John Barrymore *Nearly a King* (US 14); *The Nightingale* (US 14)
Lionel Barrymore *Free and Easy* (US 30); *Main Street to Broadway* (US 53)
Freddie Bartholomew *Sepia Cinderella* (US 47)
Jennifer Beals *Caro Diario* (It/Fr 94)
Noah Beery *Hollywood* (US 23)
Harry Belafonte *The Player* (US 92); *Prêt-à-Porter* (US 94)
Dorothy Bellew *The Kinema Girl* (GB 14)
Jean-Paul Belmondo *Les Acteurs* (Fr 00)
Jim Belushi *Last Action Hero* (US 93); *Wag the Dog* (US 97)
William Bendix *Duffy's Tavern* (US 45); *Variety Girl* (US 47)
Constance Bennett *It Should Happen to You* (US 54)
Edgar Bergen *Stage Door Canteen* (US 43); *Song of the Open Road* (US 44)
Milton Berle *Let's Make Love* (US 60); *Broadway Danny Rose* (US 84)
Jacqueline Bisset *Est & Ouest: Les Paradis Perdus* (Fr 93)
Karen Black *The Player* (US 92); *The Independent* (US 00)
Humphrey Bogart *Thank Your Lucky Stars* (US 43); *Two Guys from Milwaukee* (US 46); *Always Together* (US 47); *The Love Lottery* (US 54)
John Boles *Stand Up and Cheer* (US 34)
Ray Bolger *The Great Ziegfeld* (US 36)
Sandrine Bonnaire *A Hundred and One Nights* (Fr/GB 95)
Ernest Borgnine *Mistress* (US 92)
Clara Bow *Fascinating Youth* (US 26)
Pierce Brosnan *The Disappearance of Kevin Johnson* (US 97); *The Match* (GB 99)
Joe E. Brown *Hollywood Canteen* (US 44)
Johnny Mack Brown *The Marshal's Daughter* (US 53)
Coral Browne (as herself in 1958) *An Englishman Abroad* (GB 84)
Sandra Bullock *Famous* (US 00)
James Caan *Silent Movie* (US 76)

Nicolas Cage *Welcome to Hollywood* (US 98)
Eddie Cantor *Thank Your Lucky Stars* (US 43); *Hollywood Canteen* (US 44); *The Story of Will Rogers* (US 52)
Claudia Cardinale (who grew up in La Goulette in Tunisia): *A Summer in La Goulette* (Fr/Tunisia/Bel 96)
Jack Carson *It's a Great Feeling* (US 49)
Jackie Chan *An Alan Smithee Film—Burn, Hollywood, Burn** (US 97)
Charles Chaplin *Show People* (US 29)
Cyd Charisse *Words and Music* (US 48)
Chevy Chase *L.A. Story* (US 91); *Last Action Hero* (US 95)
Cher *Good Times* (US 67); *The Player* (US 92); *Prêt-à-Porter* (US 93)
Maggie Cheung *Irma Vep** (Fr 96)
Maurice Chevalier *L'Homme du Jour* (Fr 37) (also plays fictitious hero); *Pepe* (US 60)
Julie Christie *Nashville* (US 75)
James Coburn *The Player* (US 92); *The Disappearance of Kevin Johnson* (US 97)
Betty Compson *Hollywood* (US 23); *Hollywood Boulevard* (US 36)
Chester Conklin *Fascinating Youth* (US 26); *The Perils of Pauline* (US 47)
Sean Connery *Memories of Me* (US 88)
Eddie Constantine *Les Septs pêches capitaux* (Fr/ It 62); *Warnung vor einer Heiligen Nutte* (FRG/It 71); *Flight to Berlin* (GB 84)
Jackie Coogan *Free and Easy* (US 30)
Gary Cooper *Variety Girl* (US 47); *It's a Great Feeling* (US 49); *Starlift* (US 51)
Ricardo Cortez *Hollywood* (US 23)
Dolores and Helene Costello *How Cissy Made Good* (US 14)
Broderick Crawford *A Little Romance* (US 79)
Joan Crawford *Hollywood Canteen* (US 44);

It's a Great Feeling (US 49)
Bing Crosby *Star Spangled Rhythm* (US 42); *Duffy's Tavern* (US 45); *Variety Girl* (US 47); *Angels in the Outfield* (US 52); *The Greatest Show on Earth* (US 52); *Let's Make Love* (US 60); *Pepe* (US 60)
Finlay Currie *6.5 Special* (GB 58)
Karl Dane *Free and Easy* (US 30)
Bette Davis *Thank Your Lucky Stars* (US 43); *Hollywood Canteen* (US 44)
Sammy Davis Jr *Pepe* (US 60); *Moon Over Parador* (US 88)
Doris Day *Starlift* (US 51)
Olivia de Havilland *Thank Your Lucky Stars* (US 43)
Robert De Niro *A Hundred and One Nights* (Fr/GB 95)
Alain Delon *A Hundred and One Nights* (Fr/GB 95); *Les Acteurs* (Fr 00)
Dolores Del Rio *Torero!* (Mex 56)
Catherine Deneuve *L'Enfant de l'Art* (Fr 88); *A Hundred and One Nights* (Fr/GB 95)
Gérard Depardieu *A Hundred and One Nights* (Fr/GB 95); *Les Acteurs* (Fr 00)
Johnny Depp *L.A. Without a Map* (GB/Fr/Fin 98)
Marlene Dietrich *Follow the Boys* (US 44); *Jigsaw* (US 49)
Richard Dix *Fascinating Youth* (US 26)
Diana Dors *Allez France* (Fr 64)
Sidney Drew *Pay Day* (US 18)
Jimmy Durante *Pepe* (US 60)
Robert Englund *Wes Craven's New Nightmare* (US 94)
Douglas Fairbanks *Hollywood* (US 23); *The Kiss of Mary Pickford* (USSR 26); *Show People* (US 29)
Marianne Faithfull *Made in USA* (Fr 67)
Peter Falk *Der Himmel über Berlin* (FRG/Fr 87); *The Player* (US 92); *In Weiter Ferne, So Nah!* (Ger 93)

Jane Wyman as Jane Wyman, John Garfield as John Garfield and Bette Davis as Bette Davis in Warner Bros' Hollywood Canteen (US 44). (Kobal Collection)

STARS PLAYING THEMSELVES IN FILMS continued

William Farnum *The Perils of Pauline* (US 47); *Trail of Robin Hood* (US 51)
Felicia Farr *The Player* (US 92)
Mia Farrow *Private Parts* (US 97)
Alice Faye *Four Jills in a Jeep** (US 44)
Stepin Fetchit *Stand Up and Cheer* (US 34)
Gracie Fields *Stage Door Canteen* (US 43)
W. C. Fields *Sensations of 1945* (US 44); *Song of the Open Road* (US 44); *Follow the Boys* (US 44)
Flora Finch *How Cissy Made Good* (US 14)
Laurence Fishburne *Welcome to Hollywood* (US 98)
Carrie Fisher *Famous* (US 00)
Barry Fitzgerald *Variety Girl* (US 47)
Rhonda Fleming *The Patsy* (US 64)
Cyril Fletcher *Yellow Canary* (GB 43)
Louise Fletcher *The Player* (US 92)
Errol Flynn *Always Together* (US 47); *Cuban Rebel Girls* (US 60)

Although stars playing themselves in cameo roles is far from unusual, as this list demonstrates, there is a distinct impression that scriptwriters and directors seldom exercise much imagination in exploiting their fleeting presence to the best advantage of the story. With the director doubling as scenarist, though, the results can be telling, and all tribute to Wim Wenders for the pleasure of a scene in his *In Weiter Ferne, So Nah!* (Ger 93) in which Peter Falk, as Peter Falk, is trying to gain entry to a guarded building in Berlin. The security staff, watching on the entry-phone circuit, are thrown into confusion as they debate why an episode of *Colombo* has suddenly appeared on the monitoring screen.

Henry Fonda *Jigsaw* (US 49); *Main Street to Broadway* (US 53); *Fedora* (FRG 78)
Jane Fonda *Leonard Part 6* (US 87)
Harrison Ford *A Hundred and One Nights* (Fr/GB 95); *Jimmy Hollywood* (US 95)
Zsa Zsa Gabor *Pepe* (US 60); *Jack of Diamonds* (US 67); *California Girls* (US 85, TVM); *Smart Alex* (US 86); *The Naked Gun 2½: The Smell of Fear* (US 91); *Est & Ouest: Les Paradis Perdus* (Fr 93); *The Beverly Hillbillies* (US 93); *A Very Brady Sequel* (US 96)—record number of self portrayals.
Greta Garbo *A Man's Man* (US 29)
Ava Gardner *The Band Wagon* (US 53)
John Garfield *Thank Your Lucky Stars* (US 43); *Hollywood Canteen* (US 44); *Jigsaw* (US 49)
Judy Garland *Words and Music* (US 48)
Terri Garr *The Player* (US 92)
Greer Garson *The Youngest Profession* (US 43); *Pepe* (US 60)
Vittoria Gassman *Io sono fotogenica* (It 82)
John Gilbert *Married Flirts* (US 24); *A Man's Man* (US 29)
Paulette Goddard *Star Spangled Rhythm* (US 42); *Variety Girl* (US 47)
Whoopi Goldberg *An Alan Smithee Film— Burn, Hollywood, Burn* (US 97)
Jeff Goldblum *The Player* (US 92); *Welcome to Hollywood* (US 98)
Cuba Gooding Jr *Welcome to Hollywood* (US 98)

Elliott Gould *Nashville* (US 75); *The Muppets Take Manhattan* (US 84); *The Player* (US 92)
Betty Grable *Four Jills in a Jeep** (US 44)
Cary Grant *Without Reservations* (US 46)
Joel Grey *The Player* (US 92)

Garbo's last screen appearance? No, not *Two-Faced Woman* (US 41). It was in tacky sex movie *Adam and Yves* (US 74). She was depicted as herself walking down a street in New York— needless to say her participation was without her consent and unpaid.

Greta Gynt *I'm a Stranger* (GB 52)
Larry Hagman *I Am Blushing* (Swe 81)
Creighton Hale *Mary of the Movies* (US 23)
Monte Hale *Trail of Robin Hood* (US 51)
George Hamilton *Bulworth* (US 98)
Rex Harrison *Main Street to Broadway* (US 53)
W. S. Hart *Hollywood* (US 23); *Show People* (US 29)
Laurence Harvey *The Magic Christian* (GB 70) as self playing Hamlet
David Hasselhof *Welcome to Hollywood* (US 98); *The Big Tease* (US/GB 99)
Sessue Hayakawa *Night Life in Hollywood* (US 22)
Sterling Hayden *Variety Girl* (US 47)
Susan Hayward *Star Spangled Rhythm* (US 42)
Sonja Henie *Hello London* (GB 58)
Katherine Hepburn *Stage Door Canteen* (US 43)
William Holden *Variety Girl* (US 47)
Jack Holt *Hollywood Speaks* (US 32)
Bob Hope *Duffy's Tavern* (US 45); *Variety Girl* (US 47); *The Greatest Show on Earth* (US 52); *The Oscar* (US 66)
John Houseman *Scrooged* (US 88)
Rock Hudson *The Patricia Neal Story* (US 81, TVM)
John Hurt *Spaceballs* (US 87)
Anjelica Huston *The Player* (US 92)
Betty Hutton *Star Spangled Rhythm* (US 42); *Duffy's Tavern* (US 45)
Lauren Hutton *The Venice Project* (Aut/US 99)
Sidney James *The Beauty Contest* (GB 64)
Al Jolson *Hollywood Cavalcade* (US 39); *Rhapsody in Blue* (US 44); *Jolson Sings Again* (US 49)—scene of Jolson meeting Larry Parks and congratulating him on his portrayal of Jolson in *The Jolson Story*
James Earl Jones *True Identity* (US 91)
Boris Karloff *The Cohens and the Kellys in Hollywood* (US 32); *Bikini Beach* (US 64)
Danny Kaye *It's a Great Feeling* (US 49)
Buster Keaton *Hollywood Cavalcade* (US 39); *Sunset Boulevard* (US 50)
Sally Kellerman *The Player* (US 92)
Gene Kelly *Words and Music* (US 48); *Love is Better than Ever* (US 52); *Let's Make Love* (US 60)
George Kennedy *The Legend of Lylah Clare* (US 68); *Modern Romance* (US 81)
Sally Kirkland *The Player* (US 92)
Alan Ladd *Star Spangled Rhythm* (US 42); *Duffy's Tavern* (US 45); *Variety Girl* (US 47)
Veronica Lake *Star Spangled Rhythm* (US

42); *Variety Girl* (US 47)
Dorothy Lamour *Star Spangled Rhythm* (US 42); *Duffy's Tavern* (US 45); *Variety Girl* (US 47); *Here Comes the Groom* (US 51)
Carole Landis *Four Jills in a Jeep** (US 44)
Harry Langdon *Ella Cinders* (US 26)
Heather Langenkamp *Wes Craven's New Nightmare* (US 94)
Laurel and Hardy *Pick a Star* (US 37)
Peter Lawford *Pepe* (US 60)
Janet Leigh *Pepe* (US 60)
Jack Lemmon *Pepe* (US 60); *The Player* (US 92)
Gina Lollobrigida *A Hundred and One Nights* (Fr/GB 95)
Sophia Loren *Sophia Loren: Her Own Story** (US 80, TVM)
Peter Lorre *Hollywood Canteen* (US 44)
Bessie Love *Night Life in Hollywood* (US 22); *Mary of the Movies**(US 23)
Linda Lovelace *Linda Lovelace for President* (US 75)
Ida Lupino *Thank Your Lucky Stars* (US 43)
Jeanette MacDonald *Follow the Boys* (US 44)
Andie MacDowell *The Player* (US 92)
Malcolm McDowell *The Player* (US 92)
Sir Ian McKellen *Thin Ice* (GB 94)
Virginia McKenna *An Elephant called Slowly* (GB 69); *The Lion at World's End* (GB 71)
Shirley Maclaine *Judgement City* (US 91)
Fred MacMurray *Star Spangled Rhythm* (US 42)
Gordon MacRae *Starlift* (US 51)
Lee Majors *Scrooged* (US 88)
John Malkovich *Being John Malkovich** (GB/US 99)
Cheech Marin *The Venice Project* (Aut/US 99)
George Marshall *Variety Girl* (US 47)
Steve Martin *The Venice Project* (Aut/US 99)
Harpo Marx *Stage Door Canteen* (US 43)
Marcello Mastroianni *L'Ingorgo/Bottleneck* (It/ Fr/Sp/FRG 79)
Marlee Matlin *The Player* (US 92)
Victor Mature *Head* (US 68)
Kermit Maynard *Trail of Robin Hood* (US 51)
Virginia Mayo *Starlift* (US 51)
Adolphe Menjou *Fascinating Youth* (US 26)
Burgess Meredith *Jigsaw* (US 49)
Ray Milland *Star Spangled Rhythm* (US 42); *Variety Girl* (US 47)
Liza Minnelli *Silent Movie* (US 76); *The Muppets Take Manhattan* (US 84)
Tom Mix *The Cohens and the Kellys in Hollywood* (US 32)
Bull Montana *Hollywood* (US 23)
Yves Montand *Trois places pour le 26* (Fr 88)
Dudley Moore *The Disappearance of Kevin Johnson* (US 97)
Owen Moore *Hollywood* (US 23)

Chester Conklin, William Farnum, Creighton Hale and Snub Pollard, together with Paul W. Panzer as the oily silk-hatted villain, all played in the cliffhanger serial *The Perils of Pauline* (US 16). With the aid of deft make-up, they came together again 31 years later to play themselves in Paramount's tribute to Queen of the Serials *Pearl White The Perils of Pauline* (US 47).

STARS PLAYING THEMSELVES IN FILMS continued

Jean Moreau *The Four Hundred Blows* (Fr 58); *A Hundred and One Nights* (Fr/GB 95)

Dennis Morgan *It's a Great Feeling* (US 49)

Paul Muni *Stage Door Canteen* (US 43)

Bill Murray *Space Jam* (US 96)

Mae Murray *Married Flirts* (US 24); *Show People* (US 29)

Ornella Muti *Grandi Magazzini* (It 86)

Nita Naldi *Hollywood* (US 23)

Prem Nazir *Prem Nazarin Kanmanilla** (India 83)

Patricia Neal *It's a Great Feeling* (US 49)

Pola Negri *Hollywood* (US 23)

Paul Newman *Silent Movie* (US 76)

Anna Q. Nilsson *Sunset Boulevard* (US 50)

Nick Nolte *The Player* (US 92)

Chuck Norris *Sidekicks* (US 92)

Merle Oberon *Stage Door Canteen* (US 43); *The Oscar* (US 66)

Donald O'Connor *Follow the Boys* (US 44)

Bulle Ogier *Le Fils de Gascogne* (Fr 95)

Lili Palmer *Main Street to Broadway* (US 53); *Le Rendezvous de Minuit* (Fr 66) (also played two fictitious characters); *Jack of Diamonds* (US/FRG 67)

Larry Parks *Jolson Sings Again* (US 49)—also played Jolson

Dolly Parton *The Beverly Hillbillies* (US 93)

Luke Perry *Vacanze di Natale '95* (It 95)

Mary Pickford *Hollywood* (US 23); *The Kiss of Mary Pickford* (USSR 26), made by Sergei Komorov without Miss Pickford being aware of her own participation (see p. 82).

Walter Pidgeon *The Youngest Profession* (US 43)

Marie-France Pisier *Le Fils de Gascogne* (Fr 95)

ZaSu Pitts *Mary of the Movies* (US 23); *Make Me a Star* (US 32)

Eddie Polo *Dangerous Hour* (US 23)

Dick Powell *Star Spangled Rhythm* (US 42)

Jane Powell *Song of the Open Road* (US 44)

William Powell *The Youngest Profession* (US 43)

Robert Preston *Variety Girl* (US 47)

Dennis Price *Go for a Take* (GB 72)

George Raft *Broadway* (US 42); *Stage Door Canteen* (US 43); *The Patsy* (US 64); *Casino Royale* (GB 67); *Sextette* (US 78)

Tony Randall *The King of Comedy* (US 83)

Ronald Reagan *It's a Great Feeling* (US 49)

Wallace Reid *Night Life in Hollywood* (US 22)

Michael Rennie *The Body Said No!* (GB 50)

Burt Reynolds *Silent Movie* (US 76); *The Player* (US 92)

Debbie Reynolds *Pepe* (US 60); *The Bodyguard* (US 92)

Ralph Richardson *The Volunteer* (GB 43)

Tex Ritter *Nashville Rebel* (US 66); *What Am I Bid?* (US 67)

Joan Rivers as President of the USA Joan Rivers in *Les Patterson Saves the World* (Aus 87)

Eric Roberts *The Cable Guy* (US 96)

Julia Roberts *The Player* (US 92)

Edward G. Robinson *It's a Great Feeling* (US 49)

May Robson *How Molly Malone Made Good* (US 15)

Patricia Roc *Holiday Camp* (GB 47)

Roy Rogers *Hollywood Canteen* (US 44)

Will Rogers *Hollywood* (US 23)

Sabrina *Just My Luck* (GB 57)

Susan Sarandon *The Player* (US 92)

John Saxon *Wes Craven's New Nightmare* (US 94)

Maria Schneider *Les Acteurs* (US 00)

Arnold Schwarzenegger *Dave* (US 93); *Last Action Hero* (US 93)

Hanna Schygulla *A Hundred and One Nights* (Fr/GB 95)

Randolph Scott *Starlift* (US 51)

Tom Selleck *Open Season* (US 95)

Larry Semon *Go Straight* (US 25)

William Shatner *Free Enterprise* (US 98)

Norma Shearer *Married Flirts* (US 24)

Charlie Sheen *Hot Shots! Part Deux* (US 93); *Being John Malkovich* (US 99); *Famous* (US 00)

Martin Sheen *In the King of Prussia* (US 82); *Hot Shots! Part Deux* (US 93)

Brooke Shields *The Muppets Take Manhattan* (US 84); *Speed Zone* (US 89)

Sylvia Sidney *Make Me a Star* (US 32)

Phil Silvers *Take It or Leave It* (US 44)

Frank Sinatra *Pepe* (US 60); *The Oscar* (US 66); *Cannonball Run II* (US 83)

Suzanne Somers *Serial Mom* (US 94)

Mira Sorvino *Famous* (US 00)

Tori Spelling *Scream 2* (US 98)

Sylvester Stallone *An Alan Smithee Film – Burn, Hollywood, Burn* (US 97)

Barbara Stanwyck *Hollywood Canteen* (US 44); *Variety Girl* (US 47)

Tommy Steele *Kill Me Tomorrow* (GB 55); *The Tommy Steele Story** (GB 57)

Rod Steiger *The Player* (US 92)

Alexandra Stewart *Le Fils de Gascogne* (Fr 95)

Anita Stewart *Mary of the Movies* (US 23); *Hollywood* (US 23); *Go Straight* (US 25)

Sharon Stone *Last Action Hero* (US 93)

Edith Storey *How Cissy Made Good* (US 14)

Gloria Swanson *Hollywood* (US 23); *Airport 75* (US 74)

Blanche Sweet *Souls for Sale* (US 23)

Constance Talmadge *In Hollywood with Potash and Perlmutter* (US 24)

Norma Talmadge *In Hollywood with Potash and Perlmutter* (US 24); *Show People* (US 29)

Estelle Taylor *Mary of the Movies* (US 23); *Hollywood* (US 23)

Robert Taylor *The Youngest Profession* (US 43)

Billy Bob Thornton *An Alan Smithee Film— Burn, Hollywood, Burn* (US 94)

Lily Tomlin *The Player* (US 92)

Bill Travers *An Elephant called Slowly* (GB 69); *The Lion at World's End* (GB 71)

John Travolta *Welcome to Hollywood* (US 98)

Lana Turner *The Youngest Profession* (US 43)

Ben Turpin *Hollywood* (US 23); *Make Me a Star* (US 32)

Liv Ullman *Players* (US 79)

Peter Ustinov *Players* (US 79)

Jean-Claude Van Damme *Last Action Hero* (US 93)

Conrad Veidt *Die Grosse Sehnsucht* (Ger 30)

Vera-Ellen *Words and Music* (US 48)

Robert Wagner *The Player* (US 92)

H. B. Warner *Sunset Boulevard* (US 50)

Paul Wegener *The Golem and the Dancer* (Ger 14)

Johnny Weissmuller *Stage Door Canteen* (US 43)

Orson Welles *Follow the Boys* (US 44); *Someone to Love* (US 87)

Cornel Wilde *Main Street to Broadway* (US 53)

Michael Wilding *Hello London* (GB 58)

Bruce Willis *The Player* (US 92)

Natalie Wood *The Candidate* (US 72); *Willie and Phil* (US 81)

Monty Woolley *Night and Day* (US 46)

Jane Wyman *Hollywood Canteen* (US 44); *It's a Great Feeling* (US 49); *Starlift* (US 51)

Ed Wynn *The Patsy* (US 64)

Michael York *Fedora* (FRG 78)

Susannah York *Scruggs* (GB 66)—also played heroine; *Long Shot* (GB 78); *Diana and Me* (Aus 97)

Pia Zadora *Troop Beverly Hills* (US 90); *Naked Gun 33 1/3 The Final Insult* (US 94)

Occasionally the stars were able to impose unusual conditions on their masters, the studios. At the Warner studios in the early '30s, George Arliss's contract provided that he did not have to remain on set after 4.30 p.m., while John Barrymore's gave him the privilege of not being on set before 10.30 a.m. Moran and Mack, the *Two Black Crows*, were the only Paramount stars allowed to drive their car within the studio gates. Garbo's desire to be alone was protected by a clause preventing MGM from demands that she make any public appearances. When stage player Margaret Sullavan was persuaded by director John Stahl to accept the lead in *Only Yesterday* (US 33), she was so reluctant to enter films that she had a clause inserted in her contract to the effect that she could quit after ten days if she disliked Hollywood as much as she anticipated. Although she loathed Tinsel Town, she completed the picture and many others. Joe E. Brown's contract with Warners demanded that the studio co-operate with him in running a baseball team. Virginal Evelyn Venable's contract with Paramount in 1933 had a clause inserted by her father preventing her from being kissed on screen. The rather less virginal Clara Bow wrote into her contract with Paramount that none of the workmen or technicians were to use profane language to her or in her presence.

Even in more recent times, producers have been known to make grudging concessions if the name of the star was big enough. Roger Moore would not sign any contract unless he was guaranteed an unlimited supply of hand-rolled Monte Cristo cigars (continued p. 93)

NON-ACTORS PLAYING THEMSELVES IN FILMS

The list excludes the many bandleaders and vocalists appearing in sound movies. All roles were acted—documentary material and newsreel footage is excluded.
(* Autobiopics)

Bella Abzug, US Congresswoman *Manhattan* (US 79)

Princess Aicha Abidir *Pierrot-le-Feu* (Fr/It 65)

Frankie Albert, All-American quarterback *The Spirit of Stanford** (US 42)

Buzz Aldrin, astronaut *The Boy in the Plastic Bubble* (US 76, TVM)

Dragljub Aleksic, acrobat *Nevinost bez Zastite** (Yug 68)

Queen Alexandra *The Great Love* (US 18); *Women Who Win* (GB 19)

Muhammed Ali, heavyweight boxing champion *The Greatest** (US 77); *Body and Soul* (US 81)

Alfredo Alvarado, exhibition dancer *El Rey del Jorapo** (Ven 80)

Vijay Amritraj, Indian tennis champion *Octopussy* (GB 83)

Mario Andretti, motor-racing driver *Speed Fever* (It 78)

Duke and Duchess of Argyll *Bullseye!* (US 90)

Lady Astor, first woman MP to sit in House of Commons *Royal Cavalcade* (GB 35)

Lt-Commander Auten VC, RNR re-enacted exploit which won him VC in *Q Ships* (GB 28)

Lord Baden-Powell, defender of Mafeking and founder of the Scout movement *Boys of the Otter Patrol* (GB 18); *The Man Who Changed His Mind* (GB 28); *The Woodpigeon Patrol* (GB 30)

Max Baer, boxer *The Prizefighter and the Lady* (US 33)

Bruce Bairnsfather, creator of cartoon character 'Old Bill' *Old Bill Through the Ages* (GB 24)

Joan Bakewell, TV personality *The Touchables* (GB 67)

Sonny Barger, Hell's Angels leader *Hell's Angels on Wheels* (US 67); *Hell's Angels '69* (US 69)

Jeremy Beadle, TV prankster (as Beadle disguised as British bobby) *A Fistful of Fingers* (GB 95)

Adolf Beck, convicted of false murder charge *The Martyrdom of Adolf Beck** (GB 09)

The Duchess of Bedford *The Beauty Contest* (GB 64)

The Duke of Bedford *The Iron Maiden* (GB 62)

Alec Bedser, cricketer *The Final Test* (GB 53)

Saul Bellow, novelist *Zelig* (US 83)

Yogi Berra, baseball star *That Touch of Mink* (US 62)

Daniel and Phillip Berrigan, radical Jesuits *In the King of Prussia* (US 82)

Roy Best, warden of Canon City Penitentiary *Canon City* (US 48)

Ronald Biggs, train robber *The Great Rock 'n' Roll Swindle* (GB 80); *Honeymoon* (FRG 80)

Danny Blanchflower, soccer star *Those Glory Glory Days* (GB 83)

Jasmine Bligh, first TV announcer in Britain (1936) *Band Wagon* (GB 40)

John Wayne Bobbitt, whose penis was cut off by wife with kitchen knife *John Wayne Bobbitt Uncut** (US 94)

Ada Bodart, assisted Nurse Edith Cavell in establishing her World War I escape organisation *Dawn* (GB 28)

Evangeline Booth, Commandant of US Salvation Army *Fires of Faith* (US 19)

Lord Boothby, politician *Rockets Galore* (GB 58)

Bjorn Borg, tennis champion *Racquet* (US 79)

Horatio Bottomley, politician and financier, three times charged with fraud (convicted 1922) *Was It He?* (GB 14)

The Bowen Family of Guyra, NSW, victims of psychic phenomena *The Guyra Ghost Mystery** (Aus 21)

Jack Brabham, motor-racing driver *The Green Helmet* (GB 61)

Melvyn Bragg, adenoidal broadcaster *The Tall Guy* (GB 89)

Sir David Brand, premier of Western Australia *Nickel Queen* (Aus 71)

RSM Ronald Brittain, regimental sergeant major of ferocious demeanour *You Lucky People* (GB 55)

Dr Joyce Brothers, sexologist *Stand Up and Be Counted* (US 71); *Embryo* (US 76); *The Lonely Guy* (US 84); *Last of the Great Survivors* (US 84, TVM); *Troop Beverly Hills* (US 90); *Lover's Knot* (US 96)

Joe Brown, New York speakeasy proprietor *Dressed to Kill* (US 28)

Judge Willis Brown of Salt Lake Juvenile Court *A Boy and the Law* (US 14)

Maurice Buckmaster, spy-master *Odette* (GB 50)

Don Budge, tennis champion *Pat and Mike* (US 52)

Sir Matt Busby, football manager *Cup Fever* (GB 65)

Jeanne Marie Calment of Arles, aged 114, last person alive who knew Van Gogh *Vincent and Me* (Can 90)

José Capablanca, chess grand master *Chess Fever* (USSR 25)

Andrew Carnegie, multi-millionaire industrialist *Our Mutual Girl* (US 14)

A disclaimer before the end credits of *Players* (US 79) insisted that all the characters in the film were wholly fictitious; it was immediately followed by a cast list that included no less than 14 famous tennis personalities, including John McEnroe, playing themselves.

James Earl Carter, US President *Special Counsel* (US 88)

George Washington Carver, distinguished black scientist *George Washington Carver** (US 40)

Vernon and Irene Castle, exhibition dancers,

*Not the first Prince of Wales to act in a movie. His great uncle Edward VIII appeared in three silent pictures, but Charles was the first member of the British Royal Family to speak on screen in a fiction movie—*Grimes Goes Green *(GB 90). Here the manic John Cleese as Grimes realises that the person behind the newspaper whom he has been abusing is not who he thought it was (see p. 92). (Mail Newspapers)*

NON-ACTORS PLAYING THEMSELVES IN FILMS continued

played by Fred Astaire and Ginger Rogers in *The Story of Vernon and Irene Castle* (US 39), in *The Whirl of Life* (US 15)*

Dick Cavett, TV chat show presenter *Health* (US 80)

César, sculptor who created the César (French Oscar) *T'es folle ou quoi?* (Fr 82)

Claude Chabrol, film director *Le Fils de Gascogne* (Fr 95)

HRH Prince Charles *Grimes Goes Green* (GB 90); *The Legend of Lochnagar* (GB 93)

Michael Chow, restaurateur *Basquiat* (US 96)

Arthur Christiansen, ex-editor of the *Daily Express*, *The Day the Earth Caught Fire* (GB 61)

Cicciolina (Ilona Staller), Italian politician and former porn star *Sexploitation* (Hun 90)

M. E. Clifton-James, ex-actor who impersonated Montgomery to deceive Nazi Intelligence *I Was Monty's Double** (GB 58)

George Clinton, brother of Bill *PCU* (US 94)

Ty Cobb, baseball player *Somewhere in Georgia* (US 17); *Angels in the Outfield* (US 51)

Sir Alan Cobham, aviator *The Flight Commander* (GB 27)

William Cody, Buffalo Bill *The Life of Buffalo Bill** (US 09); *Buffalo Bill's Far West and Pawnee Bill's Far East* (US 10); *The Indian Wars* (US 13); *Sitting Bull—The Hostile Indian Chief* (US 14); *Patsy of the Circus* (US 15)

Denis Compton, cricketer *The Final Test* (GB 53)

Douglas 'Wrong Way' Corrigan, aviator *The Flying Irishman** (US 39)

Wes Craven, director of *Nightmare on Elm Street* series *Wes Craven's New Nightmare* (US 94)

Quentin Crisp, gay icon *To Wong Foo, Thanks for Everything! Julie Newmar* (US 95)

Edwina Currie MP, former junior health minister and victim of egg jokes *News Hounds* (GB 90, TVM)

Michael Curtiz, film director *It's a Great Feeling* (US 49)

Emmett Dalton, youngest of the Dalton brothers, notorious desperadoes *Beyond the Law* (US 18)

Josephus Daniels, US Secretary of the Navy *Victory* (US 13)

Clarence Darrow, criminal lawyer *From Dusk to Dawn* (US 13)

Jimmie Davis, Governor of Louisiana *Louisiana** (US 47)

Moshe Dayan, Israeli Minister of Defence *Operation Thunderbolt* (Isr 77)

Cecil B. DeMille, film producer and director *Hollywood* (US 23); *Free and Easy* (US 30); *Star Spangled Rhythm* (US 42); *Variety Girl* (US 47); *Sunset Boulevard* (US 50)

Brian De Palma, film director *Rotwang Muss Weg!* (Ger 95)

Jack Dempsey, heavyweight boxing champion *Sweet Surrender* (US 53); *Big City* (US 37); *Off Limits* (US 53); *Requiem for a Heavyweight* (US 62)

Joe Di Maggio, baseball player *Angels in the Outfield* (US 51)

Richard Dimbleby, BBC commentator *The Twenty Questions Murder* (GB 50); *John and Julie* (GB 55); *Rockets Galore* (GB 58); *Libel* (GB 59)

Georgi Dimitrov, communist revolutionary tried and acquitted in the 1933 Reichstag Fire trial, Prime Minister of Bulgaria 1946–49 *Kämpfer* (USSR 36)

Dionne quins, world's first surviving quintuplets, in *The Country Doctor* (US 36); *Reunion* (US 36); *Five of a Kind* (US 38)

Walt Disney, creator of Mickey Mouse, etc *Once Upon a Time* (US 44)

Sir Arthur Conan Doyle, novelist and creator of Sherlock Holmes *The $5,000,000 Counterfeiting Plot* (US 14)

Joni Eareckson, paraplegic *Joni** (US 80)

King Edward VIII (as Prince of Wales) *The Power of Right* (GB 19); *The Warrior Strain* (GB 19); *Remembrance* (GB 27). See box.

Sgt Arthur Guy Empsey, war hero *Over the Top** (US 18)

Godfrey Evans, cricketer *The Final Test* (GB 53)

Robert Fabian, police detective *Passport to Shame* (GB 59)

Emerson Fittipaldi, motor-racing driver *Speed Fever* (It 78)

The only British monarch to have acted in films was King Edward VIII when he was Prince of Wales. In March 1919 he performed in two patriotic war dramas—like Indian stars of today he economised on time by playing his scenes for both films at the same time. This was made easier by the fact that he was portraying himself in each and that they had remarkably similar plots. *The Power of Right* (GB 19), directed by F. Martin Thornton for Harma Photoplays, was about a colonel's son who joins the cadets and succeeds in killing an escaped German internee, while *The Warrior Strain* (GB 19) was also about a cadet, this time an earl's son, who foils a dastardly plot by a German baron to signal the enemy from Brighton. In the latter film the Prince played a scene with Sydney Wood (as the boy's father), and another in which he presents each of the members of the cadet section with a gold watch as a reward for thwarting the wicked baron. Some years later he again played himself in BIP's *Remembrance* (GB 27), a story about disabled war veterans.

Margot Fonteyn, prima ballerina *The Little Ballerina* (GB 51)

Michael Foot, leader of Labour Party *Rockets Galore* (GB 58)

John Ford, director *Big Time* (US 29)

Joe Frazier, boxer *Rocky* (US 77)

Samuel Fuller, director *Pierrot-le-Fou* (Fr 65); *Scotch Myths—The Movie* (GB 83)

Paul Gallico, novelist *Madison Square Garden* (US 32)

Haile Gebrselassie, 10,000m gold medallist, 1996 Olympics *Endurance* (US/GB 98)

Bob Geldof, rock musician *Diana and Me* (Aus 97)

Dorothy Gibson, Titanic survivor *Saved from the Titanic* (GB 12)

André Gide, writer *La Vie commence demain* (Fr 52)

Allen Ginsberg, poet *Ciao! Manhattan* (US 72)

Elinor Glyn, pioneer of the sex novel and creator of 'It' *It* (US 27); *Show People* (US 29)

Barbara Goalen, model *Wonderful Things!* (GB 58)

Pancho Gonzalez, tennis coach *Players* (US 79)

John Gorton, Prime Minister of Australia *Don's Party* (Aus 76)

Steffi Graf, tennis champion *Otto-Der Ausserfriesische* (FRG 89)

Billy Graham, American evangelist *Souls in Conflict* (GB 55); *Two a Penny* (GB 67)

Sheila Graham, journalist and mistress of F. Scott Fitzgerald (played by Deborah Kerr in biopic *Beloved Infidel* (US 59)) *College Confidential* (US 60)

Angèle Grammont, who escaped from old people's home near Lausanne *Angèle** (Swz 68)

Zane Grey, Western novelist *White Death* (Aus 36)

Grock, clown *Grock** (Ger 31)

Earl Haig, World War I Commander-in-Chief *Remembrance* (GB 27)

Ernest Haigh, ex-chief inspector of police *Leaves from My Life** (GB 21)

Giscele Halimi, defence counsel in notable 1972 abortion trial *L'Une chante l'autre pas* (Fr/Bel/Cur 76)

Jerry Hall, model, ex-wife of Mick Jagger *Diana and Me* (Aus 97)

General Sir Ian Hamilton, leader of the Gallipoli Expedition *Tell England* (GB 31)

Oscar Hammerstein, composer *Main Street to Broadway* (US 53)

Judge James Hannon, judge who tried Arlo Guthrie for throwing litter *Alice's Restaurant* (US 69)

Gilbert Harding, crusty TV personality, famous for rudeness *Simon and Laura* (GB 55); *As Long as They're Happy* (GB 55); *An Alligator Named Daisy* (GB 55); *My Wife's Family* (GB 56); *Left, Right and Centre* (GB 59); *Expresso Bongo* (GB 59)

Mickey Hargitay, ex-Mr Universe, ex-husband of Jayne Mansfield *Mr Universe* (Hun 88)

Tom Harmon, All-American quarterback *Harmon of Michigan** (US 41)

Norman Hartnell, couturier *The Beauty Contest* (GB 64)

Len Harvey, boxer *The Bermondsey Kid* (GB 33)

Ira H. Hayes, American Indian Marine who helped to raise the US flag on Suribacki (portrayed by Tony Curtis in *The Outsider* (US 62)) in *The Sands of Iwo Jima* (US 49)

Edith Head, Hollywood costume designer *The Oscar* (US 66)

Hugh Hefner, founder of Playboy empire (played by Cliff Robertson in *Star 80* (US 83)) *How Did a Nice Girl Like You Ever Get Into This Business* (FRG 70)

Graham Hill, motor-racing driver *The Fast Lady* (GB 62)

Dennis Hills, captive of Idi Amin *The Rise and Fall of Idi Amin* (Ken 81)

David Hockney, artist *A Bigger Splash** (GB 74)

Ben Hogan, golfer *The Caddy* (US 53)

Hedda Hopper, movie gossip columnist *Sunset Boulevard* (US 50); *Pepe* (US 60);

NON-ACTORS PLAYING THEMSELVES IN FILMS continued

The Patsy (US 64)

William Morris Hughes, Prime Minister of Australia *Smithy* (Aus 46)

Hubert Humphrey, US senator *The Candidate* (US 72)

James Hunt, motor-racing driver *Speed Fever* (It 78)

Len Hutton, cricketer *The Final Test* (GB 53)

Father Iliodor, rascally monk, first protégé then opponent of Rasputin *The Fall*

HRH Prince Charles made his screen acting debut opposite John Cleese in Video Arts' environmental film *Grimes Goes Green* (GB 90). He plays himself on a royal visit to a factory whose managing director Grimes considers green issues are only for the beards and sandals brigade. Cleese as Grimes fails to recognise the Prince, who is buried behind the *Daily Telegraph* in reception, and harangues him with 'Oh, another one from the Palace, eh? Well, I suppose you'll be wanting to see the drains then. Let me guess—you're the Royal Sanitary Inspector, eh?'. The Prince lowers his paper to reveal himself and Grimes instantly becomes cringingly obsequious as he listens to the Prince's formula for going green. Equally sycophantic was the reaction of most newspapers, praising the 'Clown Prince' as a 'Video King'. A striking exception was *Today*, which panned his performance with the criticism that his nerves had got the better of him, resulting in some unnatural body movement, and that his lines had been delivered so unimaginatively that even the most attentive of audiences would find their minds wandering. 'We all love him,' the paper summed up, 'but the truth is he can't act.'

---

of the Romanoffs (US 18)

David Jacobs, broadcaster *Otley* (GB 68)

James J. Jeffries, boxing champion *Pennington's Choice* (US 15)

Admiral Lord Jellicoe *Q Ships* (GB 28)

Al Jennings, convicted bank and train robber *The Bank Robbery* (US 08); *Beating Back** (US 15); *The Lady of the Dugout* (US 18)

Elton John, rock musician and composer *Diana and Me* (Aus 97)

Amy Johnson, aviatrix *Dual Control* (GB 32)

Jack Johnson, boxer *Jack Johnson's Adventures in Paris* (Fr 13); *As the World Rolls On* (US 21)

Magic Johnson, basketball player *Grand Canyon* (US 92)

Tom Jones, singer *Mars Attacks!* (US 96); *Agnes Brown* (Ire 00)

Michael Jordan, basketball player, co-starred with Bugs Bunny in *Space Jam* (US 96)

José José, alcohol and drug addicted popular singer *Gavilán o Paloma** (Mex 85)

Anatoly Karpov, chess grand master *Fool's Mate* (FRG 89)

Helen Keller, deaf-blind scholar *Deliverance** (US 19)

Don King, fight promoter *The Devil's*

Advocate (US 97)

Murray King, Long Island insurance salesman *Murray, King** (US 69)

Evel Knievel, motorcycle stuntman *Viva Knievel!** (US 77)

Edward J. Koch, mayor of New York in *The Muppets Take Manhattan* (US 84); Woody Allen's 'Oedipus Wrecks' segment of *New York Stories* (US 89)

Somchai Koonperm, village chief *Kamnan Poh** (Thai 80)

Christian Lacroix, fashion designer *Ready to Wear: Prêt-à-Porter* (US 94)

Jim Laker, cricketer *The Final Test* (GB 53)

Fritz Lang, film director (played by Marcel Hillaire in *Take the Money and Run* (US 69)); *Contempt* (Fr 64)

Nikki Lauda, motor-racing driver *Speed Fever* (It 78)

Henry Lawson, Australian poet *While the Billy Boils* (Aus 21)

Dr Timothy Leary, guru of LSD *Cheech and Chong's Nice Dreams* (US 81); *Fatal Skies* (US 90); *Cultivating Charlie* (US 94)

Spike Lee, black director 'with attitude' *Drop Squad* (US 94)

Stan Lee, cartoonist, creator of Spider-Man and the Incredible Hulk *The Ambulance* (US 91)

Suzanne Lenglen, Wimbledon tennis champion *Things Are Looking Up* (GB 35)

Oscar Levant, composer *Rhapsody in Blue* (US 45)

Bernard Levin, journalist *Nothing But the Best* (GB 63)

Prinz Eduard von und zu Liechtenstein, of the Royal House of Liechtenstein *Johann Strauss an der schönen blauen Donau* (Aut 13)

Sir Thomas Lipton, millionaire grocer and yachtsman *The Lipton Cup* (US 13)

Lord Litchfield, photographer *Mad Dogs and Englishmen* (GB 95)

Chief Lomoiro, Masai tribal leader *Visit to a Chief's Son* (US 74)

Captain James Lovell, astronaut *The Man Who Fell to Earth* (GB 76)

Joan Lowell, yachtswoman *Adventure Girl** (US 34)

Paul and Linda McCartney, ex-Beatle and photographer wife *Give My Regards to Broad Street* (GB 84); Paul only in *Eat the Rich* (GB 87)

Windsor McCay, cartoonist (*Little Nemo*, etc) and pioneer film animator *The Great White Way* (US 24)

Jem Mace, boxer *There's Life in the Old Dog Yet* (GB 08)

John McEnroe, tennis champion *Players* (US 79)

George McGovern, US senator *The Candidate* (US 72)

Marshall McLuhan, Canadian academic, expert on media and communications *Annie Hall* (US 77)

George McManus, cartoonist (*Bringing Up Father*) *The Great White Way* (US 24)

Leonard Maltin, film critic *Gremlins 2: The New Batch* (US 90)

Alice Marble, tennis champion *Pat and Mike* (US 52)

Queen Mary *Women Who Win* (GB 19)

Dan Maskell, tennis commentator *Players* (US 79)

Bob Mathias, twice winner of Olympic decathlon *The Bob Mathias Story** (US 54)

Yehudi Menuhin, violinist *Stage Door Canteen* (US 43)

George Michael, pop singer *8 Seconds* (US 94)

Cliff Michelmore, TV personality *A Jolly Bad Fellow* (GB 63)

Freddie Mills, boxer *6.5 Special* (GB 58)

Leslie Mitchell, Britain's first TV announcer (1936) and Movietone commentator *Geneviève* (GB 53)

Jim Mollison, aviator who made first east–west crossing of N. Atlantic *Dual Control* (GB 32)

Montana, fashion designer *Ready to Wear: Prêt-à-Porter* (US 94)

Gussie Moran, tennis champion *Pat and Mike* (US 52)

Stirling Moss, motor-racing driver *The Beauty Contest* (GB 64)

Malcolm Muggeridge, journalist and pundit *I'm All Right Jack* (GB 59); *Heavens Above* (GB 63); *Herostratus* (GB 67); *The Naked Bunyip* (Aus 70)

Audie Murphy, most decorated US Soldier of World War II and subsequently professional actor *To Hell and Back** (US 55)

Pete Murray, disc jockey *6.5 Special* (GB 58)

Albert Namatjira, Aboriginal artist *The Phantom Stockman* (Aus 53)

Ilie Nastase, Romanian tennis champion *Players* (US 79)

Bess Nielsen, Parisian girl given to amorous adventures *On n'est pas sérieux quand on a 17 ans** (Fr 74)

William J. Obariheim, 'Officer Obie', policeman who arrested Arlo Guthrie for casting litter *Alice's Restaurant* (US 69)

Dan O'Brien, San Francisco chief of police *Poison* (US 24)

Barney Oldfield, motor-racing driver *Barney Oldfield's Race for Life* (US 16)

Tip O'Neil, speaker of the House of Representatives *Dave* (US 93)

Ignace Paderewski, pianist, Prime Minister and later President of Poland *Moonlight Sonata* (GB 37)

Camille Paglia, feminist motormouth *It's Pat* (US 94); *The Watermelon Man* (US 97)

Arnold Palmer, golfer *Call Me Bwana* (GB 63)

Emmeline Pankhurst, suffragette leader *Eighty Million Women Want—?* (US 13)

Huang Pao-Mei, girl spinner in China's Cotton Mill No 17 *Huang Pao-mei** (Chn 58)

Michael Parkinson, TV personality *Madhouse* (GB 74)

Louella Parsons, movie gossip columnist *Hollywood Hotel* (US 37); *Stagedoor Canteen* (US 43)

Nicholas Parsons, TV personality *Mr Jolly Lives Next Door* (GB 87)

Princess Patricia *Women Who Win* (GB 19)

Floyd Patterson, boxing champion *Terrible Joe Moran* (US 84, TVM)

Lieutenant Harold R. Peat *Private Peat** (US 18)

Betty Ting Pei, Bruce Lee's lover *Bruce Lee and I** (HK 76)

Pelé, Brazilian soccer player *Young Giants* (US 83)

Shimon Peres, Prime Minister of Israel *Special Counsel* (US/Isr 88)

Marshal Pétain, French commander-in-chief World War I, Head of Vichy Government World War II *Verdun, Visions d'Histoire* (Fr 28)

Pablo Picasso, artist *La Vie commence*

NON-ACTORS PLAYING THEMSELVES IN FILMS continued

demain (Fr 52); Le Testament d'Orphée (Fr 60)

Wiley Post, first aviator to circumnavigate world solo Air Hawks (US 35)

Sally Potter, director (also directed) The Tango Lesson (GB/Fr/Arg/Jap/Ger 97)

André Previn, conductor Pepe (US 60)

Luis Procuna, matador Torero!* (Mex 56)

Yizhak Rabin, Prime Minister of Israel Operation Thunderbolt (Isr 77); Special Counsel (US/Isr 88)

Dame Marie Rambert, founder of the Ballet Rambert The Red Shoes (GB 48)

Paul Raymond, eroticist Erotica (GB 81)

Jean Renoir, film director The Christian Licorice Store (US 71)

Carlos Reutemann, motor-racing driver Speed Fever (It 78)

Robert Ripley, originator of Believe It or Not, The Great White Way (US 24)

Charlie Rivel, circus clown Scö-ö-ön* (Ger 43)

Jackie Robinson, first black to play major league baseball The Jackie Robinson Story* (US 50)

Sugar Ray Robinson, boxer Paper Lion (US 68)

Richard Rodgers, composer Main Street to Broadway (US 53)

Franklin Delano Roosevelt, Assistant Secretary to the Navy, later President The Battle Cry of Peace (US 15)

Theodore Roosevelt, ex-President of the USA Womanhood, The Glory of a Nation (US 17)

Jonathan Ross, TV presenter The Tall Guy (GB 89)

Lady 'Bubbles' Rothermere, society hostess The Stud (GB 78)

Damon Runyon, writer The Great White Way (US 24); O, Baby (US 26); Madison Square Garden (US 32)

Bertrand Russell, philosopher and pacifist Aman (India 67)

'Babe' Ruth, baseball player Speedy (US 28); Pride of the Yankees (US 42)

Gunther Sachs, millionaire industrialist and playboy Cadillac (FRG 94)

Col. Harlan T. Sanders of Kentucky Fried Chicken fame The Big Mouth (US 67); Hell's Bloody Devils (US 69)

Margaret Sanger, birth-control pioneer Birth Control (US 17)

Jean-Paul Sartre, philosopher La Vie commence demain (Fr 52)

Ronnie Scott, jazz club proprietor Doggin' Around (GB 94, TVM)

Charles E. Sebastian, ex-mayor of Los Angeles The Downfall of a Mayor* (US 17)

Mlle Segree, lover of Landru, murderer of 11 women Landru (Ger 23)

Caporal Sellier, bugler who sounded the World War I armistice, re-enacted scene in The Soul of France (Fr 28)

Mack Sennet, founder of the Keystone Kops

Hollywood Cavalcade (US 39)

Ma Sha, reformed pimp and killer The First Error Step* (Sin 79)

Dick Shafer, Playgirl Man of the Year later revealed to be gay Man of the Year* (US 95)

Alan Shearer, footballer The Match (GB 99); Purely Belter (GB 00)

Barry Sheene, world motorcycling champion, and his girlfriend Stephanie McLean Space Riders (GB 83)

William Shirer, historian The Magic Face (US 51)

Maria Shriver, Mrs Arnold Schwarzenegger Last Action Hero (US 93)

O. J. Simpson, football player The Klansman (US 74)

George R. Sims, crusading journalist gaoled in celebrated 1885 Maiden Tribute of Modern Babylon case The Martyrdom of Adolf Beck (GB 09)

Alfred E. Smith, Governor of New York (and first politician to appear on TV, 1928) The Volcano (US 19)

Sir Charles Kingsford Smith, Australian aviator Splendid Fellows (Aus 34)

Kate Smith, singer Hello Everybody* (US 33) (fictionalised biopic)

Susan Sontag, writer Zelig (US 83)

Mickey Spillane, thriller writer Ring of Fear (US 54)

Jerry Springer, TV shock-jock Austin Powers: The Spy Who Shagged Me (US 99)

Ringo Starr, ex-Beatle Give My Regards to Broad Street (GB 84)

Isobel Lillian Steele, American victim of Gestapo Captive of Nazi Germany* (US 36)

Howard Stern, radio shock-jock Private Parts* (US 97)

Oliver Stone, director Dave (US 93)

Charles Stragusa, narcotics agent who led ten-year quest to nail mobster Lucky Luciano Re: Lucky Luciano* (It/Fr 73)

Preston Sturges, film director Star Spangled Rhythm (US 42)

Anne Sullivan, who taught blind deaf-mute Helen Keller to speak and read Deliverance (US 19)

Ed Sullivan, TV personality The Patsy (US 64)

William Sulzer, impeached Governor of New York The Shame of the Empire State* (US 13)

Hannen Swaffer, journalist Spellbound (GB 41)

Fuji Takeshi, world junior welterweight boxing champion Fuji Takeshi Monogatari* (Jap 68)

Yukio Tani, martial arts exponent Ju-Jitsu to the Rescue (GB 13)

Alderman C. E. Tatham, mayor of Blackpool Sing As We Go (GB 34)

A. J. P. Taylor, historian Rockets Galore (GB 58)

Evelyn Nesbitt Thaw, beauty whose husband

murdered her lover, architect Stanford White (played by Joan Collins in The Girl in the Red Velvet Swing (US 55) and by Elizabeth McGovern in Ragtime (US 81)) The Great Thaw Trial (US 07); Redemption (US 17)

William 'Big Bill' Thompson, mayor of Chicago Is Your Daughter Safe? (US 27)

William Tilghman, marshal of Cache, Oklahoma (played by Rod Steiger in Cattle Annie and Little Britches (US 80); by Sam Elliott in biopic You Know My Name (US 99)) The Bank Robbery (US 08); Passing of the Oklahoma Outlaw (US 15).

Sir Frederick Treves, surgeon (played by Anthony Hopkins in The Elephant Man (GB 80)) The Great Love (US 18)

Lee Trevino, golfer Happy Gilmore (US 96)

Donald Trump, tycoon Another You (US 91); Across the Sea of Time (US 95)

Ivana Trump, ex-wife of Donald The First Wives Club (US 96)

Mark Twain, humorous writer A Curious Dream (US 07)

John van Druten, playwright Main Street to Broadway (US 53)

Princess Victoria Women Who Win (GB 19)

King Vidor, film director It's a Great Feeling (US 49)

Guillermo Vilas, tennis player Players (US 79)

Lech Walesa, founder of Solidarity, President of Poland Man of Iron (Pol 81)

Jimmy Walker, mayor of New York Glorifying the American Girl (US 29)

Raoul Walsh, film director It's a Great Feeling (US 49)

Cyril Washbrook, cricketer The Final Test (GB 53)

Alan Whicker, TV commentator The Angry Silence (GB 60); Whatever Happened to Harold Smith (GB 00)

Gough Whitlam, Prime Minister of Australia Barry McKenzie Holds His Own (Aus 74)

Frank Wills, Watergate security guard who discovered break-in All the President's Men (US 76)

Woodrow Wilson, President of the USA The Adventures of a Boy Scout (US 15)

Walter Winchell, influential American columnist (played by Lew Ayres in Okay America! (US 32)) Wake Up and Live (US 37); Love and Hisses (US 37); The Helen Morgan Story (US 57); College Confidential (US 60); Wild in the Streets (US 68)

Godfrey Winn, journalist Very Important Person (GB 61); Billy Liar! (GB 63)

Yo Yo Ma, cellist Sarabande* (Can 97)

Maharishi Narish Yogi, guru Candy (It/Fr 68)

Sam Yorty, mayor of Los Angeles The Candidate (US 72)

Jimmy Young, broadcaster Otley (GB 68)

Florenz Ziegfeld, impresario Glorifying the American Girl (US 29)

Adolf Zukor, film producer Glorifying the American Girl (US 29)

---

from Cuba. On one of the Bond movies, the bill for 007's cigars came to £3176.50. Audrey Hepburn also knew how to wipe the thin-lipped smile from producers' faces. Before agreeing to star in Sidney Sheldon's Bloodline (US/FRG 83), she imposed a condition that all her costumes were to be designed by Paris couturier Givenchy; and furthermore that, when filming was completed, she

would be given the $100,000 wardrobe.

Cricket fanatic Trevor Howard had a clause in his contracts relieving him of having to be on set during Test Matches, while Peter Sellers stipulated that he was to have accommodation which allowed his bed to be positioned east–west—any other way and he could not sleep. Personal vanity also has its part to (continued p. 96)

NON-ACTORS PLAYING OTHER PEOPLE IN FILMS

See also Non-Actors Playing Themselves.
* lead role

Horacio Accavallo, world flyweight boxing champion, lead in *Destino para dos* (Arg 67)

Muhammed Ali, world heavyweight boxing champion, as young fighter in *Requiem for a Heavyweight* (US 62); as Gideon Jackson, first black US senator, in *Freedom Road* (US 79, TVM)

Martin Amis, novelist, as John Thornton, child captured by pirates in *A High Wind in Jamaica* (GB 65)

Ossie Ardiles, soccer star, as p.o.w. in *Escape to Victory* (US 79)

Joe Barbera, animator, creator with Bill Hanna of *The Flintstones* TV cartoon series, as nightclub patron in *The Flintstones* (US 94)

Sydney Biddle Barrows, NY socialite who ran high-class call-girl ring, as Peggy Eaton in biopic of Barrows (Candice Bergen) *Mayflower Madam* (US 87, TVM)

Max Baer, boxer, in *The Prizefighter and the Lady* (US 33)

Paula Barbieri, the 'other woman' in the O. J. Simpson case, as abused girlfriend of drug lord in *The Dangerous* (US 94, TVM)

Mrs Morgan Belmont, society leader and member of New York's '400', played the upper crust Diana Tremont in *Way Down East* (US 20)

Peter Benchley, author of Jaws, played a reporter in *Jaws* (US 75)

Alan Bennett, playwright, author of play *The Madness of George III* and screenwriter of *The Madness of King George*, as backbench MP in *The Madness of King George* (US/GB 94)

Godfrey Binaisa, President of Uganda, bit parts in *King Solomon's Mines* (US 50) and *The African Queen* (GB 51)

Ben Bradlee, editor of *Washington Post* (played by Jason Robards in *All The President's Men* (US 81); by Henderson Forsythe in *Chances Are* (US 89)), as Senator Duffee in *Born Yesterday* (US 93).

Bricktop, black night club proprietor famous in café society, as mother figure in *Honeybaby, Honeybaby* (US 74)

RSM Ronald Brittain, Regimental Sergeant Major at Sandhurst Military Academy during 1950s, appeared (usually as a Sergeant Major) in *Carrington VC* (GB 54), *The Missing Note* (GB 61), *The Amorous Prawn* (GB 62), *Joey Boy* (GB 65) and *The Spy with a Cold Nose* (GB 66)

Dr Joyce Brothers, sexologist, in *Burnin'*

Love US 87); as baseball announcer in *The Naked Gun* (US 89); as tag team member in *Spy Hard* (US 96)

Erin Brokovich, working-class legal activist (played by Julia Roberts in film), as coffee-shop waitress in *Erin Brokovich* (US 00)

Joe Bugner, heavyweight boxing champion, as forest ranger in *Sher Mountains Killing Mystery* (Aus 90)

William Burroughs, sex writer, as a mafia don in *It Don't Pay to be an Honest Citizen* (US 85); as defrocked junkie priest in *Drugstore Cowboy* (US 89); also in *Wax, or the Discovery of Television Amongst the Bees* (US 92)

Chief Buthelesi, leader of the Zulu Inkatha movement, as Zulu leader Cetewayo (his great-grandfather) in *Zulu* (GB 64)

Shakira Caine, Guyanese wife of Michael Caine, as tribal princess Roxanne in *The Man Who Would Be King* (US 75)

Maria Callas, opera diva, in non-singing title role of *Medea** (It/Fr/FRG 70)

Naomi Campbell, supermodel and 'novelist' as cheese shopper in *The Night We Never Met* (US 93); as heroine's supportive friend in *Invasion of Privacy* (US 96)

Eric Cantona, footballer-philosopher, as rugby player in *Le Bonheur est dans le pré* (Fr 95); as Lionel in *Happiness in the Field* (Ger 95) as French ambassador in *Elizabeth* (GB 98); as boxer Joe Sardi in *Les Enfants du Marais* (Fr 99); in lead as boxer Antoine Capella in *Mookie** (Fr 99).

Truman Capote, author, leading role in detective fiction parody *Murder by Death** (US 76)

Primo Carnera, boxer, as boxer in *The Prizefighter and the Lady* (US 33); as Pyrhon Macklin in *A Kid for Two Farthings* (GB 55); as Corfa in *Casanova's Big Night* (US 54)

Georges Carpentier, boxer, as hero in *Toboggan** (Fr 34)

Viscount Castlerosse, bon viveur, as the man in the bath chair in *Kipps* (GB 41)

Fidel Castro, dictator, bit player in *Holiday in Mexico* (US 46)

Juan Chacon, trade union leader, as Mexican strike leader in *Salt of the Earth* (US 54)

Ray Charles, blind pianist, as bus driver in *Spy Hard* (US 96)

Henri Charriere, Devil's Island escapee 'Papillon' (played by Steve McQueen in *Papillon* (US 73)), as ageing gangster Marcou in *Popsy Pop** (Fr 70)

G. K. Chesterton, author, in *Rosy Rapture— The Pride of the Beauty Chorus* (GB 14)

Michael Chow, restaurateur, as underworld boss Fong Wei Tan in *Hammett* (US 82)

Roger Clinton, brother of Bill, as Agent Clinton in *Spy Hard* (US 96)

Daniel Cohn-Bendit, revolutionary, in Godard's *Vent d'est* (FRG/It 70); as friend of heroine who bemoans his resemblance to Daniel Cohn-Bendit in *Un Amour à Paris* (Fr 87)

Jackie Collins, best-selling novelist, sister of Joan, as teenager June in *All at Sea* (GB 57)

Henry Cooper, boxer, as prizefighter John Gully in *Royal Flash* (GB 75)

Carmine Coppola, composer, as man in the lift in Francis Coppola's *One From the Heart* (US 82); as street musician in *New York Stories* (US 89)

James John Corbett, heavyweight boxing champion of the world, as 'Gentleman Jim' (lead) in *The Man from the Golden West** (US 13); as Raffles in *The Burglar and the Lady** (US 14); as pugilist Kid Garvey in *The Other Girl* (US 16); also in *The Midnight Man* (US 19)

Gregory Corso, American beat poet, as 'unruly stockholder' in *The Godfather III* (US 90)

Quentin Crisp, 'one of the stately homos of England' (played by John Hurt in *The Naked Civil Servant* (GB 75, TVM)) as Polonius in *Hamlet* (GB 76); as Dr Zaklus in *The Bride* (GB 85); as partygoer in *Fatal Attraction* (US 87); as Queen Elizabeth in *Orlando* (GB 93)

Fred Demara, imposter (played by Tony Curtis in *The Great Imposter* (US 60)) as imposter impersonating actor impersonating doctor in *The Hypnotic Eye* (US 59)

Jack Dempsey, world heavy weight boxing champion, as boxer in *The Prizefighter and the Lady* (US 33)

Lt Col Hugh Dickens, CO 9th/12th Royal Lancers, as Nazi officer in *Indiana Jones and the Last Crusade* (US 89)

E. L. Doctorow, author of *Ragtime* etc, as advisor to President Cleveland in *Buffalo Bill and the Indians* (US 76)

Steve Donaghue, champion jockey, as Steve Baxter, hero of *Riding for a King* (GB 26), *Beating the Book** (GB 26), *The Golden Spurs** (GB 26) and *The Stolen Favourite** (GB 26)

Dmitri Dostoevsky, St

Spotting the ball in Escape to Victory *(US 79) were soccer stars Ossie Ardiles (far left), Bobby Moore (third from left) and Pelé (fourth from left), portraying prisoners-of-war chosen to play against the German team in a propaganda match rigged by the Nazis. (Kobal Collection)*

NON-ACTORS PLAYING OTHER PEOPLE IN FILMS continued

Petersburg tram-driver, great grandson of Fyodor Dostoevsky, in *Possessed* (USSR 90), based on Dostoevsky's *The Brothers Karamazov*

Terry Downes, boxer, as Chunky in Sherlock Holmes movie *A Study in Terror* (GB 65)

Bob Dylan, rock musician, as Alias in *Pat Garrett and Billy the Kid* (US 73); as avant-garde artist who uses buzz-saw as brush in *Catchfire* (US 90)

Gertrude Ederle, first woman to swim the English Channel, in *Swim, Girl, Swim** (US 28)

Princess Elizabeth of Toro, as the Shaman in *Sheena—Queen of the Jungle* (US 84)

Daniel Farson, Soho icon, as anonymous Colony Room habitué—he himself played in same scenes by Adrian Scarborough—in Francis Bacon biopic *Love Is The Devil* (GB 97)

Mohamed Fayed, proprietor of Harrods, as Harrods doorman in *Mad Cows* (GB 99)

Larry Flynt, publisher of *Hustler* (played by Woody Harrelson), as judge in *The People vs Larry Flynt* (US 96)

'Mad' Frankie Fraser, gangster given to torturing geezers who step out of line, as gang boss Pops Den in *Hard Men* (GB/Fr 96)

David Frost, television commentator, as reporter in *The VIPs* (GB 63)

Princess Ira von Furstenberg as femme lead Arabella in *Matchless** (It 67)

Jim Garrison, DA who investigated Kennedy assassination, as Earl Warren, president of the Warren Commission (Garrison played by Kevin Costner) in *JFK* (US 92)

Paul Getty III, grandson of oil tycoon, as film scriptwriter Dennis in *The State of Things* (US/Por 82)

Althea Gibson, black tennis star, as maid in John Ford's *The Horse Soldiers* (US 59)

Allen Ginsberg, poet, as a lawyer in *It Don't Pay to be an Honest Citizen* (US 85)

Menahem Golan, film producer, as mobster Hymie Weinstock in *Hit the Dutchman* (US/Rus 92)

Jerry Goldsmith, film composer (*Rambo, Gremlins*) as patron in ice-cream parlour in *Gremlins 2: The New Batch* (US 90)

Robert Graves, poet and novelist, as partygoer in *Deadfall* (GB 68)

Graham Greene, author, as the insurance representative in *Day for Night* (Fr 73)

Germaine Greer, women's liberationist, as Clara Bowden in *Universal Soldier* (GB 71)

Arlo Guthrie, '60s icon, as Harvey in *Roadside Prophets* (US 92)

Jerry Hall, statuesque model and former Mrs Mick Jagger, in *Running Out of Luck* (US 85); *Topo Galileo* (It 88); and as Lady Motley in *Princess Caraboo* (US 94)

Tonya Harding, banned ice-skating star, as waitress who winds up with stash of Mafia money in *Breakaway* (US 94)

Lorenz Hart, of Rodgers and Hart, played the bank teller in *Hallelujah, I'm a Bum* (US 33)

Len Harvey, British boxing champion, played a glass collector turned boxer in *Excuse My Glove* (GB 36)

Patty Hearst, kidnap victim (played by Natasha Richardson in *Patty Hearst* (US/GB 88)) as upper-crust mother in *Cry Baby* (US 90); in *Serial Mom* (US 94);

Pecker (US 98); as mother of kidnapper in *Cecil B. Demented* (US 00)

Hugh Hefner, founder of *Playboy* empire (played by Cliff Robertson in *Star 80* (US 83)) as pipe-smoking ancient Roman in *History of the World—Part I* (US 81)

Ernest Hemingway, author, uncredited bit part in *The Old Man and the Sea* (US 58)

Al Hill, mobster, as Repulsive Rogan in *The Bank Dick* (US 40)

Xaviera Hollander, prostitute and writer, lead in *My Pleasure is My Business** (Can 74)

Whitney Houston, singer, as singer-turned-actress Rachel Marron in *The Bodyguard* (US 92)

Christopher Isherwood, novelist, as partygoer in *Rich and Famous* (US 81)

Bianca Jagger, jet-setter, leads in *Flesh Colour** (US 79) and *The Great American Success Company** (US 79)

Clive James, Australian pundit, as most drunken of Bazza's mates in *Barry McKenzie Holds His Own* (Aus 77)

James Jones, novelist, as a poker player in *The Marseilles Contract* (GB/Fr 74)

Vinnie Jones, bad-boy footballer, as gangster's bagman Big Chris in *Lock, Stock and Two Smoking Barrels* (GB 98); as Bullet Tooth Tony in *Snatch* (US/GB 00)

Thomas Keneally, Australian novelist, as Father Marshall in *The Devil's Playground* (Aus 76)

Jomo Kenyatta, President of Kenya 1963–78, played an African chief in *Sanders of the River* (GB 35)

Lord Kilbracken, peer of the realm, as merchant seaman in *Moby Dick* (US 55)

Stephen King, bestselling novelist, as farmer beset by cosmic grass in *Creepshow* (US 83); as minister at funeral in *Pet Sematary* (US 89)

Jerzy Kosinsky, controversial Polish-American novelist, as Bolshevik revolutionary Zinoviev in *Reds* (US 81)

Ronnie Kray, East End gangster (played by Gary Kemp in *The Krays* (GB 90)), as boy-in-flat-cap in *The Magic Box* (GB 51)

Jake LaMotta, prizefighter (played by Robert De Niro in *Raging Bull* (US 80)); as rebel Julio in *Rebellion in Cuba* (US 61); as army deserter Joe Shenken in *House in Naples* (US 70)

Dr Emmanuel Lasker, world chess champion, played Napoleon's chess partner in Lupu Pick's *Napoléon a Sainte-Hélène* (Fr 29)

Lady Sandra Hotz Lean, wife of David Lean, as Mrs Fielding (wife of James Fox character) in *A Passage to India* (GB 84)

Dr Timothy Leary, proponent of hallucinogenic drugs, as TV evangelist in *Shocker* (US 89); as diner at 'The Nouveau Woodstock' in *Rude Awakening* (US 90); as Salvadore in *Roadside Prophets* (US 92); as Sims in *Conceiving Ada* (GB 97)

John Lindsay, mayor of New York, played Senator Donnovan in *Rosebud* (US 75)

Joe Louis, boxer, played lead as young fighter in all-black *Spirit of Youth** (US 38)

Victor Lowndes, chairman of *Playboy* UK, as Reeve Passmore in *Fledglings* (GB 65)

Patrick McCabe, novelist, author of *The Butcher Boy*, as drunken Jimmy the Skite in *The Butcher Boy* (US/Ire 98)

John McAllister, Sinn Fein activist, as Sinn Fein activist in *Hidden Agenda* (GB 90)

Tom McCall, Governor of Oregon, as news commentator in *One Flew Over the Cuckoo's Nest* (US 75)

Compton MacKenzie, author, as Capt Buncher in film of his own novel *Whisky Galore!* (GB 49); as Sir Robert Dysart in *Chance of a Lifetime* (GB 50)

Norman Mailer, writer, as 'The Prince' in *Wild 90* (US 68); as Lt Francis Xavier Pope of NY police in *Beyond the Law* (US 68); as film director and presidential candidate 'Kingsley' in *Maidstone* (US 70); as New York architect Stanford White (murdered in celebrated turn-of-century crime of passion) in *Ragtime* (US 81); as Lear (in opening scenes—Burgess Meredith then takes over) in *King Lear* (US/Swz 87); as Harry Houdini in *Cremaster 2* (US 99) based on his book *The Executioner's Song*.

Duke of Marlborough as cavalry officer in *Hamlet* (US/GB 97)

Yehudi Menuhin, violinist, in *The Magic Bow* (GB 46)

Freddie Mills, British champion boxer, in *Emergency Call* (GB 52), *Kill Me Tomorrow* (GB 55), *Fun at St Fanny's* (GB 56), *Breakaway* (GB 56), *Chain of Events* (GB 58), *Carry on Constable* (GB 60), *Carry on Regardless* (GB 61), *The Comedy Man* (GB 63), *Saturday Night Out* (GB 64)

Joan Miró, Spanish painter, played the museum curator in *El Umbracle* (Sp 73)

Lt-Cdr Ewen Montagu, Naval Intelligence officer who devised the 'Man who never was' deception prior to invasion of Sicily (played by Clifton Webb in the film), as RAF Intelligence officer in *The Man Who Never Was* (GB 55)

Bobby Moore, soccer star, as p.o.w. in *Escape to Victory* (US 79)

Stirling Moss, motor-racing driver, in *Casino Royale* (GB 67)

Benito Mussolini, Italian dictator, extra in *The Eternal City* (US 14)

Andrew Neil, journo, as newsreader in *Parting Shots* (GB 99)

Beverly Nichols, author, as the Hon. Richard Wells in *Glamour* (GB 31)

Mrs Richard Nixon, wife of ex-President Nixon, walk-on parts in *Becky Sharp* (US 36) and *Small Town Girl* (US 37)

Duke of Northumberland, proprietor of Hotspur Films (named after ancestor Henry 'Hotspur' Percy), as kidnapped tourist in *Lost in Africa* (GB 93)

HRH Nana Agyefi Kwame II de Nsein, as the mad King Bossa Ahadee in *Cobra Verde* (FRG 88)

John O'Hara, novelist, as a reporter on a train in *The General Died at Dawn* (US 36)

Charley Paddock, US Olympic athlete (played by Dennis Christopher in Chariots of Fire (GB 81)), as hero in *The Olympic Hero** (US 28)

Tara Palmer-Tomkinson, It girl, as partygoer in *An Ideal Husband* (GB 99); as girl ejected from nightclub in *Mad Cows* (GB 99)

Princess Pearl, daughter of White Rajah of Sarawak, as Princess Paula in Ruritanian romance *Everything is Rhythm* (GB 36)

Pelé, Brazilian football star, as p.o.w. in *Escape to Victory* (US 79); as soccer hero in *Hotshot* (US 87); *Solidão* (Br 89)

NON-ACTORS PLAYING OTHER PEOPLE IN FILMS continued

Paloma Picasso, daughter of Pablo, as Countess Bathory, she who bathed in the blood of virgins, in *Immoral Tales* (US 74)

Harold Pinter, playwright, as 'society man' in *The Servant* (GB 63); as lawyer Saul Abrahams in *Rogue Male* (GB 76); as bookshop customer in *Turtle Diary* (GB 85); as Sir Thomas Bertram in *Mansfield Park* (US/GB 99)

Nosher Powell, minder, in lead role as Home Secretary in *Eat the Rich** (GB 87)

Kukrit Pramoj, Prime Minister of Thailand (1974), as Prime Minister of the fictitious state of 'Sarkhan' in *The Ugly American* (US 62)

Rex Reed, film critic, as Myron Breckenridge in *Myra Breckenridge* (US 70)

Erich Maria Remarque, author of *All Quiet on the Western Front*, as the schoolmaster Pohlmann in the film of his novel *A Time to Love and a Time to Die* (US 58)

David Robinson, film critic of *The Times*, in *If* (GB 60); *Fragments of Life* (Hun 70); *Britannia Hospital* (GB 81); and as 1930s drama critic of *The Times* in *Mephisto* (Hun 81)

Sugar Ray Robinson, boxer, as Zero in *Candy* (It/Fr 68)

Babe Ruth, baseball player (played by William Bendix in *The Babe Ruth Story* (US 48)), as hero in *Headin' Home** (US 20); as ball player Babe Dugan in *The Babe Comes Home** (US 27)

Pierre Salinger, John F. Kennedy's Press Secretary, as poker player in *The Marseilles Connection* (GB/Fr 73)

Max Schmeling, boxer, as hero Max Breuer, playing opposite wife Anny Ondra, in *Knockout** (Ger 36)

Martin Scorsese, film director, as the director of the Metropolitan Opera House in *Pavlova—A Woman for All Time* (GB/USSR 83)

Erich Segal, author of *Love Story*, as Kleinberg in *Sans Mobile Apparent* (Fr 71)

Rev. Al Sharpton, rabble-rousing black pastor, as streetwise impresario in *Malcolm X* (US 92)

George Bernard Shaw, playwright, in *Rosy Rapture—The Pride of the Beauty Chorus* (GB 14)

Jean Shrimpton, model, leading lady in *Privilege** (GB 67)

Prince Sihanuk of Cambodia, ruler, in lead role opposite his wife in *Sunset** (Cambodia 64)

Wayne Sleep, ballet dancer, as the dancing master in *Elizabeth* (GB 98)

Jean Kennedy Smith, US Ambassador to Ireland, as IRA supporter (appropriately) in *Michael Collins* (US/Ire 96)

Ex-Empress Soraya in triple role as herself, Linda and Mrs Melville in *I Tre Volti** (It 65)

Earl Spencer, brother of Princess Diana, as public schoolboy in *Another Country* (GB 84)

Steven Spielberg, producer/director, as Cook County Clerk in *The Blues Brothers* (US 80)

Mickey Spillane, detective novelist, as straw-chewing sleuth in *Ring of Fear* (US 54); as his own creation Mike Hammer in *The Girl Hunters** (US 63)

Jacqueline Susann, novelist (played by Bette Midler in *Isn't She Great* (US/Ger/GB/Jap 99), as reporter in film of her own book *Valley of the Dolls* (US 67)

Dame Joan Sutherland, opera diva, as Mum in *On Our Selection* (Aus 95)

Leslie 'Squizzy' Taylor, Melbourne gangster gunned down in 1927, in race-track drama *Bound to Win* (Aus 19)

Studs Terkel, writer, as sportswriter in *Eight Men Out* (US 88)

Jim Thorpe, Oklahoma Indian who was stripped of his Olympic Gold Medals (played by Burt Lancaster in *Jim Thorpe—All American* (US 51)), as Captain of the Guard in *She* (US 35); as prisoner in *White Heat* (US 49)

Bill Tilden, tennis champion, as Joles in *The Music Master* (US 27)

Daniel Topolski, Oxford rowing coach (played by Johan Leysen in film), as Boat Race umpire in *True Blue* (GB 96)

Baroness Maria von Trapp, postulant nun, governess and *lieder* singer (played by Julie Andrews in *The Sound of Music*), as extra in *The Sound of Music* (US 65)

Franz von Trauberg, first post-war Mayor of Berlin, as kidnapped ambassador in *Guernica* (It 72)

Leon Trotsky, revolutionary and founder of the Red Army, played a bit part as a nihilist in Vitagraph's spy drama *My Official Wife* (US 14) and also appeared in *The Battle Cry of Peace* (US 15)

Margaret Trudeau, estranged wife of Premier of Canada, Pierre Trudeau, starred in *The Guardian Angel** (Can 78) and *Kings and Desperate Men** (Can 79)

Dalton Trumbo, screenwriter blacklisted during UnAmerican Activities witchhunt, as prison commandant in *Papillon* (US 73) (his first screen role and his last script assignment)

Donald Trump, tycoon, as 'Mr Speculator' in *Ghosts Can't Do It* (US 89); as rich kid's tycoon father in *Little Rascals* (US 94)

Ivana Trump, socialite, ex-wife of above, as heroine in *Pantau** (Cz 70)

Gene Tunney, heavyweight boxing champion as Marine in *The Fighting Marine* (US 26)

Ted Turner, founder of CNN and husband of Jane Fonda, as Confederate officer in *Gettysburg* (US 93)

Mark Twain, novelist and commentator, in unidentified role in his own *The Prince and the Pauper* (US 09)

King Umberto II, King of Italy for one month in 1946, as extra in *The White Sister* (US 24)

Roger Vadim, film director, as partygoer in *Rich and Famous* (US 81)

Gore Vidal, polemicist, as bearded preacher in *Gore Vidal's Billy the Kid* (US 89); as Senator Brickley Paiste in *Bob Roberts* (US 92); as pompous Harvard professor Pitkannan in *With Honors* (US 94)

Meyer Weisgal, Israeli statesman, as David Ben-Gurion in *Exodus* (US 60)

Hugh Walpole, author, as the vicar in *David Copperfield* (US 35)

Senator John Warner, ex 'Mr Elizabeth Taylor', as a fisherman in *The Mirror Crack'd* (GB 81)

Judge Joseph N. Welch, presiding judge at the McCarthy hearings, played a judge in *Anatomy of a Murder* (US 59)

Bombardier Billy Wells, British boxing champion, starred as the pilot in *The Silver Lining** (GB 19) and played the hangman in *The Beggar's Opera* (GB 53)

White Man-Runs Him, last survivor of the Battle of the Little Big Horn (at which Gen. Custer's force was massacred in 1876), played in a Ken Maynard western *The Red Raiders* (US 27)

Gough Whitlam, Prime Minister of Australia, as 'man in nightclub' in *The Broken Melody* (Aus 38); see also under Non-actors who have played themselves

Oprah Winfrey, television presenter and talk-show hostess, as bossy housewife Sofia in *The Color Purple* (US 85)

Godfrey Winn, journalist, played an announcer in *The Bargee* (GB 64) and Truelove in *The Great St Trinian's Train Robbery* (GB 65)

Jersey Joe Walcott, boxer, as 'George' in *The Harder They Fall* (US 56)

Alexander Woolcott, writer and critic, as literary sophisticate Vanderveer Veyden in *The Scoundrel* (US 35)

Brig. Gen. Chuck Yeager, first pilot to break sound barrier and US astronaut, as Fred the barman in *The Right Stuff* (US 83). Yeager portrayed in same film by Sam Shepard—one of the rare instances of a name appearing on both sides of the cast list.

Yevgeny Yevtushenko, poet, played leading role as Russian space pioneer Konstantin Tsiolkovsky in *Take-Off** (USSR 79); also in *The Kindergarten* (USSR 85)

> Alfred Hitchcock, who held that actors should be treated like cattle, on the subject of those celebrated cameo roles in his own movies: 'I've always said to the cameraman, "Make it as short as you can, so I don't suffer the indignity of being an actor too long".'

play in deal making. Warren Beatty will not sign any contract that requires him to be filmed without his shirt, while Steve McQueen imposed a condition on his employers that he *had* to be filmed naked to the waist—he claimed that otherwise women would not pay to see his pictures. Sylvester Stallone will only be shot in profile from his good side, otherwise the deal's off.

The bottom line, though, is that superstar contracts are about money—lots of it. Michael Ovitz, then Hollywood's most powerful agent, secured a unique concession for Sean Connery when he negotiated terms for the Scottish star's appearance in *The Hunt for Red October* (US 90). He demanded extra money to compensate for the dollar's decline against the pound. 'I don't think the studio had heard the argument before,' Connery confided, 'but funnily enough they came round to my way of thinking.'

Black Actors

The first black performers to appear in a motion picture were Joe Rastus, Denny Tolliver and Walter Wilkins, who were filmed at Edison's 'Black Maria' studio in East Orange, NJ, on 6 October 1894, in a 'breakdown dance' routine. It was released as *The Pickaninnies* (US 94) and described in a later catalogue as 'A scene representing Southern plantation life before the war'. The three dancers were members of a troupe called Lucy Daly's Pickaninnies which had been appearing in George Lederer's revue *The Passing Show* at the Casino Theatre in New York.

The first black actor to play a leading role in a feature film was Sam Lucas, cast in the title role of *Uncle Tom's Cabin* (US 14).

The first black actor to make a career in films was Noble Johnson, who made his debut in a Lubin western in 1914 playing an Indian chief. After arriving in Hollywood in 1915, he graduated from stunt work and bit parts with the formation of the Lincoln Motion Picture Co., an all-black production company specialising in ghetto films, of which he was president as well as leading player. Johnson starred in three Lincoln productions—*The Realisation of a Negro's Ambition* (US 16), *The Trooper of Company K* (US 17) and *The Law of Nature* (US 18)—before leaving the company to concentrate on the Universal serials he had been making between Lincoln pictures. In 1932 he had the unusual distinction of becoming the only black actor to have played a white man in a straight role (others have in comedy roles) when he appeared as a Russian 'heavy' in Radio Pictures' *The Most Dangerous Game* (US 32).

The first black performer to be awarded a studio contract was six-year-old 'Sunshine Sammy' Morrison by Hal Roach in 1919. The original two-year contract was

Brock Peters played the black American who lived in the rooming house also inhabited by Leslie Caron and Tom Bell in The L-Shaped Room *(GB 62). The casting was notable for the fact that the character could equally have been played by a white actor.* (Kobal Collection)

Until well after World War II, Hollywood was notorious for depicting black Americans as menials or rolling-eyed, shuffling halfwits. Happily there was the occasional exception, as the celebrated novelist Sinclair Lewis testified when his much acclaimed *Arrowsmith* was brought to the screen by John Ford in 1931. 'The negro doctor in it, I think, is the first one of his kind on the screen who failed to come on as a quaint or curious character. I've met dozens in Trinidad and Barbados. I presented him honestly in my book. And the movie has miraculously presented him with the same honesty.' The role of Dr Tubbs was played by Claude King, who faded back into the obscurity from whence he came. Apart from the author, no one at the time commented on the fact that for a negro to be portrayed as a professional man of skill and resource was a remarkable breakthrough. It would be many years before it was repeated.

The subject of *Arrowsmith* was an epidemic of bubonic plague in the West Indies, so it was wholly appropriate that Dr Tubbs was black. More than 30 years later the appearance of US actor Brock Peters in Bryan Forbes' *The L Shaped Room* (GB 62) made a small but significant contribution to film history. In his role as an American musician living in the next room to Leslie Caron in a seedy rooming house in Notting Hill Gate, Peters was doing something which had never been done before by a black actor in a major motion picture—playing a part where the colour of his skin was irrelevant to the character or his place in the story. The role could have equally gone to any white American actor.

Thirty years later black and white roles had become interchangeable—sometimes. Most people who saw Eddie Murphy as Axel Foley in *Beverly Hills Cop* (US 84) and its sequels would have thought of the sassy, jiveass, streetwise displaced Detroit cop as quintessentially black. Not so, as far as producers Don Simpson and Jerry Buckheimer were concerned. They had originally tagged Sylvester Stallone for the part.

later renewed and over a five-year period Sunshine Sammy appeared in 114 Hal Roach Studios comedy shorts, including 28 of the *Our Gang* series in 1922–24. As an adult Morrison worked in vaudeville before leaving showbusiness for the aerospace industry.

Britain's first black screen actor was Bermuda-born Ernest Trimmingham, who made his debut in the British & Colonial production *Her Bachelor Guardian* (GB 12).

The first black actor to play a leading role in a British film was Paul Robeson as Bosambo in Alexander Korda's *Sanders of the River* (GB 35). He also starred in *Song of Freedom* (GB 37), *Big Fella* (GB 37), *King Solomon's Mines* (GB 37) and *Jericho* (GB 37).

Most Roles

The performer who played in the most movies made for general release was Tom London (1883–1963), who was born in Louisville, Ky., and made the first of his over 2000 appearances on screen in *The Great Train Robbery* (US 03). He was given the role of the locomotive driver, which was also his job in real life. By 1919 he was playing starring roles at Universal under his real name, Leonard

Tom London in the first of 2000 roles, playing the locomotive driver in The Great Train Robbery *(US 03). He had been a locomotive driver in real life.*

Clapham, which he changed to Tom London in 1924. When he became too old for lead roles he receded comfortably into character parts, specialising in sheriffs in 'B' westerns. His last picture was Willard Parker's *The Lone Texan* (US 59).

John C. Holmes (1944–88) claimed in 1985 to have appeared in 2274 mainly hardcore sex pictures. Of these, probably not more than 200 were features, the remainder being shorts, most of them made in the 1960s, known in the trade as 'porno loops'. Holmes admitted to being arrested 13 times during his career, usually for indecency. In 1981 he was tried and acquitted of a charge of bludgeoning to death four people in Laurel Canyon, but gaoled for contempt of court.

The performer who has played the most leading roles in feature films is the Indian comedienne Manorama, who made her screen debut in 1958 and completed her 1000th film in 1985. Of the total, 999 were in Tamil and one in Hindi (a language she does not speak). Manorama worked on as many as 30 films at the same time.

The Hollywood star who played the most leading roles in feature films was John Wayne (1907–79), who appeared in 153 movies from *The Drop Kick* (US 27) to *The Shootist* (US 76). In all except 11 of these films he played leading roles. The Duke summed up his simple yet enduring qualities thus: 'I've never had a goddam artistic problem in my life, never, and I've worked with the best of them. John Ford isn't exactly a bum, is he? Yet he never gave me any manure about art.' And: 'I play John Wayne in every part regardless of the character, and I've been doing okay, haven't I?'

The international star with the most screen credits who is still performing in movies is Christopher Lee (b. London 1922), star of English, French, Spanish, German, Dutch, Italian, Swedish, Norwegian, Russian, American, Canadian, Australian and Pakistani films. The 188 feature films and TVMs and two shorts he has played in from *Corridor of Mirrors* (GB 47) to *Lord of the Rings* (US/GB/NZ 01) include nine in which he recreated his most celebrated role, that of Count Dracula, and one in which he played HRH Prince Philip.

The busiest Hollywood actor of the 1990s was Samuel L. Jackson with 36 films. Whoopi Goldberg headed the actress list with 29.

The Most Popular Actors and Actresses

The earliest recorded popularity poll was conducted by a Russian fan magazine in 1911 and was headed by dapper French comedian Max Linder, followed by Denmark's tragic actress Asta Nielsen, with another Danish star, Valdemar Psilander, in third place. America's first poll was staged by *Motion Picture Story Magazine* in March 1912 and resulted in Maurice Costello being voted most popular male star and the now forgotten Dolores Cassinelli most popular actress. By 1914 Mary Pickford, 12th in the 1912 poll, had displaced her and for the next

> Gene Hackman recalls that he and Dustin Hoffman were voted by fellow students at the Playhouse Acting School in California as the members of their class 'least likely to succeed'.

ten years 'the girl with the golden curls', otherwise known as 'America's sweetheart', topped virtually every popularity poll held throughout the world, including those conducted in Soviet Russia (where her husband Douglas Fairbanks was voted most popular male star in 1925). The most durable star of talkies would appear to be John Wayne, who featured in the annual 'Ten Top Box Office Stars' Quigley Poll 25 times 1949–74 and headed it in 1950, 1951, 1954 and 1971.

The first popularity poll confined to British-born stars was conducted by *Pictures and the Picturegoer* in 1915 with the following results: 1 Alma Taylor; 2 Elizabeth Risdon; 3 Charles Chaplin; 4 Stewart Rome; 5 Chrissie White; 6 Fred Evans. Ten years later the *Daily News* poll showed Alma Taylor and Chrissie White, both of whom had joined the Hepworth Co. as child actresses in 1908, still firmly in the public favour: 1 Betty Balfour; 2 Alma Taylor; 3 Gladys Cooper; 4 Violet Hopson; 5 Matheson Lang; 6 Fay Compton; 7 Chrissie White; 8 Stewart Rome; 9 Owen Nares; 10 Ivor Novello.

During the 1930s America's box office was dominated by children, elderly ladies and gentlemen, and a mouse. Marie Dressler topped the Quigley Poll at age 63 in 1932 and again in 1933; Will Rogers came first aged 55 in 1934; then Shirley Temple rose to the top, aged seven, and remained there for the following three years, until 1939, when Mickey Rooney, 18 years old and playing a high school kid in the *Andy Hardy* series, took the lead and held first place for three years. Mickey Mouse was not eligible for the Quigley Poll, but he beat Emil Jannings by 400,000 votes as number-one star in a popularity contest held in Australia in 1931, and knocked Wallace Beery into second place in Japan in 1936.

Bridging this period and the John Wayne era were the Bing Crosby–Betty Grable years of the 1940s. Cumulative Quigley Poll results for the 1960s give the following hierarchy of the biggest box-office draws of the decade: 1 John Wayne; 2 Doris Day; 3 Cary Grant, Rock Hudson and Elizabeth Taylor; 6 Jack Lemmon; 7 Julie Andrews; 8 Paul Newman; 9 Sean Connery; 10 Elvis Presley. (Of course no such list is definitive. Sophia Loren, who never appeared in the annual Top Ten, was nevertheless voted the most popular star in the world by the US Foreign Press Corps in 1969.) The order for the 1970s: 1 Clint Eastwood; 2 Burt Reynolds; 3 Barbra Streisand; 4 Paul Newman; 5 Robert Redford; 6 Steve McQueen; 7 John Wayne; 8 Woody Allen; 9 Dustin Hoffman; 10 Sylvester Stallone. The order for the 1980s: 1 Clint Eastwood; 2 Eddie Murphy; 3 Burt Reynolds; 4 Tom Cruise; 5 Sylvester Stallone; 6 Harrison Ford; 7 Michael J. Fox, Paul Hogan; 9 Arnold Schwarzenegger; 10 Michael Douglas. Top woman star of the decade, despite rare appearances on screen and few successes, was Jane Fonda in 11th place.

The 1990s saw only three survivors from the previous decade, including the new number one: 1 Tom Cruise; 2 Mel Gibson; 3 Tom Hanks; 4 Julia Roberts; 5 Robin Williams; 6= Arnold Schwarzenegger and Harrison Ford; 8 Kevin Costner; 9 Jim Carrey; 10 Leonardo Di Caprio.

In the 1999 Quigley Poll, Julia Roberts became the first actress to be voted the biggest box-office draw since Julie Andrews in 1967. She joined a select company whose other members were Mary Pickford (1921, 1922), Norma Talmadge (1924), Colleen Moore (1926), Clara Bow (1928, 1929), Joan Crawford (1930), Janet Gaynor (1931), Marie Dressler (1932, 1933), Shirley Temple (1935, 1936, 1937, 1938), Betty Grable (1943), Doris Day (1960, 1962, 1963, 1964) and Elizabeth Taylor (1961).

The record for the most number-one spots in the Quigley Poll is jointly held by Clint Eastwood, Burt Reynolds and Bing Crosby, with five wins apiece. John Wayne made the most appearances in the Top 10 with 23, including four number-one spots.

The largest number of members of one family to have appeared in films is 31 in the case of the Luevas of Los Angeles. Matriarch Augustina Lueva (b. La Refugio, Mexico 1852), 18 of her 21 children and 12 of her grandchildren were reported to be actively employed as film actors in 1928. Six of the children and four of the grandchildren appeared together in an unidentified film of that year.

Other films in which families have appeared together are: *Hearts of the World* (US 18), in which Bobby Harron

QUIGLEY PUBLICATIONS POLL

The annual Quigley Poll is a poll of exhibitors to determine the top box-office draws. Listed below are the top male and the top female star for each year—the rating of whichever was not number one is given in brackets after the name. For example the (12) after Meryl Streep's name for 1983 signifies that, although she was rated most popular actress, eleven male stars scored higher popularity ratings in that year.

1915	William S. Hart Mary Pickford (2)	1936	Shirley Temple Clark Gable (2)	1957	Rock Hudson Kim Novak (11)	1979	Burt Reynolds Jane Fonda (3)
1916	William S. Hart Mary Pickford (2)	1937	Shirley Temple Clark Gable (2)	1958	Glenn Ford Elizabeth Taylor (2)	1980	Burt Reynolds Jane Fonda (4)
1917	Douglas Fairbanks Anita Stewart (3)	1938	Shirley Temple Clark Gable (2)	1959	Rock Hudson Doris Day (4)	1981	Burt Reynolds Dolly Parton (4)
1918	Douglas Fairbanks Mary Pickford (2)	1939	Mickey Rooney Shirley Temple (5)	1960	Doris Day Rock Hudson (2)	1982	Burt Reynolds Dolly Parton (6)
1919	Wallace Reid Mary Pickford (3)	1940	Mickey Rooney Bette Davis (9)	1961	Elizabeth Taylor Rock Hudson (2)	1983	Clint Eastwood Meryl Streep (12)
1920	Wallace Reid Marguerite Clark (2)	1941	Mickey Rooney Bette Davis (8)	1962	Doris Day Rock Hudson (2)	1984	Clint Eastwood Sally Field (5)
1921	Mary Pickford Douglas Fairbanks (2)	1942	Abbott & Costello Betty Grable (8)	1963	Doris Day John Wayne (2)	1985	Sylvester Stallone Meryl Streep (10)
1922	Mary Pickford Douglas Fairbanks (2)	1943	Betty Grable Bob Hope (2)	1964	Doris Day Jack Lemmon (2)	1986	Tom Cruise Bette Midler (5)
1923	Thomas Meighan Norma Talmadge (2)	1944	Bing Crosby Betty Grable (4)	1965	Sean Connery Doris Day (3)	1987	Eddie Murphy Glenn Close (7)
1924	Norma Talmadge Rudolph Valentino (3)	1945	Bing Crosby Greer Garson (3)	1966	Julie Andrews Sean Connery (2)	1988	Tom Cruise Bette Midler (7)
1925	Rudolph Valentino Norma Talmadge (2)	1946	Bing Crosby Ingrid Bergman (2)	1967	Julie Andrews Lee Marvin (2)	1989	Jack Nicholson Kathleen Turner (10)
1926	Colleen Moore Tom Mix (2)	1947	Bing Crosby Betty Grable (2)	1968	Sidney Poitier Julie Andrews (3)	1990	Arnold Schwarzenegger Julia Roberts (2)
1927	Tom Mix Colleen Moore (2)	1948	Bing Crosby Betty Grable (2)	1969	Paul Newman Katharine Hepburn (9)	1991	Kevin Costner Julia Roberts (4)
1928	Clara Bow Lon Chaney (2)	1949	Bob Hope Betty Grable (7)	1970	Paul Newman Barbra Streisand (9)	1992	Tom Cruise Whoopi Goldberg (6)
1929	Clara Bow Lon Chaney (2)	1950	John Wayne Betty Grable (4)	1971	John Wayne Ali MacGraw (8)	1993	Clint Eastwood Julia Roberts (6)
1930	Joan Crawford William Haines (2)	1951	John Wayne Betty Grable (3)	1972	Clint Eastwood Barbra Streisand (5)	1994	Tom Hanks Jodie Foster (8)
1931	Janet Gaynor Charles Farrell (2)	1952	Dean Martin and Jerry Lewis Doris Day (7)	1973	Clint Eastwood Barbra Streisand (6)	1995	Tom Hanks Sandra Bullock (6)
1932	Marie Dressler Charles Farrell (4)	1953	Gary Cooper Marilyn Monroe (6)	1974	Robert Redford Barbra Streisand (4)	1996	Tom Cruise/ Mel Gibson Sandra Bullock (5)
1933	Marie Dressler Will Rogers (2)	1954	John Wayne Marilyn Monroe (5)	1975	Robert Redford Barbra Streisand (2)	1997	Harrison Ford Julia Roberts (2)
1934	Will Rogers Janet Gaynor (3)	1955	James Stewart Grace Kelly (2)	1976	Robert Redford Tatum O'Neal (8)	1998	Tom Hanks Meg Ryan (5)
1935	Shirley Temple Will Rogers (2)	1956	William Holden Marilyn Monroe (8)	1977	Sylvester Stallone Barbra Streisand (2)	1999	Julia Roberts Tom Hanks (2)
				1978	Burt Reynolds Diane Keaton (7)		

played the lead, his mother played a French woman, her two daughters Jessie and Mary played her screen daughters, and Bobby's brother Johnny played 'a boy with a barrel'; *Mr Smith Goes to Washington* (US 39) with brothers and sisters Coy, Vivian, Gloria, Louise, Harry, Billy, Delmar, Garry and Bobs Watson playing the Governor's children; and *Ein Tag ist Schoener als der Andere* (FRG 70), featuring the seven von Eichborn children, Clarissa, Justina, Evelyn, Jacqueline, Wolfram, Holger and Isabella. Peter Bogdanovich's *Paper Moon* (US 73) featured the eight Budke siblings as the children of the widowed Mrs Stanley.

So great was the popularity in his own country of Mexican comedian Cantinflas (known to wider audiences for his portrayal of the valet Passepartout in *Around the World in 80 Days* (US 56)), that the Mexican government would close all the pawnshops two days before the opening of his films lest the poor pawned their meagre possessions to buy tickets.

Charles Chaplin cast several members of his family in *Limelight* (US 52): his daughter Geraldine made her debut as a street urchin, together with siblings Michael and Josephine; one grown-up son, Sydney, played the composer Neville and another, Charles Jr, portrayed a clown; and his half-brother Wheeler Dryden appeared as a doctor.

Blake Edwards' *That's Life* (US 86) starred his wife Julie Andrews opposite Jack Lemmon, and featured his own daughter Jennifer Edwards and Jack's son Chris Lemmon, as well as Julie's daughter Emma Walton and Jack's wife Felicia Farr. When Mia Farrow starred as Hannah in *Hannah and Her Sisters* (US 86), there were no sisters around, but her mother Maureen O'Sullivan, her three children by André Prévin and four of her adopted children were all in the picture. Three generations were also represented in *Kung Fu Master* (Fr 88), with Jane Birkin's parents (mother is actress Judy Campbell) playing her parents in the film, and her children Charlotte Gainsbourg and Lou Doillon playing her on-screen daughters. Maurice, Philippe and Louis Garrel replicated their real-life relationship as grandfather, son and grandson in *Les Baisers de secours* (Fr 89) and Robert, Christopher and Bentley C. Mitchum did the same in *Promises to Keep* (US 85, TVM).

Soviet director Vladimir Basov solved the problem of the 25-year-time span in his film of J. B. Priestley's *Time and the Conways* (USSR 84) by casting four fathers and sons and three mothers and daughters to play the characters in their older and younger personas respectively.

Some film families deliberately avoided working with each other. All six McLaglen brothers were film actors, Victor in America, the others mainly in Britain. When the youngest, Leopold, tried to break into Hollywood pictures in the mid-1930s, eldest brother Victor took out an injunction restraining him. 'There's only room for one McLaglen in Hollywood,' asserted Victor.

The most generations of screen actors in a family is four in the case of the Redgraves and the Kapoors. Roy Redgrave (1872–1922), father of Sir Michael, made his screen debut in *The Christian* (Aus 11) and continued to

Crispin Bonham Carter made his screen debut in *Howards End* (GB 92), which starred his cousin Helena Bonham Carter. Not a case of family string-pulling. They met each other for the first time on set.

appear in Australian movies until 1920. Sir Michael Redgrave (1908–85) married actress Rachel Kempson (1910–), and their two daughters Vanessa (1937–) and Lynn (1943–) and son Corin (1939–) all went into movies. Vanessa's daughters Natasha and Joely made their debut in *The Charge of the Light Brigade* (GB 68) and subsequently appeared in *Dead Cert* (GB 74) and *Joseph Andrews* (GB 77), while Corin's daughter Jemima (Jemma) appeared for the first time in *Joseph Andrews*. All three actress members of the fourth generation successfully transferred to adult leading roles, Joely in *Wetherby* (GB 85), *Loch Ness* (GB 95), *101 Dalmations* (US 96) and opposite Mel Gibson in *The Patriot* (US 00); Natasha in *Gothic* (GB 86), *A Month in the Country* (GB 87), *Patty Hearst* (US/GB 88), *The Handmaid's Tale* (US/FRG 90), *The Comfort of Strangers* (GB 91), *Nell* (US 95) and *The Parent Trap* (US 98); and Jemma (her adult name) in *The Dream Demon* (GB 88) and *Howards End* (GB 92) before moving over to the small screen for the long-running drama series *Bramwell*. Their aunt Lynn brought the family back full circle to its cinematic provenance down under with her starring role opposite Geoffrey Rush in *Shine* (Aus 96).

No fewer than 24 members of the Kapoor family have been screen actors since the debut of patriarch Prithviraj Kapoor (1906–72), son of a police inspector from Peshawar, in *Be Dhari Talwar* (Ind 29), which he also directed at the precocious age of 23. Prithviraj, a revered actor, starred in India's first feature-length talkie *Alam Ara* (Ind 31). His three sons, Raj, Shammi and Shashi (married to actress Jennifer Kendal, sister of Felicity), all followed him into movies with spectacular success. The fourth generation is represented by Bollywood leading lady Karishma Kapoor, daughter of actor Daboo, son of Raj and his actress wife Babita.

The most married of many-times wedded Hollywood stars was B-movie luminary Al 'Lash' La Rue (1917–96), who went to the altar and the divorce court on ten occasions, finally ending a turbulent life—in which he had been charged with vagrancy, drunkennes, possession of marijuana (while practising as an evangelist) and stealing candy from a baby in Florida, besides scripting porno movies—unmarried.

Mums and Dads

A number of artistes have portrayed their own parents or other relatives in films. Eddy Foy Jr was cast as Eddy Foy Sr in *Yankee Doodle Dandy* (US 42). Marie Lloyd Jr played 'Queen of the Halls' Marie Lloyd Sr in *Variety Jubilee* (GB 43), while on the other side of the Channel playwright Sacha Guitry took the role of his father, actor Lucien Guitry, in *The Private Life of an Actor* (Fr 48)—he also played himself. Will Rogers Jr portrayed Will Rogers Sr in three films—*Look for the Silver Lining* (US 49), *The Story of Will Rogers* (US 52) and *The Eddie Cantor Story* (US

53). Dick Powell Jr was seen in a cameo role as lookalike father Dick Powell Sr in *The Day of the Locust* (US 74) and Marcel Cerdan Jr had a leading role as his father in *Edith and Marcel* (Fr 84), the story of Edith Piaf's love affair with middleweight boxing champion Marcel Cerdan Sr. In *Adolf Hitler—My Part in His Downfall* (GB 72), Jim Dale plays Spike Milligan, while Milligan appears as his own father.

Chynna Phillips portrayed her own mother Michelle Phillips, formerly of the 1960s pop group the Mamas and the Papas and ex live-in lover of both Jack Nicholson and Warren Beatty, in *California Dreamin'* (US 88). One of only two recorded examples of a character being played by his own brother is in Raj Kapoor's two autobiographical movies *Awara* (Ind 51) and *Shree 420* (Ind 55), with Shashi Kapoor in the roles based on Raj Kapoor. The other was *29th Street* (US 91), in which Anthony LaPaglia played the role of Frank Pesce, who won over $6 million in the first New York State Lottery in 1976, while the real Frank Pesce played his own elder brother Vito.

Yonas Yergaw from Ethiopia portrayed his uncle Haile Gebrsellassie, 10,000m gold medallist at the 1996 Olympics, as a boy in *Endurance* (US/GB 98). (Gebrsellassie played himself as an adult.) Albert Wimscheider also took the part of his own uncle in *Autumn Milk* (FRG 89), based on his wife's autobiographical story of how she ran their farm while he was away at the war. Another story of war and its aftermath, the 1989 Berlin Film Festival Silver Bear winner *The Summer of Aviya* (Isr 89), starred Gila Almagor as her own mother, a mentally disturbed Holocaust survivor.

Marie Osmond played her mother Olive Osmond while her daughter Amy Osmond appeared as Marie in *Side by Side: The True Story of the Osmond Family* (US 82, TVM). Patty Duke's brother Ray Duke portrayed their father in his sister's autobiopic *Call Me Anna* (US 90, TVM).

The Mambo Kings (US 92) reconstructs the appearance of the eponymous Cuban brothers on the *I Love Lucy* TV show, using original footage of Lucille Ball with matched footage of the actors playing the Mambo Kings and Desi Arnaz Jr playing his father and Lucille Ball's husband Desi Arnaz Sr. Pierre Schoendoeffer cast his son Ludovic as his youthful self, a war cameraman with the French army in Indo-China in 1954, in his epic battle film *Diên Biên Phú* (Fr 92).

Desi Arnaz Jr as his father Desi Arnaz Sr in The Mambo Kings *(US 92).* (Warner Bros)

Only one actor has played his own grandfather, one her own grandmother and two their great grandfathers. Stalin's grandson Eugene Djugasvili played the tyrant in *War Is War For Everyone* (USSR 90). In Richard Attenborough's *Chaplin* (US/GB 92), the subject's daughter Geraldine Chaplin was cast as her unstable Cockney grandmother Hannah. Michael Palin stars in *American Friends* (GB 91) as a middle-aged Oxford classics don based on his great-grandfather, the Rev. Edward Palin, who had to resign his post after deciding to marry a teenage American girl he met on a walking tour of Switzerland. The story was based on a few cryptic entries Palin discovered in his great-grandfather's diary. Zulu chief Mangosuthu Buthelezi, leader of the Inkatha Freedom Party, is the great-grandson of Warrior Chief Cetshwayo, whom he portrayed in Battle of Rorke's Drift epic *Zulu* (GB 64).

Largest and Smallest Cast

The largest cast of credited performers in a film was 381, including 71 major roles, in Edgar Reitz's monumental 25½-hour *The New Heimat* (Ger 92). The most in a film intended for uninterrupted showing was 260 in *Dny Zrady/Days of Treason* (Cz 72), the story of the betrayal of Czechoslovakia in 1938, including Gunnar Möllar as Hitler, Jaroslav Radimecky as Chamberlain, Alexander Fred as Goebbels, Rudolf Jurda as Goering and Vladamir Stach as Mussolini.

Sacha Guitry's *Napoleon* (Fr 54) had 101 credited roles, but was claimed to have 300 speaking parts. MGM claimed 365 speaking parts (73 credited) for *Ben Hur* (US 59), but this seems almost impossible for a 217-minute film unless it includes groups of people all speaking at once. As many as 430 speaking parts were claimed for the 188-minute *Gandhi* (GB 83), with 138 credited. The British film with the largest cast of credited performers is *Little Dorrit* (GB 87) with 211.

Other films with large casts (credited) include: *Mission to Moscow* (US 43) with 195; *Rottenknechte* (GDR 70) with 194; *A Cry in the Dark* (Aus 88) with 168; *Baron Muenchhausen* (Ger 45) with 150; *Sweden for the Swedes* (Swe 80) with 142; *Around the World in 80 Days* (US 56) with 138; *A Bridge Too Far* (GB 77) with 137; *The Women* (US 39) with 135; *Oh! What a Lovely War* (GB 69) with 125; Karl Ritter's *Pour la Merité* (Ger 38) with 102.; and *Radioland Murders* (US 94) with 'over 100'.

For the **largest cast including extras**, see pp. 82–3

The smallest cast in a live-action dramatic feature, excluding movies with an all-animal cast, is none. Kostas Sfikas' *Model* (Gre 74) had no performers, only robots seen in a single set representing a factory yard. The one hour and 45 minute film was intended as a critique of the 'implacable process that transforms mankind into negotiable goods and mere accessories of an industrial machine'.

There have been a number of movies with a cast of one. Olaf Fønns, leading Danish romantic hero of the World War I period, played alone in Fritz Magnussen's *Remorse* (Den 19), made for Dansk Astra Film. The story is of a wealthy man who is ruined and loses his mistress (represented only by a pair of arms), then returns to her in a starving condition, is rejected and kills her. He restores his fortune but, relentlessly pursued by his own accusing shadow, eventually gives himself up. In addition to its solo performance, the silent film was distinguished by having no inter-titles.

Sunil Dutt's *Yaadein/Recollections* (Ind 64), in which he starred as well as directed and produced, was a single set, solo movie about a husband deserted by his wife. At the end of the film the woman's shadow seen against a wall indicates that she has returned to him. Robert Carlisle's *Sofi* (US 68), an adaptation of Gogol's *Diary of a Madman*, had Tom Troupe as its only performer. Thierry Zeno's *Vase de noces* (Bel 73) starred Dominique Garny, who does not speak throughout the film. It tells the story of a simple man living alone among his poultry and pigs who eventually hangs himself. Danilo-Bata Stojkovic played alone as a man fleeing from imaginary pursuers in Milos Radivojevic's *Testament* (Yug 75), which was also without speech. Jean-Pierre Lefebvre's *L'Amour blessé* (*Confidences de la nuit*) (Can 75) starred Louise Cuerrier as a lonely woman spending a dull evening in her room listening to a talk show, while Britain's first single-artiste film had Monica Buferd in the rather more compelling role of *St Joan* (GB 77). James Whitmore gave a standout performance as Harry S. Truman in his solo biopic of the President's life and times *Give 'Em Hell, Harry!* (US 75).

Other examples of solo performances are by Anne Flannery in A *State of Siege* (NZ 78), Willeke van Ammelrooy in Frans Zwartje's *It's Me* (Neth 79), and by Alain Cavalier in *Ce répondeur ne prend pas de message* (Fr 79). Spalding Gray transferred his critically acclaimed stage monologues to three feature length films, *Swimming to Cambodia* (US 87), *Monster in a Box* (GB 91) and *Gray's Anatomy* (US 96).

Julie Harris played Charlotte Brontë in Delbert Mann's evocation of the author's life and times *Brontë* (US/Ire 83). Interaction with the other members of the Brontë family was conveyed by having Charlotte handle both sides of the conversation. Another powerful portrayal of a real-life character was by Philip Baker Hall as Richard Nixon in Robert Altman's *Secret Honor* (US 84), delivering an 80-minute monologue described as 'a fictional meditation'.

In *A Fine Film of Ashes* (GB 88) Steve Shill, who also directed, plays an estate agent who has returned from his father's funeral to ruminate over the ashes in the old man's living room, the only set. *Private Code* (It 88) also had a single set, the ornate flat belonging to a girl (Ornella Muti) whose rich and famous lover has flown off to a conference, perhaps with no intention of returning. Interaction with other, unseen characters is via telephone and computer. In a rare Irish solo production, Ronan O'Leary's *Fragment of Isabella* (Ire 89), Gabrielle Reidy stars as Auschwitz survivor Isabella Leitner.

Stanislaw Rojewicz's *The Body Snatchers* (Pol/Cz 89), declared by *Sight and Sound* to be the oddest film screened at the 1989 Gdansk Festival, achieved the remarkable feat of translating R. L. Stevenson's novel of the same name to the screen with only one body in evidence—that of a lively, lovely nude actress. As remarkable, and perhaps even odder, was the Belgian version of *Romeo and Juliet* in which the eponymous lovers and all the other Shakespearian characters are played by cats. The only human being in *Romeo-Juliet* (Belg 90) is an old Venetian bag-lady—played in drag by John Hurt.

Unusual Casts

- There have been five full-length feature films with casts composed entirely of American Indians, and none since the advent of talkies. The tally: *Hiawatha* (US 13), with a cast of 150 headed by Soon-goot as Minnehaha; *The Land of the Headhunters* (US 14); *Before the White Man Came* (US 20), with a cast drawn from the Crow and Cheyenne tribes; *The Daughter of Dawn* (US 20), with a cast from the Comanche and Kiowa tribes; and *The Silent Enemy* (US/Can 30), starring Chief Yellow Robe of the Obizibway Indians of Canada, one of only four members of the cast who had ever seen a motion picture.

- The only feature film with a cast composed entirely of Lapps was *The Pathfinder* (Nor 87).

- There have been three fiction films with all-Eskimo casts, *Kivalina of the Ice Lands* (US 25), *Igloo* (US 32) and *Heart of Light* (Greenland/Swe/Den/Nor 99); and three Hollywood movies with all-Balinese casts— *Virgins of Bali* (US 32), *Goona-Goona* (US 32) and *Legond, Dance of the Virgins* (US 32). One American film has been made with an all-Chinese cast, Universal's *The War of the Tongs* (US 17), starring Lee Gow and Lin Neong; one with an all-Siamese cast, *Chang* (US 27); and one with an all-Sudanese cast, *Stampede* (US 30).

- In *Sitting Bull* (US 54), the Indians and the US Cavalry were all played by Mexicans. In Samuel Fuller's war picture *Big Red One* (US 80), all the Nazi concentration camp guards were played by Jews.

- *The Writing on the Wall* (Fr/Bel 82) was a story of the Northern Ireland troubles in which all the Protestants were played by Catholics and the Catholics by Protestants.

- There have been many films about nuns, but only two in which they were actually played by nuns. *Francesca* (FRG 87) is about a fictitious star of yesteryear who was raised by nuns in Bavaria. The Mother Superior is played by real-life Mother Superior Roswitha Schneider and the nuns by the Sisters of St Mary's Convent in Niederviebach, Bavaria. One hundred cloistered nuns of the Clarissa order perform in *Invisible Things* (It 90, TVM), directed by Capuchin monk Fr Serafino Rafaiani.

- Nearly all the performers in *Amy* (US 81) were deaf— they were recruited from the California School for the Deaf at Riverside. Mentally handicapped actor Richard Mulligan was cast as the most brilliant and intellectual teacher on campus in the off-beat high-school social comedy, *Teachers* (US 84). The title role in *Annie's Coming Out* (Aus 84), based on a true story about a brain-damaged teenager, was played by real-life spastic Tina Arhondis.

- Members of the International Brigade played in André Malraux's *Man's Hope* (Sp 45), filmed from his own novel during the bombardment of Barcelona in 1938. For three Allied fliers who were shot down over Switzerland in World War II, not only was it the end of their war but the opportunity to star in a film. John Hoy and E. G. Morrison of the RAF and Ray Reagan, USAAF sergeant, were given the leading roles in the Swiss film *Last Chance* (Swz 45), playing escaped prisoners leading a party of refugees over the Alps to neutral Switzerland. The refugees, all of different nationalities, were played by real refugees.

- All the leading players in *Dionysus* (Fr 84), about a US university professor who comes to Paris to defend a thesis on Dionysus and ends up running an assembly line at Citroën, were played by real-life university professors.

- Beauty queens have often been given a chance to break into movies, but never so many all at once as in *Yankee Pasha* (US 54). A costumer about a New England girl sold into a Moroccan harem, the film's cast included the Misses USA, Japan, Panama, Norway, Uruguay, South Africa, Australia and Miss Universe, Christiane Martel.

- RKO tried an unusual experiment in 1944 with a film called *Days of Glory* (US 44), in which all 19 featured players were making their screen debut. One of the 19 went on to stardom—Gregory Peck.

- In the Jackie Chan action caper *Twin Dragons/Shuanglong Hui* (HK/US 91–98), all roles except the two female leads were played by directors, no fewer than 24 of them.

- Von Stroheim used real hookers to play the prostitutes in *The Wedding March* (US 27) and similarly the inmates of the bordello in John Huston's *Under the Volcano* (US 85) were real-life members of their calling. Not so in *Maya* (Fr 49). A set representing a red-light district was built in false perspective to give an illusion of depth. The prostitutes seen at the far end of the street were played by little girls of six to eight years old outfitted in the gaudy raiment of harlotry.

- When lesbian producer/star Nazimova starred in her own production of *Salome* (US 23), she employed only gay actors as a 'homage' to Oscar Wilde.

- The masochists receiving the punishing attentions of Bulle Ogier in *Maitresse* (Fr 79) were not actors. They were deviants who were invited to bring along their own chains and whips. In *Just Like a Woman* (GB 92) Julie Walters plays a suburban divorcee who takes a transvestite as a lodger and falls in love with him. Apart from leading man Adrian Pasdar, all the cross-dressers in the film were genuine, recruited from transvestite clubs across London.

- The extras engaged to play convicts in *Hell's Highway* (US 32) were all ex-cons themselves. Fritz Lang used real criminals to play the underworld types in his chilling study of a child murderer *M* (Ger 31). Before filming had been completed no fewer than 24 of them had been arrested for various offences.

- Woody Allen also chose real gangsters for the cast of *Bullets Over Broadway* (US 95). One of them turned out to be a contemporary from the director's high-school days, but Allen said he had not known him well: 'I was only on cowering terms with him.'

- Bhutanese monk Khyentse Norbu's *The Cup* (Aus/Bhutan 99), set in a Tibetan monastery-in-exile at the foothills of the Himalayas, had a cast of genuine monks. The auditions were unconventional by Hollywood standards, though perhaps par-for-the-

The Women *(US 39) was one of scarcely a dozen pictures with all-female casts.*

course for Buddhists. Those chosen, Norbu explained, were selected by divination.

- There have been many prison dramas and war films with all male casts, but very few films with all-female casts. Best known is probably *The Women* (US 39), whose 135 speaking roles included those played by Joan Crawford, Norma Shearer, Rosalind Russell, Paulette Goddard and Joan Fontaine. Others have been: *Mädchen in Uniform* (Ger 31) with Dorothea Wieck; *The Mad Parade* (US 31) with Evelyn Brent; *The Blossoms Have Fallen* (Jap 38), about the constraints of life in a geisha house; Esther Eng's *Women's World* (HK 40); *Cry Havoc* (US 43), starring Margaret Sullavan, Ann Sothern and Joan Blondell; *The Bitter Tears of Petra von Kant* (FRG 72) with Margit Carstensen; *Cries and Whispers* (Swe 72) with Harriet Andersson, Ingrid Thulin and Liv Ullmann; and *Friendships, Secrets and Lies* (US 79) with Sondra Locke, Tina Louise and Paula Prentiss. All-women films of the 1980s included *Black Mirror* (Can 81), a French-Canadian movie set in a women's prison, *Les Chicks* (Fr 85) and *Les Nanas* (Fr 85) with Marie-France Pisier. Cynthia Scott's *The Company of Strangers* (Can 90), seventh in a series of National Film Board of Canada features in which non-professionals play themselves in a fictitious setting, had a cast of seven elderly ladies (oldest 88) and one young one in a story of how they are marooned in an abandoned country house when their bus breaks down. The Italian all-female *A Day to Grow* (It 92), with Françoise Fabian, Flora Mastroianni and Sabrina Ferilli, is set in an orphanage run by nuns.

- Rarer still are films with all-child casts. Since the inception of talkies there have been eight features in which the children are playing children, of which the earliest was *Torn Shoes* (USSR 34)—all the performers were under 13. Next up were two films directed in Telegu by Chittajullu Pullaiah for the East India Film Co, *Ansuya* (Ind 36) and *Dhuivra* (Ind 36), made back-to-back and released as a double bill. They were based on the Hindu *Sati Ansuya* and *Bhakta Dhuvra* and were commended in reviews for their realism in scirpt and casting. Peter Brook's *The Lord of the Flies* (GB 63) was from William Golding's novel about schoolboy castaways on an uninhabited island who revert to barbarism (the 1990 Hollywood remake had an adult character), while *Leave Us Alone* (Den 75) had a similar theme of children adapting to life on a desert island. Mexico's *Poison for Fairies* (Mex 86), winner of five Ariels (Mexico's equivalent to the Oscar), is set in a girls' school and confronts the dangerous world of childhood fantasies. The only adult characters are represented by an arm or a leg seen at the side of the screen. *Maramao* (Fr/It 87) had a cast composed entirely of five to 13-year-olds, headed by Italian moppet Vanessa Grevina. In addition there have been two films in which children play adults. *Bugsy Malone* (GB 76) parodied the gangster movies of the thirties with a then unknown Jodie Foster as a 13-year-old femme fatale. The cast of *The Annunciation* (Hun 84), in which Adam, the first man, is guided through the darker passages of man's tormented history, were all between eight and 12, with the part of Satan played by a nine-year-old girl.

- All the leading roles in Shusuki Kanedo's *Summer Vacation 1999* (Jap 89), a story of teenage homosexual love at a boys' boarding school in Japan, were played by children. But the remarkable feature of this film was that all the boys were played by 14-year-old girls. Their voices were dubbed by young males.

- There have been isolated examples of children playing adults in straight dramas. Blanche Sweet played a married woman at the age of 13 in *A Man with Three Lives* (US 09) and 12-year-old Gladys Leslie took the role of a debutante in *The Beloved Imposter* (US 19). Mickey Rooney played an adult midget in *Not To Be Trusted* (US 26) at the age of five and this led to a persistent rumour that the child star was in reality a midget posing as a child. The reverse principle, of adults playing children, was not uncommon in silent days, when actresses like Mary Pickford and Lillian Gish specialised in such roles. More unusual examples are the 33-year-old Richard Barthelmess playing a six-year-old boy in the opening scenes of *The Little Shepherd of Kingdom Come* (US 28) and Bette Davis's portrayal of a 13-year-old in *Payment on Demand* (US 51) at age 43. Sally Thomsett was 22 when she was cast as 17-year-old Jenny Agutter's eight-year-old younger sister in *The Railway Children* (GB 70).

- The Neo-Nazi gang which terrorises the streets in *Luna Park* (Rus/Fr 92) were real Muscovite skinheads.

- The performers of the climactic Dance of Death in Ingmar Bergman's *The Seventh Seal* (Swe 56) were actually the crew of the film. The scene was to have

> Specialised casting agencies abound in Hollywood. Few quite as specialised as Rent-a-Gang, which is where casting directors go to hire mobs of genuine, menacing motorcycle outlaws.

been shot the following day and the actors had already gone home when a beautiful cloud appeared in the sky. Unwilling to forego such a telling background, Bergman hastily dressed his technicians and assistants in the actors' costumes and, with barely ten minutes' rehearsal, shot the scene before the light failed.

- The French convicts on Devil's Island in *Papillon* (US 73) were 600 farmers from a German settlement in Jamaica, where the film was shot. The World War I French troops in Stanley Kubrick's *Paths of Glory* (US 57) were 800 German policemen.

- The press corps in *The Right Stuff* (US 83), docudrama about America's Mercury astronauts, were played by a commedia dell'arte troup of Italian jugglers, mimes and acrobats known as I Fratelli Bologna.

- Veteran producer Mario Cecchi Gori assembled a mammoth cast for his 125th picture *The Department Store* (It 86) which included every available performer who had appeared in his previous 124 films.

Longest Careers

The longest screen career was that of Curt Bois (1900–91), who made his film debut at the age of eight in *Der Fidele Bauer* (Ger 08). Bois left Germany in 1933 on the accession of the Nazis and made his way to the US via Prague, Vienna, London and Paris. He went to New York to star in a stage play which closed after only one night and thence to Hollywood in 1938. He appeared in such notable films as *Casablanca* (US 42) and Max Ophuls' *Caught* (US 49) before returning to Berlin in the early '50s. His last screen role in a career spanning 80 years was in Wim Wenders' enigmatic story of angels come to earth, *Wings of Desire* (FRG 88), in which he played an old man who regards himself as the last story-teller of his tribe.

The British actor with the longest screen career was Sir John Gielgud (1904–2000), who made his film debut as Daniel, the young lover of a married woman, in Walter Summers' *Who Is the Man?* (GB 24), adapted from the

These menacing-looking Neo-Nazis in Luna Park *(Rus/Fr 92) were not actors. They were real Muscovite skinheads.* (Kobal Collection)

French stage play *Daniel* by Louis Verneuil, and concluded his film appearances 76 years later playing an actor who does not speak (going full circle to his silent-era debut) in David Mamet's six-minute tour de force *Catastrophe* (US/GB 00). As he reached his tenth decade, Gielgud said that he got 'terribly nervous on stage these days', but would continue to accept film roles. The beauty of cinema, he declared, is that he did not have to learn many lines and could do retakes. 'What appeals is a good part with a few good lines, a good entrance and a good exit. A bit of limelight on me and that's all I ask for.' Notable nonagenarian appearances included Professor Parker in *Shine* (Aus 96), Pream in Kenneth Branagh's *Hamlet* (GB 97), and the Pope in *Elizabeth* (GB 98). He played the Lord Chief Justice in his final feature film, *The Tichborne Claimant* (GB 99).

The actress with the longest screen career was Helen Hayes (1900–93), who made her debut in *Jean and the Calico Doll* (US 10) and performed in the religious docudrama *Divine Mercy, No Escape* (US 88) at the age of 88. Since her other screen work in the 1980s was confined to television movies, the record for the most enduring performer of the large screen goes to Lillian Gish (1893–1993). First seen as a 19-year-old in *An Unseen Enemy* (US 12), she made her last screen appearance 75 years later co-starring with Bette Davis in *The Whales of August* (US 87).

The performer with the longest screen career who is still acting and the only one to have performed in silent films is Mickey Rooney (1922–), who made his debut at the age of four in *Not To Be Trusted* (US 26) as a cigar-smoking midget. Recent appearances include starring roles in *Animals (and the Tollkeeper)* (US 98) and *Michael Kael vs the World News Company* (Fr 98). The only other active survivor from Hollywood's inter-war years is Mexican-born Anthony Quinn (1915–), who debuted in *Parole* (US 36) and 63 years later played the lead in *Oruindi* (Bra 99).

Multiple Roles

The largest number of roles played by one actor in a single film is not, as stated in *The Guinness Book of World Records*, the eight members of the d'Ascoyne family portrayed by Alec Guinness in *Kind Hearts and Coronets* (GB 49), but the 27 parts taken by Rolf Leslie in Will Barker's life story of Queen Victoria *Sixty Years a Queen* (GB 13). Others who have equalled or exceeded Sir Alec's eight roles are Lupino Lane, who played all 24 parts in *Only Me* (US 29), Joseph Henabery, cast as Abraham Lincoln and 13 other characters in *The Birth of a Nation* (US 15), Robert Hirsch, seen in 12 roles in *No Questions on Saturday* (US 64), Michael Ripper, with nine in *What a Crazy World* (GB 63), Sivaji Ganesan playing all nine roles in Tamil picture *Navarathri* (Ind 64) and Sanjeev Kumar the same nine roles in the Hindi remake *Naya Din Nayi Rat* (Ind 74), Flavio Migliaccio, who had eight parts in *Como Vai, Vai Bem* (Bra 69), Rolv Wesenlund, portraying eight characters in the comedy *Norske Byggeklosser* (Nor 71), and Eddie Murphy, whose eight roles in *Nutty Professor II: The Klumps* (US 00) included six members of the Klump family.

Perhaps the most economically casted film was *The Great McGonagall* (GB 74) which had five actors playing 34 parts between them. What might be described as a double Dutch movie, *Ongedaan gedaan* (Neths 89), did the opposite. The four principal roles were played by eight performers, each character by two actors or actresses.

The most actors to have played a single character in a movie was nine in the case of the title role of *Buddy* (US 97). The true story of an animal-loving couple in 1920s Brooklyn who saved a baby gorilla from a certain death

> The eponymous male porker in *Babe* (Aus 95) was in fact 48 different female pigs. None of which became pork. The film-makers stipulated, before returning them to their sties, that they should only be used for breeding.

and raised him as a member of their household, the film featured Peter Elliott, Mark Wilson, Lynn Robertson Bruce, Mark Sealy, Rob Tygner, Michelan Sisti, Peter Hurst, Leif Tilden and Star Townshend as Buddy. Most portraying a human character was six actresses as Rachel in *Superstarlet A.D.* (US 00), for reasons unexplained.

Actresses Who Have Played Men

Critical and box-office success *Boys Don't Cry* (US 00), in which Hilary Swank delivered an Oscar-winning performance as true-life murder victim Teena Brandon aka Brandon Teena, is one of many examples of films in which female characters disguise themselves in male attire, while in the silent days it was not uncommon for young women to play small boys, but few actresses have played adult males. Those who have:

- Francesca Bertini in the title role of *Histoire d'un Pierrot* (It 13).
- Violet Radcliffe as Long John Silver in *Treasure Island* (US 18).
- Mathilde Comont as the Persian prince in *The Thief of Bagdad* (US 24).
- Sulochana (Ruby Myers) played seven male roles, including a gardener, a policeman, a Hyderabadi gentleman, a street urchin and a banana seller, as well as a female role as a blonde European siren, in *Wildcat of Bombay* (Ind 27).
- Elspeth Dudgeon (billed as 'John Dudgeon') as the aged man in the upstairs bedroom in *The Old Dark House* (US 32).
- Virginia Engels as old man who falls down the stairs during a saloon brawl in *San Antonio* (US 45).
- Jean Arless as Warren (also as his wife Emily) in *Homicidal* (US 61).
- Sena Jurinac as Octavian in *Der Rosenkavalier* (GB 62).
- Ivy Ling Po as the hero Chang in *The Mermaid* (HK 66).
- Laura Betti as moustachioed British tourist ('his' wife

Linda Hunt playing a man, Billy Kwan, in Peter Weir's drama of the last months of the Sukarno regime in Indonesia, The Year of Living Dangerously *(Aus 82).*

played by a man) in Pasolini's segment of *Le Streghe* (It 67).

- Tanya Lopert as the effeminate emperor in Fellini's *Satyricon* (It/Fr 69)
- Caroline Johnson as the Prince of Denmark in *Hamlet* (Can 71).
- Anne Heywood as Roy, a transsexual man, in *I Want What I Want* (GB 72).
- Victoria Abril as an effeminate young man who undergoes a sex change in *I Want To Be A Woman* (Sp 77).
- Linda Hunt, 4ft 9in American actress, as the male Eurasian cameraman Billy Kwan in *The Year of Living Dangerously* (Aus 82).
- Li Ching-hsia as effeminate young man, Pao Yu, with voracious sexual (hetero) appetite in *Dream of the Red Chamber* (HK 77).
- Ethel Merman as a shell-shocked soldier suffering from the delusion he is Ethel Merman in *Airplane* (US 80).
- Eva Mattes as a male film director based on Rainer Werner Fassbinder in *A Man Like Eva* (FRG 83).
- Anne Carlisle in male and female leading roles in Slava Tsukerman's *Liquid Sky* (US 83).
- Ina-Miriam Rosenbaum as Jesus Christ in Johannes' *Hemmelighed* (Den 85).
- Vanessa Redgrave as Richard Radley, who underwent a sex change and became tennis champion Renee Richards, in *Second Score* (US 86, TVM).
- Gillian Jones as Sebastian (also Viola) in *Twelfth Night* (Aus 86).
- Debra Winger as redheaded male archangel Emmett, who is in charge of Heaven in *Made in Heaven* (US 87). (Ms Winger played the role on condition she was neither credited nor identified.)
- Theresa Russell as King Zog of Albania in husband Ken Russell's segment of portmanteau film *Aria* (GB 87).
- Lanah Pelley as black waiter-turned-revolutionary Alex in *Eat the Rich* (GB 87).
- Barbara Leary as moustachioed Russian heavy Dimitri in *9½ Ninjas* (US 91).
- Glenn Close as a bearded pirate in *Hook* (US 92).
- Tilda Swinton as Orlando in *Orlando* (GB/Ger/It/Neths/Fr/Rus 92).
- Wong Tsu Hsien as eponymous swordsman and sexual athlete in *East Is Red: Swordsman 3* (HK 92).
- Unidentified actress as male psychiatric patient in *When the Bough Breaks* (US 93).
- Carina Liu as gay Taoist swordsman Chou Po-tung in *The Eagle Shooting Heroes: Dong Cheng Xi Jiu* (HK 94).
- Claire Nebout as the cross-dressing 18th-century spy Chevalier d'Eon in *Beaumarchais l'insolent* (Fr 96).
- Fiona Shaw as the king in Deborah Warner's National Theatre production of *Richard II* (GB 97, TVM).
- Maori actess Rena Owen as cross-dressing man 'Katie' in *When Love Comes* (NZ 98).
- Talia Shire as sickly Mr Price in *Palmer's Pick-up* (US 99).
- Kathy Burke as testosterone-ridden girl-chasing teenager Perry (she aged 35) in *Kevin and Perry Go Large* (GB/US 00).

Names

The most usual reasons for actors and actresses changing their names are that those they were born with are too long, too difficult to pronounce, or simply unglamorous. It is not hard to understand why Herbert Charles Angelo Kuchacewich ze Schluderpacheru decided to drop it in favour of Herbert Lom, or why Derek Julius Gaspard Ulrich Niven van den Bogaerde thought he would go further with a name like Dirk Bogarde. Equally, Larushka Mischa Skikne had good reason to change his to Laurence Harvey and nobody complained when Walter Matuschanskayasky chose to call himself Matthau instead (though he was billed as Walter Matuschanskayasky when he played a recurring cameo role as a drunk in *Earthquake* (US 74)).

Briefer names may be just as unacceptable. Sarah Jane Fulks was distasteful to Jane Wyman, as was Alexandra Zuck to Sandra Dee and Diana Fluck to Diana Dors. Olga Kronk preferred Claire Windsor, and not surprisingly Doris Day was as relieved to be free of Doris Kappelhoff, as was Cyd Charisse not to have to answer to Tula Finklea. Burl Ivanhoe substituted Ives, while Fabian Forte Bonaparte was satisfied to get along with just his first name. Robert Taylor had rather more appeal for a romantic hero than Spangler Arlington Brugh and Septimus Ryott was undoubtedly correct in thinking that his female fans would prefer him as Stewart Rome. Austrian actor Jake Kratz doubted he would be able to play hot-blooded Latin lovers with a name like that and changed it to Ricardo Cortez. Many performers born with Latin names preferred something Anglo-Saxon: Dino Crocetti opted for Dean Martin, Margarita Carmen Cansino for Rita Hayworth, Luis Antonio Damaso de

---

The family of the late River Phoenix were surnamed Bottom. Although he began life as River Bottom, his New Age parents changed their name to Phoenix soon after he was born, not in order to spare their son trauma at school but to symbolise rising from the society they had rejected.

Alonso for Gilbert Roland and Anna Maria Luisa Italiano for Anne Bancroft. A few reversed the process, and changed Anglo-Saxon names into something more exotic: Bonar Sullivan became Bonar Colleano, Peggy Middleton assumed the more romantic Yvonne de Carlo and Muriel Harding decided that Olga Petrova held a greater air of mystery for a femme fatale.

Some actors chose names that others had discarded. Bernard Schwarz chose Tony Curtis, while the real Tony Curtis had become Italy's best loved comedian Toto. American actor Bud Flanagan changed his name to Dennis O'Keefe, while British actor Robert Winthrop altered his to Bud Flanagan. It was fortunate for James Stewart that his British namesake had already decided to change James Stewart into Stewart Granger before the other James Stewart went into movies. The Leslie Hope who starred in *First Degree* (US 95) knew she was in little danger of being confused with the screen's other Leslie Hope, who had thoughtfuly changed his name to Bob when he first entered showbusiness. Michael Keaton's real name is Michael Douglas.

Alternatively, an artiste could sometimes get away with adopting a name which already had cachet. Cambodia's leading female star before the communist takeover, Kim Nova, selected her screen name in

Casting director Paula Herold sought a 'family looka-like' to co-star with Helen Slater as her younger brother in *The Legend of Billie Jean* (US 84). When young Christian Slater was chosen for his close resemblance to Helen Slater, audiences not surprisingly assumed they were real-life siblings. In fact they are not related.

unabashed imitation of Kim Novak. In 1974 a Cambodian starlet called herself Kim Novy in imitation of the imitation. Charles Chaplin sued a Mexican comedian called Charles Amador who had changed his name to Charles Aplin, but was unable to do anything about a German comedian who appeared on screen as Charlie Kaplin. Hong Kong's Bruce Li found fame and fortune treading in the footsteps of the late Bruce Lee.

It was also perfectly possible to have several actors with a legitimate claim to the same name. There were three Robert Lees working in Hollywood during the 1920s and four Charles Macks, two of them styling themselves Charles E. Mack, and additionally a Mrs Charles Mack, who performed under that name. When Pernilla Wahlgren and Pernilla Wallgren were both cast in Bo Wideberg's *The Serpent's Way Across Helle Mountain* (Swe 86), the latter decided to change her screen name to Ostergren—her married name—to avoid confusion. After marrying director Bille August on the set of *Best Intentions* (US 92), she changed it again to August Oestegren, then dropped her second name altogether and became simply August.

Although relatively few actresses assume their husbands' names, another one who did was Ellen Burstyn. It was as well that she found a name she felt she could stick with when she met Mr Burstyn (pronounced BURST-un), because the Irish-American former model from Detroit had rejoiced in no fewer than 25 different stage names since abandoning the name she had been born with, Edna Gilhooley.

Joseph Keaton assumed the first name of 'Buster' at the age of six months when he fell downstairs and Harry Houdini, a family friend, remarked to his father: 'That's some buster your baby took!' Harry Crosby acquired 'Bing' from avid reading of a comic strip called *The Bingville Bugle* when he was at school.

Some were satisfied simply to change their Christian name: Leslie/Bob Hope; James/David Niven; William/Pat O'Brien; Clarence/Robert Cummings; Hubert/Rudy Vallee; John/Arthur Kennedy; Julius/Groucho Marx; Virginia/Bebe Daniels; Sari/Zsa Zsa Gabor; Marilyn/Kim Novak; Adolf/Anton Walbrook; Julia/Lana Turner; Ruth/Bette Davis.

Even simpler was to change a single letter of the name: Conrad Veidt (Weidt); Beulah Bondi (Bondy); George Raft (Ranft); May Robson (Robison); Ronald Squire (Squirl); Gerard Philipe (Philippe); Dorothy Malone (Maloney); Warren Beatty (Beaty); Yul Brynner (Bryner); Madeleine Carroll (O'Carroll); Paul Henreid (Hernreid); Edmund (Edmond) Lowe; Van (Evan) Heflin; Julia (Julie) Roberts. James Baumgarner was content to drop the 'Baum', Anna Maria Pierangeli split her surname down the middle and eschewed her first names, while Banky Vilma just switched to Vilma Banky. Mitchell Gordon, American star of numerous 1960s Italian sword and sandal epics, did the same, reversing his name to Gordon Mitchell.

Choice of a new name is dictated by varied circumstances. Judy Garland (Frances Gumm) took her stage surname from the theatre pages of a Chicago newspaper, whose reviews were written by Robert Garland. It was chosen by George Jessel, to whom the 11-year-old Miss Gumm had appealed for help after being billed as Glumm at the theatre where they were both appearing. Her first name came from a Hoagy Carmichael song Judy, of which she was fond. Barbara Stanwyck was named by legit producer Willard Mack, who told her that Ruby Stevens sounded like a stripper. He selected Stanwyck after glancing at an old programme listing Jane Stanwyck.

French comedian Fernandel was born Fernand Constandin. His wife called him Fernand d'elle (her Fernand). Luis Alonso selected his new name of Gilbert Roland as a tribute to the two stars he most admired,

Too bad for L.A. actor Wyatt Earp that he did not get the lead role played by Kurt Russell in the Wyatt Earp biopic *Tombstone* (US 93)—he had to settle for the rather more minor role of Billy Claiborne instead.

John Gilbert and Ruth Roland. Stepin Fetchit, the startled black manservant of '20s and '30s Hollywood movies, named himself after a racehorse which had obliged him by winning.

Marilyn Monroe's Christian name was selected for her by Fox talent scout Ben Lyon because of his admiration for Marilyn Miller—the Monroe was her mother's maiden name. Bette (Ruth) Davis took her screen Christian name from Balzac's Cousin Bette, while young Susan Weaver, daughter of NBC president Sylvester 'Pat' Weaver, was also inspired by literature. When she was sixteen she asked her family to call her Sigourney after the character of that name in F. Scott Fitzgerald's *The Great Gatsby*. Gary (Frank J.) Cooper was named after his agent's hometown, Gary, Indiana. The actor's own hometown would hardly have been appropriate—he came from Helena, Montana.

MGM ran a fan contest in 1925 to find a new name for the extravagantly named Lucille Le Sueur. The winner came up with Joan Arden, but as there was already an actress of that name in Hollywood, Miss Le Sueur adopted the name suggested by the runner-up instead—Joan Crawford. Gretchen Young had her first name changed to

> Movie fans under the impression that Ingrid Bergman was the wife of the great Swedish director Ingmar Bergman are, of course, absolutely correct. This Ingrid, though, was the Countess Ingrid van Rosen before becoming Bergman's fifth wife and perpetuating the Ingrid–Ingmar confusion for all time.

Loretta by Colleen Moore, who discovered her as a 14-year-old extra in *Her Wild Oat* (US 26). Loretta, said Miss Moore, was the name of 'the most beautiful doll I ever had'.

Bela Lugosi, real name Bela Blasko, took his screen surname from his hometown of Lugos in Hungary. Richard Burton, formerly Richard Jenkins, assumed the

> British actor Mark Lindsay was to be signed for the John Lennon role in *John and Yoko: A Love Story* (US 85, TVM), but had to surrender the part to Mark McGann when it became known that his real name was Mark Chapman—the same as the name of John Lennon's assassin.

name of his old teacher in Port Talbot. Gig Young (Byron Barr) took the name of the character he played in *The Gay Sisters* (US 42) and former child star Dawn O'Day switched to Anne Shirley to play the heroine of that name in *Anne of Green Gables* (US 34).

The story put about by her studio (and still believed in some quarters) that Theda Bara's name was an anagram of 'Arab Death' was so much hokum: the name was selected by director Frank Powell on learning that she had a relative called Barranger. Equally unromantic was Carole Lombard's (Jane Peters) decision to call herself after the Carroll, Lombardi Pharmacy on Lexington and 65th in New York. Greta Garbo might easily have become Greta Gabor. Long before meeting young Greta Gustafsson, her mentor Mauritz Stiller had cherished the dream of discovering and moulding a great star. He asked his manuscript assistant, Arthur Norden, to select a name. Norden, an historian, chose Gábor, after the Hungarian king, Gábor Bethlen. Stiller wanted something less East European, however, and amended it to Garbo. Another monarch was rather more personally involved in naming Lili Damita (Lilliane Carré). Holidaying at Biarritz in 1921 when she was 17, she attracted the attention of the King of Spain, who enquired after the *damita del maillo rojo* (young lady in a red bathing dress).

Those who retain their own names may also have cogent reasons for doing so. 'Bradford Dillman,' said that actor, 'sounded like a distinguished, phoney, theatrical name—so I kept it.'

Put Downs

Hollywood luminaries have a tendency to venerate each other, at least in public. It is reassuring to know that they do not always express such cloying sentiments in private.

Julie Andrews
'Working with her is like being hit over the head with a Valentine card.'—Christopher Plummer
'Julie Andrews has lilacs for pubic hair.'—her husband Blake Edwards

Talullah Bankhead
'A day away from Tallulah is like a month in the country.'—Howard Dietz

Diana Barrymore
'Diana is a horse's arse, quite a pretty one, but still a horse's arse.'—her father, John Barrymore

John Barrymore
'It takes an earthquake to get Jack out of bed, a flood to make him wash, and the United States Army to put him to work.'—his brother, Lionel Barrymore

Warren Beatty
'He's been famous longer than he's been a person.'—Dustin Hoffman
'He's in danger of waking up one morning in his own arms.'—Mamie Van Doren
'I like Warren. I think he's talented. He's just not fun to be with.'—Robert Altman

Ingrid Bergman
'Poor Ingrid—speaks five languages and can't act in any of them.'—Sir John Gielgud

Humphrey Bogart
'Bogey's a helluva nice guy until 11.30 p.m. After that he thinks he's Bogart.'—Dave Chasen

Marlon Brando
'Most of the time he sounds like he has a mouth full of wet toilet paper.'—Rex Reed
'His heart, it bleeds for the masses
But the people he works with
Get kicked in the asses.'—producer Alan Miller

Yul Brynner
'One of the biggest shits I've ever come across in show business. He was just a pig.'—Jeffrey Bernard

Richard Burton
'The rudest man I ever met, and unattractive—pock-marked as an Easter Island statue.'—Libby Purves

Michael Caine
'An over-fat, flatulent 62-year-old windbag, a master of inconsequence now masquerading as guru, passing off his vast limitations as pious virtues.'—Richard Harris

Capucine
Laurence Harvey to Capucine during filming of *Walk on*

Bette Davis said the best time she ever had with Joan Crawford was when she pushed her down the stairs in Whatever Happened to Baby Jane *(US 62). Kicking her in the face must have been a bundle of fun too.* (SI)

the Wild Side (US 62): 'If you were more of a woman, I would be more of a man. Kissing you is like kissing the side of a beer bottle.'

> Peter Sellers and Orson Welles had a major scene together at the gaming table in *Casino Royale* (GB 67), playing against each other. In fact they never met on the set. So strong was their mutual dislike that they acted the scene on different days, performing to doubles.

Charles Chaplin
'The best goddamned ballet dancer in the business'—W. C. Fields (who rated ballet dancers with children and animals)

Maurice Chevalier
'A great artiste, but a small human being.'—Josephine Baker

Claudette Colbert
Noël Coward to CC: 'I'd wring your neck, if you had one.'
'An ugly shopgirl.'—Marlene Dietrich

Gary Cooper
'When he puts his arms around me, I feel like a horse.'—Clara Bow
'He's got a reputation as a great actor just by thinking hard about the next line.'—King Vidor
'He is a nice, shy, quiet, modest young man, devoid of any

brains.'—Harold Nicholson, Hollywood 1933

Joan Crawford
'The best time I ever had with Joan Crawford was when I pushed her down the stairs in *Whatever Happened to Baby Jane*.'—Bette Davis
'I wouldn't piss on Joan Crawford if she were on fire.'—Bette Davis again
'There is not enough money in Hollywood to lure me into making another film with Joan Crawford.'—Sterling Hayden after co-starring with her in *Johnny Guitar* (US 54)

Tom Cruise
'He has the habit of treating you like a princess one minute and then like a piece of furniture the next.'—former girlfriend, Rebecca de Mornay

Bette Davis
'As much sex appeal as Slim Somerville.'—Carl Laemmle on BD in her youth
'I can't imagine any guy giving her a tumble.'—Carl Laemmle again
'Surely no one but a mother could have loved Bette Davis at the height of her career.'—Brian Ahearne
When I get hold of her, I'll tear every hair out of her moustache.'—Talullah Bankhead

Daniel Day-Lewis
'I knew Daniel before he was Irish.'—Stephen Frears (See also Oscar Levant on Doris Day)

Doris Day
'I knew Doris Day before she was a virgin.'—Oscar Levant
'Doris Day is as wholesome as a bowl of cornflakes and at least as sexy.'—Dwight MacDonald
'Doris is just about the remotest person I know.'—Kirk Douglas (see also Day on Douglas)

Olivia de Havilland
'I married first, won the Oscar before Olivia did, and if I die first, she'll undoubtedly be livid because I beat her to it.'—her sister Joan Fontaine

James Dean
'He was a hero to the people who saw him only as a little waif, when actually he was a pudding of hatred.'—Elia Kazan

Kirk Douglas
'Boastful, egotistical, resentful of criticism—if anyone dare give it.'—Sheilah Graham
'Kirk never makes much of an effort toward anyone else. He's pretty much wrapped up in himself.'—Doris Day
'I'm here to speak about his wit, his charm, his warmth, his talent . . . At last, a real acting job.'—Burt Lancaster at tribute to K.D.

Nelson Eddy
'The ham of hams.'—Allan Dwan

Frances Farmer
'The nicest thing I can say about Frances Farmer is that she is unbearable.'—William Wyler

Peter Finch
'I just can't bring myself to say anything nice about my father. He brought nothing but anguish and hardship to our lives.'—producer Charles Finch

Errol Flynn

'A 50-year trespass against good taste.'—Leslie Mallory

'You always knew exactly where you were with him, because he always let you down.'—David Niven

Jane Fonda

'A pain in the behind.'—Bob Evans

Harrison Ford

'An extra in a big hat.'—Ken Russell

Clark Gable

'Clark Gable took the humour and sex from the characters he played.'—Joan Crawford

'To tell the honest truth, he isn't such a helluva good lay.'—his lover, subsequently his wife, Carole Lombard

'Clark is the sort of guy, if you say "Hiya Clark, how are ya?"—he's stuck for an answer.'—Ava Gardner

Greta Garbo

'Boiled down to essentials, she is a plain mortal girl with large feet.'—Herbert Kretzmer

'The most inhibited person I've ever worked with.'—Ernst Lubitsch

'Making a film with Greta Garbo does not constitute an introduction.'—Robert Montgomery

Richard Gere

'Richard is so arrogant. I've never felt less for a co-star. What people saw on screen as pure passion was pure misery.'—Debra Winger after *An Officer and a Gentleman* (US 82)

Hugh Grant

'From my personal experience I think he is a self-important, boring, flash-in-the-pan Brit'—Robert Downey Jr.

Jean Harlow

'She was the kind of girl who climbed the ladder of success wrong by wrong.'—Mae West

David Hasselhoff

'You look much better with your clothes on.'—Princess Diana

Paul Henreid

'He looks as if his idea of fun would be to find a nice cold damp grave and sit in it.'—Richard Winnington

Katharine Hepburn

'She ran the gamut of emotions from A to B.'—Dorothy Parker on Hepburn's performance in the Broadway play *The Lake*

'She wasn't really stand-offish. She ignored everyone equally.'—Lucille Ball

'At the studio [RKO], they called her 'Katharine of Arrogance'. Not without reason, as I could tell you—but why bother?'—Estelle Winwood, who played with her in *Quality Street* (US 37)

Hepburn to John Barrymore on completion of *A Bill of Divorcement* (US 32): 'Thank goodness I don't have to act with you any more.' Barrymore: 'I didn't know you ever had, darling.'

Dustin Hoffman

'Why doesn't the boy just act? Why must he go through all this *sturm und drang*.'—Laurence Olivier

'She is good as a peasant but incapable of playing a lady'—Sophia Loren on Gina Lollobrigida, seen here not playing a lady in The Hunchback of Notre Dame *(Fr 57).*

Thousands of women swooned for Leslie Howard in his romantic roles as The Scarlet Pimpernel *(GB 34), as Romeo in* Romeo and Juliet *(US 36) and as Ashley Wilkes in* Gone With the Wind *(US 39). Harold Nicholson thought he looked like 'an assistant master at some inferior private school'.*

'My experience with Hoffman was unhappy.'—David Puttnam, producer of *Agatha* (GB 79)

Sydney Pollack, on receiving his Oscar for *Tootsie* (US 82): 'I'd give it up, if I could have back the nine months of my life I spent with Dustin making it.'

'Dustin is a professional victim ... when you put yourself in that position, you can make pre-emptive strikes against everyone and feel morally righteous. I think he does care about quality, but that's not a license for his behaviour.'—director Ulu Grosbard, former close friend

Miriam Hopkins

'Puerile and silly and snobbish.'—Edward G. Robinson

'I don't think there was ever a more difficult female in the world.'—Bette Davis (whom some reckoned a close contender)

'The least desirable companion on a desert island.'—Harvard Lampoon's citation to M.H., 1940

Leslie Howard

'He looks like an assistant master at some inferior private school. Glasses and bad teeth.'—Harold Nicholson, Hollywood 1933 (Howard's brother Arthur, who resembled him, became a household name late in life playing an assistant master at an inferior private school in TV's *Whacko!*)

Rock Hudson

'I call him Ernie because he's certainly no Rock.'—Doris Day (the implication of this remark was lost on many at the time)

'... hog lumpy.'—James Dean

William Hurt

'He promises you a bad time, and he delivers on his promise.'—Hector Babene, his director on *Kiss of a Spiderwoman* (US/Br 85)

Don Johnson

'This man is unbearable.'—Mickey Rourke

They may look lovey-dovey, but after completing Desperately Seeking Susan *(US 85) Rosanna Arquette expressed the view that Madonna should have learned to act before jumping into the movie game. (Kobal)*

Alan Ladd

'Alan Ladd is hard, bitter and occasionally charming, but he is, after all, a small boy's idea of a tough guy.'—Raymond Chandler

Burt Lancaster

'Burt Lancaster! Before he can pick up an ashtray, he discusses his motivation for an hour or two. You want to say "Just pick up the ashtray, and shut up!"'—Jeanne Moreau

Jessica Lange

'Beautiful face, no brains, big bosoms.'—Dino de Laurentis

Vivien Leigh

'She made life hell for everybody near her, unless they did everything she wished, as she wished and when she wished.'—Wolfe Kaufman

---

Among the many battles royal between stars and directors was one that raged on the set of *Santa Fe Trail* (US 40) between Raymond Massey, who played the abolitionist John Brown—executed for leading the Harper's Ferry raid—and helmer Michael Curtiz. On a day when friction between the two had reached a new high, actor Alan Hale admonished the rest of the cast: 'Don't go near Curtiz this morning. He's in an ugly mood. The front office has just told him he must fake Massey's hanging.'

Jerry Lewis

'One of the most hostile, unpleasant guys I've ever seen ... arrogant, sour, ceremonial, piously chauvinistic egomaniac.'—Elliott Gould on his childhood idol

Gina Lollobrigida

'Her personality is limited. She is good as a peasant but incapable of playing a lady.'—Sophia Loren

Sophia Loren

'Sophia is a very pretty girl but she cannot threaten me because she is incapable of playing my roles.'—Gina Lollobrigida

Steve McQueen

'You've got to realise that a Steve McQueen performance lends itself to monotony.'—Robert Mitchum

'I can honestly say he's the most difficult actor I've ever worked with.'—Norman Jewison

Madonna

'She's jumped right into the movie game ... but I think people should learn to act first, you know what I mean?'—Rosanna Arquette, her co-star in *Desperately Seeking Susan* (US 85)

'Her sex is totally contrived, but mine is natural. And I don't honestly see her as an acting rival, judging from the films she's made so far.'—Kim Basinger

'She's so hairy, when she lifted her arm I thought it was Tina Turner in her armpit.'—Joan Rivers

Lee Marvin

'Lee Marvin—Lee Moron.'—Marlon Brando, his co-star in *The Wild One* (US 54)

Victor Mature

'Hollywood's self-avowed disciple of conceit and vulgarity.'—W. H. Mooring

Marilyn Monroe
'She's just an arrogant little tail-twitcher who's learned to throw sex in your face.'—Nunnally Johnson

'A vacuum with nipples.'—Otto Preminger

'There's a broad with a future behind her.'—Constance Bennett

'A fat cow.'—Harry Cohn (given what he said about other people, this could be taken as moderately complimentary)

'A professional amateur.'—Laurence Olivier

Eddie Murphy
'I have no respect for you as an actor. You f*** me over as a friend.'—John Landis on the set of *Coming to America* (US 88)

David Niven
'An extremely mean and deeply heartless figure.'—fellow actor Peter Willes

Merle Oberon
'Amateur little bitch!'—Laurence Olivier, after she had accused him of spewing saliva at her on the set of *Wuthering Heights* (US 39)

'I'm not bitchy myself. In all my life I've only met two bitches—Wendy Barrie and Merle Oberon. They were both ex-Korda girls. Maybe that's the reason.'—June Duprez

'That Singapore streetwalker.'—Marlene Dietrich (a reference to the fact, unknown to the public, that Oberon was mixed race).

Maureen O'Hara
'She looked as if butter wouldn't melt in her mouth—or anywhere else.'—Elsa Lanchester

Michael Palin
'Michael Palin is not just one of Britain's foremost character actors; he also talks a lot. Yap, yap, yap he goes, all day long and through the night, 23 to the dozen, the ground littered with the hind legs of donkeys, till you believe it is not possible for him to go on any longer, but he does.'—fellow Python John Cleese (according to the universally popular Palin this is the most critical thing that has ever been said about him)

Mary Pickford
'That prissy bitch.'—Mabel Normand

'She was the girl every young man wanted to have—as his sister.'—Alistair Cooke

Dennis Quaid
'A giant pain in the ass.'—*Great Balls of Fire* director Jim McBride

Ronald Reagan
'I can't stand the sight of Ronnie Reagan. I'd like to stick my Oscar up his ass.'—Gloria Grahame

Robert Redford
'Well, at least he has finally found his true love—what a pity he can't marry himself.'—Frank Sinatra

Ralph Richardson
'I don't know his name but he's got a face like half a teapot.'—King George VI

Eric Roberts
'For as many people I meet who love Eric Roberts, I meet just as many who think he's a jerk.'—his sister, Julia Roberts

Mickey Rourke
'I found him incredibly boring.'—Jacqueline Bisset, who co-starred with him in *Wild Orchid* (US 90)

Meg Ryan
'The image Meg has—the innocent, dizzy girl next door—could not be further from the truth. In real life she's a cold-hearted, cruel manipulator.'—her mother Susan

Arnold Schwarzenegger
'Class will out. And a lack of it usually tells.'—columnist Marilyn Beck after a display of boorish behaviour in Calgary

'Arnold is an arch manipulator, an incorrigible womaniser, a hypocrite and a control freak, a man with a cruel streak who cannot admit to an iota of weakness.'—anonymous producer

George C. Scott
'A jerk.'—Joseph Levine

Kristin Scott Thomas
'If you've got ambitions to play Lady Macbeth, you'll have to join your local amateur dramatic society.'—her tutor at the Central School of Speech and Drama

Norma Shearer
'A face unclouded by thought.'—Lillian Hellman

'I love to play bitches, and she certainly helped me in this part.'—Joan Crawford after co-starring with her in *The Women* (US 39)

'A dead fish.'—Marlene Dietrich

Sam Shepard
'He is a very selfish, self-orientated person.'—Robert Altman, who directed him in *Fool for Love* (US 85)

Frank Sinatra
'When Frank Sinatra was down he was sweet, but when he got back up he was hell.'—Ava Gardner

'He's the kind of guy that, when he dies, he's going up to heaven to give God a bad time for making him bald.'—Marlon Brando

'Terribly nice one minute and . . . well, not so nice the next.'—HRH Prince Charles

'I think he's an ill-bred swine who operates on the level of an animal.'—David Susskind

Sylvester Stallone
'He thinks he's irresistible and expects women to fall at his feet. Maybe I should have done—his feet probably have more appeal than the rest of his body.'—Sharon Stone

'His career is more mysterious than cot death.'—critic Rex Reed

Sharon Stone
'So goddamned mean—when she's angry she knows how to say things that really hurt.'—Paul Verhoeven, who directed her in *Basic Instinct* (US 91). (To which Ms Stone countered that she and Mr Verhoeven had a love–hate relationship: 'He loves me and I hate him.')

'I would rather clean toilet bowls than make another film with Sharon Stone. Many women have given me heartache. She's the only one who gave me a heart attack.'—Bob Evans, her producer on *Sliver* (US 93)

Barbra Streisand

'The most pretentious woman the cinema has ever known.'—producer Jon Peters

Walter Matthau to B.S. during filming of *Hello Dolly* (US 69): 'I have more talent in my smallest fart than you have in your entire body.'

And on considering the matter further, Matthau again: 'She is the most extraordinarily uninteresting person I have ever met. I just find her a terrible bore.'

Elizabeth Taylor

'Elizabeth Taylor has a double chin, two short legs and a pot belly.'—her husband Richard Burton

On herself: 'I have the face and body of a woman and the mind of a child.'

Spencer Tracy

Clark Gable on hearing that Tracy was up for the lead in *Broken Lance* (US 54): 'Spence is the part. The old rancher is mean, unreasonable and vain. All he has to do is show up and be photographed.'

Lana Turner

'She is not even an actress . . . only a trollop.'—Gloria Swanson

Monica Vitti

'I fell in love with all my leading ladies. Oh, except Monica Vitti. No one could love Monica Vitti.'— Dirk Bogarde on *Desert Island Discs*

Raquel Welsh

'Silicone from the knees up.'—George Masters, make-up artist

Orson Welles

'There but for the grace of God, goes God.'— Herman Mankiewicz

Esther Williams

'Wet she's a star, dry she ain't.'—Joe Pasternak

'I can't honestly say that Esther Williams ever acted in an Andy Hardy picture, but she swam in one.'—Mickey Rooney

Bruce Willis

'The world's worst actor.'—Robert Stephens

Loretta Young

'Whatever it is this actress never had, she still hasn't got it.'—*New York Times* critic Bosley Crowther

Screen Tests

The most extensive screen tests in the history of motion pictures were held for the role of Scarlett O'Hara in *Gone With the Wind* (US 39). Producer David O .Selznick shot 149,000ft of black-and-white test film and another 13,000ft of colour with 60 actresses, none of whom got the part. Having discarded 27 hours of test film, Selznick narrowed the choice to three major stars and one unknown—Joan Bennett, Jean Arthur, Paulette Goddard and newcomer Vivien Leigh. The final tests required the four contenders to play the scenes of Scarlett getting into her corset, talking to Ashley in the

Ernest Borgnine claims to have had the shortest screen test of any aspirant film actor when he auditioned for his first motion-picture role in *Whistle at Eaton Falls* (US 51). He reported with six other candidates to director Robert Siodmark, prepared for anything except what actually happened. The only instruction from the director was 'Walk across the room and say "panhandle".' Borgnine did as bidden. 'Okay,' responded Siodmark laconically, 'see you on set.'

paddock and drunkenly proposing to Rhett Butler. Miss Leigh's successful test was actually made after shooting of the movie had commenced—perhaps the only instance of a major motion picture going into production before the star role had been cast. Total cost of the 165,000ft of tests was $105,000—approximately the budget of an average second feature at the time.

Hollywood's first nude screen tests were held for *Four for Texas* (US 63), which starred Ursula Andress and Anita Ekberg in the femme leads. Those actresses who had been unwilling to be tested need not have worried; all nude scenes were cut by the censor.

Marlene Dietrich used to introduce a song in her solo stage act which, she would say, 'brought me into pictures'. Just to confuse matters, if it was an English speaking audience she would then sing 'You're the Cream in My Coffee', whereas in Germany she would sing 'Wer Wird Denn Weinen'. Those familiar with her performances in both languages assumed she was simply romancing, but the recent chance discovery of her screen test for *The Blue Angel* (Ger 30) in an unmarked canister at the Austrian Film Archives in Vienna reveals that she was indeed speaking what would have been the truth had she said that either song 'brought her into talking pictures' (she made over 20 silents). Taken in September 1929 in Berlin, the test has Dietrich singing both songs. What makes the four-minute film especially compelling for the modern viewer is to see Dietrich losing her temper not once but three times in as many minutes. First she castigates the accompanist for failing to render 'You're the Cream in My Coffee' correctly with a few words of reproof, but when he gets it wrong a second time there is an outburst. 'What do you think you're doing, fella,' she shouts. 'You call that piano playing? I'm supposed to sing to that junk? It belongs to the wash house, not here. Get it? Dope.' A third attempt proving no better, Marlene bangs her fist on top of the piano and screams at the hapless pianist 'Good God, it doesn't go that way! Don't you get it? Some genius we lost in you.'

Going round to the front of the piano, she puts one foot on the keyboard and clambers onto the top of the piano, where she crosses her legs and pulls a rolled down stocking up her right leg. 'When you play this wrong, you get a kick,' she warns the cowed and trembling pianist, then launches into the world-weary 'Wer Wird Denn Weinen'. Fortunately for the accompanist, he knew that one and avoided a crack in the teeth with the toe of Dietrich's sharp pointed shoe. Nobody knows what happened to him; everyone knows what happened to Dietrich's career after that historic screen test.

STARS WHO FAILED SCREEN TESTS

Failing a screen test may not be a passport to stardom, but in some cases it has been no barrier. Bette Davis's first screen test was so appalling that she ran from the Goldwyn projection room screaming. Her next, with Universal, was successful enough for her to be given a job—as a stand-in girl for screen tests of male actors. Clark Gable failed a Warner screen test in 1930 because Jack Warner declared (in Gable's hearing) that he was only 'a big ape'. His next was at MGM, where his prominent ears told against him. The fact that he did it in Polynesian costume with a flower in his hair may not have helped—production chief Irving Thalberg reckoned he lacked macho appeal. Although he failed the test, MGM signed him anyway and he stayed with the studio—contributing significantly to its ascendancy—for 23 years. Another star who failed the rigours of a MGM test was Maurice Chevalier; but he was signed by Paramount in 1928 on the strength of the same test.

Shirley Temple, probably the greatest box-office attraction of all time, failed a test for the *Our Gang* series. The screen's most prestigious luminary, Laurence Olivier, was turned down for *Queen Christina* (US 33) after testing opposite Greta Garbo, though it is widely held that Garbo deliberately sabotaged the test in order that the role should go to ex-lover John Gilbert, then in decline.

François Truffaut was so enchanted with 12-year-old Jean-Pierre Léaud's screen test for *The Four Hundred Blows* (Fr 59) that he decided to incorporate it into the film—despite the fact that it consisted of an informal conversation between Léaud and the director. The scene was preserved in the film as an interview between the boy Antoine Doinel and a woman psychiatrist in a reformatory. The psychiatrist was not seen, but a female voiceover substituted for Truffaut's questioning. Fade-outs were used to cover up Léaud's explicit replies to Truffaut's intimate questions about adolescent sex, heightening the effect of disorientation.

Paramount gave the thumbs down to young British thespian Archibald Leach on account of his thick neck and bandy legs. A couple of years later Paramount head B. P. Schulberg noticed Leach in the test of an aspiring actress in which he was merely the feed. Notwithstanding his neck and his legs, he was signed at $450 a week and given a brand-new name to boot—Cary Grant.

Rock Hudson's screen test for Twentieth Century Fox was so bad it was preserved and shown to other aspirants as a classic example of how not to perform before the camera.

Occasionally it might be the candidate who said no. The talented Romy Schneider walked out of her 1955 screen test with Walt Disney, furious at being made to pose in a dirndl dress in front of a picture-postcard Tyrolean backdrop.

It was Peter O'Toole's roguish Irish humour—often directed at those who held themselves in high regard—which caused him to fail his screen test for *Suddenly Last Summer* (GB 59). Producer Sam Spiegel asked him to improvise the role of a doctor. O'Toole assumed his best bedside manner and said: 'It's all right Mrs Spiegel, your

son will never play the violin again.'

Some aspirants to stardom, however young and inexperienced, are unwilling to take 'no' for an answer. At the age of 17 going on 18 Susan George auditioned together with over 300 other teenage girls for the lead role of a 16-year-old schoolgirl in *Twinky* (GB 69) who marries a 40-year-old American writer (Charles Bronson). She was so devastated at not being even short-listed that she returned the following day wearing her school uniform, giving a false name. She won the part.

Brigitte Bardot was another teenager dreaming of stardom who found the going tough—puppy fat and spots caused her to fail a screen test with Marc Allégret when she was 16. Jane Russell also failed to pass muster. The report on her 1940 test for Fox read 'unphotogenic'. Warner's comments when she tested for them were 'no energy' and 'no spark'. Another star considered physically unsuitable was Robert Taylor. He failed his test for United Artists in 1933 because Sam Goldwyn thought he was too skinny.

Nothing was found wanting in Ava Gardner's physique. After seeing her test for MGM, Louis B. Mayer expostulated: 'She can't talk. She can't act. She's terrific.'

Less enthusiasm was expressed for Fred Astaire in a studio report on his first screen test, even if the words were much the same: 'Can't act. Can't sing. Can dance a little.'

Not even an established star could afford to be over-confident. According to Hollywood legend, at the height of her screen career Gloria Swanson took a test incognito wearing a blonde wig. She was turned down.

The Long and Short of it

The shortest adult performer in movies was 2 ft 7 in tall Tamara de Treaux (1959–90), an actress and singer from San Francisco. Tamara's most celebrated role was E.T., Steven Spielberg's lovable alien from outer space. Although in parts of the film E.T. was an electronic puppet, in others he was played by actors and actresses in costume—beside Tamara, there were 2 ft 10 in Pat Bilson and legless schoolboy Matthew de Merritt, who played the drunk scene walking on his hands inside the E.T. suit. Tamara's main scene was of E.T. shuffling into the spacecraft for his return home. Her weight—she considered she was too heavy at 2 st 12 lb—helped her to perfect what she described as 'a cute Daffy Duck waddle'. Tamara was dwarfed by seven-year-old Drew Barrymore, who towered over her by 17 in.

The shortest actor to play the leading role in a film is Filipino paratrooper and black-belt martial arts exponent Weng Weng, who has starred in *Agent 00* (Phi 81) and *For Your Height Only* (Phi 84). Weng Weng measures 2 ft 9 in.

The shortest Hollywood actor is 2 ft 8 in Verne Troyer, who played Mini-Me in *Austin Powers: The Spy Who Shagged Me* (US 99) and was also seen in *Men in Black* (US 97) and *How the Grinch Stole Christmas* (US 00).

All-dwarf casts have been used in two films—a western, *The Terror of Tiny Town* (US 38), and Werner Herzog's

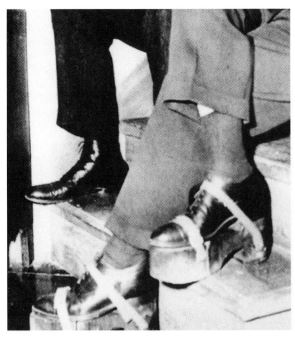

Humphrey Bogart may have been a movie giant, but he needed these platforms to bring his scrawny 5 ft 4 in body level with Ingrid Bergman's limpid eyes in Casablanca *(US 42).* (Associated Press)

The long and the short of it. A 5 ft 3 in Mickey Rooney looks skywards at 6 ft 6 in gf. Dorothy Ford in Love Laughs at Andy Hardy *(US 47).* (BFI)

Even Dwarfs Started Small (FRG 70). *The Little Cigars* (US 73) had a cast of five midgets and one full-sized actress, described as 'a busty blonde'.

The largest cast of dwarves and midgets was 116 in *The Wizard of Oz* (US 39), and an equal number in *Under the Rainbow* (US 81), which was the story of what the original Munchkins got up to on and off the set of *The Wizard of Oz* while they were staying at the Culver Hotel in 1938. (What they got up to was miniature mayhem.)

The shortest artiste to play major roles, apart from dwarves and midgets, is 4 ft 9 in Linda Hunt, who made her debut in *Popeye* (US 80) as mother of the giant, Oxblood Oxheart, and won the Academy Award for Best Supporting Actress in 1984 for her role as Billy Kwan, a male Eurasian cameraman in Indonesia, in *The Year of Living Dangerously* (Aus 82). She has since been in the Merchant-Ivory version of Henry James's *The Bostonians* (GB 84), *Dune* (US 84), *Silverado* (US 85), as Gertrude Stein's lifetime companion Alice B. Toklas in *Waiting for the Moon* (US 87), in *She-Devil* (US 89), and as vertically challenged fashion-mag honcho Regina Krumm in *Ready to Wear (Prêt-à-Porter)* (US 94).

The only leading ladies under 5 feet were silent-screen heroines Florence Turner and Marguerite Clark, each 4 ft 10 in tall, 4 ft 11 in May McAvoy, who starred opposite Al Jolson in *The Jazz Singer* (US 27), and 4 ft 11½ in Gloria Swanson. Janet Gaynor and Mary Pickford were both 5 ft exactly, as was the lesser known Edith Roberts, whose height qualified her to play the title role in *Her Five-Foot Highness* (US 20).

The shortest actor in leading roles is 5-foot-nothing Danny De Vito, veteran of a host of cameo roles before achieving stardom opposite Arnold Schwarzenegger in *Twins* (US 88). Most diminutive actor in romantic leads was 'Cuddly' Dudley Moore, who insisted that the half was not omitted from his 5 ft 2½ in. Mickey Rooney could look him in the eyebrows at 5 ft 3 in and Michael J. Fox could look down at them both from his 5 ft 4 in elevation—the same height as Humphrey Bogart. Reports that Alan Ladd was only 5 ft tall were quite untrue; he was 5 ft 6 in, which made him an inch taller than Dustin Hoffman and the same height as Al Pacino. Nevertheless, Ladd's lack of inches was proverbial in Hollywood. Sophia Loren has confirmed that he had to stand on a box for his love scenes with her in *Boy on a Dolphin* (US 57), and James Mason, when he was invited to co-star with Ladd in *Botany Bay* (US 54), told the producer that he had no intention of standing in a trench for their scenes together.

The tallest screen artiste was Clifford Thompson, claimed to be 8 ft 6 in and then the tallest man in the world, who played opposite (and above) ZaSu Pitts in Hal Roach's *Seal Skins* (US 32). No other eight-footers are recorded. Artistes of 7 feet or over include Tex Erikson, 7 ft exactly, who was featured in *Jungle Jim in the Forbidden Land* (US 52); 7 ft University of California basketball player Tiny Ron Taylor, seen as Ira in *Seven Hours to Judgement* (US 88); Kevin Peter Hall, at 7 ft 2 in the tallest of six brothers all over 6 ft 5 in, who played the space alien in *Predator* (US 87) and the eponymous apeman in *Big Foot and the Hendersons* (US 87); Johan Aasen, a 7 ft 2 in character actor who entered Hollywood pictures in 1923; Peter Mayhew, 7 ft 2 in ex-hospital porter, who played a mythical monster in *Sinbad and the Eye of the Tiger* (US 77) and the furry wookie Chewbacca in *Star Wars* (US 77); Richard Kiel, 7 ft 2 in without his size

16 shoes, who played the steel-teethed giant villain in Bond movies *The Spy Who Loved Me* (GB 77) and *Moonraker* (GB/Fr 79) and starred in the title role of *The Humanoid* (It 78) and *The Giant of Thunder Mountain* (US 91); 7 ft 2 in Masai tribesman Bolaji Badejo, the alien monster in *Alien* (GB 78); John Bloom, 7 ft 4 in, who was Frankenstein's monster in *Dracula v Frankenstein* (US 71); 7 ft 4 in 520 lb French-born wrestler André René Roussimaff as the gentle giant Fizzick in *The Princess Blade* (US 87); J. Lockard Martin, the 7 ft 7 in doorman at Grauman's Chinese Theater in Hollywood, who played the robot Gort in *The Day the Earth Stood Still* (US 51) and was so weak he was unable to lift Patricia Neal; and Jack Tarver, 7 ft 10 in, the giant in Fox's feature-length children's picture *Jack and the Beanstalk* (US 17). Latest of the tall guys to present cameramen with problems of how to keep them in frame is Romanian-born, US domiciled Georghe Muresan, who starred opposite Billy Crystal in comedy-drama *My Giant* (US 98), and at 7ft 7in is ³/₄in taller than the tallest man in Europe. His shoe size is 19.

The tallest leading men were 6 ft 7 in James Arness, who starred in *Them* (US 54) and *The First Travelling Saleslady* (US 56), and Bruce Spence, 6 ft 7 in, in *Stork* (Aus 71), which was scripted by 6 ft 7 in David Williamson, and *Wo die Grunen Ameisen Trauma* (FRG 84). Christopher Lee is the tallest major star at 6 ft 5 in, an inch taller than Clint Eastwood.

The tallest actress was 7 ft 2 in Sandy Allen of Shelbyville, Indiana, who played the arm-wrestling 'tallest woman on Earth' opposite lanky Donald Sutherland, a whole foot shorter, in Federico Fellini's *Casanova* (It 76). The tallest leading lady was Baltimore-born Tamara Dobson, the 6 ft 2 in star of Warner Bros 'blaxploitation' picture *Cleopatra Jones* (US 73), in which she played a US Government superagent ripping the guts out of an evil drug syndicate. Her father, who sold tickets for the Pennsylvania Railroad, was 6 ft 3 in and her three siblings were all over 6 ft. By an odd coincidence Tamara shared her somewhat unusual forename with the shortest-ever screen artiste (see above). Currently the tallest leading ladies are Sigourney Weaver and Geena Davis, both 6 ft exactly.

The heaviest screen artiste was Ethel Greer, who weighed 637lb when she appeared with Clara Bow in *Hoopla* (US 33). Miss Greer's 140lb husband, visiting the set, remarked of the slender 118lb Miss Bow: 'I never could see why some fellows go for these skinny girls.'

The most generously proportioned leading lady of all time was Chesty Morgan, the possessor of a 73-in bust, who starred in *Deadly Weapons* (US 75).

Play it Again

The most enduring screen team was that of Indian superstars Prem Nazir and Sheela, who had played opposite each other in 130 movies by 1975.

The Hollywood record pales by comparison. Excluding performers billed together solely in 'series' films, the most enduring screen partners were husband-and-wife team Charles Bronson and the late Jill Ireland, who co-starred in 15 films up to and including *Assassination* (US 87). Myrna Loy and William Powell played opposite each other in 13 pictures; Janet Gaynor starred with Charles Farrell and Sophia Loren with Marcello Mastroianni in 12 films; Lila Lee with Thomas Meighan in 11 films; Ginger Rogers with Fred Astaire, Judy Garland with Mickey Rooney, Katharine Hepburn with Spencer Tracy and Paul Newman with his wife Joanne Woodward in ten films; while three screen teams bring up the rear with eight films together—Jeanette MacDonald and Nelson Eddy; Greer Garson and Walter Pidgeon; and Olivia de Havilland and Errol Flynn.

The actor who has played the same role the most times in feature films is the Hong Kong actor Kwan Tak-Hing, who portrayed the great South China martial arts hero Huang Fei-Hong (1847–1924) in 77 films out of a series of 104. His first appearance was in *The True Story of Huang Fei-Hong* (HK 49) and his last in *Magnificent Butcher* (HK 80). During the 1970s, when he played in only one Huang Fei-Hong movie, Kwan Tak-Hing continued the role in a television series.

The Hollywood actor to repeat the same role the most times in feature films was William Boyd (1898–1972), a major star of the '20s whose flagging career was revived in the '30s when Paramount chose him as the gentleman cowboy Hopalong Cassidy. Dressed always in black (usually reserved for villains in 'B' westerns), Boyd rode the range as 'Hoppy' in 66 full-length films, starting with *Hop-a-long Cassidy* aka *Hopalong Cassidy Enters* (US 35) and ending with *Strange Gamble* (US 48). The films were among the first American productions aired on television in the '40s and Boyd then embarked on a long-running *Hopalong Cassidy* TV series, having already played the character in a network radio series.

The actor who played the same role the longest was Desmond Llewellyn (1914–1999), who debuted as Q, the gizmo-meister of the quartermaster's stores, in the second James Bond film *From Russia with Love* (GB 63)) and made his 17th and last appearance in the role 36 later in *The World Is Not Enough* (US/GB 99). Unlike the character he played, Llewellyn was a self-confessed technophobe baffled by automatic cash machines and plastic hotel keycards. Because he was so closely indentified with Q, he found it difficult to obtain other parts between Bond films. Successive directors contrived to extend his four days on set so that he would earn some extra money.

TYPECASTING
A number of actors established a reputation for playing particular historical characters: Charles Vanel as Napoleon, Frank McGlynn as Abraham Lincoln and Robert Watson as Hitler. Silent player Roy Travers was cast as the Prince Consort 11 times and as Charles Dickens seven times. The most appearances in one historical role was probably by Mikhail Gelovani, who portrayed Stalin in more than 20 Soviet films. The dictator was so gratified by Gelovani's rather wooden projection of him as the wise, all-seeing, noble proletarian that he was never allowed to give the parts any other dimension.

When Donald Sutherland was 16 he asked his mother whether he was good-looking. 'No ...' she answered carefully, 'but your face has a lot of character.' On graduating from the London Academy of Music and Dramatic Art he found that the downside of a face with that much character was that the only parts he could get were as psychopaths or homicidal maniacs. Eventually an opportunity arose for a different kind of role in *Three in the Morning* (GB 68), a sweet and gentle individual for which he felt he would be perfectly cast. 'They turned me down,' he recalled, 'on the basis they wanted somebody who looked like the guy next door and that I didn't look like I had ever lived next door to anybody.' Eventually it wasn't his face which made his fortune, but being a Canadian... see p. 80.

Richard Gere might easily have become typecast as a hoodlum but for the break he got in a British film, *Yanks* (GB 79). In his debut picture *Looking for Mr Goodbar* (US 77) he was cast as a violent, drug-crazed hustler who terrorises Diane Keaton with a savage knife dance. For his next outing in *Days of Heaven* (US 78) he was the rough migrant worker who stabs his lover's husband to death. Then in *Bloodbrothers* (US 78) he was an alienated high-school rebel who batters a construction worker for no very good reason. It was John Schlesinger who saw another dimension to Richard Gere's persona and gave him the chance of playing the clean-cut young G.I. Matt in *Yanks* who charms his British hosts with his gentle manners, bakes cakes for his new English sweetheart and politely but firmly declines when she offers herself to him before he leaves for the D-Day landings. Gere did not admit to playing himself in the film, but conceded that the kind, honest and open-hearted Matt was a dead ringer for his father, a World War II veteran. Those who worked with him knew that it was a case of like father, like son.

Other actors have found their niche in occupational roles. Arthur Treacher and Charles Coleman seldom played anything but butlers throughout their screen careers, Irish-American actor Tom Dugan played a slow-witted New York cop in over 100 films following his debut in 1926, while Pat O'Brien was cast as a Roman Catholic priest in at least a dozen of his movies. In 1928 Guy Oliver claimed to have been cast as a sheriff in 150 of the 230 westerns he had made and in 1931 Frank Hagney, invariably seen as a boxer, declared ruefully that he had lost the world's heavyweight title no fewer than 29 times during his career. A number of performers specialised in courtroom dramas, but none with such dedication as Hollywood character actor Richard Tucker, who is known to have played the prosecuting attorney at least 54 times.

Henry Bergman played the maître d'hôtel in virtually all the numerous Charlie Chaplin films with scenes set in restaurants. He eventually retired from the screen to become a real maître d'hôtel at Hollywood's celebrated Henri's restaurant. Another actor to turn soup-and-fish typecasting to good account was Gino Corrado, who played waiters or head waiters for 15 years in such films as *Hallelujah! I'm a Bum* (US 33), *Top Hat* (US 35), *Casablanca* (US 42), *An Innocent Affair* (US 48), *My Wild Irish Rose* (US 47) and *The Stratton Story* (US 49). On his retirement from acting in 1949 he became head waiter at the Italia Restaurant in Beverly Hills, where as many as 30 to 50 patrons a day would ask him to autograph their menus.

Some were cast against type. German-born Peter van Eyck, who became Hollywood's stock Nazi beast, only came to California because as an active anti-Nazi he was forced to flee Hitler's Germany. Hollywood character actor Mischa Auer was an authentic Russian aristocrat who made his living playing phony Russian aristocrats.

The ability to play a drunk well is a rare one, which enabled Jack Norton and Arthur Housman to specialise in amiable inebriates, seldom playing anything else. Some special talent must also have inspired producers to cast Carmen Nigro as a gorilla in 32 movies, or 33 if his claim to have played the title role in *King Kong* (US 33) can be sustained (it is generally accepted that all the gorilla scenes were acted with models). He last donned his ape suit for *Gorilla at Large* (US 54). 'Cowardly Lion' Bert Lahr was not so lucky. 'After *The Wizard of Oz*,' he declared ruefully, 'I was typecast as a lion—and there aren't all that many parts for lions.'

Versatility is harder to quantify. However, it is doubtful whether any performer ever played with a greater variety of accents than Russian-born Hollywood actor Vladimir Sokoloff, who was cast as 35 nationalities during his career, ranging from an Italian physicist in *Cloak and Dagger* (US 46) to a blind Chinese beggar in *Macao* (US 52). The only accent Sokoloff never succeeded in mastering was American.

Oldest and Youngest

The oldest performer to have played a starring role in a movie was French veteran Charles Vanel (1892–1989), who was 95 on the completion of *Les Saisons du Plaisir* (Fr 88) in August 1987. The picture also marked his 75th anniversary as a screen actor. Set during a perfume manufacturers' convention in the south of France, it relates how a centenarian perfumier (Vanel) marries a 90-year-old bride (Denise Grey, who was playing her real age) and plans to name a successor to his dynasty. Vanel's co-star in his previous film, Claude Goretta's *Si le Soleil ne revenait pas* (Fr 87), was Catherine Mouchet, who was somewhat younger than Mme Grey—by 70 years. She had made her debut the previous year in *Thérèse* (Fr 86), 74 years after Vanel had made his debut in *Jim Crow* (Fr 12).

The oldest actress to have played a starring role in a movie is Lillian Gish (1893–1993), who was 93 when she completed principal photography on *The Whales of August* (US 87), in which she co-starred with the comparatively juvenile 78-year-old Bette Davis, in December 1986. Other nonagenarian starring roles were in *Hambone and Hillie* (US 84) at the age of 90 and in *Sweet Liberty* (US 86) at the age of 92. Like Charles Vanel (see above), Miss Gish had made her screen debut in 1912. Neither, though, holds the record for the longest screen career (see pp. 104–5), M. Vanel coming second to Curt Bois as the most enduring actor and Miss Gish coming second to Helen Hayes as the most enduring actress. (Note: most reference books cite Miss Gish's year of birth as either 1896 or 1898. In 1984 the American Film Institute was ungallant enough to make public its discovery of her birth certificate, which conclusively proved a birth date of 1893—and secured her place in the record books.)

The greatest age at which anyone has embarked on a regular movie career was 84 in the case of minuscule 4 ft 9 in character actress Lydia Yeamans Titus. She made her screen debut in the Rudolph Valentino film *All Night* (US 18) and played in over 50 features before her death in 1929 aged 95.

NONAGENARIAN AND CENTENARIAN SCREEN ARTISTES

Besides Charles Vanel (1892–1989), Lillian Gish (1893–1993) and Lydia Yeamans Titus (1834–1929) (see above), other nonagenerian artistes have been A. E. Matthews (1869–1960) in *Inn for Trouble* (GB 60); Estelle Winwood (1883–1984) in *Murder by Death* (US 76); John Cromwell (1887–1979) in *The Wedding* (US 78); Catherine Nesbitt (1889–1982) in *Never Never Land* (US 80) and *The Second Star to the Right* (GB 81); Sam Jaffe (1891–1984)—who played the 200-year-old High Lama in *Lost Horizon* (US 37)—in *Nothing Lasts Forever* (US 82) and *On the Line* aka *Downstream* (US 84); and George Burns (1896–1996) in *18 Again* (US 88) and *Radioland Murders* (US 94); and Sir John Gielgud (1904–2000) in *Shine* (Aus 96), *Hamlet* (GB 97), *Elizabeth* (GB 98), *The Tichborne Claimant* (GB 99) and *Catastrophe* (US/GB 00). Matty, as A. E. Matthews was known, once observed: 'I always wait for *The Times* each morning. I look at the obituary column, and if I'm not in it I go to work.' Estelle Winwood (b. Lee, Kent, 24 January 1883) completed her role as Nurse Withers in *Murder by Death* (US 76) on her 93rd birthday. Miss Winwood was the oldest member of the Screen Actors Guild at the time of her death in California aged 101. She made her professional debut at the Theatre Royal, Manchester, in 1898 and claimed to have been the first woman in America to wear lipstick in public. Madoline Thomas (b. Abergavenny, 2 January 1890) appeared with Emlyn Williams in *Caring* (GB 87 TVM) at the age of 97. She had come to the profession late in life, having been given her first stage role by Emlyn Williams when she was 52 and her first film role, also by her compatriot, in *The Last Days of Dolwyn* (GB 49). She died in 1989 three days short of her 100th birthday. The oldest British performer to act in a film and the only centenarian was Dame Gwen Ffrancon-Davies (b. London, 25 January 1891) who played opposite Jeremy Brett as Sherlock Holmes in *The Master Blackmailer* (GB 91, TVM) at the age of 100. She died aged 101 in January 1992 a month after the film had first been aired on television.

At least two centenarians were professional extras. William H. 'Dad' Taylor, born Brownsville, Texas, 9 July 1828, appeared in Edwin Carewe's *Evangeline* (US 29) at the age of 101—a unique instance of a person born during the Georgian era playing in a talkie. The other was Walter 'Cap' Field (1874–1976), who joined the Mexican production company Ammex in 1913 and played his last role in *She's Too Hot to Handle* (US 76) when he was 101. He fondly remembered being 'killed or wounded four or five times' in various small roles in *Gone with the Wind* (US 39). The 'sage' in *The Man Who Would Be King* (US 75) was played by a 102-year-old Moroccan.

The oldest performer to have played a speaking role on screen was 114-year-old Jeanne Louise Calment (1875–1997), who appeared as herself in *Vincent and Me* (Can/Fr 90). The film is about a 13-year-old Canadian girl called Jo (Nina Petronzio), passionate about the work of Vincent Van Gogh, who sets out on a European odyssey in pursuit of art forgers and eventually travels through time to 19th-century Arles to encounter the master himself. On her return, having succeeded in her objective of making Vincent smile, she meets the last survivor of those who knew him in person, Mme Jeanne Calment, whose father kept the shop where Van Gogh bought his canvas. She used to serve behind the counter as a girl and remembers vividly how he used to roll the canvas between his fingers to see if it was of good quality. When Jo tells her that Van Gogh was kind to her, Jeanne Calment replies 'Well, good for you, because he was rude to me!'. She also remembers him as 'rough and ugly'. In the year that *Vincent and Me* was released, 1990, Jeanne Calment succeeded Mrs Carrie White of Florida as the oldest person in the world. At her death in Arles in 1997 aged 122 she was the oldest person ever with an authenticated birth certificate.

One other person is claimed to have appeared in a movie at the age of 114, though not in a speaking role as it was a silent film. She was Mammy Lou, who played an old servant at the Southern mansion depicted in Goldwyn's *The Glorious Adventure* (US 18). The location for the picture was the famous Hermitage estate near Savannah, GA, where Mammy Lou had been a slave before the Emancipation. If her reported age was genuine, she would have been already over 60 at the time she received her freedom.

The youngest performer in a feature film was Balázs Monori, whose actual birth was shown in *Kilenc Hónap/Nine Months* (Hun 76), the story of a pregnant woman (Lili Monori) torn between two men and striving to improve herself. The director, Márta Meszaros, was reported to be delighted that Balázs's screen debut was so accomplished that no second take was needed.

The youngest performer to receive star billing was Leroy Overacker, known on the screen as Baby Leroy, who was chosen at the age of six months to play the central juvenile role opposite Maurice Chevalier in *Bedtime Story* (US 33). Master Overacker's contract had to be

One of the hazards of shooting with child actors over a period of months is that they can change both in manner and appearance. When Louis Malle made *Zazie dans le Métro* (Fr 60), about one day in the life of an 11-year-old girl, he found at the end of the shoot that some of the early scenes needed reshooting. To his dismay he realised that his young star, Catherine Demongeot, had changed so much in three months that she looked manifestly older in these scenes than she did in those immediately following. It was this experience which persuaded Malle to shoot *Pretty Baby* (US 78) in strict chronological sequence. Afterwards he observed that it was as well he had done so. During the shoot 12-year-old Brooke Shields had evolved from childhood to adolescence, as her character of Violet does in the film.

signed by his grandfather, because not only the star but also his 16-year-old mother was under age. The film was about a confirmed bachelor becoming encumbered with an abandoned baby whose protruding lower lip matches his own, a circumstance which leads everyone to believe that Chevalier is the father of the motherless child. All is unscrambled when it is found that the distinctive facial feature of the baby is accounted for by nothing more reprehensible than a button lodged under his lip.

The youngest performer to win a national or international award against adult competition was four-year old Victoire Thivisol, who secured Best Actress at the 1996 Venice Film Festival for her role as the infant heroine of *Porette* (Fr 96). The youngest Best Actor was eight-year-old Lee Mete-Kingi, honoured at the 1990 New Zealand Film Awards for his performance in *Ruby and Rata* (NZ 90).

There are over 7000 registered child actors in Hollywood, keeping 70 juvenile talent agencies in business. Many find employment only rarely and even for those who do taste a measure of success, it is usually fleeting. According to Hollywood-based best-selling novelist Jackie Collins, even the most talented have a professional life which rarely exceeds six years. Once puberty robs them of the gap-toothed and freckled cuteness that made them marketable in the first place, the career is over. 'They're thrown out as yesterday's trash,' as actress Mary Crosby aptly puts it. For those who have become accustomed to the trappings of their passing success, finding themselves back in the real world, often with a cursory education and lacking basic employment skills, can be an experience they are unable to cope with. Happily, not everyone is indifferent to their fate. Former child actor Paul Petersen was one who underwent this confrontation with growing up and finding himself no longer the centre of attention. He has used part of the fortune he earned as a teenager to set up a support group for other young victims of the Hollywood dream.

The highest-paid child performer was Macaulay Culkin, who was ten years old when his success in *Home Alone* (US 90) won him a $1 million contract with Columbia to appear in *My Girl* (US 91). This began to look like small potatoes when he reprised his role as the resourceful Kevin in *Home Alone II: Lost in New York* (US 92) at $5 million plus percentage. The youthful megastar's fee for *Richie Rich* (US 95) is said to have been $8 million, which made him a hotter property than Sharon Stone and equal to Whoopi Goldberg. While *Richie Rich* failed to ring the box-office tills with the same insistent clamour, his $22 million take from the percentage deal on *Home Alone II* meant that he could face an uncertain future without too much anxiety about paying the rent. After nine movies and aged 15 he had banked $50 million and fired his agent, one Kit Culkin, also his dad.

Insurance

Insurance of stars' more notable physical accoutrements began when silent-screen comedian John Bunny

(1863–1915) insured his unlovely face for $100,000. Faces were most stars' fortunes and it was an enterprising Los Angeles underwriter, Arthur W. Stebbins, who originated the 'scarred face' policy taken out in the early 1920s by Rudolph Valentino, Douglas Fairbanks and Mary Pickford, the latter for $1 million. Some stars, though, owed their success to individual features, not always facial—Chaplin insured his feet for $150,000. Clara Kimball Young (1891–1960), often described as 'the most beautiful woman in films' at the peak of her career, c. 1918, insured her large and luminous eyes for the same amount. Cross-eyed Ben Turpin (1874–1940) insured to the tune of $100,000 against the possibility of his eyes ever becoming normal again—it would undoubtedly have cost him his career. Suave leading man Edmund Lowe (1890–1971) took out a $35,000 policy on his distinguished nose in the mid-1920s and at about the same time Kathleen Key had her lovely neck underwritten at $25,000. A decade later the most famous nose in the business carried a $100,000 risk for Jimmy Durante (1893–1980).

Average cost to an insurer when a major motion picture stops production is $600 per minute.

Alberta Vaughn took out a $25,000 policy in 1925 against the possibility of putting on 20 lb weight by 1 June 1927, while Walter Hiers—literally a Hollywood 'heavy'—insured for an equal sum against losing 45 lb. RKO insured Roscoe Ates' (1892–1962) inimitable nervous stutter in the early '30s. A year or two earlier, when sound arrived, First National had insured Corinne Griffith (1898–1979) against loss of voice. Ironically it was her unsuitability for talkies that finished her career. When Anthony Quinn (1915–) had his head shaved for the role of a Greek magician in *The Magus* (GB 68), he insured against the risk of his hair failing to grow back.

The first actress to insure her legs was Hollywood extra Cecille Evans, whose appendages were underwritten for $100,000 in 1921. Miss Evans' speciality was 'doubling' her sensational legs for those of stars less well endowed. The 'Girl with the Million Dollar Legs', Betty Grable (1916–73), actually had them insured for more than that—the sum was $1,250,000. The legs may have been incomparable, but the policy did not stand comparison with the record risk of $5 million accepted on Cyd Charisse's (1921–) long and lovely limbs. No actor has ever been described as 'The Man with the Million Dollar Legs', but Fred Astaire (1899–1987) could have claimed the title—his were insured for just that sum.

It is not only performers who have had parts of their bodies insured. In 1939 the Fleischer Studio took out a $185,000 policy with Lloyd's of London to cover the hands of the 116 animators working on the full-length cartoon feature *Mr Bug Goes to Town* (US 41).

The first artiste whose life was insured for the duration of a picture was Lillian Gish (1893–1993), covered for the sum of $1 million during the filming of *Way Down East* (US 20). The insurance company turned down director D. W. Griffith's application for insurance on the other principal players on health grounds. Had they known that Miss Gish was to be exposed on an (continued p. 123)

BIOPICS OF SCREEN STARS

Increasingly common as television movies, star biopics often concentrate on an aspect of the performer's life other than their screen career. The biopics of Diana Barrymore and Lillian Roth were concerned with their subjects' alcoholism, those of Eddie Cantor and Al Jolson dwelt mainly on their singing careers, and Annette Kellerman's on her swimming exploits, while *The George Raft* Story recounted the star's pre-Hollywood days in the gangster milieu of '20s New York. The following performers have had their life stories, in whole or in part, portrayed in feature movies:

Bud Abbott (1895–1974) and **Lou Costello** (1906–59)
Bud and Lou (US 78, TVM). Harvey Korman and Buddy Hackett in a behind-the-scenes story of the comedy duo's stormy personal relationship.

Diana Barrymore (1921–60)
Too Much Too Soon (US 58) with Dorothy Malone in the story, based on Miss Barrymore's memoirs, of how she went to Hollywood to look after her alcoholic father John Barrymore (Errol Flynn) and herself succumbed to drink.

John Belushi (1949–82)
Wired (US 89). Based on Bob Woodward's biography, with Michael Chiklis as the overweight comic genius who died of a drug overdose.

Humphrey Bogart (1899–1957)
Bogie (US 80, TVM) with Kevin O'Connor, based on Joe Hyams' biography of the same title.

Eddie Cantor (1892–1964)
The Eddie Cantor Story (US 53) with Keefe Brasselle in the name role. Cantor himself played a bit part and also sang the songs off-screen. On seeing the finished picture, he remarked: 'If that was my life, I didn't live.'

Lon Chaney (1883–1930)
The Man of a Thousand Faces (US 57) with James Cagney as the character actor and contortionist extraordinare of the silent screen.

Charles Chaplin (1889–1977)
The Life Story of Charles Chaplin (GB 26) with Chick Wango in a British attempt to cash in on the popularity of the Cockney lad who had made it in Hollywood. The first biopic of a screen star, but never released due to a threat of legal action from its subject.
    Chaplin (GB 92). Robert Downey Jr as the difficult genius with the penchant for teenage girls in one of the most faithful personifications of a star achieved in any biopic. Richard Attenborough's picture spans the whole of Chaplin's long and turbulent life up to his welcome back to America after 20 years of exile to receive an honorary Oscar. Cast includes Kevin Kline as Douglas Fairbanks, Penelope Ann Miller as Edna Purviance, Marisa Tomei as Mabel Normand and Diane Lane as Paulette Goddard. Geraldine Chaplin played her own grandmother, the unbalanced Hannah Chaplin.

Joan Crawford (1906–77)
Mommie Dearest (US 81) was based on Christina Crawford's controversial exposé of her adoptive mother, here portrayed by Faye Dunaway as an insecure but savagely egotistical woman given to beating her children with coathangers.

Dorothy Dandridge (1923–65)
Introducing Dorothy Dandridge (US 99, TVM). With Halle Berry as the *café au lait* beauty, traumatised in childhood when assaulted by her mother's lesbian lover, who rose to fame in *Carmen Jones* (US 54) as the first black to be nominated for the Best Actress Oscar. Klaus Maria Brandauer limned helmer Otto Preminger.

Fernando Ramos da Silva (1968–94)
Quem Matou Pixote?/ Who killed Pixote? (Bra 96). Cassiano Carneiro plays the 11-year old street dweller of Sao Paulo, Brazil, who achieved instant international fame in his one and only film *Pixote* (Bra 88), only to succumb to a life of crime, degradation and early death.

Marion Davies (1879–1961)
The Hearst and Davies Affair (US 85, TVM). Virginia Madsen as the chorus girl who became the lifetime lover of press baron William Randolph Hearst (Robert Mitchum)—he bought her stardom by financing her films and ballyhooing them in his newspapers. Lorne Kennedy as Charlie Chaplin.

Sammy Davies Jr (1925–90)
See SINATRA.

James Dean (1931–55)
James Dean (US 76, TVM) was scripted by the moody rebel's friend Bill Bast and recounted the story of their lives together as aspiring young actors when they were room-mates in the early '50s. Dean was portrayed by Stephen McHattie, Bast by Michael Brandon.
    Race with Destiny (US 97) Casper Van Dien portraying Dean towards the end of his life, focussing on the tormented affair with Pier Angeli.

Marlene Dietrich (1901–92)
Marlene (Ger 00). Katja Flint as the legendary German actress, depicting her rise to fame and fortune, her loves and losses.

Leila Diniz (194?–6?)
Leila Diniz (Bra 87) with Louise Cardoso as the unconventional and rebellious Brazilian star of the 1960s who became a symbol of the period before perishing in a plane crash at the age of 27.

Diana Dors (1931–84)
The Blonde Bombshell (GB 99, TVM). Keeley Hawes as the younger DD, Amanda Redman as the RADA-trained sex symbol who might have achieved the kind of roles her thespian ability merited but for the bad company she kept. But then there probably wouldn't have been a biopic.

Patty Duke (1946–)
Call Me Anna (US 90, TVM). Rare example of an autobiopic (see also SALDANA), with Patty Duke playing herself as an adult (Ari Meyers plays her as a child, Jenny Robertson as a teenager). Tele-film, based on Duke's autobiography of the same title, depicts her horrific childhood as the molested victim of monstrous foster parents, the actress's drug and alcohol abuse as an adult, and her desperate attempts to find love.

Frances Farmer (1914–70)
Committed (US 84) was an earnest black-and-white docudrama with Sheila McLaughlin in an intense performance as the overwrought, alcoholic, leftist and eventually lobotomised Hollywood beauty whose neuroses led to commitment to an asylum. The title is a play on words signifying Farmer's other commitment, to various 'progressive' causes.
    Jessica Lange underwent the strait-jacketing and lobotomy in a standout performance in Graeme Clifford's *Frances* (US 82), a version with less emphasis on politics and more on the relationship with monstrous mother Lillian Farmer, played for hisses by Kim Stanley.

Mia Farrow (1945–)
Love and Betrayal: The Mia Farrow Story (US 95, TVM). Rare example of star biopic made while the star is still alive and active, with British actress Patsy Kensit playing Mia as a sensitive, loving mother to her vast brood of adopted children and Dennis Boutzikaris playing their surrogate father Woody Allen as a mean, conniving cad with few redeeming qualities. Much to his surprise Boutzikaris received a call from Allen's casting agent while the picture was still in production inviting him to audition for a part in the director's next film.

W. C. Fields (1879–1946)
W. C. Fields and Me (US 76) with Rod Steiger in another study of a star disintegrating through drink. The 'Me' of the title was Fields's mistress Carlotta Monti (Valerie Perrine), who nursed the tyrant comic through his alcoholism to the detriment of her own career.

Errol Flynn (1909–59)
My Wicked, Wicked Ways—The Legend of Errol Flynn (US 85, TVM) with Canadian Duncan Regehr as the swashbuckling Australian. Barbara Hershey played his fiery French actress wife Lili Damita, Barrie Ingham his fellow drunk

BIOPICS OF SCREEN STARS Continued

John Barrymore and Lee Purcell the too perfect Olivia de Havilland.

Flynn (Aus 90 and 93). Guy Pearce, adulated by thousands of pre-teens as the rather wimpish teacher Mike in Aussie soap *Neighbours*, was the surprise choice to play the title role in this rampage through Flynn's early life as policeman, gold prospector, slave trader, spy and murder suspect following his departure for New Guinea from his native Australia. The reason two dates are given above is that there were two versions. The one premièred at the 1990 Cannes Film Festival had Australian actors Paul Steven and Jeff Truman in major supporting roles. The other, first shown at the 1993 Cannes Film Festival under a new title *My Forgotten Man*, had British actor/playwright Steven Berkoff and American actor John Savage in the same roles, apparently to give the picture a better chance in overseas markets. Reportedly some 40% of the film was reshot for the second version. The new footage was shot in Fiji, allegedly to prevent action by Australian Equity, who declared the replacements 'an absolute bloody disgrace'.

Annette Funicello (1942–)
A Dream is a Wish Your Heart Makes: The Annette Funicello Story (US 95, TVM) For those wanting their hearts well-warmed, Eva LaRue limns the role of the juvenile hostess of TV's *Mickey Mouse Club* who went on to cult stardom as the bikini-clad virginal heroine of early '60s beach movies and eventually became wheelchair-bound as a victim of multiple sclerosis.

Clark Gable (1901–60)
Gable and Lombard (US 76) with James Brolin struggling bravely in a generally misconceived attempt to portray 'the man rather than the star'. See also LOMBARD.

Greta Garbo (1905–90)
Moviola: The Silent Lovers (US 80, TVM). Swedish actress Kristina Wayborn played the divine one very competently—and looked sensationally beautiful—in this tele-pic of Garbo's early years in Hollywood and her celebrated on-off romance with the doomed John Gilbert. Harold Gould portrayed mogul Louis B. Mayer as a monster.

Judy Garland (1922–69)
Rainbow (US 78, TVM) Judy's early life from her days starting out in vaudeville aged ten to her triumph in *The Wizard of Oz* (US 39) when she was 17. Andrea McArdle played Judy, Moosie Drier the teenage Mickey Rooney and Johnny Doran played Jackie Cooper, who directed *Rainbow*. Probably the only occasion the director of a movie has been portrayed in it.

Ruth Gordon (1896–1985)
The Actress (US 53). The young Jean Simmons, then 24, played the even younger Ruth Gordon as a stagestruck teenager in a warm and humorous evocation of growing up in New England in the early years of the century. (Gordon was to make her screen debut in *Camille* in 1915.) The screenplay was by the actress herself, from her own autobiographical play *Years Ago*.

Corinne Griffith (1898–1979)
Papa's Delicate Condition (US 63), based on silent-screen heroine Corinne Griffith's own book, is possibly the only biopic about the infancy of a star. Linda Bruhl played the six-year-old Corrie, Jackie Gleason her inebriate father.

Jean Harlow (1911–37)
Harlow (US 65) with Carroll Baker in a travesty of the star's life of which the producer, director and screenwriter should be thoroughly ashamed.
Harlow (US 65) with Carol Lynley in a rather better attempt at the subject, released in an Electronovision version.

Rita Hayworth (1918–87)
The Love Goddess (US 83, TVM) Lynda Carter chronicled the flame-haired beauty's rise from café dancer to screen legend and her eventual meeting with husband-to-be Prince Aly Khan, played by Israeli actor Aharon Ipale. Edward Edwards essayed Orson Welles, while Terri Lynn looked suitably vacuous as Kim Novak.

Rock Hudson (1925–85)
Rock Hudson (US 90, TVM) with Thomas Ian Griffith as the homosexual star. Recounts his arranged marriage to his agent's secretary Phyllis Gates (Daphne Ashbrook) and relationship with lover Marc Christian (William Moses), to whom he never confided that he was suffering from AIDS.

Sammo Hung
Painted Faces (HK 88). Ching-ying as the martial-arts superstar of Hong Kong action-comedy films, playing opposite Sammo Hung himself as his teacher. Tells the story of Hung's early life as a pupil undergoing the gruelling training in a monastic-type martial arts/Chinese opera school where he was incarcerated from the age of seven to 17 with virtually no contact with the world outside.

Jill Ireland (1936–92)
Reason for Living: The Jill Ireland Story (US 91 TVM). Jill Clayburgh played Jill Ireland, Lance Henriksen was husband Charles Bronson, in TV movie from Ireland's book *Life Lines* about her struggle to rid adoptive son Jason of his drug habit.

Sid James (1913–76)
Cor Blimey! (GB 00, TVM) Despite the title, which suggests slapstick of the *Carry On* variety, this is a poignant and ultimately tragic study of the destructive obsession South African comedian Sid James indulged for the not-always-so-chirpy Cockney icon Barbara Windsor. Top-flight performances from lookalikes Geoffrey Hutchings and Samantha Spiro in a drama which reveals the disillusionment and despair of the team of comics typecast in one-dimensional roles in the enormously popular, but cheaply made and often poorly scripted, *Carry On* series. Adam Godley is not a lookalike for misanthropic Kenneth Williams but essays the voice as well as the self-loathing with distinction. In the final scenes Barbara Windsor plays herself with a depth never afforded her on the large screen.

Al Jolson (1886–1950)
The Jolson Story (US 46) and *Jolson Sings Again* (US 49) with Larry Parks in both highly successful films. Jolson himself did the voiceover for the songs and is also seen in long shot during the 'Swanee' sequence of the first picture.

Buster Keaton (1895–1966)
The Buster Keaton Story (US 57) with Donald O'Connor in what Leslie Halliwell has described as 'a dismal tribute'. Once again the theme is one of drink being the curse of the starring classes.

Annette Kellerman (1888–1978)
Million Dollar Mermaid (US 53) with Esther Williams playing the Australian girl who invented the one-piece bathing suit and became one of the first star actresses to appear on the screen in the nude (not depicted in the biopic).

Grace Kelly (1928–82)
Grace Kelly (US 83, TVM). Made with Princess Grace's consent and participation, shortly before her death in September 1982. Cheryl Ladd succeeded, where so many have failed in star biopics, in looking like the original. Ian McShane played Prince Rainier and there was a galaxy of star portrayals: Rita Gam (Marta DuBois); Mady Christians (Salome Jens); Raymond Massey (Paul Lambert); Clark Gable (Boyd Holister); Alec Guinness (Arthur Berggren); William Holden (Van Corwith). Lomax Stucly had the difficult task of impersonating Alfred Hitchcock.

Peter Lawford (1923–84)
see SINATRA

Bruce Lee (1940–73)
A Dragon Story/GB: *The Bruce Lee Story* (US 74) with Hsiao Lung as the Chinese-American actor who achieved international stardom in Hong Kong martial arts movies.
Dragon: The Bruce Lee Story (US 93) with Jason Scott Lee (no relation). A gamut of wholly or semi-fictitious martial arts films have also purported to portray Bruce Lee: *The Story of the Dragon* (HK 76) with Ho Tsung-tao (Bruce Li); *Bruce Lee–True Story* (HK 76) with Bruce Li; *Bruce Lee and I* (HK 76) with Li Msiu Hsien; *The Dragon Lives* (HK 78) with Bruce Li; *Bruce Lee: the Man, the Myth*

BIOPICS OF SCREEN STARS continued

(HK 78) with Bruce Li; *Bruce Lee, The Tiger of Manchuria* (HK 78) with Hang Yong Chul; *Young Bruce Lee* (HK 79) with Chuck Norris; *Sexy Isla Meets Bruce Lee in the Devil's Triangle* (Can 7?); *Bruce Lee versus the Gay Power* (Bra 7?). *The Death of Bruce Lee* (HK 76) merely invoked the name, not the character.

Vivien Leigh (1913–67) *and Laurence Olivier* (1907–90)
Darlings of the Gods (Aus/GB 90, TVM). Anthony Higgins as a somewhat wooden Sir Larry and Mel Martin as an effectively lookalike Vivien Leigh in the story of their triumphant but turbulent tour of Australia in 1948 with the Old Vic Company. As the marriage starts to collapse under the pressures of Vivien's erratic behaviour and insatiable sexual appetite, she seeks solace in the arms of young Australian actor Peter Finch (Jerome Ehlers).

Lekha
Lekha's Death, a Flashback (Ind 84). The life and death of a teenage superstar of the thriving Malayalam cinema, with Nalini as Lekha. Director K. G. George speculates on the reasons for her suicide in a partly fictional account of her escape from prostitution into the false glamour of the 'filmi' world.

Carole Lombard (1908–42)
Gable and Lombard (US 76) with Jill Clayburgh as the love of Gable's life, killed tragically in an aeroplane accident at the age of 34. The film failed to illuminate either the romantic myth of the legendary affair or the earthy reality (Lombard confided to a friend 'He's not what you'd call a helluva great lay'). Though even Hollywood could not bring itself to nominate the film for an Oscar, it did succeed in picking up Harvard Lampoon's 1976 Victor Mature Memorial Award for the most embarrassing line of dialogue. The citation read: '*Gable and Lombard*, for the screen's greatest insouciant comment following the incendiary demise of his beloved in a plane crash, as he gazes fondly over the twisted wreckage: "She should have taken the train".'

Sophia Loren (1934–)
Sophia Loren: Her Own Story (US 80, TVM). Sophia Loren as herself and as her mother in a poor girl makes good story aptly summed up by her own remark 'Everything you see, I owe to spaghetti'. John Gavin made his last screen appearance, playing Cary Grant, before his appointment by former colleague Ronald Reagan as Ambassador to Mexico.

Bela Lugosi (1882–1956)
Ed Wood (US 94) Martin Landau as the drug-addicted and alcoholic Hungarian star of early Hollywood horror movies (though this is about his later, B-movie career) and Johnny Depp as the cross-dressing 'world's worst director' Ed Wood in Disney's uncharacteristic tale of the platonic love affair between the two oddballs.

Jayne Mansfield (1932–67)
The Jayne Mansfield Story (US 80, TVM). Fictionalised biopic of the '50s platinum-blonde sex siren, played by Loni Anderson. Arnold Schwarzenegger, in his first starring role on television, played her muscle-bound second husband Mickey Hargitay.

Dean Martin (1931–95)
See SINATRA

Miroslava (1926–55*)*
Miroslava (Mex 93) with French actress Arille Dombasle in a reverential portrait of the Czech-born actress, star of some two dozen Mexican films before she killed herself aged 29, following betrayal by her lover, the Spanish bullfighter Luis Miguel Dominguin.

Marilyn Monroe (1926–62)
Goodbye, Norma Jean (US/Aus 75) with Misty Rowe, a reasonable look-alike but nothing more, in an exploitation movie that concentrates on Norma Jean Baker's seedy and often degrading existence before her metamorphosis into Marilyn Monroe Superstar.
Catherine Hicks essayed the challenging role of legendary sex goddess in *Marilyn the Untold Story* (US 80), a TVM theatrically released in Europe. Based on Norman Mailer's biography, it in fact told little that had not been told before, but then neither did the book. One unusual feature was the portrayal of living and active stars by other actors—Tony Curtis by Bruce Neckels, Jack Lemmon by Brad Blaisdell and Laurence Olivier by Anthony Gordon.
Constance Forslund starred as MM in the other tele-biopic of 1980, *Moviola: This Year's Blonde* aka *The Secret Love of Marilyn Monroe* (US 80, TVM). This one was about her relationship with the agent who launched her in the face of jibes that she was no more than 'this year's blonde'.
Goodnight, Sweet Marilyn (US/Aus 89) was both a follow-up to and a reworking of *Goodbye, Norma Jean* by the same producer/ director, Larry Buchanan. It focuses on the last day of MM's life, with extensive flashbacks taken from the Misty Rowe movie. The older Marilyn is played by Paula Lane.
In *Marilyn and Bobby: Her Final Affair* (US 93, TVM) Melody Anderson played Marilyn, opposite James F. Kelly as Robert Kennedy in a largely imaginary version of what may have transpired between the sex siren and the Attorney General of the United States. According to the movie, bedrooms romps had to play second fiddle to the serious business of running the world. After one particular night of wanton abandon, Bobby takes a call from an aide and resists MM's attempts to lure him back between the sheets with a classic TVM line: 'Seems we have a situation—Cuba needs immediate attention.'
Norma Jean and Marylin (US 96, TVM). Unusual take of the oft-told story with Ashley Judd in the Norma Jean per-

sona and Mira Sorvino as the superstar, each interacting with the other. According to this biopic, MM's death was suicide following her rejection by John F. and Robert Kennedy.
Norma Jean, Jack and Me (US 00). A biopic only in the sense that it fantasised about what life might have been like for Marilyn Monroe (Sally Kirkland) and JFK (Michael Murphy) had their reported deaths been fabricated to enable them to escape together to a new life on an otherwise uninhabited Caribbean Isle.
Latest to essay the difficult task of portraying the greatest screen legend of the second half of the 20th century is Poppy Montgomery in an adaptation of Joyce Carol Oates's best-selling fictionalised autobiography *Blonde* (US/GB 01, TVM).
See also under SINATRA.

Patricia Neal (1926–)
The Patricia Neal Story (US 81, TVM). Glenda Jackson as Patricia Neal, the actress who won an Oscar for *Hud* (US 63) but was struck down by a series of major strokes at the peak of her career. Her husband, the best-selling writer Roald Dahl, was portrayed by Dirk Bogarde and Rock Hudson played himself.

Laurence Olivier
See LEIGH.

Elvis Presley (1935–77)
Elvis (US 79, TVM) with Kurt Russell playing the Pelvis, Ronnie McDowell dubbing the songs. Theatrically released in Europe.

George Raft (1895–1986)
The George Raft Story (US 61) with Ray Danton as the professional athlete, gambler, nightclub dancer and intimate of gangsters who turned it all to good account in Hollywood.

Bill 'Bojangles' Robinson (1878–1949)
Stormy Weather (US 43) with 'Bojangles' himself in an all-black fictionalised version of his own life story. Also subject of 1979 Broadway musical *Bojangles*.

Will Rogers (1879–1935)
The Story of Will Rogers (US 50) with Will Rogers Jr playing his father in a bland homage to the celebrated crackerbarrel philosopher and latecomer movie star.

Lillian Roth (1910–80)
I'll Cry Tomorrow (US 55) with Susan Hayward as the Broadway/ Hollywood star of the early '30s whose career became another write-off to alcoholism.

Ruan Ling-Yu (1910–35)
Actress aka *Center Stage* aka *Ruan Ling-Yu* (HK/Taiwan 92). Maggie Cheung as the great tragic actress of the silent screen, known as China's Garbo, who killed herself at the age of 25, following newspaper scandal about her affair with a married man. Includes archive footage of the real Ruan.

BIOPICS OF SCREEN STARS continued

Theresa Saldana (1964–)
Victims for Victims: The Theresa Saldana Story (US 84, TVM). TS starred as herself in this recounting of the horrific attack on her by a crazed fan in 1982, shortly after she had appeared opposite Robert De Niro as Jake LaMotta's sister-in-law in *Raging Bull* (US 80), and its aftermath when she became spokeswoman for the Victims for Victims support organisation.

Frank Sinatra (1915–98)
The Rat Pack (US 98, TVM). Ensemble piece about the Voice (Ray Liotta) and his three fellow hellraisers Dean Martin (Joe Mantegna), Sammy Davis Jr (Don Cheadle) and JFK's brother-in-law Peter Lawford (Angus Mcfadyen), with Kara Unger as Ava Gardner and Barbara Niven as Marilyn Monroe. Pic focuses on Sinatra's support for Kennedy's presidential campaign and how he was subsequently shunned by the Kennedy brothers because of his association with the Mob.

Gale Sondergaard (1899–1985)
One of the Hollywood Ten (Sp/GB 00) The one of the title is not Sondergaard, winner of the first Best Supporting Actress award for her 1936 debut performance in *Anthony Adverse*, but her blacklisted husband, director Herbert Biberman (Jeff Goldblum). Sondergaard, played by Greta Scacchi, was, however, one of the mainly Jewish group of ten Hollywood figures who fell victim to the House Un-American Activities Committee hearings in 1947. The picture focuses on Biberman's heroic efforts to make his classic strike film *Salt of the Earth* (US 54) and the tension caused when Sondergaard is bypassed for the female lead. Peter Bowles limns studio boss Jack Warner.

Margaret Sullavan (1911–60)
Haywire (US 80, TVM). Based on Brooke Hayward's best-selling biography of her parents, film and stage star Margaret Sullavan, played by Lee Remick in the film, and theatrical agent/producer Leland Hayward (Jason Robards). Produced by their son William Hayward.

Kinuyo Tanaka (1910–77)
Actress (Jap 87). Sayuri Yoshinaga as one of the greatest Japanese screen actresses, star of the first successful talkie made in Japan *A Madame and a Wife* (Jap 31). Almost a potted history of the Japanese film industry, the picture includes recreated scenes of Kenji Mizogushi (played by Bunta Sugawara) directing Tanaka in his masterpiece *The Life of Oharu* (Jap 52).

Thelma Todd (1905–35)
White Hot: The Mysterious Murder of Thelma Todd (US 91, TVM) Loni Anderson as the '30s actress chiefly known to devotees of Kenneth Anger's *Hollywood Babylon*, though in her time she starred in her own series of comedies as well as in films with such legends as Laurel & Hardy and the Marx Brothers. Before her mysterious death in 1935—she was found dead in her car from carbon monoxide—she had a notorious affair with gangster Lucky Luciano.

The Three Stooges
The Three Stooges (US 00, TVM) The sole star biopic devoted to actors who only performed in short films, with Paul Ben-Victor as Moe Howard, Eran Handler as Larry Fine and Michael Chiklis as Jerome 'Curly' Howard. Linal Haft limns Columbia Pictures' monster maven Harry Cohn, under whose less than benign gaze the Stooges became the studio's blue-plate special working stiffs who thumb their noses at the respectable middle classes.

Taiji Tonayama
Sammon Yakuska (Jap 00) Naoto Takenaka as the alcoholic and womanising veteran of 250 Japanese movies in a film directed by another veteran, 88-year-old Kaneto Shindo.

Robert Tudawali (1930–67)
Tudawali (Aus 87) Ernie Dingo in a powerful performance as the first top-billed Aboriginal film star from his debut in Charles Chauvel's *Jedola* (Aus 55) through a turbulent life caught between two cultures: the glamour of the film and TV world of Sydney and the depressed existence of his fellow blacks in Darwin, Northern Territory, to which he returned to take up menial employment between assignments. Much of the film is concerned with the mysterious circumstances of his death, from being thrown into a fire, after he had become a spokesman for Aboriginal rights. Frank Wilson plays his mentor, pioneer Australian director-producer Charles Chauvel, with distinction.

Rudolph Valentino (1895–1926)
Valentino (US 51) with Anthony Dexter in a flat biopic made at a time when Hollywood's attempts to portray the '20s invariably mixed period cliché with blundering anachronisms.
The Legend of Valentino (US 75) with Franco Nero in a version billed as 'romantic fiction'—a precaution against litigation from any of the surviving personalities in Valentino's tempestuous life.
Valentino (GB 77) with Rudolf Nureyev charismatic in Ken Russell's lush and stimulating evocation of man, myth, place and period.

Hansa Wadkar (1920–71)
Bhumika (Ind 78) with Smita Patil as the popular Hindi star of the '30s and '40s. One of the few foreign-language star biopics.

Mae West (1892–1980)
Mae West (US 82, TVM). Ann Jillian in a sanitised version of the raunchy star's life from age seven until her triumphant Broadway return in *Diamond Lil* in 1948. Chuck McCann played W. C. Fields.

Pearl White (1889–1938)
The Perils of Pauline (US 47) with Betty Hutton recreating the career of the silent serial queen in uncompromisingly '40s style.

Barbara Windsor (1937–)
See JAMES.

---

ice floe in sub-zero temperatures wearing only a thin frock every day for three weeks, and that she was to be rescued by the hero just before the floe went over the falls without anytrick or stunt work, nor any safety precautions in case the rescue failed, doubtless the application on her behalf would have been refused with even greater promptitude.

When seven-year-old Shirley Temple's life (1928–) was insured with Lloyd's, the contract stipulated that no benefit would be paid if the child met death or injury while drunk.

Siobhan McKenna's insurance policy for *Of Human Bondage* (GB 64) forbade her to drive a car while the picture was in production. The first time the Irish actress had taken the wheel she had ended in a ditch, the second time against a wall, the third time up a tree.

Film-Making and Film-Makers

Animals

The first animal star to appear regularly in films was 'Hepworth Picture Player Rover', an English collie belonging to pioneer producer Cecil Hepworth who made his debut in his master's outstandingly successful low-budget (£7 13s 9d) box office hit *Rescued by Rover* (GB 05). A simple melodrama about a dog rescuing a baby who has been kidnapped by gypsies, it was in such demand by exhibitors that the negative wore out and the film had to be remade twice. Rover, whose real name was Blair, starred in at least seven other films before his death in February 1914. American historian Kenneth Macgowan dryly observed that Rover was the first screen performer who did not overact.

One of the first animals to achieve something akin to 'superstar' status was Strongheart, an ex-Red Cross dog who had served in the trenches in World War I. Strongheart was a consummate screen actor, but had an aversion to being made to howl. According to Lawrence Trimble, who directed Strongheart in most of his films, he would get so depressed that his work would be below par for several days afterwards. Once he had graduated to canine stardom, however, there was little choice but to indulge these displays of temperament. A double would be brought in to do the howling for him.

Serving on the other side of the lines in World War I was the German army dog Rin Tin Tin (1916–32), who came to Hollywood in the early '20s and became an animal 'megastar'. He was the only dog in America with a valet, a personal chef, his own limousine and a chauffeur for his exclusive use. He also had a five-room dressing room complex of his own on the studio lot.

The largest cast of living creatures in a film were the 22 million bees employed on *The Swarm* (US 78), about a 5-mile swarm of killer bees from South America who cause mass destruction before meeting their come-uppance from Michael Caine, improbably cast as an egghead scientist. A nurse equipped with bee-sting serum was on set throughout the filming of the swarm sequences and director-producer Irwin Allen was far-sighted enough, or perhaps lacking sufficient confidence in his vast airborne cast, to insure for $70 million against any deaths by bee stings. Happily the only fatal casualties were bees.

The largest number of horses ever assembled for a film was 11,000 in the case of Alexander Ptushko's *Ilya Muromets/Sword and the Dragon* aka *The Epic Hero and the Beast* (USSR 56). The Hollywood record was established the same year when King Vidor used 8000 horses in *War and Peace* (US 56).

The largest assemblage of assorted animals in a movie totalled 8552 in *Around the World in Eighty Days* (US 56), to wit: 3800 sheep, 2448 buffalo, 950 donkeys, 800 horses, 512 monkeys, 17 bulls, 15 elephants, 6 skunks and 4 ostriches.

ANIMAL CRACKERS

- There have been four full-length fiction films with all-animal casts. *Bill and Coo* (US 48), produced by comedian Ken Murray, was a comedy feature with a cast of lovebirds in miniature sets. Most of Walt Disney's True Life Fantasies were documentaries about wildlife, but *Perri* (US 57) was based on a novel by Felix Salten about the life of a squirrel. There were no credited human performers in *Jonathan Livingstone Seagull* (US 73), though some fishermen in a boat are seen in the opening sequence. Apart from this, the cast was composed entirely of seagulls. The story, adapted from the novel by Richard Bach (who also wrote the screenplay), is a mystical one of a seagull who acquires grace, is killed doing a noble act, rises from the dead and becomes a bird messiah. Kon Ichikawa's *The Adventures of Chatran* (Jap 87) had a cast of cats, dogs and farm animals with not a human in sight and became Japan's box-office hit of the year.

- The scrupulous care that film-makers take to ensure that no harm comes to animals appearing in their pictures now extends even to insects. Steven Spielberg's *Arachnophobia* (US 90), about a Californian town invaded by marauding mutant killer spiders, claimed a zero spider-mortality rate, despite one scene in which the town exterminator is seen stomping on one which is manifestly the real-life hairy horror. The trick? A cavernous, spider-sized hole crafted in the sole of his boot. The sound of crunched spider was achieved simply but effectively—with crushed potato crisps.

- The lions seen in Sydney Pollack's *Out of Africa* (US 85) were shipped out to Kenya, where the film was shot, from California. Kenyan law forbids the use of its own wild animals in films.

- The hit moppet picture *Benji* (US 74), about a dog who rescues two children from kidnappers, was shot mainly at a height of 18 inches from the ground—the camera was showing the action from Benji's viewpoint. In Samuel Fuller's *White Dog* (US 84), the story of a dog trained to attack black people, all shots through the eyes of the dog were in black and white—dogs are colour blind.

- The natural thespian abilities of Lassie had sometimes to be aided by his trainer Rudd Weatherwax. Whenever the collie scratched low at a door, Rudd was on the other side of it with a dog biscuit, whispering through the crack: 'Come and get it, come and get it.' When Lassie seemed to be gazing adoringly at Edmund Gwenn or Jeannette MacDonald he was really gazing adoringly at Rudd's left-hand pocket, which held the pieces of biscuit used to reward a scene well played. To get Lassie to open a door, Rudd covered the doorknob with a slit open rubber ball, then commanded him to 'go fetch'. And to persuade him to lick Roddy MacDowall's face in *Lassie Come Home* (US 43), the youngster's cheek was first smeared with ice cream. When Lassie limped in a scene, the studio received thousands of letters from irate animal lovers accusing them of cruelty. They were assured that the crippled effect had been achieved with nothing more disturbing than a piece of chewing gum under one paw.

- How do you stampede a herd of cattle? Gun shots may pull the trick, but are unreliable. When *Western Union* (US 41), with Randolph Scott and Gene Tierney, was being shot at Keenab, Utah, one of the wranglers remembered seeing newsreel shots of German Stukas diving on to marching troops and scattering them. The producer sent for a small squadron of aircraft and the mob of cattle was duly 'dive-bombed'.

- There are many hundreds of footprints set in the sidewalk outside Grauman's Chinese Theatre in Hollywood—also three sets of hoof-prints. They belong to Tony (Tom Mix), Trigger (Roy Rogers) and Champion (Gene Autry).

- In *The Canine Detective* (US 36), Rin Tin Tin Jr captured a whole robber band by his own unaided efforts. Shortly after the picture's release, burglars broke into the Hollywood home of his master, Lee Duncan, and made off with hundreds of dollars' worth of goods. Rin Tin Tin slept soundly through the whole episode.

- Bucking broncos and bucking steers were among the highest priced of the huge range of animals routinely hired out to the studios in the 1930s. While a common Western horse hired out for only $2.50 a day, the bucking variety would earn $15 for the first buck and $10 for each subsequent buck. Trained falling horses got $25 a fall, which is probably why many studios preferred to use untrained horses and trip wires until this cruel practice was outlawed. Elephants were let out for $100 per week, while wrestling lions and intelligent chimpanzees commanded as much as $100 per day. Least expensive of the beasts for rent were chickens and chipmunks at 25c a day. Cats earned scarcely more, though there was one remarkable cross-eyed feline belonging to a lady in Long Beach who was unwilling to let the unfortunate creature be exposed to public ridicule for less than $2 a day. But even cats sometimes played starring roles, with the salary to go with it. Whitey, the nondescript white alley cat who played opposite Katharine Hepburn in *Stage Door* (US 37), was bought by his master for a humble quarter. On the film the pampered puss was paid $300 a week.

- Nowadays the highest day rate for animal performers in Hollywood is $3500 for grizzly bears—double the rate paid for elephants. Budding Elsas are strictly in the starlet league—take-home pay for lions is only $800 per diem.

The rather doleful looking palomino ridden by Olivia de Havilland in The Adventures of Robin Hood *(US 38) became the spirited and much-loved Trigger when he teamed up with every small boy's favourite cowboy Roy Rogers.* (Pictorial Press)

- The palomino ridden by Olivia de Havilland as Maid Marian in *The Adventures of Robin Hood* (US 38) was later to become a star in his own right—as Roy Rogers' faithful steed Trigger. Similarly, the dashing white horse ridden by Thomas Mitchell as Scarlett's father in *Gone With the Wind* (US 39) secured later screen immortality as the Lone Ranger's Silver. He sometimes appeared in other films, notably in the carousel sequence of *Ziegfeld Follies* (US 46) with Lucille Ball on his back. On this occasion the stallion's owner was so furious with the studio for braiding Silver's tail and prettifying him with pink satin bows that he threatened court action.

Cameras and Camerawork

The largest number of film cameras used for a single scene was 48 for the sea battle in *Ben Hur* (US 25). Another 42 cameras were employed on the chariot-race scene. Concealed in statues, in pits in the ground, and behind soldiers' shields, the 42 operators took 53,000ft of film—equivalent to seven full-length features—in a single day.

A reputed 100 video cameras were used for each of the seven musical numbers in Lars Von Trier's Palme d'Or winner *Dancer in the Dark* (Den/Fr/Swe/Ir/Ger/Nor/Neths/Ice/Fin/US/GB), starring Icelandic pop singer Björk. Von Trier himself was credited as camera operator, though presumably not of all 100 cameras at once.

The practice of using more than one camera on a scene was introduced by D. W. Griffith, who used three for the big fight between Dorothy West and Mabel Normand in *The Squaw's Love* (US 14). The three cameramen on this occasion were Billy Bitzer, P. Higginson and

> The shower scene in Alfred Hitchcock's *Psycho* (US 60) involved 70 camera set-ups for 45 seconds of edited footage and took seven days to shoot.

Bobby Harron. The use of multiple cameras was not confined to special scenes in Hollywood's silent days. Nearly all feature films were shot with twin cameras, one supplying the master negative from which all release prints for the domestic market were struck, the other the negative for all overseas prints.

The largest number of cameras used on one film was 160 in the case of *One Day of War* (USSR 42). A feature-length documentary, the film was shot in a single day by 160 newsreel cameramen at the Russian front and behind the lines.

The widest aperture lens ever used in production of a feature film was f0.7 by cameraman John Alcott on *Barry Lyndon* (GB 75). Developed for the US space programme, the lens was fitted to a specially modified camera and employed in filming an interior scene lit only by candle-light.

The first motorised camera (professional) in series production was the all-metal Bell & Howell of 1912, manufactured in the USA with the motor as an optional fitment.

The first feature film made with a motorised camera was *A Sainted Devil* (US 24) with Rudolph Valentino, which was photographed at Famous Players' Long Island studio by Harry Fishbeck with an electrically driven camera of unidentified make. Generally cameramen continued to crank by hand throughout the silent era, due to the fact that it enabled action to be speeded up or slowed down at will. The coming of sound rendered hand-cranking impractical, since variations in film speed would have caused a corresponding and unnatural variation in the delivery of synchronised speech.

The earliest known multi-shot scene (different camera positions being used within a single scene) occurs in G.A. Smith's *The Little Doctors* (GB 1901), in which there is a cut from a shot of two children administering medicine to a sick kitten to a close-up of the kitten with the spoon in its mouth.

Prior to the rediscovery of this film (see *Sight & Sound*, summer 1978), the innovation had generally been attributed to D. W. Griffith. In *For the Love of Gold* (US 08), Griffith used a medium shot and a three-quarter shot in a card-game scene where he wanted to register the

expressions on the gamblers' faces, and this has been credited as the first use of camera movement within a scene. Another recent discovery of the use of close-up (q.v.) shots within a scene in *The Yale Laundry* (US 07), must cast doubt on whether Griffith was the pioneer of the multi-shot scene even as far as the US industry is concerned.

The first panning shots were used by Max Skladanowski in *Komische Begegnung im Tiergarten zu Stockholm* (Ger 1896), a short comedy shot on location in Sweden, and by Lumière representative Eugène Promio in *View of St Mark's Square, Venice* (Fr 1896), a panorama of the square taken from a boat on the Grand Canal.

The first 360° panning shot was made by Edwin S. Porter in *Circular Panorama of the Electric Tower* (US 1901), in which the whole of the exhibition grounds of the Pan-American Exposition at Buffalo, NY are seen as the camera slowly revolves. Porter used a geared mounting of his own design for this effect.

The first use of a 360° pan in a full-length dramatic film was by James Whale in *Frankenstein* (US 31), and the following year Rouben Mamoulian employed the technique in *Dr Jekyll and Mr Hyde* (US 32) to give an effect of vertigo during the transformation scene.

Other films with 360° pans are *Rain* (US 32), Herbert Wilcox's *Bitter Sweet* (GB 33)—notable for its double 360° pan (the second much faster than the first), *La Signora di Tutti* (It 34), *La Strada* (It 54), *Lola Montes* (Fr/FRG 55), *Vertigo* (US 58), *On the Beach* (US 59), *Judgement at Nuremberg* (US 61), *The Manchurian Candidate* (US 62), *Providence* (Fr/Swz 77), *The Swarm* (US 78), *Eagle's Wing* (GB 79), Mai Zetterling's *Scrubbers* (GB 82) and *Highlander II: The Quickening* (US 91). *Laughter in the Dark* (GB 69) was another British film with a double 360° pan, while Brian de Palma's *Obsession* (US 76) is notable for both a 360° and a 540° pan. The latter shot shows all four walls of a room entered by Genevieve Bujold, then pans on past the door to pick her up on the side opposite.

The first slow-motion film was made in 1898 by Berlin cinematographer Oskar Messter, using a specially constructed high-speed 60mm camera of his own design. Among the earliest sequences filmed with this camera was one that showed a cat falling off a wall, with a Hipp millisecond watch inset in one corner to indicate the rate of descent. This was shot at 66 frames per second—over four times normal speed—though the camera was capable of filming at speeds of up to 100 frames per second.

The technique has had its widest application in sports and scientific films. The earliest practical application of slow-motion cinematography was for the purpose of gauging the breaking strain of girders, according to Hopwood's *Living Pictures*, published in 1899.

The fastest speed at which a camera has been operated on any feature film (or the slowest slow-motion sequence) was 2500 frames per second for the giant explosion scene in *Star Trek: The Wrath of Khan* (US 82). The scene, shot by Industrial Light and Magic at the Cow Palace in San Francisco, took a single second to film but occupied 104 seconds on screen. The normal speed at which a 35mm motion picture camera operates is 24 frames per second.

The fastest camera in the world (manufactured for sale) is the digital Imacon 468, produced by DRS Hadland of Tring, Herts. Capable of filming at up to 100 million frames per second (equivalent to 77 full length feature films), each camera takes about six weeks to assemble and test and about a dozen a year are sold at £250,000 each. Imacon 468 cameras are designed for scientific research. The Los Alamos National Laboratory in New Mexico uses one to analyse the clinical potential of laser-beams to break up blood clots in the brain, while Ulm University in Germany filmed bubbles of ink exploding in an ink-jet printer to facilitate improved design. DRS Hadland announced in 2000 that they were developing a new version of the Imacon able to film at 200 million frames a second.

The time-lapse technique was pioneered by Oskar Messter of Berlin, who filmed the blooming and wilting of a flower in 1897. The lapse factor was 1500 frames per 24 hours.

The earliest known wipe appears in G. A. Smith's *Mary Jane's Mishap, or Don't Fool with the Paraffin* (GB 03), in which Mary Jane does and is blown out of the chimney. A line moving across the screen 'wiped' away the scene of her unfortunate demise and replaced it with one of her forlorn grave. Hitherto the introduction of the wipe has generally been attributed to Georges Méliès in *La Royaume des fées* (Fr 03), but Dr Barry Salt of the Slade School has established that this is a misconception. What looks like a wipe between scenes is in fact no more than the lifting of a backdrop.

The only full-length feature film to have been made without a camera was Barcelona artist José Antonio Sistiaga's remarkable 75-minute animated one-man production in Cinemascope *Ere Ereve Baleibu Icik Subua*

G ordian Maugg's black and white *Der Olympische Sommer* (Ger 93), a low-key drama of everyday life set in Berlin at the time of the 1936 Olympics, captured the atmosphere of the period with such authenticity that critics remarked on its likeness to documentary footage of pre-war Nazi Germany. This was due not only to meticulous art direction, but also to the fact that the film was shot with a 1927 Askania camera.

Arvaren/Scope, Colour, Muda (Sp 70). Completed in 17 months between October 1968 and February 1970, Sistiaga painted each frame of the film separately and single-handed direct on to the film stock.

The first close-up was a study of a man called Fred Ott sneezing, copyrighted on 7 January 1894 as Edison's *Kinetoscopic Record of a Sneeze* (US 94).

Close-ups of inanimate objects or of hands or feet were not unusual in American films of the early years of the century, particularly in the productions of the American Mutoscope and Biograph Co. (AM & B).

Examples include the fire-alarm box in Edison's *The Life of an American Fireman* (US 03), a girl's pretty foot in Edison's *The Gay Shoe Clerk* (US 03), the contents of a jewel case in AM & B's *The Great Jewel Mystery* (US 05), gifts in AM & B's *The Silver Wedding* (US 06) and a newspaper article in AM & B's *Trial Marriages* (US 07). Facial close-ups were rarer, though the opening scenes of AM & B's *The Widow and the Only Man* (US 04) introduce the two principal characters with separate close-ups. The persistent claim of D. W. Griffith to have been the only begetter of the close-up—he even went so far as to suggest he could have patented the technique—has now been rejected by most film historians, though many still credit him with having been the first to employ the interpolated facial close-up as a dramatic device to register emotion. Even this had been accomplished a year before Griffith entered the film industry. In the AM & B production *The Yale Laundry* (US 07), a comedy about students at Yale playing a jape on their professors, close-ups are used to show surprise on the faces of the victims. It is precisely this technique of advancing the narrative by means of a close-up shot that Griffith was later to claim as his innovation and his alone. There is a certain irony in the fact that it had been used earlier by an uncredited director of the very company with which Griffith was to establish his reputation. The great director also seems to have overlooked the fact that he himself was the subject of a close-up when he played the part of a clown in *At the French Ball* (US 08), a film made shortly before his directorial debut at Biograph.

Despite the pioneering efforts of the Edison Co., AM & B and 'the Brighton school' (in England), elsewhere the notion that a film should give its audience the same view as a theatre audience received of the stage persisted for many years. As late as 1911 the leading production company in Scandinavia, Nordisk Film, was using a 16ft-long pole attached to the camera as an indication to the actors that they must come no closer. Albert E. Smith recalled that about this period at Vitagraph the actors were always positioned 9 yards in front of the camera. Mary Pickford, who claimed that she had been the subject of 'the first close-up' in D. W. Griffith's *Friends* (US 12), said that the front office at Biograph had vigorously protested at the idea on the grounds that audiences were paying to see the whole of the performer, not only the top half.

The longest close-up is to be seen in *Daaera* (Ind 53) and lasts six and a half minutes.

The earliest recorded use of the telephoto lens (invented in 1891) with a cinematograph camera was by W. K. L. Dickson, the Biograph cameraman covering the Boer War in 1900. Dickson recorded in *The Biograph in Battle* (London 1901) how he had sought to film the Boer positions with a telephoto, an attempt frustrated by poor visibility caused by haze.

The first feature film to end with a freeze frame was Abel Gance's epic melodrama *La Roue* (Fr 23), in which the device was used to intensify the moment of the old railwayman Sisif's death. The earliest Hollywood feature to culminate in a freeze frame was *Poor Little Rich Girl* (US 36), with the three principals, Shirley Temple, Jack Haley and Alice Faye, arrested in motion.

The first camera dolly was used by British pioneer cinematographer R. W. Paul at the studio he built at New Southgate in 1899. In a lecture he gave before the British Kinematographers' Society in 1936, Paul recalled: 'A trolley mounted on rails carried the camera, which could thus be set at any required distance from the stage, to suit the subject. Sometimes the trolley was run to and from the stage while the picture was being taken, thus giving a gradual enlargement or reduction of the image of the film.' It is not known whether Paul's dolly dates from the opening of the New Southgate studios, but a photograph taken in 1902 shows it in use.

The first known use of a camera dolly in a feature film was for a tracking shot in the first reel of Evgenii Bauer's *The Twilight of a Woman's Soul* (Rus 13), executed by cameraman Nikolai Kozlovski of the Franco-Russian Star Film Factory. This was the innovative Bauer's first film as director. It was unlikely that he was aware that the Spanish cameraman Segundo de Chomon had developed a camera dolly while working for Pathé in Paris and that it had been patented in Italy in 1912. It was this dolly that de Chomon used for his pioneering work on Giovanni Pastrone's *Cabiria* (It 14).

The dolly arrived in America comparatively late, no examples of its use being known before 1915. Tracking shots were used in two feature films that year, by Allan Dwan on *David Harum* (US 15) to follow the hero as he walks down the street of his small hometown, and by William Bowman in *The Second-in-Command* (US 15). On this film, cameraman William F. Alder employed two dollies, one for forward and backward tracking and the other for sideways movement. This was a notable innovation which did not come to its full fruition until Chinese-born James Wong Howe introduced the 'crab dolly'—a dolly that moves in any direction, including sideways and diagonally—on *The Rough Riders* (US 27).

Britain, having pioneered the dolly, then completely forgot about it until the end of the silent era. The first use of a 'mobile camera' in a feature film was by Graham Cutts on Gainsborough-Piccadilly's *The Triumph of the Rat* (GB 26), with Ivor Novello.

Camera mobility could be achieved without the use of a dolly. F. W. Murnau overcame the problem of how to depict Emil Jannings' drunken view of the wedding feast in *The Last Laugh* (Ger 25) by mounting his cameraman on roller skates. When Sidney Franklin decided to use a hand-held Bell & Howell Eyemo camera on *Quality Street* (US 27), he emulated Murnau's example, but here the scene was not a drunken one and the camera had to be kept steady. The solution was to have an assistant pushing the roller-skated cameraman from behind. James Wong Howe also found roller-skates the answer for the prize fight scene in *Body and Soul* (US 47), but on *He Ran All the Way* (US 51) he needed higher camera angles. A squatting camera operator could not roller-skate, so Howe found another expedient—the cameraman was pushed in a wheelchair.

The earliest known use of a hidden camera was in 1916 when director George Terwilliger used this device in the making of the Van Dyke Film Corporation's *The Lash of Destiny* (US 16), starring Gertrude McCoy and Duncan McRae. Scenes which included diners and dancers at the restaurant of the Ansonia Hotel in New York were shot without the unpaid 'extras' being aware of their participation. There is no other record of the technique before 1924. In that year, concealed cameras were used by Russia's master of the newsreel, Dziga Vertov, in making his feature-length documentary about everyday life in the early Soviet state, *Kino-Eye* (USSR 24). Vertov's brother, the cameraman Mikhail Kaufman, filmed open-air scenes at Pioneer camps, in markets, at stations, etc., as well as interiors of low life in bars, cafes and thieves kitchens, without his subjects ever being aware of the camera. In America a hidden camera was used by Erich von Stroheim for the scene in *Greed* (US 24) in which Trina rushes out of the junk shop after finding a murdered body. The film was made entirely on location and

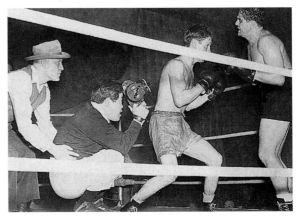

Mobile cameraman James Wong Howe found a new use for roller skates when he shot the prize fight scene in Body and Soul *(US 47).* (Kobal Collection)

it is a real street into which ZaSu Pitts dashes distractedly, grabbing the arms of real passers-by as she shrieks her awful news. The reaction of those unwittingly involved was, as von Stroheim hoped, totally believable, as they registered horror and alarm before rushing for help.

These pioneer efforts were followed by a number of other noted uses of hidden camerawork during the '20s. George Webber filmed exterior scenes for *Night Life of New York* (US 25) from a van parked in the streets of the city. Most of *Berlin, Symphony of a Great City* (Ger 27) was filmed in this way by Karl Freund, but where a van was impracticable he concealed the camera in a suitcase, using a special film stock that he had hypersensitised himself in order to shoot in poor lighting conditions. King Vidor shot most of the New York exteriors for *The Crowd* (US 28) with a hidden camera.

The first double exposure was accomplished by Georges Méliès in *La Caverne maudite/The Cave of the Demons* (Fr 98), employing the technique of 'spirit photography'. The evil inhabitants of the cave were first filmed against a black backdrop, so that the background was not exposed, then the film was wound back and the cave setting filmed. The effect was of 'ghost' characters superimposed against a solid background.

The more normal use of double exposure was to achieve the effect of two characters played by the same performer appearing on screen simultaneously. This was done by 'duplex cinematography', also pioneered by

Georges Méliès and at about the same time as the film above. Méliès adapted a technique, already well known to still photographers, by which a small frame enclosing two swing doors was mounted in front of the camera lens. When one door was opened, half the scene was exposed on film. The film was then wound back, one door shut and the other opened, and the rest of the scene shot. If the same performer was filmed each time, he or she would appear to be two characters interacting. Méliès' first attempt at this technique was in *Un Homme de tête/The Four Troublesome Heads* (Fr 1898), which shows a magician removing his head three times over and in which he used a combination of both spirit photography and duplex photography.

The first physical contact between two characters played by the same person was accomplished in *Little Lord Fauntleroy* (US 21) when Mary Pickford played both the boy and his mother 'Dearest'. Cameraman Charles Rosher used a camera loaded with 2000 lb of weights to achieve absolute steadiness between one take and the next, but the exact details of his extraordinarily advanced technique are still not known. The preparations for each double exposure were among the most meticulous and precise in the history of camerawork. It took 15 hours to shoot the scene in which the boy kisses 'Dearest'

The attempted suicide of Alex (Malcolm McDowell) in *A Clockwork Orange* (GB 71) was achieved by throwing a Newman Sinclair camera off the top of a building. On the sixth take the camera landed downward as intended. The lens was smashed, but the camera was found to be still in perfect working order

on the cheek, a take which lasts three seconds on the screen. In another scene they embrace and, in the most spectacular of all, the Little Lord runs and jumps into his mother's arms. The complexity of the operation was enhanced by the fact that Mary Pickford the mother had to be 9 inches taller than Mary Pickford the boy. For her adult role in the double exposure scenes she was given platform heels and stood on a concealed ramp, a hazardous operation since she fell off on a number of occasions.

Double exposure was temporarily abandoned when sound came in because of the difficulty of post-synching. **The first double exposure with dialogue** was a scene in Fox Movietone's *Masquerade* (US 29) in which Alan Burmingham carried on a conversation with another character also played by Alan Burmingham.

The first triple exposure was achieved by cameraman Al Siegler in Universal's *The Twins' Double* (US 14), in which Grace Cunard played the twin heroines and the villainess, their double—all three characters appearing on the screen at the same time.

Nowadays multiple exposures tend to be used for naturalistic special effects rather than the trick of showing the same person simultaneously performing more than one role. **A septuple exposure** was used in *Star Trek* (US 79) for the elaborate sequence in which the Starship Enterprise first approaches the alien invaders. The different exposures, which included shots of the spacecraft, fog, yellow lights, a star-field and cloud

effects, were combined in a scene which occupied only 30 seconds of screen time but 48 hours of filming.

The first film shot at night out-of-doors was Edwin S. Porter's *Panorama of the Esplanade at Night* (US 1901), taken at the Pan-American Exposition at Buffalo, NY, on 5 September 1901. Each frame required a ten-second exposure and it took Porter several hours to expose 27ft of film.

The first feature film containing outdoor scenes shot at night was the Balboa Feature Film Co.'s *An Eye for an Eye* (US 15), a melodrama about bigamy starring and directed by William Desmond Taylor, which was released in January 1915. A number of other examples date from the same year. The Paramount western *Buckshot John* (US 15), starring and directed by Herbert Bosworth, included a scene filmed by moonlight, believed to have been shot at Banning, CA. *The Patriot and the Spy* (US 15), released in June, had night battle scenes, while the detective mystery *The Game of Three* (US 15), released in September, took to the streets of New York for scenes shot at midnight. Another midnight scene, the meeting of the vigilantes in *A Gentleman from Indiana* (US 15), was filmed by the light of 50 radium flares and ten Windfield Koerner lamps.

Feature films which played entirely at night include *Crossfire* (US 47), *The City that Never Sleeps* (US 50), and *La Notte* (It 61). Most Philippine silent moves of the 1920s were made entirely at night, as the ill-paid part-time actors had to take day jobs to support themselves.

Back-projection was first employed successfully by special-effects maestro Willis O'Brien for a single scene in *The Lost World* (US 25). It is a technique by which outdoor scenes can be shot in the studio by placing the actors against a back-projected filmed background. The following year back-projection was used in the making of *Metropolis* (Ger 26), but it was slow to catch on because of the technical difficulties involved. The breakthrough came with the development of the Teague Back Projector, which was employed for the first time on the Fox production *Just Imagine* (US 30), a science-fiction film set in 1980. Back-projection was used to depict a city of the future, with stars Maureen O'Sullavan and John Garrick coasting along in their private aircraft in the foreground.

Back-projection in colour was first used by William Wellman on *Nothing Sacred* (US 37).

The first camera crane was used by cameraman William F. Alder for obtaining elevated shots in Metro's *The Second in Command* (US 15), with Francis X. Bushman. At about the same time Allan Dwan devised a more sophisticated elevator on tracks for use in the Babylonian sequence of D. W. Griffith's *Intolerance* (US 16). The 115ft-high structure enabled Griffith to secure a parabolic shot, commencing at the ramparts of the Palace and descending forwards over a sea of extras to ground level and a close shot of the leading players. These early uses of the crane were exceptional. It was not until F. W. Murnau introduced his 20-ton, 200-hp 'Go-Devil' on *The Four Devils* (US 29), and the appearance of an even larger 28-ton apparatus with a 60ft elevation on the set of *Broadway* (US 29), that the crane came to be regarded as standard studio equipment.

The first use of a helicopter for shooting from the air in a feature film took place on 21 August 1947, when cameraman Paul Ivano went aloft to film two sequences for the RKO production *The Twisted Road* (US 48), directed by Nicholas Ray. One showed escaped convicts being pursued through a wheatfield, the other a car chase. Ray estimated that use of the helicopter saved $10,000 in production costs.

The first camerawoman was Lucie Chapuis, who joined the Lumière Co at Lyon in 1896 and, together with her 17-year-old twin brothers, was trained as a Cinématographe operator. She made a number of actualities in and around Lyon that year, but little is known of her subsequent life and work.

The first British camerawoman was the aristocratic Mrs Aubrey Le Blond, who made the first Alpine films starting in 1900. Several of these, all taken in the Engadine valley of Switzerland, featured in Hove-based film distributor James Williamson's catalogue for 1902. They included three films of bobsleigh racing, three of tobogganing and two of skating on the Kulan rink. Mrs Le Blond became the first president of the Ladies' Alpine Club in 1907, by which time she had abandoned film-making.

The first American camerawoman was Grace Davison, who joined the Astor Film Corp. at its Long Island studios as an actress in 1915 but was taught to handle a camera by veteran Harry Fishbeck. Miss Davison photographed *The Honeymooners* (US 15), *Spring Onions* (US 15) and other one-reel comedies.

The first camerawoman to shoot a feature film was Tamara Lobova, who worked on *Suvorov* (USSR 41) together with her husband Anatolij Golovnja. First with a solo camera credit was Galina Pyshkova for *Songs of Abay* (USSR 46).

The first feature film with computerised special effects was Robert Wise's sci-fi meller *The Andromeda Strain* (US 71), also the first screen adaptation of a Michael Crichton novel, which opened on 21 March 1971. The special photo effects were credited to Douglas Turnbull and James Shourt.

The first use of morphing was in Ron Howard's *Willow* (US 88). Developed specially for the film by Industrial Light & Magic, the technique created a seamless metamorphosis of a sorceress from a goat to a tortoise to an ostrich to a tiger and finally to a woman. Morphs have since become a standard means of making a transition between images not only in feature films, but also on TV, both for commercials and comment—for example, Michael Heseltine morphing into Arthur Scargill and Bill Clinton morphing into Hillary—as well as music videos, title sequences and even on posters. Its use in feature films has now extended well beyond transformations. For instance, in *Forrest Gump* (US 94) it was this technique which enabled President Kennedy to greet Tom Hanks as the eponymous hero in the Oval Office. The image of Kennedy shaking hands with some anonymous visitor was cut out of a 16mm news clip and visual effects supervisor Ken Ralston of Industrial Light & Magic used morphing to create a convincing handshake between the President and the fictitious Forrest Gump.

The film with the most special effects was George Lucas's *Star Wars: Episode 1—The Phantom Menace* (US 99), with claims of 'over 2000' and 'about 2500' (nobody seems to have done an exact count) in its 133 minutes running time. This is some four times the number of F/X in *Titanic* (US 97). Lucas is on record as saying that the reason he waited so long to embark on the second *Star Wars* trilogy was that he did not want to do so until his F/X company Industrial Light and Magic had the technological capability for creating the effects he had dreamed of for the new series of films.

Costume

The first couturier to design screen costumes was Paul Poiret, regarded as the founder of modern French haute couture, who was responsible for dressing Sarah Bernhardt in *La Reine Elizabeth* (Fr 12).

The largest number of costumes in any one film was 32,000 for *Quo Vadis* (US 51). *Waterloo* (It/ USSR 70) used 29,000 costumes and *Cleopatra* (US 63) 26,000 costumes.

The largest number of costume changes by one performer was 201 by poet-musician-filmmaker Lee Groban of Chicago in his 85-hour duration *The Cure for Insomnia* (US 87). The most in a commercially made feature were by Joan Collins in the television movie *Sins* (US 88, TVM), who wore 87 different frocks including 30 by top couturier Valentino. The record for a theatrical feature was the 85 costume changes by Madonna in *Evita* (US 97), who also wore 39 different hats, 45 pairs of shoes and 56 pairs of earrings. While this eclipsed the 65 costumes designed by Irene Sharaff and worn by Elizabeth Taylor in *Cleopatra* (US 63), Miss Taylor's wardrobe actually comprised 105 outfits. The 40 costumes and head-dresses designed by Oliver Messel at a cost of $64,800 did not appear in the movie as released.

The largest number of wig changes was 35 by Angela Bassett in her role as soul singer Tina Turner in the Touchstone Pictures biopic *What's Love Got to Do with It?* (US 93).

The most expensive costume ever worn in a movie was the barzucine sable coat that enfolded Constance Bennett in *Madame X* (US 65). It was valued at $50,000.

The most expensive costume designed and made specially for a film was Edith Head's mink and sequins dance costume for Ginger Rogers in *Lady in the Dark* (US 44), which cost Paramount $35,000. By comparison, Elizabeth Taylor's dress of cloth-of-24-carat-gold in which she made her entry into Rome in *Cleopatra* (US 63) cost a modest $6500.

At the other end of the scale, costumes could cost next to nothing even in Hollywood's most extravagant days; except for the studios' insistence that nothing was worthwhile unless it was expensive. When a rough,

Ingrid Bergman's costume in For Whom the Bell Tolls *(US 43) may not look as if it has been specially designed for her, but the producer insisted.*

workaday costume was needed for Ingrid Bergman in *For Whom the Bell Tolls* (US 43), designer Edith Head selected an old pair of men's trousers and a shirt from the extra's wardrobe. Producer Sam Wood was incensed and demanded that Miss Head should design a new costume. She did so, copying the old garments exactly, then bleaching them and dying them to look as worn as the originals.

The record spent on costumes in relation to budget was the $1 million-plus for wardrobe in the $7 million production *Chanel Solitaire* (US 81), a biopic of the legendary French fashion designer Coco Chanel.

The largest costume collection in the world is owned by Western Costume Co. and housed in a six-storey building at 5335 Melrose Avenue, Hollywood, California. The collection consists of 2.5 million costumes.

Western Costume was established in Los Angeles in 1912. In a curious way its fortune could be said to have been founded on dietary deficiency. Business was slow until a major break came with D. W. Griffith's order for all the Civil War costumes for *The Birth of a Nation* (US 15).

The truth is now out about the most celebrated bra in history, the cantilevered job designed by Howard Hughes to give Jane Russell support where he felt she needed it most. According to Jane's autobiography, the fabled garment did really exist, but she only wore it once and that was in the privacy of her own dressing room. Hughes had used engineering principles to design the ideal brassière for the well-endowed woman. It simply did not work. Jane found it 'uncomfortable and ridiculous' and changed back into her own custom-made bra. She went on set and everyone assumed she was wearing her mentor's creation. She never let on until years after Howard Hughes's death, but there is little doubt that the legend of the cantilevered bra will long outlive Jane Russell herself.

Griffith, preoccupied with authenticity, had hoped to use genuine uniforms of the period, but found that progress in nutrition over the intervening 50 years had made the average actor of 1914 too large to fit the average soldier's uniform of the 1860s.

Later Western Costume was to supply Clark Gable's clothes for *Gone With the Wind* (US 39), Errol Flynn's for *The Charge of the Light Brigade* (US 36) and Chaplin's Führer uniform for *The Great Dictator* (US 40). In more recent times they provided all the suits for *Dick Tracy* (US 90), matched to the stark monotone colours of the original comic strip (hence the sickly yellow of Beatty's overcoat). Most unusual request, per floor manager Roger Faustino, came from Woody Allen, who wanted sperm costumes for *Everything You Always Wanted to Know about Sex* (US 72).

The highest price paid at auction for an article of costume was $666,000 for a pair of the ruby slippers worn by Judy Garland in *The Wizard of Oz* (US 39), bought by an anonymous American collector at Christie's East in New York on 24 May 2000. The blue and white gingham dress which accompanies the slippers had been sold at Christies South Kensington the previous December for £199,500, the former record. Neither the slippers nor the dress are unique—there were half a dozen identical sets worn by Miss Garland during the making of the picture, a fact of which one hopes the buyers were aware.

Jean Seberg in the diminutive suit of armour acquired from London costumiers Nathan's for her performance in Otto Preminger's Saint Joan *(US 57).* (Kobal Collection)

COSTUME PIECES

- The famous orchid percale dress worn by Scarlett (Vivien Leigh) for much of the middle part of *Gone With the Wind* (US 39) was in fact no fewer than 27 dresses which started out identical. After she and Rhett had fled Atlanta in advance of Sherman's invading army, the orchid percale was her only raiment—in the words of historical adviser Wilbur Kurtz, 'an armor for the embattled Scarlett'. As she struggled to survive in the devastated South, designer Walter Plunkett progressively bleached the various versions of the costume to make them look sufficiently worn. And if the dress was torn or burned in a scene, all the succeeding copies of it had to be torn or burned in exactly the same way. Eventually, Plunkett remembered, 'We couldn't bleach any further. The dye was just too strong. So, the last five or six were ripped apart and turned inside out because the color was weaker on the wrong side.'

- The seedy coat sported by Professor Marvel (Frank Morgan) in *The Wizard of Oz* (US 39) had belonged to Oz creator Frank Baum. It had been found in a second-hand clothing store in Chicago with his nametape inside.

- Despite her slight form, the suit of armour worn by 18-year-old Jean Seberg in the title role of Otto Preminger's *Saint Joan* (US 57) was not made for her. It had been fashioned to the design of Sir Guy Laking in 1910 and worn for the first time by his children's governess. To demonstrate its flexibility, the diminutive governess curled up in a big pie and was carried into a dinner party. Later it was worn by the actress wives of tragedians Sir Seymour Hicks and Sir John Martin Harvey when they played Joan. The armour eventually ended up in the wardrobe of Nathan's, the London theatrical costumiers. In 1956 an American offered a substantial sum to buy it from them. Fortunately they refused and a few weeks later Preminger announced his film.

- Amanda Walker's costumes as Queen Elizabeth II in ABC's telefilm *Charles and Diana: The Fairy Tale—What Happened* (US 92, TVM) included a number of actual dresses and coats which had formerly belonged to the Queen. They were obtained from a dress agency in Chelsea which had acquired them from one of Her Majesty's ladies-in-waiting. Although the outfits chosen for Tracy Balbin as the Duchess of York were not the real thing, the production's costume designer had her own means of achieving authenticity. 'We got together a lot of designer outfits and made her try them on,' she explained. 'Whichever ones just missed, we kept.'

- Faced with an acute wartime shortage of materials, Roger and Katherine Furse, costume designers on Olivier's wartime production of *Henry V* (GB 44), were greatly relieved when contemporary accounts of Henry's army revealed that his archers and bowmen had a distinct aversion to wearing shoes. They were wont, the Furses discovered, to wrap their feet in some coarse material like burlap. 'This proved a bit of all right for us,' Mrs Furse reported, 'in that it saved us from having to provide a thousand pairs of shoes which simply didn't exist.'

- The fabulous costume worn by Hedy Lamarr as Delilah in *Samson and Delilah* (US 49) was made of real peacock feathers. Each had been personally gathered by producer-director Cecil B. DeMille. He had spent ten years following moulting peacocks around at his 1000-acre ranch in order to assemble the 1900 plumes needed for Delilah's extravagant dress.

- Costume designer Herschel McCoy found a unique source for the 2600 costumes used in MGM's *The Prodigal* (US 55). The story was based on the parable of the Prodigal Son, in Luke Chapter XV, which producer Charles Schnee had decreed should be set in Syria and Palestine in the year 79 BC. This was after that territory was captured by Alexander the Great and before its conquest by Rome. Greek and Persian influences dominated the lives of the people in a land that was then the crossroads of the world. Standard 'Hollywood epic' togas would not suffice; the costumes had to reflect the Graeco-Persian culture prevailing at the time. Fortunately recent excavations at Persepolis, ancient capital of the Persian kings Cyrus and Darius, had uncovered thousands of near life-size figures representing citizens of all nations of the known world bringing tribute to Persia. Each was accurately portrayed in the dress of their own country. It was on these images of the authentic costumes of the time that McCoy's designs were based, at a record costume budget for any MGM picture made till then of over $250,000. Much to the dismay of studio accountants, none of the 650,000 costumes held in the studio wardrobe was deemed adequate to the historical integrity of MGM's monumental two-hour evocation of St Luke's brief 22 verses of scripture.

- Noël Coward wore Lord Louis Mountbatten's old naval cap for several scenes in the classic wartime flagwaver *In Which We Serve* (GB 45), a tribute to the man whom he hero-worshipped but whom he claimed, unconvincingly, was not the model for the role of Captain 'D'. The battered hat worn by Henry Fonda in *On Golden Pond* (US 81) was Spencer Tracy's. Katharine Hepburn, who surprisingly had never met Fonda in the 50 years each had spent around Hollywood, presented it to him the first day on set. John Wayne's silver and leather hatband in *True Grit* (US 69) had belonged to Gary Cooper, who gave it to the film's director Henry Hathaway. Cooper was also the source for the well-used, lived-in looking stetson worn by Mercedes McCambridge in *Giant* (US 56), after he had registered dismay at the wardrobe master's intention to provide her with a brand-new one. The Cooper hat, with its patina of honest cowboy sweat, also had the inestimable merit, according to its owner, that it had 'been pissed on by a lot of horses'.

- Dustin Hoffman's heavy 17th-century costume as Captain Hook in Steven Spielberg's *Hook* (US 92) was so hot to wear that a special air-conditioned jacket was devised for him to wear underneath it. Similar to the apparel worn by astronauts in space, the garment was electrically operated. Whenever Hoffman overheated, he was able to plug in to lower the temperature.

- One of the commonest giveaways in period films and films set in exotic locales is that the clothes of the ordinary people look brand new and probably are. Not so in Bertolucci's *The Sheltering Sky* (GB/It 90), which takes place in North Africa shortly after World War II. Art director James Acheson toured Morocco offering brand-new jellabas in exchange for well-worn ones.

- America's sweetheart Mary Pickford was beloved for her rosebud mouth and her corkscrew curls. Would the mothers of America have simpered over Mary's golden aureole of hair, had they known that wardrobe master George Westmore customarily reinforced the famous curls with tresses bought from Big Suzy's French Whorehouse in L.A.?

- Chaplin's celebrated tramp costume was devised in response to Mack Sennett's request that he 'get into a comedy make-up' for *Kid Auto Races at Venice* (US 14). Chaplin created the costume in a dressing room where Fatty Arbuckle and Chester Conklin were playing pinochle. The moustache was a scrap of crêpe hair borrowed from Mack Swain; the trousers were Fatty Arbuckle's—hence the bagginess—and the Derby came from Minta Durfee's father, Fatty's father-in-law; the cut-away coat belonged to Chester Conklin (or Charlie Avery, according to one account); the size 14 shoes were Ford Sterling's and Chaplin had to wear them on the wrong feet to keep them on. Only the whangee cane belonged to Charlie himself.

Chaplin gave the original costume to his assistant Harry Crocker in 1928 as a central exhibit in the newly opened Crocker Museum of props and costumes on Sunset Boulevard. Nearly 60 years later, in 1987, Chaplin's bowler and cane came up for sale at Christie's in London, where they were bought by Danish shopping-mall entrepreneur Jörgen Strecker for $150,000.

FASHION AND THE MOVIES

Movie costumes began to influence fashion as early as 1912, when it was reported that the natives of Tahiti had become so addicted to westerns that they had taken to wearing stetsons. A rather more far-reaching fashion was initiated by D. W. Griffith when he invented the first pair of false eyelashes in order to give Seena Owen's eyes an abnormally large and lustrous appearance for her role as Princess Beloved in *Intolerance* (US 16). They were made by a wigmaker who wove human hair through the warp of a 24-inch strip of thin gauze. Each day two small pieces were cut from the end of the strip and gummed to Miss Owen's eyelids. The use of mascara and other eye make-up was directly inspired by the example of screen vamps Theda Bara and Pola Negri, who darkened their eyelids to give themselves an air of brooding mystery. Plucked eyebrows became the rage about 1930 after Jean Harlow had hers trimmed into a slender arch. Beauty editors advised her imitators to dab ether on their brows to ease the pain of plucking out the hairs.

Bessie Barriscale caused a sensation with the backless evening gown she wore in *Josselyn's Wife* (US 19) and soon the middle classes were aping a fashion formerly displayed only by their betters. All classes followed the trend to bobbed hair, which became the style of the '20s after Colleen Moore had created the archetypal flapper role in *Flaming Youth* (US 23). Pola Negri was not only the first to go barelegged and sandalled in summer, she was

also the first to paint her toenails. She recalled that when she first did this in about 1923, using a bright red polish, a woman glanced down at her feet and shrieked 'She's bleeding'. Nevertheless, within a few weeks, Miss Negri claimed, women everywhere were lacquering their toenails. Joan Crawford was the first to go barelegged with evening clothes in 1926. She stated that she never wore stockings between then and 1930, when long dresses returned to fashion. Bare legs for ordinary 'streetwear' were pioneered by blonde starlet Rita Carewe in 1927. To preserve the proprieties, however, Miss Carewe had her legs polished to give the impression that she was wearing silk stockings.

Bejeaned teenagers might have made an earlier appearance but for the obduracy of D. W. Griffith. In about 1914, 16-year-old Dorothy Gish became the first screen star and one of the first women in America to adopt jeans. She never wore them in films, however, and only once to the studio; a stern message to her mother from Griffith prevented such a solecism from ever being repeated. Another ten years were to pass before a woman wearing trousers as an article of feminine apparel (as opposed to male impersonation costume) appeared on screen in the person of Myrna Loy in *What Price Beauty* (US 24). This seems to have had little impact upon fashion at the time and it was not until Louise Brooks took to wearing silk trousers (indoors only) in 1927 that the practice became accepted amongst the more sophisticated followers of filmdom's fashion decrees. The real breakthrough for emancipated womanhood, though, had to await the release of von Sternberg's *Morocco* (US 30), in which Marlene Dietrich concealed her celebrated legs in slacks. Von Sternberg's purpose was to emphasise the lesbian characterisation of the role, but the innovation was imitated by the women of America to an extent that suggests its implication was wholly lost on them.

Probably the single most influential trendsetter, and the star who made least effort to be one, was Garbo. The enormous fur collars of the '20s owed their genesis to the broad collar designed by Max Ree to conceal her long neck in *The Torrent* (US 26). Garbo's berets, which she wore off-screen, became a universal fashion of the '30s and made a comeback in the '60s after Faye Dunaway had worn one as the '30s female gangster in *Bonnie and Clyde* (US 67). The diagonally placed Eugénie hat, dipping over one eye, worn by Garbo in *Romance* (US 30), hastened the end of the cloche and introduced the basic configuration that was to dominate hat styles throughout the '30s. Although most fashion design of the period reflected a conscious rejection of the past, Adrian's Eugénie hat was created for a film that was set in the 1850s.

The other major trendsetter of the period was Joan Crawford, whom women fans watched spellbound as she suffered in mink. While her taste in furs was beyond the reach of the majority, the padded-shoulder costume Adrian designed for her to wear in *Today We Live* (US 33) started the vogue for tailored suits that sloped upwards from the neck. Crawford herself was so enamoured with the style that she went on wearing padded shoulders long after they had gone out of general fashion.

By this time the big studios were co-operating with the garment trade—most of the moguls had come from that industry themselves—so that the costumes designed for the new genre of 'women's pictures' could be in the shops by the time the film was released. It was another Adrian creation for Joan Crawford that began this mass-marketing of star costumes, the celebrated Letty Lynton dress which she wore in the film of the same name (US 32). Over half a million copies were sold by Macy's of New York alone. The success of the venture encouraged its development. In 1933 a leading department store in Columbus, Ohio, called Morehouse Martens 'completed an arrangement by which copies of movie stars' clothes are on sale at the store prior to, or coincident with, the opening of their pictures'. The initial offerings were a Joan Blondell double-duty dress, a Jean Arthur frock and Claire Dodd pyjamas. The same year Bamberger's of Newark, NJ, opened a 'Cinema Shop' devoted exclusively to copies of the clothes worn by stars, and their lead was followed by other major stores from coast to coast, including such noted names as the Hecht Co. of Washington, Goldsmith's of Chicago, Joseph Horne of Pittsburgh ('The Hollywood Shop') and the May Co. of Los Angeles. The desire to look like the stars was no less fervent in Britain, where a magazine devoted to the subject with the title *Film Fashionland* was started in 1934.

Generally, the adoption of a movie fashion brought fortunes either to the designer or to the entrepreneur who succeeded in adapting it to a mass market. The star who launched the style seldom derived any direct benefit, with the notable exception of Shirley Temple. The astute business sense of Mrs Temple ensured that when Fox sold the manufacturing rights to Shirley's party dresses from *Baby Takes a Bow* (US 35), it was Shirley who garnered the lion's share of the profits.

What stars did not wear could sometimes have as much impact on fashion trends as what they did wear. When Clark Gable opened his shirt to reveal a bare and matted torso in *It Happened One Night* (US 34), men's undershirt sales took a 40% dive. Mae West also enjoyed a quite unlooked-for effect on fashion, if the Kansas Restaurant Association is to be believed. In 1934 the Association publicly thanked Miss West for stemming the dieting craze stimulated by the sylph-like figures of Dietrich, Crawford and Harlow and for restoring well-rounded curves to healthy US women.

Hollywood also played its part in bringing an exotic touch to American fashion. When Dorothy Lamour wore the first of her celebrated series of sarongs in *Jungle Princess* (US 36), it generated a demand for tropical fabrics that lasted for the next ten years. The Latin-American look that swept the USA in the early '40s was instigated by Edith Head's costumes for Barbara Stanwyck in *The Lady Eve* (US 41), and Charles LeMaire's designs for Jennifer Jones in *Love is a Many Splendoured Thing* (US 55) began a trend towards oriental fashion.

After World War II, Hollywood's main fashion influence was in the direction of casual wear, though even as early as 1922 American males had been persuaded to abandon their stiff collars after heart-throb Wallace Reid had played a romantic lead wearing a soft collar. By the 1950s it was mainly teenagers who took their fashion lead from movie idols. What we now regard as standard leather-biker costume only became so after Marlon Brando had appeared looking butch and menacing in a zip-up jacket in *The Wild One* (US 54). It also inspired the leather look among gays. James Dean's windcheater in *Rebel Without a Cause* (US 55) and Elvis Presley's tight trousers in *Jailhouse Rock* (US 57) set the teenage-style of the late 1950s and early 1960s.

Footwear is less often influenced by the movies, but girls with slim ankles took to wearing slip-ons without socks or stockings after Bardot had sloughed off the conventions of the formal '50s in *And God Created Woman* (Fr 57). The sex kitten also made going barefoot acceptable—she seldom wore shoes off-screen—provided you were young and pretty. Ten years later Jane Fonda's knee-length white vinyl boots in *Barbarella* (Fr/It 67) became part of the uniform of the mini-skirt generation.

Make-up influences may be even rarer, but not unknown even in recent years. Chanel's deep blood-red 'Rouge Noir' nail polish was originally a one-off talon extravaganza for the catwalk, but after it had been sported to sensational effect by Uma Thurman in *Pulp Fiction* (US 94) women everywhere demanded it.

Hairstyles are often prone to the dictates of Hollywood, with Jean Seberg and Mia Farrow demonstrating that cropped hair went well with an elfin face. Blonde streaks in brunette hair was a fashion inspired by Audrey Hepburn in *Breakfast at Tiffany's* (US 61). Whatever it may or may not have done for the butter industry, *Last Tango in Paris* (Fr/It/US 72) gave the world frizzy hair, as exemplified by sultry Maria Schneider, and revived the neglected art of permanent waving.

Another kind of casual look, for highbrows rather than hoydens, involved wearing the kind of baggy, rumpled clothes sported by Diane Keaton with neurotic chic in *Annie Hall* (US 77). Youth and good looks were not really sufficient if you wanted to get away with this; a certain fey and anxious charm was also imperative.

The decline of the cinema as a cultural force has reduced its fashion impact in the west, but in the Orient, where cinema-going continues to increase, it appears to have broken down traditional prejudices against Western dress. Symptomatic of the trend were reports in the late '70s that jeans were being worn by Indian women once superstar Zeenat Aman began wearing them in public. It seems that the movies can even introduce fashions long since discarded in the west. When *Corset* (S.Kor 96) debuted in Seoul, this tale of the romantic tribulations of a chubby lingerie designer created an unprecedented demand for the eponymous undergarment of the title.

Crews

The largest production crew on a movie consisted of the 556 craftsmen and technicians employed by producer Sukertaru Taguchi on Kon Ichikawa's *Tokyo Olympiad* (Jap 65). The largest number on a dramatic feature was 532 for the British World War I flying story *Sky Bandits* (GB 86).

The smallest crew on a major motion picture was two for the final scenes of *Bullseye!* (GB 90), shot in Barbados with Michael Caine, Jenny Seagrove and John Cleese in January 1990. The unit consisted of director Michael Winner, who operated the camera, and cameraman David Wynn Jones who held the reflector. John Cleese moonlighted as soundman, but as he was performing at the same time (the sound recorder was concealed in a book he carried), he did not count as crew.

The first continuity girl was Sarah Y. Mason, who came to Hollywood in 1917 at the invitation of Douglas Fairbanks, after he had seen her perform in a high school play, with the idea of becoming an actress. She was to have performed in the Fairbanks starrer *Arizona* (US 18),

Unique among Hollywood's many occupational specialists of the 1930s was one David Kashner, who was paid $35 a day to whip slaves, malefactors and winsome young things with sadistic stepfathers. His art, learned as a sheep herder in Poland and Palestine, lay in an ability to crack the whiplash before it reached its victim, thus dispelling its force. He could also direct its tail to a precise spot, as when he whipped a rose from Dorothy Lamour's lips in *Road to Singapore* (US 40). Despite his uncanny accuracy, Kashner occasionally mistimed a whiplash. It was said that hungry extras in the Depression years would eagerly volunteer as targets. In the rare instances when the thong struck with full force, generous recompense from the studio would stifle complaint.

but failed to make the grade before the camera. Explaining that she was an experienced stenographer, she offered to take notes on each scene so that continuity mistakes could be avoided. The director, Alan Dwan, accepted the proposition and a new career for women was born. As well as checking for continuity, she also looked out for potential anachronisms, notorious in the films of the '20s. So much money was saved by avoiding costly retakes that the studio took her on permanently and other studios followed suit by appointing their own continuity girls. Sarah Mason later became a successful scenario writer.

Directors

The first director: the functions of director and producer were first separated for America's earliest 'spectacle' film *The Passion Play* (US 98). Rich G. Hollaman, the producer, engaged a distinguished stage director, L. J. Vincent of Niblo's Garden Theatre in New York, to direct the picture. Unfortunately, America's first movie director had never seen a movie and nothing could persuade him that the camera was capable of reproducing live action. Convinced that he had been engaged to direct a succession of lantern-slide tableaux, he would rush out on to the set whenever the performance of a scene was progressing favourably and scream 'Hold it!' The film was eventually made by subterfuge. Each afternoon cameraman William Paley would declare that the light was no longer strong enough to continue and as soon as Vincent had departed the actors would reassemble and shoot as much as possible before dark. The two-reel drama was a sensation when it was premièred at the Eden Musée on 30 January 1898, but it is difficult to know whether it would be more accurately described as the first film made by a professional director or the first dramatic film made with no director at all.

The world's first woman director, Alice Guy, on the set of her first movie La Fée aux choux *(Fr c. 1900).*

The first woman director was Alice Guy (1873–1968), originally secretary to Léon Gaumont, who was given an opportunity to direct after she had complained at the lack of variety in Gaumont productions. She made her debut with *La Fée aux choux*, about a young couple walking in the countryside who encounter a fairy in a cabbage patch and are presented with a child. The film is usually said to date from 1896, but since it is listed No. 370 in the Gaumont catalogue it seems more likely that it was made c.1900. Mlle Guy was Gaumont's sole director of dramatic films until Zecca joined the studios at La Villette in 1905. In 1907 she emigrated to the USA, and founded the Solax Co. on Long Island three years later. Between 1919 and 1922 she directed for Pathé and Metro, then returned to France. Despite her long experience, she was unable to find work as a director in her own country and made a living writing stories based on film scenarios for pulp magazines.

The first feature film directed by a woman was the Rex production of *The Merchant of Venice* (US 14), which had Lois Weber as director. Miss Weber was also the first American woman director, starting with Gaumont Talking Pictures in New York in 1907, then working for Reliance in 1908, for Rex 1909–13, for the Bosworth Co. 1914–15 and for Universal 1915–19, after which she went independent. Her best known picture was Universal's highly successful *Where Are My Children?* (US 16), a treatise on birth control. As her films became increasingly controversial, she had difficulty in obtaining distribution, and her last picture, *White Heat* (US 34), about miscegenation, was not released.

Sharon Smith, in *Women Who Make Movies* (New York 75), has listed 36 women directors who were active in the United States during the silent era and believes there were others who directed anonymously. The only one to make the transition to sound was Dorothy Arzner, whose *Manhattan Cocktail* (US 28) was the first talkie directed by a woman. At the height of her career in the '30s she was listed as one of Hollywood's top ten directors.

The first woman to direct a British production was Ethyle Batley, whose directorial debut was a one-reel comedy for John Bull Films titled *Peggy Becomes a Boy Scout* (GB 12), starring her sister Dorothy. She directed nearly 70 films before her untimely death in 1917. The first feature by a woman was Frances E. Grant's *The Sword of Fate* (GB 21), a heady melodrama in which the heroine (Dorothy Moody) proves that a mine manager had rigged the death of the mad owner's wife and framed his son, her fiancé. The first talkie was *Knowing Men* (GB 30), produced and directed by Elinor Glyn and scripted by her from her own novel. Starring Carl Brisson and Elissa Landi, it was made in English- and French-language versions and shot in colour, though released in black and white.

The most successful film directed by a woman was Amy Heckerling's *Look Who's Talking* (US 89), a TriStar production starring John Travolta and Kirstie Alley. *Variety's* prediction that it was 'destined for a short life in theaters' was proved resoundingly wrong when the picture took $68,872,000 in North American rentals alone.

Of the 7332 feature films distributed by the major Hollywood studios during the 30 years 1949 to 1979, only 14 were directed by women—less than one-fifth of one per cent.

The first director to direct himself in a full-length feature film was Harold Heath, who played the lead in Anchor Films' detective thriller *£1000 Reward* (GB 13).

The first black American to direct an American film at a major studio was former *Life* photographer Gordon Parks, who directed *The Learning Tree* (US 69) for Warner Bros.

The first black American director to direct a film aimed at multi-racial audiences was Melvin van Peebles, former San Francisco cable-car gripman, who made his directorial debut with *La Permission/The Story of a Three Day Pass* (Fr 67). Based on van Peebles' own novel, *The Pass*, it related the story of a black GI on a three-day furlough who has a brief affair with a Parisian shop girl. His first American movie was *The Watermelon Man* (US 70), in which Godfrey Cambridge portrays the white insurance salesman who wakes up one morning to find he has turned black.

The fact that Van Peebles was unable to direct his first feature in the United States was a sad reflection on the state of race relations in the Hollywood of the 'liberated' 1960s. It had not been for want of trying. When the neophyte director had taken some of his early short subjects on a round of production offices in 1964, he was offered two assignments—one as a studio elevator operator, the other as a parking lot attendant.

The only blind director has been India's Bhupat Giri, seen here on set with leading man Kadarkhan.

The first black African director was Paulin Soumanou Vieyra, born in Dahomey in 1925, who made his directorial debut with *Afrique sur Seine* (Sen 55).

The first black woman director of a mainstream Hollywood movie was Euzhan Palcy of Martinique, who ,helmed MGM's *A Dry White Season* (US 89).

The most successful film by a black director in terms of box office is *Scary Movie* (US 00), directed by Keenen Ivory Wayans for Dimension, with an estimated gross of $300 million worldwide.

The first Maori to direct a feature film was Barry Barclay, whose *Ngati* (NZ 87) was selected for Critics' Week at the 1987 Cannes Film Festival and won the award for Best Film at the 1987 Taormina Film Festival.

The first Aborigine director was Brian Syron, who made his feature-film debut with *Jindalee Lady* (Aus 91). The first female Aborigine director was Rachel Perkins, who debuted with *Radiance* (Aus 98), a melodrama about three estranged sisters reunited at their mother's funeral. Interestingly, it was not about Aborigines.

The first director to make a film on percentage was D. W. Griffith, who made *The Birth of a Nation* (US 15) while earning his regular $300 a week with Majestic and was offered $37\frac{1}{2}\%$ of net profits after the film had been completed.

The first director to earn a million dollars for a single picture was Mike Nichols for *The Graduate* (US 67).

The longest directorial career has been that of Portugal's Manoel Candido Ponto de Oliveira (1908–), who began making his debut picture *Douru, Faina Furial/Work on the River Douru* (Por 31), about the hardships of the river workers in his hometown of Oporto, in 1929. As the son of a prominent industrialist, and in his youth a successful athlete and motor-racing driver, de Oliveira was born to a life of privilege but had a compassion for his less fortunate fellow countrymen which was to inform many of his films. His first feature, *Aniki-Bobo* (Por 42), was a children's film noted for its realism and use of a cast of non-actors. It was only in his 60s that he began to acquire an international reputation, consolidating his earlier work with a series of insightful films known collectively as the 'Quartet of Frustrated Loves'. His steadily increasing output in the 1980s and 1990s, when he was already well past the normal age of retirement, was lauded with many international honours. He was aged 91 when *Word and Utopia* (Por 00) debuted at the 2000 Venice Film Festival, 71 years after he began shooting his first film.

The longest career of a Hollywood director lasted for 67 years in the case of King Vidor (1894–1982), beginning with an actuality, *Hurricane in Galveston* (US 13), filmed in the city where he grew up, and culminating in another short, a documentary about painting called *The Metaphor* (US 80). Vidor's feature-film career had begun with a Christian Science melodrama titled *The Turn of the Road* (US 18), which oddly enough had been financed to the tune of $9000 by a consortium of ten doctors. Between this and his last feature, *Solomon and Sheba* (US 59), came such notable milestones in movie history as *The Big Parade* (US 25)—the most profitable silent film ever made (see p. 31)—his greatest artistic success *The Crowd* (US 28), the all-black movie *Hallelujah* (US 29), a classic tear-jerker *The Champ* (US 31), and a beautifully crafted adaptation of A. J. Cronin's novel *The Citadel* (GB 38) with Robert Donat. Vidor was a romantic, both on and off screen. Looking for a female lead for his first, rather primitive, comedy *The Tow* (US 14), he saw a beautiful girl passing in the back of a car. When he tracked her down, her father refused to let her debase herself in motion pictures. Vidor was determined to secure her services as an actress, but he had also fallen in love with her. They married and she became a major star of the silent screen as Florence Vidor.

DIRECTORS WITH A CAREER SPANNING HALF A CENTURY:

Manoel de Oliveira (1908–) 69 years from *Douru, Faina Fluvial* (Por 31) to *Word and Utopia* (Por 00).

King Vidor (1894–1982) 67 years from *Hurricane in Galveston* (US 13) to *The Metaphor* (US 80).

Jean Delannoy (1908–) 65 years from *Paris-Deauville* (Fr 35) to *Marie de Nazareth* (Fr/Mor 00)—**longest features career.**

Abel Gance (1889–1982) 60 years from *La Digue* (Fr 11) to *Bonaparte et la Révolution* (Fr 71).

Joris Ivens (1898–1989) 60 years from *De Brug* (Neth 28) to *Le Vent* (Fr 88).

Gilberto Martinez Solares (?–1998) 60 years from *Rosario* (Mex 37) to *Crisis* (Mex 97).

Grigori Alexandranov (1903–83) 59 years from *The Battleship Potemkin* (USSR 25), co-directed with Sergei Eisenstein, to *Lubov Orlova* (USSR 84).

Yuli Raizman (1903–94) 57 years from *A Circle* (USSR 27) to *A Time for Wishes* (USSR 84).

Alexander Medvedkin (1900–89) 55 years from shorts for military film organisation Gosvoyenkino 1925 to *Madness* (USSR 80).

John Ford (1895–1973) 54 years from *Lucille Love—The Girl of Mystery* (US 14) to *Vietnam, Vietnam* (US 68).

Claude Autant-Lara (1901-2000) 54 years from avant-garde short *Faites Divers* (Fr 23) to *Gloria* (Fr 77)

Alfred Hitchcock (1899–1980) 53 years from *Always Tell Your Wife* (GB 23) to *Family Plot* (US 76).

George Marshall (1896–1975) 53 years from *The Devil's Own* (US 16) to *Hook, Line and Sinker* (US 69).

Raoul Walsh (1887–1980) 52 years from *The Life of Villa* (US 12) to *A Distant Trumpet* (US 64).

Ford Beebe (1888–?) 52 years from *The Honor of the Range* (US 20) to *Challenge to be Free* (US 72).

Sir Charles Chaplin (1889–1977) 52 years from *Caught in a Cabaret* (US 14) to *A Countess from Hong Kong* (GB 67).

Kon Ichikawa (1915–) 52 years from *A Flower Blooms, 365 Nights* (Jap 48) to *Dora-Heita* (Jap 00).

Rudall Hayward (189?–1974) 51 years from *The Bloke from Freeman's Bay* (NZ 20) to *To Love a Maori* (NZ 71).

George Cukor (1899–1983) 51 years from *Grumpy* (US 30) to *Rich and Famous* (US 81).

Mark Donskoi (1901–1981) 51 years from *Life* (USSR 27) to *The Orlovs* (USSR 78).

Michael Curtiz (1888–1962) 50 years from *Ma Es Holnap* (Hun 12) to *The Comancheros* (US 62).

William Beaudine (1892–1970) 50 years from *Almost a King* (US 15) to *Jesse James Meets Frankenstein's Daughter* (US 65).

Akira Kurosawa (1910–98) 50 years from *Sanshiro Sugata* (Jap 43) to *Madadayo* (Jap 93).

O*ther Voices, Other Rooms* (US 97), from Truman Capote's first novel about a young homosexual groping his way to maturity in a small town in the American South, was directed by the Lord Great Chamberlain of England. For David, 7th Marquess of Cholmondeley, a successful director of television documentaries, it was his first feature film. Shooting near Charleston, South Carolina, the director had to pay a flying visit back to London for the State Opening of Parliament. It is the duty of the hereditary Lord Great Chamberlain, as the custodian of the Palace of Westminster, to walk backwards before the Queen, clad in his traditional gold-braided uniform and bearing his white wand of office, as she processes towards the throne in the House of Lords. It is not recorded how he explained this temporary absence to his American crew.

The longest career of a director of animated films is that of Chuck Jones (1913–), who has made over 250 cartoons for Warner Bros since his directorial debut with the Merrie Melodie *The Night Watchman* (US 38), released 19 November 1938. His latest work is the 13-episode series of *Thomas T. Wolf* (US 00–01) for Warner Brothers Online, which debuted on the Internet in November 2000. Chuck Jones was the creator of Road Runner, Pepe Le Pew, Wile E. Coyote and Michigan J. Frog.

Hollywood's most prolific director was William Beaudine (1892–1970), who directed 182 full-length features from *Watch Your Step* (US 22) to *Jesse James Meets Frankenstein's Daughter* (US 65), of which 32 were silents and 144 were talkies. In addition he directed over 120 shorts from 1915. Runners-up are as follows:

Richard Thorpe (1896–) 179 features from *Burn 'em Up Barnes* (US 21) to *The Scorpio Letters* (US 67), of which 63 were silents and 116 were talkies.

Michael Curtiz (1888–1962) 164 features from *Ma Es Holnap* (Hun 12) to *The Comancheros* (US 62), of which 61 were made in Europe before 1926 and the remainder in Hollywood.

Sam Newfield (1900–64) 140 talkies.

Allan Dwan (1885–1981) 132 features from *Richelieu* (US 14) to *The Most Dangerous Man Alive* (US 61), plus over 200 shorts from *Brandishing a Bad Man* (US 11). Dwan

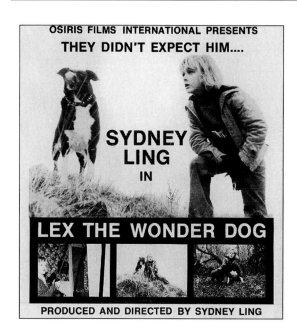

Ling the Wonder Boy was the youngest-ever director and producer of a professionally made feature film.

claimed to have been involved in the making of 1400 films since 1910 as writer, producer or director.

John Ford (1895–1973) 132 features from *The Tornado* (US 17) to *Vietnam, Vietnam* (US 68).

Note: It has been claimed that George Marshall (1896–1975) directed 425 features during his career, but only 88 full-length pictures crediting him as director can be traced for the period 1917–69. Ford Beebe (1888–?) is said to have directed over 200 westerns, 'B' pictures and serials from 1916, but only 72 known films give him director credit.

The most prolific British director was Darlington-born Maurice Elvey (1887–1967), who directed 149 full-length features from *Her Luck in London* (GB 14) to *Second Fiddle* (GB 57). In addition he directed 41 shorts (mainly two-reelers) from *The Fallen Idol* (GB 13).

The most prolific director still alive is Spanish sex-and-gore film-maker Jesus Franco, who has directed over 200 low-budget features since the late 1950s. Nearly 100 of his works are available on video.

The directors to make the most films in a single year were Sam Newfield (1900–64), who directed 17 'B' westerns for eight different 'Poverty Row' studios during 1938; and Spanish helmer Jesus 'Jess' Franco (1930–), who scored the same number in 1973.

The most co-directors on a single film was 16 in the case of *I misteri di Roma* (It 63), an anti-establishment view of 'one day in the life of the city' directed by Gianni Bisiach, Libero Bozzari, Mario Carbone, Angelo D'Alessandro, Nino del Fra, Luigi di Gianni, Giuseppe Ferrara, Ansano Giannarelli, Guilo Macchi, Lori Mazzetti, Massimo Mida, Enzo Mutti, Piero Nelli, Paolo Nuzzi, Dino Partesano and Giovanni Vento.

Deutschland im Herbst (FRG 78), *Love for Everyone* (Chn 42) and *Paramount on Parade* (US 30) each had 11 directors; *Dreams of Thirteen* (FRG/Neth 74) and *Aria*

(US/GB 87) had ten; *If I Had a Million* (US 32) and *Forever and a Day* (US 43) had seven. All the foregoing were either non-fiction or episodic fiction films. The most directors on a straight fiction film was seven for *Casino Royale* (GB 67), a Bond movie directed by John Huston, Ken Hughes, Val Guest, Robert Parrish, Joe McGrath, Richard Talmadge and Anthony Squire; and the same number for *Dungeonmaster* aka *Ragewar* (US 85), which was the collective work of Rose-Marie Turko, John Buechler, Charles Band, David Allen, Steve Ford, Peter Manoogian and Ted Nicolaou.

The youngest director of a professionally made feature film was Netherlands wunderkind Sydney Ling, who also produced, wrote and starred in his 92-minute *Lex the Wonder Dog* (Neths 73) at the age of 13. The distribution rights to the picture, which told a thrilling story of canine detection, were acquired by Scandinavian Oswald Brandaus Film and later by Osiris Film International and Cine Artists Corp.

Eleven-year-old Chaille Stovall of Florida began directing the family film *Camp Grizzly* (US i.p.), starring Dan Haggerty, for Emmett/Furla Films in October 2000.

Teenage directors have included Lev Kuleshov, who was 17½ when he embarked on his four-reel *Proyekt inzhenera Praita/Engineer Prite's Project* (USSR 18); Japan's Masahiro Makino, who made his directorial debut in 1927 at the age of 18; George Palmer, 17½, of Melbourne, Vic., who directed the railroad drama *Northbound Ltd* (Aus 26); Yuli Raizman, director of *A Circle* (USSR 27) at the age of 19; Philippe Garrel, whose feature debut *Anemone* (Fr 66), made when he was 19, starred his father Maurice Garrel; Sam Raimi, a 19-year-old who hustled the money for *The Evil Dead* (US 82) on the strength of a 30-minute pilot shot on 8mm; and 18-year-old Laurent Boutonnat, enfant terrible responsible for *La Ballade de la Feconductrice* (Fr 80). Boutannat was just old enough to be allowed to see his own film—it won an adults-only rating for its depiction of castration, child slaughter and bestiality. The only teenage female director prior to Samirah Makhmalbaf (see below) was 19-year-old French helmer Christine Ehm, who made her debut with *Simone* (Fr 87).

Youngest of the new wave of black American directors was juvenile prodigy Matty Rich. At age 17 he embarked on *Straight Out of Brooklyn* (US 91), a film about the struggles of a black working-class family which he based on true stories of people he had known. He also produced and wrote the picture, as well as performing in it. *Straight Out of Brooklyn* was released internationally by the Samuel Goldwyn Co. after winning a special jury award at the 1991 Sundance Film Festival.

The youngest woman director was Iran's Samirah Makhmalbaf, daughter of distinguished helmer Moshen Makhmalbaf, who was 17 when she made *Sib/The Apple* (Iran 98), a true-story dramatic reconstruction about two 11-year-old girls who were locked up from birth by their parents. The family, including the father who had imprisoned his daughters so that they would meet no men until of marriageable age, all agreed to play themselves.

The oldest directors are Manoel de Oliveira (b. Oporto 1908), aged 91 when *Word and Utopia* (Por 00) debuted at the 2000 Venice Film Festival (see also the longest directorial career above), and Jean Delannoy (b. Noisy-le-Sec 1908), also 91 when *Marie de Nazareth* (Fr/Mor 00) was released.

The oldest directorial debut was by 83-year-old Alain Cuny, who also acted in his screen version of the Paul Claudel play *L'Annonce faite à Marie* (Fr/Can 92).

The oldest woman director was Denmark's Astrid Henning-Jensen, who was 82 when she helmed *Bella, Min Bella* (Den 96).

The most delayed directorial comeback was by Mexican pioneer woman director Matilde Landeta, who allowed 41 years to elapse without a film between *Trotacalles* (Mex 51) and her biopic of national romantic poet *Manuel Acuna Nocturno a Rosario* (Mex 92).

The most versatile film-maker in terms of the most credits for a single film is Polish director Andrzej

As deputy Culture Minister of Armenia, Vigen Chaldranian has responsibility for activating the fledgling nation's nascent film industry. In the absence of quality film-makers, he kick-started production by making his own feature movie. In *Lord Have Mercy* (Armenia 98) he not only starred opposite femme lead Irina Karachera, but also earned the credits for director, producer, screenwriter, art director and editor. 'There just wasn't any money to pay anyone else,' he observed, noting that he had to sell his house to complete the $15,000 picture.

Kondratiuk, whose *The Four Seasons* (Pol 85) credited him as producer, director, scriptwriter, cameraman, art director, composer, soundman, props buyer, lighting-man and star. The only technical credit to someone else went to editor Maryla Orlowska. Exceptionally for a professionally made film produced in a then Communist country, *Four Seasons* was privately financed—by Andrzej Kondratiuk.

Most credits for a major motion picture went to Charles Chaplin for producing, directing, scripting, composing, editing, choreographing, costume-designing and starring in *Limelight* (US 52).

Most versatile femme film-maker is Sweden's Ann Zacharias, director, producer, scriptwriter, production designer and star of *The Test* (Swe 87).

Editing

The most edited film in terms of total negative discarded was Howard Hughes' *Hell's Angels* (US 30), which consumed 2,254,750ft of film during the four years it took to make. If all this footage had been shown unedited, it would have run for 560 hours or 23 days non-stop. The cost of the film stock was $225,475. The final release print was 9045ft (two hour 15 minute running time), a reduction in the ratio of 249:1. A single scene without actors—a brief close-up of the valves of an aeroplane

Most directors are heroically resistant to their films being cut—occasionally misguidedly. Guiseppe Tornatore's *Cinema Paradiso* (It 88) had a disastrous debut. It went on to worldwide success and the Oscar for Best Foreign Film only after a massive 32 minutes and an entire story chapter had been lopped from the director's cut.

engine—occupied 20,000 ft of film (the length of four full-length features) before Hughes was satisfied.

In more recent times Michael Cimino shot 220 hours of film for his $57 million epic *Heaven's Gate* (US 81) to produce a release print which one critic described as five hours and 25 minutes of 'staggering self-indulgence'. When the long version flopped, it was cut to two and half hours.

Other films with extravagant shooting ratios: Fritz Lang's *Metropolis* (Ger 26) was reduced from 1,960,000 to 13,165ft, a ratio of 149:1; Charles Chaplin's *City Lights* (US 31) was reduced from 975,000 to 7784ft, a ratio of 125:1; *Uncle Tom's Cabin* (US 27) was reduced from 900,000 to 13,000ft, a ratio of 69:1; Charles Chaplin's *The Kid* (US 20) was reduced from 400,000 to 6000ft, a ratio of 67:1; Leni Riefenstahl's *Olympische Spiele* (Ger 38) was reduced from 1,300,000 to 20,000ft, a ratio of 65:1; William Wyler's *Ben Hur* (US 59) was reduced from 1,125,000 to 23,838ft, a ratio of 47:1; Howard Hughes' *The Outlaw* (US 46) was reduced from 470,000 to 10,451ft, a ratio of 45:1; Erich von Stroheim's *Foolish Wives* (US 21) was reduced from

Many stars, Marilyn Monroe among them, faced the early disappointment of seeing the footage of their debut performance end up on the cutting-room floor. In only one instance have the record books had to be rewritten when what should have been a first screen appearance was later restored. Bing Crosby performed in a vocal trio which sang with Paul Whiteman's band in *The King of Jazz* (US 30), but the scene failed to make it into the release print. By the time the film was re-released several years later, Crosby was a major star. The reissue was re-edited to include close-ups of the crooner which fortuitously had been preserved by the studio—usually discarded footage was melted down to salvage the silver nitrate it contained. Posters for the reissue gave Crosby top billing.

360,000 to 10,000ft, a ratio of 36:1; William Wyler's *The Best Years of Our Lives* (US 46) was reduced from 400,000 to 16,000ft, a ratio of 25:1; Chuck Wein's *Rainbow Bridge* (US 71) was reduced from 252,000 to 10,300ft, a ratio of 24:1; three with a ratio of 23:1 were D. W. Griffith's *Intolerance* (US 16), reduced from 300,000 to 13,000ft, Sergei Eisenstein's *October* (USSR 27), also reduced from 300,000 to 13,000ft, and *Gone With the Wind* (US 39), reduced from 474,538 to 20,300ft; and *The Longest Day* (US 72), reduced from 360,000 to 17,000ft, which had a ratio of 21:1, or about twice the average.

The most edited single sequence of a movie was the chariot race scene in *Ben Hur* (US 25), for which editor

Lloyd Nosler had to compress 200,000ft of film into a sparse 750ft, a ratio of 267:1. Historian Kevin Brownlow commented: 'These 750 feet are among the most valuable in motion-picture history.'

It is not recorded how many separate cuts this involved. It is doubtful, though, that it exceeded the 181 cuts in the final three minutes of John Frankenheimer's *Black Sunday* (US 77), an average of one per second. The sequence shows a Goodyear airship armed with thousands of lethal darts gliding into the Super Bowl, which is packed with 80,000 spectators, pursued by an Israeli secret agent suspended on a rope beneath a helicopter. All 181 edits were planned and drawn on paper weeks

> In 1976 Continental Airlines started showing single- reel versions of movie classics, editing out everything except the skeleton of the plot. Commenting on the 20-minute duration edit of Tyrone Power–Ava Gardner starrer *The Sun Also Rises* (US 57), from Hemingway's novel, the *New York Times* called it 'the cinematic version of *Reader's Digest* at 35,000 feet'.

before the scene was shot and each of the four camera operators who filmed the sequences had copies of production illustrator Nikita Knatz's drawings. Some of the edits were only four frames—one sixth of a second—registering only subliminally. 'I wanted the audience overwhelmed,' Frankenheimer explained. 'I wanted them to feel a total sense of panic.'

The least edited films include D.W. Griffith's *Broken Blossoms* (US 19), which was made with no retakes of any scene and had only 200 ft trimmed from its original

length of 5500 ft; and William Wellman's *The Public Enemy* (US 31), which was reduced by only 360 ft from its original 8760 ft.

Narrative features which were released unedited include *My Hustler* (US 65); Andy Warhol's *Chelsea Girls* (US 66); and Laura Mulvey and Peter Wollen's *Penthesilea: Queen of the Amazons* (GB 74). The ultimate

> R2 D2, lovable robot hero of *Star Wars* (US 77), was named after a piece of film editors' jargon—it means 'Reel 2, Dialog 2'.

was achieved by *The Lacy Rituals* (GB 73), which was unedited to the extent of including shots of the clapperboard being clapped and even retained the director's cries of 'Cut!' on the soundtrack. More recently Mike Figgis's *Timecode* (US 00) was shot with four digital video cameras recording four interconnecting stories, each in a single, unedited 93-minute take. The stories were presented simultaneously on a quartered split screen.

The first woman editor was Viola Lawrence, who graduated from assistant editor to editor at New York's Vitagraph Studios in 1915.

NEW FILMS FOR OLD

Skilful editing can create an entirely new film from rearrangement of shots in an earlier one. This was achieved by Fred J. Balshofer, who had made a spy spoof

Bing sings in silhouette (left) in The King of Jazz *(US 30). The unknown's performance ended up on the cutting room floor when the film was first released, but was restored again for the reissue after he had become America's number-one crooner.* (Kobal Collection)

called *An Adventuress* (US 20) in which the then unknown Rudolph Valentino played a bit part, and wanted to cash in on the Latin lover's meteoric rise to stardom. The locale of the new picture, *The Isle of Love* (US 22), was switched from World War I Germany to a desert island by the simple expedient of inserting stock shots of bathing beauties on a palm-fringed beach throughout the film. The problem of expanding Valentino's minor role in the original into the lead for the new picture was overcome in a number of ways. Various shots were repeated several times; long shots were blown up into close-up and intercut with other footage; some scenes were projected on a loop, so that Valentino repeated the same motions several times over; one scene was used as a flashback; and out-takes from the original were inserted into the new film, notably discarded footage of a car ride, which so expanded the scene as to make it seem interminable. Valentino, it is hardly necessary to add, received no recompense for this unauthorised 'star performance'.

Woody Allen successfully cannibalised and transmogrified a Japanese crime melodrama into a madcap comedy. Retitled *What's Up Tiger Lily?* (US 66), the comedic effect was achieved by re-editing, deliberately mismatching the dubbed dialogue, and by Allen's zany narration.

Blake Edwards did what was in effect a reconstruction job with *The Trail of the Pink Panther* (GB 82), the only film ever to have been embarked upon after the death of its star. Peter Sellers (1925–80) was seen once again as the accident-prone Inspector Clouseau in a story knit together from clips and leftover out-takes from five

> **M**ost cuts are made to satisfy the director or the producer. The 35 minutes which were lopped off the director's cut of David Lean's epic *Lawrence of Arabia* (GB 62) was to satisfy the cost accountants. It meant that cinemas could accommodate three showings a day instead of two.

previous Pink Panther films. Linking shots were made with an uncredited lookalike filmed at a distance or heavily disguised, as in one scene where the Inspector sets off for England swathed in bandages from head to foot. When all the useable Sellers footage had been exhausted, the film resorted to flashbacks of a teenage Clouseau played by Daniel Peacock and an eight-year-old Clouseau in the person of Lucca Mezzofanti. All this ingenuity failed to pay off. The picture flopped and Sellers' widow Lynne Frederick won an award of $1,687,000 from United Artists for violation of her late husband's contractual rights; United Artists were also ordered to pay $214,000 in costs.

Film Stock

The first transparent roll film of a kind suitable for motion-picture use (though designed for still photography) was manufactured by the Eastman Dry Plate and Film Co. of Rochester, NY, in August 1889. Although Thomas Edison ordered some about this date for experiments in cinematography, it was found unsatisfactory

and the first stock used for taking films for the Edison Kinetoscope was supplied by the Merwin Hulbert firm in 50 ft rolls on 18 March 1891. In the meantime, however, Louis Aimé Augustin Le Prince of Leeds, Yorkshire, had succeeded in making experimental cinematograph films on Eastman Kodak stock that he had ordered in the autumn of 1889.

The first commercially produced films in Britain were made in 1895 by Robert Paul and Birt Acres using stock supplied by the European Blair Camera Co. Ltd of St Mary Cray, Kent. By the end of 1896, film stock specially cut and prepared for motion-picture use was being advertised by the Celluloid Co. of New York, Dr J. H. Smith & Co. of Zurich, Switzerland, the Blair Co. of Cambridge, Mass. and London, England, the Eastman Kodak Co. of Rochester, NY, and Fitch & Co. of London.

The first perforated film was used by Louis Aimé Augustin Le Prince (1842–90?) in his motion-picture experiments conducted at Leeds, Yorkshire, in 1889. The inventor's assistant Longley recalled that 'we had brass eyelets fixed in the band [i.e. film] similar to the eyelets of boots'. The projector built by Le Prince in 1889 had a wheel with pins 'for gearing into the band of pictures'. Perforated film was not used by Thomas Edison until at least three years later.

Commercially produced film stock was originally sold unperforated and it was not until 1904 that Eastman Kodak began offering perforation as an optional extra. Even as late as 1922 Richardson's Handbook of Projection states 'perforation is usually done by the producer'. Unperforated nitrate stock continued to be available from Eastman Kodak until September 1949.

The first safety film on an acetate base was introduced by Eastman Kodak of Rochester, NY, in the autumn of 1908, but its application was limited due to the fact that it tended to shrink and cockle. The negative safety stock was withdrawn in 1912, though positive safety film continued to be available for use with portable projectors in schools. Little record of production on safety film in the USA survives from this period and the earliest commercially made movie known to have been released on safety stock, a 345ft drama titled *La Vendetta del Groom* (It 09), was produced by Cines of Rome.

Substandard safety film was produced in 28mm gauge by Pathé for use with the KOK home movie projector in France in 1912 and in 22mm gauge by Kodak for use with the Edison Home Kinetoscope the same year.

Safety film continued to be confined to the substandard gauges until 1950, when Eastman Kodak reintroduced 35mm uninflammable stock, using a triacetate base immune to shrinkage. The revolution in film stock was total and immediate, so that since 1951 virtually no film has been made on the highly inflammable nitrate stock previously in use.

The largest frame format of any film stock was the 2.04 x 2.805 in. dimension used in the 70mm horizontal feed IMAX system, developed by Multiscreen Corp. of Canada. The first film produced in this 5.242 sq in format, which is nine times the size of the standard 35 mm frame, was *Tiger Child* (Can/Jap 70), presented at the Fuji Group's pavilion at Japan's Expo 70.

The first feature film in giant-screen IMAX was the Walt Disney Pictures' 75-minute *Fantasia/2000* (US 99), a reworking of their 1940 stereophonic sound production with seven new animated sequences and one original—Mickey Mouse as 'The Sorcerer's Apprentice'. After debuting with a live orchestra at New York's Carnegie Hall on 17th December 1999, the new *Fantasia* was released worldwide in 75 IMAX cinemas between 1 January and 30 April 2000, then to conventional cinemas in 35mm format. It took 30 years for IMAX to graduate to feature-length movies because the size of the film reels limited the projection equipment to subjects with a maximum duration of 45 minutes.

The first film shot in High Definition Video System (HDVS) for theatrical release was *Julia and Julia* (It 87), starring Kathleen Turner, an English-language film made by RAI of Rome. HDVS was developed by Sony and NHK to enable feature films to be shot on tape and transferred to film without loss of quality. The video image has 1125 lines, about twice the definition of a television picture. The technique is claimed to cut below-the-line production costs by 20–30%. The first HDTV feature produced in America was *Do It Up* (US 88), starring Robby Benson, which was made by the Rebo High Definition Studio, New York.

GAUGES

The standard gauge of 35mm was adopted by Thomas Alva Edison (1847–1931) of West Orange, NJ, in the spring of 1891 for use with the Kinetoscope peep-show viewing apparatus developed by his assistant W. K. L. Dickson. Edison's choice of four perforations, giving a 4 x 3 format to the image, was probably dictated by the fact that the film was designed for showing in a viewing machine, not on screen. Had he anticipated that projection would become the normal method of presenting movies, he would doubtless have opted for a wider format to give an aspect ratio approximating more closely to that of a theatre stage. The Lumière brothers of Lyon, France, who built the first commercially successful projectors, decided to conform to the gauge pioneered by Edison and it was undoubtedly their dominance of the nascent film industry in Europe that established 35mm as the standard gauge. It was officially recognised as such by international agreement in 1907.

The first use of 70mm film was by Birt Acres (1854–1918) of Barnet, Herts, for shooting scenes of Henley Regatta on 7–9 July 1896. He soon abandoned use of wide gauge film because of the high cost.

A 70mm projector was produced by Herman Caster of Canatosta, NY, and introduced into Britain as *The American Biograph* on 17 March 1897 at the Palace Theatre.

The first 70mm feature film was a special widescreen version of *Fox Movietone Follies* of 1929, premièred in the Grandeur process at the Gaiety Theater, New York, on 17 September 1929.

The smallest gauge ever employed for filming was 3mm, developed circa 1960 by Eric Berndt and used by NASA in manned space flights in the late 1960s. It had a centre frameline perforation.

The largest gauge ever employed in filming was 75 mm, by the Lumière Co. of Lyons, for special large-screen presentations at the Paris Exposition of 1900.

Flashbacks

The first flashback was used in the Lubin production *A Yiddisher Boy* (US 08) and showed the hero involved in a boyhood street-fight 25 years earlier.

The first sound flashback, in which dialogue and sounds from the past are synchronised with an image of the present in order to conjure up a distant memory, was used by Rouben Mamoulian in *City Streets* (US 31). Dialogue heard earlier in the film was repeated over a huge close-up of Sylvia Sidney's tear-stained face as she recalls the past.

The first flashback within a flashback appeared in Jacques Feyder's *L'Atlantide* (Fr 21); thereafter it was bypassed by film-makers as too confusing until Michael Curtiz challenged the audience's comprehension with a flashback within a flashback within a flashback in *Passage to Marseilles* (US 44). The experiment was repeated in John Brahm's *The Locket* (US 46) and then happily relegated to the limbo of great ideas that do not work.

UNCONVENTIONAL FLASHBACKS

These include the multiple flashbacks out of sequence employed by William K. Howard in *The Power and the Glory* (US 33) and Orson Welles in *Citizen Kane* (US 41).
Andre Antoine's *La Coupable* (Fr 16) was told entirely in flashbacks, as was *Saragossa Manuscript* (Pol 74), a Decameron-type fantasy of erotic happenings in the 18th century, which went continuously backwards in time. The original version of Sergio Leone's *Once Upon a Time in America* (US 84) jumped backwards and forwards with such confusing irregularity that *Variety*'s correspondent at Cannes actually logged the sequences: 1933—22 minutes; 1968—14 minutes; childhood sequence of indeterminate date—54 minutes; 1920s—25 minutes; 1968—seven minutes; 1920s–30s—61 minutes; 1968—30 minutes; 1933—seven minutes.

Bertolucci's first feature, *La Commare secca* (It 62), about the murder of a prostitute in Rome and the subsequent investigation, used the 'against the rules' technique of false flashbacks—deliberately intended to mislead—interspersed with true flashbacks. A charming device was adopted by Keisuke Kinoshita in *Nogiku no gotoku Kimi Nariki/She was like a Wild Chrysanthemum* (Jap 55)—about an old man revisiting his home town after 60 years and recalling boyhood scenes—when he placed all the flashbacks in an oval-shaped vignette.

Lighting

The earliest use of lighting effects for their aesthetic value is generally attributed to D. W. Griffith, who employed artificial lighting to obtain a 'fireside glow' in *The Drunkard's Reformation* (US 09), for the 'sunlight effect' in *Pippa Passes* (US 09) and the 'dim, religious light' in *Threads of Destiny* (US 10). Griffith had to overcome the resistance of his cameramen Harry Marvin and Billy Bitzer, who regarded shadows as 'amateurish'.

The first backlighting by reflectors was introduced by D. W. Griffith's cameraman Billy Bitzer on *Enoch Arden* (US 11), which opens with a superbly backlit shot of the villagers bidding the sailors goodbye. The technique had been discovered by accident. Normally the camera was never faced directly into the sun, but one day Bitzer turned it playfully on to Mary Pickford and Owen Moore as they sat at a shiny-topped table with the sun behind them. Instead of the couple appearing in silhouette, as he expected, Bitzer found that he had obtained a beautifully lit shot with the two artistes' faces bathed in radiance—suitably, since they were in love—the effect of the sun's light reflected in the table top. Bitzer devised a system whereby one mirror would reflect the sun into another, which could then be beamed to the back of a performer's head.

The most powerful lighting used on any film was the 58,000 amps that illuminated the set of *The King and I* (US 56). This is equivalent to the illumination of 258 'brute' arc lights.

The most powerful standard lighting unit currently on sale is the 350-amp Titan Molarc, manufactured by the Mole-Richardson Co. of Hollywood.

The most powerful single arc ever used was a giant 13,940 amp, 325 million candlepower lamp used by

On the set of California *(US 27) with the most powerful lighting unit in the history of motion picture.*

Colonel Tim McCoy on the western *California* (US 27). The lamp was 40 times the strength of the most powerful arc available today (see above), 54 times as powerful as the most brilliant lighthouse beam, and said to have a beam that would radiate for 90 miles.

The first feature film shot indoors without artificial lighting was Lars von Trier's *The Kingdom* (Den 95), a 4 hr 39 min 'soap noir' about the tangle of relationships in a Copenhagen hospital, which was photographed on super-sensitive film.

Locations

The first dramatic film to be shot on an overseas location was *Hiawatha* (GB 05), a one-reel rendering of Longfellow's poem directed by former Boer War cinematographer Joe Rosenthal for the Urban Trading Co of London. Filmed at Desbarats, Ont, it was also the first screen drama to be shot in Canada and at 1065ft (24 min) was one of the longest narrative films to have been released at this date.

> Starstruck sightseers are the bugbear of most location managers. A sign posted up during a 1988 shoot at New York's Café Luxembourg read: 'The name of this movie is *When Harry Met Sally*. No one famous is in it and you can't be in it either. Thanx. Soon at a theater near you.'

HOLLYWOOD THE WORLD OVER
Hollywood made 4805 feature films set in 129 identifiable foreign countries during the period 1912–99. Comparatively few of these films were shot in the locales they represented, as overseas location shooting was exceptional before the 1950s. The table overleaf, therefore, lists the 25 countries most often depicted in American movies, not necessarily the countries in which the films were actually shot. The most popular overseas locale over the whole period surveyed has been the UK with 900 films or 18.7% of the total, followed closely by France, with 830 films or 17.3%.

Hollywood's love affair with Britain, though, underwent a sharp decline from the 25% of all overseas settings in the 1930s and 1940s to a mere 8.2% (less than France) in the 1980s. Fuelled by Jane Austen and Shakespeare, and also by sometimes simplistic pro-IRA films, the UK returned to favour as a locale in the 1990s with 16.1% of overseas settings.

WHERE IT'S AT
* The railway station where romance blossomed for Celia Johnson and Trevor Howard in David Lean's *Brief Encounter* (GB 45) was called Milford Junction and was supposed to be in Kent. The actual station was at Carnforth, Lancs and was chosen because it was the only railway junction far enough removed from the flight path of German bombers for blackout restrictions to be lifted for the film-makers. (Although filmed in the last year of the war, *Brief Encounter* was set in the last year of peace.) Today Carnforth is a sorry relic of the last days of steam. Now no longer in

use, the only recognisable features from the film are the passageway where the lovers kiss before running to catch their different trains and the station clock which ticked away their stolen hours together. The refreshment room, pivot of the story, has long since vanished. British Rail replaced it with a foul-smelling room furnished only with a Klix drinks dispenser and a battered dustbin. Hope, however, is at hand. A trust has been formed to restore the station in tribute to the British film most frequently honoured in lists of the all-time greats.

- The filming of *The Great Gatsby* (US 73) took place not in Long Island, where F. Scott Fitzgerald set his 1920s novel of doomed love amongst the ultra rich, but in Newport, Rhode Island. The reason was simple: even in the 1970s Newport people still led the kind of life enjoyed in the most select resorts of Long Island in the 1920s, with houses, furniture and works of art to match. The main set, standing in for Jay Gatsby's mansion, was Rosecliff, hired from Mrs George Henry Warren of the Preservation Society of Newport County for a reported $50,000. For a below-stairs scene the kitchen of The Breakers, Cornelius Vanderbilt's mansion, was used, and some bedroom and other upper-storey shots were filmed at William K. Vanderbilt's mansion Marble House. Outdoor scenes of Jay Gatsby (Robert Redford) arriving at the Tom Buchanan home were shot at Hammersmith Farm, the estate of Mrs Hugh Auchincloss (mother of Jacqueline Kennedy), where a façade was built on to the carriage-house to represent the house. Other great houses of Newport contributed antiques and furniture for set dressing, though critic Judith Crist was to observe that the film 'leaves us more involved with six-and-a-half-million dollars worth of trappings than with human tragedy'. Some 700 gilded denizens of Newport appeared on screen as $20 a day extras, representing guests in the celebrated party scenes filmed at Rosecliff. Although 6800 candidates were interviewed, it was only those with what the casting director described as 'the Gatsby look' who were successful. It was, he explained, 'an air, an attitude of bored arrogance'.

- Harem scenes have been a standby of erotic movies and saucy comedies since the earliest days of movie making. None had been filmed in a real harem, though, until 1989. And perhaps surprisingly, the loca-

HOLLYWOOD FILMS SET IN OVERSEAS LOCALES

	1912–19	1920–29	1930–39	1940–49	1950–59	1960–69	1970–79	1980–89	1990–99	Total
UK	256/21.7%	166/21.4%	160/25.4%	134/25.3%	53/10.7%	24/7.7%	11/9.7%	22/8.2%	74/16.1%	900/18.7%
France	264/22.4%	174/22.51%	119/18.9%	63/11.9%	83/16.8%	54/17.3%	16/14.2%	24/18.9%	33/7.2%	830/17.3%
Canada	196/16.6%	99/12.8%	45/7.1%	25/4.7%	20/4.0%	4/1.3%	4/3.5%	9/3.5%	16/3.5%	418/8.7%
Mexico	53/4.5%	23/3.0%	46/7.3%	32/6.0%	35/7.0%	21/6.7%	12/10.6%	18/6.7%	19/4.1%	259/5.4%
Italy	43/3.7%	20/2.6%	18/2.9%	13/2.5%	30/6.0%	38/12.1%	7/6.2%	13/4.8%	17/3.7%	199/4.1%
Germany	29/2.5%	11/1.4%	20/3.2%	36/6.7%	18/3.6%	22/7.0%	8/7.1%	10/3.7%	17/3.7%	170/3.5%
Russia	52/4.4%	30/3.9%	21/3.3%	9/1.7%	4/0.8%	6/1.9%	6/5.3%	7/3.5%	21/4.6%	156/3.2%
China	15/1.3%	27/3.5%	31/4.9%	21/3.4%	9/1.8%	8/2.6%	1/0.9%	6/3.0%	10/2.2%	128/2.7%
Spain	21/1.8%	31/4.0%	9/1.4%	9/1.7%	11/2.2%	16/5.1%	2/1.8%	7/2.6%	9/2.0%	115/2.4%
India	35/3.0%	20/2.6%	11/1.7%	6/1.1%	15/3.0%	3/1.0%	0/–	2/1.0%	4/0.9%	96/2.0%
Austria	2/0.2%	15/1.9%	27/4.3%	12/2.3%	5/1.0%	7/2.2%	4/3.5%	4/1.5%	0/–	76/1.6%
Ireland	20/1.7%	11/1.4%	9/1.4%	5/1.0%	2/0.4%	3/1.0%	3/2.7%	2/0.7%	21/4.6	76/1.6%
Japan	23/2.0%	4/0.5%	0/–	7/1.3%	3/0.6%	12/3.8%	2/1.8%	8/3.0%	6/1.3%	66/1.4%
Egypt	19/1.6%	13/1.7%	8/1.3%	9/1.7%	6/1.2%	1/0.3%	0/–	2/0.7%	5/1.1%	63/1.3%
Vietnam	0/–	2/0.3%	2/0.3%	2/0.4%	6.1.2%	2/0.6%	4/3.5%	27/10.0%	14/3.1%	59/1.2%
Philippines	9/0.8%	2/0.3%	2/0.3%	11/2.1%	7/1.4%	12/3.8%	3/2.7%	5/1.9%	3/0.7%	54/1.1%
South Africa	18/1.5%	14/1.8%	3/0.5%	3/0.6%	3/0.6%	1/1.0%	1/0.9%	3/1.1%	5/1.1%	51/1.1%
Switzer-land	8/0.7%	6/0.8%	9/1.4%	6/1.1%	5/1.0%	3/1.0%	1/0.9%	4/1.5%	3/0.7%	45/0.9%
Cuba	4/0.3%	9/1.2%	5/0.8%	5/1.0%	12/2.4%	1/0.3%	2/1.8%	1/0.4%	4/0.9%	43/0.9%
Brazil	1/0.1%	5/0.6%	3/0.5%	9/1.7%	6/1.2%	3/1.0%	1/0.9%	4/1.5%	7/1.5%	39/0.8%
Korea	0/–	0/–	0/–	0/–	29/5.9%	6/1.9%	1/0.9%	2/0.7%	1/0.2%	39/0.8%
Morocco	4/0.3%	4/0.5%	2/0.3%	9/1.7%	13/2.6%	3/1.0%	1/0.9%	0/–	3/0.7%	39/0.8%
Algeria	10/0.8%	9/1.2%	10/1.6%	1/0.2%	3/0.6%	2/0.6%	0/–	0/–	1/0.2%	36/0.7%
Hungary	3/0.3%	10/1.3%	8/1.3%	5/1.0%	5/1.0%	1/0.3%	0/–	4/1.5%	0/–	36/0.7%
Belgium	20/1.7%	1/0.1%	1/0.2%	2/0.4%	1/0.2%	6/1.9%	0/–	1/0.4%	3/0.7%	35/0.7%
Others	73/6.2%	69/8.9%	58/9.2%	92/17.4%	110/22.3%	57/18.2%	23/20.0%	84/31.2%	110/24.0%	676/14.1%
Total	1178	775	627	526	494	316	113	269	459	4805

Percentage figures represent the proportion of all US productions with overseas locales which are set, wholly or in part, in the countries named.

tion was the Soviet Union. The international co-production *The Battle of the Three Kings* (Morocco/USSR/Sp/It 90), a 16th-century costumer about charismatic Arab leader Abdel-malek, went to Soviet Bachiserai to shoot the scene in an ancient harem which had been preserved by a local Turkish community over the centuries.

- Lindsay Anderson approached the headmaster of his old school, Cheltenham College, for permission to use it as the location for *If* (GB 68), his memorable tale of pupils rebelling against the system which ends with a group of boys machine-gunning the parents and masters on speech day. The headmaster enquired what kind of story it was. Similar to *Tom Brown's Schooldays* perhaps?, he suggested helpfully when Anderson hesitated. The director assured him that 'certain features' of the story might be compared with Thomas Hughes' Victorian classic (in which authority is upheld as always right) and permission was willingly granted for a location fee said to have been only £100. Lindsay Anderson was not invited as a distinguished Old Boy to hand out the prizes at any subsequent Cheltenham Speech Days.

- The race around the Great Court of Trinity College, Cambridge between Harold Abrahams (Ben Cross) and Lord Lindsey (Nigel Havers) in *Chariots of Fire* (GB 81), in which the Olympic athlete Abrahams becomes the first man to complete the circuit in less time than the 44 seconds it takes the 400-year-old Trinity clock to strike noon, actually took place far from Cambridge. The ultra-conservative Trinity College council, ironically similar to the stuffy dons portrayed in the film, were not prepared to be associated with anything as vulgar as moving pictures, and the scene was filmed in the courtyard of Eton College instead. Lack of an authentic location might have mattered more had the race really taken place, but in fact Abrahams never ran round Trinity Great Court to beat the clock. Nor did Lord Lindsey, because he was a fictitious character, though loosely based on champion athlete Lord Burghley.

- The cornfield which the Iowa farmer played by Kevin Costner turned into a baseball diamond in *Field of Dreams* (US 89) lies just outside Dyersville, Iowa. 'People will come,' Ray Liotta as Shoeless Joe Jackson says to Costner in the movie. 'They'll come to Iowa for reasons they can't fathom. They'll arrive at your door, innocent as children, longing for the past.' And come they did, more than 10,000 during the summer following the release of the film, just to see a featureless stretch of grass which had stirred their dreams.

- *Loch Ness* (GB 95), in which Ted Danson plays an American marine biologist trying to prove or disprove the existence of the monster, was filmed some 90 miles distant from Loch Ness. The loch in the film is Loch Diabig, which runs off Loch Torridon in Wester

The Yorkshire Moors in Wuthering Heights *(US 39) . . . 50 miles from Hollywood.* (BFI)

Ross. The producers decided it looked more romantic than Loch Ness itself. But anyone wanting to prop up the bar at the cosy Moffat Arms, where Danson romances inn-keeper Joely Richardson, will be disappointed. The building, in the village of Diabig, is really a holiday cottage called Cadha na Hearba which the art director extended and decorated to look like a traditional Scottish fishing inn.

- On the other hand, young lovers who would like to emulate Charles (Hugh Grant) and Carrie (Andie MacDowell) in *Four Weddings and a Funeral* (GB 94) and sleep together for the first time at the romantic Boatman hotel of the film can in fact do so. Its real name is the Crown and it is in Amersham, Buckinghamshire. The Queen Elizabeth Suite where Charles and Carrie consummated their love will cost them £165 a night during the week and £186 at weekends, but they are advised to behave with decorum. The management threw the cast and crew out because they were said to be disturbing other guests. The suite was rebooked to a real-life honeymoon couple and the final shots of the hotel scenes had to be completed at Shepperton Studios.

- The château with the myriad pointed towers in Richard Lester's *The Three Musketeers* (Pan 73) was the Alcazar, perched on a hill above Segovia some 75 miles north of Madrid. If it looks familiar to those unacquainted with old Castile, it could be because it was also the model for the Sleeping Beauty castle at Disneyland.

- The Yorkshire Moors in *Wuthering Heights* (US 39) were replicated on a 540-acre tract in the Canejo Hills, a topographical duplicate of the moors lying some 50 miles from Hollywood. The land had to be cleared of the native wild lilac and greasewood, and in their place went 14,000 tumbleweeds which had been gathered by schoolboys at 1c each. Each weed was anchored to the earth and the whole sprinkled with purple sawdust so that in the longshots it resembled heather. For close work a thousand heather plants were brought from florists, but transporting them to the location presented a problem because it necessitated crossing a county line with a plant embargo. The authorities were only persuaded to relax the ban when the heather was fumigated for scale, treated for bugs and the seed pods sterilised. Total cost of recreating Yorkshire in California was $100,000.

- During the Cold War years it was usual for scenes set in Soviet cities to be shot in Vienna or Helsinki. Much has changed. In gangster movie *Mad Dog Coll* (US 92) Moscow stood in for 1920s New York.

- Roads present logistical problems for period movies— they need to be cleared of modern vehicles. No such difficulties lay in Universal's way when they chose Mackinac Island in Michigan for the location of *Somewhere in Time* (US 80), in which Christopher Reeve travels back in time to 1912 to encounter the long-dead actress (Jane Seymour) whose photograph has captivated him. The 3-mile-long island, at whose shores Lake Michigan and Lake Huron converge, has a ban on automobiles. Nor was it necessary to bring horses to the location, as there were already 600 of them on Mackinac, including Percherons, hackneys, American saddlebreds and Kentucky high-steppers.

Moreover, the 92-year-old Grand Hotel, which provided accommodation for cast and crew as well as serving as the principal set, was able to provide its own carriages for the production. One other feature made Mackinac the perfect location. Despite existing in an Edwardian time-warp (guests still have to dress for dinner at the Grand), the island boasts its own fully equipped movie studio, built by the Moral Rearmament Campaign who have their headquarters there.

- *Oklahoma!* (US 55) was shot in . . . *Arizona!* Location scouts reported that the state celebrated in the title afforded hardly a vista without an oil derrick and where there were no derricks there were invariably noisy aircraft overhead. Arizona, they declared, had the great benefit of reliable weather—dry and sunny. But during the shoot it rained so relentlessly that, whenever big limos bearing anxious studio executives hove into sight, the crew broke into song with 'The mud is as high as a Cadillac's eye'.

- The Antarctic setting for Captain Scott's march homeward from the South Pole in *Scott of the Antarctic* (GB 48) was in fact close to the Arctic Circle—almost as far from the true locale as it was possible to get. The main location was the vast glacier close to the small Norwegian town of Finse. Director Charles Frend and star John Mills were amazed to find that many of the citizens of Finse had personal memories of Captain Scott. The explorer had used the glacier in 1909 for trials of the motor sledges he took with him on his final and fatal expedition.

- Milos Forman's *One Flew Over the Cuckoo's Nest* (US 75) was filmed in the actual setting of Ken Kesey's cult novel of the same name, the Oregon State Mental Hospital at Salem. Although the story, a savage satire on life in an asylum, could hardly be considered as complimentary to Oregon State Mental Hospital, permission was granted to the film-makers after hospital director Dr Dean Brooks had over-ruled the more faint-hearted of his staff. The opportunity for many of the patients to work on the film as crew members or as extras was of such therapeutic value, he argued, that it was well worth the disruption to the closely regulated life of the wards. He did, however, insist that the film should be set at the time of the novel, 1963, rather than the present, and that there should be a disclaimer to the effect that it was not a factual representation of life in a mental ward. The strong-willed and very capable Dr Brooks himself played the role of the weak-willed and not very capable hospital administrator Dr Spivey and various of his less deranged patients were engaged to play themselves alongside professional actors. The difference, Dr Brooks drily observed, was not discernible.

- Kevin Smith's ribald, ultra-low-budget ($27,000) comedy *Clerks* (US 93), a hit at the 1993 Sundance Festival, is about one Dante Hicks, a clerk stuck in a dead-end job at a New Jersey convenience store. The pic was shot where it was most convenient—in the store at Asbury Park, NJ, where Smith himself served behind the counter by day while shooting the film evenings and weekends.

- One of the first films to have interior domestic scenes shot on location, rather than in the studio, was Tony

Richardson's *A Taste of Honey* (GB 61). Occasionally mansions or stately home interiors had been used as settings before, but the locale of Shelagh Delaney's grittily realistic drama was a small, cramped flat in grimy Salford, her home town. Exterior location scenes were shot in Salford and Manchester, but the actual flat itself was on the top floor of 74, Elm Park Gardens, a crumbling grey-brick Victorian house at World's End, the unfashionable part of London's Chelsea. Cameras and crew had to be accommodated together with the action in a living room measuring 20 x 18 ft, a small bedroom of only 12 x 12 ft, and an even smaller combined bathroom and kitchen. In a scene between Jo (Rita Tushingham) and her mother (Dora Bryan), Tony Richardson directed from the end of the bed, just out of camera range (and carefully avoiding reflection in the dressing-table mirror), while cameraman Walter Lassally crouched between the bed and the wall. The soundman stood outside. Not only did the location lend authenticity—one of the improbabilities about studio-built interiors meant to represent poverty is that they are invariably too spacious—it was also cheap. Woodfall Productions hired the whole decaying house for £22 ($60) a week, using the other four floors as production offices, art department, wardrobe and canteen. The cost of filming at a studio would have been about £1750 a week.

- When Dino De Laurentis decided to shoot *Hurricane* (US 79) on the French Polynesian island paradise of Bora Bora, standing in for 1920s American Samoa, the first major problem he encountered was that its two small hotels were fully booked for tour parties several years ahead. With the panache for which he was renowned, De Laurentis simply built his own hotel, the Marara, comprising 65 luxury bungalows surrounding the island's lagoon, a cinema, a discotheque and kitchens presided over by two Italian chefs ready to serve dinner for 300 with a choice of 12 brands of champagne and 18 of brandy. The cost at $4.5 million represented nearly a quarter of the film's budget and exceeded the total salary bill for De Laurentis himself and his associate producer, the director (Jan Troeil), screenwriter (Lorenzo Semple) and the leading actors (Jason Robards, Mia Farrow, Max von Sydow, Trevor Howard and Timothy Bottoms). Purse-lipped production accountants who watched the picture's budget spiral from $15 million to well over $20 million—De Laurentis bought a 265ft freighter and a $1 million transport aircraft to provision his hotel—need not have lost any sleep. Even before shooting commenced the magnificent spender had received several offers for the Hotel Marara which not only covered its cost but afforded a comfortable margin of profit.

The largest number of different locations used on a motion picture was 168 in the case of Sergei Bondarchuk's four-part *War and Peace* (USSR 1963–67), of which the most prominent were the Battle of Borodino sequence, filmed at Borodino; the 'Moscow on Fire' sequence, filmed at Volokolamsk; and the 'Hunting in Otradnoye' sequence, filmed in the village of Boguslavskiy, near Kashira.

The largest number of locations in a Hollywood

Sometimes the original setting for a story does not conform sufficiently to stereotype. When director Jack Cardiff filmed D. H. Lawrence's autobiographical *Sons and Lovers* (GB 60), he wanted to use the actual miner's dwelling in Eastwood, Notts, where the Lawrence family lived at the time of the events depicted. Unfortunately, it turned out to be a three-storey house, far more substantial than the audience was likely to find realistic. Instead he found a modest two-up, two-down cottage of the kind non-miners would expect a mining family to inhabit.

motion picture were the 140 worldwide for Mike Todd's *Around the World in 80 Days* (US 56).

The most frequently used US location outside of Los Angeles or New York is claimed to be the small town of Sonora, California, which lies 363 miles north of Hollywood. Over 300 films have been shot there since the first in 1913, a W. S. Hart western of which none of the citizens could recollect the title when quizzed on the matter by a *New York Times* reporter in 1947.

The provincial city most often used for film settings in Britain is Liverpool, which has been featured in 56 films to date: *Her Benny* (GB 20); *Grass Widowers* (GB 21); *A Girl in Every Port* (US 28); *Old English* (US 30); *The House of the Spaniard* (GB 36); *Souls at Sea* (GB 37); *Penny Paradise* (GB 38); *Spare a Copper* (GB 40); *Atlantic Ferry* (GB 41); *It Happened One Sunday* (GB 44); *Waterfront* (GB 50); *The Magnet* (GB 50); *These Dangerous Years* (GB 57); *The Key* (GB 58); *Violent Playground* (GB 58); *Sapphire* (GB 59); *In the Wake of a Stranger* (GB 59); *Ferry Across the Mersey* (GB 64); *The Little Ones* (GB 64); *Charlie Bubbles* (GB 67); *The Reckoning* (GB 69); *Children* (GB 76); *Madonna and Child* (GB 80); *Death and Transfiguration* (GB 83); *Letter to Brezhnev* (GB 85); *No Surrender* (GB 86); *Coast to Coast* (GB 86); *Business as Usual* (GB 87); *The Fruit Machine* (GB 88); *The Dressmaker* (GB 88); *Distant Voices, Still Lives* (GB 88); *Appuntamento a Liverpool* (It 88); *Wonderland* (GB 89); *Shirley Valentine* (US 89); *The Man from the Pru* (GB 90, TVM); *Dancin' Thru the Dark* (GB 90); *Blonde Fist* (GB 91); *Hear My Song* (GB 92); *The Long Day Closes* (GB 92); *A Little Bit of Lippy* (GB 92); *The Bullion Boys* (GB 93, TVM); *Priest* (GB 94); *Dark Summer* (GB 94); *An Awfully Big Adventure* (GB 95)—shot in Dublin; *Land and Freedom* (GB/Sp/Ger 95); *Butterfly Kiss* (GB 95); *Under the Skin* (GB 97); *Downtown* (GB 97); *Julie and the Cadillacs* (GB 97); *Peggy Su!* (GB 98); *Swing* (US/GB 99); *Liam* (GB/Ger 00); *Going Off Big Time* (GB 00); *Shooters* (GB 00, TVM); *51st State* (US 01); *My Kingdom* (GB 01). Thirty films have been set in Glasgow, 21 in Edinburgh, 19 in Blackpool, 16 in Brighton, and 13 in Oxford. Liverpool evidently does not intend to rest on its laurels. In 1994 it became the first local authority in the UK to appoint a full-time films officer responsible for promoting the city to prospective producers and arranging facilities.

Make-up

Little attention was paid to make-up in films before the advent of the close-up (q.v.). **The earliest motion**

picture in which it is apparent that the actors are wearing make-up (other than black-face or whiskers) is Edwin S. Porter's *The Whole Dam Family and the Dam Dog* (US 05), in which the cast are made up to create the illusion of a family resemblance. The pioneer of special make-up techniques for film as opposed to stage performances was D. W. Griffith, who began experiments to achieve a more naturalistic appearance for his performers at Biograph in about 1910. Stage actress Olga Petrova recalled of her film debut in *The Tiger* (US 14): 'I noticed immediately that my co-workers wore a make-up much darker, almost a beige, whereas I wore the usual light Leichner's 1.' There was a good reason for her co-workers' departure from stage practice. The orthochromatic film stock used at this date was insensitive to the red end of the spectrum (scarlet registered as black) and consequently a heavy application of yellow make-up was necessary to create an impression of natural skin tone on screen.

Max Factor at work in his backroom laboratory in Hollywood soon after he had originated the first screen make-up in 1914.

The advent of super-panchromatic film in the late 1920s gave new opportunities to the lighting cameraman, but posed fresh challenges to the make-up artist. Requiring a third less light than formerly, it meant that much more detail was visible on screen. Cecil Holland, make-up chief at MGM, explained in 1933 that previously beards had been made of crêpe wool, but with the improved film stock this gave a cottony effect. For ordinary beards the use of real human hair provided the answer. Coarse beards were another matter. Eventually a solution was found, all the way from Tibet—yak's hair.

The first make-up specifically for on-screen use was Supreme Greasepaint, introduced by Polish immigrant Max Factor in 1914. The need for special make-up was dictated by the increasing use of artificial lighting for filming from 1912 onwards. Freckles and skin blemishes photographed black, pink cheeks a murky grey, and skin tones a deathly white.

The first studio make-up department was established at the Selig Studio in Hollywood by Isle of Wight-born George Westmore in 1917. His first real break was transforming Billie Burke when he created a wholly new facial look for her by the skilful application of make-up designed to fit particular lighting conditions. Other studios began to take notice and by 1920 all the majors had their own make-up departments. George Westmore had six sons, all of whom followed him into the business and variously headed up the make-up departments of Triangle, Eagle-Lion, First National, Paramount, RKO, Selznick International, Twentieth Century Fox and several others during their careers. They were known as 'the Marrying Westmores', as they succeeded in marrying no fewer than 18 wives between them. The eldest, Monty, is remembered for his supreme achievement of making Vivien Leigh's blue eyes appear to be green in her role as Scarlett in *Gone With the Wind* (US 39).

The longest make-up job ever performed on a single performer was the tattooing applied to Rod Steiger in Warner Bros' *The Illustrated Man* (US 69). It took make-up artist Gordon Bau and his team of eight assistants ten hours to complete the torso and another full day was spent on the lower body, hands and legs. Bau's longest job previously had been Charles Laughton's make-up for the title role of *The Hunchback of Notre Dame* (US 39), which he finished in a mere five and a half hours.

Other marathon make-up jobs have included the four hours daily spent by Wally Westmore on Fredric March's Hyde in *Dr Jekyll and Mr Hyde* (US 32); four hours for Boris Karloff's monster in *Frankenstein* (US 31), and a similar time for Jean Marais' make-up in *La Belle et la Bête* (Fr 45); four and a half hours on Bull Montana's apeman in *The Lost World* (US 25) and the same for Lon Chaney in *The Hunchback of Notre Dame* (US 23); five hours for the principal apes in *Planet of the Apes* (US 68) and also for the 121-year-old character played by Dustin Hoffman in *Little Big Man* (US 70); Klaus Kinski's Dracula make-up for *Nosferatu* (FRG 79) also took five hours daily to apply. Rick Baker's conversion of svelte Eddie Murphy into the 300lb eponymous hero of *The Nutty Professor* (US 96) was a six-hour job.

Boris Karloff's make-up for *The Bride of Frankenstein* (US 35), an elaboration of Jack Pierce's origi-

The red hair that Jane Fonda sported as the Los Angeles TV reporter Kimberly Wells in *The China Syndrome* (US 79) was her own idea and based on personal observation. According to Miss Fonda, only one of the female TV reporters in LA did not have dyed hair. 'I don't think it's a personal proclivity,' she explained, 'It's part of the reason these women are hired.' They were mainly former models or actresses, she said, 'who never read newspapers'. She was originally going to dye her hair bimbo blonde, but changed her mind after husband Tom Haydon remarked that he had never had a relationship with a red-head and had always wanted one.

nal monster make-up for the 1931 *Frankenstein*, took seven hours to complete each day. Shooting of scenes involving Karloff—he was in most—had to be delayed until 1 p.m. In the same film Elsa Lanchester's make-up as the female monster was so rigid she had to be fed lunch through a tube. John Hurt was unable to eat at all after the seven-hour ordeal of having his head monstrously deformed for the title role in *The Elephant Man* (GB 80). It was so exhausting that the full make-up could only be applied every second day. Nick Maley's transformation of 37-year-old Francesca Annis into the 100-year-old Widow of the Web for *Krull* (GB 82) took eight and a half hours daily and involved 11 layers of latex compound on her face as well as 12 layers on her hands. The mask extended inside her mouth and prevented eating.

Robert De Niro's make-up for The Creature in *Mary Shelley's Frankenstein* (US 94) took seven and a half hours for head and face and 12 hours for the full body, transforming him into what one critic described as 'a cross between the victim of a particularly nasty knifing and the *Elephant Man*'.

Producers

The youngest producer of a feature film was Netherlands-born Sydney Ling, whose *Lex the Wonder Dog* (Neths 73) he also scripted, directed and starred in at the age of 13. It was released by Scandinavian Oswald Brandaris Film and later by Osiris Film International.

America's youngest producer was Matty Rich, who was 17 when he began preproduction of his award-winning drama of black working-class life *Straight Out of Brooklyn* (US 91). He also directed.

Britain's youngest producer was 19-year-old Genevieve Jolliffe, who claimed that her 'slam-bang action picture' *The Runner* (GB 91) was turned down for financing by the British Film Institute Production Board because they were only willing to subsidise films which lost money. With start-up backing from Prince Charles's Youth Business Trust, Ms Jolliffe's Living Spirit Pictures raised production money from accountants and dentists with surplus funds at their disposal and the balance of the £100,000 budget came from a small-time distributor whose advertisement she had seen in the trade press. Shooting of what the tyro producer claimed was a million dollar American production made on an island off the coast of Canada actually took place in Nantwich, Cheshire, with some underground tunnel scenes shot at a colliery in Wales. The American leading man, Terence Ford, was Harrison Ford's younger brother, desperate to get out of soap opera into feature films. On the first day of shooting, the 22-year-old director Chris Jones, who had seen the completed script for the first time, asked how many of the 22-strong crew had been on a set before and was somewhat dismayed when no one put up their hand. *The Runner* was premièred at BAFTA in the presence of the Prince of Wales, who presented Living Spirit Pictures with an award for the 'most tenacious' business established in 1989 by the Youth Business Trust. It was subsequently sold for cinema, TV or video release in Germany, France, Spain, Portugal, Benelux, Yugoslavia, Poland, Turkey, Mexico, Venezuela, Colombia, Argentina, Korea, Japan, Australia, Canada, the US and the UK.

The first woman producer was Alice Guy (see p. 133), who founded the Solax Co. at Flushing, New York, on 7 September 1910. The first of nearly 300 short films produced by her in the next three years was *A Child's Sacrifice* (US 10), starring 'The Solax Kid' (Magda Foy), which was released on 21 October 1910.

The first feature film produced by a woman was Eros Films' *The Definite Object* (GB 20), a gangster movie set in New York produced by Countess Bubna.

The first talkie produced by a woman was Elinor Glyn's Talkicolor production *Knowing Men* (GB 30), with Carl Brisson and Elissa Landi. She also directed. **The first Hollywood talkie by a woman** was Elsie Janis's *Paramount on Parade* (US 30), which was released in April 1930, two months after Miss Glyn's picture.

The first woman to become an executive producer at a major Hollywood studio was former child star and scenarist Virginia Van Upp, who assumed responsibility for some 12 to 14 big-budget films a year at Columbia in January 1945. All the associate producers working for her were men. She was selected by the notoriously male chauvinist studio head Harry Cohn despite the fact that there were ten other in-house producers, all male, for him to choose from. Only one of them called Von Upp to congratulate her on becoming the most senior woman executive in Hollywood and he was the only one Cohn retained on the payroll.

The two most successful producer/directors in terms of box-office revenue are George Lucas and Steven Spielberg, who between them are responsible for many of the highest grossing movies of all time. Spielberg has to his credit, as both producer and director, the blockbusters *E.T. The Extra-Terrestrial* (US 82), the two *Jurassic Park* pictures (US 93 and 97) and *Saving Private Ryan*, as well as co-producing *Back to the Future* (US 85) and directing *Jaws* (US 75), which was the first picture to break the $100 million barrier in North American rentals, and the Indiana Jones blockbusters *Raiders of the Lost Ark* (US 81), *Indiana Jones and the Temple of Doom* (US 84) and *Indiana Jones and the Last Crusade* (US 89). These three were produced by George Lucas, who also directed *Star Wars* (US 77) and produced *The Empire Strikes Back* (US 80) and *Return of the Jedi* (US 83). Latterly Lucas has produced prequel *Star Wars: Episode 1—The Phantom Menace* (US 99), which is second only to *Titanic* in the list of biggest-grossing movies with a worldwide box office of $927 million.

Variety has estimated that Spielberg's personal earnings from *Jurassic Park* were some $200 million, since he was an equal partner with Universal after direct costs, interest and distribution fees had been deducted. This established a new record for individual payment for a single film, the highest amount hitherto being the $50–$60 million it is estimated Jack Nicholson earned for his performance in *Batman* (US 89). When the final accounting of *Phantom Menace* is done, Lucas may well have exceeded Spielberg's jackpot.

The longest career as a producer was by Pierre Braunberger (1905–90), who started producing silent pictures in Paris in 1924 with Jean Renoir's *La Fille de l'eau* (Fr 24) and produced his last film, *Knights of the Round Table* (Fr 89), 65 years later. Among his notable productions were Louis Buñuel's controversial debut film *Un Chien Andalou* (Fr 29), Renoir's *Une Partie de campagne* (Fr 36), Truffaut's *Tirez sur le pianiste* (Fr 60) and Godard's *Vivre sa vie* (Fr 62). Many of the French nouvelle vague directors began their careers with his Films de la Pléiade production outfit. He was the only producer to have been awarded the prestigious Louis Delluc Prize on three occasions.

The most co-producers on a film was 14 in the case of Robert Redford's *Quiz Show* (US 94), of whom 11 were credited and three opted for anonymity (Richard Goodwin; Barry Levinson; Mark Johnson). Redford was one of the many producers but the sole director. Richard Donner's *Assassins* (US 95) had 11 producers and six associate producers. *Girl* (US 99), starring Dominique Swain, has 13 producers credited.

David Mamet's *State and Main* (US 00) had a mere seven producers, executive producers and co-producers credited, but an end credit offered: 'A complete list of this film's associate producers is available on request.' Lars Von Trier's *Dancer in the Dark* (Den/Fr/Swe/Ir/Ger/Nor/Neths/Ice/Fin/US/GB 00), as befits a film made by 36 production outfits from 11 different countries, credits producer, executive producer, two co-executive producers, two line producers and nine associate producers.

Props

The most valuable assemblage of props ever to be brought together on a single set was the $10 million worth of paintings and sculptures used for the art-gallery scenes in Universal's *Legal Eagles* (US 86), starring Robert Redford. They included works by Willem de Kooning, Roy Lichtenstein, Alexander Calder and Pablo Picasso.

The most expensive single prop ever used on a movie was the full-scale replica of a Spanish galleon built for Roman Polanski's *Pirates* (US/Tun 86) at a cost of £7 million. Designed by Pierre Guffrey, its construction kept 2000 Maltese shipyard workers in jobs for a whole year.

In Merchant-Ivory's *Jefferson in Paris* (US 95) there is a scene which concerns the American Minister's dispute with the naturalist Buffon, who had insisted that the harshness of the American climate stunted the growth of its indigenous mammals. Jefferson proved him wrong by having a moose shot and the skeleton sent over to France. For the props master the task of locating an available moose skeleton in Europe was a difficulty, but eventually one was traced in a natural history museum. It was only when it arrived on set that someone noticed a label attached to the wheeled platform on which the skeleton was mounted. It stated that the moose was a gift to the people of France from the Americans, with the date: 1787. This was indeed the very moose that Jefferson had brought over to confound Buffon.

The largest land-based prop ever constructed for a movie was the 60 foot long, 40 foot high Wooden Horse of Troy used in Robert Wise's *Helen of Troy* (US 54). It weighed 80 tons, and 30 full-grown trees and over 1000lb of nails were needed to build it. A modern air-conditioning system was fitted to save the twenty-five occupants from heat prostration.

The most often used single prop in movies was the Imperial Necklace owned by jewellers Joseff of Hollywood. By the end of 1950 it had been featured in 125 films.

The monstrous and menacing computer of Stanley Kubrik's *Dr Strangelove: Or How I Learned to Stop Worrying and Love the Bomb* (GB 64) was not the fantasy creation of a hypercharged art director. It was the real computer 7090 at IBM's London headquarters, the only interior in the film that was not shot in the studio. And 7090 was no run of the mill computer. It was the same data processor which calculated where pioneer US astronaut John H Glen Jr would descend into the ocean after his 1962 orbit of the Earth.

The highest price realised by a prop sold at auction was $275,000 for James Bond's Aston Martin from *Goldfinger* (GB 64) at Sotheby's New York on 28 June 1986.

The first product placement has yet to be established. The practice of movie studios doing deals with manufacturers for the placement of their products as props dates back at least as far as 1958, when United Artists arranged with a number of different companies to display appropriate items in their David Niven–Mitzi Gaynor starrer *Happy Anniversary* (US 59). The quid pro quo was for the beneficiaries to pay for tie-in advertising for the movie. Not everyone was enamoured of the innovation. One female cinema patron wrote to United Artists: 'I go to the movies to get away from commercials.'

In the days before props men were entitled to a screen credit, one Irving Sindler ensured that his name was seen in every picture he worked on. In *Wuthering Heights* (US 39) there was a gravestone inscribed 'I. Sindler. A Good Man.'. In *Intermezzo* (US 39) there was a Swedish bakery owned by Sindler & Son and in *Raffles* (US 39) a newspaper insert noted that 'Lord Sindler has just returned from a big game hunting expedition'. Sindler's name was prominent over a delicatessen in *Dead End* (US 37) and also when it appeared in Chinese characters across a banner in *The Adventures of Marco Polo* (US 38). In a tribute to his mother he engineered a sign labelled 'Ma Sindler Home Cooking' over a small eatery in *The Westerner* (US 40). Sindler's first and only failure to secure the recognition he felt he deserved occurred on *The Long Voyage Home* (US 40). Not for want of trying. He tacked a 'Sindler & Son' sign over a low Limehouse dive in which Thomas Mitchell and John Wayne were scheduled to have a brawl, but director John Ford played spoilsport and shot the exterior with Sindler's calling card out of frame.

In 1931 Twentieth Century Fox established what they called 'The Garden of all Nations'. The garden consisted of trees, shrubs and flowers from all over the world, most of them unfamiliar to California. A particular source of pride was a Brazilian pitcher plant, a flower which captures and devours insects. Plants were transplanted on to a 'living stage' as required, the first production to draw on its resources being the Spencer Tracy starrer *Society Girl* (US 32).

Props went to war in 1991. Authentic World War II military hardware, including tanks and trucks, from Jadran Film's studio in Zagreb, Croatia, were drafted into service by the Croat forces and used in combat against federal troops of a fragmenting Yugoslavia. They had previously taken to the movie battlefield not only in local productions but in such Hollywood mini series as *Winds of War* and *War and Remembrance*.

FOOD FACTS

- When a mock-up aircraft was needed for studio scenes in *Coastal Command* (GB 42), the problem was rivets. Real rivets were too precious to spare in wartime, so the Ministry of Information officer assigned to the film wrote to his opposite number at the Ministry of Food, explaining that for the purpose of simulating rivets 'there is nothing more suitable than large grey continental lentils which will be glued and painted over. Permission is sought to purchase 7 lb of these'. Lest such a quantity should seem extravagant, he assured the Food Ministry that it was 'unlikely that the whole of the 7 lb would be used, but as the lentils are not of uniform size some selection would be necessary, and any balance would be handed over to the canteen'. An Assistant Divisional Food Officer at the MoF replied a week later: 'I have asked the Food Executive Office, Westminster, to supply you with an authority to purchase, and Gennaros of Old Compton Street to supply.'

- The telephone Harpo Marx ate in *The Coconuts* (US 29) was made of chocolate and the bottle of ink he drank was Coke. The boots eaten by Charlie Chaplin in *The Gold Rush* (US 24) were made of licorice.

- The raindrops in *Singin' in the Rain* (US 52) had milk added so that they would register better on film. Milk was also used for the nasal spray used by Shirley MacLaine in *The Apartment* (US 60). Real nasal spray would not have shown up on screen.

- The snow blanketing the small town of Gentryville in *Elmer the Great* (US 33) consisted of 1 ton of bleached cornflakes and 45 tons of powdered gypsum and salt in equal proportions. Garden rollers were used to pack down the cornflakes to the consistency of snow, while the salt in the gypsum gave the crisp sparkle of snow which has newly fallen.

- In one of the most memorable scenes in Sergio Leone's elegiac *Once Upon a Time in the West* (US 69), Jack Elam has a fly crawling on his face. This was achieved by plastering Elam's beard with marmalade. After many takes and repeated applications of marmalade, the thespian fly did as it was bidden.

- The blood in the celebrated scene in *Psycho* (US 60) in which Janet Leigh is stabbed in the shower was actually chocolate sauce. In Roman Polanski's aptly titled *Repulsion* (GB 65) the gore was a mixture of cochineal and Nescafé shot from a bicycle pump.

- The dank green slime that covered Natasha Richardson as she writhed on the muddy floor of a crypt in *Gothic* (GB 86) was boiled spinach, while the human flesh consumed by the zombies in George Romero's *Night of the Living Dead* (US 68) was really lamb entrails from a slaughter house in Evans City, PA, where the film was shot. The monster's revolting drool in *Alien* (GB 79) was innocuous K-Y Jelly.

- The green vomit that gushed out of the possessed child Nancy Anglet (Linda Blair) in *The Exorcist* (US 73) was realistic enough to make some spectators throw up themselves. It was in fact only a simple concoction of split-pea soup and oatmeal. In the spoof sequel *Repossessed* (US 90) Linda Blair as Nancy grown up is now a suburban housewife who prepares her family split-pea soup for supper.

- The excrement which a 'John', played by Luis Bunuel's son, throws over the part-time high-class prostitute played by Catherine Deneuve in *Belle de Jour* (Fr 67) was soft cheese.

- In *The Picture of Dorian Gray* (US 45), from Oscar Wilde's novella, the portrait of Dorian Gray progressively alters to depict the physical effects of the character's depravity, while its subject remains ever-youthful and untrammelled by his dissolute life. Twin artists Ivan and Malvin Albright painted four versions of the changing portrait. For the last one, which is seen in a flash of Technicolor in the otherwise black and white movie, they eschewed scarlet pigment in favour of fresh chicken blood.

Schedules

The longest production schedule for a completed feature movie was the 28 years it took London-based Canadian animator Richard Williams to complete *An Arabian Knight* (GB 95). For most of this time Williams financed the film from a combination of backers and his own resources, more than half the $20 million spent on it being money earned from his masterpiece *Who Framed Roger Rabbit* (US 89) as well as the proceeds of TV commercials and main-title animation for such features as *What's New, Pussycat?* (US/Fr 65), *Murder on the Orient Express* (GB 74) and the two Pink Panther movies. A distribution deal was signed with Warner Bros which guaranteed financing through the Completion Bond Co. to complete the picture. In June 1992 it was reported that Warner Bros had pulled out because there was still no sign of the film six months past the deadline. The Completion Bond Co. bailed out Williams to the tune of $18 million and acquired the rights, which were eventually sold to Miramax. The picture opened on 25 August 1995 to a box-office response which brought little reward to its indefatigable creator.

The longest production schedule for a dramatic film in terms of start date and completion date was 13 years for Leni Riefenstahl's *Tiefland* (FRG 53) and the same length of time for *Dr Bethune* (Chn 77), the Chinese tribute to the Canadian chest surgeon who gave his life while serving as a volunteer with the Red Army in 1939. In the case of *Tiefland*, production of what promised to be the most expensive talkie then made was suspended in 1942 after expenditure of 5 million Reichsmarks and the complete breakdown of the director's health. At the end of the war Riefenstahl was banned from working in the film industry, but following her de-Nazification in 1952 she succeeded in reassembling the original cast and completed the film. It recouped its cost but Riefenstahl, dissatisfied with her work, then withdrew the picture from distribution and it has not been shown since.

The longest production schedule for a British film was the eight years 20 days (6 May 1956–26 May 1964) it took Kevin Brownlow and Andrew Mollo to complete their fantasy of a Nazi-occupied Britain, *It Happened Here* (GB 66). The picture, which occupied a cumulative shooting schedule of ten weeks, started as an amateur production by a group of enthusiastic teenagers and ended as a professional film with a West End release.

Other protracted production schedules have included 27 years for Paul Grimault's animated *Le Roi et l'oiseau* (Fr 80); 18 years for Alvaro Henriques Goncales' *Presente de Natal* (Bra 71), made singlehandedly; 12 years for Désiré Ecaré's story of women's role in modern African society *Visages de Femmes* (Ivory Coast 85); 11 years (1925–36) for Ladislas Starewitch's animated puppet film *Le Roman de Rénard* (Fr 40); 11 or possibly 12 years for *Pakeezah* (Ind 71), which was so long in the making that the original hero aged too much and had to be recast as the heroine's father; ten years for Michael and Andy Jones's Newfoundland comedy *The Adventures of Faustus Bidgood* (Can 86), which called on the services of almost every actor and actress in the province; nine years for the Indian historical epic *Mughal-e-Azam* (Ind 60); seven years for Harry Hoyt's *The Lost World* (US 25), Fred Zinnermann and Walter Mirisch's *Hawaii* (US 66), Michael Kohler's *The Experiencer* (US) and *Flame Top* aka *Down to Earth* (Fin 81), a biopic of the enigmatic Finnish folklorist Maiju Lassila; five and a half years for Edgar Reitz's *Heimat* (FRG 84), which perhaps is not surprising for a film nearly 16 hours long; and seven years for the 25½ hour sequel *Die Zweite Heimat* (Ger 92); five years for George Stevens's *The Greatest Story Ever Told* (US 65) and David Lynch's *Eraserhead* (US 77), declared to contain 'one of the most repugnant scenes in film history'; and four years for Mel Ferrer's *Vendetta* (US 50), Rudall Hayward's *On the Friendly Road* (NZ 36), which would have been New Zealand's first talkie if he had managed to finish it a year earlier, Francis Ford Coppola's *Apocalypse Now* (US 79), Joseph L. Mankiewicz's *Cleopatra* (US 63) and Terence Young's Korean War epic *Inchon* (Kor/US 81), starring Laurence Olivier as General MacArthur. Sir Richard Attenborough's monumental biopic of *Gandhi* (GB 82) had a schedule of 20 months from the start of pre-production to delivery of prints, with 26 weeks spent on shooting. The gestation of the movie, however, lasted 17 years from the start of the first of 12 draft screenplays to the pre-production date. Attenborough estimated that during this time he gave up some 40 acting parts and a dozen directorial assignments in order to realise what he described as 'my love affair with this project'.

Not even this represents the ultimate in patience and fortitude. Screenwriter Ted Allan, whose *Bethune: The Making of a Hero* (Can/Chn 90) is based on his own recollections of the Canadian doctor venerated in China for his services on the Long March, first took the project to Darryl F. Zanuck at Fox in 1942. The film went into pre-production with Canadian star Walter Pidgeon signed to play Bethune. When the deal fell through, Allan continued his fight to get the story of his hero on to the screen. Both Columbia and Warner picked up the option and Robert Redford and Paul Newman were among those canvassed for the title role. After various independent companies had toyed with the project, Allan finally saw his efforts rewarded when Bethune went before the cameras in China in April 1987 as a Canadian/ French/Chinese co-production starring Donald Sutherland, some 45 years after he had initiated it. Even then there were further delays. Shooting was suspended after five months and not resumed until November 1988. The picture eventually premièred at the Montreal World Film Festival on 27 August 1990 but did not go on release until 1993, 51 years after its inception.

The longest shooting schedule was 557 days on set for Edgar Reitz's 25½ -hour epic of German post-war life *Die Zweite Heimat* (Ger 92).

The longest shooting schedule for a Hollywood movie was 220 days for Kevin Costner's record-budgeted $175 million *Waterworld* (US 95), including a month spent shooting a single scene involving power-boats, jet-skies and 175 actors. Disasters of every kind known to man or film crew culminated in the huge floating set sinking to the bottom of Hawaii's Kawaihae Harbor.

The shortest shooting schedule of all time was the one day for Paul Vecchialli's 80-minute feature film *Trou de Mémoire* (Fr 85). Starring Françoise Lebrun and Vecchialli himself, the picture was shot with film stock left over from a documentary he had been commissioned to make.

Other directors who haven't stood around on the job are Rob Nilsson, whose *Heat and Sunlight* (US 87), about a fortyish photographer obsessed with a beautiful dancer, was shot in 60 hours, and Roger Corman, who completed his cult movie *The Little Shop of Horrors* (US 60) in just two days and three nights. Frank Oz's 1986 remake, by contrast, took seven months to shoot.

Also shot in two days (and a couple of hours) was Emile de Antonio's *In the King of Prussia* (US 82), a reconstruction of the attack on the General Electric warhead plant in the Midwest township of King of Prussia by anti-nuclear demonstrators and their subsequent trial. Starring Martin Sheen as himself, and with the defendants, known as the 'Plowshares Eight', as themselves, the film had to be shot in 50 hours to meet the deadline before the defendants had to report for sentencing.

The fastest shoot of a film with an 'all star cast' was Wayne Wang's *Blue in the Face* (US 94), starring Roseanne Arnold (now simply Roseanne), Harvey Keitel, Lily Tomlin and Michael J. Fox. A Miramax production, it took just three days from first positions to wrap.

The shortest production schedule for a full-length feature film was 13 days from the start of scripting to the première in the case of *The Fastest Forward* (GB 90), directed by John Gore and produced by Russ Malkin in aid of the Telethon '90 fund-raising event. The 75-minute comedy-thriller was scripted in five days, shot in three and edited in five. It was completed on 27 May 1990, the day of the première at the Dominion, Tottenham Court Road. The volunteer cast included Caroline Bliss, Maurice Denham, Phil Daniels, Fiona Fullerton, Jenny Seagrove, Jerry Hall and veteran character actor Michael Ripper. Fastest time from the inception of a feature film till its general release was achieved by the makers of *Twist Around the Clock* (US 61), which opened 28 days after Chubby Checker reached number one in the charts and gave Sam Katzman the idea of shooting an instant movie to cash in on the new dance craze. Chubby Checker starred.

The shortest time between completion of shooting and the première of a feature film was five hours in the case of Alfred Rolfe's racing drama *The Cup Winner* (Aus 11). The final scenes, consisting of footage of the Melbourne Cup shot by six cameramen, were filmed on 7 November 1911 and the completed drama edited and processed in time for a simultaneous opening at five Melbourne cinemas the same night. It opened in Sydney, 640 miles away, the following day.

Sets

The largest film set ever built was the 1312 by 754 ft Roman forum designed by Veniero Colosanti and John Moore and built on a 55-acre site at Las Matas, outside Madrid, for the last great Hollywood epic of the ancient world, Samuel Bronston's production of *The Fall of the Roman Empire* (US 64). Commencing 10 October 1962, 1100 workmen spent seven months laying the surface of the forum with 170,000 cement blocks, erecting 22,000ft of concrete stairways, 601 columns and 350 statues, and constructing 27 full size buildings. The highest point on the set was the Temple of Jupiter, whose bronze equestrian statues surmounting the roof soared 260ft above the paving of the Forum.

The largest indoor set was the UFO landing site built for the climax of Steven Spielberg's *Close Encounters of the Third Kind* (US 77). With a height of 90ft, length of 450ft and 250ft breadth, the set was constructed inside a 10 million cubic feet dirigible hangar at Mobile, Alabama, which had six times the capacity of the largest sound stage in Hollywood. The structure included 4 miles of scaffolding, 16,900 square feet of fibreglass, 29,500 square feet of nylon canopy and 'enough concrete to make a full-scale replica of the Washington monument'.

The largest single structure ever built as a movie set was the 882ft long replica of the *Titanic*, built for James Cameron's *Titanic* (US 98) at Fox Studios Baja, just south of Rosarito in Baja California, Mexico. The vast structure was full scale in length and height with the exception of some redundant sections on the superstructure, a 10% reduction in the funnels and the omission of the forward

well deck to allow it to fit in the 17 million gallon tank. The height from the base of the tank to the main deck was 90ft. Construction coordinator Les Collins observed 'This one set alone is the equivalent of building a 70-storey skyscraper on its side'.

IT'S FOR REAL

Some of the wonder of the movie-going experience has been diminished by the formidable screen literacy of modern audiences, who assume that every marvel depicted on celluloid is contrived by F/X, matte shots, highly skilled stuntmen or other artifice. Sometimes what is shown on screen is more genuine than cinema patrons expect or believe.

- John Ford was determined that all the misadventures which befell the native hero of *Hurricane* (US 37) should be portrayed without artifice. As it was unlikely that any established star would consider the unprecedented demands, he proposed to make on his leading actor, Ford hired a young man called Jon Hall who had applied for a job as a stand-in. In the convict scene it took five men to lift the bag of stones Hall was forced to carry under a blazing sun. He had to dive from the top of a ship's mast and fight a shark—a real one. And when the guards fire at the hero swimming away from the island prison, Ford insisted that real bullets were used. Probably the worst ordeal for Hall was the flogging scene. Ford persuaded him that it would not be possible to replicate the violent contortions of a man's body under the lash unless the whipping was genuine. A horsewhip was applied to Hall's bare back until it bled and for two nights afterwards he was obliged to sleep on his stomach. When the censors had had their way with the footage, nothing was left which could not have been adequately conveyed with some greasepaint weals and good sound effects.

- In Werner Herzog's *Heart of Glass* (FRG 76) a whole community, when given the secret of making a precious glass, takes leave of its senses and wanders away in a dreamlike trance. Their hypnotic state was not acting. The cast had all been hypnotised by the charismatic Herzog himself.

- When D. W. Griffith put out a casting call for actors exactly 6 ft in height for the role of Washington in *America* (US 24), historical purists complained that the Father of the Nation was being diminished—all the standard biographies recorded his height as 6 ft 2 in. Not so, declared the meticulous Griffith. He had consulted no less an authority than the order books of Washington's London tailor and it was the biographies which had his height wrong, not the film.

- Ice-skating duo Natalie (Charlotte Avery) and Steffi (Sabra William) are seen competing and winning at the international Gay Games in Fiona Cunningham Reid's cross-racial lesbian romance *Thin Ice* (GB 95). The scene was shot at the real Gay Games in New York and the two actresses were competing for real. And they really won.

- When Gregory LaCava was assigned by RKO in 1937 to bring *Stage Door* to the screen, he came to the conclusion that there was little reality in the way the individual stories of the aspirants to stardom at Mrs

Orcutt's boarding house had been portrayed in Edna Ferber's and George S. Kaufman's Broadway play. Abandoning the text, he turned several stenographers loose on the town with pencil and notepad to ride on buses, sit in studio reception rooms and talk to bit players on sets. One moved into the Studio Club, where she lived with girls whose real-life stories became part of the film version of *Stage Door*. The stenographers took down word-for-word the conversations of the struggling actresses and these were adapted into the script. LaCava declared that the result was not only more truthful but also more dramatic than the dialogue of the play.

- The restaurant scene in *Kramer versus Kramer* in which Dustin Hoffman smashes a glass against the wall was not scripted. The camera was running when Hoffman threw a tantrum, as he frequently does on set. The occasion of his wrath was co-star Meryl Streep's rewriting of her own lines, to which Hoffman reacted with his customary pugnaciousness. 'Next time you do that I'd appreciate you letting me know', snapped Streep as she picked shards of glass out of her hair. Director Robert Benton hugged himself with delight that the mutual antipathy of leading man and leading lady so exactly mirrored that of the couple they were playing and he told the cameraman to print the unscheduled take.

- *Alexander Graham Bell* (US 39) was one of the few Hollywood biopics of the '30s to stick to the facts, in an era notorious for the liberties taken with history by semi-literate producers. Director Irving Cummings had to fight every inch for authenticity, including a set-to with the Twentieth Century Fox casting office. In the early days of telephones, switchboard operators were boys; only when there were growing numbers of complaints about their impertinence were young ladies substituted. Cummings ordered 30 boys for the scene in the telephone exchange, but casting objected that they had a number of stock girls on salary and in any case they did not believe audiences were well enough versed in social history to know the difference. The director did what few contract directors would dare to do; downed megaphone and refused to proceed with shooting. Historical truth prevailed over studio parsimony and Cummings got his men.

- Few cinema patrons may have bothered to focus on the books lining the shelves in Jim Garrison's study in New Orleans as depicted in Oliver Stone's *JFK* (US 91). Nor, had they done so, would they have known that the titles represented the actual books on Garrison's own shelves. Set decorator Crispian Sallis photographed ranks of the District Attorney's books and then scoured second-hand book shops to replicate them title by title. He allowed himself one departure from actuality. Garrison had a miniature set of Shakespeare on his desk. Sallis, an Englishman, decided it would be more appropriate to the mood of the film if he substituted a set of the speeches of Abraham Lincoln.

- Charles Chaplin, living up to his title role in *The Great Dictator* (US 40), insisted that his wife Paulette Goddard, who played the scrubwoman, should scrub the floor of the entire set in order to get the proper sweep of the brush. Miss Goddard rebelled and walked off the set. Chaplin countered by dismissing the rest of the cast and withdrawing himself until Miss Goddard submitted to his will. With the set scoured from end to end, and his leading lady's wrist action conforming to what Chaplin deemed true to the character's humble calling, filming was able to resume.

- The gunfire heard in Oja Kodar's *Vrijeme Za . . ./A Time For . . .* (Croatia/It 94), a drama about the war in Croatia, was not a sound effect. Lensed in besieged towns and on real battlefields, the guns heard on the soundtrack were those of the opposing Serb and Croatian batteries while filming proceeded in the midst of the conflict.

- On occasion, even a studio set can be the real thing. When René Clément was making *Gervaise* (Fr 57), his screen adaptation of Zola's *L'Assommoir*, he was delighted to find that the actual Paris lavoir or public wash-house, which Zola had used as the scene of a women's battle, was not only still intact but was for sale. He bought it, dismantled it brick by brick, and had the whole edifice re-erected in the studio.

- The distinguished Iranian director Abbas Kiarostami's *Through the Olive Trees* (Iran 94) is about a film crew making a feature film in Northern Iran following the earthquake which devastated the region. In an early scene the fictitious director is shown holding a casting call of local non-professionals to fill the role of the young heroine. The audition seen on screen was also the audition for casting the leading role in Karostami's film, a part won by a girl called Tahereh.

- A chance encounter on the set of *The Phenix City Story* (US 55) not only enhanced the actuality of the events portrayed but also provided the evidence which resulted in the conviction of assassins. Phil Karlson's film was about the slaying of anti-vice crusader Albert Patterson in Phenix City, Alabama on 17 June 1954 and he began shooting even while the trial was in progress. The murder scene was shot where it happened, with the actor playing Patterson (John McIntyre) wearing the very clothes the dead man had worn. Despite the director's meticulous attention to documentary detail, during the filming a young man of 18 or 19 came up to him and said 'Mr Karlson, that isn't the way it was'. Karlson asked him how he knew and the youth explained that he had been an eyewitness. The director immediately summoned John Patterson, the murdered man's son who was also prosecuting attorney, and declared 'Here is your key witness. He saw the whole thing'. He then changed the script and shot the scene to accord with the young man's convincing account of events. Later in court the surprise witness's testimony was instrumental in securing a guilty verdict.

- The role of Chris, a young dancer dying of AIDS, is played in *The Last Supper* (Can 96) by Ken McDougall, who was dying of AIDS as he made the film. The 'last supper' of the title was the last for the actor as well as the character he portrayed: McDougall died four days later.

- It is not unusual for actors playing particular professions to spend time 'on the job' to get the feel of it, but Anthony Perkins went one further when he was invited by Ken Russell to play a clergyman in *Crimes of Passion* (US 84). He had himself ordained a minister of the Universal Church of America in order not only to feel the part, but actually be the part. Although he continued in the acting business after this film, he would occasionally moonlight as a parson at the request of friends, as when he officiated at Ken Russell's marriage aboard the *Queen Mary* at San Francisco.

● Stjepan Sabljak's film of the war in Croatia *Encircled* (Croatia 97) not only used real war veterans playing the soldiers but also real bullets. The micro-budget of $5000 would not run to blanks.

● Truffaut's *Day for Night* (Fr 73) has been hailed as the most realistic film ever made about film-making. The director (who also played the director of *Meet Pamela*, the film in production in the film) used a simple but unusual device to achieve a workaday look to his representation of life on set. The cameraman started turning over on a secret signal from Truffaut and the actors playing cast and crew of *Meet Pamela* seldom knew whether they were being filmed or not.

● When Walt Disney posted a notice on the studio bulletin board one day in the late 1930s which asked 'Will anyone who has had any circus experience please see Walt?', he was resigned to the fact that it was unlikely to produce any very useful response. Indeed, most of those who made a prompt appearance at his office door were staff who had cherished an ambition to work in a circus since childhood and surmised that the boss was about to go into the Barnum & Bailey business. They were disappointed to learn that he wasn't, and that the notice was a prelude to the start of a new cartoon feature about circus life called *Dumbo* (US 41). Over the next few days, however, a line-up of people who really knew the Big Top from inside the ring made their appearance. Assistant director Larry Lansburgh proudly proclaimed his former calling of trick rider, while a quiet, unassuming animator called Ivy Carol Van Horn timidly confessed to having been a high-wire walker. Studio guide Joe Jameson proved his former vocation as a juggler by keeping a paperweight, a book and an ashtray from Walt's desk rotating in the air all at once and animator Ward Kimball marched into the office at the head of a high-stepping brass quintet which had once been a circus band. Greatest surprise of all was when a modest little typist from the publicity department was coaxed into revealing that she was formerly a lion tamer. With his in-house team of professional circus talent, Disney was able to ensure that *Dumbo* was faithful to the spirit of the sawdust ring.

● Three of the Texas small-town banks robbed by Clyde Barrow (Warren Beatty) and Bonnie Parker (Faye Dunaway) in *Bonnie and Clyde* (US 67) were the actual banks raided by the outlaw pair 33 years earlier. They had all closed down during the Depression, but were carefully restored to their 1930s appearance for the picture.

● The 12 jurymen and jurywomen in Richard Brooks' screen adaptation of Truman Capote's *In Cold Blood* (US 67) were the real jury who had convicted Kansas killers Perry Smith and Dick Hicock seven years earlier. The trial scene was re-enacted at the Finney

County Court House in Garden City where the actual trial had taken place.

● If the actors looked cold in *Batman Returns* (US 92) it was because they were cold—even in the heat of a Los Angeles summer. The story plays in Gotham (a comic-book New York) in winter and to facilitate the non-method actors in the cast the six huge sound stages at the Warner Bros studios were kept at a constant 4°C during shooting. There was also the practical consideration that the low temperature made the performers' breath realistically visible as they exhaled. The cost of the extra electricity used added some $750,000 to the budget.

● Although *Billy the Kid* (US 41), in which Robert Taylor was improbably cast as the ugly and evil little outlaw William Bonney, owed almost everything to legend and scarcely anything to history, MGM made one particular concession to what they believed to be verisimilitude. The research department had turned up a photograph of Bonney handling his gun—with his left hand. It was decreed that the right-handed Robert Taylor should play the part as a southpaw. Somewhat dismayed, but obedient to the holders of his contract, the actor spent weeks in practice until he could draw as swiftly with his left hand as his right. Then he visited the retired cowboy star William S. Hart, an authority on the Old West. Hart had the same photograph of Bonney as the MGM research department, but his showed Bonney with the gun in his right hand. One of the photographs had been printed in reverse, but nobody could establish which. Eventually, it was decided that as Taylor had expended so much effort in learning to shoot with his left hand, he had better go ahead and play the role that way—at least the studio could claim credit for its meticulous attention to historical detail, even if the movie was a lot of hokum.

● Anthony Hopkins was well tutored for his role as the passionless butler Stevens in *Remains of the Day* (GB 93). Technical adviser on the production was Cyril Dickman, 50 years a member of the Royal Household

---

Detective Constable Simon Weigold of Sheffield Police borrowed an idea from an Al Pacino movie he had seen to effect the arrest of 31 elusive criminals. In *Sea of Love* (US 89), Pacino succeeds in rounding up the villains by inviting them to a party hosted by a baseball team. Baseball being of limited appeal to the Yorkshire underworld, Weigold adapted the sting to local conditions. In February 1995 he had a letterhead printed in the name of a fictitious market research company, Mison Giewold (an anagram of his own name), and sent out invitations to a prize draw for free television sets and videos in return for filling in a questionnaire about viewing habits. Those who turned up at the fake company offices in the hope of receiving a television without the bother of having to steal it were wanted for offences which included burglary, theft and perverting the course of justice. By the end of the day 26 men and five women had been arrested, one of them an escaped prisoner who had been on the run for six months. Some were so impressed by the ingenuity by which they had been apprehended that they congratulated the police on 'a bloody good scam'. It is reasonable to suppose that none had seen *Sea of Love*.

and a former steward to the Queen. It was Dickman's task to show Hopkins 'how things were done in a big house years ago', including how to lay a table using a ruler for exact place settings and the art of ironing newspapers—our forefathers believed you could catch a dangerous chill from handling a damp newspaper. Dickman's verdict on Hopkins' abilities as a butler was that he was 'a natural'.

- Many actors will make thorough preparations to 'get into' a part, but few with the fervour of Daniel Day-Lewis for his role as wrongly convicted IRA suspect Gerry Conlan in *In the Name of the Father* (GB/Ire 93). He went without sleep for several nights in order to experience real sleep deprivation; lived in a specially constructed cell on set and ate only cold porridge for breakfast and prison slops for lunch; and had himself interrogated for hours by a pair of real detectives. The actor, British-born but now a naturalised Irish citizen, also hired four Dublin heavies to harass him by regularly kicking the door of his cell, shouting abuse and throwing buckets of freezing water over him as allegedly happened to Gerry Conlan while he was in police custody.

    This dedication to the reality of the role was nothing new for Day-Lewis. For his Oscar-winning performance in *My Left Foot* (GB/Ire 89), the story of cerebral palsy victim Christy Brown, he refused to move on the set and insisted that his inert body should be lifted by stage-hands. At meal-breaks he demanded that he be spoon-fed by members of the crew just as Christy Brown had been fed by members of his family. Totally contrasting was his role as Newland Archer, the prim, socially prominent attorney in 1870s Manhattan that he played in *The Age of Innocence* (US 93). Among his many and varied preparations for this departure from his more familiar parts as victims of outrageous circumstance was experimenting with 14 miniature bottles of cologne, specially prepared to 19th-century formulae, to find precisely the right scent for his character. It is perhaps as well that he turned down the role of the vampire Lestat in *Interview With the Vampire* (US 94) which subsequently went to Tom Cruise. What his efforts to find insight for that character might have been is something it may be better not to contemplate.

- The sinking of the Orca by the giant shark in *Jaws* (US 75) was not faked. Although Jaws was a steel-framed model, covered in polyurethane and not a real shark, it proved to be sufficiently monstrous to scuttle the vessel unintentionally. The camera crew were rescued from the water but divers had to retrieve the camera from the ocean bed 30ft below the surface. The exposed film was immediately flushed with fresh water and developed. Fortunately, it had survived its ordeal by sea water and the sequence was able to be used in the completed picture.

- *The Brinks Job* (US 78) was the story of 'the crime of the century', the legendary $2.7 million heist of the Brink's safe by small-time Boston hoods in 1950. When Peter Falk is seen picking the lock of the Brink's garage in six seconds flat, that was no ready-picked lock. Standing just out of camera range, whispering instructions, was a corpulent man known to the film crew, and the Boston underworld, as Spanish

Eddie. It took long hours of instruction and then eleven takes before Falk succeeded in picking the lock in the six seconds Spanish Eddie had decreed was all the time a professional like himself would need. Also real was the massive 3ft thick door of the safe which forms the centrepiece of the picture, recovered from its last resting place somewhere in Idaho and shipped to Boston at a cost of $16,000. And appearing as Brink's guards was a troupe of Brink's guards, originally hired to guard the $500,000 of genuine currency used as the contents of the safe but kept on as extras.

After his spell in legitimate employment as technical adviser on *The Brinks Job*, Spanish Eddie—later revealed to be one Edward Q. Colombani—reverted to his former vocation. In June 1979 he was charged with plotting to rob an armoured security van of $2 million at La Guardia Airport—and yes, the van belonged to Brink's.

- The darkening of the skies that heralded the termination of the agony of the Crucifixion was achieved in *Barabbas* (US/It 62) without resort to artificial lighting. Director Richard Fleischer arranged for the crucifixion scene to be shot on location at the village of Roccastrada, 120 miles north of Rome, when an eclipse of the sun was due—the only occasion on which a genuine eclipse has been featured in a dramatic film.

- Normally any actor seen at the controls of an aeroplane is strictly at ground level—the sky is back projected. Not so in *The Spirit of St Louis* (US 57), the story of Lindbergh's 1927 solo flight across the Atlantic. James Stewart, who played Lindbergh, was an experienced pilot who had led combat missions during World War II as commander of a USAAF bomber squadron stationed in England. The replica *Spirit of St Louis* flown by Stewart in the film was fitted with six camera mounts which recorded the actor's reactions automatically as he simulated the elation, anxiety and numbing tiredness experienced by Lindbergh during his 33½-hour flight from Long Island to Paris.

- *All The President's Men* (US 76), the story of *Washington Post* reporters Bernstein and Woodward's investigation of the Watergate affair, was an ephemerist's dream picture. All the accumulation of paper littering the huge 33,000 square foot replica of the *Washington Post* newsroom—several tons of it—was genuine trash, shipped to the Warner Bros Studios at Burbank from the actual WP newsroom. Another piece of reality in the picture was in the casting of Frank Wills, the security guard who discovered the Watergate break-in, as himself.

- The scene of a rhino charging in W. S. Van Dyke's *Trader Horn* (US 30) was unscripted. The camera car had been following the rhino when it suddenly turned and came straight towards the vehicle. Fortunately, the camera operator had the presence of mind to leave the camera running while he and the rest of the crew fled literally for dear life. An African employed on the film who was in front of the vehicle was struck by the beast and tossed in the air. According to John McClain, a journalist present, the man was 'either too frightened or too stupid to step out of the way'. Meanwhile, a hunter sitting on the back of the truck fell off as the driver accelerated, but had the presence of mind to jump to his feet and fire at the rhino from the hip. The bullet hit the animal in the mouth and in the film it is seen spitting teeth. As for the unfortunate African, McClain had little sympathy to spare. 'The native who'd been hit wasn't damaged,' he told the *New York Times*, 'but he ducked work and we let him knock off for two weeks. They're the laziest people in the world and they'll do anything to get out of a job.' Including lazing around in front of a charging rhino, presumably.

There were other respects in which *Trader Horn* failed to measure up to current standards of political correctness. All the animals seen being slaughtered—a prodigious number—died for real, sacrificial victims to a god called box office.

- Walter Plunkett, costume designer on *Gone With the Wind* (US 39), was meticulous not only about historical accuracy but also about the integrity of the story. At the outset of the Civil War, Scarlett O'Hara is married in her mother's wedding gown. According to Margaret Mitchell's novel, Ellen O'Hara had been married in 1844. The costume had the full, balloon sleeves of that era, not the close-fitting sleeves of the 1860s, the time of the story. Plunkett then insisted that the dress should be too long for Scarlett. Barbara O'Neal, who played Scarlett's mother Ellen, was a good deal taller than the diminutive Vivien Leigh. Given the rushed wedding, with the men preparing to leave for their units, Plunkett reasoned that the O'Haras would have had insufficient time to tailor and shorten the dress. It is doubtful whether any of *Gone With The Wind*'s adoring female fans noticed any of this attention to verisimilitude, particularly as they invaded the department stores in droves to purchase 'authentic' replicas of Scarlett O'Hara's wedding dress.

- The Yorkist monarch's limp in *Richard III* (GB 55) made few demands on Laurence Olivier's prodigious acting talent. During the filming of the very first sequence of the shoot, the Battle of Bosworth, a trained stunt archer failed to implant his arrow into the side padding of Olivier's horse and it was buried in the great man's left calf instead.

On another occasion, Sir Laurence voluntarily submitted to a painful ordeal in the interests of his art. The leering professional grin of Archie Rice, the broken-down seaside comic of *The Entertainer* (GB 59), was not achieved by the deft application of make-up to Olivier's teeth. Although the theatrical knight had been content to have just one front tooth blacked out when he played the part on stage, for Tony Richardson's film version he underwent the grim experience of having his teeth filed in order to give them the jagged appearance he deemed essential to the character.

- In his stage directions for *Pygmalion*, George Bernard Shaw wrote that the Cockney flower girl Eliza's hair needed washing rather badly. 'Its mousy colour can hardly be natural,' he observed. For the film version *My Fair Lady* (US 64), director George Cukor prescribed a mess of Vaseline and Fuller's earth to ensure that Audrey Hepburn's normally elegant coiffure should be sufficiently disgusting. Miss Hepburn

submitted, but insisted on one concession. Once her hair had been messed into an abandoned tangle and daubed with Cukor's pungent concoction, she sprayed the whole with de Givenchy perfume and appeared on set smelling, if not looking, every inch a lady.

Studios

The first film studio in the world was Thomas Edison's Black Maria, a frame building covered in black roofing-paper, built at the Edison Laboratories in West Orange, NJ, and completed at a cost of $637.67 on 1 February 1893. Here Edison made short vaudeville-act films for use in his Kinetoscope, a peep-show machine designed for amusement arcades. The building was so constructed that it could be revolved to face the direction of the sun.

Iran has a permanent battle set devoted to the shooting of war films. Demand for feature films about the 11-year Iran–Iraq war is so great in a country where few foreign films are allowed that the Sacred Defence War Movies Township was established on a 700-hectare site off the Tehran-Qom expressway in 1995. It can accommodate three 60-strong film crews at a time and the managing director claimed that it would continue to serve as a production centre for Iran–Iraq war films for at least 20 years.

The first studio in Europe and the first in the world in which films were made by artificial light was opened by Oskar Messter at 94a FriedrichStrasse, Berlin in November 1896. For illumination Messter used four Körting & Matthiessen 50 amp arc-lamps on portable stands. His earliest productions by artificial light included *From Tears to Laughter* (Ger 1896) and *Lightning Artist Zigg* (Ger 1896). The first artificially lit studio in the USA, the Biograph Studio at 11 East 14th Street, New York, was not opened until 1903.

The first film studio in Britain was built at the back of the Tivoli Theatre in the Strand in 1897 by the Mutosope & Biograph Co. Like Edison's Black Maria, the studio was mounted on a cup-and-ball fixture that enabled it to be turned in the direction of the sun. It could also be rocked to and fro for 'storm at sea' sequences and similar effects. The glass panels that made up the sides of the studio could be dismantled for 'outdoor' scenes.

The first purpose-built sound stage was Stage Three at Warner Bros Studios, Sunset Boulevard, Hollywood, erected in April 1927. Shooting of *The Jazz Singer* (US 27) commenced on Stage Three the following month.

The oldest film studio still operating is the Babelsberg Film Studio, East Berlin, known as DEFA during the dark decades of communism and as Ufa in the '20s and '30s. It opened with the first day of shooting of *Der Toten Tanz* (Ger 12), starring Asta Nielsen, on 12 February 1912. The 7700 feature films produced at Babelsberg include such classics as Fritz Lang's *Metropolis* (Ger 26) and Josef von Sternberg's *The Blue Angel* (Ger 30). The present-day complex houses 120 independent media companies, including the reconstituted Ufa. Facilities include a $60 million F/X centre, opened in March 1999.

Babelsberg soon after it opened in 1912. (Stiftung Deutsche Kinemathek)

The largest studio in the world is Ramoji Film City, near Hyderabad, India, opened in September 1997 and capable of hosting up to 100 productions simultaneously. The 1000-acre site accommodates 40 sound stages, state-of-the-art post-production facilities, 250 make-up rooms, its own electric power station, kitchens capable of producing 2000 meals at a time, a 5-star and a 3-star hotel, an in-house travel agency and a nursery cultivating tens of thousands of flowering plants from all parts of the world. Standing sets include city streets, an airport, railway stations, a fort, a palace, and a replica of Dharavi, Asia's biggest slum. Among the 5000 staff are a thousand set builders, and the props department occupies a six-storey building. 'A producer can walk in with a script and walk out with the canned film,' claims founder Ramoji Rao.

The largest Hollywood studio is Universal City, California, whose 34 sound stages and other buildings cover an area of 420 acres. As many as 6000 staff are employed at times of peak production. Built by Carl Laemmle, the studio was originally opened on a 230-acre lot on 15 March 1915 and had the unique distinction of being a municipality in its own right. Besides the outdoor stages, indoor studio, prop stores, processing labs, zoo and stables, Universal City had its own town hall, fire station and police department.

The largest studio stage in the world is the 007 stage at Pinewood Studios, Buckinghamshire, England, which was built in 1976 at a cost of £350,000. It is 336ft long by 139ft wide and 41ft high. Designed by Ken Adam and Michael Brown, the stage was originally built for the James Bond film *The Spy Who Loved Me* (GB 77) and accommodated 1.2 million gallons of water, a full-scale 600,000-ton oil-tanker and three nuclear submarines. The 007 stage is owned by MGM-UA and Eon Productions and is rented out to other film production companies.

The largest tank for water-based shoots is at Fox Studios Baja at Rosarito, Baja California Norte in Mexico. With an uninterrupted background vista of the Pacific Ocean, the tank holds 17 million gallons (US) of water and was originally constructed for shooting the exterior scenes of *Titanic* (US 97).

Stunts

The first stuntman was ex-US cavalryman Frank Hanaway, who won himself a part in Edwin S. Porter's *The Great Train Robbery* (US 03) for his ability to fall off a horse without injuring himself.

The first professional stuntwoman was Helen Gibson, who doubled for Helen Holmes in the first 26 episodes of Kalem's serial *The Hazards of Helen* (US 14). Trained as a trick rider and married to cowboy star Hoot Gibson, she was chosen for her ability to do stunts on horseback but proved herself adept at other hair-raising exploits, including jumping a speeding motorcycle on to a fast-moving locomotive. Unlike most stunt people, she achieved stardom in her own right, replacing Helen Holmes' successor Elsie McCleod as the lead in the long-running *Hazards of Helen*. Generally at this period, actresses were doubled in dangerous scenes by men in drag. Since the introduction of the Sexual Equality Act in the USA, it is illegal for stuntmen to double for actresses unless no stuntwoman is willing to take on the assignment.

THE STUNTMAN AS STAR

The claim made by many stars that they performed all their own stunts seldom amounted to anything more than press agents' ballyhoo. Apart from Helen Gibson (see above), the only star who really did all his own stunting was Richard Talmadge (1896–1981). The reasons were twofold—he was an accomplished stuntman himself; and he never became so valuable a star that the studio feared the consequences if he was put out of action. Perhaps the star most often trumpeted as his own stuntman was Douglas Fairbanks; ironically, it was Talmadge who did most of his stunts, including the celebrated slide down the sail in *The Black Pirate* (US 26). Present-day stars also like to cultivate a macho image by pretending to do stunts performed by professionals. No doubts need to be entertained though about Mel Gibson's claim to have done his own stunts in *Mad Max Beyond Thunderdrome* (Aus 85), since the credits list his name twice: as leading man and as one of the stuntmen.

> Clint Eastwood's *The Rookie* (US 90) had the rare distinction of featuring more stuntmen than actors—indeed more than twice as many. The men of action outnumbered the ones who just do the talking by 87 to 37.

The only stuntman who stands in for children is Bobby Porter, who at 4 ft 9 in often substitutes for little girls as well as little boys. Among his more spectacular appearances was the title role of *Annie* (US 82), in which he hung suspended from a 20-storey-high drawbridge as stand-in for nine-year-old Aileen Quinn.

The greatest height from which a stuntman has leaped in a free fall was 1170ft, a stunt performed for *Highpoint* (Can 79) by Los Angeles parachutist Dar Robinson from a ledge at the summit of the CN Tower in Toronto. Robinson opened his chute out of shot at a height estimated at 300–350ft from the ground after six seconds of freefalling, one of reaction time and two for releasing the canopy. The fee, an unconfirmed $150,000, is believed to be a record payment for a single stunt.

The highest jump without a parachute by a movie stuntman was 232ft by A. J. Bakunas, who was doubling for Burt Reynolds in *Hooper* (US 78). He fell on to an air mattress.

The longest leap in a car propelled by its own engine was performed by stunt driver Gary Davis in *Smokey and the Bandit II* (US 81). Davis raced a stripped-down Plymouth up a ramp butted up against the back of a double-tiered car-carrier at 80 mph and described a trajectory of 163ft before landing safely on the desert floor.

Takes and Retakes

The longest take in a movie shot on film comprises the whole of the second reel of Andy Warhol's *Blue Movie* (US 68) and consists of a 35-minute uninterrupted scene of Viva and Louis Waldon making love.

The longest take in a commercially made feature movie is a 14-minute uninterrupted monologue by Lionel Barrymore in *A Free Soul* (US 31). Since a reel of camera film only lasts ten minutes, the take was achieved by using more than one camera. Alfred Hitchcock's *Rope* (US 48), the story of two homosexual college men who kill a third for the intellectual thrill of it, was shot in eight ten-minute takes (apart from one cut to the housekeeper in

the first reel). The effect was of one continuous shot, since the action of the story occupied the same period of time—80 minutes—as the length of the film.

Mike Figgis's *Timecode* (US 00), made in digital video, consists of four parallel stories each shot in one continuous 93-minute take and played out in real time. The four stories, recounting the overlapping experiences of a group of Hollywood actors and actresses, are shown simultaneously on a quartered screen. No editor is credited.

The greatest number of retakes of a single scene was 342 for the episode in Chaplin's *City Lights* (US 31) in which a blind flower girl (Virginia Cherrill) sells the little tramp a flower under the misapprehension he is a rich man. Chaplin kept reshooting the scene because he was unable to find a satisfactory way of making the blind girl think that the tramp was wealthy. Finally he found a simple yet perfect solution. Chaplin is trying to cross a street jammed with traffic. Unable to reach the sidewalk, he sees a limousine parked by the kerb, gets in at one door and out at the other. The girl hears the door close and assumes it is the owner getting out. She hands him the flower, takes his last quarter, and keeps the change.

Difficult dialogue is the most common reason for prodigious numbers of retakes. One scene in *Dr Strangelove* (GB 63) was shot 48 times because Sterling Hayden, playing the mad base commander, fluffed his line 47 times. Marilyn Monroe did 59 takes of a scene in *Some Like It Hot* (US 59) in which her only line of dialogue was 'Where's the bourbon?'. Hollywood rebel Dennis Hopper had an early run-in with veteran director Henry Hathaway when he was made to repeat a scene in *From Hell to Texas* (US 57) no fewer than 85 times. 'Kid' Hathaway growled at the moody Method actor after the 85th take, 'You'll never work in this town again.' It was in fact some ten years before Hopper was offered another worthwhile role. Robert Mitchum claims he stopped taking Hollywood seriously when it took his co-star Greer Garson 125 times to say 'No' in *Desire Me* (US 47). (The picture was such a catastrophe it was released without director credit.)

Other reasons for retakes can be simply the difficulty of working up the right emotional response on demand, or it may be the perpetual problem of making inanimate objects do the director's bidding. Both occurred on Steven Spielberg's *Hook* (US 92). British actress Caroline Goodall, who played Mrs Peter Pan, was required to break down in tears no less than 28 times on the first day of shooting.

It took 342 takes to get this scene in City Lights *(US 31). Chaplin spent 534 days making the movie, including 368 days when he shot nothing at all as he sought a way of showing that the girl, who couldn't see, thought the tramp, who never spoke, was a wealthy tycoon.*

Stenographic transcript of Russian director Gregory Ratoff at work on *The Rose of Washington Square* (US 39).
Ratoff: Cut! Cut it! Cut. Cut. Cut. (As an afterthought): Cut.
Tyrone Power, Alice Faye and Al Jolson (expectantly): Well?
Ratoff (with deliberation): Wary excellent. Wa-a-a-ry, wa-a-a-a-ry excellent, but it's not colossal.
Power, Faye and Jolson (wearily): Okay.
They do the scene.
Ratoff (leaping from chair and doing a pas seul): Sansational . . . but sa-a-ansational! Now, let's do it again.

After the first couple of dozen takes she no longer needed to act. Rather more takes were required for a scene in which leaves are blowing in through a window and one is supposed to land on Miss Goodall's shoulder. The special effects team attempted to direct the leaf by fixing it on the end of a fishing line. After they had muffed the first 30 takes, director Steven Spielberg seized the rod and tried to work the trick himself. He succeeded on the 52nd take.

Recalling the hazards of working with Stanley Kubrick on *A Clockwork Orange* (GB 71), Malcolm McDowell says that the perfectionist director demanded 25 takes of the scene in which the parole officer spits in McDowell's face. 'Stanley shouted out to the crew, "Does anyone want to spit at Malcolm?" They all came over and took turns.'

The record number of takes for a dialogue sequence is claimed to be the 127 demanded by Stanley Kubrick of a scene with Shelley Duval in *The Shining* (US 80).

Even this total has been greatly exceeded in a song sequence. Josef von Sternberg did 236 takes of Marlene Dietrich singing 'Falling In Love Again' for the English-language version of *The Blue Angel* (Ger 30), because the word 'moths' constantly came out as 'moss' in the actress's German accent. Eventually, after two days' filming von Sternberg gave up and simply heightened the background noise of the night club patrons in order to drown out the offending word.

ONE SHOT DIRECTORS

At the other end of the scale, there have been those who earned themselves reputations as 'one-shot' directors, notably G. W. Pabst, Cecil B. DeMille, W. S. 'One-Shot Woody' van Dyke, and D. W. Griffith. According to Lillian Gish, Griffith's masterwork *The Birth of a Nation* (US 15) was made with only one retake of one scene. The single repeat shot was necessitated, much to Mr Griffith's displeasure, by the fact that Mae Marsh forgot to drape herself in the Confederate flag for her suicide scene.

Lewis Gilbert filmed *Alfie* (GB 66), the film which brought Michael Caine to international stardom, in single takes for a simple reason—the $350,000 budget did not allow for retakes.

> Some scenes can only be performed in a single take. One such was the episode in John Waters' notorious *Pink Flamingos* (US 74) where a dog exudes a turd and 300lb drag artiste Divine picks it up and eats it. There was no cut and the scene was played for real. As Divine swallowed the steaming 'hot-dog do', he gagged and, in John Waters' own words, 'the whole world gagged with him'.

Blunders

The most frequent mistakes made in movies are microphone booms visible within the frame, and camera crews reflected in plate-glass windows. Other blunders are manifold. Some of the choicest include:

● Balthazar Getty as Ralph uses the short-sighted

This fire in Lord of the Flies *(US 90) would have remained unlit. Glasses for short-sightedness like Piggy's do not converge the sun's rays.*

Piggy's glasses to light a fire from the sun in Harry Hook's remake of *Lord of the Flies* (US 90). But glasses to correct short-sightedness do not converge rays of light and in reality the fire would have remained unlit. The error, though, has a literary legitimacy. William Golding made the same mistake in the original novel.

● In Alfred Hitchcock's *Vertigo* (US 58), James Stewart leaps from one rooftop to another. As he hangs from the edge, the distance has widened to that of a city street.

● When Kevin Costner is on the run in *Robin Hood Prince of Thieves* (US 91) printed 'wanted' posters are displayed—in the 12th century.

● The bewitching Julia Roberts kicks off her shoes at a polo match in *Pretty Woman* (US 90), revealing the fact—nothing to do with the storyline—that each of her big toes is encircled by sticking plaster. Arriving back at her hotel she sheds her shoes again and a close-up of her bare feet betrays the absence of the plasters.

● The police announce that the haul from the first bank robbery in *The Thomas Crown Affair* (US 68) totals $2,660,527.62. Later a secretary enumerates the denominations of the missing bank notes—16,240 $20 bills, 19,871 $10 bills, 34,645 $5 bills and 129,000 single dollar bills. Added together, a grand total of only $825,735.

● *The Madness of King George* (GB 95) had all the attention to precise historical detail associated with the Merchant-Ivory team. Except for the opening shot. This shows the oaken gates of Windsor Castle in 1788, the year in which George III first became mad. Windsor Castle being unavailable for filming, the actual gates were those of Eton College. They are scored with the imprint of initials and graffiti from the clasp-knives of generations of Eton boys, the most prominent of these incisions being an unmistakable date: 1862.

● Some blunders are eliminated at the 11th hour. *The*

You would have thought that with a budget of $43 million the makers of Cleopatra *(US 63) might have avoided having a 25c plastic sponge from the corner drug store floating in the royal bath.* (BFI)

Great Ziegfeld (US 36) was given a sneak preview before release and one of the report cards completed by a paying patron noted that while Ziegfeld's hair grew naturally greyer and thinner as the showman became older, his long-serving valet's hair remained untrammelled by age. A panic meeting back at the MGM lot resulted in retakes of all the later scenes in which Ernest Cossart as the valet appeared.

- Eponymous pig Babe in *Babe: Pig in the City* (US/Aus 98) is purported to be male. One injudicious close-up reveals that the star is a porcine actress, not an actor.

- As the hoodlum in *Angels with Dirty Faces* (US 38), James Cagney engaged in a prolonged battle with large numbers of New York's Finest without ever once having to reload his gun. There were so many protests from the public about this patent lack of realism that when he made his next picture, *The Oklahoma Kid* (US 39), Cagney insisted that he must not be seen to fire more than six shots in any scene.

- When an army officer is shot in the Sherlock Holmes adventure *The Master Blackmailer* (GB 92, TVM), a police detective is seen picking up the discarded weapon in a handkerchief. Not Scotland Yard practice in the mid-1890s, when the film is set. The use of fingerprinting for detection was not adopted in Britain until 1901.

- During the celebrated car chase up and down the San Francisco hills in *Bullitt* (US 68), the Dodge Charger pursued by Steve McQueen loses three hubcaps. Eventually it crashes into a wall and three more hubcaps spin into the air.

- In *Braveheart* (US 95) Robert the Bruce is characterised as 'the 17th Earl of Bruce'. No one could have been a 17th earl in the 12th century: earldoms had not been in existence for seventeen generations. In fact he was Lord of Annandale and Earl of Carrick.

- When some Confederate officers escape by balloon in the Jules Verne story *Mysterious Island* (GB 61), they

are caught in a downpour *above* the clouds.

- Katharine Hepburn received a solo credit for *State of the Union* (US 48) which occupies at least half the screen—a fitting tribute but for the fact that her first name is wrongly spelled Katherine. And while [Sir] Alec Guinness may have been deemed worthy of an Oscar for his performance in *The Bridge on the River Kwai* (GB 57), he was not honoured by having his name spelled correctly in the credits—it appears as Guiness.

- Perhaps even more culpable than spelling the names of the stars wrong is spelling the title wrong, as in *Brylcream Boulevard* (Belg 96). The hair gel with which the Battle of Britain pilots went to war is *Brylcreem*. Truffaut's *nouvelle vague* film *La Sirène du Mississipi/Mississippi Mermaid* (Fr 69) may have reflected his passion for all things American, but insufficiently to spell the name of the gulf state correctly.

- A blunder that could easily have been averted was the name of the railway company on the Austrian railway carriage in the train scene of *Goodbye Mr Chips* (GB 39). Austrian actor Paul Henreid, who played the German schoolmaster, pointed out to director Sam Wood that the name of Austrian Railways had been different in the 1890s. Wood considered the error unimportant and not likely to be noticed by anyone except Austrians, hardly a key element of the audience. He regretted being so dismissive when hundreds of railway buffs wrote to the studio decrying the solecism.

- Some directors have been wholly unapologetic for their mistakes. Writing in the *New York Times*, Sir

Check the prison number of Elvis's prison uniform in these two scenes from Jailhouse Rock *(US 57)—there's something wrong here.* (Kobal Collection)

Laurence Olivier said of his tour de force rendering of Shakespeare's *Richard III* (GB 56): 'Americans who know London may be surprised to find Westminster Abbey and the Tower of London practically adjacent. I hope they'll agree with me that if they weren't like that, they should have been.'

- Lily Tomlin is stopped by a motorcycle cop in *9 to 5* (US 80) because one of the rear lights of her car is out and the other is blinking. When she drives on her way, both lights are working perfectly.
- Fluffed lines seldom survive on the soundtrack, as it is easy enough to correct them. A notable exception is Cary Grant's spondurgle in Hitchcock's *North by Northwest* (US 59), when he picks up a photograph from a dressing table and says, 'Look who's here . . . Our friend who's assembling the General Assembly this afternoon.' (The script said addressing.)
- Another soundtrack error that failed to be eliminated occurred in *Abe Lincoln in Illinois* (US 40). Raymond Massey as Abraham Lincoln is on his way from his native Illinois to Washington for his inauguration as President. As the train pulls out of the railroad station, the crowd of well-wishers wave their hats in the air and call out 'Goodbye Mr Lincoln!'. All but one, who cries 'Goodbye Mr Massey'.
- The sponge floating in Elizabeth Taylor's bath in *Cleopatra* (US 63) was a plastic one of the kind readily available from the corner drug store.
- *Indiana Jones and the Last Crusade* (US 89) is cherished by blunder buffs. Set in 1938, the film has Indy crossing the Atlantic by airliner a year before the first transatlantic passenger service began, and starting back by airship a year after transatlantic airship services ceased. In the airport lounge two passengers are reading identical copies of the same German newspaper—fine except that the papers date from 1918, 20 years earlier.

While in Germany, Indy encounters Hitler and asks for his autograph. In a sequence lasting only a few seconds, twin blunders are made—Hitler signs himself Adolph instead of the correct Germanic Adolf and he does so with his right hand. The Führer was left handed.

But the classic 'how-come-no-one-noticed-that-before-release' humdinger of a howler is an intertitle reading 'The Republic of Hatay', followed immediately by a scene in which the ruler of the 'republic' is addressed as 'Your Royal Highness'.

- Michael Curtiz's biopic of George M. Cohans *Yankee Doodle Dandy* (US 42) contained two blunders of the kind easily avoided. Cohan's luggage bears a label with a picture of London's Nelson's Column in Trafalgar Square and the legend 'Nelson Square Hotel'. When the sinking of the Lusitania occurs, a newspaper report is illustrated with a photograph of a liner with two funnels. The *Lusitania* had four funnels.
- The uniform worn by Elvis Presley in *Jailhouse Rock* (US 57) bears his prison number 6239. Later he is seen wearing a uniform with the number 6240.
- Some errors are unavoidable. Yak fanciers were swift to spot that the beasts seen in *Seven Years in Tibet* (US 97) were not genuine Tibetan yaks. The reason was that the picture was shot in the province of Mendoza in Argentina, a mountainous region of the Andes which closely resembles Tibet. The Argentine authorities refused permission for the import of Tibetan yaks on health grounds. They eventually allowed in the more hygienic type of yak found in Wyoming.

- All the cars seen in the London street scenes in the Danny Kaye movie *Knock on Wood* (US 54) are left-hand drive. In another Danny Kaye film, *Merry Andrew* (US 58), a London bus is progressing along the right-hand side of the road.

- The teenage boy played by Charlie Shattner in *The Delinquents* (Aus 89) receives a severe whipping from his brutal stepfather. The same evening he strips down to make love to girlfriend Kylie Minogue and there is not a mark on his body.

- When Anthony Dowson attempts to throttle Grace Kelly in Hitchcock's *Dial M for Murder* (US 54), she picks up a pair of scissors and stabs him in the back. Even before she strikes, though, a pair of scissors already embedded in his back is momentarily visible to any keen-eyed member of the audience.

- The action of *The Sound of Music* (US 65) is set in the 1930s, yet in one scene an orange box can be discerned, stamped 'Produce of Israel'.

- Anachronisms are usually visual or in the dialogue. In *The Draughtsman's Contract* (GB 83) it is a background noise that dispels, at least for ornithologists, the illusion of the film's 17th-century setting. The gentle cooing of a collared dove is not a sound that would have fallen on Jacobean ears. The species was unknown in Britain until 1955.

- The makers of *Unforgiven* (US 92) missed by a much smaller margin. Richard Harris shoots at pheasants from a train in 1881. Pheasants were introduced into America the following year.

- Moviegoers confronted with any filmic version of *Genesis* should spare a glance at Adam's midriff. If, as in *The Bible* (US 66), he has a navel—well, he shouldn't, should he?

- This one could be described as a 'deliberate mistake', because director John Schlesinger was fully aware of it. In *Billy Liar* (GB 63) the eponymous hero (Tom Courtenay) fantasises about being a general reviewing his victorious troops. The girl at his side on the balcony is not the girl who features in all his other fantasies, played by Julie Christie. She was played by the actress originally cast in the inamorata role, but who fell ill just a few days into production and had to be replaced. The budget was too tight to allow for the march-past to be shot again with Miss Christie at Tom Courtenay's side.

- Another intentional error was the costuming of the Irish nationalists who seized the Dublin GPO in the Easter Rising depicted in *Michael Collins* (US/Ire 96). Under the misapprehension that their Gaelic forbears had worn kilts, a number of the rebels attired themselves in this way. The film-makers, fearful that historical accuracy would be mistaken for historical solecism, costumed them in sober suits.

- In Chris Newby's *Anchoress* (GB/Bel 93) apples are harvested from a pine tree.

- The trial of the farmer Sommersby (Richard Gere) in the 1993 film of the same name takes place in a Tennessee court presided over by a black judge (James Earl Jones). The story is set in the Reconstruction period (1865–77) following the American Civil War and it is true that there were black judges in the South at that time. The problem is that they did not sit in judgement in white courts;

there were separate black courts in the so called 'skid-aways', self-governing black communities set up by federal agency the Freedman's Bureau. Casting a black actor as the judge in *Sommersby* seems, therefore, to have been a concession to political correctness at the expense of historical accuracy.

- The fallacy that the orchestra was playing 'Nearer My God to Thee' as the *Titanic* went down was fuelled by three film treatments of the disaster—*Titanic* (US 53), *A Night to Remember* (GB 58) and James Cameron's mighty *Titanic* (US 97). In fact the musicians were struggling with the hymn 'Autumn' as the giant liner slipped into an ever steeper angle.

- Joe Pesci and Brendan Fraser are seen crossing Harvard Yard, the latter on crutches, in *With Honors* (US 94). At mid-point in the scene the negative has been reversed, with the result that Fraser's plaster cast switches from his right leg to his left and the legend on Pesci's sweatshirt reads ᗡЯAVЯAH.

- In Martha Coolidge's *Joy of Sex* (US 84), a pair of high-school students are making out in room 319 of a motel when someone takes an axe to the door to get in. Pity that the broken door displays the number 302.

- *Emma* (GB 96) brought to the screen Jane Austen's 1815 novel and from the costumes and décor there is no reason to suppose that it is set any further on in time. Except for the anachronisms, which would suggest a Victorian rather than a Georgian setting. First off is a scene in which the bewitching but exasperating Emma is seen decorating the parish church, with Mr Knightley in attendance, for the Harvest Festival. It is a common error to suppose that Harvest Festival is an ancient celebration; as a religious festival, however, it dates only from 1854. A little later Emma and Mr Knightley partake of afternoon tea, complete with sandwiches, in an arbor. Afternoon tea as a modest repast bridging the long hours between lunch and dinner is not recorded before 1840. In Jane Austen's time it was customary to dine around mid-afternoon. A dramatic scene of attempted larceny occurs at a gypsy encampment replete with gypsy caravan. Gypsies did not take to caravans till much later; the earliest known reference dates from 1873. Jane Austen's gypsies would have occupied bender tents. These are mistakes which probably only the most didactic of social historians would have noted. But many people spotted the glaring error in the picture where the wild strawberries gathered from the hill-side are not the small wild variety at all, but large cultivated ones.

- The basic premise of Sir Carol Reed's *The Third Man* (GB 49) that black marketeer Harry Lime (Orson Welles) is able to evade arrest by moving around Vienna's labyrinth of sewers is a false one. In fact the sewers do not interconnect in the way suggested in the film. Even the stairs from the Karplatz which Harry Lime races down in his doomed escape lead only to overflows and the underground Wien river. But then, if scriptwriter Graham Greene had been a stickler for accuracy, the film which many consider Britain's greatest screen classic could never have been made.

- According to Hoxton shoplifter Shirley Pitts, a close friend of the Kray Twins, the way that Billie Whitelaw was costumed in post-war utility frocks for the role of heart-of-gold mum Vi Kray in *The Krays* (GB 90) was totally wrong. 'Violet,' she declared, 'was a very smart woman . . . She used to love Tricosa and other makes from the White House in Bond Street.' Shirley should know. She it was who stole Vi's designer-label dresses for her.

- As the decrepit private eye (Art Carney) and his ageing flower-child partner (Lily Tomlin) emerge from a cemetery in the final scene of *The Late Show* (US 77) they pass a large sign by the gate with the words 'Hollywood Cemetary'. Director Robert Benton only spotted the unconventional spelling in the final rushes, by which time it was too late to do anything but hope that audiences were no better spellers than all those who had observed the sign on set.

- The young Clarice in *The Silence of the Lambs* (US 91) has brown eyes. The elder Clarice, played by Jodie Foster, has blue eyes.

- One of the corpses on the battlefield at Agincourt in Kenneth Branagh's *Henry V* (GB 89) starts to grin as the camera tracks past him.

- Jim Sheridan's powerful political polemic about the Guildford Four *In the Name of the Father* (GB/Ire 93) was criticised for its economy with the truth. But apart from imaginative treatment of the facts of the case, there was one key scene which was simply not possible. At the climax of the appeal against the Guildford Four's conviction on terrorist charges, Gerry Conlan's solicitor (Emma Thompson) secures the release of the prisoners when she harangues the court with fresh evidence. In fact she (or rather he in reality) never presented the case at all. Solicitors do not do that because they do not have the Right of Audience in the Court of Appeal.

- In a scene set in London shortly after World War II, Meryl Streep as the heroine of *Plenty* (US 85) apologises to guests that the omelette she has cooked for them is made from dried egg powder. Only moments earlier she had been depicted whisking fresh eggs in a bowl.

- When Al Pacino visits Penelope Ann Miller at the strip joint where she works in *Carlito's Way* (US 94), the music in the background is the Bee Gee's 'You Should Be Dancing'. The picture is set in 1975. Too bad the song did not come out until 1976. Another 'just too early' anachronism occurs in the Kevin Costner starrer *A Perfect World* (US 94). The Jolly Joes candy being consumed in 1963 could not have been—it was introduced in 1966.

- Kevin Kline as the stand-in for the President in *Dave* (US 93) watches *The Tonight Show* at the White House. The clock on the wall shows the time to be 11.05 p.m. The programme goes out at 11.35 Eastern Standard Time. In a scene in which Kline and the First Lady (Sigourney Weaver) take a drive she is holding a bag of groceries. But it is not until later that Kline is seen buying the self-same groceries. In fact the script had been changed—originally the shopping episode was supposed to have been before the drive.

- It is unfortunate that the leaves of the trees showing in the background at the high-school graduation in the Harvey Keitel–Faraiza Balk starrer *Imaginary Crimes* (US 94) are turning to autumnal umber when

the ceremony is one that takes place as the buds of spring are breaking forth. In Robert Altman's *Ready to Wear (Pret-a-Porter)* (US 94) some of the outdoor Paris scenes show the trees in the boulevards bare of leaves (correctly for the time of year the Ready to Wear collections are shown), while others reveal paths and gardens lavish with flowers in bloom and the trees in full foliage.

- One and the same sartorial error occurs in Michael Reeves' *Witchfinder General/US: The Conqueror Worm* (GB 68) and Michael Winner's remake of *The Wicked Lady* (GB 83). Both are set in the 17th century and each features Anglican ministers—in the latter film the minister accompanies the condemned highwaywoman in the tumbril taking her to be hanged at Tyburn. Unfortunately, the costume worn by the actors is that of a 17th-century bishop, not an ordinary clergyman—the giveaway is the billowing lawn sleeves. John Fraser, historical adviser on *The Wicked Lady*, says that both productions rented their costumes from Berman & Nathan and suggests that the bishop's robes have been wrongly labelled. Wardrobe masters take note!

- The Americans have always tended to think of Britain as a small offshore island, but their concept of distance can sometimes seem a little understated to the natives. In *Robin Hood Prince of Thieves* (US 91), Robin (Kevin Costner) and his majestic black 'buddy' (Morgan Freeman) escape from incarceration in the Holy Land and eventually arrive, many months later, on a sandy beach at Dover (which has a pebble beach, but let that pass). Robin kisses the sand and declares to his faithful henchman that they will be home at Sherwood by nightfall. Sherwood Forest in Nottinghamshire is a good 150 miles from Dover.

- A simple special effect in *Interview With the Vampire* (US 94) fails to come off as intended. Stephen Rea, doing a vampire vaudeville routine in a Parisian backstreet, is seen to walk upside down beneath a brick arch. This was achieved by the simple technique of building the brick arch upside down, having Rea walk across it upright, and printing the film image the wrong way up. Regrettably the game is given away by the fact that the voluminous cloak worn by the actor appears to be defying gravity by hanging straight up in the air.

- Steven Spielberg committed a solecism on the soundtrack of *Schindler's List* (US 93) which was only noticed at the charity première in aid of the Simon Wiesenthal Centre. It could not have been a worse occasion. It is Orthodox Jewish practice never to say or write the word 'God', but to use respectful allusions such as 'the Holy One' or 'the Almighty' instead. In the film an Orthodox rabbi speaks the forbidden word in a Sabbath ceremony, an error which most of the audience at the première were well qualified to draw to Spielberg's attention. Hundreds of prints were rapidly doctored at great expense and with considerable technical ingenuity in order that the offence should not be repeated.

- The historical detail of the films made by Ismail Merchant and James Ivory is normally impeccable, but Thomas Jefferson scholar Dan Jordan of the University of Virginia accused them of 'howling errors of fact' in *Jefferson in Paris* (US 95). The most reprehensible, in Mr Jordan's view, was the representation of America's first ambassador to Paris as someone unable to speak or understand French. In fact, Jefferson was proficient not only in French but in five other foreign languages as well. Director James Ivory explained that the script had to be rewritten to suggest that Jefferson was monoglot because the actor playing him, Nick Nolte, was unable to manage a single word in French. Mr Jordan conceded, however, that Merchant-Ivory were entitled to portray Jefferson in any way they liked. 'It's their Jeffersonian right to free expression.' he said pointedly.

Less excusable was an easily avoidable anachronism. Jefferson goes to a draper's shop in Paris to buy a length of cloth to make up a dress for his favourite slave, Sally Hemings. He asks for 10 metres; Maria Cosway accompanying him, says 8 metres is sufficient for simple servant's dress. The episode takes place before the French Revolution in 1789. The metric system was devised by a commission appointed at the behest of the revolutionary Constituent Assembly in 1790 and the metre, as the key measure, introduced by law on 7 April 1795.

- The castle of Louis XIV (1638–1715) in *The Man in the Iron Mask* (US 98) contains a magnificent portrait of his great-grandson Louis XV (1710–74). At the time the story takes place, Louis XIV is about the same age as protagonist Leonardo Di Caprio—half a century before his successor was born!

Home Movies

The first home-movie outfit was the 35mm Motorgraph projector-cum-ciné camera offered for sale at 12 gns (£12.60) by W. Watson & Sons of High Holborn and advertised for sale in *The British Journal of Photography Almanac* in November 1896. Like most early amateur projectors, it was designed to be used in conjunction with a magic lantern as light source. The machine itself was tiny, measuring only 6 x 4 x 5½ in and was undoubtedly the first camera small enough to be held in the hand.

However, due to the wide arc of the turning handle—the name Motorgraph was a misnomer, as it was not motorised—it would have been unsteady unless mounted on a tripod. Used as a projector, the film ran through the gate into the basket, since there was no take-up spool; for use as a camera, film magazines were fitted to the top and bottom. Watson's also supplied a range of about 100 films available for home-viewing.

The first substandard gauge home-movie outfit was the Birtac, also a combined camera and projector, which was designed by pioneer film-maker Birt Acres and marketed in Britain in 1898 at a price of 10 gns (£10.50), or 12 gns (£12.60) including a developing and printing outfit. The film used was 17.5mm gauge, chosen because it could be produced by simply slitting standard 35mm film down the middle. It was supplied in 20ft daylight-loading cartridges at 2s 6d (12½p) a roll. For projection illumination an upright Welsbach mantle fed from the domestic gas supply was used, the gas being pressurised in a bag with weights loaded on to it. Picture size was claimed to be up to 3 x 4ft.

An astonishing range of home-movie outfits was available to the Victorian amateur cinematographer. Besides the Motorgraph (1896), the Birtac (1898) and the Biokam (1899), English enthusiasts had the choice of the Cynnagraph projector, marketed at 5 gns (£5.25) in September 1898, the French-made Pocket Chrono of 1899 at £7 or the La Petite—British-made despite its name—offered at £5 10s (£5.50) in 1900. Across the Channel, Oskar Messter of Berlin listed an Amateur-Kinetograph, plus library of films for home viewing, in his October 1897 catalogue. In the same year, Reulos & Goudeau of Paris produced the Mirographe and it was they who were to coin the term 'amateur cinematography' for the hobby in 1900. In 1899 Faller's cinematographe des familles was introduced.

Considering the number of home movie outfits which were available by 1900, it is surprising how little is recorded about the pioneer amateur film-makers themselves. None of their films are known to survive and few of their names have come down to us.

The earliest known surviving home movies were taken by Ella Lewenz (1888–1954), the daughter of an eminent Jewish banker and philanthropist, who, between 1914 and the 1950s, filmed her home life in Germany and many of the distinguished friends of her family (including Einstein, Walter Gropius, actress Brigitte Helm, author Gerhard Hauptmann), as well as travels in Europe and Egypt. The earliest footage includes scenes in the streets of Berlin at the outbreak of World War I. In the 1930s Ella Lewenz began to use Agfacolor, making striking films of a Berlin festooned with the emblems of Nazidom. Her granddaughter Lisa Lewenz edited the material as a 62-minute documentary *A Letter Without Words*, which was presented at the Berlin Film Festival in 1998. A particular fascination of the film is that Ms Lewenz had engaged a lip reader to transcribe what was being said by the people depicted in the silent footage.

CHAPTER 8

Colour, Sound and Scope

Colour

The first commercially successful natural colour process was two-colour Kinemacolor, developed by George Albert Smith of Brighton for the Urban Trading Co., London. Smith made his first colour film by this process outside his house at Southwick, Brighton, in July 1906. It showed his two children playing on the lawn, the boy dressed in blue and waving a Union Jack, the girl in white with a pink sash.

The first commercially produced film in natural colour was G. A. Smith's *A Visit to the Seaside* (GB 08), an eight-minute short featuring the White Coons pierrot troupe and the Band of the Cameron Highlanders which was trade shown in September 1908. Taken at Brighton, it showed children paddling and eating ice-cream, a pretty girl falling out of a boat, and men peeping at the Bathing Belles changing in their bathing machines. The first public presentation of Kinemacolor before a paying audience took place at the Palace Theatre, Shaftesbury Avenue, on 26 February 1909 and consisted of 21 short films, including scenes taken at Aldershot, sailing at Southwick, the Water Carnival at Villefranche and the Children's Battle of Flowers at Nice.

The first dramatic film in natural colour was the Kinemacolor production *Checkmated* (GB 10), directed by Theo Bouwmeester, who also played the lead role of Napoleon.

The first American dramatic film in natural colour was Eclair's Kinemacolor production *La Tosca* (US 12), with Lillian Russell. A total of 54 dramatic films were produced in Kinemacolor in Britain from 1910–12. In the USA there were only three dramatic productions in

Kinemacolor besides *La Tosca*. These were *Mission Bells* (US 13), *The Rivals* (US 13) and *The Scarlet Letter* (US 13), the latter starring D. W. Griffith's wife Linda Arvidson.

The first full-length feature film in colour was a five-reel melodrama, *The World, the Flesh and the Devil* (GB 14), produced by the Union Jack Co. in Kinemacolor from the play by Laurence Cowen. Starring Frank Esmond and Stella St Audrie, it opened at the Holborn Empire on 9 April 1914 billed as 'A £10,000 Picture Play in Actual Colours' in '4 parts and 120 scenes'. Like most of the Kinemacolor dramas, the acting and direction (F. Martin Thornton) were execrable, the colour impressive.

Kinemacolor was an additive process in which both filming and projection were done through red and green filters. The drawbacks were the cost of the special projector used and the wear on the film, which passed through the projector at twice normal speed. Nevertheless, it was installed at some 300 cinemas in Britain and achieved success overseas as well, notably in the United States and Japan. On the production side Kinemacolor was limited in its application because it could not be used for indoor work. There was also a virtue to this, since it encouraged location shooting at a time when black-and-white productions were becoming progressively more studio-bound. One enterprising Kinemacolor venture was **the first colour western**, Theo Bouwmeester's *Fate* (GB 11), set in Texas but filmed in Sussex! Kinemacolor was particularly well suited for films of pageantry, two of the most successful releases being a newsreel of King Edward VII's funeral in May 1910—at which no less than nine kings were present—and a spectacular two-hour presentation of the 1912 Delhi Durbar. Others included the Coronation of King George V, the Naval Review of June 1911 and the Investiture of the Prince of Wales at Caernarvon. Production came to a halt when Charles Urban, the guiding spirit behind Kinemacolor, left for the US in 1914 to propagate the British war effort through films.

Little survives today to commemorate the world's first successful natural colour film process. But on the south side of the Brighton–Hove railway line near to Hove Station is an undistinguished shed which formed part of the Smith & Urban's studio from 1910. On it can still be discerned the faded lettering which spells out the word KINEMACOLOR.

The first colour talkie was Frans Lundberg Films' *Vals ur Solstrålen* (Swe 11), directed by Ernst Dittmer and starring Rosa Grünberg, which was premièred at the Stora Biografteatern in Malmö, Sweden, on 1 May 1911. The 215ft short was made by the Biophon synchronised disc sound process. The colour process is not recorded, but it was probably stencilled.

The first all-colour talkie feature was Warner Bros' two-colour Technicolor musical *On With the Show* (US 29), directed by Alan Crosland with Betty Compson and Joe E. Brown, which was premièred at the Winter Garden, New York, on 28 May 1929.

The first British talking feature in colour was BIP's *A Romance of Seville* (GB 29), which was originally shown as a silent in 1929 but had sound added in July 1930. The first film made as a talkie to be released in colour was BIP's *Harmony Heaven* (GB 30), a musical about a composer (Stuart Hall) who wins fame and the hand of his girl (Polly Ward) despite the attentions of a flirtatious socialite (Trilby Clark).

The first Technicolor film was *The Gulf Between* (US 17), a five-reeler starring Grace Darmond and Niles Welch, produced by the Technicolor Motion Picture Corporation in a two-colour additive process and premièred at the Aeolian Hall, New York, on 21 September 1917. It was **the first full-length colour feature produced in the USA** and the third in the world.

The first film in three-colour Technicolor was Walt Disney's Silly Symphony cartoon *Flowers and Trees* (US 32), premièred 17 July 1932 at Grauman's Chinese Theater, Hollywood. The first dramatic subject was *La Cucaracha* (US 34), released at the RKO-Hill Street Theater, Los Angeles, on 15 November 1934 and the first three-colour Technicolor sequence in a feature was in MGM's *The Cat and the Fiddle* (US 34).

The first feature made entirely in three-colour Technicolor was Rouben Mamoulian's *Becky Sharp* (US 35) with Cedric Hardwicke and Miriam Hopkins. Not everyone appreciated the innovation. A critic for *Liberty* magazine wrote that the performers looked like 'boiled salmon dipped in mayonnaise'. The first in Britain was *Wings of the Morning* (GB 37), a race-track drama starring Henry Fonda and French actress Annabella, which opened at the Capitol, Haymarket, in May 1937.

The most widely used colour process: Technicolor held almost a monopoly of the three-colour field from 1932 until 1952, when *Royal Journey* (Can 52) was released in Kodak's new Eastman Color process. Within three years Technicolor had fallen into second place, with 112 films being produced in Eastman Color in 1955 against 90 in Technicolor. Eastman Color is now used for virtually all colour films produced in the West. Metrocolor, Warnercolor and De Luxe are all processes using Eastman Color stock and films credited 'Color by Technicolor' are generally made with Eastman Color negative but printed by Technicolor laboratories.

The colour values of Van Gogh's celebrated painting of a cornfield are not true to nature, according to director Vincente Minnelli. When he made *Lust for Life* (US 56), there was a scene in which Van Gogh is seen painting the picture (the original was used in the film), followed by a dissolve to an actual cornfield. In order to make the real corn match the colours rendered in the painting, Minnelli was obliged to spray the entire field with golden dye.

The shortest colour sequence consisted of two frames of Alfred Hitchcock's *Spellbound* (US 45). Towards the end of the film, a split-second scene of a gun blast was presented in vivid red Technicolor.

DECLINE OF BLACK-AND-WHITE FILMS
Not surprisingly the USA was the first country to produce more films in colour than black and white, with 157 out of a total of 237 full-length features being shot in colour in 1954. Rather more surprisingly, monochrome made something of a comeback in the later 1950s, with nearly 80% of 1959's releases being in black and white, but from 1962 onwards colour remained in the ascendant. The number of monochrome releases fell dramatically from

COLOUR AND BLACK-AND-WHITE PRODUCTION IN THE US AND UK, 1920–70

| | Full Colour | | Part Colour | | Black and White | | | |
	US	UK	US	UK	US	%	UK	%
1920	0	0	0	0	797	100	155	100
1921	0	0	2	0	852	99.8	137	100
1922	2	1	0	1	746	99.7	108	98.2
1923	2	1	1	1	573	99.5	66	97.1
1924	1	1	5	0	577	99.3	48	98.0
1925	0	0	14	0	578	97.6	33	100
1926	1	0	19	0	731	97.4	33	100
1927	0	0	6	0	677	99.1	48	100
1928	1	0	9	0	638	98.6	80	100
1929	5	1	31	0	552	94.4	80	98.8
1930	14	1	21	1	481	95.6	73	97.3
1931	5	0	0	0	496	99.0	93	100
1932	1	0	0	0	488	99.8	110	100
1933	1	0	2	0	504	99.4	115	100
1934	0	0	3	0	477	99.4	145	100
1935	2	0	1	0	522	99.4	165	100
1936	4	0	0	0	518	99.2	192	100
1937	8	0	2	0	530	98.1	174	98.9
1938	10	3	0	0	445	97.8	131	97.8
1939	10	3	1	0	472	97.7	81	97.6
1940	16	1	1	0	460	96.4	49	98.0
1941	17	0	1	0	474	96.3	46	100
1942	15	1	0	0	473	96.9	38	97.4
1943	19	1	0	0	378	95.0	46	97.9
1944	26	1	1	0	374	92.3	34	97.1
1945	22	2	0	0	328	93.7	37	94.9
1946	30	6	0	0	348	92.1	35	85.4
1947	40	3	1	0	328	88.9	55	94.8
1948	58	7	0	0	308	84.2	67	90.5
1949	52	6	1	0	303	85.1	95	94.1
1950	61	5	0	0	322	84.1	76	93.8
1951	78	7	1	0	312	79.8	68	90.7
1952	108	14	0	0	216	66.7	87	86.1
1953	144	14	0	0	200	58.1	88	86.3
1954	157	32	0	0	80	33.8	78	70.9
1955	138	33	0	0	98	41.5	62	65.9
1956	134	35	0	0	139	50.9	56	61.5
1957	99	31	1	0	203	67.0	84	73.0
1958	91	23	2	0	164	63.8	88	79.3
1959	80	24	1	0	96	79.3	75	75.8
1960	77	20	0	0	74	49.0	90	81.8
1961	72	32	1	0	78	51.7	77	70.0
1962	67	25	1	0	60	46.9	101	80.2
1963	76	31	0	0	54	41.5	76	63.5
1964	80	34	0	0	58	42.0	41	54.7
1965	88	46	0	0	50	36.2	34	42.5
1966	115	58	0	0	24	17.3	11	15.9
1967	136	84	2	0	7	4.8	6	6.7
1968	170	72	1	0	9	5.0	1	1.4
1969	171	86	2	0	4	2.3	0	0
1970	227	103	3	0	1	0.4	3	2.8

Since 1970 nearly all production in the US and UK has been in colour.

year to year until in 1970 there was but a single black and white production. Elsewhere, the changeover took a little longer, delayed perhaps by a feeling that colour was inappropriate to naturalistic, 'social realism' films or to subjects of serious concern. In Britain colour became predominant in 1965, when 46 colour films were produced against only 34 monochrome. Only three years later monochrome production was down to a single picture, with 72 colour releases. 1969 was the first year in which British production was 100% colour. France, long the bastion of grainy monochrome effects, had succumbed by 1967, when only four out of 120 films were shot in black and white. Japan had reached a 50–50 stage by 1965, but within three years the proportion of monochrome features had dropped to 25%. Italy maintained some black-and-white feature productions up to 1968, when seven out of 153 films were shot in monochrome, but very few after that.

In the Far East the changeover was generally slower. Out of the total of 763 films produced in India in 1982, 43 were black and white. All Burmese films were black and white before 1983, the year a colour laboratory was established in Rangoon processing Fuji Colour.

The first feature film shot in black and white to be converted to full colour was *Yankee Doodle Dandy* (US 42), biopic of George M. Cohan starring James Cagney. The special prints with their computer-applied colour were released by MGM on 4 July 1985. 'Colorisation', as it is known, has become a controversial issue in the industry, with many directors and stars vehemently opposed to the practice on the grounds that it diminishes the visual quality of films never intended to be in colour. Nevertheless, it appears to be popular with a large section of the public—the colour version of *Miracle on 34th Street* (US 47) achieved the highest ratings of any film on US television in 1985. Color Systems Technology, the company which developed the system, claims that it goes to great trouble to preserve the integrity of the films given their treatment, even maintaining a research department whose sole function is to ascertain the true colour of props, buildings, vegetation, costumes and such physical attributes as hair and eyes.

Sound

The first presentation of sound films before a paying audience was made by Oskar Messter at 21 Unter den Linden, Berlin, in September 1896. The sound system employed synchronised Berliner discs, but there is no record of the titles of the films or the performers in them. **The first artistes known to have performed in a sound film** were Giampetro and Fritzi Massary, who appeared in a scene from an operetta filmed by Max Skladanowski, probably before the end of 1896.

The earliest-known talking films were presented by Clément Maurice of the Gaumont Co. at the Phono-Cinéma-Théâtre of the Paris Exposition on 8 June 1900. They included: Sarah Bernhardt and Pierre Magnier in the duel scene from *Hamlet*, playing Hamlet and Laertes respectively; Coquelin and Mesdames Esquilar and Kervich in Molière's *Les Précieuses Ridicules*; Felicia

Mallet, Mme Reichenberg and Gabrielle Réjane of the Comédie Française in scenes from *Madame Sans-Gêne* and *Ma Cousine*. In addition there were synchronised opera films and ballet films.

The earliest-known talking film with original dialogue was *Lolotte* (Fr 1900), a comedy written and directed by Henri Joly and premièred at the Théâtre de la Grande Roue at the Paris Exposition. The scene takes place in a hotel bedroom and is played by three characters, a newly married couple and the patron of the hotel, the latter performed by Joly himself. The dialogue script survives.

The first sound films produced in Britain were a series of song subjects made by Walter Gibbons in the autumn of 1900 under the name of Phono-Bio-Tableaux Films. They included Vesta Tilley singing *The Midnight Son*, *Algy the Piccadilly Johnny* and *Louisiana Lou*, and G. H. Chirgwin giving a soulful rendering of *The Blind Boy*. There was also an actuality with sound effects titled *Turn Out the Fire Brigade*. **The earliest British talking film** was Hepworth's Vivaphone version of *Cinderella* (GB 13) with Gertie Potter.

The first sound-on-film process was patented by French-born Eugene Lauste of Stockwell, London, on 11 August 1906. It was not until 1910, however, that Lauste succeeded in recording and reproducing speech on film, employing an electromagnetic recorder and string galvanometer. He used a French gramophone record, selected at random, for the initial trial, and by coincidence the first words to be heard in the playback were 'J'entends très bien maintenant' ('I hear very well now'). A colleague in the film business, L. G. Egrot, recalled visiting Lauste at his home in Benedict Road about this time: 'He had already started building his camera to take pictures and sound together, the front part of the camera allowing to test the different systems he was experimenting with for sound recording . . . Very often on a Sunday, a bandmaster friend of his, Mr Norris, would come along with his band and play in the garden of the house where, in 1911, Mr Lauste had had a wooden building erected as an experimenting studio. The machine was taken out, with all leads, some pictures would be made and some sound recorded.'

Lauste completed his sound-on-film projector and reproducing apparatus in 1913, and was about to embark on the commercial exploitation of the process when war broke out. In 1916 he went to the USA with the idea of obtaining financial backing, but the entry of America into the war the following year put an end to his hopes.

The first sound-on-film productions to be presented in public were shown at the Alhambra Kino in Berlin on 17 September 1922 before an invited audience of a thousand people. The films were made by the Tri-Ergon process developed by Joseph Engl, Joseph Massolle and Hans Vogt and included **the first sound-on-film dramatic talkie.** Titled *Der Brandstifter/The Arsonist* (Ger 22), and adapted from Von Heyermann's play of the same name, it had a cast of three with Erwin Baron playing seven of the nine parts. The other films were mainly orchestral with vocal accompaniment. Press reaction was mixed, criticism being made not so much against the level of technical achievement, but at the notion of talking films, which it was said would destroy the essential art of the motion picture—mime—and detract from the cinema's international appeal.

The first American sound-on-film motion picture was *Lincoln's Gettysburg Address* (US 22), a monologue delivered by Ellery Paine, made by Polish-born Prof. Joseph Tykocinski-Tykociner, research professor of electrical engineering at the University of Illinois, and presented in the Physics Building on 9 June 1922. The film was not released commercially.

When primitive sound-on-disc 'talkies' were introduced during the Edwardian era, volume was sometimes considered rather more important than quality. William Haggar, proprietor of a cinema in Aberdare, Wales, advertised that his films 'can be heard two miles away'.

The first presentation of sound-on-film productions before a paying audience took place at the Rialto Theater, New York, on 15 April 1923, when Lee De Forest showed a number of singing and musical shorts made by the Phonofilm process. The sound films formed a supporting programme to the main (silent) feature, *Bella Donna* (US 23) with Pola Negri. During the following 12 months, 34 cinemas in the eastern United States were wired for Phonofilm sound. The films made at the De Forest Studios between 1923 and 1927 included monologue numbers by Eddie Cantor, George Jessel and Chic Sale; dialogues between Gloria Swanson and Thomas Meighan and between Weber and Fields; Folkina's Swan Dance; playlets with Raymond Hitchcock; and orchestral subjects featuring Ben Bernie, Paul Sprecht and Otto Wolf Kahn.

The year 1924 saw three notable sound-on-film 'firsts' from Phonofilm. President Coolidge was filmed delivering a campaign speech on the White House lawn, **the first time that a President of the USA had spoken from the screen**; **the first Technicolor film with a soundtrack** was made, the subject being Balieff's Chauve Souris danced in the open air; and **the first dramatic talkie film to be released commercially**, *Love's Old Sweet Song*, a two-reeler directed by J. Searle Dawley with Mary Mayo and Una Merkel in the leading roles. Although the first to exploit sound-on-film commercially, De Forest failed to establish talking pictures as a major entertainment medium and the Phonofilm patents were eventually taken over by William Fox together with those of the Tri-Ergon system.

The first public demonstration of sound-on-film in Britain took place at the Finsbury Park Cinema on 14 June 1923, when a programme of Phonofilm shorts was trade shown. The *Bioscope* reported: 'Several pictures were projected, including a vocalist rendering a song from *Carmen*, a dancer imitative of Pavlova with dying swan musical effects, and others. The synchronisation was as near perfect as possible, but the articulation sounded to me somewhat throaty.'

One of the effects of the introduction of talkies in the USA was to kill off the theatrical stock companies. In 1929 there were still two hundred companies playing stock; by 1939 there were five.

The first sound-on-film production shown before a paying audience in Britain was the Technicolor dance subject *Chauve Souris* (US 24), which was shown with musical soundtrack at the Tivoli in London in the summer of 1925. **The first talking film seen by a paying audience** introduced a programme of Phonofilm singing and orchestral shorts premièred at the Empire, Plumstead on 4 October 1926 and consisted of Sidney L. (later Lord) Bernstein explaining how Phonofilm worked. **The first sound-on-film talkie produced in Britain** was De Forest Phonofilms' *The Gentleman* (GB 25), a comedy short directed and scripted by William J. Elliott. The following year four short dramas were produced at the Clapham Studios by the De Forest Phonofilm Co. of Great Britain and in 1927 there were films of Edith Sitwell reading her own poems and Sybil Thorndike in a scene from Shaw's *Saint Joan*.

The first full-length feature film with sound (in part) was D. W. Griffith's *Dream Street* (US 21), a United Artists release. Described by one cinema historian as 'a dreadful hodgepodge of allegory and symbolism', it was a total failure when originally presented as an all-silent picture at the Central Theater, New York, in April 1921. After it had closed, Griffith was persuaded by Wendell McMahill of Kellum Talking Pictures to add a sound sequence. On 27 April the star, Ralph Graves, was brought to the Kellum Studios on West 40th Street to record a love song on synchronised disc, and this was included when the film reopened at the Town Hall Civic Centre on 1 May. A fortnight later a second sound sequence was added, consisting of the shouts and whoops of Porter Strong shooting craps together with other background noises, and this version opened in Brooklyn on 29 May 1921.

The only other feature movie with vocal sound prior to *The Jazz Singer* (see below) was José A. Ferreya's *La Muchacha del Arrabal* (Arg 22), starring Lidia Lis.

The first talking feature film (in part) was Warner Bros' Vitaphone (sound-on-disc) production *The Jazz Singer* (US 27), directed by Alan Crosland and starring Al Jolson, which opened at the Warner Theatre on Broadway on 6 October 1927. The initial, historic talking sequence takes place in Coffee Dan's, where Jack Robin (Al Jolson) has been singing *Dirty Hands, Dirty Face*. Amid the applause, Jolson holds up his hands and urges: 'Wait a minute. Wait a minute. You ain't heard nothin' yet! Wait a minute, I tell you. You ain't heard nothin'. You wanna hear "Toot-toot-tootsie"? All right. Hold on.' Turning to the band, Jolson says: 'Now listen: you play "Toot-toot-tootsie". Three choruses, you understand, and in the third chorus I whistle. Now give it to 'em hard and heavy. Go right ahead...'

The second and only other talking sequence was longer and involved a conversation between Jack Robin and his mother (Eugenie Besserer). In view of the many conflicting claims concerning the amount of dialogue in *The Jazz Singer*, it is worth recording that exactly 354 words are spoken in the two talking sequences, 60 in the first and 294 in the second. Jolson speaks 340, Eugenie Besserer 13 and Warner Oland (as the father) one—'Stop!' The dialogue sequences were unscripted, because Warner Bros had only intended to make a film with synchronised music and singing, not a talkie. Jolson, however, ad libbed—the famous line 'You ain't heard nothin' yet' was in fact a catchphrase he used in his stage performances—and studio head Sam Warner liked the snatches of talk enough to keep them in.

> When the talkies came to the island of Malta in 1930 with the Valetta première of *Broadway Melody* (US 29), the manager of the Royal Opera House asked all his patrons to wear tennis shoes to lessen the noise of late arrivals. Such precautions were not sufficient to make the innovation the success it had been in other parts of the world. The sound-on-disc system got out of sync, so that the men talked in women's voices and vice versa. Come the halfway interval, the show had to be abandoned because a man was found dead in the stalls.

The first all-talking feature was Warner Bros' *Lights of New York* (US 28), which was premièred at the Strand Theater, New York, on 6 July 1928. Starring Helene Costello, the picture was so determinedly all-talking that the dialogue continued non-stop from opening credits to end title. Warner's billed it as '100% Talking!'; *Variety* commented '100% Crude'.

The first sound-on-film feature was Fox's *The Air Circus* (US 28), with Louise Dresser and David Rollins, which opened at New York's Gaiety on 1 September 1928. The dialogue sequence lasted 15 minutes. **The first all-talking sound-on-film feature** was Raoul Walsh and Irving Cummins' Fox western *In Old Arizona* (US 28), with Edmund Lowe and Warner Baxter, which was also **the first talkie shot outdoors.** It opened 26 December 1928 at the Criterion, Los Angeles.

The first British talking feature was Marshall Neilan's *Black Waters* (GB 29), a melodrama about a mad captain posing as a clergyman to murder people aboard a fogbound ship. Starring John Loder and Mary Brian, the picture was produced in the USA by Herbert Wilcox for British & Dominions Sono Art World Wide.

The first feature-length talkie made in Britain was Alfred Hitchcock's *Blackmail* (GB 29), produced by British Int. Pictures at Elstree with Anny Ondra and John Longden and premièred at the Regal, Marble Arch, on 21 June 1929. The first reel had incidental sound and music only, but the characters began to speak in the second as the plot unfolded. It was billed as '99% talking', a pardonable exaggeration. The posters also carried the slogan 'See and Hear It—Our Mother Tongue As It Should Be Spoken'—a sideswipe at the American-English that had dominated the screen hitherto.

Britain's first all-talking feature was *The Clue of the New Pin* (GB 29) adapted from the Edgar Wallace novel of the same name and produced by British Lion in association with British Photophone. The film was directed by

Arthur Maude, starred Donald Calthrop and Benita Hume, and was released on 16 December 1929. An undistinguished production, the film is chiefly memorable for the fact that a rising young stage performer called John Gielgud played a bit part in it.

The first dubbed film was Lee De Forest's Phonofilm production *Love's Old Sweet Song* (US 24). The film contains one exterior scene, in which Una Merkel is strolling down a street when she hears the title song being sung by Mary Mayo from indoors. Since the exterior footage had to be shot silent, the song was dubbed in afterwards.

Cantor Joseph Rosenblatt sang in the synagogue scenes of first feature talkie *The Jazz Singer* (US 27) while Swedish actor Warner Oland, playing Al Jolson's father, the cantor, lip-synched.

> When a restored version of Stanley Kubrick's *Spartacus* (US 60) was planned for release in 1991, the restorers were confronted with the problem of a scene in which the soundtrack had been destroyed. Not difficult to dub, but for the fact that the distinguished thespian speaking in the scene was the late great Sir Lawrence Olivier. Who could possible replicate such a distinctive voice? An audience was sought with Oliver's widow, Joan Plowright, to seek her advice. 'Anthony Hopkins,' she declared unhesitatingly, 'he used to mimic him to his face at cocktail parties.'

The first occasion on which another actor's voice was substituted for that of a member of the cast was in *The Patriot* (US 28). The performer concerned, Emil Jannings, threatened legal proceedings if the new soundtrack was not erased, and the dubbed voice was removed.

The first film released with a substitute voice was *The Wolf of Wall Street* (US 29), in which the heavily accented Hungarian actor Paul Lukas played a partner in a firm of stockbrokers. His dialogue was dubbed by Lawford Davidson. Happily Lukas's accent did not hinder the development of his career—he continued to play major roles in Hollywood pictures for another 40 years.

The first British film to be dubbed was Alfred Hitchcock's *Blackmail* (GB 29). The female lead, Czech actress Anny Ondra, spoke almost no English and her voice was dubbed by Joan Barry (later the mother of heiress Henrietta Tiarks). This was done by the novel method of having Miss Barry read Miss Ondra's lines into a microphone while the latter was performing.

> While a number of British and particularly Scottish films have been partly dubbed for American release, *Trainspotting* (GB 96) is believed to be the only one in one in which the dialogue was actually rewritten into American English. 'Rubbish' was changed into 'garbage' and 'O levels' into 'semester grades'. (Are US audiences really incapable of relating to any culture but their own?) Curiously the title was left unchanged—there are no anoraked trainspotters in America.

The first artificial sound effect used in a film was created by a small cylinder and piston mounted on a flat board, together with a 9-inch piece of copper tubing set in an upright position. By turning a crank and blowing into the tube, an unknown hero, who was probably unaware that he had just created the new profession of sound-effects man, was able to simulate the sound of a train in motion for the benefit of his employers, Warner Bros, and the verisimilitude of their first all-talking pro-

> Lauren Bacall sings in *To Have and Have Not* (US 44), or rather she is seen to sing, because her voice needed to be dubbed. The problem was that she had such a deep speaking voice, no female singer could be found who could match it convincingly. The solution lay in choosing a male singer and the voice heard emanating from Lauren Bacall's lips is actually that of Andy Williams.

duction *Lights of New York* (US 28). Following this first experiment, Warner Bros established its own library of prerecorded sound effects, starting with just five—the gurgle of water, the squeak of a new pair of shoes, a train whistle, an automobile horn and the crash of glass. Within three years it had grown to nearly one million feet of film.

Many of these effects were natural, while some had to be contrived. Talking to the *New York Times* in 1935, Universal's sound effects chief Jack Foley revealed some of the secrets of his trade. Fire sounds, for example, were simulated by crumpling thin paper in front of the microphone, while a smack in the jaw was conveyed by means

If you thought that was Lauren Bacall singing in To Have and To Have Not *(US 44), you're wrong. It was none other than Andy Williams!*

of one technician rolling up his sleeve and another hitting him on the soft flesh of the forearm. Foley's pride and joy was his Niagara Falls sound effect. The mighty rush of waters was captured on the soundtrack by playing a 3-inch hose against a big tin advertising signboard.

Natural sound effects, on the other hand, sometimes gave the producers of early talkies special difficulties. The crude microphones of the day tended to amplify sound to unnatural proportions, so that the tramping of shoes on gravel would register as a buffalo stampede. The solution in this instance was quite easy—rubber soles. Police sirens produced a deafening effect on the eardrums and had to be wrapped in blankets to attain a normal decibel level on the soundtrack.

The click of long fingernails on a nervous hand registered with unbecoming clarity and actresses like Nita Naldi who favoured the talon look were enjoined to pare their nails to delicate ovals. One of the most tricky problems was the rustling of a newspaper, which Paramount's Head of Sound Roy Pomeroy likened to the firing of a Gatling gun. After much experimentation, he cracked the problem by dampening the newspaper before use.

> If the crowd noises used in the scenes of gladiators fighting to the death in *Spartacus* (US 60) sound like the howls of a savage people baying for blood, it is because that is more or less what they were. The recording was made at a football game played between arch-rivals Notre Dame and Michigan State in October 1959. In Chaplin's *The Great Dictator* (US 40), however, the sound of the massed ranks of the politically faithful cheering their fanatical leader was created by nothing more sinister than grapenuts juddering on a tin tray over a vibrating machine.

The scream of the demon being exorcised from the child played by Linda Blair in *The Exorcist* (US 73) was a recording of the terrified squeals of pigs being driven to slaughter.

The noises made by the dinosaurs in *Jurassic Park* (US 93) were a combination of the screams of a dolphin, the hiss of a goose and the hoot of a mating tortoise.

The first film with stereophonic sound was the re-edited version of Abel Gance's *Napoleon Bonaparte* (Fr 27), which was presented with added dialogue and sound

In *Singin' in the Rain* (US 52) Jean Hagen plays a spoiled silent screen star whose voice is too déclassé for talkies. The producers secretly have her voice dubbed by well-spoken ingénue Debbie Reynolds. In reality Miss Reynolds' voice was not considered classy enough and so the voice heard on the soundtrack of the film-within-a-film is not hers at all. It was Jean Hagen's own, speaking in her normal voice.

effects at the Paramount Cinema, Paris, in 1935. The stereophonic process used had been patented by Gance and André Debrie three years earlier.

The first American productions with stereophonic sound were the Warner Bros' productions *Santa Fe Trail* (US 40) and *Four Wives* (US 40), presented in Vitasound. The first successful system of stereophonic musical accompaniment was Fantasound, developed by Walt Disney Studios in association with RCA and first employed for the soundtrack of Disney's feature-length cartoon *Fantasia* (US 41), with music by the Philadelphia Orchestra under the direction of Leopold Stokowski.

The first use of overlapping dialogue—The talking picture borrowed the stage convention, far removed from reality, whereby no more than one character speaks at once. Credit for introducing overlapping dialogue in the interests of naturalism is usually given to Orson Welles for *Citizen Kane* (US 41), but in fact the technique had been used a year earlier in Howard Hawks' wild and witty *His Girl Friday* (US 40), with Cary Grant and Rosalind Russell.

DOLBY SOUND

Dolby is a noise-reduction system designed to eliminate hiss from recorded sound—as its originator has expressed it, 'real high fidelity means reproducing the silence as accurately as the sound'. It was developed by American-born Ray Dolby in an old dressmaking factory in Fulham, where Dolby laboratories were established in May 1965 with four employees and a refusal of credit from the bank. The first practical application was by Decca for disc recording, the units being known as the S/N Stretcher because they were for stretching the signal-to-noise ratio. After Ray Dolby had heard some engineers at Pye referring to his equipment as 'a Dolby', he decided to change the name to his own. **The first film with Dolby sound** was Stanley Kubrick's *A Clockwork Orange* (GB 71). This

used Dolby noise reduction on all pre-mixes and masters, though the release prints had a conventional optical soundtrack. The first film with a Dolby encoded mono soundtrack was *Callan* (GB 74) and the first with a Dolby encoded stereo optical soundtrack was Ken Russell's *Lisztomania* (GB 75). At this point Dolby began to take off; less than ten years later there were 6000 cinemas worldwide equipped to take the new system. The thousandth film with a Dolby stereo soundtrack, *Heartbreak Ridge* (US 86), was released in 1986. Since 1977 all the films winning the Oscar for Best Achievement in Sound have been recorded on Dolby. There are now some 45,000 cinemas worldwide equipped with Dolby Sound and more than 8000 films have been recorded with Dolby soundtracks.

The first commercial play-off of a movie with digital sound took place at the Plitt Century Plaza Theater in Century City, California over a four-week period during February and March 1985. A specially recorded version of Disney's 1941 cartoon feature *Fantasia* (US 41) was used for the presentation, with the sound emanating from a digital audio playback unit synchronised with the projector. The process allows for the exact reproduction of sound. The first feature to be made in digital sound was Disney's *Dick Tracy* (US 90), released on 15 June 1990. Five Los Angeles cinemas, as well as the Embassy I and Loew's 84th Street Sixplex in Manhattan, were fitted with Optical Radiation's Cinema Digital Sound, a playback system providing six-track optical stereo from special 70mm release prints of the Warren Beatty movie. A specially developed film stock, Eastman Digital Sound Recording Film 2374, had been developed by Kodak to accommodate the newly designed optical soundtrack.

The first audio-described film for the blind was *Hear My Song* (GB 92), charming whimsy about a quest for the missing Irish tenor Josef Locke, which was adapted with special voiceover by the RNIB. The technique lies in the pauses—it is important that gaps in the dialogue should not be filled with non-stop description of what is happening on screen.

As early as 1901 there had been an attempt to produce silent films for the blind. In February of that year Dr Dussaud of the Psychological Institute in Paris demonstrated a machine which passed a band of images in relief under the fingers of the blind 'viewer'. Each image being in a position minutely advanced from the previous one, as on an ordinary cinematograph film, the user was supposed to obtain a tactile illusion of movement.

The last wholly silent film (i.e. without a soundtrack) **produced in America** for general distribution was George Melford's *The Poor Millionaire* (US 30), with Richard Talmadge (who played both the hero and the villain) and Constance Howard. It was released by Biltmore Pictures on 7 April 1930, just 30 months and a day after the presentation of the first talkie feature. Only four other silents had been issued in 1930, all of them low budget westerns. The following year there were no silents but four films with synchronised music and sound effects only, including Chaplin's *City Lights* and F.W. Murnau's *Tabu*. Silent production in America, however, was not finished for good. In 1950 Georges Sadoul reported that silent features in colour were being produced in San Francisco for the Chinese population of the United States.

The last British silent feature was Argyle Art Pictures' *Paradise Alley* (GB 31), starring John Argyle and Margaret Delane, the story of a miner who takes the blame when his brother shoots a man during a robbery. It was released in March 1931.

European production had made virtually a complete changeover to sound by the end of 1931. Elsewhere, the last silent feature from Soviet Russia—Alexander Medvekin's *Schastye/Happiness*—was released in 1935 and the last seven Indian silents were issued the same year. Japan took longer to make the change. In 1937, 209 out of 524 movies were without dialogue—50 with sound effects and music, 159 silent. The following year saw the virtual demise of the silent, with 16 'sound effects only' films and 15 wholly silent. As late as 1952 in Burma, where only two of the 22 production companies were equipped to make sound films, production totalled 40 silents and six talkies.

The last silent feature films for commercial distribution were produced in Thailand at the end of the 1960s. Although talkies had been produced in the 1930s, World War II totally disrupted both the Thai economy and its film industry and subsequently all films were shot silent on 16mm stock until 1965. Dialogue was supplied by actors and actresses 'live dubbing' in cinemas from a cubicle next to the projection booth. After 1965 the popularity of Indian-style musicals stimulated producers to shoot sound song-and-dance sequences on 35mm stock for interpolation with otherwise silent 16mm footage. According to the Thai Motion Picture Producers' Association 'by 1970 all Thai films were shot on 35mm with sound'.

Languages

Hollywood's foreign-language output was confined principally to the early talkie period, the largest proportion being in Spanish for the Latin American market. Beginning with a dubbed version of RKO's *Rio Rita* (US 29), a total of 96 Spanish-language movies were produced in the USA during the ensuing six years, the majority by Fox, and another 17 were made by Paramount at their Joinville studios in France 1930–33. **The first foreign language feature made in America with live dialogue** was *Sombras de Gloria/Blaze of Glory* (US 30). It was a Sono Art-World production.

During the period 1930–35 a total of 63 French language pictures were produced by MGM, First National, Paramount, Warner Bros, RKO, Universal, Fox, Columbia and Twentieth Century. The Paramount productions were made at Joinville, outside Paris, where they also produced in Spanish, German, Italian, Swedish, Portuguese, Romanian, Polish, Czech and Dutch.

Chinese-language production in the US began with Esther Eng's *Golden Gate Girl* (US 41), produced by the Hong Kong Grandview Film Co after they had relocated to San Francisco just prior to the invasion of Hong Kong by the Japanese. A total of 18 Cantonese films were made by Grandview before the end of the war, when the company returned to Hong Kong.

The first foreign-language talkie to be subtitled in English was *Two Hearts in Waltz Time* (Ger 29). The titles were written by Herman G. Weinberg (an American), who subtitled a record number of over four hundred films during the ensuing 40 years.

> Bingham Ray of October Films, US distributors of foreign-language pictures: 'America doesn't like to read. And it certainly doesn't like movies it has to read.'

The first talkie produced in different language versions was British International Pictures' tri-lingual *Atlantic* (GB 29), which was released with separate English, French and German soundtracks. Besides its overseas release, the German version was shown at the Alhambra, Leicester Square, to cater for the large German population living in London prior to World War II.

Multilingual films in which foreign characters speak in their own language were comparatively rare before *The Longest Day* (US 62) broke with former Hollywood practice by having the Germans speaking German and the French speaking French. There had been occasional examples, however, from the earliest days of sound, starting with G. W. Pabst's *Westfront 1918* (Ger 30), with dialogue in French and German. Others included Pabst's *Kameradschaft* (Ger 31), about a mining disaster involving French and German miners; Luis Trenker's *Der verlorene Sohn/The Prodigal Son* (Ger 34), in German and English; Jean Renoir's *La Grande Illusion* (Fr 37), in French, English and German; Nyrki Tapiovaara's *Stolen Death* (Fin 38), a thriller in Finnish, Swedish and Russian; *Carl Peters* (Ger 41), in German and English; *Die Letzte Chance* (Swz 34), in German and French; Guy Hamilton's *The Colditz Story* (GB 54), in English and German; *La Chatte* (Fr 58), in French and German; and Jean-Luc Godard's quadrilingual *Le Mépris/Contempt* (Fr/It 63), in which Michel Piccoli spoke Italian, Brigitte Bardot spoke French, Jack Palance spoke American and Fritz Lang spoke German, the need for subtitles being effectively reduced by Giogia Moll's role as the interpreter.

A more recent example is Jim Jarmusch's *Night on Earth* (US 91), an episode film recounting five different stories about cabbies. Each has dialogue in the language of its setting: American for Los Angeles and New York, Finnish for Helsinki, French for Paris, Italian for Rome.

Even silent films could be multilingual. Rex Ingram stated in *Motion Picture Directing* (New York, 1922) that when making films with foreign settings, he made his principals speak the language of the country. Explaining that 'it helps them materially in keeping to the required atmosphere,' he admitted ruefully 'few of them like to go to this trouble . . .'

The most multilingual film producing country is India, which has produced films in the following 61 languages since 1931: Angami Naga, Arabic, Assamese, Avadhi, Badaga, Bengali, Bhojpuri, Bodo, Brijbhasha,

Bundeli, Burmese, Chattisgadhi, Coorgi, Dogri, English, Farsi, French, Garhwali, German, Gorkhili, Gujarati, Gujjar, Haryanavi, Hindi, Kannada, Karbi, Kashmiri, Khasi, Kodava, Kok Borok, Konkani, Kumaoni, Lambani, Magadhi, Maithili, Malay, Malayalam, Malvi, Manipuri,

> In the days when any Continental film was likely to cause the American censors to reach for their scissors, the subtitles did not always transcribe what was being spoken. The scene in which a girl and her lover indulge in physical intimacy in Jacques Deval's *Club de Femmes* (Fr 36) had an English subtitle conveying the idea that the couple were married. For anyone able to follow the French dialogue, it was abundantly clear that they were not. The reverse could also happen. The dialogue in *Her Jungle Love* (US 38) emphasised that the romantic liaison between Ray Milland and Dorothy Lamour during their two weeks alone on a desert island was entirely platonic—as Miss Lamour was supposedly of Asian blood, it had to be to satisfy American susceptibilities. In the dubbed version of the film released in France the steamy French dialogue left no doubt that their relationship was anything but.

Marathi, Marwari, Nagamese, Nagpuri, Nepalese, Nimadi, Oriya, Punjabi, Pushtu, Rajasthani, Sadri, Sambalpuri, Sanskrit, Sindi, Sinhalese, Swahili, Tamil, Telegu, Thai, Tibetan, Tulu, Urdu.

In 1999 Hindi was the most prolific language for Indian films with 166 features, followed by Tamil (153) and Telegu (132). Six were in English.

The only film made in Latin was Derek Jarman's *Sebastiane* (GB 76), a homophile interpretation of the legend of St Sebastian. The translator, Jack Welch, used ingenious shifts to put Roman barrack-room language of the third century AD into comprehensible Latin, but in one instance had to resort to a Greek word, rendering the epithet *Motherfucker* as *Oedipus*. *Sebastiane* enjoys the unique distinction of being the only English film ever to have been released in Britain with English subtitles.

The only feature film made in Esperanto was *Incubus* (US 65), whose star William Shatner is familiar to TV viewers as Capt Kirk of *Star Trek*. The avowed purpose of using Esperanto dialogue was to give the movie an air of the supernatural. It is one of the few American films to have been released with English subtitles.

The first talking film made in dialect was *Mieke* (Bel 30), a comedy made in Antwerp by Felix Bell (Gaston Schoukens) in the Anversois patois.

The first feature film in Irish was Bob Quinn's *Poitín/Poteen* (Eire 78), with Cyril Cusack as a poteen maker attempting to evade the attentions of the Garda in Connemara.

The first feature film in Welsh to go on general release was *Coming Up Roses* (GB 86), which opened at the Cannon, Cardiff, on 6 March 1987 and then crossed the borders of the principality to charm the English (in a subtitled version) with its engaging story of a fleapit cinema in the valleys which staves off demolition when the pro-

jectionist (Dafydd Hywell) and usherette (Iola Gregory) turn it into a mushroom farm.

The first feature film in Gaelic was Barney Platts-Mills' *Hero* (GB 82), a medieval fable about sorcery and magic in a remote corner of the Scottish highlands.

The first feature film in Breton was Gerard Guerin's *Lo Pais* (Fr 73), starring Olivier Bousquet and Nada Stangcar, about a young man trying to make his way to Paris and finally deciding to go home to help his own people. It was premièred at the Cannes Film Festival in 1973.

The first full-length feature film made in pidgin English was *Wokabout Bilong Tonten* (Aus 73), filmed in New Guinea with Anton Sil and Taruk Wabei in the lead roles.

The first feature film in a Native American language was *Windwalker* (US 80), starring Trevor Howard, which was made entirely in the Cheyenne and Crow languages.

The first feature film in Sanskrit (an ancient Indian language) was *Sankaracharya* (Ind 82).

The first feature film in Frysian, a language spoken in part of North Holland, was *De Droom* (Neth 85).

The first feature film in Okinawan, the language of Okinawa in the Ryuku Is, was *Paradise View* (Jap 85).

The first feature film in Iban, the language of Sarawak, was *Bejalai* (Malaysia 87).

The first feature film in Lapp was Nils Gaup's *Ofelas* (Nor 87), starring Mikkel Gaup, Ailu Gaup and Sara Marit Gaup. A tale of Lapps resisting Tchude marauders in the Arctic North 800 years ago, it was filmed in temperatures of up to 40° below zero.

The first feature film in Aymara, Amerindian language of Bolivia, was Jorge Sanjinés' *Ukamau* (Bol 66).

The first feature film in Quechua, Amerindian language of Bolivia, was Jorge Sanjinés' *Yawar mallku/Blood of the Condor* (Bol 69).

The first feature film in Nahuatl, the ancient language of the Aztecs no longer spoken, was *In Necuepaliztli in Aztlan* (Mex 90).

The first feature film in Papiamentu, the language of Curaçao (Dutch West Indies), was Felix de Rooy's *Ava & Gabriel, Un Historia di Amor* (Curaçao 90), starring Nashaira Desbarida and Cliff San-A-Jong.

The first feature film in the Gypsy language Romanes was Emir Kusturica's *Time of the Gypsies* (Yug 90), with Davor Dujmovic as an awkward young man growing up in a squalid Gypsy ghetto outside Skopje and his survival in the criminal underworld of Milan.

The first feature film in Faroese was *Atlantic Rhapsody* (Faroes 89).

The first feature film in Kurdish was *Klamek Ji Bo Beko/A Song for Beko* (Ger 92), directed by and starring Kurdish actor-poet exile Nizamettin Aric.

The first feature film in Mongolian was *Son of Mongolia* (USSR 36), a Lenfilm production with players from the State Theatre of Ulan-Bator.

The first feature film in Latgalian, the dialect of East Latvia, was *Cilveca berns/The Child of Man* (Latvia 91).

The first feature film in Berber to be released was Belkacem Hadjadj's *Once Upon a Time* (Algeria 95). Previously Berber films had been banned by the Algerian authorities, though Mouloud Mammeri had made *The Forgotten Hillside* in Berber in 1992.

The first feature film in Tlingit (Alaskan Indian) was Alaskan Nomad Co's *Kusah Hakwaan* (US 99).

The first feature film in Inuit (Eskimo) was Jacob Gronlykke's *Lysets Hjerte/Heart of Light* (Greenland/Den/Nor/Swe 99), which was also the first feature shot entirely in Greenland.

Wide Screen

The first wide-screen process used for a feature film was Panoramico Alberini, devised by Filoteo Alberini in 1914, which was employed by Enrico Guazzoni for a sequence of *Il Sacco di Roma* (It 23).

The first wide-screen system to employ the use of an anamorphic lens—a lens that squeezes a wide image on to standard gauge film as in Cinemascope (see below)—was Henri Chrétien's Hypergonar, used by Claude Autant-Lara in making *Construire un feu* (Fr 27).

The first feature film in wide screen throughout was *Fox Movietone Follies* (US 29), premièred in the 70mm Fox Grandeur process on a 35 x 17½ft screen at the Gaiety, New York, on 17 September 1929.

The first wide-screen system to incorporate both wide gauge film and the anamorphic lens was Todd-AO, which was originally employed on *Oklahoma!* (US 55)

CINEMASCOPE
This was developed by the French inventor Henri Chrétien from his original anamorphic Hypergonar system of 1927. Fox bought the patent rights in 1952 and **the first Cinemascope feature film**, *The Robe* (US 53), was premièred at Grauman's Chinese Theater in Hollywood on 24 September 1953. **Britain's first Cinemascope production** was also her first wide-screen feature: MGM's *Knights of the Round Table* (GB 54), with Robert Taylor and Ava Gardner. Cinemascope was an immediate success, so much so that by the end of 1955 over 33,000 cinemas throughout the world were equipped to show films shot in the process. About half of these were in the US and Canada.

> '**A** wide screen just makes a bad film twice as bad.'—Sam Goldwyn

The peak year for wide screen Hollywood releases was 1957 with 102 or 32% of the total. Of these, 64 were in Cinemascope, 17 in Regalscope, 16 in VistaVision, 4 in Technirama and one in SuperScope. Wide screen achieved its highest proportion of all releases as early as 1955, with 38%. Out of the total of 96 wide-screen films, 72 were in Cinemascope.

CINERAMA
This was developed by self-taught inventor Frederick Waller of Huntington, New York, who had originated the idea as early as 1939 for an oil exhibit at the New York's Fair. His intention had been to project moving pictures all over the interior surface of the oil exhibit building, but technical difficulties persuaded him to compromise with a half-dome, using 11 16mm projectors to cover the vast area of screen. After the war he resumed work on the process, reducing the number of projectors to three and adopting a wide-screen ratio of almost 3:1. **The first production in the perfected process** was *This is Cinerama* (US 52), which opened in New York on 30 September 1952 and ran for 122 weeks. **The first full-length dramatic feature in Cinerama** was MGM's *The Wonderful World of the Brothers Grimm* (US 62). Only three Cinerama Cinemas now retain the classic three-panelled curved screen format, projecting the film from three separate projectors: in Seattle, Ohio and England.

The widest wide-screen system ever was Raoul Grimoin-Sanson's Cinéorama, presented at the Paris Exposition of 1900. Ten synchronised projectors threw a 360° image on to a screen 330ft in circumference. The audience sat on the roof of the projection booth, which was designed to simulate the basket of a giant balloon. The hand-coloured film took the audience on an aerial voyage of discovery, looking down on the great capitals of Europe. Unfortunately, the show had to be terminated after three performances, since the heat of the ten projectors constituted a fire risk. The concept of 'cinema-in-the-round' was not revived until Walt Disney introduced Circarama at the Brussels World Fair in 1958, though this time on a screen of a more modest circumference.

Smellies

The first film made as a 'smellie' was the feature-length *Mein Traum/My Dream* (Swz 40), starring Paul Hubschmid and Gerda Foster, which was premièred at the Swiss Pavilion of the New York World's Fair on 10 October 1940. Produced by Pro Film Zurich for Odorated Talking Pictures of Zurich, the Director of Smells was Hans E. Laube, who had developed a fragrancy process which he claimed could reproduce over 4000 different odours. Those smelt in the 70-minute film included flowers, forest, tea, honey, smoked meat, encaustique, petrol, tar, medicaments, etc.

Whatever sensation the film may have created in its

native Switzerland, most of the rest of the world had more pressing matters on its mind over the next five years and the small peaceful nation so often traduced for having only the cuckoo clock as its contribution to western civilisation failed to win international recognition for this one. There were no further smellies until 1959, when a wide-screen travelogue about China called *Behind the Great Wall* (US 59), filmed in Totalscope, DeLuxe Color, stereophonic sound and the new wonder of Aromarama, opened in New York, accompanied by a range of 72 smells that included incense, woodsmoke, burning pitch, oranges, spices and a barnyard of geese. Unlike most novelty films, *Behind the Great Wall* had the smell of success even without the gimmicks. It won two awards when it was shown at the Brussels Film Exposition unaccompanied by Aromarama.

Mainstream Hollywood scented money and Michael Todd Jr released his 70mm Technicolor feature *Scent of Mystery* (US 60) in the miracle of Smell-O-Vision. The scents used—ocean ozone, pipe tobacco, garlic, oil paint, wine, wood shavings, boot polish, etc.—were piped to each individual cinema seat on cue from the 'smell-track' of the film.

Away from the mainstream, a less sophisticated technique was used to waft the scents of Odorama to spectators of the 'sickie smellie' *Polyester* (US 82), which starred the outsize transvestite Divine playing an all-American housewife whose life stinks. Each member of the

The Todd AO widescreen system had a 128° field of vision and was claimed to eliminate all viewing distortions. The first production using the technique was South Pacific *(US 58), with Mitzi Gaynor as Navy nurse Nellie Forbush.* (Kobal Collection)

audience was given a card numbered from one to ten. When a number was flashed on screen, the spectator scratched the card with a coin, releasing a revolting odour appropriate to whatever disgusting activity was taking place before his eyes.

Three Dimensional Films

The first presentation of 3-D films before a paying audience took place at the Astor Theater, New York, on 10 June 1915. The programme consisted of three one-reelers, the first of rural scenes in the USA, the second a selection of scenes from Famous Players' *Jim, the Penman* (US 15), with John Mason and Maria Doro, and the third a travelogue of Niagara Falls. The anaglyphic process used, developed by Edwin S. Porter and W. E. Waddell, involved the use of red and green spectacles to create a single image from twin motion-picture images photographed 2½ inches apart. The experiment was not a success, for much the same reason that 3-D failed 40 years later. Lynde Denig wrote in *Moving Picture World*: 'Images shimmered like reflections on a lake and in its present form the method couldn't be commercial because it detracts from the plot.'

The first 3-D feature film was Nat Deverich's 5-reel melodrama *Power of Love* (US 22), starring Terry O'Neil and Barbara Bedford, premièred at the Ambassador Hotel Theater, Los Angeles, on 27 September 1922. Produced by Perfect Pictures in an anaglyphic process developed by Harry K. Fairall, it related the adventures of a young sea captain in California in the 1840s. The only other

American feature in 3-D prior to *Bwana Devil* (US 52) was R. William Neill's *Mars* aka *Radio Mania* (US 22), with Grant Mitchell as an inventor who succeeds in making contact with Mars via television. It was produced in Laurens Hammond's Teleview process.

The first feature-length talkie in 3-D was Sante Bonaldo's *Nozze vagabonde* (It 36), starring Leda Gloria and Ermes Zacconi, which was produced by the Società Italiana Stereocinematografica at the Cines-Caesar studios. The 3-D cameraman was Anchise Brizzi.

> Alfred Hitchcock on the shortlived fad for 3-D in the early '50s: 'A nine-days' wonder—and I came in on the ninth day.'

The first feature-length talkie in colour and 3-D was Alexander Andreyevsky's Soyuzdetfilm production *Robinson Crusoe* (USSR 47), starring Pavel Kadochnikov as Crusoe and Y. Lyubimov as Friday. The process used, Stereokino, was the first to successfully dispense with anaglyphic spectacles. Developed by S. P. Ivanov, it employed what were known as 'radial raster stereo-screens'—a corrugated metal screen with 'raster' grooves designed to reflect the twin images separately to the left and right eye. The most difficult technical problem encountered during the production of *Robinson Crusoe* was persuading a wild cat to walk along a thin branch towards the camera. After five nights occupied with this one scene, the cameraman succeeded in getting a satisfactory shot. The effect, according to accounts, was riveting, the animal seeming to walk over the heads of the audience and disappear at the far end of the cinema.

The first 3-D feature with stereophonic sound was Warner Bros' *House of Wax* (US 53). When it was premièred at the Paramount Theater, New York, with 25 speakers, the Christian Science Monitor was moved to deplore the 'cacophony of sound hurtling relentlessly at one from all directions'. André de Toth, director of the movie, may have been able to hear the cacophony, but was unable to see the 3-D effect, as he only had one eye.

3-D OUTPUT
During the 3-D boom that began with the low-budget *Bwana Devil* (US 52), over 5000 cinemas in the USA were equipped to show 3-D movies, but the fad was short-lived. 3-D production figures were: 1952—1; 1953—27; 1954—16; 1955—1. In addition there were 3-D movies produced in Japan, Britain, Mexico, Germany and Hong Kong, but many of these (as well as some of the US productions) were released flat.

Sporadic production resumed in 1960 with the first Cinemascope 3-D movie *September Storm* (US 60), since when there have been about 60 further three-dimensional films.

The first dramatic film in 3-D IMAX technology was Sony's *Wings of Courage* (US 95), starring Val Kilmer, Tom Hulce and Elizabeth McGovern. The $15m movie had a maximum universe of the 120 IMAX cinemas worldwide.

HOLOGRAPHY
The first successful demonstration of holographic film was given by Professor Victor Komar on 7 October 1976 at the Cinema and Photo Research Institute in Moscow. It was the first true three-dimensional system in that individual members of the audience saw a differently angled image according to their position in relation to the screen. Komar's method involved the deployment of laser beams to create a representation of objects in depth based on wave interference. No anaglyphic spectacles were required as in conventional 3-D systems. The first, experimental holographic film was shot in 70mm colour and showed a woman with a bunch of flowers held in front of her face advancing towards the audience. It lasted for 47 seconds. The maximum audience was eight, four sitting on one side of the screen and four on the other.

CHAPTER 9
Music

Cinema music is almost as old as cinema. Felicien Trewey's presentation of films at the Regent Street Polytechnic in February 1896, the first before a paying audience in Britain, had a piano accompaniment described in a contemporary newspaper report as 'a trifle meagre'. It was not long before presenters began to recognise the virtue of appropriate music, though whether the quartet of saxophones engaged by the Cinématographe Lumière when it opened in the Boulevard Saint-Denis, Paris, in March 1897 was able to produce something apposite for every item on the programme is not recorded. In America, Albert E. Smith of Vitagraph recalled that the first of their productions to be shown with musical accompaniment was a news film of the burial of the victims of the sinking of the USN *Maine*, premièred at a disused opera house on Lexington Avenue, New York, in March 1898 with an orchestra playing a funeral dirge. Similarly, Henry Hopwood recorded in his book *Living Pictures* (1899) that a news film of the Albion launch disaster, screened only 30 hours after the event, was accompanied by an orchestra playing *Rocked in the Cradle of the Deep*.

The resident cinema orchestra is recorded as early as 1901, when Britain's first picture house, Mohawk's Hall, in Islington, appointed the 16-piece Fonobian

This is one of the few surviving photographs of a cinema pianist accompanying a film. The year was 1913, the picture was Mabel's Dramatic Career. *(BFI)*

Orchestra under the direction of Mr W. Neale. This remained rare, though, until the advent of the super-cinemas after 1914, which generally employed large orchestras under competent, if not distinguished, conductors. At the smaller houses, a single pianist would do the job, sometimes far from competent, but occasionally brilliant—Shostakovich supported himself while writing his first symphony in 1924 by playing the piano in an 'old, draughty and smelly' backstreet cinema in Leningrad. (He lost the job a year later because he stopped playing during an American comedy to roar with laughter.) About the same time, less brilliant at the keyboard, but later to achieve celebrity status in another walk of life, was the pianist at the Market Street Cinema in Manchester. She was Violet Carson, the hairnetted Ena Sharples of television's *Coronation Street*.

Picture houses that could not afford even the meagre wages of a pianist might fall back on the humble phonograph, which was adequate only if there was no intention that the music should relate to the mood of the film being shown. The manager of the first cinema in Leicester, opened in 1906, recalled that he installed a gramophone (later replaced by a mechanical organ) operated by the girl in the paybox, but that the choice of records bore no relation to the action on the screen, their only purpose being to drown the noise of the projector.

Inappropriate music could easily destroy the enjoyment of an otherwise meritorious picture, and in the USA the usual practice was for production companies to issue

'cue sheets' of suitable mood music with screen cues, an idea inaugurated by the Edison Co. in 1910 and copied by Vitagraph the following year. The consequence of leaving the choice of music to individual accompanists could be disastrous. Paul McCartney's father Jim McCartney recalled leading a small orchestra providing the music for *The Queen of Sheba* (US 21) when it was presented in Liverpool. For the chariot-race sequence they played *Thanks for the Buggy Ride* and for the tragic culmination of the picture, the death of the Queen, they chose *Horsey Keep Your Tail Up.*

The first purpose-built cinema organ (i.e. a unit organ) was designed by Robert Hope-Jones, a Liverpudlian who joined the Wurlitzer Co. of North Tonawanda, New York, in 1910 and killed himself four years later after his employers, exasperated at the expense incurred by his constant improvements in design, had locked him out of the factory on full salary. The first Wurlitzer cinema organs were installed in theatres in 1911.

The first cinema organ in Britain was built by Jardine & Co. to the specification of organist George Tootell in 1913 and installed at the Palace Cinema in Accrington, Lancashire.

Britain's first Mighty Wurlitzer was a Model D Unit Orchestra Organ, with six units on two manuals, installed at the Picture House, Walsall, Staffs, in January 1925. Although removed in 1955, the organ is still in use at the Congregational Church at Beer, South Devon.

The largest cinema organ in the world was the Wurlitzer installed at Radio City Music Hall, New York, in 1932. Still in use, it has 58 ranks of pipes controlled from either or both of the twin four-manual consoles.

The largest organ ever installed in a cinema in Britain was a Christie 4/30 (30 units on four manuals), installed at the Regal (now Odeon), Marble Arch and first played by Quentin Maclean in 1928. It incorporated a piano and a carillon, the latter feature being unique.

The first film music to be specially composed for the screen was commissioned from Hermann Krüger of Berlin, who composed a score for the nine films premiered by the Skladanowsky brothers at the Berlin Wintergarten on 1 November 1895. The first specially composed music to accompany narrative films was by Romolo Bacchini for the Cines productions *Malia dell'Oro* (It 06) and *Pierrot Innamorato* (It 06).

Italy was the first country whose major films were regularly supplied with an original score, a practice that did not become widespread elsewhere until the 1920s.

The majority of cinema organs which have survived are now in the hands of collectors or preservation societies. Some, though, have been put to practical use. One of the less probable last resting places of a cinema organ is the Chapel of St Francis in Wormwood Scrubs Prison, where the prisoners are uplifted by the strains of the Ealing ABC's Compton.

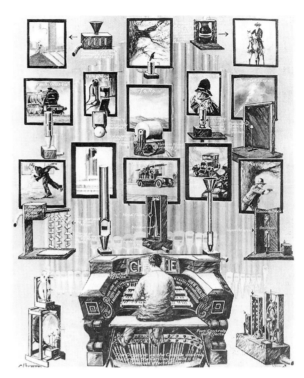

The mammoth 2500-pipe Christie organ at the Regal Theatre, Marble Arch, could create all the effects illustrated. It would also simulate most orchestral instruments as well as a 32-note carillon and a 25-note cathedral chime. But it was too late: the year was 1929 and already movies were being made with all the sound effects recorded on film. (ILN)

Notable early examples were *Lo Schiavo di Cartagine* (It 10), with music by Osvaldo Brunetti, *La Legenda della Passiflora* (It 11), for which Mazzuchi composed the music, and rival scores by Walter Graziani and Colombio Aron for the two simultaneous productions of *The Last Days of Pompeii* (It 13). Pizetti's *Fire Symphony* was written to accompany the sequence in *Cabiria* (It 13) in which the young maidens are sacrificed to the fire god Moloch. Mario Costa wrote a distinctive score for *Storia del Pierrot* (It 13) and Tosti lent prestige to *A marechiare ce sta 'na fenesta* (It 15).

The first composition for a French film was written by Camille Saint-Saëns for Film d'Art's inaugural production *L'Assassinat du Duc de Guise* (Fr 08). This was an arrangement for piano, two violins, viola, cello, bass violin and harmonium. Other pioneer film composers were: Mikhail Ippolitov-Ivanov, who composed scores for *Stenka Razin* (Rus 08), Russia's first dramatic film, and for Vasili Goncharov's *Song About the Merchant Kalashnikov* (Rus 08); R. N. McAnally, whose composition, originally thought to be for the Salvation Army's *Soldiers of the Cross* (Aus 00), is now believed to have been for their similarly titled religious feature *Heroes of the Cross* (Aus 09); the Brazilian Costa Junior, composer of a score for *Paz e Amor* (Bra 10), a two-reel 'talkie' with dialogue spoken by actors behind the screen; and V. Strizhevsky, who wrote the music for *Zaporozhskaya Syetch* (Rus 11).

America and Britain trailed behind the countries mentioned above. **The first original score to**

accompany an American production was composed by Manuel Klein for the All Star Feature Corporation's production of *The Jungle* (US 14), based on Upton Sinclair's 'muckraker' novel of the same title about exploitation of immigrant workers in the Chicago stockyards. Starring George Nash and Gail Kane, with Upton Sinclair playing himself, the picture opened in New York on 25 May 1914.

The first composer to write music for a British film was Sir Edward German, who was paid 50 gns by W. G. Barker for 16 bars of music to accompany the Coronation scene in *Henry VIII* (GB 11). It was reported at the time that Barker 'personally supervised rehearsals of special music which he thinks important in adding to the effectiveness of the subject', which suggests that there may have been a rather more complete score than the single theme by German.

The first film music composed for a sound film was commissioned by Erich Pommer, Gaumont mana-ger for Central and Eastern Europe, for *Les Heures* (Fr 13) aka *Die Stunden*, a 55-minute non-acted 'visual impression' of a day—morning, noon and night. The score was recorded on disc and synchronised with the film. The name of the composer is not known.

The first sound-on-film score was Hugo Riesenfeld's music for Fritz Lang's *Siegfried* (Ger 22), recorded on Phonofilm for its presentation at the Century Theater, New York, in 1925. This was a year earlier than the sound-on-disc Vitaphone accompaniment to Warner Bros' *Don Juan* (US 26), usually claimed as the first synchronised sound feature film.

The first film in which the music was dubbed (i.e. post-recorded) was *Innocents of Paris* (US 29), a Maurice Chevalier confection whose success was mainly due to the theme song 'Louise'.

The first concert devoted exclusively to film music was *Music of the Cinema*, held at the Hollywood Bowl on 2 August 1938.

The first song specially composed for a motion picture was 'Mother I Still Have You', written by Louis Silvers and sung by Al Jolson in *The Jazz Singer* (US 27).

The first hit-song from a movie was 'Sonny Boy', also an Al Jolson number, from *The Singing Fool* (US 28), composed by Buddy De Sylva, Lew Brown and Ray Henderson. Within nine months of the film's release, the sales of 'Sonny Boy' records had reached 2 million and sheet music 1¼ million.

The first record of a song from a movie was 'Mother o' Mine' from *The Jazz Singer* (US 27), sung by Al Jolson and released on the Brunswick label on 6 October 1927 concurrently with the film's première.

The first golden disc awarded for a record selling one million copies was presented to bandleader Glenn Miller on 10 February 1942 for 'Chattanooga Choo Choo', the hit song he and his orchestra had performed in the Fox musical *Sun Valley Serenade* (US 41).

The biggest-selling record of a song from a movie is Irving Berlin's 'White Christmas', performed by Bing Crosby in *Holiday Inn* (US 42), which has sold over 30 million copies to date. Crosby, a devout Catholic, tried to have 'White Christmas' excised from the film, because he thought it would further commercialise what should be a religious festival. Persuaded to perform it, he was amazed at the public response, which coincided with the darkest days of World War II when people wanted sentimental reminders of home. In the event he was to reprise the song every Christmas on television and he also rendered it in *Blue Skies* (US 46) and *White Christmas* (US 54).

The biggest-selling soundtrack album is of Bee Gees Barry, Robin and Maurice Gibb's pastiche of disco dancing music for *Saturday Night Fever* (US 77), which *Variety* castigated with the observations that it 'lurches through predictable travail and treacle, separated by phonograph records (or vice versa)'. Despite their stricture that 'the topical disco milieu is a slapdash backdrop to the worst in teenage exploitation rehash', the music was such a hit with exploited teenagers that the album has sold in excess of 27 million copies. The most successful non-vocal album is of James Horner's symphonic score for *Titanic* (US 98), which had sold 25.3 million copies to April 2000 and seems set to overhaul the now venerable record holder.

The first and probably the only soundtrack album to outgross the movie was Curtis Mayfield's score to Gordon Parks' *Superfly* (US 72), a Warner Bros 'blaxploitation' film about New York cocaine dealers in which the music was the only redeeming feature.

The most prolific songwriter for the screen is Tamil lyricist Vali, who is reputed to have composed 6500 songs since his debut film, *Azhagarmalai Kalvan* (Ind 59).

The longest movie song title was 'How Could You Believe Me When I Said I Loved You When You Know I've Been a Liar All My Life', sung by Fred Astaire and Jane Powell in *Royal Wedding*/GB: *Wedding Bells* (US 51).

> As late as 1937 the *New York Times* was able to refer to composing film music as 'one of the obscurest jobs in Hollywood'. This was echoed by Hollywood composer Erich Korngold, who observed: 'A movie composer's immortality lasts from the recording stage to the dubbing room.'

The first sound film with a full symphonic score was RKO's *The Bird of Paradise* (US 32), with music by Viennese composer Max Steiner. It was also **the first complete film score to be issued on disc**, released by RCA Victor as an album of 78s. Formerly producers had been unwilling to have music coming from an unidentified source, on the premise that audiences would be confused by hearing music where there was no visible orchestra. Hence, early sound films tended to confine the musical accompaniment to the front and end credits or to passages of the action where it could be clearly seen to emanate from a radio or gramophone. There is no evidence that audiences were confused, for once Steiner had established the symphonic score as integral to certain types of movie the source was never questioned. The symphonic score fell into disfavour in the 1960s with the rise of pop and jazz accompaniments, but after a slow climb back in the 1970s reached its apogee with John Williams's Oscar-winning music for *Star Wars* (US 77).

The first major motion picture in which all the music was performed live to camera was Robert Altman's *Nashville* (US 75). Composer Richard Baskin spent 15 weeks in Nashville before and during the shoot arranging most of the songs and writing about half of them—the others were written by the actors themselves (see The Star as Composer, below). He also featured in the picture, appearing in the opening scene when Haven Hamilton (Henry Gibson) is recording the song '200 Years' in a local studio. The highly hirsute Baskin plays Frog, the hapless pianist who keeps missing his cues. Eventually Haven Hamilton gives up in despair, dismissing the offender with the words 'Frog, get a haircut. You don't belong in Nashville'.

The most prolific film composer was and is the Tamil musician Ilaiyaraja, who has over 500 credits since his debut on *Annakkili* (Ind 76). He currently commands fees equalling those of the highest-paid Tamil actors and is an independent star attraction, one of the rare composers who can add to the box office potential of a movie on his name alone.

The most prolific composer for Hollywood films was Max Steiner (see above), with a total of 306 feature film scores from his debut on RKO's *Symphony of Six Million* (US 29). His output during his seven years with RKO and 30 years with Warner Bros included the scores for *King Kong* (US 33), *Gone With the Wind* (US 39), and his three Oscar-winning movies *The Informer* (US 35), *Now Voyager* (US 42) and *Since You Went Away* (US 44).

Britain's most prolific film composer was the Northampton-born William Alwyn (1905–85), second cousin of Gary Cooper, who received an estimated 80 credits on feature films. He worked frequently for Carol Reed and the Frank Launder-Sidney Gilliat partnership. Before embarking on features, he had been in demand as a composer for documentaries, including Hamphrey Jennings' World War II classic *Fires Were Started* (GB 43).

The only time an orchestra composed entirely of strings has been used to record the musical accompaniment to a movie was for *Psycho* (US 60). Hitchcock wanted music that would help to terrify the audience and composer Bernard Herrman responded with what he described as a black and white sound to complement a black and white film of a black and white story. The shrieking violin strings played a significant part in making *Psycho* the film that many people remember as the most frightening they have ever seen.

The first use of electronic music on a soundtrack was for *L'Idée* (Fr 34). The score by Arthur Honegger (1892–1955) was for an orchestra which included an electronic instrument called the Theremin.

The first film with an all-electronic score was MGM's *Forbidden Planet* (US 56), with 'electronic tonalities' by Louis and Bebe Barron.

The first feature-length rock concert film was Lee Robinson's *Rock 'n' Roll* (Aus 59), an all-star performance from Sydney Stadium.

The most successful concert film was Paramount's *Eddie Murphy Raw* (US 87), which grossed $50 million at the US box office.

The first woman film composer was Jadan Bai, founder of the Sangeet Film Co. and mother of India's superstar Nargis, who made her musical debut with the score of *Talash-e-Huq* (Ind 35).

Contrary to popular belief, the plaintive and slightly sinister Harry Lime Theme, perhaps one of the most evocative theme tunes of all time, was not composed especially for Sir Carol Reed's *The Third Man* (GB 49). The director happened to be having a drink with friends at a café in Sievering, a village outside Vienna, when he heard a man playing a zither, an instrument unfamiliar to him. Enraptured by its haunting strains, Reed determined to engage the instrumentalist for the musical accompaniment to his new film. The café entertainer was a man named Anton Karas and it transpired that he did not read or write music. This did not deter Reed, who had him flown to London so that he could simply play his zither to the film while he was recorded. It was scriptwriter Graham Greene's idea that his character of Harry Lime (Orson Welles), a racketeer in postwar Vienna, should have his own theme tune. Reed asked Karas if he could compose one, but the zither player shyly suggested he should play a tune he had made up many years earlier. This was to be The Harry Lime Theme and Karas became a rich man as the result of it. He used the money to open his own restaurant in Sievering, where of course the music of an evening always included a reprise of the proprietor's most celebrated composition.

The first woman composer to write a complete score for a Hollywood feature was Elizabeth Firestone, daughter of tyre magnate Harvey S. F. Firestone, who scored the Robert Montgomery comedy *Once More, My Darling* (US 47).

The first woman to compose for a British feature was Elizabeth Lutyens, whose score accompanied the Christopher Lee–Diana Dors low-budget thriller *Penny and the Pownall Case* (GB 48).

The most successful film composer of all time—in terms of scoring the music for box-office hits—is former Boston Pops resident conductor John T. Williams (1932–) who has composed the scores of many of the highest-earning films in history: *Jaws* (US 75), *Close Encounters of the Third Kind* (US 77), *Star Wars* (US 77), *Superman* (US/GB 78), *The Empire Strikes Back* (US 80), *Raiders of the Lost Ark* (US 81), *E.T.* (US 82), *Return of the Jedi* (US 83), *Indiana Jones and the Temple of Doom* (US 84),

Indiana Jones and the Last Crusade (US 89), *Home Alone* (US 90), *Jurassic Park* (US 93), *Saving Private Ryan* and *The Lost World: Jurassic Park* (US 97). He has won five Oscars for Best Original Score, the latest for *Schindler's List* (US 93) and been nominated 38 times up to and including *Angela's Ashes* (US/Ire 00).

Stewart Granger was given violin lessons so that he could play the role of Niccolo Paganini at least half convincingly in biopic *The Magic Bow* (GB 46). It was not intended that the music which emanated from his strings should actually adorn the soundtrack; that was to be replicated by Yehudi Menuhin playing in synch in the background. Unfortunately, Granger's fingering and bow work proved unequal to the task. The actor was instructed to hold his hands behind his back while an assistant director held the scroll of the violin and propped the other end under Granger's chin. As one professional violinist ran his left hand up and down the fingerboard, his body out of camera, another similarly disembodied musician performed the deft bow movements demanded by the composer's capricious music. Together the quartet, ably supported by Menuhin, produced sight and sound to the required virtuoso standard.

MUSIC ON SET

Providing music on set to create 'mood' for the performers, a common practice during the production of silent dramas, is usually said to have originated with D. W. Griffith's *Judith of Bethulia* (US 14), though the star of the film, Blanche Sweet, says she has no recollection of it. In fact the idea had originated in Europe at an earlier date, pioneer woman director Alice Guy playing a gramophone on set to assist the actors in emoting during the production of *La Vie du Christ* (Fr 06).

On occasions the practice got out of hand. Garbo was not satisfied with unadorned orchestral music and insisted on being sung to on set, it was reported in 1927. A soloist would join the studio orchestra and serenade her through a megaphone. Another demanding star caused an even greater onslaught of melody, though not entirely of her own volition. During an epic feud between Pola Negri and Gloria Swanson, whose respective egos were too great to be accommodated together in one studio, Swanson's director Allan Dwan hired a 70-strong brass band to drown the noise being made on Negri's adjacent set and persuade his opposite number to control the temperamental Polish star. In another instance the practice was itself instrumental in inflating a performer's ego to the point of affecting his career. Erich von Stroheim had commanded that whenever Anton Wawerka, who played the Emperor Franz Josef in *The Merry-Go-Round* (US 22) and in *The Wedding March* (US 28) appeared on set, the orchestra should strike up the Austrian national anthem. The custom even prevailed off set, all the Hollywood restaurants honouring Wawerka with the anthem whenever he entered their doors. The actor became so accustomed to this regal treatment that he suffered a breakdown when *The Wedding March* was completed and his imperial privileges withdrawn.

THE STAR AS COMPOSER

Charles Chaplin composed the score for all his films from *City Lights* (US 31) onwards. Noël Coward produced, directed, scripted and starred in *In Which We Serve* (GB 42) as well as composing the music. Less well-known instances are: Robert Mitchum's composition of the music for the songs 'The Ballad of Thunder Road' and 'Whippoorwill' in *Thunder Road* (US 58); the use of a portion of Lionel Barrymore's symphony *Tableau Russe* in *Dr Kildare's Wedding Day* (US 41); David McCallum's theme song for *Three Bites of the Apple* (US 67); teenager John Rubinstein's score for *All Together Now* (US 75, TVM)—son of legendary pianist Artur Rubinstein, he also starred; and Brazilian soccer star Pelé's score for his autobiopic *Pelé* (Mex 78); the eight songs written and performed by Robert Duvall playing an ex-alcoholic country-and-western singer in *Tender Mercies* (US 82); Kris Kristofferson's title song for *Trouble in Mind* (US 85), in which he starred as an ex-cop and ex-con. Jeff Bridges composed some of the music for the Dustin Hoffman–Mia Farrow movie *John and Mary* (US 69), but did not appear in it. Half of the songs in Robert Altman's *Nashville* (US 75) were composed by members of the cast, including Keith Carradine's hit single 'I'm Easy' which was nominated for an Oscar as Best Original Song. Phil Collins, who starred as Great Train Robber Buster Edwards in *Buster* (GB 88), wrote three of the songs for the picture (in collaboration with Lamont Dozier), including the hit 'Two Hearts' which soared to the No. 1 spot in the American Top Ten. The jazz solo performed by Richard Gere on the piano in *Pretty Woman* (US 90), prior to his performance with the irresistible Julia Roberts on top of the instrument itself, was the star's own composition. The only musical composed by its star, in an age when musicals were supposed to be dead, was *Dancer in the Dark* (Den/Fr/Swe/Ir/Ger/Nor/Neths/Ice/Fin/US/GB 00), with Icelandic pop singer turned actress Björk contributing the score to director Lars von Trier's lyrics.

CHAPTER 10

Titles and Credits

Titles

THE TWELVE LONGEST FILM TITLES

- *Night of the Day of the Dawn of the Son of the Bride of the Return of the Revenge of the Terror of the Attack of the Evil, Mutant, Hellbound, Zombified, Flesh-Eating, Sub-Humanoid Living Dead—Part 4* (US 93).

- Lina Wertmüller's *Un Fatto di sangue nel commune di Siciliana fra due uomini per causa di una vedova si sospettano moventi politici. Amore Morte Shimmy. Lugano belle. Tarantelle. Tarallucci é vino.* (It 79). The English-language title was *Revenge.*

- *The Persecution and Assassination of Jean-Paul Marat as Performed by the Inmates of the Asylum of Charenton under the Direction of the Marquis de Sade* (GB 66).

- *Les yeux ne veulent pas en tout temps se fermer ou peut-être qu'un jour Rome se permettra de choisir à son tour* (Fr/FRG 70).

- *Why Do I Believe You When You Tell Me That You Love Me, When I Known You've Been a Liar All Your Life* (GB 83).

- *La' il cielo e la terra si univano, la' le quattro stagioni si ricongiungevano la' il vento e la pioggia si incontravano* (It 72).

- *Mais qu'est-ce que j'ai fait au Bon Dieu pour avoir une femme qui boit dans les cafés avec les hommes?* (Fr 80).

- *I Killed My Lesbian Wife, Hung Her on a Meat Hook and Now I have a Three-Picture Deal at Disney* (US 95)

- *Those Magnificent Men in Their Flying Machines: or, How I Flew from London to Paris in 25 Hours and 11 Minutes* (GB 65).

> '**I**t is an axiom of cinema history, one admitting of few exceptions, that the longer the film's title the likelier it is to be an outright dud.'—Gilbert Adair

- *Film d'amore e d'anarchia, ovvero stamattina alle 10, in via dei Fiori, nella nota casa di tolleranza* (It 72).

- *Izrada i otkrivanje spomenika velikom srpskom satiricaru Radoju Domanovicu kao i druge manifestacije povodom 100-godisnjice njegovog rodenja* (Yug 75).

- *Caffeteria or How Are You Going to Keep Her Down on the Farm after She's Seen Paris Twice* (US 73). Described as 'the short and sweet story of a girl and her 26 cows', this film runs for precisely one minute.

THE SHORTEST FILM TITLES

These have all had one letter or digit (an asterisk signifies a feature movie): *A* (Fr 64); *A* (It 69); *A* (Jap 99)*; *B* (It 69); *C* (It 70); *D* (It 70); *E* (Can 82)*; *E* (GB 93)*; *F* (US 80); *F* (Jap 98)*; *G* (US 72); *G* (GB/FRG 74)*; *G* (Swe 83)*; *H* (US 60); *H* (Can 90)*; *H* (Sp 97)*; *I* (Rom 66); *I* (Swe 66)*; *K* (US 18)*; *K* (Hun 89)*; *K* (Fr 97)*; *M* (Ger 31)*; *M* (US 51)*; *M* (Cz 64); *M* (US 00)*; *O* (GB 32); *O* (Jap 75); *O* (US 00)*; *P* (Neth 64); *Q* (Fr/It/Bel 74)*; *Q* (US 83)*; *S.* (Bel 98); *V* (It 68); *V* (US 83, TVM)*; *W* (US 73)*; *W* (Phi 85)*; *X* (Ger 28)*; *X* (Swe 57); *X* (US 62); *X* (S. Kor 82)*; *X* (Nor 86)*; *X* (Jap 00)*; X (Sp 01)*; *Y* (Swe 87)*; *Y* (Col 92)*; *Z* (Fr/It 68)*; *$* (US 72)*; *3* (US 56); *3* (US c.80); *3* (It 96); π (US 98)*.

The average number of letters used in a film title is 17.

ODD TITLES

Writing in *Films and Filming*, David McGillivray nominated *Betta, Betta in the Wall, Who's the Fattest Fish of All* (US 69) and *She Ee Clit Soak* (US 71) as 'the most preposterous movie titles ever conceived'. Other unusual titles include *Ojojoj* (Swe 66); *RoGoPaG* (It 63); *I-Ro-Ha-Ni-Ho-He-Yo* (Jap 60); *Ha, Ha, Hee, Hee, Hoo Hoo* (Ind 55); *Sssssssss* (US 73); *Phffft* (US 54). Rather more comprehensible curiosities are *Telephone Girl, Typist Girl or Why I Became a Christian* (Ind 25); *After the Balled-Up Ball* (US 17); *In My Time Boys Didn't Use Hair Cream* (Arg 37); *The Film That Rises to the Surface of Clarified Butter* (US 68) and *How to Make Love to a Negro Without Getting Tired* (Can/Fr 88), but some explanation might be needed for *Egg! Egg?* (Swe 75) and *Cash? Cash!* (Bel 69). *Yes* (Hun 64) was followed by *No* (Hun 65) and the situation remained equally unclear with *Yes No Maybe Maybe Not* (GB 75), though things get less indecisive with *Certain, Very Certain, As a Matter of Fact . . . Probable* (It 70). *I Go Oh No* (Tai 84) invites the injunction *Hurry, Hurry* (Sp 81), but then the answer will probably be *I Can't . . . I Can't* (Ire 69). The response to *I Know that You Know I Know* (It 82) might be *Okay Okay* (It 83) or perhaps *Augh! Augh!* (It 80), while *I'm Married. Ha Ha* (Mex 62) might elicit something more sympathetic like *Come to My Place, I'm Living at My Girl Friend's* (Fr 81) if the problem is *Feudin', Fussin' and A-Fightin'* (US 48). No answers were vouchsafed to the important questions *Who Created the Yoyo? Who Created the Moon Buggy?* (Phi c.80), though another, unspoken question met with the response *No Thanks, Coffee Makes Me Nervous* (It c.81).

> **T**he longest single word in a movie title, and undoubtedly the most unpronounceable occurs in *Schwarzhuhnbraunhuhnschwarzhuhnweisshuhnrothuhnweiss oder Put Putt* (FRG 67)

Some odd titles make more sense than first appears. *P'Tang Yang Kipperbang* (GB 83) is a recurring phrase in the film's dialogue, representing part of the codes and rituals of teenagers at school in the 1940s. A sci-fi comedy called *Recharge Grandmothers Exactly!* (Cz 84) was about robot grandmothers who take over the running of households. *Down by Law* (US 86) was released in Italy as *Daunbailò*. No, that isn't an Italian dialect word—that's *Down by Law* spelt phonetically. Similarly, *Nocaut* (Mex 84) is not an unfamiliar word in Spanish, but simply the phonetic spelling of 'Knockout'—the picture is about boxing.

Another example is *Bezness* (Fr/Tunisia 92), the Tunisian corruption of 'Business', meaning in this context the activity of young gigolos who sell their charms to tourists of both sexes, while *Krush* (Ind 92) simply means 'crush', as in the relationship of passionate schoolgirls before they graduate to hunks, or in this case the love life of Indian lesbians. It might be reasonable to suppose that if a German movie is called *Schtonk* (Ger 92) then '*Schtonk*' is a German word. In fact it is one of the nonsense words used by Chaplin in *The Great Dictator* (US 40) when he is pretending to speak German.

The title of Akira Kurosawa's *Dodes'kaden* (Jap 70) had no meaning in Japanese: it was an approximation of the rumble of tram wheels on the tramway.

Andy Bausch's *A Wopbopaloobop A Lopbamboom* (Lux 89) means about as much in Luxembourgish as it does in any other language, while possibly *Beautiful Lady Without Neck* (S. Kor 66) sounded less odd in Korean.

The Sexual Life of the Belgians (Bel 94), which was directed by the curator of the Brussels Museum of Underpants, evokes memories of that old parlour favourite 'Name six famous Belgians'. Contrary to rumour, the picture was not a one-reeler.

Brad Pitt starrer *Se7en* (US 95) is not the only film with a numeral interspersed in the letters of a word. Released the same year was *O Qu4trilho* (Bra 95). The Thais have since come up with *6ixtynin9* (Thai 00).

The title of Carlo Vanyina's *Io No Spik Inglish* (It 95) may have presented translation problems for Italian cinemagoers who no spik Inglish.

There have been several films whose titles consisted simply of a number. One of the more intriguing was *23:58* (Fr 94), the story of a stadium holdup during the Le Mans 24-hour motorcycle-race. The title is based on the premise that the event never lasts the full 24 hours—the last lap cannot be run to the finishing line because spectators invariably invade the track.

> Totally *F***ed Up* (US 93), Gregg Akari's picture about gay and lesbian teenagers in contemporary LA, is one of the very first feature films in which the title does not appear on screen. With a discretion not wholly allied to its subject matter, the film announced itself with the title spoken by lead player James Duval.

Wordless titles include Warhol's well-known **** (US 67); . . . (Arg 71)—the English-language title was *Dot Dot Dot*; and Michael Snow's ↔ (Can 69). Rather less inventive, but eminently explicit, is *A 100% Brazilian Film* (Bra 87), which is a 100% Brazilian film. Casting about for an apt title for an animated film, Aleksander Skrocynski made an inspired choice with *An Animated Film* (Pol 84), while Netherlands producer Jos Stelling figured that if you are trying to sell a Dutch movie, you might as well call it that, so *Dutch Movie* (Neth 84) it was. *Film Without Title* (FRG

47) was the title of a Rudolph Jugert movie, but it was not apparent whether Vincenzo Ferrari's *Untitled* (It 73) had one or not. The makers of *Don't Worry, We'll Think of a Title* (US 65) evidently had trouble in doing so. Less confidence was displayed by the makers of *Still Lacking a Good Title* (Yug 88).

HOME TOWN

Most of the world's big cities and many of the smaller ones have been used in movie titles. This list is confined to titles which consist only of the names of towns.

Aberdeen (Nor/GB 00); *Abilene* (US 00); *Abilene Town* (US 46); *Albuquerque* (US 48); *Aspen* (US 93); *Atlantic City* (US 44) (Can/Fr 81); *Bagdad* (US 49); *Baghdad* (India 52 x 2—different films) (Ind 60); *Bar-cel-ona* (Sp 87); *Barcelona* (US 94); *Baton-Rouge* (Fr 85); *Belfast, Maine* (US 00); *Bengazi* (US 55); *Benghazi* (It 42); *Berlin* (Ger 27) (Jap 95); *Bilbao* (Sp 78); *Birdsville* (Aus 86); *Bombay* (Ind 49) (India 95); *Cairo* (GB 42) (GB 63) (Egypt 91); *Calcutta* (US 47); *Canon City* (US 48); *Caracas* (AUT 89); *Carson City* (US 52); *Casablanca* (US 42); *Casablanca, Casablanca* (It 85); *Chartres* (Swz 90); *Cheyenne* (US 47); *Chicago* (US 27); *Coronado* (US 35); *Dallas* (US 50); *Dimboola* (Aus 79); *Dodge City* (US 39); *El Paso* (US 49); *Fargo* (GB 97); *Fort Worth* (US 51); *Fresno* (US 86, TVM); *Guadalajara* (Mex 43); *Guatanamera* (Cuba/Sp/Ger 95); *Haifa* (Palestinian/Neths/Ger/Fr 96); *Havana* (US 90); *Havre* (Fr 86); *Honolulu* (US 39); *Houston, Texas* (Fr 81); *Istanbul* (US 57) (Bel 84); *Jakarta* (US 88); *Jerusalem* (Swe 96); *Kalamazoo* (Can 87); *Kansas City* (Fr/US 95); *Karachi* (Nor 88); *Khartoum* (GB 66); *Lahore* (Ind 53); *L.A.NEWYORKPARIS-ROMEHELSINKI* (US 91); *Laramie* (US 49); *Lisbon* (US 56) (Sp/Arg 98); *London* (GB 26); *Madrid* (Sp 87); *Malacca* (Swe 86); *Malaga* (GB 54); *Managua* (Can 87); *Manaos* (It/Mex/Sp 80); *Mandalay* (US 34); *Manila* (Sp 92) (Ger 00); *Maracaibo* (US 58); *Marbella* (It 86); *Matewan* (US 87); *Memphis* (US 92, TVM); *Mexico City* (US 00, TVM); *Miami* (US 24) (US 94) (US 99); *Minas, Texas* (Bra 89); *Monte Carlo* (US 26) (US 30); *Montevideo* (FRG 52) (FRG 64); *Moscow* (Rus 00); *Naples and Sorrento* (It 30); *Nashville* (US 75); *New Delhi* (Ind 56) (Ind 87); *New Orleans* (US 29); *New York* (US 16) (US 27); *New York, New York* (US 77); *Ostende* (Fr 91); *Palm Beach* (Aus 79); *Palm Springs* (US 36); *Paris* (US 26) (US 29); *Paris-Deauville* (Fr 35); *Paris, France* (Can 93); *Paris–New York* (Fr 40); *Paris, Paris* (Ind 88); *Paris, Texas* (FRG 84); *Paris–Tombuctu* (Sp 99); *Pasajes* (Sp 96); *Philadelphia* (US 93); *Phoenix* (US 95); *Plymouth* (GB 91, TVM); *Port Arthur* (Cz 37); *Port Said* (US 48); *Prague* (Cz 85) (GB/Fr 92); *Quebec* (US 51); *Reno* (US 23) (US 30) (US 39); *Rimini, Rimini* (It 87); *Rio* (US 39); *Rome* (It 71); *Saigon* (US 48) (US 88); *Saint Tropez Saint Tropez* (It 93); *Salome, Where She Danced** (US 44); *San Antonio* (US 97) (US 45); *San Francisco* (US 36) (Bel 83); *Santiago* (US 56); *Santa Fe* (US 51) (Aut 88) (US 97); *Sarajevo* (US/GB 97); *Sausalito* (HK 00); *Shanghai* (US 35); *Shiraz* (Ger/Ind 28); *Singapore* (India 60); *Sioux City* (US 94); *Sofia* (US 48); *Soweto* (GB/Nigeria 88); *Stalingrad* (Ger 93); *Suddenly*** (US 54); *Talpa* (Mex 57); *Tangier* (US 46); *Teheran* (GB 47); *Tel Aviv–Berlin* (Isr 87); *Texas City* (US 52); *Timbuctoo* (GB 33); *Timbuktu* (US 59); *Tobruk* (US 66); *Tombstone* (US 42) (US 93); *Tucson* (US 49); *Tulsa* (US 49); *Twin Falls Idaho* (US 00); *Union City* (US 80); *Valencia* (Ger 27); *Valparaiso* (Chile 94); *Valparaiso, Valparaiso!* (Fr

71); *Vegas* (US 78, TVM); *Venice/Venice* (US 93); *Vera Cruz* (US 54); *Versailles, Nevada* (US 97); *Virginia City* (US 40); *Warsaw* (Fr/Ger 92); *Washington* (Iran 83); *West Beirut* (Fr/Leb/Belg/Nor 98); *Wetherby* (GB 85); *Wichita* (US 55); *Yuma* (US 71, TVM).

* Yes, this is the name of a town. It was originally a settlement in Arizona called Drinkmens Wells. According to legend a Mexican dancer called Salome (played by Yvonne de Carlo in the film) danced to hold the attention of a band of outlaws while the citizenry assembled to organise the defence of their homes. The name of the town was changed to Salome, Where She Danced in her honour.

** Suddenly is a small town in California.

DATE TITLES

*1492** (GB/Fr/Sp 92); *1514* (Hun 62); *1740* (Can 77); *1776* (US 06); *1776* (US 72); *1778* (Fr 78); *1789* (Fr 73); *1793* (Fr 14); *1810* (Arg 60); *1812* (Rus 12); *1812* (Ger 23); *1812* (USSR 44); *1812* (GB 65); *1812* (Hun 73); *1814* (Fr 11); *1848* (It 48); *1848* (Rom 80); *1857* (India 46); *1860* (It 32); *1861* (US 11); *1866* (It 33)—English-language title; *1870* (It 72); *1871* (GB 90); *1880* (Fr 63); *1881* (Ger 94); *1884* (GB 83); *1895* (Estonia 95); *1897* (GB 91); *1900* (US 72); *1900* (It/Fr/FRG 77); *1905* (USSR 52); *1907* (Rom 76); *1913* (Bul 85); *1914* (GB 15); *1914* (Ger 31); *1915* (Aus 82); *1917* (GB 70); *1918* (Fin 55); *1918* (USSR 58)—English-language title; *1918* (US 85); *1919* (Sp 83); *1919* (GB 85); *1921* (India 88); *1922* (Gre 79); *1925* (Bul 76); *1929* (Cz 74)—English-language title; *1929* (Fin 79); *1931* (GB 32); *1933* (Can/US 67); *1936* (It 81); *1936* (Jap 87); *1939* (Swe 90); *1941* (US 41); *1941* (US 79); *'42* (India 49); *1945* (Ger 45); *1945* (Ger 84); *1948* (Fr 48); *1958* (Nor 80); *1967* (US 67); *1968* (US 68); *1969* (US 88); *1970* (US 70); *1971* (Ven 71); *1972* (FRG 73); *1972* (Bra 00); *1983* (GB 83); *1984* (GB 56); *1984* (GB 84); *1985* (US c.70); *1996* (GB 89, TVM); *1999* (US 98); *1999* (US 00); *2000 AD* (HK/Singapore 00); *two thousand and none* (Can 00); *2010* (US 84); *2040* (HK 00); *2084* (Aus 85).

*Australian title of *1492: Conquest of Paradise*.

Battle Shock (Isr 87) starring Alon Abouthoul is not to be confused with *Battle Shock* (Isr 87) also starring Alon Abouthoul. Two entirely different movies, one was directed by Yossi Zomer, the other by Yoel Sharon.

TITLE CHANGES

- *Livingstone* (GB 25) was reissued in America in 1933 as *Stanley*. (Livingstone was British; Stanley an American citizen.) Numerous British films have needed title changes for the USA—*Carleton Browne of the F.O./US: Man in a Cocked Hat* (GB 59) and *Never Take Sweets from a Stranger/US: Never Take Candy from a Stranger* (GB 60) are two obvious examples, but there is only one recorded instance of a simultaneous title change within Britain. *This England* (GB 41), a wartime flagwaver with Emlyn Williams and Constance Cummings, was retitled *Our Heritage* for release in Scotland.

- *Peyton Place* (US 57) played in Paris as *The Pleasures of Hell*, in Munich as *Glowing Fire Under the Ashes* and in Hong Kong as *The Cold and Warmth in the Human World*. *Guys and Dolls* (US 55) was *Heavy Youths and Light Girls* in Germany. Indonesia changed *I'll Cry Tomorrow* (US 55) to *To Relieve Yourself From the Grief of Your Passions*, while Hong Kong looked for something catchier than *Not as a Stranger* (US 55) and came up with *The Heart of a Lady as Pure as a Full Moon Over the Place of Medical Salvation*. *The Rebel Novice Nun* was the Mexican title of *The Sound of Music* (US 65).

- The Tokyo office of United Artists translated *Dr No* (GB 62) as *We Don't Want a Doctor*. The solecism was noticed just in time to stop the posters being printed. No such last-minute rescue prevented *Eine Nacht in London* (Ger/GB 34) from being released in Britain as *One Knight in London*.

- In China *The Full Monty* (GB 96), about unemployed steelworkers in Sheffield who become strippers for a night, was renamed *Six Naked Pigs*, while Oliver Stone's *Nixon* (US 95) became *The Big Liar*. The Chinese may have believed that Anthony Minghella's doom-laden *The English Patient* (US/GB 96) was a ribald comedy when it was released under the title *Do Not Ask Me Who I Am—Ever!*. Rather more subtlety went into the renaming of the Coen brothers' *Fargo* (GB 97), which took its title from the wintry snowed-in North Dakota town where it is set. It became *Mysterious Murder in Snowy Cream*: the last two words in Cantonese are pronounced *fah go*.

- *Chicago, Chicago* was not the Midwest release title of *New York, New York*, but the Spanish title of Norman Jewison's *Gaily, Gaily* (US 69).

- The Spanish word for *Grease* (US 78) is grasa, but this translates literally as 'fat'. In Spain the movie was released as *Brillantina/Brilliantine* and in Venezuela as *Vaselina/Vaseline*.

- *Dennis the Menace* (US 93), live-action moppet movie based on Hank Ketcham's Stateside newspaper cartoon, became plain *Dennis* in Britain to avoid trademark infringement of the D. C. Thompson character of the same name who wreaks havoc in the *Beano*. So which has precedence? By an extraordinary coincidence the American Dennis the Menace and the British Dennis the Menace, wholly unconnected other than both being juvenile mischief-makers, each made his debut in print on opposite sides of the Atlantic on the same day, 17 March 1951.

- Roland Joffé's *Fat Man Little Boy* (US 89) opened with that title, but the intended audience for this drama about the building of the atom bomb stayed away because they thought the picture was a slapstick comedy. Business picked up under the new title *Shadow Makers*.

- *Whisky Galore* (GB 48) was changed to *Tight Little Island* in the US because the Hays Office would not allow alcohol to be named in a film title.

- Before the war it had been the British who were uptight about 'improper' titles. Dorothy Arzner's *Merrily We Go to Hell* (US 32) became *Merrily We Go to ----* for its British release. Similarly *Woman, Wife and Whore* (Malaysia 93) was refused certification in its own country until the final word was dropped in favour of *Woman, Wife and...*

- The screen version of Christopher Hampton's play *Les Liaisons Dangereuses* was changed to *Dangerous Liaisons* (US 89) after a street poll in the US revealed that only 2% of respondents were prepared to see a film with a foreign title.

- Miramax maven Harvey Weinstein also decided that foreign titles did not feel good in America when he changed Robert Altman's *Pret-a-Porter* to *Ready to Wear (Pret-a-Porter)* (US 94). Unfortunately, Columbia Records, having paid $350,000 for the record rights, had released the soundtrack under its original title. Just to confuse things more, the title as seen on screen consists of *Pret-a-Porter* in logo form and *Ready to Wear* in brackets underneath. In France, of course, the title remained unchanged (except for the missing accents). Otherwise it would have translated as *Prêt à Porter (Prêt à Porter)*.

- Darryl F. Zanuck changed the title of *32 Rue Madeleine* to *13 Rue Madeleine* (US 46) because he reckoned 13 was his lucky number.

- *The American Success Co* (US 79) started out under that title without much success, so was recut and re-released in 1983 as *American Success*. American it may have been . . . Three years later the distributors tried again with another cut, this time titled simply *Success*. When that did not bring in the crowds either they just had to accept that for them *Success* meant failure.

- The title of *Saturday to Monday* was changed to *Experimental Marriage* (US 19) because exhibitors believed that patrons might be misled into thinking that the picture was only playing over the weekend.

- Paramount considered 250 alternative titles for the American release of Australian smash-hit *Crocodile Dundee* (Aus 86). After rejecting them all, the distributors decided on one small change for US consumption—the first word was put in quotes, as they felt *'Crocodile' Dundee* would help to avoid the misconception that the film was about crocodiles.

- Changing English-language titles does not always help their prospects in overseas markets. *City Slickers* (US 91) did good business everywhere except in France, where it was known as *Life, Love and Cows*. Another film which bombed in France after scoring well in other territories was the Aussie sleeper *Strictly Ballroom* (Aus 92), which could have had a lot to do with changing its title to the prosaic *Ballroom Dancing. Wayne's World* (US 92) was a hit worldwide except in Taiwan, where it was released as *The Rambunctious and Clever Ones*. Equally, some titles may be improved. The basketball picture *White Men Can't Jump* (US 92) clicked at the Italian box office under its new title *White Men Don't Know How to Stick It In.*

- How do you translate *Sense and Sensibility* (US/GB 96) into Russian? The Russkies went for *Reason and Feeling*. . . near, but not quite what Miss Austen had in mind.

- Although *The Pope Must Die* (GB 91) was a ribald comedy, newspapers and TV webs in America refused to accept advertising for the film in case militant Protestant fundamentalists mistook the title for a call to arms. Portly star of the picture Robbie Coltrane, who played a humble priest accidentally elevated to the papacy, found the solution. He had noticed that someone had been embellishing the posters for the film on the Underground by adding a 't' to the end of the title immediately above his picture. So for US release it became *The Pope Must Diet.*

- Stripper Gypsy Rose Lee's novel *The G-String Murders* was to have been brought to the screen under its original title, until Universal commissioned a poll to find out how many people could correctly identify the eponymous garment. While a majority of the male population of Providence, Rhode Island were well informed about such matters—56% of them anyway—only 29% of their women were familiar with the object. In Richmond, Va. the women proved more knowing than the men, but only by a meagre 8% to a derisory 4%. Most people figured it meant 'a string of a violin, a fiddle or some such instrument'. The Barbara Stanwyck vehicle was released as *Lady of Burlesque* (US 43) in the US and a little more explicitly as *Strip-tease Lady* in the UK.

- *The Devil is a Sissy* (US 36) became *The Devil Takes the Count* for its British release, because at that time in England 'sissy' was a euphemism for homosexual. *Encino Man* (US 92) became *California Man* in Britain for the benefit of those Brits unfamiliar with West Coast topography and in the process lost the delicate play on words which made the original title far more apt for a story about a prehistoric man revived in the present time.

- Legendary producer Joe Levine, barely literate yet a master of the spoken word, listed as number one of his regrets in life that he had let Dore Schary, head of the Anti-Defamation League, talk him into changing the title of Mel Brooks' first film into the scarcely compelling *The Producers* (US 67). Unpressured, Levine would have stuck with the original title, which survived only as the ever-to-be-remembered 'play-within-a-play' *Springtime for Hitler.*

- Chaplin's *The Great Dictator* (US 40) was to have been released as *The Dictator*. It was then discovered that Paramount held the screen rights to Richard Harding Davis's novel of that title. Paramount demanded $25,000 for the name. Chaplin called the fee 'outrageous' for just two words and secured them for nothing by interpolating 'Great'.

- The original title of Woody Allen's *Annie Hall* (US 76) was *Anhedonia*, defined as the chronic inability to experience pleasure. The change of title, made only three weeks before release, reflected Allen's decision at the cutting-room stage to alter the whole concept of the film from a study of anhedonia to a more intimate exploration of personal relationships, based on his own affair with Diane Keaton. Hall was Miss Keaton's real name. Whether the alteration helped to sell the movie is a moot point—Allen later reflected ruefully that it had taken less at the box office than any previous winner of the Academy Award for Best Picture.

- A number of commentators took issue with Steven Spielberg's decision to change the name of Thomas Keneally's *Schindler's Ark* to *Schindler's List* for his 1993 film version, one supercilious British critic suggesting it was because Americans did not understand the meaning of 'ark'. In fact the film title is the more subtle of the two for those with a knowledge of Yiddish or German. In both languages 'ein List' can mean either 'a list' or 'a cunning trick'.

- Most inexplicable title change? A strong candidate

must be the Alexander Korda picture of derring-do in British India *The Drum* (GB 38), released in America as *Drums*.

- In 1933 publicist Arthur L. Mayer spent weeks training 70 parrots to squawk in unison the title of Paramount's latest Mae West starrer *It Ain't No Sin*. Then the studio changed it to *I'm No Angel*...

- Hollywood studios have been putting movie titles into research for several decades. The sequel to *Jaws* (US 75) was to have been called *More Jaws*, but the research showed that people thought this was a comedy take-off of the original and the more prosaic *Jaws II* (US 78) was substituted instead. It is surprising that Universal bothered to put *The Blarney Cock* into research and even more so that they were shocked to find that most people came up with meanings for the last word of the title which had nothing to do with doodle-doo. Or to put it in the words of Universal's research director Willett Klausner, 'several suggestive connotations which were entirely misleading'. The startled studio honchos rapidly changed it to *Swashbuckler* (US 76) instead. Sometimes though the studios have the wit to ignore the numbers. Pretesting of the title for a 20th Century Fox sci-fi pic showed that prospective audiences were turned off by what they thought was another wartime combat movie. George Lucas said 'What the heck?' and called it *Star Wars* (US 77) anyway.

- There is only one country where it was possible to see the movie titled *The Punisher 2*. Malaysia, notorious for the most stringent censorship in Asia, had rejected the Dolph Lundgren starrer *The Punisher* outright. The cynical but ingenious local distributor simply bided his time, then resubmitted the picture with a 2 tacked on to the title. It passed the censors without a single cut.

- *Fucking Åmål* (Swe 98), chosen as Sweden's entry for the 1999 Oscars, had to undergo a title change to the anodyne *Show Me Love* before it could be accepted.

- There are two versions of the story of why the title of *The Madness of King George* (US/GB 95) was changed from *The Madness of George III*, the title of Alan Bennett's original play. The more prosaic is that recounted by the star of both play and film, Nigel Hawthorne. He was asked to go to Arundel Castle to be photographed for the film poster as the mad king. On arrival he was dismayed to find that the substance of the picture was to be conveyed by having him pose in a nightshirt and crown with an orb in one hand and a piglet in the other. When he complained to executive producer Samuel Goldwyn Jr, he was told that the crude symbolism was necessary to indicate to the less historically minded that George III was a king as well as mad. 'Well, why don't we call it *The Madness of King George*,?' suggested Hawthorne and Goldwyn willingly acquiesced.

Much more engaging, and therefore to be preferred, is Sam Goldwyn's version. According to the producer, not only are US audiences unfamiliar with the names of English monarchs (even the one who lost the American colonies), but they believe that any title with a figure in it is a sequel. Rather than lose the patronage of those who might be reluctant to see *III* if they had missed *The Madness of George* and *The*

Probably the largest number of alternative titles considered for a film was the 422 possibles devised as a substitute for *The Pinnacle*, the title of the novel by Erich von Stroheim which he himself adapted for the screen. Producer Carl Laemmle reckoned this 'too deep' and invited New York exhibitors to vote from a shortlist of eight. They chose *Blind Husbands* (US 19). Von Stroheim was so incensed that he took a full page advertisement in *Motion Picture News* to protest against 'a name which I would have rejected in disgust had it been submitted to me'. Carl Laemmle responded with another full-page the following week, saying of the old title: 'I've even heard it accented pee-nokkle in a joking manner, a thing which would kill your picture deader than a salt mackerel.' The picture triumphed as *Blind Husbands*, but Laemmle failed to outlive a persistent Hollywood legend that he had changed the title because he thought that *Pinnacle* was the name of a card-game.

Madness of George II, Goldwyn decided on the title switch.

- *The Lion King* (US 94) was originally to be titled *King of the Jungle*. Then someone told the Disney people that lions do not actually live in the jungle.

STAR TITLES

When a performer's name was billed above the title, that meant real stardom. But an even greater accolade of fame is for a star's name to appear *in* the title—particularly when the star is not in the movie. (Where the title is marked with an asterisk, the star did appear—often only in a cameo.) Omitted from this list are star biopics (see pp. 120–3) and also titles containing the names of performers like Abbott and Costello who always played a fictitious version of themselves. The first title listed, therefore, is on account of Karloff rather than the comedy duo.

Abbott and Costello Meet the Killer, Boris Karloff (US 48)*; *Adolf and Marlene* (FRG 77)—with Margit Carstensen as Marlene Dietrich; *Bacall to Arms* (US 46)—Warner Bros Merrie Melodie; *Le Bassin de John Wayne* (Fr 92); *Being John Malkovich* (US 99)*; *Bela Lugosi Meets a Brooklyn Gorilla* (US 52)*; *The Black Dragon Revenges the Death of Bruce Lee* (HK 75); *Buster's Bedroom* (Ger/Can/Por 91)—refers to Buster Keaton; *Chaplin! Who Do You Cry* (Jap 32)—porno; *Charlie Chaplin and the Kung Fu Kid in Laughing Times* (HK 81); *Charlie Chaplin Na Vitoscia* (Bul 24); *CID Nazir* (Ind 71)*—starring Prem Nazir; *Come Back to the 5 and Dime, Jimmy Dean, Jimmy Dean* (US 82); *The Curse of Fred Astaire* (US 84); *Dear Brigitte* (US 65)*; *Elvis and Marilyn* (It 98); *F comme Fairbanks* (Fr 75); *Garbo Talks* (US 86); *Gary Cooper, Who Art in Heaven* (Sp 81); *Ginger and Fred* (It 86); *The Gracie Allen Murder Case* (US 39)*; *Happy Birthday, Marilyn!* (Hun 81)—Yes, it does refer to MM; *In Like Flynn* (US 85); *Ist Eddy Polo Schuldig* (Ger 28)*; *Kim Novak is on the Phone* (It 94); *The Kiss of Mary Pickford* (USSR 26)*—shot clandestinely without the star knowing she was in it; *The Little Valentino* (Hun 79); *The Man with Bogart's Face* (US 80); *Moonlight and Valentino* (US 95); *My Dear Tom Mix* (Mex 91); *My Love Mary Pickford* (Rus 96); *Prem Nazirine Kanmanilla* (Ind 83)*; *Travolta et Moi* (Fr 93); *Sabu and the Magic Ring* (US 57)*; *The Semester We Loved Kim*

Novak (Sp 80); *Shirley Temple se enamora* (Mex 38); *Valentino Returns* (US 86); *The Woman Who Married Clark Gable* (Ire 85); *To Wong Foo, Thanks for Everything! Julie Newmar* (US 95)*; *You Elvis, Me Monroe* (FRG 90).

Garbo (Aus 92) was not a homage to the Divine One with the supposedly large feet. It was a nifty little melodrama about garbage collectors, known as 'Garbos' in the Australian vernacular.

MEANINGLESS OR MISLEADING TITLES

- *The Bible* (It 13) was not a biblical epic as its title suggested, but a six-reel melodrama which included a riot in a theatre, a revolver fight on stage, a car chase, a motorcycle blowing up, and people falling out of trains, fighting to the death in rivers, and kidnapping children. Somewhere among all this activity a Bible was worked into the plot. Warner's *Tracked by the Police* (US 27) was a Rin Tin Tin vehicle whose title was decided before the script was written. The completed film was certainly about tracking, but the tracker was Rin Tin Tin with never a policeman in sight from first reel to last. Edgar Ulmer's *The Black Cat* (US 34) had nothing to do with the Poe story of the same name (despite a credit to Poe) and nothing to do with a black cat other than the fact that a cat crept in and out of a few scenes, to justify the title.

- *The Axe* (US 77) was released in Britain as *California Axe Massacre*, though it was set nowhere near California. *Big Hand for a Little Lady* (US 66) had its title changed in Britain to *Big Deal at Dodge City*. Whoever thought this one up had not seen the picture. It was set in Laredo. *Exiled To Shanghai* (US 37) was not about anyone being exiled and the story did not play in Shanghai, while *Roundup Time in Texas* (US 37) was about roundup time on the South African veldt and *Adventures in Iraq* (US 43) was set in Syria. *The Malibu Bikini Shop* (US 86) is about a boardwalk swimsuit store in Venice, California, not in Malibu.

- Dore Schary, head of production at MGM and RKO in the 1940s and 1950s, recalled that in his early days in Hollywood at Columbia, it was customary to assign a writer a title and expect him to develop an appropriate story. His first assignment was to devise a plot for the title *Fury and the Jungle* and this was followed by *Fog, The Most Precious Thing in Life* and *Man of Steel*. The titles were deliberately kept general enough to admit of almost any plot line.

- *Never Say Never Again* (GB 83), the film in which Sean Connery made his reluctant comeback as James Bond, was so called because the Scottish star had said 'Never again' after *Diamonds Are Forever* (GB 71).

- Roger Corman's *The Beast with 1,000,000 Eyes* (US 55) was produced ultra quickly on an ultra low budget. Unfortunately, Corman ran out of money before the appearance of the opticular beast of the title. Fortunately, his assistant Sam Arkoff was a man of resource. He poked holes in an aluminium tea kettle, which was then shot close to disguise its shape. Nobody, Arkoff figured, would actually count the eyes.

- Gene Wilder's *Haunted Honeymoon* (US 86) is about an engaged couple staying in a spooky old house. Story ends well before the honeymoon.

- Rather confusingly *As You Like It* (Bul 85) is based on

Romeo and Juliet.

- In the early 1930s, piracy of ideas was rife in the Indian film industry and director Dhiren Ganguly was wont to evade questions about the title of his next film with a courteous 'Excuse me, Sir' before hastily switching to another topic. After a while people began asking him when *Excuse Me, Sir* was due to be released, so he decided to call his current project by that title. *Excuse Me, Sir* (Ind 31), released in Hindi and Bengali versions, was one of the most successful prewar Indian comedies.

- Equally meaningless, and for not dissimilar reasons, was the title of a Warner movie starring Errol Flynn. During the 1930s there was a Hollywood convention of using the wholly fictitious title of *Another Dawn* for films purportedly showing at any cinema in a film story. When Warner's ran out of ideas for something catchy to title the somewhat slender story for Flynn's next exhibition of sexual bravura, they tagged it *Another Dawn* (US 38).

- Universal executives admitted that they had no idea what relevance *You Can't Cheat an Honest Man* (US 39) had on the subject matter, nor what writer-star W. C. Fields meant by this scarcely tenable aphorism.

- *The Man With No Name* (It 73) had one. Clint Eastwood is identified in the credits as 'Joe'.

- *Assault on Precinct 13* (US 76) was actually about an assault on Precinct 9.

- In *Her Twelve Men* (US 54), Greer Garson played a teacher in charge of a class of 13 boy pupils. The original story by Louise Baker, on which the film was based, was called *Miss Baker's Dozen*, which aptly and accurately tallied the 13 young men.

> In November 1988 strong winds in London's predominantly Jewish suburb of Golders Green blew off the final letter of the film being advertised on the canopy of the Cannon Ionic cinema. The title read *Who Framed Roger Rabbi.*

- Steven Spielberg's *1941* (US 79) was based on an incident which took place on 23 February 1942 when a Japanese submarine surfaced off Santa Barbara and attempted to bombard as much of Southern California as came within its limited range. Notable as the only armed attack on the Pacific Coast during World War II, the episode caused widespread panic in Los Angeles when it was rumoured that the submarine was launching attack aircraft to bomb the city. Spielberg's not very persuasive reasoning for changing the year was that the date 'automatically leads you to think of Pearl Harbor and makes meaningful the fantasy-hysteria that follows'.

- The title of Stanley Kubrick's notorious *A Clockwork Orange* (GB 72), based on Anthony Burgess's novel of the same name, was not quite as meaningless as some people have supposed. During World War II Burgess had overhead an elderly Cockney in a London pub say that someone was 'as queer as a clockwork orange'—meaning they were mad. The author recalled the phrase 20 years later when he wanted a title for a story about mind control. In the book the violent young gangleader Alex eventually turns from evil of his own volition, but in the film, as played by Malcolm McDowell, he is brainwashed into total submission.

- *The Amorous Prawn* (GB 62) was about a general's wife who opens their official home in the Highlands to American paying guests. In America the title was changed to *The Playgirl and the War Minister*, despite the fact that there was no playgirl and no War Minister in the film—the date explains the choice, since 1962 was the height of the Profumo Affair. Similarly *Marilyn and the Senator* (US 75) had nothing to do with Marilyn Monroe and Senator Kennedy, despite its promotors' obvious intention to mislead, and the girl entangled with a senator is not even called Marilyn.

- Many people who saw and enjoyed Hitchcock's fast-moving thriller *North by Northwest* (US 59) left the cinema wondering what the title had to do with the story. Those of a literary bent may have divined that it was a reference to the character played by Cary Grant, who feigns madness. The words in the title are slightly misquoted from Hamlet: 'I am but mad north-northwest; when the wind is southerly, I know a hawk from a handsaw.'

- Horror pic *Frogs* (US 72) was actually about marauding toads. Frogs will not stay out of the water long enough to take direction.

- Matthew Barney's cult movie *Cremaster 4* (US 94) was actually the first in a cycle of five films on a common theme (that every foetus is potentially double-sexed—the cremaster muscle raises and lowers a man's testicles in response to cold or fear). The fourth film in the cycle was titled *Cremaster 2* (US 99).

- UA's 16th Bond movie *Licence to Kill* (US 89) was to have been called *Licence Revoked*, a title which would have made a good deal more sense. The story-line has Bond's double-0 'licence to kill' revoked by M as he embarks on a personal vendetta to revenge the slaying of his CIA friend Felix Leiter's wife. It is, therefore, the only Bond movie in which the agent does *not* have a licence to kill. But when UA discovered that less than 20% of the American public knew the meaning of 'revoked', they decided to go for the simpler, even though contradictory, alternative.

- Malcolm McDowell may be the eponymous *Gangster No. 1* (GB 00) of that film's title, but he is identified as Gangster 55 in the credits.

The title of James Bond caper *The World Is Not Enough* (US/GB 99) is a straight translation of *non sufficit orbis*, the motto of the Bond family of Wareham, Dorset. It was Ian Fleming's own declaration, in *On Her Majesty's Secret Service*, that this was James Bond's family motto. It raises, however, an issue about 007's own provenance. According to his creator he was a Scot and educated at Tony Blair's alma mater Fettes (Sean Connery, in his first job as a milkman, used to deliver milk there). Now it would appear that he was English after all and a member of a family described by its present head, Martin Bond, as 'a pretty drab bunch, although always respectable'. With the exception, perhaps, of its one black sheep.

- *South of Rio* (US 49) took place well north of it and *Krakatoa, East of Java* (US 68) wasn't. Krakatoa was 200 miles *west* of Java.
- *Special Effects* (US 85) didn't have any.
- *Remake* (Sp 97) wasn't.

Credits

The first screen credits went to André Heuzé for the films he wrote for the French production company Pathé Frères from 1906.

The first person to receive screen credits in the USA was G. M. Anderson, as the leading man of the *Broncho Billy* westerns in 1908. As producer and author of the films, and part-owner of the Essany studio, Anderson was in a strong position to promote his own name. Generally performers in American films did not receive screen credit until 1911, when the Edison Co. and Vitagraph Co. led the way.

The first British film known to have included screen credits was the Gaumont Co.'s *Lady Letmere's Jewellery* (GB 08), with Maisie Ellis in the title role. The credits were pictorial, each leading character being portrayed next to a card bearing his or her name and role. It is possible that Gaumont had adopted the practice of screen credits earlier the same year when they released a now lost film version of the Lyceum Theatre production of *Romeo and Juliet* (US 08), with Godfrey Tearle and Mary Malone. In this case the cast had been billed in the advertising for the film.

The film-maker with most screen credits was Cedric Gibbons (1893–1960), whose name appeared as art director on over 1500 films between 1917 and 1955. The feat was achieved by Gibbons' insistence on a clause in his 1924 contract with MGM to the effect that every film produced by the studio in the USA would credit him as art director. In practice the art direction for the majority of these films was in the hands of his subordinates.

The first pre-credit sequence was in Ben Hecht and Charles MacArthur's *Crime Without Passion* (US 34), which opens with an extreme close-up of the barrel of a gun. The gun fires and blood drips on to the floor. The three Furies of Greek mythology ascend from the puddle of blood in flowing robes and fly over a modern metropolis inciting various crimes of passion. One of the Furies sweeps her arm over the face of a skyscraper, shattering the window glass, which showers down until it forms the words *Crime Without Passion*.

The record for the longest pre-credit sequence is shared by Dennis Hopper's *The Last Movie* (US 71) and Pere Portabella's *Pont De Varsoria* (Sp 90), both movies running for a full half-hour before the credits roll. Portabella's film opens with the award ceremony for a literary prize won by a book with the same title as the movie. The credit sequence begins after 30 minutes of this prologue, which concludes with the book's author deciding to summarise the plot for a guest at the reception. The remainder of the picture, after the credits, consists of scenes from the award-winning novel.

The record for the longest credit sequence is shared by Sergio Leone's *Once Upon a Time in the West* (It/US 68) and Richard Donner's *Superman* (GB 78), each movie running the credits for 12 minutes. Leone disposed of them all at once, Donner in bite-size chunks of five

---

In June 1942 the US Government's Film Conservation Committee voted unanimously for the abolition of all screen credits. The only remaining wording would be the title and 'The End', a measure that was estimated to save 10 million feet of film a year and help save America for democracy. Nothing stood in the way of this patriotic endeavour ... except the massed ranks of producers, directors, actors, writers, tunesmiths, gownsmiths, art directors, editors, first assistant directors, second assistant directors, third and fourth ditto, key grips, best boys, clapper loaders, assistants to the assistant to ... The rest was a footnote to history.

---

minutes at the start and seven at the end. But Donner's took up more of the movie—9% of the running time against 7% for the longer Leone picture.

The largest number of names credited was 1468 in Tadashi Imai's *Senso to Seishin/War and Youth* (Jap 91), but 1421 of these were 'citizen producers', otherwise backers, who had put up $740 each towards the budget in exchange for a credit. The most credits for people involved in the actual making of a film was 1,178 cast and crew credited by Warner Bros for *Space Jam* (US 96), the part live-action, part animated caper starring baseball star Michael Jordan and (uncredited) superrabbit Bugs Bunny. Highest number on a non-animated movie was 599 for *Star Wars: Episode 1—The Phantom Menace* (US 99), many of them for computerised special effects.

When Spencer Tracy insisted on top billing in *Adam's Rib* (US 49), the producer, rightly fearing the reaction of fiery co-star Katharine Hepburn, discreetly asked whether he had not heard of 'ladies first'. Tracy gave him a level stare. 'This,' he growled, 'is a movie, not a lifeboat.'

UNUSUAL CREDITS

In *The Terror* (US 28), the novelty of sound inspired Warners to have the credits spoken by a caped and masked Conrad Nagel. Other films in which the credits have been spoken rather than written include Orson Welles' *The Magnificent Ambersons* (US 42), Truffaut's *Fahrenheit 451* (GB 66), Tony Richardson's *Hamlet* (GB 69) and Robert Altman's *M*A*S*H* (US 70). The last named had a recurring theme of the front-line field hospital's nightly film show being announced over the Tannoy. The last film to be so announced is *M*A*S*H* itself, with full credits. A film called *Episode* (Aut 35) was released with conventional credits at home, but with spoken credits in Nazi Germany. In this case the reason was more sinister than a mere desire for novelty. The director of the picture, Walter Reisch, was Jewish. The credits were spoken against a musical background and when Reisch's name

was reached, the music swelled to make it inaudible.

One of the few recorded examples of sung credits features in *Por que te engana tu marido/Why Does Your Husband Deceive You* (Sp 69). The vocalists are a priest and his choirboys. The credits were sung also on *Don Juan, My Dear Ghost* (Sp 90).

Credits for *Leap of Faith* (US 92), in which Steve Martin plays a dodgy faith-healing evangelist, includes one for the 'cons and fraud consultant'.

A mystery credit on *True Blood* (US 89), to the Wyoming Film Commission, remains unexplained. The picture is not set in Wyoming and was not filmed there.

The Bear (Fr 89) has four casting directors credited. Yet the cast consisted of three people, one non-speaking and the others hardly speaking. The credits also included a credit for the credits.

If I Ever See You Again (US 78) had several credits to dentists, for no obvious reason other than the fact that leads Joe Brooks and Shelley Hack had teeth of the gleaming perfection seemingly unique to the state of California.

Martin Scorsese paid tribute to the therapeutic talents of his analyst, Dr Robert Kahn, in the closing credits of his breakthrough movie *Mean Streets* (US 73).

One of the few films which managed to spell its star's name wrong in the credits was *The Bit Part* (Aus 87), with topliner Chris Haywood billed as 'Heywood'. Probably unique was the film which managed to spell the director's name wrong. Max Ophül's name appeared in the credits of Universal's *Letter from an Unknown Woman* (US 48) as Opuls.

In Mike Snow's curiously titled ↔ (Can 69), the credits appear in the middle of the film. Steven Soderbergh's *Schizopolis* (US 96) has no credits at all, either front or rear, and no title sequence. The only evidence of the film's identity is a copyright notice at the very end.

A notorious credit for *The Taming of the Shrew* (US 29) bore the attribution 'by William Shakespeare, with additional dialogue by Sam Taylor'. Gus Van Sant's *My Own Private Idaho* (US 93) reversed the Sam Taylor principle, by crediting Shakespeare with 'additional dialogue'. The director claimed that Prince Hal in *Henry IV* was a major inspiration for the character of the male prostitute played by Keanu Reeves.

Fritz Lang's *Hangmen Also Die* (US 43) is probably the only film with credits distinguishing the scriptwriter who wrote the script that was used (Fritz Lang) from the scriptwriter who wrote the script that was not (Bertolt Brecht). Incensed that Lang had departed so far from his intended ideas, Brecht won a court decision that allowed him a credit disassociating his script from the shooting script.

Adrian Lyne's *Fatal Attraction* (US 87) boasts one of the odder script credits with 'screenplay, James Dearden, for the screenplay based on his original screenplay'. This last was the screenplay for a 45-minute film called *Diversion* (US 79), rescripted and reshot as a full-length feature under a new title.

Escapade (US 35) ended with William Powell speaking to camera to tell the American public about his co-star, newcomer Luise Rainer, and MGM's high hopes for her Hollywood career. Miss Rainer herself then appeared and was introduced to the audience by Powell.

The role of Crystal Kingsby in *The Lady in the Lake*

(US 46) is given as Ellay Mort. In fact the character never appears, because she is dead. Ellay Mort is 'elle est mort'. Story credit for *Lt Robin Crusoe USN* (US 66) went to the somewhat obscure Retlaw Yensid. Reversed it reveals the rather better known Walt Disney.

The sombre Australian melodrama *In Search of Anna* (Aus 78), featuring a pooch called Billy, had a closing credit which informed audiences that 'Billy eats Loyal Dog Food'. Dusan Makavejev's *The Coca Cola Kid* (Aus 85) contained an unusual testimonial in the credits: 'Catering—Kaos (Highly recommended by the whole cast and crew)'. What appears to be an Australian preoccupation with comestibles stimulated another testimonial at the end of *The Marsupials: The Howling III* (Aus 87), which has a credit to director Philippe Mora for his Eggs Benedict. Credit for catering on *Cactus* (Aus 86) was to Cecil B. DeMeals.

Hollywood feminism is even taking over the credits. The Best Boy on *Slam Dance* (US 87) is credited as 'Electrical Best Person'. In politically incorrect *The Adventures of Priscilla, Queen of the Desert* (Aus 94), an extravagant tale of drag artistes in the Aussie outback, playful crew member Matt Inglis receives his credit as 'Naughty Best Boy'.

David Mamet's *State and Main* (US 00) cocked another snook at Hollywood political correctness with a credit reading 'Only two animals were harmed in the making of this motion picture'.

Diangaka (SA 65) had a credit which read 'Original African music composed by . . .', followed by a number of European names.

The Merchant-Ivory production *Mr and Mrs Bridge* (US 90) has an end credit which reads 'Shakespearean tutor to Mr Newman: Sen. Bob Dole'. This refers to the Kansas politician's reading of *Romeo and Juliet* to Paul Newman to assist him in his characterisation of Kansas City lawyer Walter Bridge.

Only a movie as pretentious as *Patti Rocks* (US 89), with its avowed purpose of 'questioning patriarchal language' and 'equalising nudity', could have a credit to the 'Spiritual Adviser'. On a more down-to-earth level there was also a credit for 'Skunk Wrangler'. *The Dark Half* (US 91) has a credit for 'Sparrow Wranglers'. In the finale the villain is attacked by hordes of these vicious little creatures (sparrows, not wranglers).

The making of *The Cotton Club* (US 85) involved so much litigation that the credits even included one for the law firm representing the successful litigants.

> *Variety*, Hollywood's showbiz bible, does a regular facts-and-figures breakdown of the movie business in different countries. Normally the categories are much the same for each country, but for their 1992 appraisal of Japan they added a new one, headed 'Biggest movie-viewing cultural difference'. It read: 'Entire audience sits through the credits.'

'Tail by Dunlop'. Glynis Johns in Miranda *(GB 47).* (British Film Institute)

There are some credits that the credited might prefer omitted. George Huang's debut picture, *The Buddy Factor* (US 94), was about the relationship of a humble development assistant in Hollywood with his monstrous boss, a senior studio executive. This maven routinely abuses his assistant by throwing things at him, stealing credit for his ideas and belittling him before his peers. Among those in Hollywood at the time who had a reputation for imperious behaviour was Columbia Pictures head of production Barry Josephson. Huang was formerly Josephson's assistant. In the credits for his film, the fledgling director 'thanks' his former mentor for the inspiration he provided.

Some have more worthy reasons for preferring anonymity. Two short Anglo-French wartime dramas directed by Alfred Hitchcock for the Ministry of Information in World War II Britain had no credits except for one leading player, John Blythe. The casts of *Aventure Malgache* (GB/Fr 44) and *Bon Voyage* (GB/Fr 44) were made up of members of the Molière Players, a troupe of French actors who had fled to England from occupied France. As the subject of the two films was the Resistance, the performers asked not to be identified in order to protect their friends and relatives from reprisals by the occupying Nazi authorities.

Unique credit on a unique version of *Casablanca* (US 43) is 'Copyright Infringements by Joao Luiz Albuquerque'. Brazilian cinéaste Albuquerque recut the classic movie for a private showing at the 1987 Rio Film Festival. In the celebrated airport scene Ingrid Bergman does not get on to the plane leaving Casablanca and comes back into the arms of Bogey.

'Diversions by Irving Schwartz' among the credits for

The Sand Pebbles (US 66) was, apparently, in tribute to a mysterious, unknown correspondent whose letters proved a morale booster to cast and crew during trying location work in Hong Kong and Taiwan.

Other unusual credits include one for the 'Roach Wrangler' on George Romero's *Creepshow* (US 59)—the film contains a scene involving thousands of cockroaches; for the 'Technical Consultant on Vampire Bats' on *Chosen Survivors* (US 74); for 'Ant Consultant' in *Empire of the Ants* (US 77); for 'Orgy Sequence Adviser' on *Solomon and Sheba* (US 59); for the perfume worn by the leading players in *Marjorie Morningstar* (US 58); for the shoe polish brightening the cast's shoes in *Scent of Mystery* (US 60); for 'Tail by Dunlop' on *Miranda* (GB 47)—Miranda was a mermaid; for cobbles in *Michael Collins* (US/Ire 96) – credited to The Cobble Crew; for the 'Second Second Assistant Director' on *Reform School Girls* (US 86); for Assistant Second Second Assistant Director on *Lolita* (US 98); for the 'Assistant to the Assistant to the Unit Publicist' on *The Greek Tycoon* (US 78); and to Frederico Fellini, who was not on the picture, 'for encouragement at the right time' in *The World's Greatest Lover* (US 77). Gary Graver's low-budget horror pic *Trick or Treats* (US 82) credits Orson Welles as 'Magical Consultant'. 'Fangs by Dr Ludwig von Krankheit' in Polanski's *Dance of the Vampires* (GB 67) should probably be taken with a pinch of garlic salt.

CHAPTER 11
Censorship

The first film known to have been suppressed was taken by Lumière cameraman Francis Doublier in Moscow in the summer of 1896 and showed Prince Napoléon dancing with the 'lady of his affections', a professional dancer. The film was seized by the Russian police and destroyed.

Later the same year *Delorita's Passion Dance* (US 1896) became **the first film to be banned in the USA** when it was prohibited from exhibition in Atlantic City, NJ, by order of the Mayor.

The first film to be banned for political reasons was Georges Méliès' *L'Affair Dreyfus* (Fr 1899), a 12-scene re-enactment of the arrest, trial, degradation and imprisonment on Devil's Island of Alfred Dreyfus, the Jewish army officer convicted of betraying French military secrets to the Germans. Méliès was passionately pro-Dreyfus, and this was so manifest in the film that at the premiere fighting broke out between the Dreyfusards and their opponents. So riven was France at this time by conflicting attitudes to the case that there was fear for the authority and stability of the state. Méliès' film was suppressed by the government together with the shorter version by Pathé. The Dreyfus Affair remained so controversial that the ban on films about it was not lifted until 1950.

The world's first regulated film censorship was introduced under a Chicago City Council Ordinance of 4 November 1907 'prohibiting the exhibition of obscene and immoral pictures'. Effective 19 November 1907, the Ordinance required that every film be shown to the Chief of Police before it was exhibited publicly and an exhibition permit obtained. Penalty for violation was a fine of $50–100 (£10–20), each day of exhibition without a permit to be regarded as a separate offence. One of the first films to fall foul of the censorship in Chicago was a Vitagraph production of Shakespeare's *Macbeth* (US 08), banned by a zealous police lieutenant on the grounds that 'Shakespeare is art, but it's not adapted altogether for the five cent style of art'. He explained: 'The stabbing scene in the play is not predominant. But in the picture show it is the feature.'

The first country to establish a State Censorship Board was Sweden. The Statens Biografbyra was founded on 4 September 1911 and all films released in Sweden after 1 December 1911 were required to be certified by the Board.

Censorship USA
The USA is one of four countries where the film industry has a self-regulatory censorship independent of government (the others are Britain, Germany and Japan). The following is a brief chronology of American censorship as regulated by the Motion Picture Producers of America (MPPA).

1922 The Motion Picture Producers and Distributors of America founded March under the presidency of former Postmaster General Will H. Hays in an attempt to regulate the industry from within and combat growing demands for government intervention. At this date there were already eight State Censorship Boards (Maryland, New York, Florida, Ohio, Pennsylvania, Virginia, Kansas, Massachusetts) plus 90 municipal boards of varying degrees of severity.

Roscoe 'Fatty' Arbuckle, the world's highest-paid entertainer, became **the first screen star to be banned**. The announcement was made by Will H. Hays of the MPPDA on 18 April, six days after Arbuckle had been acquitted of the manslaughter of 'good-time girl' Virginia Rappe. Shortly afterwards Hays drew up a list of 200 people considered morally dangerous whom it was intended to bar from the industry. Heading the list was Wallace Reid, probably the most popular male star in America prior to Fairbanks' ascendancy, whose

A scene cut from Mervyn LeRoy's I Am A Fugitive From A Chain Gang *(US 32). The rule about floggings was that you could show the impact of the whip but not the sound of the blow; or you could have the sound, but not the sight of the whip falling. In the version of the film as released the camera tracked along the faces of the other convicts as they listened to the thud of the heavy belt.*

drug habit was to finish his career before the MPPDA was able to finish it for him.

1924 The 'Hays Formula' introduced—members agreed to submit scripts in advance for comment and guidance. Few did so unless the script was known to be innocuous.

The 'Index' of forbidden books and plays was introduced.

1927 Hays' list of 'Don'ts' and 'Be Carefuls' adopted in June. Eleven 'Don'ts' included 'any licentious or suggestive nudity', 'miscegenation', 'ridicule of the clergy', 'any inference of sex perversion' and 'the illegal traffic of drugs'. 'Be Carefuls' included 'brutality and possible gruesomeness' and 'the sale of women, or of a woman selling her virtue'. Largely ineffective.

1930 First Production Code—known as 'The Hays Code'—drawn up by Martin Quigley, publisher of Motion Picture Herald, and Fr Daniel A. Lord of St Louis University. Introduced 31 March. No penalties for evasion.

1931 Prior submission of scripts made binding on members.

1934 Production code Administration Office established in June. 'Resolution for Uniform Interpretation' required producers to abide by Code. Penalties for evasion introduced.

First Seal of Approval granted by Hays Office to Fox's *The World Moves On* 11 July.

1943 Howard Hughes caused the first serious breach of the Code when he exhibited *The Outlaw* (US 43) without a Seal of Approval. Billy the Kid, a criminal and moral transgressor, and his girl Rio, a moral transgressor only, were able to ride off into the sunset without reaping any of the just deserts demanded by the Code. (Or by history—in reality Billy the Kid was shot.)

1954 Code seriously breached when Preminger distributed *The Moon is Blue* without a Seal of Approval. He had refused to remove the phrase 'professional virgin' from what was otherwise a wholly innocuous sex comedy.

1955 *The Man With the Golden Arm* awarded Seal despite explicit treatment of drug addiction.

1956 Revised Code introduced. Nudity, profanity and obscenity remained forbidden in all circumstances. Most other former prohibitions modified.

1961 *The Children's Hour* granted Seal despite theme of sexual deviation—in this case lesbianism.

1964 Sidney Lumet's *The Pawnbroker* was passed uncut with a scene showing a woman naked to

Some cities in the US had local ordnances banning the depiction of guns on movie posters. This censored poster advertised Douglas Fairbanks in The Nut *(US 20).*

the waist. This was the first time nudity had been allowed on screen since the setting up of the Production Code Administration Office 30 years earlier.

1966 The 'blue language' barrier finally crashed by *Who's Afraid of Virginia Woolf*, the Production Code Administration agreeing to give it a Seal (with audiences restricted to over 18s) because it reflected 'the tragic realism of life'.

Code revised again, with no positive prohibitions remaining. Approved films were now divided into 'general audience' and 'mature audience'.

1968 Production Code Administration defied when they refused to approve two British films which contained scenes of oral sex: Michael Winner's *I'll Never Forget Whatshisname* (GB 67) and Albert Finney's *Charlie Bubbles* (GB 68). They were released through subsidiary companies of the intending distributors which were not members of the Association. This device enabled any major distributor to circumvent the Administration and hastened its end.

Code replaced by ratings system under the Motion Picture Association of America Ratings Board, effective 1 November. Four classifications: G = General Audience; M = Mature Audience; R = Restricted (children under 16 to be accompanied by an adult); X = over 16 only.

1970 M was replaced by GP (General Patronage) as 'mature' was being misinterpreted as X+. R was changed to accompanied children under 17 and GP became PG (Parental Guidance).

1981 The last State Censorship Board—Maryland—dissolved after 65 years of activity. During its last full year of operation, the Maryland Censor Board viewed 559 movies and banned eight.

The poster on the left was designed to promote The Lady is Willing *(GB 33), starring Leslie Howard. In America the Production Code Administration threw a fit at the position of the hero's hand and the poster was redesigned as shown right.*

1984 A new PG-13 rating introduced 27 June to designate films which require 'special guidance' from parents for children under 13.

1990 Following increasing dissatisfaction with the X-rating, which impeded the distribution of films of artistic merit but explicit sex content, a new NC-17 rating was introduced by the MPPA to signify no children under 17. At the beginning of October the first film to be released under the new rating, Universal's prestigious *Henry and June* (US 90), was banned unseen in Dedham, Mass. A selectman justified the banning with the statement that an X-

---

HOW THE RATINGS RATE

A poll conducted by Gallup in 1994 revealed that more American filmgoers would opt for an R-rated picture—restricted to those over 17 unless accompanied by an adult—than any other rating. The breakdown by preference:

R	39%
PG–13	27%
PG	16%
NC–17	7%
G	6%

Variety, who commissioned the poll, opined that the 39% opting for R (even higher at 42% among 'frequent patrons') are convinced that such pictures are more honest and credible. 'It seems clear,' said an editorial, 'rather than setting off warning bells in moviegoers, the R is a lure.' Of those under 17, no fewer than 37% admitted to attending R-rated movies illegally.

These preferences do not necessarily translate into box office. According to a survey by Paul Kagan Associates, PG-rated films are twice as likely to gross $60 million and three times as likely to gross $100 million as R-rated pictures.

rated film by any other rating remains an X film.

1993 The last local censorship board in the US, Dallas Motion Picture Classification Board, was disbanded in August.

CENSORSHIP GB

The British Board of Film Censors (BBFC) was inaugurated by the Kinematograph Manufacturers' Association in October 1912 with powers effective from 1 January 1913. The moving spirit behind the venture was the film producer Will Barker, who was concerned at the increase in the number of films being produced 'for the smoking room', which he considered would bring the whole industry into disrepute. Together with Col. A. C. Bromhead and Cecil Hepworth, two leading pioneer film-makers, he persuaded the Kinematograph Manufacturers' Association that it was up to the trade to put its own house in order, and with the approval of the Home Secretary the Board was established under the Presidency of G. A. Redford, formerly a playreader for the Lord Chamberlain.

The original classification was into 'U' (Universal) and 'A' (Adult). **The first U Certificate** was granted to the Barker production *Mary of Briarwood Dell* (GB 13) and **the first A Certificate** to the Clarendon picture *A Strong Man's Love* (GB 13), both on 1 January 1913. The A Certificate was originally advisory only. It was not until 1923 that the London County Council prohibited unaccompanied children under 16 from attending 'A' films. Most other local authorities in England and Wales followed suit by the end of the decade, though in Scotland the 'A' Certificate always remained advisory only.

The BBFC began its life with only two firm prohibitive rules: no film depicting the living figure of Jesus Christ and no film which contained scenes of nudity would be granted a Certificate. During the first year of operation, the Board examined 7510 films (6861 'U'; 627 'A'), of which only 22 were rejected outright. Reasons included 'indelicate or suggestive sexual situations', 'holding up a Minister of Religion to ridicule', 'excessive drunkenness' and the portrayal of 'native customs in British lands abhorrent to British ideas'. In 1917 the new Chairman, T. P. O'Connor, declared that he would not grant a Certificate to any film in which crime was the dominant feature and warned producers that no criminal was to be portrayed as a victim of social deprivation. By 1925 the following were also among the 'Don'ts': 'Women fighting with knives'; 'Animals gnawing men, women and children'; 'Insistence upon the inferiority of coloured races'; and 'Salacious wit'.

An 'H' Certificate was introduced in January 1933 to designate 'horrific' films. This was originally advisory only, but from June 1937 became mandatory and as such the first certificate to ban children from cinemas. 'X' for 'Adult Only' followed in 1951. A revised rating system took effect in 1970 with the A Certificate reverting to advisory status, a new AA classification signifying a minimum admission age of 14, and a raising of the admission age from 16 to 18 for X films. It was found that few people understood the status of A and AA films and by the end of the '70s Britain was one of the only countries still using X for respectable adult films, often of artistic merit; elsewhere it was being used solely as a label for pornography. The current ratings system, introduced in December 1982, retained the U for Universal, but replaced A with PG (Parental Guidance) and AA and X with a simple numerical classification of 15 and 18 respectively to denote the minimum age for admission. It also added an 18R category to classify porno and violent films only for showing in specially licensed cinemas.

The Board's function and powers have remained fundamentally unchanged since its inception, despite modification of its criteria for certification in line with changing social and moral standards. An aide-mémoire states: 'The power of censorship is in the hands of local authorities. The BBFC exists to act as an intermediary between local authorities and the film industry. Its success or failure can be measured simply in terms of the acceptability of its judgements to the majority of local authorities in Britain.'

Local authorities have the power to alter the Certificate issued by the BBFC or to permit the showing of an uncertified film. They also remain the only agency with the power to refuse the right of exhibition.

Censorship was extended to home-video movies in Britain in 1985. Unlike cinema films, where the BBFC classification is advisory only, and can be changed on resubmission, the ratings given to video movies were statutory and could not be altered. The move was generally welcomed, as it meant the end of 'video nasties', but there have been two particularly controversial decisions. The BBFC banned the 20-minute video *Visions of Ecstasy* (GB 89) on grounds of blasphemy, the first occasion any film production had been refused for this reason. The film included scenes of the 16th-century Spanish nun St Theresa of Avila embracing the crucified Christ with more than spiritual devotion and episodes of lesbian fantasy. The Board was legally bound to reject any film which it believed to be in violation of Britain's 17th-century blasphemy law, but its decision was bitterly opposed by libertarians. The following year the Board banned distribution of the video of *International Guerillas* (Pak 90) on the grounds that it might be criminally libellous. The Pakistani film portrayed Salman Rushdie, author of *The Satanic Verses*, as a drunken playboy who tortures and murders Muslims as part of an international plot, before being struck down by Allah with a bolt of lightning. Mr Rushdie himself declared that he was against the ban.

Less controversial was the original refusal of a video certificate to *The Exorcist* (US 73). Explained the BBFC: 'Showings of this film have resulted in severe emotional problems for a small but worrying number of adults . . . We feel uneasy about being a party to this sort of psychological damage.' It has now been certified.

No cinema film has been permanently banned outright by the BBFC since 1976, when it refused certification to *Ai No Corrida* (Fr/Jap 76) in which a servant girl cuts off the penis of her master after an intense affair. *The Story of O* (Fr/Ger 75) had been banned in 1975, but was eventually released in 1999.

A new '12' certificate (no children under 12 admitted) was introduced by the City of Westminster, which covers London's West End, in 1989. First film to be awarded the new rating was *Madame Sousatska* (GB 89). It was adopted by the BBFC in August of the same year.

Under the Criminal Justice Act 1994 the BBFC was given retrospective powers to change video classifications or to cut or ban a video which had already been classified. The purpose of the measure is to allow the Board to respond to pressure of public opinion after a video has been released, though the then BBFC director James Ferman warned those who might misconstrue this as a license for indiscriminate banning that he was more likely to revise ratings downward than upward.

In September 2000 the BBFC unveiled new, less stringent guidelines for films restricted to audiences 18 or over. In future the Board will only demand cuts where sexual violence is portrayed or 'instructive detail of drug use'. Straightforward and unrelated sex and violence, other than hardcore pornography, will escape the censors' scissors. At the same time the Board declared it would be 'more relaxed' about the sexual content of films rated 15, but tougher on drug scenes and profanity.

The first cut made by censors in a soundtrack was of offensive words sung by Winnie Lightner in a 1927 Vitaphone short produced by Warner Bros.

The first film to receive an X-rating (adults only) under the British Board of Film Censors system of classification was *La Vie commence demain/Life Begins Tomorrow* (Fr 50), which opened in London on 9 January 1951. The reason for the X Certificate was a sequence dealing with artificial insemination. Previously the film would have had to have been either banned or cut. By the end of the permissive 1960s the number of X films had surpassed the number of A and U films combined.

The first film to receive an X-rating under the Motion Picture Association of America system of classification was Brian de Palma's anti-establishment *Greetings* (US 68) with Robert De Niro, which opened in New York on 15 December 1968.

The first film containing a scene of sexual intercourse to be passed fit for juvenile (accompanied) audiences in Britain was *Siddhartha* (US 72), starring Shashi Kapoor and Simi Garewal and based on the Hermann Hesse bestseller.

RIPE FOR CENSORSHIP

The first demand for censorship in Britain came from the cheese industry in 1898, when Charles Urban released one of his scientific films taken through a microscope which revealed the bacterial activity in a piece of Stilton.

The largest number of cuts known to have been made in any film was the 150 required by the MPAA ratings board for Oliver Stone's *Natural Born Killers* (US 94) to secure an R-rating. In Britain chief censor James Ferman actually asked Stone to restore a violent scene excised by the MPAA. After a bout of energetic sex with his girlfriend (Juliette Lewis), the serial killer played by Woody Harrelson menaces a bound and gagged woman. Ferman was disturbed that her subsequent unscreened killing failed to be separated from the glamour of sex. Inserting the edited-out murder in its full horror, he reasoned, would make the act of killing repugnant to audi-

ences who might otherwise dismiss it among the general mayhem of the film.

The most banned film is open to dispute, but one contender is *Make Them Die Slowly* (US 83), billed as 'The Most Violent Ever'. Publicity for the picture proudly proclaimed that it had been banned in 31 countries.

The country to have imposed the most outright bans is Abu Dhabi with a cumulative total of over 3000. Most of the films affected were declared obscene, anti-Islamic or favourable to Jews.

In the US cinema patrons can now telephone before deciding to see a picture to find out why it has been given a restricted rating. The Parents Guide service was launched in October 1994 by the National Association of Theatre Owners, the Motion Picture Association of America (who run the ratings board) and MovieFone to offer parents an opportunity to say 'No' to films that contain elements they consider unsuitable for their children. Thus in the first week of the scheme they might learn that *The Mask* (US 94) was rated PG–13 for 'stylised violence', while *The Client* (US 94) received the same rating for 'kids in jeopardy and language'.

The first country to abolish censorship of films was Russia under the Kerensky government in March 1917. It was formally reimposed in 1922, though, in practice, there had been a strong measure of control since the accession of the Bolsheviks to power. In the Stalinist era the Soviet censorship became the most rigorous in the world, to the point of nearly extinguishing the film industry in the 1950s. It remained so until glasnost.

The brief flowering of liberty in the revolutionary Russia of 1917 had resulted in nothing more stimulating than a spate of anti-Tsarist films, most of them centring on the depraved monk Rasputin as the architect of decay. When Germany abolished censorship in December 1918, the worst fears of its upholders were confirmed by the rash of sex films that followed. Their titles in no way belied their content: *Frauen, die der Abgrund verschlingt/Women Engulfed by the Abyss* (Ger 18), *Verlorene Töchter/Lost Daughters* (Ger 19), *Die Prostitution* (Ger 19), *Hyänen der Lust/Hyenas of Lust* (Ger 19), etc. Homosexuality (q.v.) was also treated on the screen for the first time. It is doubtful whether anything so explicitly sexual was encountered again in films until the 1960s. Censorship was restored by the National Assembly in May 1920.

No other country abolished censorship for adult audiences until 1969, when Denmark took a lead which was to be followed in the 1970s by Austria, Uruguay, Portugal and Upper Volta and in the 1980s by Panama, Argentina, Peru, Brazil, Hungary and, most remarkably of all, the Soviet Union. Belgium is unique in never having exercised any censorship of films for adults.

The Unkindest Cut

The vagaries of censorship have taken many forms. Here are some of them.

- The State of Illinois demanded excision of the scene in *The Kid* (US 21) in which Jackie Coogan smashes windows. For similar reasons the censorship board of Ohio tried to ban *Treasure Island* (US 20) altogether lest it should encourage children to piracy.
- *The Muppet Movie* (US 79) was cut by the New Zealand censor on grounds of gratuitous violence. The offending scene showed Fozzie Bear being menaced by a drunken sailor with a broken bottle. Sweden banned *E.T.* (US 82) for children under 11 because it was claimed the film showed parents being hostile to their offspring.
- The films of Libertad Lamarque, one of Argentina's major stars of the '30s, were banned in Argentina when Perón came to power in 1945. The reason was that Senorita Lamarque had slapped the face of Perón's mistress Eva Duarte—Evita—on the set of *Circus Cavalcade* (Arg 43) because the aspiring actress had sat in the star's personal chair. When Eva Duarte became the nation's First Lady as Eva Perón, Libertad Lamarque had to flee into exile.
- All Grace Kelly's films are prohibited in Monaco, by order of Prince Rainier. This is out of respect, whereas the royal ban imposed on all Peter Sellers films in Nepal was more a matter of personal pique. Eton-educated King Bivendra took grave exception to Sellers' portrayal of the Indian doctor in *The Millionairess* (GB 60), which happened to resemble the monarch in manner as well as appearance.
- *Tarzan of the Apes* (US 31) was banned in Hitler's Germany as contrary to Nazi doctrine on 'hereditary biology'.
- *Kish Island* (Iran 99) was a six-episode omnibus with contributions by six leading Iranian directors. It debuted at the 17th Fajr International Film Festival without the episode by Rakshan Barni-Etemad. This was blocked by state censors who asserted that too much hair was peeping out from under the scarf of the 13-year old heroine.
- Chahine's *The Emigrant* (Egypt 94) was banned by an Islamic court after a fundamentalist lawyer had personally sued the director on the grounds that the film depicted the Biblical character of Joseph, whom Muslims revere as a prophet. The credits had a disclaimer to the effect that the story was wholly fictitious and did not portray real persons or events. Unfortunately for Chahine a subtitle in French stated that it was based on the story of Joseph, prophet of God, son of Jacob.
- On occasion censorship can have precisely the opposite effect to that intended. The French secret service arranged for every reference to its notorious S.A.C. unit (Service d'Action Crimique) in Yves Boisset's *Le juge Fayard, dit le Shierif* (Fr 76) to be bleeped out. This only drew attention to the existence of the shadowy unit and the result was that Boisset's film, about political corruption in high places, hastened its dissolution.
- Roger Corman, 'King of Movie Schlock', made one film out of an output of over 200 which was not a camped-up horror, sex or disaster picture but a straight drama with a serious message. *The Intruder* (US 62) was intended to alert the nation to the obstruction of school desegregation which was then taking place in the southern states. This impeccably politically correct film, which starred William Shatner as a young rabble rouser stirring up racial hatred in a town about to integrate its schools, fell victim to the political correctness of the MPP code. It was refused a Motion Picture Production Code seal of approval because of the frequent repetition of the word 'nigger' by the redneck bigots and the Code administration was unmoved by Corman's reasoned line of argument that it was only possible to portray racial intolerance if the intolerant spoke in the idiom of their bigotry. The picture remained effectively banned.
- *Twister* (US 96) was rated PG 13 in the US (special guidance for children under 13) for 'intense depiction of very bad weather'.
- *Air Force One* (US 97) and *Independence Day* (US 96) were both nixed by the Chinese censors for too much 'American spirit'.
- At a time when the authorities of Andhra Pradesh felt threatened by revolutionary elements, the censor board demanded the removal of a scene in the Telegu film *Nirupedalu* (Ind 54) which showed a 'Keep Left' traffic sign.
- *Monty Python's Life of Brian* (GB 79) was banned for blasphemy by the local council of Runnymede—until some spoilsport pointed out that they did not have any cinemas in their jurisdiction.
- It is not often that a film is banned at the behest of a private citizen, but Karl Lagerfeld succeeded in having the release of Robert Altman's *Pret-a-Porter* (US 95) blocked in his native Germany because the designer played by Forest Whitaker refers to him as a 'thief'.
- *Die Hard With a Vengeance* (US 95) was banned in Malaysia on the grounds that it showed the villains making fun of the police.

Sunrise Family Video of American Fork, Utah, offered a new twist to the snip—self-censorship. For $5 they offered to doctor copies of PG-13 rated *Titanic* (US 97) to render them fit for Mormon family viewing. Scenes cut out were the ones of Kate Winslett in the nude and another in which it is implied that she and Leonardo Di Caprio have sex. Any other scenes that parents found objectionable could be deleted for an extra $3. Over 58 customers dropped off their copies of the video for the snip on the first day of offer. A heated Paramount spokesman declared the service to be illegal.

- The Egyptian censors were thrown into confusion by *Sommersby* (US 94). No scenes of adultery are allowed in films released in Egypt. The story is of a soldier (Richard Gere), presumed dead, returning to the woman he claims as his wife (Jodie Foster). But is he her husband or is he an impostor? Only if he is an impostor is he committing adultery.
- An unusual ban, which applied only to 12 just men and women, was imposed by Federal Judge Jan E.

DuBois when he instructed the jury in a trial about international money laundering not to see *Lethal Weapon 2* (US 89) until after the verdict. The picture is about international money laundering by foreign envoys protected by diplomatic immunity. The judge had been requested to impose the ban by one of the defendants, a foreign envoy but presumably not immune. He successfully contended that plot similarity might influence the jurors.

- The eight-reel Josephine Baker picture *Folies Bergère* (US 35—French-language version) lost a whole reel to the local censors before it opened at the Odeon in Shanghai, though according to the local society journal *Town and Country* it still held sufficient allure to entice 'many a tired businessman' back for a second or even a third viewing. After two years on release in the interior, it returned to Shanghai again, but considerably shortened. 'Censors all over China had spotted other things that the local censors had missed,' reported *Town and Country*, 'and the film had been reduced to a three-reel affair.' Later it went to Manila where further cuts were made. It returned to Shanghai for a third time in 1937, but scarcely a shot of the lightly clad Miss Baker survived intact—the full-length feature had been reduced to a single reel.

- Captain Renault (Claude Rains), the devious Police Chief of *Casablanca* (US 42), was conceived by the scriptwriters as a man who sold visas to desperate women seeking escape in exchange for sexual favours. One piece of dialogue found unacceptable by the Hays Office was this, between a subordinate and the Police Chief:

    'By the way, another visa problem has come up.'
    'Show her up.'

Another was 'The girl will be released in the morning', which had to be changed to 'The girl will be released later'.

- Ireland has always been notorious for the vigilance of its censors. Surprisingly, though, Roman Polanski's debut picture *Knife in the Water* (Pol 62), a film with strong homosexual overtones, passed unscathed. It was argued that homosexuality was quite unknown to the Irish and what they did not understand could not harm them. An earlier generation of censors had been less tolerant. The Marx Brothers' *Monkey Business* (US 31) was banned lest it provoke the Irish to anarchy.

- *Going My Way* (US 44), with Bing Crosby in an Oscar-winning role as an easy-going priest, was banned in several Latin American countries because the cleric wore a sweatshirt and baseball cap.

- When the script of *Zaza* (US 39) was returned from the Hays Office, a line in which the heroine screams at the villain 'Pig! Pig! Pig! Pig! Pig!' had noted in the margin against it: 'Delete two pigs.' The Hays Office permitted the saloon queen Frenchie (Marlene Dietrich) to push money down her cleavage in *Destry Rides Again* (US 39), but insisted on the deletion of the accompanying line 'There's gold in them thar hills!'.

- *La Coquille et le Clergyman* (Fr 28), the surrealist fantasy directed by Germaine Dulac, was banned by the British Board of Film Censors with the comment: 'This film is so cryptic as to be almost meaningless. If there is a meaning, it is doubtless objectionable.'

- In 1964 the Peking Cinema Institute banned, along with *Hamlet* (GB 48), *Othello* (US/Fr 51) and *The Three Musketeers* (US 48), an educational film titled *Elementary Safety in Swimming in Rivers, Lakes and Seas*. The safety element was considered a bourgeois tendency, likely to undermine revolutionary daring.

- No films depicting two-piece bathing suits were allowed on Malta's screens before 1964; a similar ban on bikinis applied to Malta's beaches. In that year an English tourist was charged with indecent exposure for having revealed her midriff while sunbathing, but was found not guilty. The court ruling had an immediate effect on film censorship. A large number of banned youth movies, including the whole Elvis Presley repertoire, were given the censor's seal of approval.

- *The Wicked Lady* (GB 45), in which Margaret Lockwood played a high-born lady highwayman, had to be almost entirely reshot for the USA due to the depth of Miss Lockwood's décolletage.

- In New Zealand, two of Shakespeare's works were barred from the University of Wellington's Shakespearian Film Festival in 1985—*The Merchant of Venice* for 'anti-Semitism' and *The Taming of the Shrew* for 'sexism'. Doubtless the organisers would have approved of the Act of Parliament passed by the Indian government in 1986 which prohibits the denigration of women in films. Penalty for infringement is up to two years in jail and a fine equivalent to $200.

- Joseph Strick's *Ulysses* (GB 67), from the long-banned novel by James Joyce, was only passed by the British Board of Film Censors with the deletion of the more outrageously obscene dialogue from the soundtrack. Strick then took the film to the GLC, who as the licensing body for London could ignore the Board's decision. The GLC passed the film without a single cut. It was later revealed that the sound reproduction in the GLC projection room was so faulty that none of the censors had heard a word of the dialogue.

- Mickey Mouse was banned in Romania in 1935 on the grounds he was frightening to children.

- *The Grapes of Wrath* (US 40) was allowed to be shown in the USSR, because the authorities considered it painted a sufficiently unattractive picture of the life of the American proletariat during the Depression. It was later banned when they found that audiences were immensely impressed by the fact that the itinerant family of the story, intended to represent America's dispossessed, owned an automobile.

- The censors demanded that Hitchcock should remove the split-second glimpse of Janet Leigh naked in the celebrated shower scene in *Psycho* (US 60). Unwilling to acknowledge the need to keep it secret that people shower without their clothes on, the master simply returned the sequence to the board, without having cut so much as a frame. Assuming that he had done as they had commanded, they approved it without further ado.

- *The Adventures of Barrie McKenzie* (Aus 73)—funded by the Australian government—fell foul of the New

Zealand censor, who said he could pass it if one cut was made—'from the beginning to the end'.

● When *The Sound of Music* (US 65) opened at the City Palast in Munich it was with about one third of its running time eliminated. Everything about the Anschluss and the Von Trapp family's daring escape from the Nazis had vanished from the screen. Munich, cradle of the Nazi Party, preferred not to confront that part of the story. The film ended abruptly and bewilderingly immediately after the marriage of Maria to the Baron Von Trapp.

The deletion of 'unpersons' from Soviet encyclopaedias and the retouching of historical photographs to eliminate 'enemies of the state' like Trotsky were familiar practices in the Soviet Union before glasnost. Evidence reached the West that a similar revision of history was undertaken with classic films during the Brezhnev era. Writing in *Sight and Sound*, Alexander Sesonske reported how he showed Mikhail Romm's distinguished *Lenin in October* (USSR 37) to a class of film students in 1983. The original film, as Sesonske knew, had attributed to Stalin a leading role in the October Revolution second only to that of Lenin himself; and in nearly every scene depicting Lenin, the tyrant was shown at his right hand, dispensing wise advice and supporting him loyally in committee against Trotsky and other revisionists. The print shown to the students had not a single image of Stalin; he had been eliminated from the film entirely. Some shots had been simply deleted, others cut at the point that Stalin should have appeared. The majority, however, had been skilfully doctored by back projecting the film, then rephotographing the images after placing a large foreground figure, usually a Baltic sailor, to block out Stalin from view. Ironically the revised version of *Lenin in October* is far closer to historical truth than Romm's original.

● At a point in *The Grass is Greener* (GB 60) where the English peer played by Cary Grant has the gravest doubts about his wife Deborah Kerr's behaviour with American visitor Robert Mitchum, the couple play a game of Scrabble. In the original script, the noble lord pointedly added to the word 'conduct' the prefix 'mis'. The censor threw a fit and drew heavy lines in blue pencil. Director Stanley Donen first substituted 'adult', with Grant adding 'ery', then had a brainwave and wrote in 'infidel' with 'ity' as the suffix. The censor passed the revision on the nod.

● Pubic hair is not allowed to be visible in pictures released in Japan. No such rule is required in Iran, where the eventuality is unlikely to arise, but women of 'extraordinary and seductive beauty' are banned from the screen. It is also prohibited for the female lead to be more prominent than the male lead, and women can never be billed first in the credits.

● There was a wide disparity between what was acceptable language in English movies for an English audience and what was deemed legitimate by the Hays Office for the sensitive ears of American audiences. In *The Way to the Stars*/US: *Johnny in the Clouds* (GB 45), Rosamund John as landlady of a pub good-naturedly sees off a roisterer who has imbibed one too many with the words 'Get the hell out of here'. In the US it had to be dubbed as 'Get the heck out of here'. Laurence Olivier offended the moral guardians of America with the expressive 'Norman bastards!' in Shakespeare's *Henry V* (GB 44). He was obliged to rerecord the soundtrack for America with 'Norman dastards'.

● Monster movies presented the censors with problems on both sides of the Atlantic, but what they wanted to protect the public from was not always the same. In the States they were preoccupied with bosoms. For *The She Monster* (US 58), B-pic producer James Nicholson wanted to create as repulsive a creature as possible. 'She had a long scaly tail; a body covered with green armor plate like an armadillo, and fangs framed in the face of a gargoyle', he recalled. 'When we submitted our script to the Johnston Office [successor to the Hays Office], the general content was approved, but we were cautioned to be certain that in our depiction of this female monstrosity, we watch the cleavage.' In Britain, where censorship was more concerned with cruelty than cleavage, difficulties arose over another Nicholson production: *It Conquered the World* (US 56). The British Board of Film Censors had strict rules against scenes depicting brutality to humans or, more importantly, in a nation where you could thrash a child but not a dog, against animals. The scene which gave officials high anxiety showed the hero sensibly destroying the evil monster with a blowtorch. After profound deliberations, the Board ruled that monsters from outer space are neither human nor animal and therefore not subject to the constraints affording protection to more familiar beings.

● *A Day at the Races* (US 37) was banned in Latvia on the grounds that it was 'worthless', much to the huge delight of the Marx Brothers. They were even more enchanted when *Duck Soup* (US 33) was prohibited in Italy on the personal orders of Benito Mussolini, who believed Groucho's portrayal of dictator Rufus T. Firefly to have been a mirror image of himself.

- The National Legion of Decency rated the biopic of Gypsy Rose Lee, *Gypsy* (US 62), as objectionable because they claimed it attempted 'to rationalise a morally questionable occupation'. Audiences eager to judge the moral issue for themselves flocked to see the film, though many were disappointed that Natalie Wood failed to outrage them by stripping to the buff.

- Stalin took personal command of the censorship of Soviet films in the years following World War II. Among the directors whose films fell victim to the tyrant's capricious whim was Sergei Yutkevich. After his film *Light Over Russia* had been screened in Stalin's private cinema in the Kremlin in 1947, he was presented with a list of the film's ideological faults and told it would not be released. In his memoirs, Yutkevich recalled this dialogue between a Goskino official and himself:

    Aide: 'Comrade Stalin didn't like the film at all.'
    Yutkevich: 'So these are his comments?'
    Aide: 'No, he didn't say anything. But Comrade Bolshakov, who was sitting behind him as usual, took note of Comrade Stalin's snorts of disapproval. Then he took these notes on Comrade Stalin's reactions to Comrade Zhdanov and they deciphered them and wrote out the conclusions you have read.'

    Comrade Yutkevich was more fortunate than many who incurred Stalin's disapproval. He survived to tell the tale.

- The performance of the haunting song 'Tomorrow Belongs to Me' by a young Nazi in *Cabaret* (US 72) was so compelling that it was cut from the German release prints lest it arouse latent far-right nationalism.

- The Hays Office insisted that an English translation of the made-up mumbo-jumbo language of the natives in *King Kong* (US 33) should be submitted to them for approval.

- One of the complaints of the smaller studios in the days when the rule of the Hays Office was inviolate was that the censors did not apply their strictures consistently. Republic objected strongly when they were ordered to cut the number of slayings in their low-budget western *West of Cimarron* (US 42) from 13 to 'seven or eight'. Even when the censors conceded that the balance could be made up with serious woundings, the studio responded that their customers wanted straightforward killings and cited a Memphis exhibitor who was reluctant to book any western with less than ten violent deaths. Most galling of all, though, was that over on the Warner Bros lot Frank Capra was directing *Arsenic and Old Lace* (US 42) without interference, despite the fact that the charming Brewster sisters were despatching their 12 lonely gentlemen boarders to a better world and had every intention of doing away with the 13th.

- The US Navy banned *From Here to Eternity* (US 53) from its movie screens on the grounds that it was 'derogatory to a sister service', the Army. The US Army approved it for showing at its bases throughout the world.

- Self-censorship was applied by the Hollywood studios themselves. In the Joan Fontaine film *From This Day Forward* (US 46) a character remarks 'I didn't sleep well last night. It must have been those two cups of coffee I drank'. The second sentence was deleted by RKO's adviser on foreign affairs, who cautioned that 'the suggestion of harmful effects of coffee would be resented by coffee-raising Brazil'.

- *Extase* (Cz 32), the sensational film in which a pre-Hollywood Hedy Lamarr appeared as nature intended, was banned in New York on the grounds that it was 'indecent, immoral and would tend to corrupt morals within the meaning of Section 1082 of the Educational Law'. In Nazi Germany, where the naked form was much celebrated in art and sculpture, the picture enjoyed a widespread popular and critical success. Until the authorities discovered that Miss Lamarr was a Viennese Jewess. Then it was promptly banned.

- If the censors will not prevent a controversial film from being shown, sometimes ordinary citizens will take matters into their own hands. When James Stewart starred in *Anatomy of a Murder* (US 59), his father was so disgusted by his son's exposure in what Stewart *père* considered 'a dirty picture' that he took an ad in the local newspaper advising his neighbours not to go and see it.

- The Mexican government used to assign a 'Licenciado' from the government cinematographic office to act as on-the-spot censor for Hollywood films shot south of the border. On Robert Rossen's *The Brave Bulls* (US 50), Licenciado Juan Barona

Joseph I. Breen, chief censor of the Production Code Administration, better known as the 'Hays Office', resigned in 1941 to become head of production at RKO. A year later he decided to resume his former office. Among his duties was censoring his own recent production.

objected to a brief scene in which a real railway worker was shown oiling the wheels of a locomotive. The reason Barona gave was that the man was too ugly. Asked if that meant he was deformed, the Licenciado replied: 'No. He is just ugly. He is not representative of our railways.'

- The Danish Film Institute found an ingenious, if questionable, way of blocking production of Jens Jörgen Thorsen's controversial project *The Return of Jesus*. Following worldwide protests that the way in which Thorsen planned to portray Jesus would be blasphemous, but unwilling to be seen to be denying the right of free speech, they revoked their subsidy on the grounds that the script violated the copyright of the authors of the *New Testament*.

- Horace Horsecollar's sweetheart Clarabelle the Cow caused the censors a severe attack of the scissors on more than one occasion. In 1930 a Mickey Mouse cartoon was banned in Ohio because she was seen reading a copy of Elinor Glyn's notorious novel *Three Weeks*. The Hays Office was even more incensed by the exposure of Clarabelle's udder to the public gaze and it was decreed that in future she should be decently attired in a skirt. And if animated cows could inflame the passions, the prospect of displaying real live ones on screen put the censors into severely moralistic mode. RKO's *Little Men* (US 40) fell foul of the Production Code when they wanted to feature the Borden Milk Company's amiable mascot Elsie the Cow. Code Administrator Joseph Breen wrote to the producer that 'dialogue about milking is extremely dangerous'. He also insisted that all shots of the provocative process itself should be eliminated. Despite all this, RKO considered Breen would be a valuable acquisition for the studio—see box above.

- The American censors allowed a scene in *La Maternelle* (Fr 33) in which a streetwalker picks up a man in a café watched by her small daughter, but insisted that a sequence in which the woman and the man touch hands beneath the table should be scissored.

- Sometimes censorship may involve adding a scene rather than cutting one out. In *The Blue Lagoon* (GB 49), young lovers Donald Houston and Jean Simmons have their baby out of wedlock for the simple reason that they have been castaways on a desert island since childhood. The British accepted this with equanimity—the episode in its literary form had failed to shock the delicate sensibilities of Edwardian readers when H. de Vere Stacpoole's novel first came out in 1909. But American audiences were judged to be unready for such a moral dilemma. It was solved to the satisfaction of the US censors by having the youngsters read the wedding service to each other from the Prayer Book.

- In 1973 a US Supreme Court ruling which allowed greater freedom for individual states and cities to make their own censorship decisions on what constitutes obscenity threw the major, Hollywood studios into a spin. Martin Scorsese, then preparing to make *Alice Doesn't Live Here Anymore* (US 74), was on the receiving end of a five-page list of admonitions from a Warner Bros executive. One of the choicest read: 'Love scenes must show "taste" and not show lovers.'

- In 1994 the New York Transit Authority decided to impose its own censorship on movies that portrayed the subway as the first circle of hell. Henceforth, it decreed, the only film crews allowed access below ground would be those making wholesome family fare. 'We want to protect our investment and increase ridership,' Transit Authority spokesman Jared Lebow told the *New York Times*. 'We don't want bullets whizzing around subway cars. We don't want bloody bodies strewn over subway cars.' The announcement was met with outrage not only from film-makers, who pointed out that production in the Big Apple brought the city some $1.3 billion a year, but also New Yorkers who take a perverse pride in the horror beneath their streets, the Kosovo of subway systems. The Transit Authority was adamant and *The Times* of London opined: 'One thing is for sure, the deranged subway rider armed to the teeth and out for blood is no more: except, of course, in reality.'

- In Italy Bernardo Bertolucci's *Last Tango in Paris* (Fr/It 72) was first banned and then charged in the courts with 'obscene content offensive to public decency, characterised by an exasperating pan-sexualism for its own end, presented with excessive self-indulgence, catering to the lowest instincts of the libido, dominated by the idea of stirring unchecked appetites for sexual pleasure, permeated by scurrilous language—with crude, repulsive, naturalistic and even unnatural representation of carnal union, with continued and complacent scenes, descriptions and exhibitions of masturbation, libidinous acts and lewd nudity—accompanied offscreen by sounds, sighs and shrieks of climax pleasure'. In other words, smut.

- In Japan the censors cut the crucial scene in *The Crying Game* (GB/Ire 93) in which Jaye Davidson as the supposed girlfriend is revealed to have a penis. A survey of patrons leaving the cinema after seeing the film revealed that many of them thought that Stephen Rea ran retching to the bathroom because he had found that Jaye Davidson's character had a loathsome disease.

- In 1914 pioneer features director Hobart Bosworth brought to the screen Jack London's novel *John Barleycorn* (US 14), based on the author's own experiences as an alcoholic. According to papers found 60 years later in the London Collection, a group of liquor companies offered Bosworth $25,000 to delay release until after referenda on prohibition had been held in six states. Bosworth refused the bribe, but influence was brought to bear on Pennsylvania's chief censor J. Louis Breitinger, who had what was discreetly referred to as 'professional connections with several breweries'. Breitinger employed delaying tactics to hold up certification, but defiant exhibitors in Pennsylvania, outraged at such shameless manipulation of the censorship system to serve commercial interests, ignored the censorship board and showed the film illegally.

- *Shock Corridor* (GB 63) was rejected by the British Board of Film Censors for suggesting that residence in a mental hospital could induce insanity.

- Steven Spielberg's *Schindler's List* (US 93), a moving account of German industrialist Oskar Schindler's heroic efforts to save victims of the concentration camps, was banned in Malaysia for favouring the Jews. The chief censor wrote to Spielberg: 'The story reflects the privilege and virtues of a certain race only. The theme of the film is to reveal the brutality and cruelty of the Nazi soldiers to the Jews. It seems the illustration is propaganda with the purpose of asking for sympathy as well as to tarnish the other race.' The resulting outcry internationally brought the matter to the notice of the Malaysian Government's cabinet, who decided the film could go out with 25 cuts amounting to 15 minutes of screen time. Spielberg responded by pulling not only *Schindler's List* from distribution, but every other Amblin Entertainment production past and present.

- French director Barbet Schroeder claimed to have been the only film-maker in history for whom acceding to a demand for cuts in a film was literally a matter of life or death. When his feature documentary *General Idi Amin Dada* (Fr 74) was screened before its subject, the ruthless dictator instructed him to cut three sequences totalling a minute and 15 seconds of screen time: a public execution, with the commentary noting that Amin had ordered the deaths of thousands since he came into power; a cabinet meeting at which he screams at his foreign minister because he did not 'make the world love Uganda enough'—the commentary stated that the minister's body was found floating in the Nile ten days later; and a personal statement by the director at the end in which he declared that it was 'partly a deformed image of ourselves that Idi Amin sends back to us'. Schroeder demurred, on grounds of his personal integrity. The dictator acted swiftly and characteristically. He rounded up all the French citizens in Kampala and threatened to have the 150 hostages executed unless Schroeder complied. Faced with this ultimatum the director did so. After the censored film had been released Amin told the French ambassador in Kampala that the film-maker would be very welcome to return to Uganda whenever he wished. Schroeder observed drily: 'I wouldn't want to test the welcome.'

• The only film banned by its own director was *A Clockwork Orange* (GB 72), which Stanley Kubrick withdrew from circulation in Britain following a spate of copycat crimes based on the violent outrages shown on screen, some of them carried out by young delinquents dressed in the bowler hat and single false eyelash sported by gangleader Alex (Malcolm McDowell) and his 'Droogs'. The only occasion it was seen in Britain during Kubrick's lifetime was a one-night special showing at the Scala cinema in London in 1992, for which the programme manager was convicted of breach of copyright and ordered to pay £1000 in costs. Strangely, Kubrick did not seek to ban the film in other countries, despite similar outbreaks of violence attributed to it, but he refused Malcolm McDowell permission to include it in a retrospective of the star's films held in Moscow in aid of the victims of Chernobyl. It was only in March 2000, a year after Kubrick's death, that *A Clockwork Orange* was re-released in Britain.

• When the Royal Flying Corps aviator played by Fredric March in *The Eagle and the Hawk* (US 33) returns to the Front from leave, he has spent the night with his sweetheart (Carole Lombard). This was delicately represented by a gardenia, which he had been wearing, left on her pillow. The censors demanded the scene be reshot—with the gardenia left on her bedside table.

• One of the most notorious examples of oppressive censorship occurred not at the hands of a censorship board but what might be loosely described as a 'pressure group'. The picture was *The Godfather* (US 72),

those who were affronted were the Mafia, and the pressure group was the Italian American Civil Rights League, headed by Joseph Colombo. When the League attempted to halt production of the film, producer Albert S. Ruddy decided it would be in the interests of his personal wellbeing and prospects of longevity to meet Mr Colombo and others of its representatives for a full and frank exchange of views. After protracted negotiations, during which the League asserted that the Mafia did not exist and was a figment of collective hysteria, they made him an offer he couldn't refuse. The film could go ahead with no fear of retribution from a non-existent Italian underworld brotherhood provided the word 'Mafia' was wholly excised from the script. Ruddy declared that he had no wish to cast a slur on the blameless lives led by New York's Italian-American community and agreed to the League's suggestion. As it happened Joseph Colombo was slain before the picture started shooting, by persons alleged to belong to an organised crime syndicate comprised of citizens of the same national origin as himself.

The Godfather (US 72) was a sensation and became the top-grossing film of 1972 even without the word 'Mafia' uttered anywhere on the soundtrack. But those who decried what they believed was a craven compromise with the Mob were mistaken in their criticism. Mario Puzo, author of the original novel and scriptwriter of the film, wryly observed: 'I must say that Ruddy proved himself a hard bargainer, because the word "Mafia" was never in the script in the first place.'

• Only one film has been banned for an alleged spelling mistake—Ousmane Sembene's *Ceddo* (Sen 78) or, if you prefer the Senegal government's version, *Cedo*. The controversy over the title waxed furious, both parties to the dispute parading linguistic experts in their defence and both asserting that their only concern was the Senegalese people should be properly instructed in the correct form of the Wolof language. To support his case Sembene, Africa's foremost film director, sent a three-page open letter to 'all Senegalese and to the President of the Republic of Senegal', defending the two d's in Ceddo—a term meaning the common people in a feudal society which had also included royalty, slaves, warriors, historians and artisans. The film-maker declared that he could afford to wait 'for another generation or more for the Government to change its mind'. In the meantime *Ceddo* with two d's opened at the Museum of Modern Art's Senegalese film festival in New York to the acclaim of non-Wolof speaking Americans.

CHAPTER 12
Animation

The first animated film using the stop-motion technique to give the illusion of movement to inanimate objects was Vitagraph's *The Humpty Dumpty Circus* (US 1898). Albert E. Smith, who conceived the idea, borrowed his small daughter's toy circus and succeeded in animating the acrobats and animals by shooting them in barely changed positions one frame at a time—the same principle as that used for animated cartoons.

The first animated cartoon film—J. Stuart Blackton's Humorous Phases of Funny Faces *(US 06).*

The earliest known British example of animation is an untitled advertising film made by Arthur Melbourne Cooper of St Albans, Herts, for Messrs Bryant & May. Dating from 1899, it consists of an appeal for funds to supply the troops in South Africa with matches, as it seems this was something the Army authorities had overlooked. The animated 'performers' are matchstick men who climb up a wall and form themselves into the legend: 'Send £1 and enough matches will be sent to supply a regiment of our fighting soldiers'.

Some years later, Melbourne Cooper made two charming films featuring animated toys, *Noah's Ark* (GB 08) and *Dreams of Toyland* (GB 08). Strutting teddy bears were featured in the latter to particularly engaging effect.

Meanwhile, in the United States, J. Stuart Blackton, Albert E. Smith's co-partner at Vitagraph, had produced an unusual novelty with *The Haunted Hotel* (US 07), in which furniture moved about seemingly by its own agency.

The following year Pathé pioneered the animation of paper cut-outs in *Paper Cock-a-Doodle* (Fr 08)—the cut-

outs being in the shape of exquisitely wrought birds. The pioneer of animation in Russia was Ladislas Starevitch, who applied the stop-motion technique to bring dead insects 'alive' in *The Grasshopper and the Ant* (Rus 11) and *The Stag Beetles* (Rus 11).

Back in Britain the Natural Colour Kinematograph Co. pioneered with the first animated film in colour, *In Gollywog Land* (GB 12), using animated puppets combined with live action, and the first claymation film, *Modelling Extraordinary* (GB 12), also in colour. Both were released in December 1912, the former also distributed in the US under the title *Gollywog's Motor Accident.*

The first cartoon film was J. Stuart Blackton's *Humorous Phases of Funny Faces* (US 06), produced for the Vitagraph Co. of New York. Like nearly all early American film cartoonists, Blackton used the technique of showing an artist drawing a still picture which then magically came alive and moved. Most of the illusions were created by means of cardboard cut-outs, but a few genuinely animated drawings featured at the beginning of the film, showing a man and a woman rolling their eyes and the outline of a gentleman with bowler and umbrella apparently drawing himself.

The first British cartoon film was *The Hand of the Artist* (GB 06), made by Walter Booth for the Charles Urban Trading Co and released in April 1906. It was clearly inspired by Blackton's *Humorous Phases of Funny Faces* (see above).

The first cartoon film to tell a story was Emile Cohl's *Fantasmagorie* (Fr 08), which was premièred at the Théâtre du Gymnase in Paris on 17 August 1908. Cohl made the film for Léon Gaumont, by whom he was employed as a scenarist. Prior to this, nearly all cartoon films were of the artist-drawing-a-living-picture genre. Robert Desnos has described Cohl as the first to 'cut the umbilical cord which still linked the life of the characters on the screen with the secretions of the fountain pen'. He made about 100 cartoons between 1908 and 1918 and can thus be regarded as **the first professional screen animator.**

The first cartoon series was inaugurated by Emile Cohl with the debut of his character Fantôche, a kind of matchstick man combatting the cruel world, in *Le Cauchemar du Fantôche* (Fr 09). **The first cartoon series in America**, also inaugurated by Cohl, was Eclair's *The Newlyweds*, starting with *When He Wants a Dog, He Wants a Dog* (US 13). Based on the popular cartoon characters originated by George McManus in the *New York World*, the series gave a new descriptive term to the vocabulary of film-making. It was an advertisement for *The Newlyweds*, appearing in *Moving Picture World* for 15 February 1913, that contained **the first use of the term 'animated cartoon'.**

The first British cartoon series was *Adventures of Slim and Pim* (GB 18), drawn by Leslie Dawson for Charles Urban's Kineto Co. Slim and Pim were two characters prone to Laurel and Hardy-type misadventures. First to feature animal characters was *The Wonderful Adventures of Pip, Squeek and Wilfred* (GB 21), 26 one-reel episodes based on the popular children's strip in the *Daily Mirror* by A. B. Payne and B. J. Lamb. The series was drawn by Lancelot Speed for Astra Films.

The longest cartoon series was Harry 'Bud' Fisher's *Mutt and Jeff*, which began as a 'Comic Supplement' to *Pathé's Weekly* with the issue of 10 February 1913 and continued as separate weekly reels from 1 April 1916 to 1 December 1926. Allowing for a gap in 1923–4 when no titles have been traced, there were at least 323 *Mutt and Jeff* films. Several have been colorised and synchronised for video release, making them the oldest cartoon films still in regular distribution. A list of all known titles is contained in Denis Gifford's *American Animated Films: The Silent Era, 1897–1929* (McFarland, 1990).

The longest series of talkie cartoons for the cinema was Max Fleischer's *Popeye The Sailor Man*, with 233 one-reelers and a single two-reeler (*Popeye the Sailor Meets Sinbad the Sailor* (US 36)) between 1933 and 1957. There were another 220 Popeye cartoons for television produced by King Features in the 1970s. For the first few weeks of the original cinema series Popeye was voiced by William Costello; then for the next 45 years (including the TV cartoons) by Jack Mercer.

The first animal cartoon series featuring an animal character was *Old Doc Yak*, a tail-coated billy-goat in striped pants, who was brought to the screen by *Chicago Tribune* cartoonist Sidney Smith in a Selig Polyscope series started in July 1913. It was the much-loved animal cartoon characters who eventually gave animated films a distinct appeal of their own as suitable entertainment for children. This development can best be dated from the advent of Pat Sullivan's Felix the Cat in Paramount's *Feline Follies* (US 20), an animal who 'kept on walking', and who was the first cartoon character to attain the celebrity of a human star. Felix was also **the first animated cartoon character to be merchandised** when Margaret Winkler (who had become the first woman producer and distributor of cartoons in 1922 at the age of 25) issued licences in the US and UK in 1924. Used first as an image on packaging, Felix became a phenomenally successful cuddly toy two years later. Although his star has waned in the west, in Japan Felix is rated as one of the three most popular cartoon characters (the others are Snoopy and Mickey Mouse). A feature-length movie, *Felix the Cat: The Movie* (US 89), failed to catch on in its home market but was enormously popular with the Japanese.

The first cartoon film based on a comic strip was Winsor McCay's *Little Nemo* (US 11), a Vitagraph production derived from the artist's *Little Nemo in Slumberland*.

The earliest known use of cartoon animation in a pornographic movie occurs in *The Virgin with the Hot Pants* (US c.24), which opens with a cartoon woman being

> The rarest and most sought-after cartoon film of all time was rediscovered in 1998 when a 16mm film, bought in London for £2 from the disposal of the Wallace Heaton Film Library in the late 1970s, was identified as the only known copy of Walt Disney's first-ever production, the 7-minute-long *Little Red Riding Hood* (US 22). It was made at Disney's Laugh-O-Gram Films, a small animation studio he established in Kansas City and which went bankrupt within a year. *Little Red Riding Hood* is particularly notable to Disney buffs because, unlike the later Hollywood cartoons such as Mickey Mouse, it was drawn by the 21-year-old fledgling film-maker himself. The reason that the unique print remained unidentified for so long was that the pirated copy bought by silent-movie collector David Wyatt had been retitled *Grandma Steps Out*. Only when he took it to the Disney company 20 years later was it finally revealed that the holy grail of animated films had been found at last.

pursued round a room by a cartoon penis-and-testicles. The pursuer finally catches and penetrates her while she hangs from a chandelier. The next sequence introduces that classic duo of cartoons, the cat and mouse double act, to the world of the dirty movie. In this case the cat is victim, caught and ravished by a mouse with a giant penis.

The first cartoon talkie for theatrical release was Max Fleischer's Song Cartune *Come Take a Trip in my Airship* (US 24), which opens with a 25-second sequence in which the animated figure of a woman in a white dress speaks some patter as the lead-in to the song. The sound-on-film synchronisation was by DeForest Phonofilm.

The first all-talking cartoon was Paul Terry's 'Aesop's Film Fable' *Dinner Time* (US 28), produced by Van Beuren Enterprises in the RCA Photophone sound system and premièred at the Mark Strand Theater in New York on 1 September 1928. Walt Disney dismissed it as 'a lot of racket and nothing else'. His own initial venture in talkies, *Steamboat Willie* (US 28), presented at New York's Colony Theater on 18 November 1928, was more auspicious; it marked the debut of the most successful cartoon character of all time, Mickey Mouse.

The first British cartoon talkie was *The Jazz Stringer* (GB 28), with 'Orace the 'Armonious 'Ound, made at Wembley Studios by Joe Noble and his brother George ('Orace's voice) for British Sound Productions and premièred at the Tivoli Cinema in the Strand on 15 December 1928. It was claimed that it was 'the first lip synchronised cartoon in the world'.

The first colour cartoon was *The Debut of Thomas Kat* (US 20), a Paramount release produced by the Bray Pictures Corporation of New York in the Brewster natural-colour process. The drawings were made on transparent celluloid and painted on the reverse, then filmed with a two-colour camera. An unfortunate kitten, Thomas Kat, had been taught by his mother to catch mice, but inadvertently mistook a rat for the smaller breed of rodent.

The first cartoon series in colour was *The Red Head Comedies* (US 23), each a lampoon of an historical event produced by the Lee-Bradford Corporation. Colour process not known.

The first colour cartoon talkie was a three-minute sequence in Universal's *The King of Jazz* (US 30). Made by Walter Lanz in two-colour Technicolor, it depicted a cartoon version of bandleader Paul Whiteman on a big game hunt in Africa. First complete film was Ub Iwerks' two-colour Technicolor *Fiddlesticks* (US 31), featuring Flip the Frog, which was copyrighted on 24 April 1931. Disney's original colour cartoon was not, as often claimed, the world's first, but it was the first in a three-colour process. A Silly Symphony titled *Flowers and Trees* (US 32), the Technicolor short premièred at Grauman's Chinese Theater on 15 July 1932.

Britain's first cartoon talkie in colour was *On the Farm* (GB 33), produced in Raycol Colour and animated by Brian White, Sid Griffiths and Joe Noble from designs by Punch cartoonist H. M. Bateman.

The first animated film for theatrical release with computerised colouring was Fox's *The Diner* (US 92), a short produced by Amblin Entertainment. The digital system used cuts the ink-and-paint workload by about 70%. A technician colours about one cell in four and a computer matches the paintwork on the rest. The first feature with computerised colour was Universal's *We're Back* (US 93), also an Amblin production.

The first feature-length cartoon film was Don Frederico Valle's 60-minute *El Apostol* (Arg 17), premièred at the Select-Suipacha in Buenos Aires on 9 November 1917. Based on the book by Alfredo de Lafarrere, the film was a political satire on Argentina's President Irigoyen. The team of five animators was headed by Diogones Tabora, a well-known caricaturist, and between them they produced 58,000 drawings for the film over a period of 12 months. No prints survive.

> Louis B. Mayer, notwithstanding the advice of MGM studio executives, refused to put aspiring cartoon-maker Walt Disney under contract in 1928 after seeing a preview of the first Mickey Mouse movie because he thought that pregnant women would be frightened of a 10ft-high rodent on the screen.

The first full-length cartoon talkie was also surprisingly produced in Argentina. Made by Quirino Cristiani in 1931, *Peludopolis* was another satire on President Irigoyen and used the Vitaphone sound-on-disc system of synchronised sound. Running time was one hour. These two Argentinian cartoon features, and an Italian production *The Adventures of Pinocchio* (It 36), preceded the film which has generally been hailed as the world's first full-length cartoon feature. In fact Walt Disney's *Snow White and the Seven Dwarfs* (US 37) was only the first American cartoon feature, though it was the world's first to be made in both sound and colour.

Britain's first feature-length cartoon made for commercial release was Halas and Batchelor's *Animal Farm* (GB 54), from George Orwell's savage satire on Soviet repression.

> Naming Disney's seven dwarfs is a cinch for most trivia-quiz contestants. Real movie buffs, though, should try this one: who were the other four dwarfs who were developed by the huge team of 750 animators working on *Snow White and the Seven Dwarfs* (US 37) but did not make it into the final cut? The names which never became immortal were Deafy, Dirty, Awful and—wait for it—Biggo Ego.

The first feature film in which live action was combined with animation throughout was Disney's *The Three Caballeros* (US 44), premièred in Mexico City on 21 December 1944. Starring Donald Duck opposite Aurora Miranda (sister of Carmen), the story unrolled chiefly in idealised Brazilian and Mexican locales at a time when it was essential to the US war effort that Latin American countries were wooed from any accommodation with Nazi Germany. Whether encouraged by the goodwill overtures of ambassador Donald Duck or not, Brazil was the only country south of the Rio Grande to send an expeditionary force to Europe.

Donald Duck trips the light fantastic with Aurora Miranda in the first feature movie to combine live action with animation, The Three Caballeros *(US 44).* (BFI)

The first X-rated British cartoon (adults only) was *Henry 9 Till 5* (GB 70), a British Lion production about a henpecked computer who spent all his working hours fantasising about cyber-sex.

The first X-rated American cartoon was Ralph Bakshi's *Fritz the Cat* (US 72), based on R. Crumb's anarchic and libidinous feline comic-strip hero, which debuted at the Fine Arts and United Artists East, New York on 28 April 1972.

The first 3-D cartoon was Norman McLaren's abstract subject *Around is Around* (Can 51).

The first full-length animated feature in 3-D was the Australian science-fantasy rock musical *Abracadabra* (Aus 82), directed by Alexander Stitt.

The first giant-screen IMAX 3-D animated film was *The Old Man and the Sea* (US 99), from Ernest Hemingway's novella of the same title. Animator Alexander Petro painted each of the 29,000 images in the 22-minute film by applying slow-drying oil paint on glass with his fingertips.

The first cartoon films made for television were Alex Anderson and Jay Ward's syndicated series *Crusader Rabbit*, produced in San Francisco as five-minute episodes from 1948 to 1951. For some reason the films were made in colour, despite the fact that there was no colour television.

The first CinemaScope cartoon feature was Disney's *The Sleeping Beauty* (US 59); there were none others until Twentieth Century Fox's *Anastasia* (US 98).

The first computer-animated character in a movie was the sea creature in James Cameron's waterlogged sci-fi pic *The Abyss* (US 89). It comes aboard a crippled nuclear sub and changes shape to mimic the looks on the faces of the crew.

The first animated feature generated by computer was John Lasseter's *Toy Story* (US 95), a Walt Disney Pictures/Pixar production with Tom Hanks voicing cowboy-puppet Woody and Tim Allen his toy-cupboard rival Buzz Lightyear. The picture took four years to complete. *Sight and Sound* commended the technical achievement of the film with the observation that 'Ordinary cel animation cannot achieve the density of colour, or the believability of these lighting effects, and can rarely match the fluidity of "camera" movement on display here', adding 'the photo-realistic quality of the rendering on the toys and surroundings is breathtakingly sharp and fine-grained'. Each of the 110,000 frames of the movie was made up of 1,416,192 pixels enabling the variables of lighting, background, character movement, reflectance, surface textures and colour which gave the action a verisimilitude never achieved in animation before. The finished print took a total of 800,000 computer hours, at 300 megabytes per frame.

The most costly animated film was Walt Disney Pictures' *Dinosaur* (US 00), which at $200 million was one of the five most expensive motion pictures to date. The budget represented a huge increase on any other animated production, the previous record having been $60 million for DreamWorks' *The Prince of Egypt* (US 98).

The highest gross for a cartoon film was $772.3 million worldwide for Walt Disney's *The Lion King* (US 94). It was Disney's 32nd animated feature and the first to be based on an original story. Directed by Roger Allen and Rob Minkoff, the all-animal African saga featured songs by Tim Rice and Elton John and voiceovers by a galaxy of stars including James Earl Jones, Jeremy Irons and Whoopi Goldberg.

Clarence Nash (1904–85), the immortal voice of Donald Duck, may have been incomprehensible quacking in his native American, but he could be equally hard on the ear in French, Spanish, Portuguese, Japanese, German and Chinese. None of these languages could he understand—Nash had the words written out phonetically and gabbled them in Duckspeak for the delight of audiences from Paris to Peking.

The longest cartoon ever made was Osamu Tezuka's erotic feature *A Thousand and One Nights* (Jap 69), which had a running time of 2 hr 30 min in the original Japanese version.

The highest price paid for an animation cell at auction was £171,250 at Christie's in 1989. The black and white drawing, from Disney's *Orphans Benefit* (US 34), depicted Donald Duck being punched by an orphan.

FEATURE CARTOON OUTPUT
Up to the end of 2000, a total of 762 fully animated cartoon features (excluding compilations) had been produced by 45 countries. The most prolific country was Japan, with 229 full-length cartoon features, followed by the USA (174), France (49), Germany (48), Italy (30), Hungary (27), UK (27), Australia (21), Spain (20), Russia (18), Belgium (17), Canada (17), Denmark (15), Czechoslovakia (11), Sweden (12), China (10), S. Korea (8), Romania (5), Norway (5), Hong Kong (5), Cuba (4), Finland (4), Eire (4), Poland (4), Argentina (4), Brazil (4), Bulgaria (3), Colombia (3), Netherlands (3), Iraq (2), Malaysia (2), Mexico (2), Austria (2), Israel (1), Thailand (1), New Zealand (1), Switzerland (1), former Yugoslavia (1), Taiwan (1), Luxembourg (1), Singapore (1), Monaco (1), Estonia (1), Syria (1) and the United Nations (1).
N.B. Co-productions are counted under each participating country.

Cartoon Debuts

BETTY BOOP Max Fleischer's boop-boop-a-doop flapper of the '30s debuted in *Dizzy Dishes* (US 30). Betty started life as a small dog with long ears and only became a human girl in *Any Rags* (US 32). She was the creation of 'Grim' Natwick, later responsible for animating Snow White in *Snow White and the Seven Dwarfs* (US 37), who died at the age of 100 in 1990. He based her on the singer Helen Kane, whose hit song 'I Wanna Be Loved By You' launched the boop-boop-a-doop catchphrase. The Betty Boop series ran for seven years, her baby-talk voice being dubbed by five different actresses, of whom Little Ann Little (who spoke in boop-boop-a-doop language in real life) and Mae Questel were the best known. Miss Questel reprised the voice when Betty made a welcome return in *Who Framed Roger Rabbit* (US 88). While all the other 'toons' were portrayed in colour, she remained in period—in black and white.

Early Bugs in his pre-Brooklyn bunny persona. The then unnamed 'wabbit' made his debut in Porky's Hare Hunt *(US 38).*

BUGS BUNNY Started as a hare rather than a 'wabbit' in Ben Hardaway and Cal Dalton's Looney Tune *Porky's Hare Hunt* (US 38). The character only began to assume his real Brooklyn-bunny persona in Tex Avery's *Wild Hare* (US 40). Bugs was originally going to be called Happy Rabbit. He was named after his creator Ben Hardaway, whose nickname was 'Bugs', at the suggestion of Mel Blanc, the rabbit's voice and author of the classic line 'Eh, What's up Doc?' (originally scripted as 'Hey, what's cookin'?'). By 1962 Bugs had appeared in 159 films, including the 3-D *Lumberjack Rabbit* (US 53), and won an Oscar for *Knightly Knight Bugs* (US 58). Following a guest appearance in *Who Framed Roger Rabbit* (US 88), in which he teamed up with Mickey Mouse to play a low-down trick on a plummeting Bob Hoskyns with a snafu parachute, the irrepressible Bugs made a comeback in his own starring vehicle *Box Office Bunny* (US 90). He came back to the big screen in *Space Jam* (US 96), playing opposite a live-action Michael Jordan in an adventure that included a galaxy of other Warner 'toons' – Daffy Duck, Porky Pig, Sylvester and Tweetie etc. The 'wascally wabbit' has also been hyperactive on the box. *Life* asserted: 'For 30 years, Bugs has starred in more programs, on more channels—and has been number one in the ratings more often—than any other artist in the history of television.'

DAFFY DUCK Tex Avery's Looney Tune *Porky's Duck Hunt* (US 37). After disappearing from cinema screens with his 126th movie in 1964, Daffy made his comeback 23 years later but not a day wiser in WB's *The Duxorcist* (US 87). His voice, originally based on film actor Hugh ('Woo-Woo') Herbert, was later given a raspberry lisp by Mel Blanc. Under the direction of Warner Bros' Chuck Jones, Daffy brought his scatty persona to a range of

detective and heroic roles with splendid incongruity.

At the 1989 Santa Barbara Film Festival, Chuck Jones was asked by a grimly earnest cartoon buff a long and rambling question about the nature of Daffy's true being. The veteran animator scratched his head awhile and then drawled, 'I guess I always thought of him as Everyduck.'

DONALD DUCK Walt Disney's *The Wise Little Hen* (US 34). His opening (and only) words were: 'Who—me? Oh no! I got a bellyache!' Clarence Nash, always Donald's voice, recalled: 'I had an ambition to be a doctor and somehow or other I became the biggest quack in the country.' He was still quacking 49 years later in *Mickey's Christmas Carol* (US 83) and made another return to the big screen in *Duck Tales the Movie—Treasure of the Lost Lamp* (US 90).

DROOPY DOG Created by Tex Avery in MGM's *Dumb-Hounded* (US 43). Voice by Bill Thompson.

FELIX THE CAT Inspired by Kipling's *The Cat that Walked by Himself* in the *Just So Stories* (1902); created for Pat Sullivan by animator Otto Messmer. Prototype Felix, as yet unnamed, debuted in Paramount's *Feline Follies* (US 20). First of the anthropomorphic animal characters to attain the kind of celebrity accorded to human stars; also first to be merchandised (see p. 27). TV debut WXB2S New York 1930.

GOOFY Walt Disney's *Mickey's Revue* (US 32). Originally called Dippy Dawg and always voiced by Pinto Colvig. Had the honour of starring in the very last of the regular Walt Disney cartoon shorts, *Goofy's Freeway Trouble* (US 65). Returned 30 years later in his own feature *A Goofy Movie* (US 95).

MICKEY MOUSE Born 18 November 1928 with première of *Steamboat Willie*. The artist for the MM cartoons was not Disney but Ub Iwerks, though Walt himself did Mickey's voice. By 1934 the Mouse was receiving more fan mail than any other Hollywood star and the following year Soviet director Sergei Eisenstein declared that he was 'America's one and only contribution to world culture'. There were a total of 119 MM cartoons, of which the majority—87—were made in the 1930s. There was a 30-year interval between *The Simple Things* (US 53) and the Mouse's triumphant return in *Mickey's Christmas Carol* (US 83). Mickey was voiced in his Dickensian role by Wayne Allwine, who was born the year of the previous Mickey Mouse film.

MM made another comeback, this time on the small screen, aged 71 and as feisty as ever, with ABC's *Mickey Mouse Works* in 1999. Showbiz bible *Variety* gave the thumbs-up for a series which will undoubtedly carry the Mouse franchise well into the new Millennium.

MR MAGOO UPA's *Ragtime Bear* (US 49). Created by John Hubley and Millard Kaufman and voiced by Jim Backus, he stumbled his way through 52 shorts and a feature, *1001 Arabian Nights* (US 59). Hubley had originally intended to base the character's physical appearance on W. C. Fields, but decided in favour of Canadian novelist, scriptwriter and fellow animator Leo Salkin (1913–93) as his model.

PLUTO Walt Disney's *The Chain Gang* (US 30).

POPEYE Debuted in Max Fleischer's *Popeye the Sailor Man* (US 33); head animator Seymour Kneitel. The voice was that of William Costello, better known as Red Pepper Sam, whose experience as a talking gorilla on a radio show was thought to qualify him for the role. Success went to his head and he was fired as too temperamental, so Jack Mercer, an artist at the Fleischer Studio with a bent for imitations, took over. Popeye's friend Wimpy gave his name to an unappetising type of British hamburger.

PORKY PIG Warner Looney Tune *I Haven't Got a Hat* (US 35). Creator Bob Clampett; voice Mel Blanc.

ROAD RUNNER Together with the Coyote, created by Chuck Jones and Michael Maltese in *Fast and Furry-ous* (US 48). Recently revived in Warner Bros' *Chariots of Fur* (US 94).

SPEEDY GONZALES The Fastest Mouse in all Mexico debuted in Warner Bros' Oscar-winning *Speedy Gonzales* (US 55). Voice: Mel Blanc.

SYLVESTER Warner Bros' *Kitty Kornered* (US 45). His constant prey Tweety Pie had preceded him on screen (see below). Voice of both adversaries was Mel Blanc.

TOM AND JERRY Hanna-Barbera's *Puss Gets the Boot* (US 39). Tom was called Jasper and Jerry was as yet unnamed. The love–hate relationship of the amiable adversaries was condemned in the '70s for its 'mindless violence'. A full-length feature *Tom and Jerry: The Movie* was released in 1992 and for the first time in their screen lives the cat and mouse were heard to speak to each other.

TWEETY PIE Warner Bros' *Birdie and the Beast* (US 44). American essayist S. J. Perelman held Tweety Pie personally responsible for what he regarded as a reprehensible British habit of referring to all felines as 'puddy tats'.

WOODY WOODPECKER *Knock Knock* (US 40). The distinctive woodpecker voice was that of Grace Stafford, wife of Woody's creator Walter Lanz, though it was Mel Blanc who recorded the signature tune which went to the top of the hit parade. The series of 192 films lasted until 1972, making Woody the last of the great big-screen 'toon' stars.

CHAPTER 13

Shorts and Documentaries

Advertising Films

The first advertising films were made in France, Britain and the USA in 1897. The single surviving American example of that year was copyrighted by the Edison Co. of West Orange, NJ, on 5 August 1897. The Library of Congress Catalogue records: 'The film shows a large, poster-type backdrop with the words "Admiral Cigarettes". Sitting in front of the backdrop are four people in costume: Uncle Sam, a clergyman, an Indian, and a businessman. To the left of the screen is an ash-can size box that breaks apart and a girl, attired in a striking costume, goes across the stage towards the seated men and hands them cigarettes. Then she unfolds a banner that reads, "We all Smoke".'

Advertising films were also made that year by the International Film Co. of New York, who were the first company to specialise in such productions. Their clients included Haig Whisky, Maillard's Chocolate and Pabst's Milwaukee Beer, and the films advertising these products were interspersed with entertainment films, in the manner of modern TV commercials, in a grand open-air free movie show in the centre of New York. The giant screen was set on top of the Pepper Building at 34th Street and Broadway and the films rear projected with a powerful Kuhn & Webster 'Projectorscope'. The projectionist was Edwin S. Porter, later to achieve fame as director of *The Great Train Robbery* (US 03). On this occasion, however, the only fame he achieved was in the police court, where he was charged with being a public nuisance and causing an obstruction by encouraging people to block the sidewalk.

Three different advertising films are known to date from 1897 in Britain. Walter D. Welford made a film called *The Writing on the Wall* for John Samuel Smith and Co. of Borough High Street, Southwark, manufacturers of bicycle tyres. This was shot in Tottenham and showed a man painting the words 'Ride Smith Tyres' on a brick wall. Rather more ambitious was a production by Arthur Melbourne Cooper of St Albans, which brought to light a contemporary poster for Bird's Custard. An old man is seen walking downstairs bearing a large tray of eggs. He misses his footing, trips, and the eggs cascade on to the floor. Cook has no need to worry, though, because she has a liberal supply of Bird's Custard Powder. The company made an agreement with Melbourne Cooper that he should be paid £1 for every copy of the film distributed. The third example comes from Nestlé and Lever Bros, who joined forces in 1897 to purchase 12 Lumière Cinématographes for a combined promotional exercise. Their initial effort was called *The Sunlight Soap Washing Competition* and was available free to showmen. Besides producing their own advertising films, Lever Bros and Nestlé also sponsored films with no advertising content. On 7 February 1898 they premièred a film of the recent Test Match in Australia at the Alhambra, Leicester Square. This was so successful that it was followed in March by films of the Cambridge crew in training for the Boat Race and later by the Boat Race itself. Mellin's Baby Food also began giving 'advertising entertainments' with the cinematograph the same year.

The most sophisticated of the pioneer advertising films were made by the great French innovator Georges Méliès, who also made the earliest trick films and the earliest 'blue movies'. Méliès' first advertising film, made at his studio at Montreuil-sous-Bois, was for Bornibus mustard. The scene was a restaurant. Two diners get into an argument that grows so heated that they begin to pelt each other with mustard. The camera then cuts to a black table top on which a jumble of white letters are scattered at random. The letters are seen to form themselves into the slogan '*Bornibus, sa moutarde et ses cornichons à la façon de la mère Marianne*'—all except the 's' of '*Bornibus*', which is unable to find its correct place and keeps bumping into the other letters. Méliès recalled that the erratic 's' was always greeted with gales of laughter.

The earliest known cartoon advertising film was made for Kineto Kino-Ads of London by Walter R. Booth in 1916 and advertised Waterman's Ideal Ink.

The earliest known advertising film in colour was *Das Wunder/The Wonder* (Ger 25), an animated cartoon coloured directly on to the prints by means of a stencilling process. Directed by Julius Pinschewer, the two-minute film advertised 'World-renowned Kantorwicz Liqueur' and was notable not only for its colour but also its use of expressionism in the animated designs, some of them wholly abstract, of animator Walter Ruttmann.

The first British all-colour advertising film was *It's An Ill Wind* (GB 29), made for Tintex Dyes of London. The film related the drama of an office boy emptying a bottle of ink over the typist heroine's jumper. However, with the aid of Tintex Colour Remover and Tintex Dye, the jumper is made like new in the latest fashionable colour.

The first talkie advertising film was *Die Chinesische Nachtigall/The Chinese Nightingale* (Ger 28), an animated silhouette version of the Hans Andersen fairy tale made by the Tri-Ergon Co. of Berlin to advertise a new process they had developed for disc recording. Although the use of synchronised discs was common to many early sound-film systems, the process Tri-Ergon were promoting had

The world's most beautiful woman? Nobody would have said so when this 16-year-old appeared in an advertising short called How Not to Wear Clothes *(Swe 21), but they did when she conquered Hollywood as Greta Garbo.*

no apparent connection with film-making, their advertising talkie being made by the sound-on-film process they had pioneered six years earlier.

The tyranny of maladjusted sound on screen ads—alternately too loud for comfort, too soft to hear—should be over. From 1 January 2000 the first blessing of the new Millennium was an internationally agreed standard of 82 decibels for all cinema commercials released by members of the Screen Advertising World Association.

The largest collection of advertising films (including TV commercials) in the world belongs to Jean-Marie Boursicot of Paris, who has amassed 350,000 examples from 42 countries which he stores in an old telephone exchange. He adds to the collection at the rate of 8000 a year, concentrating on the best and worst of the genre—the worst, he claims, come from Canada. He started it in the mid-1960s, when as a boy in Marseilles he used to beg pieces of discarded film from the projectionist of his local cinema. Most were advertising films, predominantly for ice cream. The oldest film in the collection was made by the Lumière Bros in 1904 for Moët et Chandon champagne. Others include a 1917 promotion for holidays in Brittany—while a World War was raging in one corner of France, French Railways were enticing people to vacation in another. A recruitment film for the SS extols the opportunities offered by that organisation for sporting activities and cultivation of the arts. Also in the collection is one of

the shortest advertising films ever made—for Camel cigarettes, it lasts just one second. The Camel logo appears and the beast winks. Boursicot takes choice examples from the collection on tour with a seven-hour non-stop programme entitled 'Nuit des Publivores', or in English 'Night of the Ad-eaters'. The line-up of 450 films changes from year to year except for one perennial. This is a 1975 Perrier advertisement which shows a quarter-litre bottle responding to the caress of a woman's hand until it has enlarged to litre size. Then the cap blows off and the liquid spills over. When it was originally shown, the film had to be withdrawn after five days of mounting protest.

Documentary

The term 'documentary' was first used by Edward Sheriff Curtis, director of *In the Land of the Head Hunters* (US 14), in a prospectus he issued about 1914 for the Continental Film Co., a Seattle-based venture for the making of films about Amerindian lore and life. It did not pass immediately into the language, only catching on after John Grierson had used it in his February 1926 review of Robert Flaherty's *Moana* (US 26) for the *New York Sun*. Flaherty is generally acknowledged as the first to have brought form and structure to documentary films, commencing with his study of Eskimo life *Nanook of the North* (US 22); while Grierson himself is regarded as the father of Britain's between-the-wars 'documentary movement'.

The first documentary film: Many pre-1900 films were actualities, but the first of sufficient length to be considered a legitimate documentary record of its subject was *The Cavalry School at Saumur* (Fr 1897), at 1330ft or 20 minutes. At around the same time Joseph Perry of the Salvation Army's Limelight Division at Melbourne, Australia, began shooting some 2000ft of film illustrating the social work of the Salvation Army. Melbourne had been the first place in the world where the Salvation Army embarked on an organised programme of social work in addition to its traditional evangelism.

The first feature-length documentaries were Paul Rainey's eight-reel *African Hunt* (US 12); a dramatised production in five reels called *One Hundred Years of Mormonism* (US 12); and Akaky Tsereteli's *Journey Along the Racha and Lechkhuma* (Rus 12) by the Georgian director Vasily Amashukeli.

The first sound documentary to be released was Tri-Ergon's *Life in a Village* (Ger 23), premièred at Berlin's Alhambra in September 1923.

The most successful documentary film at the box office was the IMAX large-screen production *The Dream Is Alive* (Can 85), produced and directed by Graeme Ferguson in association with NASA and with a commentary by veteran broadcaster Walter Cronkite. The 37-minute film, much of it shot in space by 14 space-shuttle astronauts, grossed over $86 million. The most successful documentary released in conventional cinemas was the Sunn Classic production *In Search of Noah's Ark* (US 77). *Variety* said of the $55.7m grosser: 'Here is a low-budget, pseudo-scientific pseudo documentary proving conclusively that Noah existed 5000 years ago and took that famous cruise to Mt Ararat, and the ark is still in existence in the remote mountains of Turkey. The pic has about as much credibility as a Sunday tabloid scandal sheet.'

In the concert documentary *Woodstock* (US 69), a telephoto lens picks up a young man and a young girl wandering off into the long grass together. Lingering on the reposeful scene, the film records first the grass swaying, then some turbulence, next the abandoned threshing of golden limbs. A vignette of the permissive generation, unlikely to cause offence in the enlightened twilight of the 1960s—or so Warner Bros thought until they found themselves served with a writ. The litigant was the young man in the long grass. He was, he deposed, a hairdresser in Montreal. His reputation and livelihood depended on his female customers assuming him to be gay—the film had revealed his closely guarded secret, that he was really straight.

News Films and Newsreels

The first news film was made by photographer Birt Acres of High Barnet, Herts, on the occasion of the opening of the Kiel Canal by Kaiser Wilhelm II (1859–1941) on 20 June 1895. Besides the arrival of the Kaiser at Holtenau aboard his yacht *Hohenzollern*, Acres took films of the laying of a memorial stone, and of a number of other events held as part of the celebrations, including scenes of the Kaiser reviewing his troops at Hamburg and leading a procession through the streets of Berlin. He also filmed a charge of Uhlan Lancers at the Tempelhof Feld in Berlin, starting a news cameraman's tradition of taking risks in the cause of film reportage by arranging with their commander that the horsemen should charge directly at the camera. Seized with the desire to run for his life as the troops thundered towards him with drawn lances, he nevertheless continued to grind the handle of his camera and was afterwards congratulated by the CO as 'the pluckiest fellow he had ever met'. The first screening took place before the Royal Photographic Society on 14 January 1896.

The first British monarch to be filmed was Queen Victoria (1819–1901) during her autumn holiday at Balmoral in 1896. She recorded the event in her diary for 3 October: 'At twelve went down to below the terrace, near the ballroom, and we were all photographed by Downey by the new cinematograph process—which makes moving pictures by winding off a reel of film. We were walking up and down, and the children jumping about. Then took a turn in the pony chair, and not far from the garden cottage Nicky and Alicky planted a tree.'

Downey was the Royal Photographer. 'Nicky and Alicky' were the Emperor Nicholas II (1868–1918) and the Empress Alexandra Feodorovna (1872–1918) of Russia, who had arrived at Balmoral for a visit ten days earlier. The film was 'premièred' in the Red Drawing Room at Windsor Castle on 23 November 1896.

The first American President to be filmed was Grover Cleveland (1837–1908), outgoing President on the occasion of President-designate William McKinley's inauguration at Washington DC on 4 March 1897. The inaugural parade, covered by Edison, Biograph and Lumière cameramen, and by one E. H. Amet, included shots of Cleveland, then in the last hour of his Presidency. The previous year (1896), McKinley had been filmed as Presidential candidate at his home in Canton, Ohio, by W. K. L. Dickson, assistant to Thomas Edison and the man chiefly responsible for the invention of moving pictures.

The first newsreel was *Day by Day*, produced by Will G. Barker and presented at the Empire Theatre, Leicester Square, in 1906. It was issued daily except when fog prevented filming.

The first newsreel produced for general distribution was *Pathé-Faits Divers*, founded in Paris early in 1908 under the direction of Albert Gaveau. The name was soon changed to *Pathé-Journal*. Japan's *Daimai News* is variously claimed to have been founded in 1908 and 1909. This was literally intended as a moving-picture newspaper, having been established by the influential daily *Osaka Mainichi*. *Pathé-Journal* did a reverse operation, founding a weekly illustrated newspaper of the same name in November 1912. The photographic news reportage consisted of stills from the newsreel.

The first sound newsreel was *Movietone News*, presented at the Roxy Theater, New York, on 28 October 1928. The subjects covered included Niagara Falls, the Army–Yale football game, 'Romance of the Iron Horse', and Rodeo in New York. Regular weekly issue of *Movietone News* to cinemas throughout the USA commenced 3 December 1928.

The first British sound newsreel was *British Movietone*, commencing with an issue showing the Derby and the Trooping of the Colour which was released on 9 June 1929. It survived as the last remaining newsreel produced in Britain.

The first unscheduled event to be captured by the sound newsreel camera was the assassination attempt on Prince Humbert of Italy on 24 October 1929. Cameraman Jack Connolly of *Movietone* had hidden himself behind the Tomb of the Unknown Warrior in Rome in order to secure forbidden pictures of the Prince and Princess paying tribute to the Italian war dead. He had just been discovered by the police when a shot was fired at the Prince, but fortunately the camera was still running and the sound equipment operating.

The first newsreel footage of an execution was taken by *Universal Newsreel*'s Cuban cameraman Abelardo Domingo, who happened to walk into a prison yard with his camera one day in 1935 just as bandit Jose Costiello y Puentas was about to face the firing squad. Domingo shot the grisly scene unobserved and shipped the film over to New York for inclusion in the newsreel. As soon as it was released in Cuba, Domingo was arrested and condemned to death—also by firing squad. He was released only after Universal's manager in Cuba had paid the appropriate financial sum.

The Pathé brothers pioneered the newsreel in 1908. (Kobal Collection)

During World War II one of Winston Churchill's prime sources of information about what was really happening at the front was the censored footage of the official newsreel for release in neutral countries, *British Olympic Newsreel*. Much of the footage was provided by the 150 Paramount cameramen accompanying the British forces and, according to Par's UK chief David Rose, about 50% of it was impounded by the government. Churchill would often drop into the Ministry of Information projection room to see the rushes before they were censored. Among the most revealing was the 500,000ft of film of the Battle of Britain which was banned as too horrifying for public consumption.

The last newsreel in the United States was *Universal Newsreel*, founded as *Universal Animated Weekly* in 1913, of which the final issue was released on 22 December 1967. At its peak it was showing in 3300 cinema theatres, but with the competition of television declined to 1100.

FAMOUS OUTLAWS
CLYDE BARROW
Terror of the Southwest and his Gun Moll
"BONNIE" PARKER
Modern tigress, fast shooting, cigar smoking, blond Jezebel
MEET DEATH AT GIBSLAND, LA.
ACTUAL AUTHENTIC PICTURES
Taken immediately after the death of these murderous lovers at the hands of the law.

See the Texas Cop Killers - Slayers of 10 men
— Extra Feature —
'BEYOND THE RIO GRANDE'
WITH 5 FAMOUS WESTERN STARS--- Featuring Jack Perrin, Buffalo Bill Jr.,
Pete Morrison, Franklin Farnum, Edmund Cobb and Starlight, the Wonder

It was not often that the newsreel was billed above the feature. In this case though the slaying of Bonnie and Clyde took precedence over any horse opera.

The last newsreel in Britain was *Movietone News*, founded as *British Movietone* in 1929 (see above), which suffered a decline from its circulation of over 2000 a week at the peak in World War II to only 200 a week when the final issue was released on 27 May 1979. The sign-off items were the Chelsea Flower Show, 'Our Capital City' (London from the air) and 'Highlights of Fifty Years'.

The major remaining producer of newsreels is China, with over 20 studios devoted to their production.

The most costly newsreel ever made was the Gaumont British edition of 24 October 1934, which included scenes of the Centenary Air Race shot at Melbourne, Victoria. The Australian footage was transmitted to Britain frame by frame by beam wireless for 68 hours at a cost of some $4000 a foot or $30,264 for the brief sequence of 160 frames. It was shown in 1500 cinemas within 48 hours of transmission.

The only woman newsreel cameraman was Dorothy Dunn, a member of the *Universal Animated Weekly* crew in America during World War I.

Serials

The first serial was the 12-episode Edison production *What Happened to Mary* (US 12), starring Mary Fuller as a foundling seeking her lost inheritance, of which the first episode was released on 26 July 1912. It has been claimed that the film was not a true serial, but a *series* of episodes, each complete in itself. Although it is true that the cliffhanger element, an essential element of later serials, was missing from *What Happened to Mary*, in fact the denouement was not revealed until the final episode, and the various adventures were all part of a continuing storyline. *The Adventures of Kathlyn* (US 13) added the missing ingredient, leaving audiences in an agony of suspense at the end of each episode until the final triumph of the heroine.

The first talkie serial was Mascot Pictures' ten-episode jungle yarn *King of the Kongo* (US 29), starring Jacqueline Logan, Walter Miller and Boris Karloff.

The longest serial was *The Hazards of Helen*, directed in 119 one-reel episodes by J. P. McGowan and James Davis for Kalem, and starring Helen Holmes (episodes 1–26), Elsie McLeod (episodes 27–49) and Helen Gibson (episodes 50–119). The first episode was released on 7 November 1914; the last on 24 February 1917. The complete picture had a running time of over 31 hours.

The last Hollywood serial was Columbia Pictures' unremarkable *Blazing the Overland Trail* (US 56), directed by Spencer Bennet.

SERIAL OUTPUT
During the 44-year life of the episode film, American studios put out an estimated 350 silent serials and 231 talkies.

War Films

The first war to be filmed was the Graeco–Turkish War of 1897. Sole cameraman in the field was British war correspondent and pioneer cinematographer Frederick Villiers (1852–1922), who filmed the Battle of Volo in Thessaly, Greece, in April. He wrote in his memoirs: 'Luckily I was well housed during the fighting in front of Volo, for the British consul insisted on my residing at the consulate. To me it was campaigning in luxury. From the balcony of the residence I could always see of a morning when the Turks opened fire up on Valestino Plateau; then I would drive with my camera outfit to the battlefield, taking my bicycle with me in the carriage. After I had secured a few reels of movies, if the Turks pressed too hard on our lines I would throw my camera into the vehicle and send it out of action, and at nightfall, after the fight, I would trundle back down the hill to dinner.' These first historic war films were destined never to be seen by the public. When he finally arrived back in London, Villiers found to his consternation that Star Films of Paris had already flooded the market with dramatised reconstructions of the campaign and there was no demand for the genuine article. He was equally unlucky the following year when he filmed the Battle of Omdurman from a gunboat on the Nile. As the gunboat's battery opened up, the camera tripod collapsed and Villiers' camera hit the deck, the magazine fell out and the film was exposed to the light.

Villiers was not the only cinematographer present at Omdurman. The other one, old Etonian John 'Mad Jack' Benett-Stanford, succeeded in bringing back footage of the battle and at least one of his films, *Alarming Queens Company of Grenadier Guards at Omdurman*, was exhibited in Britain in November. No prints of this are known to survive, and it is another of Benett-Stanford's films which is the earliest genuine war footage in existence. Shot on 12 November 1899, it consists of scenes of the 5th Northumberland Fusiliers at Orange River, South Africa, during the Boer War of 1899–1902. It is preserved in the National Film Archive.

The first war films in colour were taken by James Scott Brown of Kinemacolor, who accompanied the Greek forces in the Balkan War of 1912–13.

In the days when newsreel reportage was as important a means of communication as television news today, it was not unknown for battles to be delayed pending the arrival of the cameramen. On 3 January 1914 the Mexican bandit General Pancho Villa signed a contract with the Mutual Film Corporation assigning them the rights to all battle coverage and undertaking that, whenever possible, battles would be fought in daylight hours and at such times as were convenient to the Mutual cameramen. Villa was as good as his word. He postponed his attack on the city of Ojinaga until the camera operator, engaged elsewhere, arrived to record the victory.

CHAPTER 14
Press and Print

The first book on cinematography was *The History of the Kinetograph, Kinetoscope and Kineto-Phonograph*, by W. K. L. and Antonia Dickson, New York, 1895. Dickson was Thomas Edison's assistant and the inventor of the Kinetoscope 'peep show' motion-picture apparatus and Kinetograph camera patented in his employer's name. The book was published in Britain in October of the same year.

The first poem to mention the cinema was in the British journal *Truth* on 30 July 1896. Titled 'The St Stephens Music Hall', it was about the various attractions to be found at this mythical establishment, including the new-fangled films:

> Then, of course, of 'Living Pictures' there are some at which to laugh,
> And repeated presentations of 'The Animatographe'.

The first work of fiction about the cinema was Maxim Gorky's 1896 short story *The Revenge*. It was inspired by Gorky's first experience of film when he attended a café concert, which included a programme of Lumière films, at the All-Russian Fair of Industry and Art in Nizhiny Novogorod on 30 June or 1 July 1896. This was presented by the Algerian-born impressario Charles Aumont, whose theatrical shows were notorious as a front for prostitution. It was the attempted suicide of one of Aumont's girls, Lily Darteau, that stimulated Gorky to write his story of a prostitute who kills herself after witnessing the unobtainable domestic happiness displayed in the Lumière film *Repas de bébé* (Fr 95).

The first British work of fiction about the cinema was *Our Detective Story* from the *Referee*, a London newspaper, of 24 January 1897. Written by G. R. Sims under the pseudonym 'Dagonet', it centres around a husband whose suspicions are aroused when his wife temporarily disappears in Spain. He has almost forgotten the incident when, some time later, he and she are watching a series of actuality films of Spain at a music hall. Suddenly a lady and gentleman appear on screen arm in arm. It is the wife with the husband's partner: 'The woman was looking up into the man's face . . . His arm stole round her waist—she put up her face—he stooped and kissed her. The audience yelled with laughter.' The husband is outraged and a divorce follows, the films being produced as evidence in court.

Researching the early fiction of the cinema, film historian Stephen Bottomore has identified some 15 short stories published before 1912 that deal with films. Of these, strangely enough, all but two or three deal with a similar theme to 'Dagonet's', i.e. the revelation of some hitherto hidden facts through the showing of a film. The facts in question are usually to do with marital infidelity, but sometimes reveal the perpetrator of a more serious crime.

This constant theme in the fiction of early cinema may have had some basis in reality. As early as January 1897 the well-known British detective Henry Slater was advertising that he would employ the 'Animatographe' for surveillance 'in all cases and . . . produce the pictures in Court in evidence. Consultations free.' In subsequent years there were persistent reports of husbands or wives seeing their spouses two-timing them in newsreel pictures.

The first novel based on a movie was Harold MacGrath's *The Adventures of Kathlyn*, published in Indianapolis with stills from the film in 1914. It was derived from the Selig Polyscope 27-part serial starring Kathlyn Williams, of which the first episode was released on 29 December 1913. Gilson Willets had written the scenario for the film.

The first original work of literature based on a film was Stuart Edward White's *Oil on Troubled Waters*, published in the *Saturday Evening Post* in 1913. Director Allan Dwan had written the film scenario and approached White, a distinguished novelist, with the idea of paying him simply for the use of his name as the supposed author. White was so impressed with the plot, however, that he decided to turn it into a genuine short story for publication. One of the most notable examples of literature derived from a motion picture is Budd Schulberg's novel *On the Waterfront*, adapted from the screenplay of his 1954 film. Novels had been written from screenplays before, but as with cheap paperback adaptations today this was simply a means of publicising a film at the same time as producing a book with high readership potential. Schulberg's 'book-of-the-film' was probably the first to be conceived as a serious work of literature exploring themes beyond the capacity of the movie camera.

Another book born of a film was *The Jazz Singer*. In this case a newspaper serial was adapted from the novel (by Arline De Haas), which was based on the film script (by Alfred A. Cohn) of the 1927 talkie, which in turn was a rendering of the Broadway show (by Samson Raphaelson), which had been dramatised from a short story called *The Day of Atonement* (also by Samson Raphaelson).

Not even Shakespeare is immune. Huddersfield

Economically, the book-of-the-film is seldom more than a subsidiary merchandising operation. In what is believed to be a unique case, however, respecting the Faye Dunaway starrer *The Eyes of Laura Mars* (US 78), the highly successful paperback is reputed to have made a larger profit than the lacklustre movie.

Theatre Royal advertised *Hamlet* in April 1952 as 'The Play of the Famous Film'.

The best-selling book-of-the-film was William Kotzwinkle's *E.T. The Extra-Terrestrial in his Adventure*

> I an Fleming's 1961 James Bond novel *Thunderball* was based on a movie script which Irish director Kinn McClory and British writer Jack Whittingham had written in 1959–60 in collaboration with the author. The project failed to secure financing and Fleming turned the story into a novel without acknowledgement to the two scripters who had been principally responsible for its inception. McClory sued and the courts awarded him the film rights to the novel, which he assigned to Cubby Broccoli and Harry Salzman's Eon Productions in return for a slot as executive producer on the successful Sean Connery-starred 1965 movie. Two decades later he reworked it for Warner Bros as *Never Say Never Again* (GB 83), persuading Sean Connery to reprise the Bond role despite the actor's declaration 'Never again' (hence the title).

on *Earth*, published in 1982 by MCA Publishing in the US and by Sphere Books in the UK, which has sold over 11 million copies. The Steven Spielberg movie of the same year held the box-office record for 11 years from 1983 until 1994.

The first film script to be published in book form was by Carl Mayer for Lupu Pick's *Sylvester* (Ger 23), about a grocer (Eugen Knopfer) who is unable to resolve the jealousy between his wife and his mistress and hangs himself, which was published in Berlin in 1924.

The first dialogue film script to be published in book form was Henri Ette's *The North Pole*, described as 'A 100% Tone and Speaking Picture with Songs, Choruses and Dances', issued by Ette Publications, Faroe Isles, 1931.

The first autobiography of a star was Pearl White's *Just Me*, published by Doran of New York in 1916. It is a lively and wholly unreliable account of her rise as the Queen of the Silent Serials.

> W hile successful films based on novels usually generate hugely increased sales for the book, the idea that a movie might stimulate sales of poetry is one which would not occur to many producers or publishers. Certainly neither the makers of *Four Weddings and a Funeral* (GB 94) nor W. H. Auden's American and British publishers were expecting the extraordinary demand for the poet's work following the reading of his 'Funeral Blues' in the funeral scene by Scottish actor John Hannah, playing the partner of the deceased (Simon Callow). As soon as the film opened in America, copies of the Auden volume containing 'Funeral Blues' began leaving bookshop shelves and the publishers, Vintage of New York, rushed into print a $6 paperback comprising the elegy from the film and nine other Auden poems, followed by a similar compilation published in Britain by Faber & Faber. Published under the title *O Tell Me the Truth About Love*, no fewer than 150,000 copies were sold in the year following the film, a huge figure for any volume of poetry by a single poet.

The star with the largest number of biographies is Charles Spencer Chaplin (1889–1977), whose life and art have been expounded in over 377 book-length works to date. For this information we are indebted to Lennart Eriksson of Västerås, Sweden, who owns 321 of these works dating back to *The Charlie Chaplin Scream Book* of 1915.

The youngest screen performer to have had a full-length autobiography published is Drew Barrymore (1975–), who shot to instant fame as a seven-year-old in *E.T. The Extra-Terrestrial* (US 82). Her book *Little Girl*

> P erhaps the most unusual of the technical books on film is Stephen Ziplow's *Film Maker's Guide to Pornography* (1977), which provides a useful checklist of all the sexual acts capable of being reproduced on screen together with hints on the best ways to shoot them.
> Cunnilingus, Ziplow advises, presents particular problems for the cameraman, as the man's head tends to get in the way, whereas orgies are great film fare but beware of the cost. The book also reveals what must be the most specialised job in the movie industry—the 'fluffer'. This is a girl who sits behind the camera on porn movies and whose responsibility it is to have the male performers erect on cue.

Lost, published in 1990 when she was 15, chronicled misspent years as a tragic Hollywood wild child. Daughter of alcoholic John Barrymore Jr, she took to drink at age nine and to drugs a year later. At 14 she dried out and returned to film-making.

The largest book on cinema is *Variety Film Reviews 1907–1998* in 25 volumes. The longest by a single author is Jamal Omid's 2-volume *The History of the Iranian Cinema* at 2700 pages.

America's first fan magazine was *Motion Picture Story Magazine*, founded by J. Stuart Blackton of Vitagraph as a monthly in February 1911.

The highest circulation of any film journal was achieved by the Chinese publication *Popular Film*, with a readership peak estimated at 100 million in 1980. Since then it has declined as cinema attendance has slumped, but is probably still read by more people than any other movie magazine in the world.

The first cartoon about the cinema was published in France in the satirical newspaper *Le Charivari* on 19 April 1896. It shows a man giving a cinematograph camera to a couple of newlyweds and advising them cynically: 'In 45 years time you'll be able to see again the only agreeable moment of your marriage.'

The first painting on a cinematic theme is an oil of 1907 by American artist John Sloan (1871–1951) titled *Movies, five cents*. It shows a nickelodeon audience watching a film of a couple kissing and is in a private collection in New York. See p. 23 (Museums: Thailand) for the only gallery devoted to cinematic paintings.

CHAPTER 15

Audiences and Exhibitors

Cinemas

The first cinema was the Cinématographe Lumière at the Salon Indien, a former billiard hall in the Grand Café, 14 boulevard des Capucines, Paris, opened under the management of Clément Maurice on 28 December 1895. The proprietors of the show were Auguste and Louis Lumière, the pioneer cinematographers whose films made up the programme. The opening performance included *Le Mur, L'Arrivée d'un train en gare, La sortie des Usines Lumière, Le goûter de Bébé, La pêche des poissons rouges, Soldats au manège, M. Lumière et le jongleur Trewey jouant aux cartes, La rue de la République à Lyon, En mer par gros temps, L'Arroseur arrosé* and *La destruction des mauvaises herbes.* Returns from the box office on the day of opening were disappointingly low, as only 35 people had ventured a franc to see the new form of entertainment. This barely covered the rent of 30 francs a day, and the owner of the Grand Café, M. Borgo, doubtless congratulated himself that he had refused Maurice's offer of 20% of the receipts in lieu of rent. Later he was to come to regret his decision, when the Cinématographe Lumière became the sensation of Paris and box-office receipts rose to 2500fr a day. Most historians have assumed that the Cinématographe Lumière at the Grand Café was simply a temporary show and consequently it has usually been claimed as the first presentation of films before a paying audience (which it was not) instead of the first cinema. Although the exact date of its closure is not known, there is contemporary evidence that it was still functioning as late as 1901. The fact that it operated continuously for at least five years should be sufficient to justify any claim based on permanence.

The first cinema in the United States was Vitascope Hall, opened at the corner of Canal Street and Exchange Place, New Orleans on 26 June 1896. The proprietor of the 400-seat theatre was William T. Rock and his projectionist was William Reed. Most of the programme was made up of short scenic items, including the first British film to be released in America, Robert Paul's *Waves off Dover* (GB 95), but there was sometimes more compelling fare, such as *The Irish Way of Discussing Politics* (US 96) or *The Lynching Scene* (US 96). A major attraction was the movie *May Irwin Kiss* (US 96), which may be said to have introduced sex to the American screen. Admission to Vitascope Hall was 10c and for another 10c patrons were allowed to peep through the door of the projection room and see the Edison Vitascope projector. Those possessed of a liberal supply of dimes could also purchase a single frame of discarded film for the same price.

The first cinema in Britain: The earliest attempt at establishing a cinema in Britain was made by Birt Acres, whose Kineopticon opened at 2 Piccadilly Mansions at the junction of Piccadilly Circus and Shaftesbury Avenue on 21 March 1896. The manager was Mr T. C. Hayward. The opening programme (admission 6d) consisted of *Arrest of a Pickpocket, A Carpenter's Shop, A Visit to the Zoo, The Derby, Rough Seas at Dover* (original title of *Waves off Dover* mentioned above), *The Boxing Kangaroo* and *The German Emperor Reviewing his Troops.* After only a few weeks operation, Acres' cinema was gutted by fire.

The first cinema in Britain of any permanence was Mohawks' Hall, Upper Street, Islington, opened by the Royal Animated & Singing Picture Co. on 5 August 1901. The manager was Henry N. Phillips. Principal attractions of the inaugural programme were *The Rajah's Dream or The Enchanted Forest* (Fr 1900), billed as 'the finest mysterious picture ever placed before the public', and a number of primitive 'talkies' featuring vocalists Lil Hawthorne, Vesta Tilley and Alec Hurley. There were also war films from South Africa and China, scenes of rush hour at the Angel, a 'graphic representation of the sensational sporting spectacle *Tally Ho* taken at the London Hippodrome', a newsreel of King Edward VII presenting medals to the South African war heroes, and scenes of a motor car explosion, Count Zeppelin's airship and 'a visit to a spiritualist'. The show was nightly at 8 p.m., with matinées on Thursdays and Saturdays, and prices of admission were 6d, 1s, 2s and 3s—considerably more than the average of 3d or 6d that most cinemas charged at the time of World War I. The Mohawk, though, was an ambitious enterprise, for while later cinemas were content to offer a piano accompaniment to the films, the Royal Animated & Singing Picture Co. engaged the 16-piece Fonobian Orchestra under the direction of Mr W. Neale. Within a few days of opening, The Mohawk advertised that it was 'besieged at every performance'. Evidently the cinema-going public was fickle, for within a few months The Mohawk had been forced to close its doors. After a period as a music hall, it was reopened as a cinema in 1908 as the Palace, changed hands ten years later to become the Blue Hall Cinema, and finally became a Gaumont before closing in 1962. The building was demolished in 1985 to make way for the Business Design Centre.

USA AND UK CINEMAS FROM 1945 (TOTAL NUMBER OF SCREENS)

	USA	UK		USA	UK
1945	20,457	4723	1973	14,650	1530
1946	19,019	–	1974	15,384	1535
1947	18,607	–	1975	15,969	1530
1948	18,395	4706	1976	15,976	1525
1949	18,570	4800	1977	16,554	1547
1950	19,016	4584	1978	16,755	1563
1951	18,980	4581	1979	16,965	1604
1952	18,623	4568	1980	17,372	1590
1953	17,965	4542	1981	18,144	1562
1954	19,101	4509	1982	18,295	1439
1955	19,200	4483	1983	18,772	1327
1956	19,003	4391	1984	19,589	1226
1957	19,003	4194	1985	21,145	1311
1958	16,354	3996	1986	22,765	1289
1959	16,103	3414	1987	23,555	1295
1960	16,999	3034	1988	23,234	1416
1961	–	2711	1989	23,132	1559
1962	–	2421	1990	23,689	1685
1963	12,652	2181	1991	23,814	1789
1964	13,750	2057	1992	25,214	1845
1965	14,000	1971	1993	25,626	1890
1966	14,350	1847	1994	26,586	1969
1967	13,000	1736	1995	27,805	2003
1968	13,190	1631	1996	26,960	2116
1969	13,480	1581	1997	30,623	2207
1970	13,750	1529	1998	31,640	2638
1971	14,070	1482	1999	32,992	2825
1972	14,370	1450			

FIRST CINEMAS WORLDWIDE

The cinemas listed below were the first to be established permanently (or intended to be permanent) in their respective countries.

Argentina (1901) 467 Calle Maipu, Buenos Aires

Australia (Dec 1896) Salon Cinématographe, 237 Pitt Street, Sydney

Austria (1903) Münstedt-Kino, the Prater, Vienna

Belgium (1897) Théâtre de Cinématographie, boulevard du Nord, Brussels

Brazil (31 Jul 1897) Salão de Novidades, 141 Rua do Ouvidor, Rio de Janeiro by Paschoal Segreto

Bulgaria (1908) The Modern Theatre, Sofia

Canada (Oct 1902) The Edison Electric Theatre, 38 Cordova Street, Vancouver by John A. Schulberg

China (1903) estab. Shanghai by Antonio Ramos

Cuba (c.1904) Florodora, Palationo, Havana

Czechoslovakia (1907) Blue Pike, Prague

Denmark (7 Sept 1904) Kosmorama, Copenhagen

Egypt (1904) Pathé Cinema, Cairo

Finland (1901) Kinematograph International, Helsinki

France (28 Dec 1895) Cinématographe Lumière, 14 boulevard des Capucines, Paris

Germany (Jul 1896) 21 Unter den Linden, Berlin

Greece (1907) Constitution Square, Athens

Hong Kong (c.1909) Bi Zhao Cinema

Iceland (1906) Biógraftheater, Reykjavik

India (1907) Elphinstone Cinema, Calcutta

Iran (1905) Avenue Cheráq Gaz, Teheran

Ireland (Eire) (1909) Volta Cinema, Dublin (manager: James Joyce)

Italy (late 1896) by Vittorio Calcina at former charity hospital in Via Po, Turin

Japan (Oct 1903) Denkikan, Asakusa

Korea (1910) Kyungsung Kodeung Yeon Ye Kwan, Seoul

Lebanon (1909) Zahret Sourya, Beirut

Mauritius (1912) Luna Park, Port Louis

Mexico (1901) Salon Pathé, 5 Calle de la Profesa, Mexico City

New Zealand (19 Mar 1910) King's Theatre, Wellington

Norway (1 Nov 1904) Kinematograf-Teatret, 12 Storthingsgd, Oslo

Portugal (1904) Salão Ideal, Lisbon

Romania (May 1909) Volta, Bucharest

Russia (1903) The Electric Theatre, Moscow

South Africa (19 Dec 1908) New Apollo Theatre, 39 Pritchard Street, Johannesburg

Spain (c. 1897) Salón Maravillas, Glorieta de Bilbaô, Madrid

Sweden (27 Jul 1902) Arkaden Kino, Gothenburg

Switzerland (11 May 1906) Grand Cinématographe Suisse, 17 Croix d'Or, Geneva

Syria (1916) Janak Kala'a, Damascus

Thailand (1907) The Bioscope, Bangkok

Tunisia (16 Oct 1908) Omnia Pathé, Tunis

Turkey (1908) Pathé, Istanbul

United Kingdom (5 Aug 1901) Mohawk's Hall, Upper Street, Islington

United States (26 Jun 1896) Vitascope Hall, Canal Street, New Orleans

Yugoslavia (Croatia) (1900) Znasstveno Umjetnicko Kajilste, Zagreb

Zimbabwe (Rhodesia) (4 Aug 1910) Empire Electric Theatre & Picture Palace, Salisbury.

It is apparent from this list that the oft-repeated claim that the first cinema in the world was the Nickelodeon opened by Harry Davis in Pittsburgh, PA, in June 1905 is wholly without foundation.

The first purpose-built cinema was the Cinéma Omnia Pathé, on the boulevard Montmartre, Paris, which opened with *Le Pendu* (Fr 06) and supporting programme on 1 December 1906. The world's first luxury cinema, and the first with a raked floor so that everyone could see above the heads in front, it was decorated in classical style with columns and Grecian friezes. The screen, measuring 20 by 13ft, was one of the largest ever installed in a cinema at that time. Admission for the two-hour show ranged from 50c to 3fr—prices at other cinemas were generally in the range of 25c to 2fr.

The first purpose-built cinema in Britain was established by Joshua Duckworth of the Premier Picture Co., a former magic-lantern showman and kinetoscope proprietor, whose Central Hall, Colne, Lancs, was erected at a cost of £2000 and opened on 22 February 1907. At first Duckworth presented both films and variety, but abandoned the latter when he found that pictures alone were a sufficient attraction. In his two-hour programme, he always liked to 'include an educational or travel subject; this I find gives dignity to the show. Good drama and pathetic subjects are always appreciated. The greatest difficulty is experienced in satisfying an audience to which you are playing week after week, with humorous and comic subjects—breaking crockery, tumbling over furniture, or running against the banana cart fails to draw a smile if not positive disapproval' (*Kinematograph Weekly*

2.7.08). The building continued in operation as a cinema until 1924, then became a spiritualist chapel and later an engineering training workshop. It now houses the Robotics Division of Cleveland-Guest Engineering Ltd, but the exterior remains unchanged from when it was first built.

The first British cinema with a sloping floor was the Picture Palace at St Albans, Hertfordshire, opened by Arthur Melbourne Cooper of the Alpha Trading Co. in 1908. It was also the first to depart from standard theatre practice by charging more to sit at the back of the stalls than the front. The Bioscope reported: 'This arrangement was somewhat resented at first by patrons of the higher-priced seats, but when they found the specially raised floor gave them a better view than could be got from the front, they appreciated the innovation.' The idea was suggested to Melbourne Cooper by his usherette, whom he later had the good sense to marry.

The first cinema to erect a neon sign was the West End Cinema in Coventry Street, London in 1913. It was also the first building of any kind in Britain to be emblazoned with neon and remained the only one for another ten years.

The first air-conditioned cinema was the Central Park Theater in Chicago, opened in 1917 by former nickelodeon operators Abraham and Barney Balaban and their partner Sam Katz. The carbon-dioxide cooling system was specially designed for them by the Kroeschell Bros Ice Machine Co of Chicago. Icicles were hung from newspaper advertisements to entice prospective patrons suffering from the blistering Chicago summer heatwaves. When air conditioning was also installed at the Riviera, Tivoli and Chicago theatres, the Public Health Commissioner of the city declared that Balaban & Katz cinemas had purer air than Pike's Peak and that anyone with a lung disease or women in the final trimester of pregnancy should attend the movies regularly. Whether other patrons relished the idea of sitting next to TB patients is not recorded.

The first arts cinema, specialising in minority-interest films of artistic merit, was the Cinéma d'Avant Garde, opened in Paris in 1924 by Jean Tadesco.

The first arts cinema in the United States was the Fifth Avenue Playhouse, opened by Michael Mindlin in 1927.

The first arts cinema in Britain was established by Elsie Cohen when she took over the Palais de Luxe in London's Great Windmill Street in 1929. The following year it was converted into the Windmill, one of the rare instances of a cinema becoming a theatre.

The first cinemas to sell popcorn were Balaban and Katz Theaters, a Chicago chain one of whose managers, David Wallerstein, thought of this way of vastly increasing profits in 1928. According to Hollywood's most durable director (67 years), King Vidor, audiences at silent movies were too engrossed to do anything but gaze enraptured at the silver screen. 'Popcorn and necking only came into pictures with the talkies,' he asserted.

SOCIAL ACCEPTANCE OF THE CINEMA

Although the cinema was primarily a proletarian form of entertainment in the USA and UK prior to World War I, elsewhere it achieved social acceptance at an earlier date. The first countries in which this was manifest were Russia and Japan, a phenomenon partly accounted for by high admission charges. In Japan seat prices of the earliest cinemas (c.1903) were generally in a range equivalent to 6d (12c)–3s 9d (90c), well out of the reach of peasants or artisans. The respectability of the cinema in Russia was attested by the fact that the exclusive Hotel Metropole in Moscow saw fit to open its own cinema in 1906. The interest of the Tsar and Tsarina in films—the court photographer was kept constantly employed filming the Royal Family at leisure—did much to make movies fashionable. An American wrote to a US trade publication in 1913 that the audiences he saw in Russia were of a far better class—and the seats more expensive—than elsewhere in Europe. Cinemas were attended, he said, even by 'very high officials in uniform'.

In France the stage-bound but much admired productions of Film d'Art, with casts drawn from the illustrious Comédie-Française, catered from 1908 for the kind of audiences who looked to film as a silent record of great theatre drama. Around 1910, at a time when even minor American players would only deign to appear in films under the strictest cloak of anonymity, the fact that the leading stars of the Budapest National Theatre were prepared to be seen on screen gave the Hungarian cinema its artistic imprimatur. In Germany *Der Andere* (Ger 12), directed by Max Mack with the distinguished stage actor Albert Basserman in the lead, was the first film to receive serious critical attention in the press and consequent patronage from a new type of cinema audience. The emergence of Denmark's Asta Nielsen as the first star specialising in tragic roles had a profound influence on the cinema in Scandinavia and Central Europe from 1910 onwards, demonstrating the drawing power of original screen drama and 'name' stars to middle-class audiences. As the artistic quality of motion pictures improved, new luxury cinemas opened, designed to accommodate the kind of audiences at which these films were aimed. Foremost was the giant Gaumont-Palace in Paris (1911), with a seating capacity of 5000; others included Berlin's 2000-seat Alhambra Platz (1911), the Panellinion in Athens (1911), also with 2000 seats, and Copenhagen's majestic 3000-seat Palads-Teatret (1912).

In America the era of the 'super-cinema' began a little later, dating from the opening of the Regent on 116th Street and 7th Avenue in February 1913 and the Vitagraph Theater and the Strand on Broadway in 1914. There has been a tendency to oversimplify American film history by suggesting that the cinema remained a primitive entertainment controlled by unlettered immigrants and largely aimed at immigrant audiences until the advent of D. W. Griffith, whereupon, it is said, the movies became an art form. In fact the influence of Griffith in making the cinema socially acceptable is probably less significant than the emergence of the feature-length film in the United States in 1912–13, a development that took place later than it did in Europe. While the simple one-reeler remained standard, the primitive nickelodeon was an appropriate showplace. The rise of the full-length drama, which was contemporary with the creation of the 'star system', broadened the appeal of the movies and stimulated the erection of theatres adequate to their presentation in an atmosphere of 'comfort and refinement'.

In Britain the feature film was also late in supplanting the modest one-reel melodramas and comedies of predominantly backstreet picture houses. Significantly the humour weekly *Punch*, generally alert to social trends, did not publish its first cartoon about cinema-going until 1912. By that date artist Charles Pears was able to show what was clearly intended to represent a sophisticated, middle-class audience. Few of the 4000 cinemas estimated to be operating in Britain by 1912, however, would have aspired to such a level of patronage unless they

> In the US before World War II, cinemas which had contracted to show a film had the right to pull out within a specified period. The number of cancellations for a big picture could be as few as 20, sometimes as high as 50. A spectacular new record was established by Warner Bros' *A Midsummer Night's Dream* (US 35) with no fewer than 2971 scratched contracts. It seemed that the booking agents had failed to reveal that this was a fairy story by a scripter from London, England, who had written it '300 and somp'n years ago for Chrissake'.

were of the standard of London's first luxury cinema, Cinema House in Oxford Street (1910), with its oak-panelled auditorium, adjoining restaurant, and seats upholstered in a 'delicate shade of Rose du Barri velvet'. Generally speaking, middle-class cinema-going in Britain came in with World War I and was due to a combination of circumstances: the relaxation of chaperonage, the provision of better-appointed and more luxurious cinemas, the feverish desire for entertainment by officers home on leave, and not least, the vastly improved standard of film-making after 1914.

> Patrons of the recently opened Magic Johnson Theatres, catering to upscale Afro-American and Chicano audiences in their own neighbourhoods, are subject to a rule unique to any chain of cinemas: no baseball caps worn back to front. Explanation, as per the manager of the Magic Johnson 12-plex in the black middle-class suburb of Baldwin Hills, is to deter gang members looking for a rumble. The other rule is no guns.

The largest cinema ever was the Roxy, built in New York at a cost of $12 million and opened under the management of Samuel Rothapfel (after whom it was named) on 11 March 1927. With an original seating capacity of 6214, the Roxy employed a total of 300 staff, including 16 projectionists and 110 musicians. It closed on 29 March 1960.

Europe's largest-ever cinema was the Gaumont Palace, opened in Paris with a 6000-seat auditorium in 1931. It was closed on 31 March 1972 and subsequently demolished.

The largest cinema auditorium in Britain is the Odeon, Leicester Square, with 1930 seats. The largest

number of cinema seats in one building is 3996 at the 12-screen Warner multiplex in Bury, Lancs.

The smallest cinema in the world to operate as a regular commercial venture was the Miramar at Colon, Cuba, which was reported in 1926 to have 25 seats.

The smallest cinema in the USA was the Silver Star Theater in Silver Star, Montana, which had a seating capacity of 26 in 1925. Silver Star, population 75, boasted two cinemas, with a total seating capacity (126) exceeding the number of citizens. Only eleven of the 15,000 cinemas operating in the US at that date had under 100 seats, of which five were in the State of Montana.

The smallest licensed cinema in Britain is the 30-seat CBA Cinema Toftwood in Dereham, Norfolk. Owned by the CBA group (ABC backwards), which arguably can claim to be Britain's smallest cinema chain—it runs one other cinema in Dereham—it has a 6 x 10ft screen, cherry-red drapes on the walls, and a miniature cinema organ which rises from below the floor to serenade arriving patrons. Four flavours of Aldous ice cream, a Norfolk speciality, are available at 25p a cornet.

The smallest auditorium in a multiple cinema is in the six-screen Biohoellin at Reykjavik, Iceland, which seats 17.

The highest cinema attendance in the world is in China, with 14,428,400,000 admissions in 1998. China has the second-highest number of attendances per capita at 13.1, though far behind the number-one spot held, according to UNESCO figures, by Lebanon with a prodigious 35.3. The United States figure pales by comparison at 6.4, while the highest in Europe is the 4.5 scored by Iceland. The UK figure is 2.4 attendances per capita.

The highest number of admissions for a film per capita of population was achieved by the historical epic *Khan Asparoukh* (Bul 82), of which the first of three parts was seen by 6.5 million of Bulgaria's 8.5 million population, equal to 76.5%. Total admissions for the first run of all three parts (shown separately) were 12 million.

SPECIAL AMENITIES FOR CINEMA PATRONS

Extra facilities were offered by some exhibitors from an early date. A correspondent of the *Kinematograph Weekly* reported in 1907 that it was customary for Italian cinemas to be furnished with a reading-room stocked with the current newspapers and illustrated journals for the benefit of patrons waiting for their friends.

Berlin's first super-cinema, the 2000-seat Alhambra Platz of 1911, served beer during the performance. Each seat had a tip-up tray on the back, similar to those on airliner seats, for the person behind to rest his tankard on. The first air-conditioned cinema was opened in America in 1917, but in hot countries efforts had been made to keep the patrons cool before that date. China Theatres Ltd, which operated a chain of cinemas in the Chinese Treaty Ports, provided cold towels for the audience's comfort. *Moving Picture World* recorded: 'The picture is stopped about every reel for an interval to permit him (the Chinaman) to whizz his towel across to the attendant

USA AND UK WEEKLY CINEMA ATTENDANCE (MILLIONS)

	USA	UK		USA	UK
1922	40	–	1961	42	8.6
1923	43	–	1962	43	7.6
1924	46	–	1963	44	6.9
1925	46	–	1964	–	6.6
1926	50	–	1965	44	6.3
1927	57	–	1966	38	5.6
1928	65	25.2	1967	17.8	5.1
1929	95	–	1968	18.8	4.6
1930	90	–	1969	17.5	4.1
1931	75	–	1970	17.7	3.7
1932	60	–	1971	15.8	3.9
1933	60	–	1972	18	3.0
1934	70	18.3	1973	16.6	2.6
1935	75	–	1974	19.4	2.7
1936	88	–	1975	19.9	2.2
1937	85	–	1976	18.4	2.0
1938	85	–	1977	20.2	2.1
1939	85	–	1978	21.7	2.4
1940	80	–	1979	22.1	2.5
1941	85	25.2	1980	19.8	2.0
1942	85	28.7	1981	20.5	1.6
1943	85	29.6	1982	22.4	1.2
1944	85	30.3	1983	23.0	1.3
1945	90	30.5	1984	22.9	1.0
1946	90	31.4	1985	20.3	1.4
1947	90	28.1	1986	21.8	1.4
1948	90	29.1	1987	23.8	1.5
1949	87.5	27.5	1988	20.9	1.6
1950	60	26.8	1989	21.8	1.8
1951	54	26.2	1990	20.4	1.9
1952	51	25.2	1991	18.9	2.0
1953	46	24.7	1992	22.6	2.0
1954	49	24.5	1993	22.7	2.2
1955	46	22.7	1994	23.3	2.4
1956	47	21.2	1995	24.2	2.2
1957	45	17.6	1996	25.8	2.4
1958	40	14.5	1997	26.8	2.7
1959	42	11.2	1998	28.5	2.6
1960	40	9.6	1999	30.8	2.7

in the aisle, who immediately wets it in icy water and whizzes it back.'

Many American cinemas have provided a crèche where mothers could leave their babies, the earliest recorded being at the Alhambra, Milwaukee in 1913. The Strand, opened in New York in April 1914, would take telephone calls for patrons, who were asked to notify the Captain of Ushers, in advance, where they were sitting. In the '30s, London's Cameo cinema allowed patrons to telephone out for nothing, besides giving them free cups of tea and free pre-stamped postcards.

A New York cinema which opened in 1925, the Knickerbocker, had a separate 'Carriage Entrance' for the kind of wealthy clientele the movies were beginning to attract. A resident chiropodist ministered to patrons of the Capitol, NY, in the 1920s. Club-like amenities existed at New York's Little Carnegie Theater, which opened in 1928 with a ping-pong room, a bridge salon and a dance floor. The Fox, San Francisco, contained an art gallery with paintings personally selected in Europe by Mrs Fox.

Nothing could compare with the 6000-seat Roxy in New York, with its permanent choir of 100 voices, 50-strong ballet troupe, lavishly appointed drawing room, its own broadcasting station and a fully equipped hospital with separate male and female wards. No fewer than 12,900 cases were treated in the Roxy's first year (1927–8) and it was claimed that eight lives were saved. There was also the Bilmarjac Seat Indicator System, which consisted of aisle boxes with a row of discs corresponding to the seats. When a seat was vacated, the disc lit up.

After the Roxy, anything offered elsewhere seemed tame by comparison. However, a Paramount representative who visited Australia in the 1940s was particularly impressed with the 'Crying Rooms', in which mothers nursing infants could watch the film from behind a soundproof glass screen. In addition, there would often be a similar room with glass screen for the use of private parties, a facility that the Paramount representative thought highly desirable as Australians visiting the cinema in a group were often drunk.

The Crying Room was revived in the 1990s at the Roseville Cinema in Sydney. Manager Susan Van Pinxten was unaware that this amenity had existed earlier—she was inspired by the memory of her younger sister being christened in a crying room at church. At Roseville it is not only used by families with infants. Miss Van Pinxten revealed that the crying room is also patronised by 'people with neurological and mental problems'.

In 1926 Warner Bros made special provision for the blind at three New York cinemas, the Warner's Theatre, the Capitol and the Colony. Fifty seats in each were fitted with headphones to supply descriptive commentaries on the films shown.

In 1979 the Edmonds Theatre, Seattle, made a determined pitch for the teenage market by ripping out 40 seats and installing a dance floor. Live bands played for dancing after each performance, the $3 admission covering both the picture and the rock session.

Open-air cinemas are common in Mediterranean countries, but until recently the Oriente cinema in Barcelona enjoyed the special seasonal amenity of a sliding roof which enabled audiences to sit beneath a starstudded sky in summer—and, less romantically, enabled urchins to lob dead cats over the walls.

Nowadays cinemas tend to concentrate on state-of-the-art stereo systems, crystal-clear projection on wide, curved screens, computer-controlled temperature and humidity, stadium seating and automatic ticketing to pack in the crowds. The 20-screen Marcus Ultrapax opened in Addison, Illinois, in 1997 had all these, but they also borrowed an old and very low-tech idea from early - 18th-century English coffee houses: the free use of umbrellas for patrons departing in the rain.

The first cinema to present a double bill of feature films was the Glacarium in Melbourne, Australia, on 15 May 1911. The programme for the week was *The Lost Chord* (Aus 11) and *The Fall of Troy* (It 10).

During the 1950s small cinemas in Japanese villages would show up to six features on a single programme. This invariably arose from competition between two rival cinemas, one with a triple feature, the other outbidding with a quadruple, and so on.

The longest non-stop presentation of films took place at Le Cinéma Parallele in Montreal between midnight on

11 June 1992 and dawn on 22 June, when 136 features were unspooled in a 250-hour marathon at the 100 Years of Cinema Festival. The only member of the audience to survive the complete programme was 21-year-old McGill political-science student Laura Denison, who won C$2500 in recognition of her qualities of endurance.

Perhaps the most distinguished film ever to grace the bottom half of a double bill was Orson Welles' now much lauded *The Magnificent Ambersons* (US 42). After unfavourable previews RKO cut the picture from 128 minutes to 88 while Welles was safely out of the way in South America, then demonstrated how they rated a work of cinematic art by releasing it as the supporting feature to low budget B picture *Mexican Spitfire Sees a Ghost* (US 42).

The oldest cinema in the world *still remains elusive after six editions of this book. The author invites nominations predating Moscow's Judogestveni Theatre, which opened in 1909.*

The oldest cinema in Britain with its original fabric substantially intact is the Electric Cinema, Portobello Road, London, which opened in February 1911. It is now a Grade II listed building. Among its other distinctions is the fact that mass murderer Reginald Christie (played by Richard Attenborough in *10 Rillington Place* (GB 71) worked there as a relief projectionist. Closed in the mid-1990s, the Electric reopened in November 2000.

The oldest building ever converted to use as a cinema was the Music Hall Cinema, Chester, which was in service as a 'common hall' as early as 1280 and as a place of entertainment by 1616. The building was converted into a legitimate theatre in 1773 and a music hall in 1855. Films were first exhibited there in 1910, but only in 1921 was it reconstructed as a permanent cinema. It closed in 1962 to undergo yet another conversion, this time an ignominious transformation into a supermarket.

The National Croatian Film Festival, formerly the Yugoslavian Film Festival, has been held annually since 1954 in a 13,000-capacity 1st century AD Roman arena at Pula on the northern Adreatic.

The largest cinema chain in the world is Regal Cinema of Knoxville, Te, which at the start of the new millennium had 4180 screens at 404 sites in 30 states. Carmike Cinemas, with a lower screen count, has the largest number of sites at 507.

The largest cinema chain in Britain is Odeon Cinemas, which had 643 screens at 135 sites following the merger with ABC Cinemas in February 2000, or nearly 23% of the total screens. It includes the flagship Odeon Leicester Square, Europe's largest single-auditorium cinema.

The oldest cinema chain is the 108-screen Wehrenberg Corp. of St Louis, Mo., which was established in 1906.

The last silent cinema in Britain was the Electra at Royton, Lancs, run by the Progress Film Co. In contrast to their name the proprietors refused to countenance anything so new-fangled as talkies and only closed down in 1935 when the renters were unable to maintain a supply of silent films.

Elsewhere the silent cinema survived longer. According to US statistics, there were 36 silent picture houses remaining in 1937, though it is possible that some of these were buildings still licensed to show films, but which had ceased to operate. Finland is said to have had some silent houses running during World War II and as late as 1952 only 50 out of the 150 cinemas in Burma were wired for sound. Thailand continued to produce silent films until the mid-1960s (see p. 173).

The longest continuous run of any film at one cinema was 10 years 8 months in the case of *Emmanuelle* (Fr 74), which opened at the Paramount City, Paris, on 26 June 1974 and closed on 26 February 1985. In this time it was seen by 3,268,874 patrons.

The longest continuous run at one cinema in Britain was 4 years 9 months for the double bill *Young Frankenstein* (US 74) and *The Rocky Horror Picture Show* (GB 75) at the Times Centre in Baker Street, London, from January 1981 until October 1985. *South Pacific* (US 58) ran at the much larger Dominion, Tottenham Court Road, for 4 years 22 weeks, ending on 30 September 1962.

The shortest run of any film with a general release was that of *The Super Fight* (US 70), a feature-length movie of a mock championship fight between the then two undefeated heavyweight champions of history, Rocky Marciano and Muhammad Ali, which was released globally on 20 January 1970. In accordance with conditions laid down by the distributor, bonded guards collected all prints after a single showing and took them to be incinerated.

The first feature film presented in digital was Wavelength Releasing's terror-in-the-woods chiller *The Last Broadcast* (US 99), which premiered at the Directors Guild of America Theater in New York on 15 May 1999 and was subsequently exhibited at the Cannes Festival and in London, Dublin and Stockholm. It was projected with Power Display projection equipment from Digital Projection. The pic was shot in digital by Stefan Avalos and Lance Weiler.

The first use of digital projection for a mainstream release followed a month later when *Star Wars: Episode I −The Phantom Menace* (US 99) was presented by Lucasfilm in New York and Los Angeles on 18 June 1999 using equipment provided by Texas Instruments DLP Cinema. The main benefit of digital in its present stage of development is the saving on print costs—a mainstream worldwide release can require as many as 8000 prints at up to $3000 each. Digital reproduction is, at its best, close to the standard of projection with film.

The longest name ever given to a cinema was conferred on a mobile picture show operated by Spanish showman José Fessi Fernandez in the Bordeaux region of France around 1902. It rejoiced in the name of the Lentielectroplastiscromomimocoliserpentographe.

The shortest name ever given to a cinema was borne by the K in Mattoon, Ill., in 1925.

UNUSUAL CINEMA NAMES

These have abounded since the Cabbage opened in Liverpool in 1914 and the Decadence in Harbin, China, the same year. A Bradford clergyman, the Rev. S. Thomas, opened The World's Window about this date and while Brussels offered High Life, Moscow promised Magic Dreams. Brno, Czechoslovakia made an honest declaration with The Illusion, while Estonia's Bi-Ba-Bo may have meant anything at all, even in Estonian. A name which definitely cloaked a secret was the 555 at Brown's Bay, New Zealand, owned by Mrs Olga Brown—it was 'a private family joke, believed to concern cards'. The first cinema in Peking to show talkies was inappropriately called the Peace and Quiet. The Yank Theatre was located far from any indigenous Yanks in the Grand Duchy of Luxembourg, and it was unnecessary to travel to Milan to attend La Scala when there was one in the Irish village of Letterkenny, Co. Donegal. Greenland Theatre was nowhere near Greenland, but in Palacode, India. The image of suburban gentility conjured up by Bristol's Kosy Korner Kinema was matched by Mon Repos, only the latter was located in the untamed frontier atmosphere of Russia's Baku oilfield in 1916. In India many cinemas are still called 'Talkies', such as Swastika Talkies in Bihar, Tip Top Talkies at Gopichettipalayam, Jolly Talkies in Muttom and Molly Talkies in Nedunganpara, or Baby Talkies, Thiruvarar. English Talkies in Ahmedabad shows movies in Gujarati, not English. The Roxy, now no more than a fading memory to New Yorkers, lives on in Motihari, Champaran, Bohar, and Bombay. The White Elephant and the Black Cat both belonged to World War I Glasgow, as did a Cinerama, long before today's wide-screen spectacle was ever thought of. The Buffalo in Ashington, Northumberland, opened about 1912, was so named because it specialised in westerns.

The oddest names were undoubtedly those found in the United States: Amusu (Lincolntown, Ga.); Hobo (Shawneetown, Ill.); The No Name (Moreauville, La.); Tootles (St Joseph, Mo.); U-No-Us (Rensselaer Falls, NY); Muse-Us (Dayton, Ohio); Tar Heel (Plumtree, NC); Dazzleland (Philadelphia); Glory B (Miami, Okla.); C-It (Ashtabula Harbor, Ohio); The Vamp (Barnwell, SC); Fo To Sho (Ballinger, Texas); Ha Ha (Minneapolis); Hoo Hoo (Doucette, Texas); The Herring (Winton, NC); Cinderella (Detroit); OK (Simpson, Ill.); My (Indianapolis); Your (Detroit); Our (Sparta, Mich.); Why Not (Greenfield, Ind.); It (Huntingdon, W. Va.); Try-It (Buffalo, NY); Hi-Art (Lockport, NY); Good Luck (Seattle, Wash.); Sour Wine (Brazil, Ind.); Oh Gee (Edwardsville, Ill.); Happy Jack (Abilene, Texas); Uses Pictures (Butlerville, Ind.); No Home (Dalton City, Ill.); Pa and Ma's (Cobsden, Ill.); Red Apple (Omak, Wash.); Fattie's (Winchester, Texas); Silent Prayers (Sprigg, W. Va.); Za Za (Plainfield, Ind.); Zim Zim (Cumberland, W. Va.). The Norka in Akron and the Idol in Lodi were simply the town name spelt backwards. In Thibodaux, La., there were two cinemas before the war. The larger was the Grand. Its smaller rival was the Baby Grand.

The largest number of cinemas in one city was 986 in New York in 1913.

The post-war record was held by Tokyo, which had over 600 cinemas in 1958, two and a half times as many as New York.

The largest number of cinemas showing the same film in the same city at the same time was 246 in New York when the sensational sex film *Traffic in Souls* (US 13) was first released.

The country with the largest number of cinemas is the United States with 32,992 or 1 to every 8500 head of population. The biggest relative increase of the last decade has been in New Zealand, where the total nearly tripled from 106 in 1990 to 315 in 1999.

The first multiplex cinema was the Regal Twins, Manchester, opened in 1930. Studio 1 and 2 in London's Oxford Street followed in 1936. The present nationwide movement into multiplexes began with the twinning of the Odeon, Nottingham, in July 1965. First in the USA was the Alhambra Twin at Alhambra, Calif., in 1939.

A choice of films at the same cinema was not unknown even before the advent of the multiplex. In 1926 the Spanish correspondent of the German film journal *Lichtbildbühne* reported that he had visited a cinema in Cairo with twin screens in one auditorium showing two different films at the same time.

The first triplex was the Burnaby Theater in Burnaby, British Columbia, opened by Taylor Twentieth Century Theaters in 1965. Britain's first triplex was the ABC Lothian Road in Edinburgh, opened on 29 November 1969.

The first quadriplex was the Metro Plaza in Kansas City, Mo., opened by the Durwood family (forerunners of the present American Multi-Cinema chain) in 1966. This was followed by a six-plex in 1969.

The largest multiplex in the world is the 31-screen complex opened by Spean Bridge at Barra de Tijuca, Rio de Janeiro, in 1999.

The largest multiplex in Britain is the 30-screen Warner Village opened at Birmingham's Star City in 2000. Six of the screens are dedicated to Bollywood movies, reflecting the significance of the Asian audience in the UK's 'second city'.

The northernmost cinema in the world is the 329-seat Nord Norsk Filmsenter at Honningsvag (pop. 5000), Norway, which lies on latitude 71°, 300 miles north of the Arctic Circle.

The southernmost cinema in the world is run by the Argentine Navy at their base in Ushuaia (pop. 2200), Tierra del Fuego, just north of latitude 55°. Although primarily for naval personnel and their families, it is also open to the paying public.

UNUSUAL CINEMAS

Cinemas have been located in odd places ever since someone thought of putting one on top of Mt Portofino, Genoa, in 1907. Motion pictures entered the Arabian harem the same year when one Mehdi Russi Khan persuaded Shah Mohammed Ali to allow him to relieve the boredom of the many royal wives with a 'ladies only' cinema showing Pathé films imported from France.

Meanwhile in the less exotic atmosphere of one of London's ancient churches, St Mary Axe, the Rev. Wilson Carlisle was relieving the ennui of his parishioners by introducing elevating and instructive movies into his Sunday services. Some years later, in the early 1920s, the Crawford Memorial Methodist church at 218th Street, New York, began doubling as a cinema. The Rev. Lincoln Caswell was worried about dwindling congregations and started up Saturday-night cinema performances with full-length features plus a supporting programme of comedies and a newsreel, borrowing the films for nothing from an obliging neighbouring theater. The following night he would preach on the moral highlighted by the 'big picture'. As a further inducement the stars themselves were invited along, one notable patron being Lillian Gish.

There have been occasional misguided attempts to establish open-air cinemas in Britain, among them the Garden Cinema at Hull, which opened for business on a balmy summer's night in July 1912. Patrons sat on deck chairs in an open-sided marquee. Not surprisingly the cinema was forced to close with the onset of winter and never reopened again. Another attempt was made in 1915

> Cinemas in Kazakhstan are oval. Audiences prefer them this shape as they resemble the traditional yurts in which the nomadic Kazakhs lived.

when a roof-top cinema seating 150 was established by Pathé Frères on a building in Wardour Street, London. Two years later an open-air cinema was inaugurated in the middle of Trafalgar Square for the benefit of soldiers and sailors on leave.

In 1913 Secretary of State William Jennings Bryan established a cinema inside the State Department, Washington, for the leisure-time entertainment of the staff.

There is no record of cinemas in prisoner of war camps, but Allied civilians interned at Ruhleben Internment Camp during World War I enjoyed the benefit of a well-appointed picture house.

One Nazi concentration camp is known to have had a cinema. In November 1944 a barracks at Dora, a concentration camp adjacent to Buchenwald, was converted into a cinema as a special privilege for the slave labourers engaged on the assembly of Hitler's V1 and V2 rockets.

In England during World War II, Chislehurst Caves were converted into shelters at the height of the blitz, special trains being run nightly from London. Some people even moved in with their own furniture and a cave cinema was operated to keep the temporary refugees amused during the long winter evenings.

A number of cinemas have been devoted to the films of a single star. The Crystal Hall on 14th Street, New York, showed only Chaplin movies for nine years, 1914–23, with the exception of one week when they decided to vary the programme. Business was so bad they reverted to Chaplin. In Moscow in 1925 there was a cinema devoted entirely to old Clara Kimball Young movies, despite the fact that Miss Young's career was already over by this date. (She had refused to diet when the fashion for slim figures overtook America. In Russia the rotund look

never went out.) There were two cinemas which showed only Bond movies—the Camera cinema in Berlin and the Kolosseum Kino in Vienna. The 007 pictures were shown strictly in rotation, each one for a week three to four times a year. In Madras there is a cinema which shows only Sivaji Ganesan movies.

In May 1931 the Grand Cinema in Auckland, New Zealand, changed its name to the London and initiated a policy of showing only British films 'for the first time in the whole Empire'. It was also the last time.

The Hitching Post Theatre was opened in 1946 in exclusive Beverly Hills solely for the exhibition of western double bills. Its habitués included director Mervyn LeRoy and western star Randolph Scott as well as the comedy duo Bud Abbot and Lou Costello, who would bring their cronies to bet on the number of white horses there would be in the inevitable pursuit to 'head 'em off at the pass'. Less distinguished patrons included numerous small boys, corralled in a special section with unupholstered seats impervious to attack with jack-knives. According to the rules of the house, all weapons were supposed to be surrendered at the cashier's window. Although these were predominately cap pistols, on occasion genuine guns, brought in on the hips of real ranch-hands visiting from the valleys to check on Hollywood's version of their workaday world, would be left in the custody of a tremulous cashier.

Cinemas catering to minorities have included one for lepers opened in Trinidad in 1921 and Britain's first and only cinema for negroes, established in Cardiff in 1935. A public cinema for children called Smile was run in the dying days of the Soviet empire by the pupils of a boarding school at Almetievsk in the Republic of Tatarstan. The Harmonic cinema in Frankfurt has women-only performances once a fortnight—the films shown are either

> The only cinema in the world which has never had a change of programme is Screen 6 of Atlanta's CNN Centre 6, which shows *Gone With the Wind* (US 39) twice a day every day of the year.

made by women or specifically about women. Another cinema with a female bias is the Kineca Omori in Tokyo, which is run by and located in a supermarket. It specialises in European films and silent classics: the people most attracted by such fare in Japan are female and over 25, so supermarket shoppers are a prime target audience.

Britain's only hospital cinema was established at St. Thomas's Hospital, London, in 1999 for the entertainment of the patients of the children's wards.

The first cinema in a train was established on the Trans-Siberian Railway by a French company in 1913. Admission was 50 kopeks (12½c or 1s). In Britain cinema coaches on trains were introduced by the LNER on the *Flying Scotsman* between Kings Cross and York in March 1924. The premier presentation was *Ashes of Vengeance* (US 23) with Norma Talmadge. 'Talkie Trains' were inaugurated by the LNER in May 1935 and continued in service till the outbreak of war.

A floating cinema was instituted in the USA on the Erie Canal between Troy and Newark, NY, in 1907. Called the *Star Floating Palace*, it was a converted canal boat with a 'wainscoted inside' which plied the canal towns giving shows at each. The idea was later borrowed by Soviet Russia. When the 'agit-steamboat' *Red Star* was dispatched on a propaganda tour down the Kama and Volga Rivers in 1919, Molotov and Lenin's wife Krupskya, who were in charge, arranged for the construction of a 800-seat cinema on a barge, which was towed behind the *Red Star*.

The Globe Cinema, a 300-seat picture house in Norwich, was built in 1934 by 14-year-old Alfred Warminger on a £1500 loan from his father. Alfred himself was manager and projectionist, while his two sisters acted as usherettes, with a boy to sell chocolates. There were two shows a night, the cost of admission to the 5 o'clock performance being a penny and to the 7 o'clock performance twopence.

A cinema called the Fly-In was opened at Asbury Park, NJ, in 1948 with space for 500 cars and 50 aeroplanes.

There is nothing unusual about watching movies in the air, but cinemas are curiously rare at airports. The only one in Europe is at Prague, where it is greatly appreciated by those subjected to the haphazard scheduling of East European airlines. There was another cinema in Prague never visited by foreign travellers. Located in the Praha Hotel, its existence was only revealed with the ending of 40 years of communist dictatorship in 1989. Open exclusively to top party officials, it showed only western-made films prohibited for exhibition to the people of Czechoslovakia.

The world's only silent-movie cinema, The Silent Movie Theater in Los Angeles, reopened in November 1999 after shutting down two years earlier following the murder of its proprietor. Earmarked for demolition to create a parking lot, the unique cinema was rescued by 32-year old songwriter Laurence Austin who charged up to $750,000 to his credit cards to raise the ante. He admitted that he 'had driven by thousands of times, but never went in'.

The American Classic Indoor Drive-In Movie is a hardtop simulated drive-in of the '50s at Dezerland on Manhattan's West Side. Patrons sit in classic cars of the period under a sky forever starry while viewing B-movies and newsreels of the period.

While many cinemas used to have cafés, there is now a gourmet restaurant in Manhattan with its own cinema. The Screening Room, opened by three college chums in August 1996, offers a $30 prix fixé menu which includes a no-charge cinema ticket. The clientele of the Screening Room Restaurant does not seem to be as movie-fixated as might be expected. Only 15% of diners check out the picture, though the 132-seat cinema grosses an average of $6000 a week from non-dining patrons.

Over-air-conditioned cinemas can be chilly, but there is no movie house colder than the one situated at the Arctic Hotel in Kiruna, northern Sweden, 200 km north of the Arctic Circle. Like the hotel itself, the cinema is built of snow and ice and the auditorium has an average temperature of −3°C. It melts by the end of June and is rebuilt at the start of each winter.

Whereas a number of luxury hotels have boasted their own cinemas, there has been only one cinema-hotel where the sole purpose of visiting was to watch films. This was opened in Deauville in 1977 by Claude Lelouche and managed by his Swedish wife, a former model. There was a menu of 200 different films, constantly updated, and guests were able to view them round the clock, interrupted only by breaks for the finest of French cuisine. Too bad for the Lelouches that only a year or so later a new idea would burst upon the world—video rental.

The first children's Saturday matinées were inaugurated by Sidney Bernstein (later Lord Bernstein) of the Bernstein Group of Theatres (later Granada Theatres) with a performance at the Empire, Willesden, on 23 March 1928. Two thousand children paid 3d each to attend a programme which included *Robinson Crusoe* (GB 27), a *Topical Budget* and two shorts.

The first gaol to institute film shows for prisoners was Goulburn Gaol, Sydney, New South Wales, commencing on 3 January 1911 with a programme presented by the Methodist chaplain, the Rev. J. H. Lewin. The *Melbourne Argus* reported: 'Some of the long-sentence prisoners had never previously seen moving pictures and they more especially enjoyed the entertainment. The pictures were of course of an elevating character, including *Waterways of Holland*, *Dogs of Various Countries*, and *The Visit of the American Fleet*.'

In Britain the first regular film shows for gaol inmates were instituted on a weekly basis at Maidstone Prison in November 1937. The inaugural programme was rather dauntingly described as 'three hours of educational and cultural films, specially selected for reformative treatment of prisoners'. The shows were held in the 100-seat prison chapel, admission according to a three-weekly rota (Maidstone held 350 prisoners) being permitted to inmates who had earned a certain number of good conduct marks. The projector was operated by 'lifers'.

The first drive-in cinema was the Camden Automobile Theater, opened by chemical manufacturer Richard Hollingshead on a 10-acre site off Wilson Boulevard, Camden, NJ, on 6 June 1933 with a presentation of *Wife Beware* (US 33), with Adolphe Menjou. The screen

This Snö-in-Bio in Northern Sweden is a drive-in for snowmobiles. (Kenneth Pålsson)

measured 40 x 30ft and there was accommodation for 400 cars. The sound came from high-volume screen speakers provided by RCA-Victor. Admission cost 25c per car and 25c for each occupant.

Hollingshead, a home-movie buff, had been inspired with the idea one hot summer night at his home in Riverton, NJ, when he set up a screen in front of his garage to watch a movie in the open air on his 16mm projector. As he needed somewhere to sit, he sat in his car. Then it occurred to him that it only needed a bigger screen for hundreds of people to sit in their cars watching a movie.

The expansion of drive-ins began very slowly; 12 years after the opening of the Camden there were still only 60 in the whole of the United States. The growth years were the same as for television, for no clear reason. In 1949 there were 1000 drive-ins and the peak was reached in 1958 with 4063 against 12,291 hard-tops. There are now only 800 remaining.

The first in-flight movie was First National's production of Conan Doyle's *The Lost World* (US 25), shown during a scheduled Imperial Airways flight from London to the Continent in April 1925.

America's first in-flight presentation was a more modest affair consisting of a Universal Newsreel and a couple of cartoon shorts shown aboard a transcontinental Air Transport Inc. Ford transport aircraft on 8 October 1929.

Airlines are sensitive about scenes in movies which may alarm the passengers. In *Rain Man* (US 88), Dustin Hoffman as the autistic genius recites a scarifying catalogue of airline disasters ... in the big-screen version. For in-flight entertainment the scene was discreetly excised by all the airlines but one. Australia's national carrier QANTAS, confident that their perfect safety record was well known to passengers, took pride in leaving it in.

Birth of the in-flight movie—Imperial Airways, April 1925. (Backnumbers)

The first airline to introduce regular in-flight movies was TWA, commencing with the presentation of *By Love Possessed* (US 61), with Lana Turner and Efrem Zimbalist Jr, in the first-class section during a scheduled New York–Los Angeles flight on 19 July 1961.

The first cinema aboard a liner was a feature of the 16,000-ton Italian vessel *Patra*, which left Naples for her maiden voyage across the Atlantic in the spring of 1914.

The world's airlines are estimated to spend about $50 to $60 million per annum on acquiring rights to films. A major airline like Australia's QANTAS pays in the region of $35,000 per picture, with a minimum of about 350 showings. The average age of the in-flight audience is about 20 years older than theatrical audiences, hence films that do well at the box office do not necessarily meet the same response a mile up in the air. Conversely a film like *Raise the Titanic* (US 80), which bombed at the box office, won plaudits from air passengers. According to specialist distributor Entertainment in Motion, a blockbuster picture can earn an extra $1 million on the wing.

NUMBER OF CINEMAS WORLDWIDE

This list is necessarily selective as not all countries have up-to-date figures.

AFGHANISTAN	0*
ARMENIA	1
ARGENTINA	899
AUSTRALIA	1528
AUSTRIA	699
BAHAMAS	4
BAHRAIN	10
BANGLADESH	946
BARBADOS	3
BELGIUM	495
BELIZE	5
BERMUDA	3
BHUTAN	6
BOLIVIA	129
BRAZIL	1350
BRUNEI	2
BULGARIA	600
BURKINA FASO	42
CAMBODIA	6
CANADA	2200
CHILE	222
CHINA	4639
COLOMBIA	320
COOK ISLANDS	1
COSTA RICA	68
CROATIA	147
CUBA	531
CYPRUS	17
CZECH REPUBLIC	848
DENMARK	345
DOMINICA	1
DOMINICAN REPUBLIC	80
EGYPT	450
EIRE	310

EL SALVADOR	67
ESTONIA	134
FINLAND	340
FRANCE	4764
GERMANY	4651
GREECE	180
GREENLAND	2
GUYANA	18
HAITI	10
HONDURAS	99
HONG KONG	185
HUNGARY	c.600
ICELAND	49
INDIA	12,867
INDONESIA	2163
IRAN	295
ISRAEL	219
ITALY	3020
JAMAICA	31
JAPAN	2221
JORDAN	15
KAZAKHSTAN	1580
KENYA	50
KOREA, S.	507
KUWAIT	6
KYRGYZSTAN	343
LAOS	2
LATVIA	35
LIECHTENSTEIN	2
LITHUANIA	105
LUXEMBOURG	25
MACEDONIA	36
MALAYSIA	131
MALTA	9
MAURITIUS	40
MAYOTTE	1
MEXICO	1979
MOLDOVA	49
MONACO	3
MOROCCO	250
NETHERLANDS	475
NEW CALEDONIA	12
NEW ZEALAND	315
NICARAGUA	127
NORWAY	398
OMAN	20
PAKISTAN	657
PANAMA	55
PARAGUAY	100
PERU	123
PHILIPPINES	1200
POLAND	822
PORTUGAL	268
PUERTO RICO	115
RÉUNION	17
ROMANIA	306
RUSSIA	1650
SAMOA	3
SAINT HELENA	1
SAN MARINO	4
SEYCHELLES	1
SINGAPORE	169
SLOVAKIA	250
SLOVENIA	113

SOUTH AFRICA	519
SPAIN	3082
SRI LANKA	130
SURINAME	2
SWAZILAND	5
SWEDEN	1132
SWITZERLAND	403
TAIWAN	569
TAHITI	4
TAJAKISTAN	159
TANZANIA	27
THAILAND	215
TRINIDAD & TOBAGO	26
TUNISIA	50
TURKEY	358
UK	2825
UKRAINE	800
URUGUAY	67
USA	32,992
VENEZUELA	266
YUGOSLAVIA	164
ZAMBIA	8

* The Taliban closed all cinemas in August 1996.

Tickets

The most expensive cinema ticket was $1000 for admission to the benefit premières of *Star Wars: Episode 1—The Phantom Menace* (US 99), held at 11 sites throughout the US on 16 May 1999. Skinflints could sit in the cheap seats for a paltry $500.

The most expensive admission prices in the world are in Japan, where the average price of a cinema ticket in downtown cinemas is $16.66 and the cost of reserved seats in the centre of the auditorium is $25.

In December 1940 the Globe Theatre on Broadway in New York accepted firearms in lieu of cash for admission to Michael Powell's *Contraband*/US: *Blackout* (GB 40). The weapons were shipped to Britain for use by the Home Guard.

The lowest seat price recorded was a farthing ($\frac{1}{16}$p) by a cinema in London's Whitechapel Road in 1909, though the concessionary admission applied only to four children purchasing tickets together. The regular price for children at the Star Kinema in Newcastle upon Tyne about the time of World War I was $\frac{1}{2}$d, but admission could be obtained by presenting a clean glass jam jar instead. In 1925, during a temporary slump in moviegoing, a desperate cinema manager in Covington, La., admitted patrons in exchange for empty beer bottles. He took $23 and 1812 empties. The cheapest seats noted in the Report of the Indian Cinematograph Committee (1928) were priced at one anna—slightly over a penny. These were 'seats' in a figurative sense, since the lowly price meant only a lowly place on the ground. In the late 1930s some cinemas in Karachi were wont to give free shows, consisting of shorts and long trailers, when their rivals were showing a blockbuster. A cinema opened in Cardiff in 1935 for 'coloured people' only charged a flat rate admission of 1d. Even cheaper was a picture house on Sixth Avenue, New York, which advertised circa 1912 a movie of a negro lynching for 1c. On at least one occasion any price for a seat has been accepted. In Victoria, BC, a cinema manager running *The Luck of Ginger Coffey* (Can 64) allowed patrons to pay whatever they thought the film was worth.

Currently the lowest admission prices are in Cuba: average cost of a ticket in the capital, Havana, is 10c.

The first cinema to accept credit-card bookings was the Rivoli, New York, starting with *Around the World in 80 Days* (US 56) on 18 October 1956. The only card in issue at the time was Diners Club.

The first ATMs (Automatic Ticketing Machines) for use with credit cards or debit cards were introduced in 1994 by Canadian cinema chain Famous Players.

The first online booking in the UK was introduced by Odeon Cinemas via the Internet (*odeon.co.uk*) on 26 May 1998.

The first season tickets in the UK were launched by Virgin in 1999. A £15 pass allowed patrons unlimited access to the circuit (excluding the West End) for four weeks.

Audiences

The largest audience ever to view a film simultaneously in the same locale was 110,000 on the occasion of the screening of D. W. Griffith's *Boots* (US 19) at the Methodist Centenary celebration held at the Oval Amphitheater, Columbus, Ohio, on 4 July 1919. Fifty thousand of the audience were accommodated in the stands, the remainder in

---

Unruly audiences are now a major problem in the US, despite statistics purporting to prove that in any average multiplex a patron is three times as likely to sit next to a college graduate as a high-school dropout. The American Multi-Cinema complex in Washington's renovated Union Station has issued an edict against which there is no appeal: 'Two shushes and you're history.' After the first warning, alienated college graduates or other offenders who continue to be noisy are ejected without a refund. Ushers trained in self defence perambulate each of the nine auditoria once every 20 minutes.

It would seem that the problem is not a new one. Surrealist director Luis Buñuel confessed that as one given to making loud remarks during film performances, he was not the ideal person to sit nearby. On one occasion he was hissed out of a picture house showing Nicholas Ray's reverential *King of Kings* (US 61). The scene which caused the commotion was the Temptation of Christ, in which the Devil offers the Redeemer a dazzling, golden city in the desert, full of minarets and cupolas. 'My God', exclaimed Buñuel in ringing tones, 'He's offered Christ Disneyland!'

---

the arena. The film was projected on a giant screen, with a picture size of 100 x 75ft.

The highest number of times a patron has seen the same film is 940 by Mrs Myra Franklin of Cardiff, Wales, whose favourite picture can only be *The Sound of Music* (US 65).

The film seen by the most cinemagoers: There are no reliable figures to authenticate the most popular film of all time in terms of the highest number of paying patrons. However, *Mother India* (Ind 57), which has been on almost continuous release in various parts of India since 1957, is claimed by some authorities on Indian cinema to have been seen by more cinemagoers than *Gone With the Wind* (US 39). This in turn is challenged by the Chinese. Official government statistics give the cumulative audience for *Taking Tiger Mountain by Strategy* (China 70) as 7.3 billion up to the end of 1974. This seemingly impossible figure—it represents over seven admissions per head of population, including babies—could just be true. In the rural areas, where most of the population of China lives, there were an average of ten film shows per year in each village in the early 1970s. As only eight new films were released in China during the Cultural Revolution 1966–73, and nearly all others were banned, the same films had to be shown over and over again. Non-attendance at film shows was regarded as a mark of political deviation.

More Pakistani children saw *Jurassic Park* (US 93) than all the films released in Pakistan in the previous 45 years.

Fan Mail

Mail began to be sent to the uncredited performers of the early silents even before the advent of named stars. Mary Pickford recalled an occasion at the Biograph Studios in about 1912 when she enquired about a letter she was expecting, and was told that it had probably been thrown away together with the hundreds of other letters addressed simply to 'The Girl with the Curls' or 'The Biograph Girl'. She was amazed to learn that people she had never met should feel impelled to write to someone who had no more substance for them than a mute shadow on a silver screen. Biograph's high-handed method of disposing of unsolicited correspondence did not long survive the onslaught of the fan magazines, which soon took to publishing the stars' studio addresses in response to eager enquiries from the fans. Producers came to realise that a mail count was one method of assessing a rising star's popularity and consequently his or her box-office potential, while the stars themselves knew that it was in their own interest to maintain a devoted fan following, even at the cost of the $250 a week it was estimated in the '20s that a major star would need to spend on photographs and postage.

The most numerous fan mail of the immediate post-World War I period was received by 'America's Sweetheart' Mary Pickford, with an average of 18,000

But for the power of fan mail, Vivien Leigh might never have played the most celebrated heroine in movies in *Gone With the Wind* (US 39). Originally Norma Shearer was cast as Scarlett O'Hara. She announced her withdrawal from the role in July 1938, citing as her reason the amount of fan mail she had received telling her she was unsuitable for the part. Whether these were mainly from fans of Margaret Mitchell's book, aghast at the prospect of the rather wooden Canadian-born actress as the Southern spitfire Scarlett, or fans of Miss Shearer who feared for her dignity, was not apparent. She herself described Scarlett as 'a difficult and thankless role'. Given her lack of dramatic range, Miss Shearer's decision probably saved *Gone With the Wind* from becoming another run-of-the-mill costume drama.

letters a month. It was maintained that Miss Pickford employed a fleet of 18 secretaries to answer them.

Mary Pickford's popularity began to decline in the 'flapper era' and in 1927 it was reported that Colleen Moore was leading the fan-mail league table with 15,000 letters a month. Miss Moore was obliged to dispatch an average of 12,000 photographs of herself monthly at a cost of 12c each, including postage. A year later she had been overtaken by Clara Bow, whose count for the month of April 1928 was no less than 33,727 items of mail. The cost of replying was $2550 including $450 for three full-time secretaries. The most popular male star at that time was, somewhat surprisingly, Charles 'Buddy' Rogers, with 19,618 letters. Douglas Fairbanks, generally thought of as the most consistently popular male star of the 1920s, rated only 8000 letters, which gave him equal place in the league table with a dog, Rin Tin Tin. Chaplin, who had once created a fan-mail record with 73,000 letters in the first three days of his return home to London in 1921, could muster no more than 5000.

The coming of sound virtually ended the screen careers of Colleen Moore and Clara Bow, but ushered in a host of new stars, one of whom was to create a fan-mail record which has never been broken. Mickey Mouse, reported Walt Disney at the end of 1933, had received 800,000 letters that year, an average of 66,000 a month. He stressed that all these communications had been addressed to Mickey personally, and not to his creator.

In that heady period of Hollywood history known as 'the era of the Great Stars', neither Gable nor Garbo could compete with a mouse, a child and a singing cowboy. By 1936 seven-year-old Shirley Temple was receiving just over 60,000 letters a month, an all-time record for a mere human being. As age crept up on the golden-curled moppet, the fickleness of film fans once again asserted itself. By the time she had reached the mature age of ten, Miss Temple was no longer at the top. Her place had been taken by the guitar-strumming cowboy Gene Autry, though it may have been some consolation that his peak of 40,000 letters a month came nowhere near her best.

Donald O'Connor made six films with Francis the Talking Mule but surrendered his leading role to Mickey Rooney when he discovered the mule was getting more fan mail than he was.

World War II brought a new element into star appeal with the advent of the pin-up picture, and it is probable that a high proportion of the dogfaces who wrote from far-away places to the new record holder, the fighting forces' own Betty Grable, had never seen any of her films. The attraction of her million-dollar legs, however, was attested by the average of 30,000 letters a month they inspired.

Fan mail reached its apogee at the end of World War II. The record for any star in a single month was 74,852 fan letters received by Roy Rogers in July 1945. Even his horse Trigger received over 200.

The nature of the fan-letter writer has seldom been examined, but in April 1927 *Variety* published the results of a survey in which they reported that 10% of all fan mail sent from within the USA came from Poles (or people with Polish names), while 8% of the 32,250,000 letters received annually from fans worldwide by Hollywood studios originated from South American countries. The greater proportion of requests for photographs, said *Variety*, came from people who never went to the movies—'they are of the poor kind who cannot afford it and simply pick up coupons or read names on billboards of the various stars . . .'. An analysis made the following year at Paramount, the studio which received the most fan mail, revealed that 75% of the correspondents were women, despite the fact that female stars received more letters than men.

Ten years later another survey, this time of all the major Hollywood studios, showed a remarkable consistency, still with three-quarters of the fan letters coming from women. Of the remaining quarter, some 40% were men proposing marriage or asking for dinner dates. Even after her wedding had been announced in 1938, Myrna Loy received 79 proposals in a single week.

Nowadays much of the fan-mail received by Hollywood stars is handled by Studio Fan Mail, founded by picture-postcard photographer Jack Tamkin in 1962. With offices in Los Angeles, and Big Bear Lake, California, Tamkin and his 16 staff respond to between 100,000 and 200,000 letters a month. While the fans are worldwide, about 80–85% are children or adolescents. They receive a postcard portrait with a signature in a hand-addressed envelope. All letters are read, in case they are from sick children or young people who need help. These are referred to the stars or their agents for personal handling. Potentially threatening letters are recorded on a database and sent on to the LAPD, the only police force with a special unit devoted to stalkers.

Fan mail being traditionally associated with film stars, it is worthy of note that no actor or actress has received in the course of a career the number of letters delivered to Charles Lindbergh following his transatlantic flight—a total of 3,500,000.

Space precludes more than the briefest selection of the last 80 years of fan mail:

- To Kathlyn Williams 1916: 'Dear Miss Williams, You are my favourite moving picture actress. I would appreciate it so much if you would give me one of your old automobiles, any one, I wouldn't care how small.'
- To Enid Bennett 1920: 'I am making a collection of pictures of the most notorious actresses. Please send me yours.'

- To Emil Jannings (whose looks were certainly subordinate to his artistry) 1928: 'Dear Miss Jannings, You are my favourite actress. I go to see all your pictures because I like the way you wear your clothes. To me you are the best-dressed actress on the screen, as well as the most beautiful. I try to imitate your clothes and your stylish way of wearing your hair.'
- To Una Merkel (following a request for a signed photo) 1933: 'Do not send picture. Am moving and decided I don't want it.' Miss Merkel to fan: 'Picture is sent. You'll take it and like it.'
- To Glenn Ford 1946: 'I am 22, pretty, but I never saved my money. You did. That is the real reason I would like to marry you. Please let me know soon, as I have also written to Dick Powell and Larry Parks.'
- To Virginia Mayo from Arab Sheik 1948: 'You are the surest proof to me of the existence of God.'
- To Marlon Brando from Miss Jean Seberg of Marshalltown, Iowa, aged 13 (five years before being picked by Otto Preminger from 18,000 aspirants to play the title role in *Saint Joan* (US 57), in 1951: 'Dear Mr Brando, I know how hard it must be with all those photographers and reporters chasing you around, so if you would like to come and stay at my home, my family would like you to come and stay as long as you like.' Mr Brando never answered.
- To Frank Sinatra, from girl fan proposing marriage 1956: 'We've never met, but I'm a singer and I feel I can do so much for your career.'

Paul Newman has discovered that not all his fans revere him for his many notable screen performances. The actor runs a spare-time business venture for charity called 'Newman's Own', producing salad dressing, spaghetti sauces and popcorn—his handsome features adorn the packaging. On one occasion a traffic cop pulled Newman over and began writing out a ticket. About to hand it over, he happened to glance at the driver. 'My God, it's Newman!' he exclaimed, crunching the speeding ticket into a ball. 'Wait'll I tell my wife. Take off! We eat your popcorn every night.'

Film Fans, Famous amd Infamous

Royalty have been among the most fervent supporters of the cinema since its earliest days. At a time when 'animated pictures' had scarcely moved out of the fairground, Queen Victoria was enjoying frequent film shows at Windsor Castle. An ardent film fan, the Queen had a special predilection for movies about children and her favourite was said to be a Riley Bros production called *The Pillow Fight* (GB 98), in which four mischievous schoolgirls bombarded each other with pillows in their bedroom.

The first royalty with private cinema theatres in their palaces were the Crown Prince of Siam and Tsar Nicolas II, both in around 1913. When war broke out and the Tsar took command of his forces in the field, he missed his cinema at the Tsarkoye Selo palace so much that he had another one installed at the Stavka, headquarters of the Russian Army. The Tsar's favourite film was *The Exploits of Elaine* (US 14), a cliffhanger-type serial which he watched weekly at Stavka throughout the second half of 1916. The deposed Emperor of China, Henry P'u Yi, had a cinema built at the Palace of Established Happiness about 1920, where a steady flow of Charlie Chaplin and Fatty Arbuckle films were maintained, until the emergence of Harold Lloyd, who displaced them as Imperial Favourite. The Emperor's owlish horn-rimmed glasses were said to have been acquired in tribute to the American comedian.

Queen Alexandra's favourite film was *True Heart Susie* (US 19), in which Lillian Gish played the kind of simple, joyful country girl the Queen sometimes wished she could have been. A private print of the film was kept at Buckingham Palace. Queen Mary's taste, on the other hand, ran to rather more robust fare, her favourite star being the romantic and extremely athletic hero of Hollywood adventure movies Eddie Polo. (Reputedly Queen Mary was the only member of the Royal Family who was not a Charlie Chaplin fan—the reason, according to one fan-magazine writer, being the fact that she was not endowed with a very developed sense of humour.) The Queen was said to be the Royal Family's most enthusiastic filmgoer and during World War II, when living at Badminton, she gave a weekly film show for servicemen. Sometimes her enjoyment of the movies proved troublesome for her entourage, as when she made a rare visit to a public cinema in November 1945 to see *The Wicked Lady* (GB 45), a lusty period drama with Margaret Lockwood in drag as a female highwayman. Two ladies-in-waiting went first to see if it was suitable and were shocked by some of the indelicate language used, which they considered wholly improper for royal ears. As the formidable old Queen refused to cancel her visit, it was arranged (without her knowledge) for the sound to be turned so low every time there was a racy bit that the offending words were inaudible.

Queen Mary's youngest son, the Duke of Kent, seems to have rivalled her in his passion for the pictures. When he married Princess Marina in 1934, the Earl of Dudley had a squash court converted into a cinema at his seat, Himley Hall, where the royal couple were to spend their honeymoon. During the 12 days of their stay, the Duke and Duchess watched 18 feature films, nine comedies, an unspecified number of documentaries, five newsreels and a specially made life story of His Royal Highness. Every night of the honeymoon was spent at the movies reported an ecstatic Gaumont-British, who had supplied the 202 reels of film shown.

Both the Duke's brothers shared his delight in the cinema. The Duke of York, later King George VI, was reported in America to have a particular weakness for the films of Nancy Carroll. A greater sensation, though, was the revelation in Photoplay in 1931 that the Prince of Wales (later Edward VIII) was in the habit of making incognito

---

'I stopped believing in Santa Claus at an early age. Mother took me to see him in a Hollywood department store and he asked me for my autograph.'
—Shirley Temple Black

visits to one of London's less exclusive suburban cinemas, the Grand in Edgware Road, at least once or twice a week. The Prince always attended with the same girl, it was alleged, she taking her seat at 8.45 p.m. and he slipping into his at precisely 9 p.m., after the house lights had gone down.

No recent information is available about HM The Queen's taste in films, the Palace being prepared to say only that 'she most often asks to see those of which she has read favourable reviews'. According to a newspaper report of the late 1950s, however, her favourite stars were then Gary Cooper, Laurence Olivier and Dirk Bogarde. Curiously Her Majesty does not have a private cinema. At Sandringham the shows are held in the Ballroom, at Balmoral in the Large Drawing Room and at Windsor Castle in the Waterloo Room. Films are not shown at Buckingham Palace. Royal film shows are the responsibility of the Equerry in Waiting, who selects the films unless the Queen has made a particular request.

Before her separation, the late Princess of Wales frequented the Odeon in Kensington High Street. She usually attended with girlfriends—the so-called 'Throne Rangers'—and joined the queue for tickets with humbler patrons, often paying herself. She always sat in the back row of the stalls for privacy. In her giddy days as a teenage bride who loved disco-dancing her favourite star was said to be John Travolta. With maturity and a growing commitment to good causes, her favourite film was reported to be *Rain Man* (US 88), in which Dustin Hoffman played an autistic. The condition was one of Princess Diana's special concerns.

Prince Charles has a long-held regard for Barbra Streisand, whom he arranged to meet after being entranced by her performance in *Funny Girl* (US 68). 'People look at me in amazement when I say she is devastatingly attractive and with a great deal of sex appeal (all based on one film!),' he confided in his diary at the time. 'But I still contend she has great sex appeal after meeting her.' They met many times subsequently, including on his visit to Los Angeles in November 1994 when she came to tea with him.

The Prince is not alone in having revealed a wholly unexpected predilection for a particular lady. Or in the case of the Viennese philosopher Wittgenstein, particular ladies, since he doted on two of them—Betty Hutton and Carmen Miranda. Whenever one of their films came to Cambridge, where he was Professor of Philosophy, the austere genius would indulge himself with a seat in the front row of the stalls, the better to observe their pulchritudinous charms, and a pork pie to munch during the show.

World leaders have also been in the forefront of the world's film fans. Both Stalin and Churchill named *Lady Hamilton* (GB 42) as their favourite film, the British Prime Minister seeing it four times and Stalin, according to former British Ambassador to Moscow Sir Frank Roberts, no fewer than 38 times. Churchill's passion for films was not shared by all his wartime colleagues, a number of whom have testified to their displeasure at the PM's habit of breaking off the evening's work to watch the ritual movie and then expecting them to match his alertness and vigour as top-level discussions continued until three in the morning. At Kremlin film shows, according to Khrushchev, Stalin 'used to select the movies himself. The

films were usually what you might call captured trophies: we got them from the West. Many of them were American pictures. He liked cowboy movies especially. He used to curse them and give them their proper ideological evaluation but then immediately order new ones.'

Hitler's favourite movie at the time he became Chancellor of Germany was *The Blue Angel* (Ger 30), of which he had a private print. Trenker's *The Rebel* (US 33), was said to be his favourite American film. *The Blue Angel* was later displaced in his affections by Willi Forst's *Mazurka* (Ger 35), which he watched as often as two or three times a week in the small hours of the morning when he was suffering from insomnia. Such was the Führer's devotion to the film, a rumour spread that its star, the bewitching Pola Negri, was under his special protection. In fact Miss Negri had never met Hitler, but found that whenever she went to Nazi Germany she was treated with the kind of privileged deference accorded only to intimates of the Reich's Chancellor. (She later won a libel action against the French cinema magazine *Pour Vous*, which alleged she was Hitler's mistress.)

The Führer is said to have indulged in film shows of a less conventional kind. Pauline Kohler, who served on the staff at Berchtesgarten, claimed that Hitler had a special film made of a prominent German star stripping and exhibiting 'various exercises' which 'threw a terrible light on the perversity of Hitler's sexual desires'. This was shown in the Führer's private cinema at Berchtesgaden, where a selected group of staff were invited to view it on Christmas Day 1937.

The silent-screen vamp Lina Basquette, widow of Sam Warner, claimed to have been invited to Berchtesgarten that same year, following a correspondence which had begun in 1929 when the leader of the Nazi Party had written her a fan letter declaring she was his favourite Hollywood star. Basquette said that Hitler pressed his attentions on her, but she was repelled. 'He had terrible body odour; he was flatulent,' she recalled, adding, however, that he had a sweet smile. It was not sweet enough, though, for Miss Basquette, who related how she had sought to dampen his ardour with a kick in the groin. That did not prove effective, so she told him she was partly Jewish. That did.

In Romania the hated dictator Ceaucescu and his evil wife Elena spent at least one evening a week seeing the same film over and over again in their velvet-lined private cinema. It was *The Great Gatsby* (US 74), from Scott Fitzgerald's novel of reckless hedonism in the 1920s. They both adored the luxurious lifestyle portrayed in the film and ignored the subversive message that excessive riches render such privileged people wholly heartless.

When the hitherto secret records of the Soviet State

When Douglas Fairbanks and Mary Pickford, the 'King and Queen of Hollywood', visited England in 1922 they were mobbed by 20,000 fans in Hyde Park. On the edge of the crowd was a Daimler Barouch discreetly bearing the royal insignia on its coachwork. In the back sat King George V, rubbernecking Hollywood's royalty together with his subjects.

Film Committee were examined by the Russian investigative weekly *Argumenty i Fakhty* in 1992, it was revealed that Leonid Brezhnev's favourite movie fare included *Dirty Harry* (US 71), *Magnum Force* (US 73), *Taxi Driver* (US 76) and the soft-porn *Emmanuelle* (Fr 74), while his successor Yuri Andropov liked all the Bond movies, as well as *The Godfather* (US 72) and anything else about violent crime. Needless to say, none of these films was considered fit for the eyes of ordinary Soviet citizens; nor, of course, were the blue movies that the State Film Committee despatched to the seaside dachas of the Politburo for their delectation in the summer holidays.

Pope John Paul II had a penchant for pouting blonde child-woman Patsy Kensit. He asked to meet her after she had starred in *Il Ragazzo delle Crociette* (It 89). Said a breathless Miss Kensit of the encounter: 'I felt holy for a week afterwards.' Another fan, from the opposite end of the social spectrum, was gangland boss Reggie Kray (played by Martin Kemp in *The Krays* (GB 90)), a longtime friend of her family. His opportunities to see her films were limited, as he was serving a life sentence in a maximum-security gaol, but for many years they wrote to each other regularly.

President Mandela's favourite star is Elizabeth Taylor, whom he first met at an awards ceremony in Spain shortly before becoming the first black president of South Africa. Ten years earlier, on Robben Island, prisoner number 466/64 had watched her ruling a nation when *Cleopatra* (US 63) was shown to the convicts on a makeshift outdoor screen.

American Presidents have been enjoying films at the White House since June 1914, when Giovanni Pastrone's epic *Cabiria* (It 14) was screened before President Wilson and his Cabinet. The President's favourite star was the statuesque Katharine MacDonald, known as 'The American Beauty'. If FDR had any preferences when it came to the ladies, he was not letting on to his wife. Eleanor Roosevelt confided that 'the President never has an evening of his own planning without at least one Mickey Mouse film'. It is not recorded whether President Truman was obliged to sit through *The Scarlet Pimpernel* (GB 34) the 16 times his daughter Margaret—a devotee of Leslie Howard—had it screened at the White House. Eisenhower's favourite films while President were *Angels in the Outfield* (US 52)—described by Leslie Halliwell as 'unamusing, saccharine whimsy'—*Springfield Rifle* (US 52), *To Catch a Thief* (US 55), and *Rear Window* (US 54). The latter two starred his favourite actress, Grace Kelly. President Kennedy left the selection of films to aide Arthur Schlesinger, who arranged a show every Sunday evening at the White House. But he was the only President known to have gone to the movies incognito at a public cinema during his term of office. He slipped out of the White House one night to see *Spartacus* (US 60), in which Kirk Douglas played a charismatic leader who inspires his people with a new vision of liberty but dies an early and violent death.

A President's predilection for a particular movie could have sinister overtones. Richard Nixon had repeated private screenings of *Patton: Lust for Glory* (US 69) shortly before ordering American bombers into Cambodia. He said of the Vietnam conflict 'I will not go down in history as the first American President to lose a war'. The line came out of *Patton*. (Oliver Stone actually shot a scene about this for *Nixon* (US 95), with Nixon going with his family to see the film for the seventh time, but it was vetoed by George C. Scott who held the *Patton* licensing rights.)

President Carter was too discreet to mention a favourite film, but it did not escape attention on the other side of the Atlantic that he was enrolled as an honorary member of Britain's Errol Flynn Fan Club. It also behoved Hollywood's own incumbent of the White House not to be too forthcoming about his personal preferences, but in answer to the obvious question, the President's Director of Media Relations revealed that Mr Reagan had 'viewed one of his own films at the request of his staff'. Among films not starring Ronald Reagan which he admired, one was certainly the Gary Cooper American Civil War drama *Friendly Persuasion* (US 56). It was a copy of this movie which he presented to Mikhail Gorbachev during his visit to Moscow in 1988.

William Jefferson Clinton admitted to having been an inveterate filmgoer since childhood and used to see two movies a day whenever he could. His favourite movie of all time was *High Noon* (US 52), which he has seen no fewer than 20 times. He cited the Kevin Costner starrer *Field of Dreams* (US 89), about an Iowa farmer who creates a baseball diamond out of his cornfield, as the film he wanted everyone in America to see, quoting the inspirational line 'If you build it, people will come . . .'. Favourite star was Meryl Streep, while Nick Nolte was his selection for the lead role in a Bill Clinton biopic—before the Lewinsky revelations. Special mention also went to Jodie Foster, whom he believed represents 'hope for our generation'. President Clinton also sought political inspiration from the movies, if a story circulating in Washington is to be believed. Together with top adviser James Carville he was watching Ivan Reitman's comedy of shenanigans in the White House *Dave* (US 93) when, so the story goes, the two men's attention was drawn by the episode in which the incorruptible Vice President (Ben Kingsley) is removed out of harm's way by being sent on an extended state visit to Burundi. It so happened that at the time Senator Bob Krueger, a Democrat from Texas, was causing the White House trouble by refusing to toe the party line on NAFTA and the Budget. Removal not only from the Senate but to somewhere far, far distant from Washington seemed like a very attractive idea. Thus the legend. What is indisputable is that shortly afterwards Senator Krueger was appointed United States Ambassador to Burundi.

George Bernard Shaw named Sir Cedric Hardwicke as his fifth favourite actor. The distinguished thespian was preceded in Shaw's regard by the Marx Brothers.

Premières

The largest audience to attend a world première were the 100,000 beneficiaries of the Walt Disney Co.'s offer of free tickets for the first presentation of its 33rd animated feature *Pocahontas* (US 95) on the Great Lawn of Central Park in New York on 10 June 1995. Eight projectors were used to beam special 70mm prints of the film on to four eight-storey-high screens in the 13-acre viewing area. More than 150 sound speakers were used, equal to five amphitheatre concert audio systems. It was the largest-ever audience for a sound movie (see also Audience, largest).

The largest indoor première took place at the 12,000-seat Madison Square Garden on 5 June 1915 with the presentation of Pierce Kingley's *Silver Threads Among the Gold* (US 15). It starred operatic tenor Richard José, who sang the title song on stage.

The most simultaneous world premières took place on 11 December 1992, when Rob Reiner's *A Few Good Men* (US 92), starring Tom Cruise and Jack Nicholson, opened in over 50 nations around the world.

The largest number of simultaneous openings was for *Godzilla* (US 98), which opened on 7363 North American screens on 19 May 1998. This represented some 23% of all US and Canadian screens.

UNUSUAL PREMIÈRES

Not all premières take place in glittering and star-studded surroundings. *Oliver Twist* (US 22) had its British première at London's historic Foundling Hospital, presumably in tribute to the protagonist's orphan origins; while the world première of MGM's Agatha Christie whodunnit *Murder at the Gallop* (GB 63) took place in a tent at a church garden party in rural Cheshire. The Barbara Stanwyck starrer *My Reputation* (US 46) was premièred in a Nissen hut on an airfield 'somewhere in England'. After this somewhat downbeat launch, it went on to become a major box-office success in America.

There was only one place to hold the world première of *Dodge City* (US 40). The last of the real razzmatazz preems before the austerities of war, the celebration began with a special train bringing 150 Warner Bros executives and stars, including the movie's topliners Errol Flynn and Olivia de Havilland, which was escorted into Dodge City by an aerial fleet of 50 private aircraft. Overnight the little Kansas town underwent a temporary population explosion from 10,000 to 15,000.

At the conclusion of the world première of *Gone With the Wind* (US 39) at the Loew's Grand in Atlanta on 14 December 1939, Mayor Hartsfield took to the stage and asked the distinguished audience for a round of applause for 'the Negro members of the cast'. Those so honoured were unable to respond. They had been barred from attending as the Loew's Grand was a whites-only cinema. After her death, it was revealed that Vivien Leigh was of Indian blood. Had it been known at the time, would the screen's immortal Scarlett have been equally unwelcome to attend?

There was no problem in accommodating everyone who wanted to come to the world première of *King of the Coral Sea* (Aus 54), an adventure story about pearlers in the South Seas. It took place on the tiny Pacific atoll of Thursday Island. With a population of less than a thousand, everyone was invited.

Three films have been premièred off-shore. John Ford's *The Informer* (US 35) was presented for the first time aboard the French transatlantic liner *Normandie*, while *Valley of the Dolls* (US 67) had its inaugural screening aboard the Italian cruise ship *Princess Italia*.

When Warner Bros wanted to give the world première of their film version of Jack London's *The Sea Wolf* (US 41) aboard the SS *America*, officials of United States Lines expressed doubts about the dignity of such an occasion. Warner Bros assured them that everything about it would be so dignified, nothing could bring the shipping line into disrepute. They had reckoned without the weather. A storm on the Central California Coast set the liner pitching and bucketing during the dinner preceding the unveiling of the film. Stars Jane Wyman and Priscilla Lane made their entrance to the ship's cinema with faces a distinct shade of green. When the film began and the *Sea Wolf* of the film's title was seen lurching and rolling through monstrous waves, a number of members of the cast were seen rolling or lurching towards the exit. They were followed by a bevy of reporters, heading for the radio room to file reports which amply fulfilled all the steamship executives' worst expectations.

The première of *The Incredible Mr Limpet* (US 64) was held underwater. The oddball story of a man who turned into a fish, the picture was preemed by Warner Bros on the ocean floor with a submerged screen at Weeki Wachi, Fla. The invited audience of 250 sat in a glass tank 20ft below the surface.

Three world premières have been held in the air. The first was Universal's *So Goes My Love* (US 46), starring Myrna Loy and Don Ameche, which premièred in mid-Atlantic on a Pan-American Clipper Fight between NY and London on 15 April 1946. Master showman Joseph E. Levine held the first showing of Lewis Gilbert's *The Adventurers* (US 70), a glitzy filmisation of the Harold Robbins novel, in a jet airliner crossing the USA. The other was *Crimson Pig* (Jap 92), an animated picture about an airforce pilot who turns into a pig and fights air pirates. It was first shown on Japan Airlines flights before opening at 200 cinemas in Japan on 18 July 1992. Some 25% of the $4.7 million budget for *Crimson Pig* was provided by the airline and they helped to promote the movie with the sale of porcine dolls at their airport stores.

Far-flung simultaneous openings are not so rare, but when Stanley Kramer decided to hold the world première of *On the Beach* (US 59) on both sides of the Iron Curtain at the same time there was certainly no precedent. Based on Nevil Shute's novel about the doomed survivors of a nuclear holocaust, the film opened in 17 cities on 17 December 1959, including New York, Moscow and the city in which the story was set, Melbourne.

If Kramer's intent was to stimulate peace among nations, very different sentiments must have actuated the Nazis' decision to première Veit Harlan's epic *Kolberg* (Ger 45) in the besieged fortress of La Rochelle. Kolberg was about the fortitude of the inhabitants of the Baltic town of that name during the Napoleonic Wars; the staging of its première in such unpropitious circumstances a symbolic act. Since the print could not be brought through the lines of the besieging army, it was dropped into the town by parachute.

Robert Warwick, star of *Alias Jimmy Valentine* (US

15), promised the inmates of Sing Sing that they would see the picture before anyone else, as they had helped him with the scenes shot in the 'Big Pen' of the notorious gaol. The world première took place before an audience of murderers, gangsters and rapists on 14 February 1915. It was another 60 years before the next prison première, this time at the New York City Correctional Institution for Women, when Lech Kowalski's study of drug addiction *Gringo* (US 85) was shown for the first time.

The première of *The Jeweller's Shop* (Can 88) was held in the rather more grandiose setting of the Vatican's magnificent Paul VI Hall. Reason for such a privilege was to honour the playwright whose work had been adapted for the screen—none other than Pope John Paul II. He had written the drama in 1960 when he was Bishop of Cracow.

The most belated première of a feature film took place in London in November 1996 when Maurice Elvey's *The Life Story of David Lloyd George* (GB 18) was released 78 years after its completion. Starring Norman Page as Lloyd George, Alma Reville (later Mrs Alfred Hitchcock) as Megan and Ernest Thesiger as Joseph Chamberlain, the film had been made with the Prime Minister's blessing but, for reasons which remain obscure, then suppressed. Long considered a lost film, it was rediscovered by accident in 1994 and restored by the Wales Film & TV Archive.

Film Criticism

This was born with a brief review of *May Irwin Kiss* (US 1896) in the *Chap Book* for 15 June 1896: '. . . absolutely disgusting'.

The first regular film critic was Frank Woods, who began reviewing for the *New York Dramatic Mirror* with the issue of 1 May 1909. Woods used the pen-name 'Spectator'. His salary was $20 a week.

None of the performers were identified in early reviews. *Variety* seems to have been the first to discard this anonymity, the issue for 21 January 1911 referring to Mary Pickford's 'cute ways and girlish manner' in *The Italian Barber* (US 11).

The first newspaper to carry film reviews was *Vilag* (World), a Budapest daily, which engaged Sándor Kellner as its critic in August 1912. Kellner's sojourn with the paper was brief, since he was determined to get into the production side of the movie business, which he did with spectacular success as (Sir) Alexander Korda.

The first American newspaper to employ a regular film critic was the *Chicago Tribune* with the appointment of John Lawson in 1914. Lawson was killed in an accident soon after and his place was taken by Miss Audrie Alspaugh, who wrote under the byline 'Kitty Kelly'. Movie historian Terry Ramsaye recalled: 'Kitty Kelly could make or break a picture in the Middle West . . . Her column was a large success, and she became the best disliked name in the world of the film studios.'

The longest-serving film critic was London-based Dilys Powell (1901–95), who joined the *Sunday Times* in 1924, where her first job was composing Greek and Latin couplets for the 'Atticus' column, and began reviewing films for the paper in April 1939. Among her earliest reviews were those she wrote on *Only Angels Have Wings* (US 39) and *Stagecoach* (US 39). When *Gone With the Wind* (US 39) was reissued in 1989, Miss Powell was the only critic whose 'reassessment' was in relation to a review written when it was first released. She decided that Clark Gable's performance was really rather better than she had given him credit for half a century earlier. Until 1992 Dilys Powell spent Mondays and Tuesdays at press shows, always sitting in the third row of the viewing theatre and entering precisely two minutes late. Her arrival was the signal for the picture to start. She then semi-retired, doing a weekly round-up of the films being shown on television for the *Sunday Times* arts section; her last review, for Kubrick's *Barry Lyndon* (GB 75), appeared 56 years after her first on 4 June 1995. She had died just before it was published.

STAY AWAY CRITS
Verbal annihilation has been the stock in trade of the film critic ever since the very first review. Here are a few intimations that the critic did not think the picture deserved his unqualified approval.

- Anthony Slide on Marguerite Duras's *India Song* (Fr 75) 'Without question the most boring, pretentious feature ever foisted on the general public'.
- Alan Brien of the *Sunday Times* on Irwin Allen's *The Swarm* (US 78) 'Simply the worst film ever made'.
- *Variety* on *The Gong Show Movie* (US 80) 'Bong-g-g-g-g-g'.
- Vincent Canby on the $48-million *Inchon* (US/Kor 82) 'The most expensive B-movie ever made'.
- *Variety*: 'Lonesome Cowboy is Andy Warhol's best movie to date, which is like saying a three-year-old has graduated from smearing faeces on the wall to the occasional use of finger paints.'
- Anonymous critic on *Cleopatra* (US 63) 'Elizabeth Taylor is the first Cleopatra to sail down the Nile to Las Vegas'.
- *New York Daily News* on *Hawk of Powder River* (US 48) 'Eddie Dean's latest is in black and white rather than color but the improvement is hardly noticeable; you can still see him'.
- Pauline Kael on *Dances with Wolves* (US 90) 'A New Age Social Studies lesson'.
- Judith Crist on *The Agony and the Ecstasy* (US 65) 'All agony, no ecstasy'.
- *Variety* on *Way Back Home* (Bel 81) 'So poor that it gives amateurism a bad name'.
- Gary Arnold of the *Washington Post* on Ken Russell's biopic of Tchaikovsky *The Music Lovers* (GB 71) 'Awful . . . the worst experience I ever had in a cinema'.

'Don't pay any attention to the critics—don't even ignore them.'—Samuel Goldwyn

- *Variety* on *Les Enfants du Paradis* (Fr 44)—which is probably the most universally admired foreign-language film of all time—'Downright dull'.
- Leslie Felperin Sharman of *Sight & Sound* on *Bad Girls* (US 94) 'The Office of Fair Trading should be notified about the title, which ought to be *Girls Who Are Quite Nice Really*.'
- Nigel Andrews, *Financial Times*, on *Thunderheart* (US 91) 'A stupefying slab of political piety about America's treatment of the Indian . . . It should be sub-titled "Bury My Brain at Wounded Knee"'.
- Colin Bennett of the *Melbourne Age* on Australia's first sexploitation movie *The Set* (Aus 70) 'At last my 18-year search for the worst film ever made has ended'.
- Alan Parker on *The Draughtsman's Contract* (GB 83) 'A load of posturing poo poo'.

Michael Winner, director of the *Death Wish* films and restaurant critic, reviewing London's five-star Lanesborough Hotel after paying £499 for a Chateau Lafitte-Rothschild 1996 to accompany his kedgeree: 'So awful as to be almost indescribable.'

Geoffrey Gelardi, managing director of the Lanesborough, as guest critic reviewing Michael Winner's *Dirty Weekend* (GB 93): 'So awful as to be almost indescribable.'

- John Simon on *Camelot* (US 67) 'This film is the Platonic idea of boredom, roughly comparable to reading a three-volume novel in a language of which one knows only the alphabet'.
- James Agee on *You Were Meant For Me* (US 48) 'That's what you think'.
- 'Cart' of *Variety* on *Lovelines* (US 84) 'Ought to be advertised with the warning that anyone who arrives after the beginning will miss the best part: the Tri-Star logo'.
- Desson Howe, *Washington Post*, on *Howards End* (GB 92) 'English lawns grow faster than this inert, 140-minute film . . .'
- *Variety* on *Movie Movie* (US 78) 'Awful Awful'.

Quotes from favourable reviews in a movie ad can be a powerful persuader to go and see the film. So can quotes from unfavourable reviews—used out of context. Critic Andy Klein of the *Los Angeles Reader* wrote a review of *Elvira, Mistress of the Dark* (US 88) which said that even when the star was 'supposed to be coming across as charmingly exuberant, she is only obnoxious'. The ad for the picture boasted 'Charmingly exuberant!' Merrill Shindler, critic of the *Los Angeles Herald Examiner*, recalls a review he wrote which contained the damming indictment 'The burning of this movie would be a boon to mankind'. Trumpeted the ad 'A boon to mankind'.

- David Aasen of *Newsweek* on *A Dream of Passion* (US 78) 'As one endures the spectacle of Mercouri bearing

her soul . . . it seems one has wandered into the home movies of a demented culture maven'.
- C. A. Lejeune on *No Leave No Love* (US 46) 'No Comment'. (This was the complete review.)
- *Variety* on *The American Prisoner* (GB 29) 'Save for direction, story, dialogue, acting and being a period picture, this is a good one'.
- *The Reporter* magazine on *Guess Who's Coming to Dinner* (US 67) 'Abie's Irish Rose in Blackface'.
- *New Yorker* review of *Greystoke—The Legend of Tarzan Lord of the Apes* (GB 84) 'A unique mixture of pomposity and ineptitude'.
- 'Cart' of *Variety* on *The Lion with the White Mane* (Cz 87) 'All concerned should run and hide . . .'
- Pauline Kael on *Blue Collar* (US 78) 'Jukebox Marxism'.
- Christopher Tookey of the *Sunday Telegraph* on *Desperate Hours* (US 91) 'Cimino's direction is innocently unfettered by notions of taste, proportion or suspense, while the screenplay is so criminally inept that its improbabilities are too numerous to mention. This is one of those films which should never have been released, even on parole. It's a danger to itself.'

'No reviewer has ever illuminated any aspect of my work for me.'—Stanley Kubrick

---

- *Variety* on Vadim's *And God Created Woman* (Fr 57), which became the most successful foreign film ever released in America, 'Just average for any US possibilities . . . questionable attributes of the new star here, Miss Bardot'.
- *France Soir* on philosopher Bernard-Henri Levy's debut picture, the Alain Delon/Lauren Bacall starrer *Le Jour et la Nuit* (Fr 97)—'Does for cinema what the sweat from socks does for espresso coffee.'
- David Wilson of the *Monthly Film Bulletin* on every semiologist's favourite film *Persona* (Swe 66) 'Bergman talking to himself again'.
- David Denby of *New York* magazine on Sylvester Stallone's *Cobra* (US 86) 'Senselessly crude, laughably unbelievable . . . unimaginably degraded'.
- *Newsweek*: 'The Sentinel* is the perfect film for those who like to slow down and look at traffic accidents.'

In Orson Welles' *The Other Side of the Wind* (US 76), Susan Strasberg played a character based on the critic Pauline Kael, renowned for her ability to read rather more into a movie than the director may have intended. Miss Strasberg recalled: 'There was a scene with a bus. At one point, the cameraman inside the moving bus could not avoid photographing a large red sign with a cross on it which loomed up. Somebody said, "Let's cut that sign out, it doesn't fit into the story." And Orson said, "No, no, leave it in the shot. Pauline Kael will write paragraphs about the symbolism in that red cross!"'

- Pauline Kael, on Stanley Kubrick's classic *2001 A Space Odyssey* (GB 68) 'It's a monumentally unimaginative movie'.

- The *Observer* on Disney's triumph *Snow White and the Seven Dwarfs* (US 37) 'Has all the roughness and error of a first try'.
- Alexander Walker, *Evening Standard*, on *Buffy the Vampire Slayer* (US 92) 'To enjoy this moronic rubbish, you'd need to put your IQ into total unconsciousness'.
- The *New York Times* on *Lawrence of Arabia* (GB 62) 'Just a huge thundering camel-opera . . .'
- Alan Stanbrook of *7 Days* on *Dick Tracy* (US 90) '. . . a charter for the illiterate'.
- Joseph McBride, *Variety*, on *Stay Tuned* (US 92) 'A picture with nothing for everybody.'
- Reggie Nadelson *You*, on *The Bridges of Madison County* (US 95): 'Jumbopopcorn.'
- Pauline Kael, *McCall's Magazine*, on *The Sound of Music* (US 65) 'Will probably be the single most repressive influence on artistic freedom in movies for the next few years'. (Kael was fired from *McCall's* for this review.)
- Philippe Garnier of *Liberation* (Paris) on *The Doors* (US 91): '*gross merde*'.
- H.G. Wells in the *New York Times* on Fritz Lang's science-fiction classic *Metropolis* (Ger 26) '. . . unimaginative, incoherent, sentimentalising . . . I do not think there is a single instant of artistic creation, or even of intelligent anticipation, from first to last in the whole preposterous stew'.
- Geoffrey Macnab, *Sight & Sound*, on *The Flintstones* (US 94) 'Theme-park film-making'.
  And others on the same picture:
  'Yabba Dabba Dud'—*N.Y. Daily News*
  'Yabba Dabba Don't'—*USA Today*
  'Yabba Dabba Boo'—*Washington Post*
  'Yabba Dabba Dumb'—*Boston Globe*
  'Yabba Dabba Doo-doo'—*Philadelphia Enquirer*
- Val Lewton on *Gone With the Wind* (US 39) 'Ponderous trash'.
- Vincent Canby on *Gandhi* (GB/Ind 82) '. . . a laboriously illustrated textbook'.
- Dann Gire, *Chicago Daily Herald*, on Brian DePalma's *Raising Cain* (US 92) 'DeFicient, DeRivative, DeTestable, DePalma'.
- Nigella Lawson, *Daily Telegraph* on Oz eco-animation pic *Ferngully . . . The Last Rainforest* (Aus 92) 'Infantile environmentalism'.
- Brian Lowry, *Variety*, on *True Lies* (US 94) 'Overlong, overproduced and overbudgeted'.
- Elvis Mitchell, *New York Times*, on John Travolta starrer *Battlefield Earth* (US 00) '. . . may well turn out to be the worst movie of this century'.

THE GOOD NOTICE GUIDE

Leading showbusiness trade paper *Variety* publishes weekly lists showing the number of favourable, unfavourable and mixed notices received by films reviewed in five main centres: New York, Los Angeles, Washington DC, Chicago and London. The table below shows the percentage of each during calendar 1999 and is presented in rank order of cities giving favourable notices. The total number of reviews surveyed was 11,200,

of which 4770 appeared in New York, 2317 in London, 1794 in Los Angeles, 1747 in Chicago and 572 in Washington.

	Favourable %	Unfavourable %	Mixed %
Chicago	47.8	21.8	30.4
Los Angeles	44.4	21.8	33.8
New York	42.1	30.4	27.5
Washington	40.4	30.0	29.5
London	39.3	34.9	25.9
All	42.8	28.5	29.4

According to the figures, distributors wanting a clutch of favourable reviews to quote in their ads stand a better chance if they open in Chicago. Much has changed among the scribes of the Windy City. Last time we published this survey, covering 1990–1, Chicago had the lowest score for favourable reviews at only 27.0%.

Perhaps even more remarkable is the fact that the percentage of favourable reviews in all five cities has significantly increased. Are the movies getting better or have the critics got softer? Chicago has moved from only 27.0% favourable to 47.8%, while unfavourable notices have plummeted from 48.5% to only 21.8%—level with Los Angeles, where condemnation of a movie is more likely to have an adverse effect on invites to A-list events.

Hard-boiled London critics, with the second-highest score of favourable reviews in 1990–1, now lie at the bottom of the league table, perhaps reflecting frustration at the hegemony of Hollywood and a lesser inclination to indulge indulgences like *Patch Adams*.

The most-lauded movie of the year, and all the more notable for being a sequel, was John Lasseter's computer-animated funfest *Toy Story 2*. The critics of the five key cities garlanded it with no fewer than 44 favourable notices, no unfavourable ones and only a single ambivalent review. (Mr Lasseter may have taken consolation from the fact that this emanated from the *Orange County Register*.)

Arguably the worst-reviewed movie in a decade' opined *Variety*'s Peter Bart of John Travolta starrer *Battlefield Earth* (US 00). The figures seem to bear this out. Out of 38 reviews by New York, Los Angeles, Chicago and London critics, 36 were unfavourable. A brace of generous Chicago scribes penned mixed reviews. Not one gave a thumbs-up to the film adumbrated in the *New York Times* as likely to turn out to be the worst movie of the 21st century.

Screens

The largest screen in the world measures 126 ft by 94 ft 3 in at the Panasonic IMAX Theatre, Darling Harbour in Sydney, Australia. It is the height of an eight-storey building.

Prior to the introduction of state-of-the-art IMAX technology, no screen size had exceeded the record set by Louis Lumière in 1898 at the Galérie des Machines on the site of the forthcoming Paris Exposition with a picture measuring 99 ft x 79 ft 2 in. The distance from the projector was 650 ft and the screen was kept wet to increase its reflection of light, a task undertaken by the Paris Fire Brigade, who trained their hoses on the mammoth sheet before the show began.

The largest screen in Britain measures 84 ft 6 in x 65 ft and is at the BFI IMAX Cinema at Waterloo, South London.

The widest screen ever used for projecting motion pictures was erected at the Palais d'Electricité et de la Lumière at the Paris Exposition of 1937 for showing Henri Chrétien's hypergonar films, the precursor of Cinerama. The concave screen had a breadth of 195 ft and was 32 ft 6 in high. By comparison the Cinerama screen size was 90 x 26 ft.

The widest screen in use today was installed at the Mercury Cinema, Paris, in 1981 and measures 133 ft in breadth.

360° screens, with the audience wholly surrounded by the projected image, exist at the China Pavilion of Walt Disney's EPCOT Center in Florida, where the system is called 'Circle Vision'; and at the L'Espace Gaité cinema in Paris, which presents the 'Panrama' system on a 350 square metre screen.

Small Screen

The first full-length feature film shown on television was *Police Patrol* (US 25), transmitted in six daily episodes by W2XCD Passaic, NJ, 6–11 April 1931. Directed by Burton King for Gotham Productions, it related the story of a New York policeman (James Kirkwood) who arrests a girl thief (Edna Murphy)—the exact double of his sweetheart (also Edna Murphy).

The first film made for television was *Wer fuhr IIA 2992?/Who Was Driving Car Number 2992?* (Ger 39), a thriller scripted by Gerhart W. Göbel of the Reichspost and produced by UFA in Berlin. Göbel devised the plot after seeing a police announcement on television appealing for help in a murder case. The scenario centred around a hit-and-run driver, since the Nazi Propaganda Ministry would not allow murder as a theme for films to be shown abroad. The film was first shown during television demonstrations in Bucharest and Sofia in 1940 and was also used after the war when the German Post Office resume experimental transmissions in 1950.

The highest price paid for TV rights to a movie was $80 million in June 1997 by the Fox network for Steven Spielberg's *The Lost World: Jurassic Park* (US 97).

The first video films were offered for hire by Sears, Roebuck in the USA at $3–6 each in the spring of 1972. Titles included *Stagecoach* (US 39), *Hamlet* (GB 48), *High Noon* (US 52), *The Bridge on the River Kwai* (GB 57), *Cactus Flower* (US 69) and *The Anderson Tapes* (US 71). They were for showing on the Avco Cartavision video player, which retailed at $1600. The first video films for sale were put on the market by Andre Blay of the small Michigan-based company Magnetic Video, who acquired the rights to 50 Fox productions in 1977. The initial titles, which included *M*A*S*H*, *Hello Dolly* and *Patton*, sold for $50 per cassette.

The first film produced expressly for the video market (excluding pornography) was *Tangier* (GB 82), starring Billie Whitelaw.

The highest-selling video of a movie was Buena Vista's animated *The Lion King* (US 94) at 55 million units, of which 20 million left the shelves in the first six days of release.

The first commercially made film for Internet release was Eugenio Zanetti's 32-minute, $3 million *Quantum Project* (US 00), billed as 'a story of two electron-crossed lovers' (Stephen Dorff and Fay Masterson), with John Cleese as a drunken World Wide Web pioneer. It could be downloaded from *SightSound.com* for $3.95 starting at midnight on 5 May 2000.

The first interactive movie on the Internet was Interactive Motion Picture Corporation's contemporary thriller *Running Time* (GB 00), launched on *www.itsyourmovie.com* in May 2000. The film was produced in 20 five-minute segments at the rate of two a week, each being shot only after the audience had voted via e-mail on the various options for the storyline to take. Set in London's East End, the lead character KJ (Anna Bolt) is a pretty, streetwise cycle courier who returns to her Hoxton flat one night to find it stripped bare—and her twin brother vanished with no clues as to how or why. Her frantic search for him throws her into a world of industrial espionage and eco-terrorism, principal writer Simon Beaufoy, who scripted *The Full Monty*, developing the plot in line with viewer response. In addition to interacting with the creative team, viewers could also watch the film being shot by clicking an 'On Set' button.

CHAPTER 16
Awards and Festivals

The first film awards were made in respect of a festival which opened in Monte Carlo on New Year's Day 1898. The competition was open to professionals and amateurs alike but subjects had to be taken in Monaco. The first prize was worth £80, and there were two others worth £40 and £20. The winner was Clément-Maurice for his *Monaco vivant par les appareils cinématographiques* (Fr 1897). The following year the competition was expanded. Prize money was increased to a total of £1200 (30,000 francs) plus a number of honourable mentions and this time it was purely for amateurs. It was organised by the Societé des Bains de Mer who stipulated that each competitor must send in three films of any place or subject which should never previously have been exhibited. The jury was to be composed of 'artists and amateurs' and films were judged on 'originality, artistic merit and photographic quality', according to the *British Journal of Photography*. The prizes were awarded in February 1900 by the Prince of Monaco and the winning entries were shown at the Palais des Beaux Arts. The titles of the winning films are not recorded.

The first award-winning drama was Giovanni Vitrotti's *Il Cane riconoscente* (It 07), an Ambrosio production which won a gold plaque awarded by the Lumière brothers at an international contest held in Italy in 1907.

The first award made to a feature film was also won by Ambrosio. The Grand Prix of 25,000 francs at the

> **T**he only film to have recouped its entire costs from a single festival prize award was Garin Nurgroho's *Letter to an Angel* (Indonesia 94), which won the Young Cinema Gold Prize of $200,000 at the 1994 Tokyo Film Festival. The picture's budget was $180,000.

International Exhibition at Turin in 1912 went to *After Fifty Years* (It 12), a historical drama set in the Austro–Italian War of 1859.

The first annual awards and the oldest extant were instituted in 1917 by America's National Board of Review of Motion Pictures.

Britain's first film festival was the International Festival of Women's Films, held in London in 1928. The first prize went to Dorothy Arzner's *Fashions For Women* (US 27). The only other pre-war festival on record was a non-competitive event held at Malvern in 1931, notable chiefly for the pre-release presentation of the first Bernard Shaw talkie, *How He Lied to Her Husband* (GB 31) with Edmund Gwenn.

The first regular film festival was held as part of the Venice Biennale and took place at the Hotel Excelsior from 6 to 21 August 1932, the purpose behind it being an

> **I**n 1999 there were 332 movie awards ceremonies worldwide and 3182 awards.

attempt to revive the Depression-hit tourist trade. A total of 18 pictures were entered by Germany, the USA, France, Italy and the UK, three of them directed by women. No awards were made.

Academy Awards

The Academy Awards were instituted by the Academy of Motion Picture Arts and Sciences and first presented on 16 May 1929. The awards that year were to dignify the efforts of film-makers during the 12 months August 1927 to July 1928—and at the same time to dignify, the Academy hoped, the somewhat tarnished reputation the

Casting the Oscars at the Southern California Trophy Company in 1949. The 'high hats' were knocked off before the figures were dipped in a bath of liquid gold. (Popperfoto)

film industry had earned itself in the Roaring Twenties

Oscar, the Academy Award trophy, is the figure of a man with a crusader's sword standing on a reel of film. It was designed by MGM art director Cedric Gibbons, who was to receive it no fewer than 11 times himself (see below). Until 1931 it was known simply as 'The Statuette', but in that year Academy librarian Margaret Herrick chanced to remark 'He looks like my Uncle Oscar' and the name stuck. Plated in 24-carat gold, Oscar has always stood 13½ inches tall, except in war time when the trophy consisted of a gold-plated plaster plaque with the Oscar figure in relief. The value of an Oscar is $295. Recipients pledge never to sell their statuette except back to the Academy, who will pay $1 for it (but see p. 243). Double Oscar-winning scriptwriter Frances Marion said that she saw the statuette as 'a perfect symbol of the picture business: a powerful athletic body clutching a gleaming sword, with half of his head, that part which held his brains, completely sliced off'.

The largest number of films qualifying for consideration for an Academy Award was 264 for the 47th Awards in 1974. During the 1980s the figure fluctuated around the 250 mark, representing a little less than half the films released annually in the USA. To qualify a film has to have played publicly in Los Angeles for at least a week within specified dates.

The most awards in any category have been won by Walt Disney (1901–66), as the producer of films honoured with 22 competitive awards. He also received three special trophies and the Irving G. Thalberg Award.

The most awards for individual creative achievement are the 11 won by Cedric Gibbons (1893–1960) of MGM for art direction; the most won by a woman are the eight by costume designer Edith Head (1907–81).

The most honoured living recipients, each with eight statuettes, are special-effects cameraman Dennis Muren of Industrial Light & Magic, including awards *for E.T. The Extra-Terrestrial* (US 82), *The Abyss* (US 89), *Terminator 2* (US 91) and *Jurassic Park* (US 93); and composer-songwriter Alan Menken.

The individual with the most nominations of all time was Walt Disney with 60, though the majority of these were for animated films produced under his banner rather than for personal creative contribution. Most nominations for individual creative achievement went to composer Alfred Newman with 45, while the most achieved by anyone still alive are the 38 honouring composer John Williams. The most nominations for an actress have been 12 for Katharine Hepburn (won four times) and for Meryl Streep (won twice), and the most for an actor 11 for Jack Nicholson (won twice).

The individuals to have received the most nominations without a win are composer Alex North and art director Roland Anderson, each with 15.

The most awards won by any one film were 11 for *Ben Hur* (US 59) and *Titanic* (US 97). *Ben Hur* won Best Picture; Director; Actor; Supporting Actor; Cinematography; Art Direction; Sound; Music Score; Film Editing; Special Effects; Costume. *Titanic* won Best Picture; Director; Cinematography; Costume Design; Art Direction; Editing; Dramatic Score; Original Song; Sound; Visual Effects; Sound-Effects Editing.

The most awards won by a British film went to *Gandhi* (GB 83) and numbered eight: Best Picture; Actor; Director; Original Screenplay; Cinematography; Film Editing; Art Direction; Costume Design.

Only three films have won 'The Big Five' major awards—Best Picture; Best Director; Best Actor; Best Actress; Best Screenplay. They are: *It Happened One Night* (US 34)—Frank Capra; Clark Gable; Claudette Colbert; Robert Riskin; *One Flew Over the Cuckoo's Nest* (US 75)—Milos Forman; Jack Nicholson; Louise Fletcher; Lawrence Hauben and Bo Goldman; and *The Silence of the Lambs* (US 91)—Jonathan Demme; Anthony Hopkins; Jodie Foster; Ted Tully (Best Screenplay Adaptation).

The only films to have won in every category in which they were nominated were *Gigi* (US 58) and *The Last Emperor* (It/GB/Chn 87), both with nine awards.

The most nominated films to receive no awards were *The Turning Point* (US 77) and *The Color Purple* (US 86), each with 11 nominations.

The most nominated films were *All About Eve* (US 50) and *Titanic* (US 97), each with 14 noms. The big boat won 11 (see above), *Eve* six.

The most Best Director awards were made to John Ford, who won four times: *The Informer* (US 35); *The Grapes of Wrath* (US 40); *How Green was my Valley* (US 41); *The Quiet Man* (US 52).

The first director to have won an Oscar for his first film was Delbert Mann for *Marty* (US 55). The others have been Jerome Robbins for *West Side Story* (US 61)—shared with Robert Wise; Robert Redford for *Ordinary People* (US 80), James L. Brooks for *Terms of Endearment* (US 83); Kevin Costner for *Dances with Wolves* (US 90); and Britain's Sam Mendes for *American Beauty* (US 99).

The most Best Actor awards have been won by seven actors, each with two Oscars: Spencer Tracy for *Captains Courageous* (US 37) and *Boys Town* (US 38); Fredric March for *Dr Jekyll and Mr Hyde* (US 32) and *The Best Years of our Lives* (US 46); Gary Cooper for *Sergeant York* (US 41) and *High Noon* (US 52); Marlon Brando for *On the Waterfront* (US 54) and *The Godfather* (US 72); Dustin Hoffman for *Kramer vs Kramer* (US 79) and *Rain Man* (US 88); Tom Hanks for *Philadelphia* (US 93) and *Forrest Gump* (US 94); and Jack Nicholson for *One Flew Over the Cuckoo's Nest* (US 75) and *As Good As It Gets* (US 97). Tracy, though, received nine Best Actor nominations during his career, against seven for Brando, six for Hoffman and five each for March and Cooper. Sir Laurence Olivier equalled Tracy's nominations, but won only a single Best Actor award for *Hamlet* (GB 48). Perhaps Tracy should also take first place by virtue of the fact that Katharine Hepburn is on record as saying that one of her Academy Awards was doubtless intended for both of them.

The most Best Actress awards have been won by Katharine Hepburn, whose four Oscars were awarded for *Morning Glory* (US 33), *Guess Who's Coming to Dinner* (US 67), *The Lion in Winter* (GB 68) and *On Golden Pond* (US 81). Miss Hepburn also enjoys the distinction of having received the most nominations of any performer (equal with Meryl Streep—12), and of having the longest award-winning career, spanning 48 years.

The performer with the most nominations before winning was Geraldine Page who had been nominated seven times before she was honoured with the Best Actress award for *The Trip to Bountiful* (US 85).

The performers with the most nominations and no wins were fellow Celts Richard Burton (Welsh) and Peter O'Toole (Irish) with seven noms each. The most frequently disappointed actress was another Celt, Deborah Kerr (Scots), with 6 noms.

The first co-stars to win Best Actor and Best Actress award were Clark Gable and Claudette Colbert, for *It Happened One Night* (US 34). Miss Colbert was so sceptical of her chances of winning the Oscar that she decided not to postpone a trip to New York on a train scheduled to leave on the evening of the ceremony. She was just stepping into the carriage when officials of the Academy arrived to tell her she had won. A motorcycle escort

The youngest and the oldest performers to have won regular Oscars—nine-year-old Tatum O'Neal in Paper Moon *(US 73) and 80-year-old Jessica Tandy in* Driving Miss Daisy *(US 89). (Kobal Collection)*

rushed her to the Biltmore Bowl to receive the award, still dressed in her travelling clothes.

Other co-stars in dual wins have been: Jack Nicholson and Louise Fletcher: *One Flew Over the Cuckoo's Nest* (US 75); Peter Finch and Faye Dunaway: *Network* (US 76); Jon Voight and Jane Fonda: *Coming Home* (US 78); Henry Fonda and Katharine Hepburn: *On Golden Pond* (US 81); Anthony Hopkins and Jodie Foster: *The Silence of the Lambs* (US 91); Jack Nicholson and Helen Hunt: *As Good As It Gets* (US 97).

The shortest performance to win an acting Oscar was by Dame Judi Dench, whose bravura eight minutes on screen as Queen Elizabeth in *Shakespeare in Love* (US/GB 98) secured her the Best Supporting Actress award.

The first Oscar-winning debut performance was by Gale Sondegaard in *Anthony Adverse* (US 36), for which she won the Best Supporting Actress award. First neophyte in the Best Supporting Actor category was Harold Russell for *The Best Years of Our Lives* (US 46).

Others who have won Best Supporting awards for a debut performance have been Mercedes McCambridge for *All the King's Men* (US 49), Jo Van Fleet for *East of Eden* (US 55), Miyoski Umecki for *Sayonara* (US 57), Estelle Parsons for *Bonnie and Clyde* (US 67), John Houseman for *The Paper Chase* (US 73), Tatum O'Neal for *Paper Moon* (US 73), Timothy Hutton for *Ordinary People* (US 80), Dr Haing S. Ngor for *The Killing Fields* (GB 84) and Anna Paquin for *The Piano* (Aus 93).

The first Best Actress award for a debut performance went to Shirley Booth for *Come Back, Little Sheba*

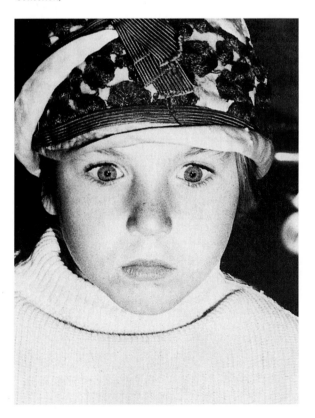

(US 52). Others to have won for their first film were Barbra Streisand for *Funny Girl* (US 68) and Marlee Matlin for *Children of a Lesser God* (US 86). There has been no Best Actor award for a debut performance.

The first performer to win an acting award for a foreign-language film was Sophia Loren for *Two Women* (It/Fr 60). The first to win Best Actor for a foreign-language film, and the only other foreign-language performance to win an Oscar, was Roberto Benigni for *Life is Beautiful* (It 98).

The only Best Actor/Actress winners to have directed themselves were Laurence Olivier in *Hamlet* (GB 48) and Roberto Benigni in *Life is Beautiful* (It 98).

The youngest Oscar winner was Shirley Temple, who won a Special Award at the age of six for 'her outstanding contribution to screen entertainment during the year 1934'.

The youngest person to receive a regular Academy Award was nine-year-old Tatum O'Neal, who won the Oscar for Best Supporting Actress for her role in *Paper Moon* (US 73). The youngest nominee was eight-year-old Justin Henry for *Kramer vs Kramer* (US 79). The winner that year was 78-year-old Melvyn Douglas for *Being There*—establishing another record with a 70-year span between oldest and youngest nominees.

The oldest performer to win an Oscar was British-born Jessica Tandy, who was 80 years and eight months old when she was awarded Best Actress for her stand-out role in *Driving Miss Daisy* (US 89). She was five months older than George Burns was when he won his Best Supporting Actor award for *The Sunshine Boys* (US 75). Miss Tandy might have won a Best Actress Oscar a lot earlier if she had not been the only member of the New York cast of Tennessee Williams' play *A Streetcar Named Desire* who was not brought to Hollywood to appear in the 1951 film version. Vivien Leigh, who substituted for her in the superlative role of Blanche Dubois, carried off the Academy Award for Best Actress.

The oldest nominee was Gloria Stuart, 87, as Best Supporting Actress for *Titanic* (US 97). She was also the nominee who has had to wait longest for this recognition, having made her screen debut 66 years earlier.

The oldest performer to win a Best Actor award was 76-year-old Henry Fonda for *On Golden Pond* (US 81).

The youngest performer to win in the Best Actor/Actress categories was 21-year-old Marlee Matlin for *Children of a Lesser God* (US 86). Janet Gaynor, the first Best Actress winner, was 22. Youngest to be nominated was ten-year old Jackie Cooper for *Skippy* (US 97). No juvenile has won either award and the youngest Best Actor winner was the 30-year-old Richard Dreyfuss for *The Goodbye Girl* (US 77).

The first black Oscar winner was Hattie McDaniel, who was awarded Best Supporting Actress for her role as Mammy in *Gone With the Wind* (US 39). Twenty-four years elapsed before another black performer won a reg-

ular Oscar: Sidney Poitier was awarded Best Actor for *Lilies of the Field* (US 63).

OSCAR ODDITIES
- The only occasion on which no film won more than one Oscar was the second Academy Awards in March 1930.
- Scriptwriter Robert Towne was so dissatisfied with the liberties he reckoned Hugh Hudson had taken with his script for *Greystoke—The Legend of Tarzan, Lord of the Apes* (GB/US 84) that he had his name replaced on the credits with that of his sheepdog, an animal called P. H. Vazak. The dog was nominated for an Oscar.
- No film has ever won all four acting categories. Two have taken three Awards: *A Streetcar Named Desire* (US 51) with Best Actress going to Vivien Leigh, Best Supporting Actor to Karl Malden and Best Supporting Actress to Kim Hunter; and *Network* (US 76) which won Best Actor and Best Actress in the persons of Peter Finch and Faye Dunaway and Best Supporting Actress for Beatrice Straight.
- The only actors to have won Oscars for playing the same character are Marlon Brando and Robert De Niro as Vito Corleone (the title role) in *The Godfather* (US 72) and *The Godfather II* (US 74) respectively.
- The highest amount paid for an Oscar statuette was $1,540,000 by Michael Jackson at Sotheby's New York in 1999 for David O Selznick's Best Picture award won for *Gone With The Wind* (US 39). The highest paid for an acting Oscar was the $607,500 by Steven Spielberg for Clark Gable's Best Actor Oscar for *It Happened One Night* (US 34), which he bought at Christie's in December 1996 and presented to the Academy. When Claudette Colbert's matching Best Actress Oscar for the same film went up for sale at Christie's a few months later there were no bids.
- No woman has won the Best Director award. Two have been nominated: Italy's Lina Wertmuller for *Seven Beauties* (It 75) and New Zealand's Jane Campion for *The Piano* (Aus 93). The latter was also nominated for Best Picture. Three other femme-helmed pix have been nominated for Best Picture: Randa Haines' *Children of a Lesser God* (US 86), Penny Marshall's *Awakenings* (US 90) and Barbra Streisand's *The Prince of Tides* (US 91), but none of the ladies' films won the accolade.
- One of the oddities of the Oscars is that the male or female lead in a picture can be nominated in the Best Supporting categories. First such to win in these circumstances was Eve Marie Saint for *On The Waterfront* (US 54). Others have been Goldie Hawn for *Cactus Flower* (US 69), Jessica Lange for *Tootsie* (US 82), Geena Davis for *The Accidental Tourist* (US 87) and Marisa Tomei for *My Cousin Vinny* (US 82). No men! Uniquely, Barry Fitzgerald was nominated as Best Actor *and* Best Supporting Actor for one and the same role in *Going My Way* (US44). He won the latter but lost out to his co-star in the picture, Bing Crosby, for Best Actor.
- Eight actresses have won Oscars for playing hookers; only one for playing a nun—Susan Sarandon in *Dead Man Walking* (US 95).
- Nowadays embarrassment at the Academy Awards is

usually occasioned by the outpourings of the honoured, but in the early days of the Oscars ceremony overenthusiastic presenters could also cause a hiatus. In 1934 Frank Lloyd and Frank Capra were amongst those up for Best Director. When Will Rogers opened the envelope he did not announce the winner, but called out 'Come and get it, Frank!'. Capra was halfway to the podium before he realised Lloyd had also risen from his seat. When Rogers clarified that the latter was the winner for *Cavalcade*, Capra had to return to his table unhonoured in what must have seemed the longest walk of his life. Happily he won the following year for *It Happened One Night*. Lloyd won again the next year. Academy members became accustomed to voting for directors called Frank—in the first ten years of the awards, seven of the Oscars for Best Director went to Franks.

- The first and only year in which all ten performers nominated for Best Actor and Best Actress were American-born was 1985. William Hurt won for *Kiss of the Spider Woman*, against competition from Harrison Ford, James Garner, Jack Nicholson and Jon Voight; while Geraldine Page took the honours for *The Trip to Bountiful* versus Whoopi Goldberg, Jessica Lange, Anne Bancroft and Meryl Streep.

- The first and only year in which all five nominations for Best Director went to non-Americans was in 1988: Bernardo Bertolucci (It) for *The Last Emperor* (It/GB/Chn 87); John Boorman (GB) for *Hope and Glory* (GB 87); Adrian Lyne (GB) for *Fatal Attraction* (US 87); Lasse Hallström (Swe) for *My Life As a Dog* (Swe 87); and Norman Jewison (Can) for *Moonstruck* (US 87). The winner was Bernardo Bertolucci.

- Three Best Picture winners have received no other awards: *Broadway Melody* (US 28), *Grand Hotel* (US 31) and *Mutiny on the Bounty* (US 35). *Grand Hotel* had the unique distinction of no other nominations.

- The longest haul for an Oscar was by John Wayne, who was eventually honoured with Best Actor for *True Grit* (US 68), his 141st film. His only previous nomination had been for *The Sands of Iwo Jima* (US 49), despite stand-out performances in *Stagecoach* (US 39), *Red River* (US 48), *She Wore a Yellow Ribbon* (US 49), *The Quiet Man* (US 53), *The Searchers* (US 56) and *The Man Who Shot Liberty Valance* (US 62).

- Reality failing to mirror art: Maggie Smith won an Academy Award for her role in *California Suite* (US 78) playing an English actress nominated for an Academy Award but failing to win it.

- The only film for which the entire cast was nominated for Oscars was *Sleuth* (GB 72). Laurence Olivier and Michael Caine lost out to Marlon Brando for *The Godfather* (US 72) and Joel Grey for *Cabaret* (US 72).

- The only person to have won an Oscar in one of the regular categories without being nominated was Hal Mohr, who received the Best Cinematography Award for Warner Bros' *A Midsummer Night's Dream* (US 35). Under a new rule write-in votes were allowed and Jack Warner had given instructions to all the Academy members on the Warner lot that they were to vote the Warner ticket whether their films had been nominated or not.

- The oldest combination of winners in the acting awards was in 1982, when 77-year-old Henry Fonda and 72-year-old Katharine Hepburn took the Best Actor and Best Actress Oscars for *On Golden Pond* (US 81), 77-year-old John Gielgud was honoured with the Best Supporting Actor award for *Arthur* (US 81) and 56-year-old Maureen Stapleton won best Supporting Actress for *Reds* (US 81)—average age 70½.

- The shortest Academy Awards ceremony was the first held at Hollywood's Roosevelt Hotel in 1929—Academy President Douglas Fairbanks handed over the statuettes in just 4 min 22 secs. Media coverage was rather more than muted—there wasn't any. The longest was the 72nd Academy Awards in 2000 at 4 hrs 9 min.

- Oscars in the Best Acting categories have a marked tendency to go to performers playing characters who are severely disabled or suffering from a terminal disease. They are also won by those who have experienced personal physical distress. Elizabeth Taylor scored her sole Academy Award (Best Actress) for her less than lustrous performance as a call girl in *Butterfield 8* (US 60) and it was generally reckoned around Hollywood that she had won the sympathy vote following her recent recovery from a near-fatal attack of pneumonia. 'I lost,' observed fellow nominee Shirley MacLaine, 'to a tracheotomy.'

- The Oscar won by Joseph Farnham was unique. He was honoured in the first year of the Awards for Best Title Writing (i.e. subtitles), an art which had become redundant by the time the second Awards were made in March 1930.

- The third Academy Awards ceremony in November 1930 was the first in which the names of the winners were supposed to be kept secret until the night. The atmosphere of suspense was somewhat depleted by the fact that Best Actor winner George Arliss and Best Actress winner Norma Shearer had both posed for photographers with their statuettes two days earlier.

- The last occasion on which the names of the Oscar winners were leaked before the ceremony was in 1940, when the *Los Angeles Times* broke its word to the Academy and hit the streets with the results—given to them under strict embargo—two hours before the announcements. This was the year in which *Gone With the Wind* (US 39) won nearly every award going, as expected, so the impact was not so harmful as in a cliffhanger year. Nevertheless, the following year the practice of sealed envelopes containing the names of the winners was introduced. Since then nobody, not even the President of the Academy, has known the results in advance—apart from the grey eminences from Price-Waterhouse who count the votes.

- Only two non-professionals have won acting Oscars: Canadian-born war veteran Harold Russell for his role as the handless ex-soldier (Russell himself had had his hands blown off) in *The Best Years of Our Lives* (US 46), and Cambodian refugee Dr Haing S. Ngor for his moving performance as a victim of Cambodia's Pol Pot regime in *The Killing Fields* (GB 84). Marlee Matlin was a non-professional before her Oscar-winning debut role as the deaf mute (she herself is deaf) in *Children of a Lesser God* (US 85), but then turned professional. (Continued p. 245.)

BEST FILM AWARDS

THE ACADEMY AWARD FOR THE BEST FILM

Dates given are year award was made (NB: no ceremony in 1933)

1929 *Wings* (US)
1930 (March) *Broadway Melody* (US)
1930 (Nov) *All Quiet on the Western Front* (US)
1931 *Cimarron* (US)
1932 *Grand Hotel* (US)
1934 *Cavalcade* (US)
1935 *It Happened One Night* (US)
1936 *Mutiny on the Bounty* (US)
1937 *The Great Ziegfeld* (US)
1938 *The Life of Emile Zola* (US)
1939 *You Can't Take It With You* (US)
1940 *Gone With The Wind* (US)
1941 *Rebecca* (US)
1942 *How Green was My Valley* (US)
1943 *Mrs Miniver* (US)
1944 *Casablanca* (US)
1945 *Going my Way* (US)
1946 *The Lost Weekend* (US)
1947 *The Best Years of Our Lives* (US)
1948 *Gentlemen's Agreement* (US)
1949 *Hamlet* (GB)
1950 *All the King's Men* (US)
1951 *All About Eve* (US)
1952 *An American in Paris* (US)
1953 *The Greatest Show On Earth* (US)
1954 *From Here to Eternity* (US)
1955 *On The Waterfront* (US)
1956 *Marty* (US)
1957 *Around the World in 80 Days* (US)
1958 *The Bridge on the River Kwai* (GB)
1959 *Gigi* (US)
1960 *Ben Hur* (US)
1961 *The Apartment* (US)
1962 *West Side Story* (US)
1963 *Lawrence of Arabia* (GB)
1964 *Tom Jones* (GB)
1965 *My Fair Lady* (US)
1966 *The Sound of Music* (US)
1967 *A Man For All Seasons* (GB)
1968 *In The Heat of the Night* (US)
1969 *Oliver!* (GB)
1970 *Midnight Cowboy* (US)
1971 *Patton* (US)
1972 *The French Connection* (US)
1973 *The Godfather* (US)
1974 *The Sting* (US)
1975 *The Godfather, Part II* (US)
1976 *One Flew Over the Cuckoo's Nest* (US)
1977 *Rocky* (US)
1978 *Annie Hall* (US)
1979 *The Deer Hunter* (US)
1980 *Kramer vs Kramer* (US)
1981 *Ordinary People* (US)
1982 *Chariots of Fire* (GB)
1983 *Gandhi* (GB)
1984 *Terms of Endearment* (US)
1985 *Amadeus* (US)
1986 *Out of Africa* (US)
1987 *Platoon* (US)
1988 *The Last Emperor* (It/GB/Chn)
1989 *Rain Man* (US)
1990 *Driving Miss Daisy* (US)
1991 *Dances with Wolves* (US)
1992 *The Silence of the Lambs* (US)
1993 *The Unforgiven* (US)
1994 *Schindler's List* (US)
1995 *Forrest Gump* (US)
1996 *Braveheart* (US)
1997 *The English Patient* (US/GB)
1998 *Titanic* (US)
1999 *Shakespeare in Love* (US/GB)
2000 *American Beauty* (US)

THE BERLIN FILM FESTIVAL AWARD FOR BEST FILM

The Berlin Film Festival was established 1951. There was no overall Best Film award in the first year and from 1952–5 the films were voted for by the audience. The Golden Bear award for Best Picture was inaugurated 1956.

1952 *She Danced for the Summer* (Swe)
1953 *The Wages of Fear* (Fr)
1954 *Hobson's Choice* (GB)
1955 *The Rats* (FRG)
1956 *Invitation to the Dance* (GB)
1957 *Twelve Angry Men* (US)
1958 *The End of the Day* (Swe)
1959 *The Cousins* (Fr)
1960 *Lazarillo de Tormes* (Sp)
1961 *La Notte* (It)
1962 *A Kind of Loving* (GB)
1963 *Oath of Obedience* (FRG); *The Devil* (It) =
1964 *Dry Summer* (Tur)
1965 *Alphaville* (Fr)
1966 *Cul de Sac* (GB)
1967 *Le Depart* (Bel)
1968 *Ole Dole Doff* (Swe)
1969 *Early Years* (Yug)
1970 No award
1971 *The Garden of the Finzi-Continis* (It)
1972 *The Canterbury Tales* (It)
1973 *Distant Thunder* (Ind)
1974 *The Apprenticeship of Duddy* Kravitz (Can)
1975 *Orkobefogadas* (Hun)
1976 *Buffalo Bill and the Indians* (US)—award declined
1977 *The Ascent* (USSR)
1978 *The Trouts* (Sp); *The Words of Max* (Sp) =
1979 *David* (FRG)
1980 *Heartland* (US); *Palermo Oder Wolfsburg* (FRG) =
1981 *Di Presa Di Presa* (Sp)
1982 *Die Sehnsucht der Veronica Voss* (FRG)
1983 *Ascendancy* (GB); *The Beehive* (Sp) =
1984 *Love Streams* (US 84)
1985 *Wetherby* (GB); *Die Frau und der Fremde* (FRG) =
1986 *Stammheim* (FRG)
1987 *The Theme* (USSR)
1988 *Red Shorghum* (Chn)
1989 *Rain Man* (US)
1990 *Music Box* (US); *Larks on a String* (Cz) =
1991 *House of Smiles* (It)
1992 *Grand Canyon* (US)
1993 *The Woman from the Lake of Scented Souls* (Chn); *The Wedding Banquet* (Tai/US) =
1994 *In the Name of the Father* (GB/Ire)
1995 *Fresh Bait* (Fr)
1996 *Sense and Sensibility* (US/GB)
1997 *The People vs Larry Flynt* (US)
1998 *Central Station* (Bra)
1999 *The Thin Red Line* (US)
2000 *Magnolia* (US)

BRITISH FILM ACADEMY

Best British Film Award (1948–68)

1948 *Odd Man Out*
1949 *The Fallen Idol*
1950 *The Third Man*
1951 *The Blue Lamp*
1952 *The Lavender Hill Mob*
1953 *The Sound Barrier*
1954 *Genevieve*
1955 *Hobson's Choice*
1956 *Richard III*
1957 *Reach for the Sky*
1958 *The Bridge on the River Kwai*
1959 *Room at the Top*
1960 *Sapphire*
1961 *Saturday Night and Sunday Morning*
1962 *A Taste of Honey*
1963 *Lawrence of Arabia*
1964 *Tom Jones*
1965 *Dr Strangelove*
1966 *The Ipcress File*
1967 *The Spy who Came in from the Cold*
1968 *A Man for All Seasons*

Best Film Award (1969–)

1969 *The Graduate* (US)
1970 *Midnight Cowboy* (US)
1971 *Butch Cassidy and the Sundance Kid* (US)
1972 *Sunday Bloody Sunday* (GB)
1973 *Cabaret* (US)
1974 *La Nuite Americaine/Day for Night* (Fr)
1975 *Lacombe, Lucien* (Fr)
1976 *Alice Doesn't Live Here Anymore* (US)
1977 *One Flew Over the Cuckoo's Nest* (US)
1978 *Annie Hall* (US)
1979 *Julia* (US)
1980 *Manhattan* (US)
1981 *The Elephant Man* (GB)
1982 *Chariots of Fire* (GB)
1983 *Gandhi* (GB)
1984 *Educating Rita* (GB)
1985 *The Killing Fields* (GB)
1986 *The Purple Rose of Cairo* (US)
1987 *A Room with a View* (GB)
1988 *Jean de Florette* (Fr)
1989 *The Last Emperor* (It/GB/Chn)
1990 *Dead Poets' Society* (US)
1991 *GoodFellas* (US)
1992 *The Commitments* (US/GB)
1993 *Howards End* (GB)
1994 *Schindler's List* (US)
1995 *Four Weddings and a Funeral* (GB)
1996 *Sense and Sensibility* (US/GB)
1997 *The English Patient* (US/GB)
1998 *The Full Monty* (GB)
1999 *Shakespeare in Love* (US/GB)
2000 *American Beauty* (US)

CANNES FILM FESTIVAL

Palme d'Or for Best Film

1946 *La Bataille du Rail* (Fr)
1947 *Antoine et Antoinette* (Fr)
1948 No festival
1949 *The Third Man* (GB)
1950 No festival
1951 *Miracle in Milan* (It); *Miss Julie* (Swe) =
1952 *Othello* (Mor); *Two Cents Worth of Hope* (It) =
1953 *Wages of Fear* (Fr)

BEST FILM AWARDS (continued)

1954 *Gate of Hell* (Jap)
1955 *Marty* (US)
1956 *World of Silence* (Fr)
1957 *Friendly Persuasion* (US)
1958 *The Cranes are Flying* (USSR)
1959 *Black Orpheus* (Fr)
1960 *La Dolce Vita* (It)
1961 *Viridiana* (Sp); *Une aussi longue absence* (Fr) =
1962 *The Given* Word (Bra)
1963 *The Leopard* (It)
1964 *The Umbrellas of Cherbourg* (Fr)
1965 *The Knack* (GB)
1966 *A Man and a Woman* (Fr); *Signore e Signori* (It) =
1967 *Blow-Up* (GB)
1968 Festival disrupted; no awards
1969 *If* (GB)
1970 *M*A*S*H* (US)
1971 *The Go-Between* (GB)
1972 *The Working Class Goes to Paradise* (It); *The Mattei Affair* (It) =
1973 *Scarecrow* (US); *The Hireling* (GB) =
1974 *The Conversation* (US)
1975 *Chronicle of the Burning Years* (Alg)
1976 *Taxi Driver* (US)
1977 *Padre Padrone* (It)
1978 *L'Albero Degli Zoccoli* (It)
1979 *The Tin Drum* (FRG); *Apocalypse Now* (US) =
1980 *All That Jazz* (US); *Kagemusha* (Jap) =
1981 *Man of Iron* (Pol)
1982 *Missing* (US); *Yol* (Tur) =
1983 *The Ballad of Narayama* (Jap)
1984 *Paris, Texas* (FRG)
1985 *When Father Was Away On Business* (Yug)
1986 *The Mission* (GB)
1987 *Under the Sun of Satan* (Fr)
1988 *Pelle the Conqueror* (Den)
1989 *sex, lies and videotape* (US)
1990 *Wild at Heart* (US)
1991 *Barton Fink* (US)

1992 *Best Intentions* (Swe)
1993 *Farewell My Concubine* (Chn); *The Piano* (Aus) =
1994 *Pulp Fiction* (US)
1995 *Underground* (Fr/Ger/Hun)
1996 *Secrets and Lies* (GB)
1997 *The Eel* (Jap); *The Taste of Cherries* (Iran)
1998 *Eternity and a Day* (Gce/It/Fr)
1999 *Rosetta* (Bel/Fr)
2000 *Dancer in the Dark* (Den/Fr/Swe/Ir/Ger/Nor/Neths/Ice/Fin/US/GB)

VENICE FILM FESTIVAL

Best Foreign Film Award (1934–42)

1932 No official award
1933 No festival
1934 *Man of Aran* (GB)
1935 *Anna Karenina* (US)
1936 *Der Kaiser von Kalifornien* (Ger)
1937 *Un Carnet de Bal* (Fr)
1938 *Olympia* (Ger)
1939 No award
1940 *Der Postmeister* (Ger)
1941 *Ohm Kruger* (Ger)
1942 *Der grosse König* (Ger)
1943–45 No festival

Best Film Award (1946–68)

1946 *The Southerner* (US)
1947 *Sirena* (Cz)
1948 *Hamlet* (GB)
1949 *Manon* (Fr)
1950 *Justice is Done* (Fr)
1951 *Rashomon* (Jap)
1952 *Forbidden Games* (Fr)
1953 No award
1954 *Romeo and Juliet* (It/GB)
1955 *Ordet* (Den)
1956 No award

1957 *Aparajito* (Ind)
1958 *Muhomatsu no Issho* (Jap)
1959 *Il Generale della Rovere* (It)
1960 *Le Passage du Rhin* (Fr)
1961 *Last Year at Marienbad* (Fr)
1962 *Childhood of Ivan* (USSR)
1963 *Le Mani sulla città* (It)
1964 *Red Desert* (It)
1965 *Of a Thousand Delights* (It)
1966 *Battle of Algiers* (It)
1967 *Belle de Jour* (Fr)
1968 *Die Aristen in der Zirkuskuppel* (FRG)

Jury and award system discontinued 1969–79

Golden Lion for Best Film (1980–)

1980 *Gloria* (US); *Atlantic City* (Fr/Can) =
1981 *Die Bleierne Zeit* (FRG)
1982 *The State of Things* (FRG)
1983 *Prénom Carmen* (Fr/Swz)
1984 *Year of the Quiet Sun* (Pol)
1985 *Sans toit ni loi aka Vagabonde* (Fr)
1986 *Le Rayon Vert* (Fr)
1987 *Au Revoir les Enfants* (Fr)
1988 *The Legend of the Holy Drinker* (It)
1989 *A City of Sadness* (Taiwan)
1990 *Rosencrantz and Guildenstern Are Dead* (GB)
1991 *Urga* (USSR/Fr)
1992 *Qiu Ju Da Guansi* (Chn)
1993 *Short Cuts* (US); *Three Colours Blue* (Fr) =
1994 *Before the Rain* (Macedonia)
1995 *Cyclo* (Fr/Vietnam)
1996 *Michael Collins* (US/Ire)
1997 *Hana-Bi* (Jap)
1998 *The Way We Laughed* (It)
1999 *Not One Less* (China)
2000 *The Circle* (Iran)

- Vivien Leigh's Oscar for her performance as the incomparable Scarlett O'Hara in *Gone With the Wind* (US 39) was sold in 1993 for a then record $510,000. Had the actress known its prospective value, she might have treated it with greater respect. A friend recalled dining at her house in Eaton Square in 1958 and noticing that the statuette was being used as a doorstop—for the lavatory door. At Notley Abbey, her husband Laurence Olivier's Oscar for *Hamlet* (GB 48) had been placed in the same position.

- Most people think of the Oscars as the quintessential Hollywood in-fest. In fact *American Beauty*'s win in 2000 was the first Best Picture since *Rocky* in 1977 to be majority-lensed in the movie capital. In the early days of the Academy Awards, virtually every Best Picture winner originated on Hollywood sound stages, but as the studio system began to disintegrate in the 1950s that became increasingly rare.

- Remarkably Britain has had two Oscar nominees for Best Foreign Language Film, both in Welsh: *Hedd Wynn* (GB 93) and *Solomon and Gaenor* (GB 99), the latter a romance between Jewish boy and Welsh girl in the Rhondda Valley, starring Maureen Lipman as a Jewish matriarch.

- The only tie for Best Actor was between Wallace Beery in *The Champ* (US 31) and Fredric March in *Dr Jekyll and Mr Hyde* (US 31). The only tie for Best Actress was between Barbra Streisand in *Funny Girl* (US 68) and Katharine Hepburn in *The Lion* in *Winter* (GB 68).

- Some winners' sense of gratitude has bordered on the excessive. Probably the longest roster of people thanked by a gushing Oscar winner was the 27 named by Olivia de Havilland when she won Best Actress for *To Each His Own* (US 46).

- The longest speech was made by Greer Garson on receiving the Best Actress award for *Mrs Miniver* (US 42) and lasted for 5½ minutes. (The author extends posthumous apologies to Miss Garson for repeating, in earlier editions of this book, the canard that she rambled on for over an hour.) Acceptance speeches were restricted to 45 seconds for the first time at the 1990 awards ceremony. After 25 seconds a red light flashes a warning. If the recipient is still thanking co-workers, friends, relatives and therapists after the allotted three quarters of a minute, loud music intervenes.

Index

Julie Christie failing her screen test with Michael Winner for West 11 (GB 63). Winner recalled: 'In 1962 I tested three girls for the lead in a film called West 11. One of these was Kathleen Breck, another was Julie Christie, and another whose name I have forgotten. When the tests came on the screen, I said: "It's Julie Christie, no doubt at all!" The producer turned to me and said: "She's a B-picture actress, who'd want her?" "I would," I said. "Who'd want to sleep with her?" he asked incredulously. "I would," I replied cheerfully. The same man turned down Sean Connery for the other lead because he, too, was a B-picture actor, and James Mason for the villain because he was past it. We ended up with Alfred Lynch (an excellent actor, but not Sean Connery), Kathleen Breck (an excellent actress, but not Julie Christie) and Eric Portman, who was so good I didn't mind. (Picture and text courtesy of Michael Winner.)

*For other stars who have failed screen tests, **see p. 114**.*

Cinderella has been remade more times than any other movie story—there have been 103 versions in 103 years, including cartoon, musical, ballet, operatic, parody and at least two pornographic productions. Sinderella (GB 72), above, was one of the latter. **See p. 29.**

'Most of the time he sounds like he has a mouth full of wet toilet paper,' said critic Rex Reed of Marlon Brando. Looks like it too. For other put-downs of the stars **see pp. 108–13.**

The largest film set ever built—the Roman forum created for Samuel Bronston's 1964 epic The Fall of the Roman Empire. **See p. 153.**

SUBJECT

The earliest surviving advertising film, made in the US in 1897. **See pp. 210–11.**

The first ever book-of-the-film, 1914.
See p. 216.

Director Gregory Cava reckoned that the legit version of Stage Door *(above) was insufficiently true to life and sent out teams of stenographers to transcribe verbatim the tales they heard from struggling young actresses. The result was a screen version (below) which was much more realistic, including the sordid conditions in which the young people lived. For other examples of truth in film-making,* **see It's For Real, pp. 153–7.**

The Girl with the $5 Million Legs. Cyd Charisse's long and lovely limbs were insured for that sum. For other stars whose features or appendages were underwritten against loss or damage, **see pp. 119–23.**

TITLES

The long and short of it—Johan Aasen, 7 ft 2 in Norwegian actor from Minneapolis, cowers above a threatening Harold Lloyd in Why Worry *(US 23). For the tallest, shortest and heaviest screen artistes,* **see pp. 114–16.**

Gloria Swanson as herself in *Airport 75 (US 74)*. More than half a century earlier she had also played herself in Hollywood *(US 23)*. For other stars playing themselves, see pp. 87–9.

Katharine Hepburn holds the record for the most Best Actor/Actress Academy Awards with four. The first was for Morning Glory *(US 33) (above), the last for* On Golden Pond *(US 81) (below) nearly half a century later.* **See p. 241.**

ADDENDA

The character most frequently portrayed in horror films (see p. 62): with the release of the Manetti Brothers' *Zora la vampira* (It 00) the total number of representations of Count Dracula on screen is 168. Toni Bertorelli donned the cape and fangs.

The most successful documentary film (see p. 211): *In Search of Noah's Ark* has now been overtaken at the wickets by Destination Cinema's *Mysteries of Egypt* (US 98), with a worldwide gross to end 2000 of $70 million.

US Presidents (see pp. 56–7): Bruce Greenwood played John F. Kennedy in *Thirteen Days* (US 00), a dramatisation of the Cuban missile crisis.

President Alessandri of Chile was so besotted with the infant Shirley Temple that he had her adopted by the Chilean navy as their official mascot. For statemen's, royalty's and the Pope's particular predilections, **see Film Fans, Famous and Infamous, pp. 231–3.**

The three-minute scene in John Frankenheimer's Black Sunday *(US 77) in which the Super Bowl is threatened with a shower of lethal darts from an airship involved no fewer than 181 edits—an average of one per second.* **See p. 140.**